brief contents

contents

Chapter 7 ● ●

Managing Human Resources 154

Chapter 8 ● ●

Managing the Diverse Workforce 180

Chapter 9 ● ●

Leadership 206

Chapter 10 ● ●

Motivating People   228

Chapter 11 ● ●

Teamwork   252

Chapter 12 ●●

Communicating   272

Chapter 13 ●●

Managerial Control   294

Chapter 14 ●●

Innovating and Changing   318

management

1

Managing

Get the Real Scoop

on what today's managers really do. Listen to what Sarah and Joe have to say about their management positions on the book Web site.

A small player in the struggling global auto market, California-based start-up Tesla Motors is trying to revolutionize its industry. Headed by chief executive Elon Musk, Tesla has an ambitious vision: to mass-produce electric cars that end Americans' dependence on fossil fuels and cut greenhouse gas emissions. The South African-born Musk predicts that by 2030, the majority of cars made in the United States will be electric. A bold prediction? Maybe. But Elon Musk is a skilled manager who has already led two successful Internet companies: Zip2 (later sold to Compaq) and X.com (which morphed into what is now known as PayPal). Tesla's success depends in large part on Musk's management and leadership abilities.[1]

Of course, not every manager or organization succeeds. In a recent story of failure, reporters investigating the Walter Reed Army Medical Center in Washington, D.C.—among the nation's top military hospitals—discovered that in some facilities, wounded soldiers were coping with mold, roaches, rodents, and damaged walls and doors, as well as red tape

Planning and organizing are crucial to running an efficient store. I make sure all the activities or store changes to our week are planned out at the beginning of every month—such as when we do markdowns weekly, or when we change the floor from month to month. Once everything is planned, then I can make sure everything is set and organized with a manager and associates to make sure everything is done in a timely manner.

—Sarah Albert, Clothing Retail Manager

The first hour of my day is planning and organizing before employees report to work. The rest of the day is spent training and instructing people to do assigned tasks, such as loading specific trailers.

—Joe Kubinski, Operations Supervisor

●● learning **OBJECTIVES**

After studying Chapter 1,
you should be able to:

LO1 Summarize the major challenges of
managing in the new competitive
landscape.

LO2 Describe the sources of competitive
advantage for a company.

LO3 Explain how the functions of management are
evolving in today's business environment.

LO4 Compare how the nature of management
varies at different organizational levels.

LO5 Define the skills you need to be an effective
manager.

LO6 Identify the principles that will help you
manage your career.

that snarled their efforts to receive services. General Richard A. Cody, the Army's vice chief of staff, admitted fundamental management problems: "Our counselors and case managers are overworked, and they do not receive enough training. We do not adequately communicate necessary information. Our administrative processes are needlessly cumbersome. . . . Our medical holding units are not manned to the proper level, and we do not assign leaders who can ensure a proper accountability, proper discipline and well-being."[2] Fortunately, these problems are correctable, and they are now being addressed.

Companies, like individuals, succeed or fail for a variety of reasons. Some of these reasons are circumstantial. Most are personal and human and include the decisions managers make and the actions they take.

3. The importance of knowledge and ideas
4. Collaboration across organizational "boundaries"

Business operates on a global scale

Far more than in the past, today's enterprises are global, with offices and production facilities all over the world. Corporations such as General Electric and Nestlé transcend national borders. A key reason for this change is the strong demand coming from consumers and businesses overseas. Companies that want to grow often need to tap international markets where incomes are rising and demand is increasing. GE, which became a massive and profitable corporation by selling appliances, light bulbs,

> ❝**Management means, in the last analysis, the substitution of thought for brawn and muscle, of knowledge for folklore and tradition, and of cooperation for force.**❞
>
> —Peter Drucker

In business, there is no replacement for effective management. Companies may fly high for a while, but they cannot do well for long without good management. It's the same for individuals: *BusinessWeek*'s Managers of the Year succeed by focusing on fundamentals, knowing what's important, and managing well. The aim of this book is to help you succeed in those pursuits.

(L)(O) 1 **WHAT YOU NEED TO KNOW . . .**
Can you summarize the major challenges of managing in the new competitive landscape?

MANAGING IN THE NEW COMPETITIVE LANDSCAPE

When the economy is soaring, business seems easy. Starting up an Internet company looked easy in the 1990s, and ventures related to the real estate boom looked like a sure thing during much of the past decade. Eventually, investors grew wary of dotcom start-ups, and the demand for new homes cooled. At such times, it becomes evident that management is a challenge that requires constantly adapting to new circumstances.

What defines the competitive landscape of today's business? You will be reading about many relevant issues in the coming chapters, but we begin here by highlighting four key elements that make the current business landscape different from the past:

1. Globalization
2. Technological change

and machinery to U.S. customers, recently announced that it expected its foreign sales to equal its sales within the United States. GE's biggest foreign customers are in Europe, but sales volume in China and India is rising fast.[3]

Globalization also means that a company's talent can come from anywhere. As with its sales, half of GE's employees work outside the United States.[4] Cisco, a leader in equipment for computer networking, considers maintaining operations in India to be an essential tactic for staying competitive. Besides thousands of technology employees, many senior executives of the San Jose–based company work in Bangalore, India. Their presence helps Cisco serve the fast-growing Indian Internet market at a crucial time: the furious growth in demand is attracting low-cost competition from Chinese businesses.[5]

Another force that is making globalization both more possible and more inevitable is the Internet. Now that more than a billion users have come online, more and more of the new users are in developing nations such as China, India, Russia, and Brazil.[6] As people in developing nations turn to the power of the Web, they become a force to develop content in their own languages and suited to their own means of access, such as cell phones and inexpensive laptops. Although some countries' governments have limited the content available to their residents (e.g., France and Germany forbid neo-Nazi content, and China blocks material seen as unfavorable to the government), the Internet is largely a force for connecting people without regard to time and space. Companies can get their message to users on every continent and often are expected to provide service anytime, anywhere. This can affect how and when people work. Laura Asiala, a manager for Dow Corning, based in Midland, Michigan, supervises employees in Tokyo, Seoul, Hong Kong,

Shanghai, and Brussels. To keep in touch with them, she starts working at 5:00 a.m. some days and ends as late as midnight. She takes a break from 3:30 to 9:30 each day, and technology lets her communicate from home.[7]

 The global reach of the Internet pushed Mitch Free to expand his business, MFG.com, into China. MFG.com runs a Web site where manufacturers that need parts post their specifications online, and suppliers bid to provide those parts. The suppliers pay an annual fee for the right to submit bids. Free, who grew up in a small town in Georgia and had barely traveled outside the United States, had never planned to be an international manager, but Chinese suppliers soon began submitting requests to participate. At the same time, manufacturers were pressing MFG.com to include Asian suppliers, which often could offer the best prices.

So Free traveled to Shanghai, China, to meet some of the interested suppliers. He learned about the business culture, such as the importance of cultivating business relationships and networks. After a difficult search, he made a key hiring decision: general manager James Jin, who speaks fluent English, studied global management, and has experience in manufacturing both in the United States and in China. The effort was well rewarded. Jin has helped Free navigate the fast-growing business landscape of his native China. Sales in China accounted for more than 10 percent of MFG.com's total annual sales and are growing faster than the company's overall sales.[8]

> # Google search sites span the Internet in more than 100 languages.

Successful CEOs know that the change from a local to a global marketplace is gaining momentum and is irreversible.[9] PepsiCo's chief executive, Indra Nooyi, brings a much-needed global viewpoint to a company whose international business has been growing three times faster than sales in the United States. Nooyi, who was raised in India and educated there and in the United States, has steered the company toward more "better for you" and "good for you" snacks by acquiring smaller companies such as a nut packager in Bulgaria and a hummus producer in Israel.[10]

Smaller firms are also an important part of globalization. Many small companies export their goods. Many domestic firms assemble their products in other countries. And companies are under pressure to improve their products in the face of intense competition from foreign manufacturers. Firms today must ask themselves, "How can we be the best in the world?"

For students, it's not too early to think about the personal ramifications. In the words of chief executive officer (CEO) Jim Goodnight of SAS, the largest privately held software company in the world, "The best thing business schools can do to prepare their students is to encourage them to look beyond their own backyards. Globalization has opened the world for many opportunities, and schools should encourage their students to take advantage of them."[11]

Technology is advancing online and off

The Internet's impact on globalization is only one of the ways that technology is vitally important in the business world. Technology both complicates things and creates new opportunities. The challenges come from the rapid rate at which communication, transportation, information, and other technologies change.[12] Until recently, for example, desktop computers were a reliable source of income, not only for computer makers but also for the companies that make keyboards and a whole host of accessories like wrist rests and attachable shelves for storing pens and DVDs close at hand. But after just a couple of decades of widespread PC use, customers are switching to laptop models, which require different accessories and are used in different ways.[13] Any company that serves desktop users now has to rethink its customers' wants and needs, not to mention the possibility that these customers are now doing their work at the airport or a local Starbucks outlet, rather than in an office.

Later chapters will discuss technology further, but here we highlight the rise of the Internet and its effects. Why is the Internet so important to business?[14]

Will Wright, creator of "The Sims" video games, poses with a computer image of the game. His newest creation, "Spore," will undoubtedly build on the success of "The Sims."

- It fulfills many business functions: it is a marketplace, a means for manufacturing goods and services, a distribution channel, an information service, and more.
- It drives down costs.
- It speeds up globalization. Managers can watch and learn what competitors, suppliers, and customers are doing—on the other side of the world.
- It provides access to information, allows better-informed decisions, and improves efficiency of decision making.
- It facilitates design of new products, from pharmaceuticals to financial services.

While these advantages create business opportunities, they also create threats as competitors capitalize on new developments.

At the beginning, Internet technology dazzled people with financial returns that seemed limitless. Today, investors and entrepreneurs have learned that not every business idea will fly, but many profitable online businesses have become a part of our day-to-day lives. Just a few years ago, it was novel to go online to order plane tickets, read the news, or share photos. Some online success stories, such as Amazon, Monster, and Google, are purely Internet businesses. Other companies, including Barnes & Noble and Office Depot, have incorporated online channels into an existing business strategy.

The Internet's impact is felt not only at the level of businesses as a whole but also by individual employees and their managers. Just as globalization has stretched out the workdays of some people, high-tech gadgets have made it possible to stay connected to work anytime, anywhere. This ability is both a convenience and

a potential source of stress. Cell phones, personal digital assistants (PDAs, such as the BlackBerry), smart phones (combinations of the two), and laptops let people use wireless connections to connect to the Internet. Wi-Fi hotspots make the connections available in stores, restaurants, hotels, airports, and libraries. Software lets users download and read files and e-mail over their phones and PDAs.

The stress comes when employees or their supervisors don't set limits on being connected. Facilities manager Cherri Chiodo loves the convenience of her BlackBerry but finds that it sometimes replaces face-to-face communication with family members. Real estate broker Ted Helgans calls his BlackBerry a "traveling office" and a valuable tool for getting and sharing information. Helgans emphasizes that users can and should decide when to turn off the devices.[15] Jean Chatzkey, an editor for *Money* magazine, found that she constantly interrupted whatever she was doing to check e-mail on her Palm Treo. Realizing that the device had become more of a distraction than a help, Chatzkey began reminding herself that the messages were not emergencies.[16] Thus, using technology effectively is more than a matter of learning new skills; it also involves making judgments about when and where to apply the technology for maximum benefit.

Knowledge is a valuable resource to be managed

Companies and managers need good, new ideas. Because companies in advanced economies have become so efficient at producing physical goods, most workers have been freed up to provide services or "abstract goods" like software, entertainment, data, and advertising. Efficient factories with fewer workers produce the cereals and cell phones the market demands; meanwhile, more and more workers create software and invent new products. These workers, whose primary contributions are ideas and problem-solving expertise, are often referred to as *knowledge workers*.

Managing these workers poses some particular challenges, which we will examine throughout this book. For example, determining whether they are doing a good job can be difficult, because the manager cannot simply count or measure a knowledge worker's output. Also, these workers often are most motivated to do their best when the work is interesting, not because of a carrot or stick dangled by the manager.[18]

Because the success of modern businesses so often depends on the knowledge used for innovation and the delivery of services, organizations need to manage that knowledge. **Knowledge management** is the set of practices aimed at discovering and harnessing an organization's intellectual resources—fully utilizing the intellects of the organization's people. Knowledge management is about finding, unlocking, sharing, and altogether capitalizing on the most precious resources of an organization: people's expertise, skills, wisdom, and relationships. Knowledge managers find these human assets, help people collaborate and learn, help people generate new ideas, and harness those ideas into successful innovations. Typically, knowledge management relies on software that lets employees contribute what they know and share that knowledge readily with one another. As a result, knowledge management may be the responsibility of an organization's information technology (IT) department, perhaps under the leadership of a chief information officer or chief knowledge officer.

In hospitals, important knowledge includes patients' histories, doctors' orders, billing information, dietary requirements, prescriptions administered, and much more. With lives at stake, many hospitals have embraced knowledge management. At Virginia Commonwealth University (VCU) Health System, a single information system lets doctors write prescriptions, look up patient information and lab results, and consult with one another. Billing also is automated as part of VCU's knowledge management system, making the process more efficient and connecting with patient data so that it can remind the physician of all the conditions being treated—and billed for.[19] Hospitals may also give patients access to the knowledge management system so they can schedule appointments, request prescription refills, and send questions to their doctors.

Collaboration is toppling performance-restraining boundaries

One of the most important processes of knowledge management is to ensure that people in different parts of the organization collaborate effectively. This requires communication among departments, divisions, or other subunits of the organization. For example, British Petroleum tries to create "T-shaped" managers who break out of the traditional corporate hierarchy to share knowledge freely across the organization (the horizontal part of the T) while remaining fiercely committed to the performance of their individual business units (the vertical part). This emphasis on dual responsibilities for performance and knowledge sharing also occurs at pharmaceutical giant GlaxoSmithKline, large German industrial company Siemens, and London-based steelmaker Ispat International.[20]

Toyota keeps its product development process efficient by bringing together design engineers and manufacturing employees from the very beginning. Often, manufacturing employees can see ways to simplify a design so that it is easier to make without defects or unnecessary costs. Toyota expects its employees to listen to input from all areas of the organization, making this type of collaboration a natural part of the organization's culture. The collaboration is supported with product development software including an online database that provides a central, easily accessible source of information about designs and processes. Along with this information, employees use the software to share their knowledge—best practices they have developed for design and manufacturing.[21] At Toyota, knowledge management supports collaboration, and vice versa.

Collaboration across former "boundaries" occurs even beyond the boundaries of the organization itself. Companies today must motivate and capitalize on the ideas of people outside the organization. How can a company best use the services of its consultants, ad agencies, and suppliers? To obtain the product development software that supports collaboration between manufacturing and design, Toyota collaborated with a software developer, PTC. Toyota and PTC together identified how software could support the company's strategy of "lean product development," and the relationship continues with regular meetings to continue improving the software. This collaboration not only helped Toyota obtain better software but also helped PTC improve the value of the products it offers to its other customers.[22]

Collaboration with investors helped a pair of entrepreneurs launch their company in the seriously risky business of making games. When Richard Tait and Whit Alexander developed their unusual board game Cranium, they felt certain that the combination of acting, singing, sculpting, and spelling backward would generate not only laughter, but sales. They confidently ordered 20,000 units from a Chinese manufacturer before winning any orders from retailers. Tait and Alexander were confident, but retailers generally are reluctant to take a chance on new products. The solution was to collaborate with a different kind of distributor. Some of the start-up funds for Cranium had come from an investment group whose participants included Howard Schultz, chairman of the Starbucks coffee chain. Schultz thought the game was great, so he let Tait and Alexander place samples of Cranium in Starbucks outlets, where customers could try playing it. Those who liked the game could buy their own copy. Customers loved it. Thanks to its track record at Starbucks, Cranium became not only the first game sold at Starbucks but also the first board game sold on Amazon.com, which had earlier turned it down. That success enabled Cranium the company to launch a dozen more games, now sold in 30 countries.[23]

Customers, too, can be collaborators. Companies still need to focus on delivering a product and making the numbers, but above all they must realize that the need to serve the customer drives everything. Best serving the customer can start with involving the customer more in company decisions. Procter & Gamble has been getting customers to think creatively and talk with one another online to come up with new product and service ideas.[24] Tapping into the popularity of social networking Web sites like Facebook and MySpace, P&G has set up two Web sites aimed at bringing its customers together. One site, the People's Choice Community, provides content about the winners of the People's Choice Awards, along with opportunities to join a "community" of people who want to share messages about those celebrities. The other site, called Capessa, is a discussion group for women, where they can trade thoughts about health and other concerns. Although both sites offer advertising opportunities, P&G intends to use them primarily as a way to learn more about consumers' attitudes.[25]

Globalization, technological change, the monumental importance of new ideas, collaboration across disappearing boundaries—what are the effects of this tidal wave of new forces? The remainder of this chapter and the following chapters will answer this question with business and management principles, real-world examples, and insights from successful managers and leaders.

Innovation and collaboration are the key factors in the phenomenal success of Cranium. This board game was the fastest selling game in history when it was released in 1998, with 100,000 units sold within seven months. Creators Richard Tait (left) and Whit Alexander are shown here demonstrating their highly successful board game.

L O 2 WHAT YOU NEED TO KNOW . . .

Can you describe the sources of competitive advantage for a company?

MANAGING FOR COMPETITIVE ADVANTAGE

The rise of the Internet turned careers (and lives) upside down. People dropped out of school to join Internet start-ups or start their own. Managers in big corporations quit their jobs to do the same. Investors salivated, and invested heavily. The risks were often ignored, or downplayed—sometimes tragically, as companies went under. Or consider an earlier industry with similar transforming power: automobiles. Out of at least 2,000 car makers, now only three U.S. car companies are left in the United States. In recent years, even these three—Ford, Chrysler, and

General Motors—have struggled to stay afloat as sales declined. Despite plant closings, layoffs, and other belt-tightening measures, the financial status of General Motors and Chrysler have remained so shaky that, even with reorganization through bankruptcy, President Obama assured the country that the U.S.-based auto industry would not "vanish."[26]

From the failures in these important transformational industries, we can see that a key to understanding the success of a company is not how much the industry in which it operates will affect society or how much it will grow. The key is the competitive advantage held by a particular company and its ability to sustain that advantage. Good managers know that they are in a competitive struggle to survive and win.

To survive and win, you have to gain advantage over your competitors and earn a profit. You gain competitive advantage by being better than your competitors at doing valuable things for your customers. But what does this mean, specifically? To succeed, managers must deliver the fundamental success drivers: innovation, quality, service, speed, and cost competitiveness.

Innovation keeps you ahead of competitors

Google's search engine quickly became a hit, and investors bid up the stock price of the company when it went public. But now that the free search service is used around the world, what can the company do next? Microsoft is working hard to take away some of Google's share of the market. Management at Google knows that it needs to come up with the next big idea, so it requires all its engineers to devote one-fifth of their time to special projects of their own.[27]

Innovation is the introduction of new goods and services. Your firm must adapt to changes in consumer demands and to new competitors. Products don't sell forever; in fact, they don't sell for nearly as long as they used to, because so many competitors are introducing so many new products all the time. Likewise, you have to be ready with new ways to communicate with customers and deliver products to them, as when the Internet forced traditional merchants to learn new ways of reaching customers directly. Globalization and technological advances have accelerated the pace of change and thus the need for innovation.

Sometimes the most important innovation isn't the product itself but the way it is delivered. Borrowing an idea that has proved popular in Europe, Opaque–Dining in the Dark has collaborated with the Braille Institute of America to present dining events at the Hyatt West Hollywood in total darkness. Diners select gourmet meals from a menu in a

People enter the Dans le Noir (In the Black) restaurant in Paris where they will enjoy a dining experience in complete darkness as if they were blind. Blind waiters serve as guides. The concept is an innovative approach to fine dining, and restaurants such as this are spreading around the globe.

lighted lounge and then are led into a dark banquet room by blind or visually impaired waiters. The attraction is that diners experience the meal in a completely new way because they are forced to concentrate on their senses of taste, smell, and touch.[28]

Innovation is today's holy grail.[29] And like the other sources of competitive advantage, innovation comes from people, it must be a strategic goal, and it must be managed properly. Later chapters will show you how great companies innovate.

Quality must continuously improve

When Spectrum Health, a hospital chain based in Grand Rapids, Michigan, asked patients how well they were served, the hospital learned that it had a problem. Patients rated staff low on helpfulness and their attitude toward visitors and said they didn't get good information about the procedures they received in the hospital or the way they were supposed to take care of themselves after being released to return home. Spectrum responded to the survey results by setting up an advisory council of patients and family members, making visiting hours more flexible, getting patient input into who was allowed to hear medical information and make decisions about treatment, and calling discharged patients at home to make sure they understood the directions they had received. Within two years of conducting the survey and beginning to make these changes, satisfaction scores of Spectrum patients improved dramatically.[30]

Spectrum Health's efforts reflect a commitment to quality. In general, **quality** is the excellence of your product. The importance of quality and the standards for acceptable quality have increased dramatically. Customers now demand high-quality goods and services, and often they will accept nothing less. In the hospital industry, the government is contributing to that trend. To receive full reimbursement from Medicare, hospitals must participate in a national program of patient satisfaction surveys. Results of these surveys are posted on the Department of Health and Human Service's Medicare information Web site, hospitalcompare.hhs.gov, so patients can compare the rankings of hospitals in their area when choosing services.[31]

Historically, quality pertained primarily to the physical goods that customers bought, and it referred to attractiveness, lack of defects, reliability, and long-term dependability. The traditional approach to quality was to check work after it was completed and then eliminate defects. But then W. Edwards Deming, J. M. Juran, and other quality gurus convinced managers to

● **SERVICE** The speed and dependability with which an organization delivers what customers want.

● **SPEED** Fast and timely execution, response, and delivery of results.

● **COST COMPETITIVENESS** Keeping costs low to achieve profits and be able to offer prices that are attractive to consumers.

take a more complete approach to achieving *total* quality. This includes several objectives:

- *Preventing* defects before they occur
- *Achieving zero defects* in manufacturing
- *Designing* products for quality

The goal is to solve and eradicate from the beginning all quality-related problems and to live a philosophy of *continuous improvement* in the way the company operates. Deming and his ideas were actually rebuffed by U.S. managers; only when he found an audience in Japan, and Japan started grabbing big chunks of market share from the United States in autos, computer chips, and TVs, did U.S. managers start living his quality philosophy.[32]

Although these principles were originally applied to manufacturing tangible goods, the experiences of Spectrum Health remind us that service quality is vital as well. Quality is also enhanced when companies customize goods and services to an individual consumer's wishes. Choices at Starbucks give consumers literally thousands of variations on the drinks they

University of Pennsylvania School of Medicine determined that a patient's risk of dying was not significantly less at hospitals that scored well on Medicare's quality measures.[35] But certainly, if you enter a hospital, you hope to come out alive! Only when you move beyond broad, generic concepts like "quality" and identify specific quality requirements can you identify problems, target needs, set performance standards more precisely, and deliver world-class value.

The service economy touches all industries

As we noted in the discussion of quality, important quality measures often pertain to the level of service customers receive. This dimension of quality is particularly important because the service sector now dominates the U.S. economy. The value of services produced in the United States is much more than one and a half times the value of tangible goods produced.[36] The total number of jobs in service companies—not including retailing, wholesaling, and government workers—is nearly five times the number in manufacturing companies. And that pattern is expected to intensify. The Bureau of Labor Statistics projects that the fastest-growing job categories will be almost entirely services and retailing jobs, and the jobs expected to see

> " "The most valuable commodity isn't soybeans but service . . . The human touch is what's going to propel our 'commodified' business models into the next century and beyond. I feel terribly privileged to be alive at such an exciting time in history."
>
> —Jonathan Hoenig, founder, Capitalistpig Asset Management[38]

can order, whether it's half-caff or all caffeine, skim milk or soy milk, or shots of espresso and any of a variety of flavored syrups. Car buyers can go online to choose from hundreds of features to "build their own" Mini Cooper, down to the color of the light for the speedometer. And for a premium price, candy lovers can select M&M's candies bearing the message of their own creation.[33]

Providing world-class quality requires a thorough understanding of what quality really is.[34] Quality can be measured in terms of product performance, customer service, reliability (avoidance of failure or breakdowns), conformance to standards, durability, and aesthetics. At the beginning of this section, we mentioned how hospitals are using patient surveys to measure quality. However, a recent study conducted by the

the greatest declines are almost all in manufacturing.[37] Services include intangible products like insurance, hotel accommodations, medical care, and haircuts.

In a competitive context, **service** means giving customers what they want or need, when and where they want it. So service is focused on continually meeting the needs of customers to establish mutually beneficial long-term relationships. Service is also an important offering for many companies that sell tangible goods. Software companies, in addition to providing the actual programs, may help their customers identify requirements, set up computer systems, and perform maintenance. Stores offer a shopping environment and customer service along with the goods on their shelves. To improve service for a wider customer base, Best Buy adjusted its store environment so it would be more inviting to female shoppers. The chain's loud music and emphasis on high-tech features had been aimed at young men, but the store found that women influence 9 out of 10 consumer electronics purchases. Best Buy lowered the volume, dimmed the lighting, and trained staff to discuss what customers want the technology to do for them, rather than merely pointing out bells and whistles. The chain is also trying to hire more female salespeople.[39]

An important dimension of service quality is making it easy and enjoyable for customers to experience a service or to buy and use products. The Detroit Institute of Arts recently hired Sven Gierlinger, a manager from the Ritz-Carlton hotel chain, noted for its exceptional level of service, to be its vice president of museum operations. As the art museum prepared for a grand reopening following a major renovation, Gierlinger analyzed the types of customer interactions that occur in a museum, identifying ways to make the experience more pleasant. He also developed programs to train the staff in customer service and worked with his staff to identify ways to customize services, such as offering tours tailored to the interests of particular groups.[40]

Do it better *and* faster

Google constantly improves its search product at a rapid rate. In fact, its entire culture is based on rapid innovation. Sheryl Sandberg, a Google vice president, once made a mistake because she was moving too fast to plan carefully. Although the mistake cost the company a few million dollars, Google cofounder Larry Page responded to her explanation and apology by saying he was actually glad she had made the mistake. It showed that Sandberg appreciated the company's values. Page told her, "I want to run a company where we are moving too quickly and doing too much, not being too cautious and doing too little. If we don't have any of these mistakes, we're just not taking enough risks."[41]

While it's unlikely that Google actually favors mistakes over money-making ideas, Page's statement expressed an appreciation that in the modern business environment, **speed**—rapid execution, response, and delivery of results—often separates the winners from the losers. How fast can you develop and get a new product to market? How quickly can you respond to customer requests? You are far better off if you are faster than the competition—and if you can respond quickly to your competitors' actions. Speed isn't everything—you can't get sloppy in your quest to be first. But other things being equal, faster companies are more likely to be the winners, slow ones the losers.

Speed is no longer just a goal of some companies; it is a strategic imperative. Speed combined with quality is a measure that a company is operating efficiently. In the auto industry, getting faster is essential just for keeping up with the competition. A recent study found that the top assembly plant in the United States was Ford's Atlanta facility, where employees needed just 15.4 hours to assemble a vehicle. Compare that with the 1980s, when GM employees needed 40 hours to assemble a vehicle.[42] Another important measure of speed in the auto industry is the time the company takes to go from product concept to availability of the vehicle in the showroom. During the 1980s, that time was about 30 or 40 months. Today Toyota has cut the process to an average of 24 months; it needed just 22 months to launch its Tundra pickup.[43]

Low costs help you price to sell

Walmart keeps driving hard to find new ways to cut billions of dollars from its already very low distribution costs. It leads the industry in efficient distribution, but competitors are copying Walmart's methods, so the efficiency no longer gives it as much of an advantage. To stay on top of the game, Walmart has urged its suppliers to use radio-frequency ID (RFID) tags on products for instantaneous identification, but so far this high-tech tracking system has not delivered on its promised savings.[44] Walmart also has sought to keep costs down by scheduling store employees more efficiently. It recently introduced a computerized system that schedules employees based on each store's sales, transactions, units sold, and customer traffic. It compares seven weeks' worth of data in those areas with the prior year's performance and uses the results to determine how many employees will be needed during which hours. The system is intended to schedule just enough workers, with full staffing only at the busiest times of day and days of the week, so it requires more flexibility from Walmart's employees.[45]

Walmart's efforts are aimed at **cost competitiveness**, which means keeping costs low enough so that the company can realize profits and price its products (goods or services) at levels that are attractive to consumers. Toyota's efforts to trim product development processes are also partly aimed at cost competitiveness. Making the processes more efficient through collaboration between design and manufacturing employees eliminates wasteful steps and procedures. Needless to say, if you can offer a desirable product at a lower price, it is more likely to sell.

As Paul Graham has seen personally, start-up firms typically practice cost competitiveness out of necessity. Graham's company, Y Combinator, provides seed funding to start-ups, and he observes how new companies keep their expenses down because they simply don't have much to spend. A start-up's total information technology could be just a few laptops connected to the Internet and running free Web-based software. Graham says lean times can remind managers to think about whether all their expenses are necessary: "You may as well use [a slowdown] as an excuse to clean out all the expensive crap you have lying around."[46] Money can be wasted in countless ways, and savings can come from the most unexpected places. You want everyone in the company looking for new ways to keep costs under control.

Managing your costs and keeping them down requires being efficient: accomplishing your goals by using your resources wisely and minimizing waste. Little things can save big money, but cost cuts involve trade-offs. That explains some of the growth in the market for private jets. Flying on a private jet is more expensive than buying a ticket on a commercial airline. But for a highly paid, frequently traveling business executive, the time spent hanging around an airport can become more costly than the cost of a jet. If the company can arrange to participate in a service such as NetJets, where the company buys only shares in a jet with the rights to use it, this can trim the price and make the arrangement even more beneficial.[47]

 One manager with a reputation for meeting this challenge skillfully is Mark Hurd, chief executive of Hewlett-Packard. For Hurd, operating efficiently is the main goal of a necessary and ongoing effort to look hard at all the company's numbers and identify areas where the company can get the job done with less. For example, HP improved the efficiency of its information technology (IT) group by cutting the number of its software applications from 6,000 to 1,500, reducing the number of data centers from 85 to 6, and laying off 11,000 of its 19,000 IT staffers. Similarly, if any new initiative doesn't promise adequate returns, it also gets the ax.

Critics question whether HP under Hurd is investing enough in innovation for the future, but at least in the short term, the drive for efficiency has positioned Hewlett-Packard to handle difficult times. In the recent recession, HP forecasted a sales decline but expected its profits would actually rise. That's not so strange when you consider that even as HP reduced staffing in support departments like IT, it was increasing its sales force and helping them target HP's most profitable goods and services.[48]

One reason every company must worry about cost is that consumers can easily compare prices on the Internet from thousands of competitors. PriceGrabber, mySimon, and Froogle are only a few of the search tools that can generate lists of prices at which a product is available from various suppliers. Consumers looking to buy popular items, such as cameras, printers, and plane fares, can go online to research the best models and the best deals. If you can't cut costs and offer attractive prices, you can't compete.

The best companies deliver all five advantages

Don't assume that you can settle for delivering just one of the five competitive advantages: low cost alone, or quality alone, for example. The best managers and companies deliver them all.

Virginia Mason Medical Center, like many hospitals, felt challenged in delivering low costs along with high quality and superior services. Virginia Mason has a reputation for high-quality care, but it was losing money treating certain patients. Complicated, high-tech procedures generate higher fees, but they aren't necessarily what a patient needs the most. Some patients may benefit more from a simple doctor visit, but that's not as profitable. So Virginia Mason collaborated with Aetna, an insurer that pays for 10 percent of the medical center's business, and with local employers that provide coverage for their employees through Aetna. Together, the companies renegotiated the standard procedures physicians would follow and the rates Aetna would pay so that some of the most expensive conditions could be treated in ways that were ultimately more economical to insure but paid for at higher rates that would be profitable for Virginia Mason. The facility presented the plan to its department heads, helping them pay attention to how their decisions affect the cost of care. Virginia Mason has also improved quality through measures that enhance speed—in this case, cutting waiting times for patients, such as a reduction in the four-hour wait for chemotherapy to 90 minutes.[49]

Trade-offs may occur among the five sources of competitive advantage, but this doesn't need to be a zero-sum game where one has to suffer at the expense of another. Avon focused on cost savings when it contracted with IBM Global Services to handle human resources tasks such as payroll and benefits management. Turning over those responsibilities to a company that specializes in performing them efficiently also frees Avon to concentrate on innovating in areas it knows best: direct selling cosmetics to new customers. Like many executives, Avon's CEO, Andrea Jung, is well aware of China's potential. In 1998, that country lifted a ban on door-to-door selling, and Jung has since launched an effort to sell cosmetics to Chinese consumers through hundreds of thousands of representatives who are licensed with the government.[50] Avon also has tapped into the trend toward customization by introducing the Hook Up Connector, a packaging product that allows consumers to snap together items of their choice, such as a lipstick and mascara.[51]

Ⓛ Ⓞ 3 **WHAT YOU NEED TO KNOW . . .**

How are the functions of management evolving in today's business environment?

THE FUNCTIONS OF MANAGEMENT

Management is the process of working with people and resources to accomplish organizational goals. Good managers do those things both effectively and efficiently:

- To be *effective* is to achieve organizational goals.

- To be *efficient* is to achieve goals with minimal waste of resources, that is, to make the best possible use of money, time, materials, and people.

Some managers fail on both criteria, or focus on one at the expense of another. The best managers maintain a clear focus on both effectiveness *and* efficiency. These definitions have been around for a long time. But as you know, business is changing radically. The real issue is what to *do*.[52]

Although the context of business and the specifics of doing business are changing, there are still plenty of timeless principles that make great managers, and great companies, great. While fresh thinking and new approaches are required now more than ever, much of what has already been learned about successful management practices remains relevant, useful, and adaptable, with fresh thinking, to the 21st-century business environment.

In the business world today, the great executives not only adapt to changing conditions but also apply—fanatically, rigorously, consistently, and with discipline—the fundamental management principles. These fundamentals include the four traditional functions of management: planning, organizing, leading, and controlling. They remain as relevant as ever, and they still provide the fundamentals that are needed in start-ups as much as in established corporations. But their form has evolved.

Planning puts you on course to deliver value

Planning is specifying the goals to be achieved and deciding in advance the appropriate actions needed to achieve those goals. Planning activities include analyzing current situations, anticipating the future, determining objectives, deciding in what types of activities the company will engage, choosing corporate and business strategies, and determining the resources needed to achieve the organization's goals. Plans set the stage for action and for major achievements.

For the new business environment, the planning function is more dynamically described as *delivering strategic value*. **Value** is a complex concept.[53] Fundamentally, it describes the monetary amount associated with how well a job, task, good, or service meets users' needs. Those users might be business owners, customers, employees, society, and even nations. The better you meet those needs (in terms of quality, speed, efficiency, and so on), the more value you deliver. That value is "strategic" when it contributes to meeting the organization's goals. On a personal level, you should periodically ask yourself and your boss, "How

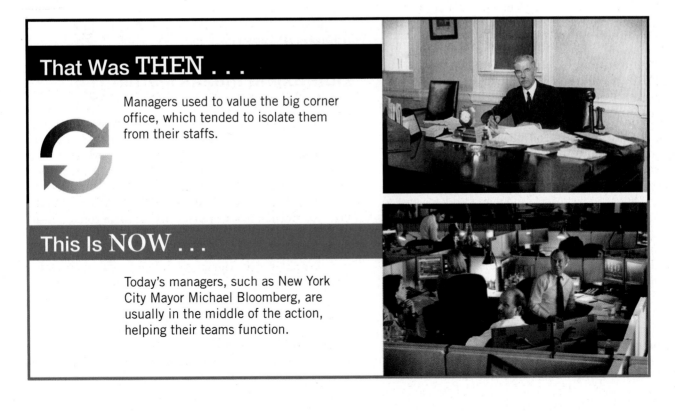

That Was THEN . . .

Managers used to value the big corner office, which tended to isolate them from their staffs.

This Is NOW . . .

Today's managers, such as New York City Mayor Michael Bloomberg, are usually in the middle of the action, helping their teams function.

can I add value?" Answering that question will enhance your contributions, job performance, and career.

Historically, planning was a top-down approach in which top executives establish business plans and tell others to implement them. Now and in the future, delivering strategic value is a continual process in which people throughout the organization use their brains and the brains of customers, suppliers, and other stakeholders to identify oppor-

> Shona Brown of Google makes decisions about organizing. She says, "The company's goal is to determine precisely the amount of management it needs—and then use a little bit less."

tunities to create, seize, strengthen, and sustain competitive advantage. This dynamic process swirls around the objective of creating more and more value for the customer. Effectively creating value requires fully considering a new and changing set of stakeholders and issues, including the government, the natural environment, globalization, and the dynamic economy in which ideas are king and entrepreneurs are both formidable competitors and potential collaborators. You will learn about these and related topics in Chapter 3 (ethics and corporate social responsibility), Chapter 4 (planning and strategic management), and Chapter 5 (entrepreneurship).

Organizing brings together the resources you need

Organizing is assembling and coordinating the human, financial, physical, informational, and other resources needed to achieve goals. Organizing activities include attracting people to the organization, specifying job responsibilities, grouping jobs into work units, marshaling and allocating resources, and creating conditions so that people and things work together to achieve maximum success.

The organizing function's goal is to *build a dynamic organization*. Historically, organizing involved creating an organization chart by identifying business functions, establishing reporting relationships, and having a personnel department that administered plans, programs, and paperwork. Now and in the future, effective managers will be using new forms of organizing and viewing their people as their most valuable resources. They will build organizations that are flexible and adaptive, particularly in response to competitive threats and customer needs. Progressive

human resource practices that attract and retain the very best of a highly diverse population will be essential aspects of the successful company. You will learn about these topics in Chapter 6 (organization structure), Chapter 7 (human resources management), Chapter 8 (managing the diverse workforce), and Chapter 14 (innovation and change).

Leading mobilizes your people

Leading is stimulating people to be high performers. It includes motivating and communicating with employees, individually and in groups. Leaders maintain close day-to-day contact with people, guiding and inspiring them toward achieving team and organizational goals. Leading takes place in teams, departments, and divisions, as well as at the tops of large organizations.

In earlier textbooks, the leading function described how managers motivate workers to come to work and execute top management's plans by doing their jobs. Today and in the future, managers must be good at *mobilizing people* to contribute their ideas—to use their brains in ways never needed or dreamed of in the past.

Today's managers must rely on a very different kind of leadership (Chapter 9) that empowers and motivates people (Chapter 10). Far more than in the past, great work must be done via great teamwork (Chapter 11), both within work groups and across group boundaries. Underlying these processes will be effective interpersonal and organizational communication (Chapter 12).

Controlling means learning and changing

Planning, organizing, and leading do not guarantee success. The fourth function, **controlling**, monitors performance and implements necessary changes. By controlling, managers make sure the organization's resources are being used as planned and that the organization is meeting its goals for quality and safety.

Control must include monitoring. If you have any doubts that this function is important, consider some control breakdowns that caused serious problems. After an explosion at BP's Texas oil refinery caused the deaths of 15 people, investigations suggested that widespread failure to implement safety measures was behind the tragedy. Investigators reported that management at BP had been focused on cost-cutting measures, which contributed to unsafe working conditions. Despite a year of record profits, BP's chief executive announced plans to retire early, and his bonus was cut almost in half.[55] Other lapses in controlling can hurt customers. A recent outbreak of salmonella infections—which can cause fever, diarrhea, dehydration, and even death—was traced to Peter Pan and Great Value peanut butter made by ConAgra Foods in its Sylvester, Georgia, factory. Processing the peanuts generally kills salmonella and other germs, so the likely culprit was contamination of jars or equipment. ConAgra quickly announced a recall, but more than 400 people in 44 states reported being infected, and 71 of them had to be hospitalized. The recall alone was expected to cost ConAgra at least $50 million; lawsuits, cleanup of the facility, and damage to the brands' reputation are adding to those costs.[56]

When managers implement their plans, they often find that things are not working out as planned. The controlling function

of the company's workforce. But Musk also was responsible for raising $55 million of capital from investors, and the Roadster is now in full production.[57]

Successful organizations, large and small, pay close attention to the controlling function. But today and for the future, the key managerial

In a recent nationwide survey, employees had mixed reviews of their manager's leadership skills. As a result, a manager who excels in leadership is especially valuable.[54]

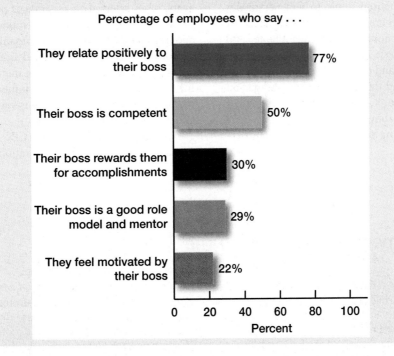

Percentage of employees who say . . .

They relate positively to their boss — 77%

Their boss is competent — 50%

Their boss rewards them for accomplishments — 30%

Their boss is a good role model and mentor — 29%

They feel motivated by their boss — 22%

Percent (0, 20, 40, 60, 80, 100)

makes sure that goals are met. It asks and answers the question, "Are our actual outcomes consistent with our goals?" It then makes adjustments as needed. Elon Musk of Tesla Motors has applied this function to make needed changes at his firm. Like many start-ups, Tesla has hit a few potholes along the way. Conflicts with the firm's founder and technical problems during development pushed back the launch of the company's first car by more than a year, causing cash flow problems. Musk was forced to close one office and lay off nearly 25 percent

challenges are far more dynamic than in the past; they involve continually *learning and changing*. Controls must still be in place, as described in Chapter 13. But new technologies and other innovations (Chapter 14) make it possible to achieve controls in more effective ways, to help all people throughout a company and across company boundaries—including customers and suppliers—to use their brains, learn, make a variety of new contributions, and help the organization change in ways that forge a successful future.

Managing requires all four functions

As a manager, your typical day will not be neatly divided into the four functions. You will be doing many things more or less simultaneously.[58] Your days will be busy and fragmented, with interruptions, meetings, and firefighting. There will be plenty of activities that you wish you could be doing but can't seem to get to. These activities will include all four management functions.

Some managers are particularly interested in, devoted to, or skilled in one or two of the four functions. But you should devote enough attention and resources to *all four* functions. You can be a skilled planner and controller, but if you organize your people improperly or fail to inspire them to perform at high levels, you will not be realizing your potential as a manager. Likewise, it does no good to be the kind of manager who loves to organize and lead but doesn't really understand where to go or how to determine whether you are on the right track. Good managers don't neglect any of the four management functions. Knowing what they are, you can periodically ask yourself whether you are devoting adequate attention to *all* of them.

The four management functions apply to you personally, as well. You must find ways to create value; organize for your own personal effectiveness; mobilize your own talents and skills as well as those of others; monitor your performance; and constantly learn, develop, and change for the future. As you proceed through this book and this course, we encourage you not merely to do your "textbook learning" of an impersonal course subject but to think about these issues from a personal perspective as well, using the ideas for your own personal development.

L O 4   WHAT YOU NEED TO KNOW . . .

How does the nature of management vary at different organizational levels?

MANAGEMENT LEVELS AND SKILLS

Organizations—particularly large organizations—have many levels. In this section, you will learn about the types of managers found at three different organizational levels:

- Top level
- Middle level
- Frontline

Top managers strategize and lead

Top-level managers are the organization's senior executives and are responsible for its overall management. Top-level managers, often referred to as *strategic managers*, are supposed to focus on long-term issues and emphasize the survival, growth, and overall effectiveness of the organization.

Top managers are concerned not only with the organization as a whole but also with the interaction between the organization and its external environment. This interaction often requires managers to work extensively with outside individuals and organizations.

The chief executive officer (CEO) is one type of top-level manager found in large corporations. This individual is the

Women Helping Women One Bead at a Time

Several years ago, three women—Torkin Wakefield, her daughter Devin Hibbard, and friend Ginny Jordan—were traveling in the African nation of Uganda when they met women who were making colorful bead jewelry from recycled paper. The craftswomen would find scraps of paper—magazines, newspapers, or brochures—and roll them tightly into beads. Then they dipped the beads in several coats of varnish to make them glossy and hard. From the beads, they crafted necklaces and bracelets. The Ugandan craftswomen had all the makings of a business but no market for their products.

The three American women recognized an opportunity to market the Ugandan women's jewelry and help them work their way out of war-torn poverty. So they founded BeadforLife, an organization that sells the jewelry through "bead parties" at host homes, much like Tupperware storage containers and Tastefully Simple gourmet food mixes. Proceeds go back to the Ugandan women, who use the money for health care, education, home ownership, and training for new careers.

For BeadforLife to succeed, its founders must be strong leaders. They must be able to communicate their vision in two directions: to the Ugandan craftswomen and to the American party hosts. As motivators, they establish links between the groups of women to inspire them. The founders have past experience in leadership roles—in health care and other not-for-profit organizations. So they understand the

importance of connecting and mobilizing all members of an organization.

In Uganda, Torkin Wakefield conducted classes for the craftswomen to help them improve the quality of the jewelry and develop new styles to appeal to Western consumers. In the United States, Devin Hibbard and Ginny Jordan planned and organized a marketing strategy. They spread the word about the Ugandan women and their bead jewelry, and U.S. women responded.

As the plan for selling the jewelry directly through home events took shape, the three founders added new elements to the home parties. BeadforLife now provides not only the jewelry to sell but also educational materials, Ugandan recipes, biographies of the primary strategic manager of the firm and has authority over everyone else. Others include the chief operating officer (COO), company presidents, vice presidents, and members of the top management team. As companies are appreciating the potential of technology and knowledge management to help them achieve and maintain a competitive advantage, more are creating the position of chief information officer (CIO). At defense contractor Northrop Grumman, CIO Tom Shelman used to focus on managing the company's computer systems. But in the last few years, he has become directly involved with strategy; Shelman's job includes meeting with customers to help identify ways the company can use its technology to serve them better and help the company grow.[59]

Traditionally, the role of top-level managers has been to set overall direction by formulating strategy and controlling resources. But now more top managers are called on to be not only strategic architects but also true organizational leaders. As leaders, they must create and articulate a broader corporate purpose with which people can identify—and one to which people will enthusiastically commit.

Middle managers bring strategies to life

As the name implies, **middle-level managers** are located in the organization's hierarchy below top-level management and above the frontline managers. Sometimes called *tactical managers,* they are responsible for translating the general goals and plans developed by strategic managers into more specific objectives and activities.

Traditionally, the role of the middle manager is to be an administrative controller who bridges the gap between higher and lower levels. Middle-level managers take corporate objectives and break them down into business unit targets; put together separate business unit plans from the units below them for higher-level corporate review; and serve as linchpins of internal communication, interpreting and broadcasting top management's priorities downward and channeling and translating information from the front lines upward.

> In a recent poll of chief information officers, half said their responsibilities extend beyond information technology to include top-level concerns such as developing the company's strategy.[60]

craftswomen, African music CDs, and a motivational DVD about BeadforLife's founders. All of these products help bring the organization's members to life with those from half a world away and allow customers to participate and interact with the craftswomen.

BeadforLife is actually changing lives. "One of the things I've been thinking about recently is the difference between charity . . . and programs that are more about empowerment," says Torkin Wakefield. "And I like to think that BeadforLife is really about helping hardworking people become individuals who can sustain themselves into the future long after Beadfor-Life is a fond memory."

 **Discussion Questions**

- BeadforLife's founders face a unique challenge: guiding and inspiring two distinct and separate workforces on two very different continents. Describe ways in which they might accomplish this and suggest possible future programs they could use.
- As the BeadforLife organization grows, how do you predict the roles of its three leaders might change?

SOURCES: Organization Web site, http://www.beadforlife.org, accessed May 15, 2009; "BeadforLife Program Helps Lift Ugandans Out of Poverty," *Online News Hour,* Public Broadcasting Service, April 16, 2009, http://www.pbs.org; Shari L. Berg, "Beads Project Helps Ugandans," *Pittsburgh Post-Gazette,* December 4, 2008, http://www.post-gazette.com.

As a stereotype, the term *middle manager* connotes mediocrity: unimaginative people defending the status quo. But middle managers are closer than top managers to day-to-day operations, customers, and frontline managers and employees, so they know the problems. They also have many creative ideas—often better than their bosses'. Good middle managers provide the operating skills and practical problem solving that keep the company working.[61]

Frontline managers: the vital link to employees

Frontline managers, or *operational managers,* are lower-level managers who supervise the operations of the organization. These managers often have titles such as *supervisor* or *sales manager.* They are directly involved with nonmanagement employees, implementing the specific plans developed with middle managers. This role is critical, because operational managers are the link between management and nonmanagement personnel. Your first management position probably will fit into this category.

Traditionally, frontline managers were directed and controlled from above, to make sure that they successfully implemented operations to support the company strategy. But in leading companies, the role has expanded. Operational execution remains vital, but in leading companies, frontline managers are increasingly called on to be innovative and entrepreneurial, managing for growth and new business development.

Managers on the front line—usually newer, younger managers—are crucial to creating and sustaining quality, innovation, and other drivers of financial performance.[62] In outstanding organizations, talented frontline managers are not only *allowed* to initiate new activities but are *expected* to by their top- and middle-level managers. And they receive the freedom, incentives, and support to find ways to do so.[63]

Table 1.1 elaborates on the changing aspects of different management levels. You will learn about each of these aspects of management throughout this course.

Today's working leaders shoulder broad responsibilities

The trend today is toward less hierarchy and more teamwork. In small firms—and in large companies that have adapted to the times—managers have strategic, tactical, *and* operational responsibilities. They are *complete* businesspeople; they have knowledge of all business functions, are accountable for results, and focus on serving customers both inside and outside their firms. All of this requires the ability to think strategically, translate strategies into

TABLE 1.1	Transformation of Management Roles and Activities		
	Frontline Managers	**Middle-Level Managers**	**Top-Level Managers**
Changing Roles	From operational implementers to aggressive entrepreneurs	From administrative controllers to supportive coaches	From resource allocators to institutional leaders
Key Activities	Creating and pursuing new growth opportunities for the business	Developing individuals and supporting their activities	Establishing high performance standards
	Attracting and developing resources	Linking dispersed knowledge and skills across units	Institutionalizing a set of norms to support cooperation and trust
	Managing continuous improvement within the unit	Managing the tension between short-term purpose and long-term ambition	Creating an overarching corporate purpose and ambition

SOURCE: Adapted from C. Bartlett and S. Goshal, "The Myth of the Generic Manager: New Personal Competencies for New Management Roles," *California Management Review* 40, no. 1, Fall 1997, pp. 92–116.

specific objectives, coordinate resources, and do real work with lower-level people.

In short, today's best managers can do it all; they are "working leaders."[64] They focus on relationships with other people and on achieving results. They don't just make decisions, give orders, wait for others to produce, and then evaluate results. They get dirty, do hard work themselves, solve problems, and produce value.

What does all of this mean in practice? How do managers spend their time—what do they actually do? A classic study of top executives found that they spend their time engaging in 10 key activities or roles, falling into three categories:[65]

1. **Interpersonal roles:**
   - *Leader*—Staffing, training, and motivating people
   - *Liaison*—Maintaining a network of outside contacts who provide information and favors
   - *Figurehead*—Performing symbolic duties (ceremonies and serving other social and legal demands)

2. **Informational roles:**
   - *Monitor*—Seeking and receiving information to develop a thorough understanding of the organization and its environment; serving as the "nerve center" of communication

● **FRONTLINE MANAGERS** Lower-level managers who supervise the operational activities of the organization.

● **TECHNICAL SKILL** The ability to perform a specialized task involving a particular method or process.

● **CONCEPTUAL AND DECISION SKILLS** Skills pertaining to the ability to identify and resolve problems for the benefit of the organization and its members.

● **INTERPERSONAL AND COMMUNICATION SKILLS** People skills; the ability to lead, motivate, and communicate effectively with others.

- *Disseminator*—Transmitting information from source to source, sometimes interpreting and integrating diverse perspectives
- *Spokesperson*—Speaking on behalf of the organization about plans, policies, actions, and results

3. **Decisional roles:**
   - *Entrepreneur*—Searching for new business opportunities and initiating new projects to create change
   - *Disturbance handler*—Taking corrective action during crises or other conflicts
   - *Resource allocator*—Providing funding and other resources to units or people; includes making or approving significant organizational decisions
   - *Negotiator*—Engaging in negotiations with parties outside the organization as well as inside (for example, resource exchanges)

Even though the study was done decades ago, it remains highly relevant as a description of what executives do. And even though the study focused on top executives, managers at all levels engage in all these activities. As you study the list, you might ask yourself, "Which of these activities do I enjoy most (and least)? Where do I excel (and not excel)? Which would I like to improve?" Whatever your answers, you will be learning more about these activities throughout this course.

Ⓛ Ⓞ 5 **WHAT YOU NEED TO KNOW . . .**
Can you define the skills you need to be an effective manager?

Managers need three broad skills

Performing management functions and roles, and achieving competitive advantage, are the cornerstones of a manager's job. However, understanding this fact does not ensure success. Managers need a variety of skills to *do* these things *well*. Skills are specific abilities that result from knowledge, information, practice, and aptitude. Although managers need many individual skills, which you will learn about throughout the text, consider three general categories:[66]

- Technical skills
- Interpersonal and communication skills
- Conceptual and decision skills

First-timers greatly underestimate the challenges of the many technical, human, and conceptual skills required.[67] But when the key management functions are performed by managers who have these critical management skills, high performance results.

A **technical skill** is the ability to perform a specialized task that involves a certain method or process. Most people develop a set of technical skills to complete the activities that are part of their daily work lives. The technical skills you learn in school will give you the opportunity to get an entry-level position; they will also help you as a manager. For example, your accounting and finance courses will develop the technical skills you need to understand and manage an organization's financial resources.

Conceptual and decision skills involve the ability to identify and resolve problems for the benefit of the organization and everyone concerned. Managers use these skills when they consider the overall objectives and strategy of the firm, the interactions among different parts of the organization, and the role of the business in its external environment. As you acquire greater responsibility, you must exercise your conceptual and decision skills increasingly often. You will confront issues that involve all aspects of the organization and must consider a larger and more interrelated set of decision factors. Much of this text is devoted to enhancing your conceptual and decision skills, but experience plays an important part in their development.

Interpersonal and communication skills influence the manager's ability to work well with people. These skills are often called *people skills*. Managers spend the great majority of their time interacting with people,[68] and they must develop their abilities to lead, motivate, and communicate effectively with those around them. Your people skills often make the difference in how high you go. Management professor Michael Morris explains, "At a certain level in business, you're living and dying on your social abilities. . . . [Knowledge of a particular field] gets you in the door, but social intelligence gets you to the top."[69] Supporting this view, a survey of senior executives and managers found that more than 6 out of 10 said they base hiring and promotion decisions on a candidate's "likeability." Almost as many (62 versus 63 percent) said they base these decisions on skills, presumably referring to technical skills.[70]

Professor Morris, quoted in the previous paragraph, has helped teach people skills to MBA candidates at Columbia Business School. He emphasizes that it is vital for future managers to realize the importance of these skills in getting a job, keeping it, and performing well, especially in the 21st century, when so many managers supervise independent-minded knowledge workers. He explains, "You have to get high performance out of people in your organization who you don't have any authority over. You need to read other people, know their motivators, know how you affect them."[71]

● **EMOTIONAL INTELLIGENCE** The skills of understanding yourself, managing yourself, and dealing effectively with others.

The importance of these skills varies by managerial level. Technical skills are most important early in your career. Conceptual and decision skills become more important than technical skills as you rise higher in the company. But inter personal skills are important throughout your career, at every level of management.

Several biomedical companies in California's Orange County collaborated to provide training because they observed that managers originally hired for their technical expertise needed to develop their people skills so that they could handle higher-level assignments. In scientific companies like these, managers are often scientists and are more comfortable conducting and evaluating research projects than communicating with and motivating people. However, as they tackle management jobs, they need to lead a team of experts in various disciplines, who may be more interested in the advancement of their science and the respect of their peers than the strategy of their employer. Orange County's training program, called the Leadership and Management Program for Technology Professionals, teaches leadership skills and jargon-free communication, as well as other management skills such as budgeting.[72]

ⓁⓄ **6 WHAT YOU NEED TO KNOW . . .**

Can you identify the principles that will help you manage your career?

YOU AND YOUR CAREER

At the beginning of your career, your contribution to your employer depends on your own performance; that's all you're responsible for. But on becoming a manager, you are responsible for a whole group. To use an orchestra analogy, instead of playing an instrument, you're a conductor, coordinating others' efforts.[73] The challenge is much greater than most first-time managers expect it to be.

Throughout your career you'll need to lead teams effectively and influence people over whom you have no authority, so human skills are especially important. These days, businesspeople talk about **emotional intelligence**,[74] or "EQ"—which combines three categories of skills:

1. Understanding yourself—including strengths and limitations

2. Managing yourself—dealing with emotions, making good decisions, seeking and using feedback, exercising self-control

3. Dealing effectively with others—listening, showing empathy, motivating, leading, and so on

One manager with these skills is Rita Burns, vice president of communications and marketing at Memorial Health System in Colorado Springs. Self-knowledge led Burns to pursue a career that brings together her talent for listening (she earned a degree in journalism) and her love of health care (as a young volunteer in hospitals, she realized that although she loved the hospital environment, she got too emotionally attached to be an effective nurse). Burns says she finds it easy to appreciate other points of view: "No matter where I am or what the situation is, I can find something to have a conversation about." Her boss, senior vice president Ron Burnside, describes her as a talented communicator, and a colleague at the American Heart Association says Burns possesses a "collaborative spirit," which helps her see how Memorial Health System can cooperate with the association on joint projects.[75]

A common complaint about leaders, especially newly promoted ones who had been outstanding individual performers, is that they lack what is perhaps the most fundamental of EQ skills: empathy. The issue is not lack of ability to change (you can), but the lack of motivation to change (you should decide to do so as necessary).[76] William George, former chair and CEO of Medtronic, says some people can go a long way in their careers based on sheer determination and aggressiveness, but personal development including EQ ultimately becomes essential.[77] Research has found that executives who score low on EQ are less likely to be rated as excellent on their performance reviews, and their divisions tend not to perform as well.[78] A vice president at an aerospace company underwent a program to improve her EQ after colleagues kept complaining that she was overly demanding and put people down. An assessment found that she was self-aware but lacked social awareness. The vice president learned to respond only after calming herself, as well as to explore colleagues' ideas rather than demeaning them. Before long, her colleagues began to appreciate the change, and her career took a more successful path.[79]

What should you do to forge a successful, gratifying career? You are well advised to be both a specialist and a generalist, to be self-reliant and connected, to actively manage your relationship with your organization, and to be fully aware of what is required not only to survive but also to thrive in today's world.

Be both a specialist and a generalist

If you think your career will be as a specialist, think again. Chances are, you will not want to stay forever in strictly technical jobs with no managerial responsibilities. Accountants are promoted to accounting department heads and team leaders, sales representatives become sales managers, writers become editors, and nurses become nursing directors. As your responsibilities increase, you must deal with more people, understand more about other aspects of the organization, and make bigger and more complex decisions. Beginning to learn now about these managerial challenges may yield benefits sooner than you think.

It will help if you can become both a specialist and a generalist.[80] Seek to become a *specialist:* you should be an expert in something. This expertise will give you specific skills that help you provide concrete, identifiable value to your firm and to customers. And over time, you should learn to be a *generalist,* knowing enough about a variety of business disciplines so that you can think strategically and work with different perspectives.

Patricia Calkins broadened her focus gradually and ambitiously from specialties in the sciences, expanding first to engineering and then to management. She started her career with AT&T's Western Electric subsidiary as a chemist. When she was considering a master's degree in chemistry, she heeded advice to develop her career opportunities by studying engineering. Once Calkins had her master's degree in civil and environmental engineering, the company saw her management talent and wanted to promote her. So she returned to school for another master's degree, this time in business administration. She developed her generalist skills by consulting and from that work moved to her current—and favorite—position as vice president of environment, health, and safety at Xerox.[81]

There's another advantage to being both a specialist and a generalist: it can allow you to indulge in the causes or activities you care about most. For example, Josh Ruxin, a professor and founder of Access Project, a program that applies management systems to hospitals in Rwanda, got started on his career path when he traveled to Ethiopia as a teenager. "That changed the rest of my life," Ruxin recalls. "I

couldn't believe that people so desperately poor were living on the same planet as we were." Ruxin earned a doctorate in medical history and joined a management consulting firm, where he honed his management skills. When he got a chance to follow a spin-off venture focusing on economic development in underdeveloped regions, he took it.

In Africa, "I realized health care there had to get fixed before these economies had a chance," says Ruxin. So he formed Access Project. Now he uses both his general and his specialized skills to help improve the health care system in Rwanda.[82]

what is your EQ?

Patricia Calkins, VP of Environment, Health, and Safety at Xerox, became successful by being both a specialist and a generalist. She developed her specialty skills in the sciences and in business administration, and then acquired her generalist skills as a business consultant. What steps do you need to take to become a specialist and a generalist?

Be self-reliant

To be self-reliant means to take full responsibility for yourself, your actions, and your career, as Patricia Calkins did when she furthered her education and tackled consulting assignments that applied her technical knowledge to the business world. You cannot count on your boss or your company to take care of you. A useful metaphor is to think of yourself as a business, with you as president and sole employee. Based on her experience with

Sun Microsystems, Vicky Farrow offers the following advice to help people assume responsibility for their own careers:[83]

- Think of yourself as a business.
- Define your product: What is your area of expertise?
- Know your target market: To whom are you going to sell this?
- Be clear on why your customer buys from you. What is your "value proposition"—what are you offering that causes your customer to use you?
- As in any business, strive for quality and customer satisfaction, even if your customer is just someone else in your organization—like your boss.
- Know your profession or field and what's going on there.
- Invest in your own growth and development, the way a company invests in research and development. What new products will you be able to provide?
- Be willing to consider changing your career.

Jordan Edelstein took ownership of his career; for him, that meant taking a leap into an industry he loved. After graduating from college, Edelstein had seized the first opportunity that came his way, as an analyst for Marketing Corporation of America, where he researched marketing strategies for a variety of clients. He realized he would rather be part of the companies that could actually implement those strategies, so he earned a master's degree in business and interned at General Mills. The company hired him as an assistant marketing manager.

Edelstein was successful, but during a business trip, as he was reading about Electronic Arts and its game Sims Online, he realized that this was an industry he felt passionate about, because it was "culturally relevant" and fun. Edelstein began researching jobs in the industry. When an opening came at Electronic Arts, Edelstein prepared for extensive interviews at the Orlando studio and California headquarters. He had to persuade dozens of people that his marketing expertise made up for his lack of experience with high-tech products. Evidently, Edelstein has real marketing talent: he landed what he identified as his dream job.[84]

To be self-reliant, find new ways to make your overall performance better. Take responsibility for change; be an innovator.[85] Don't just do your work and wait for orders; look for opportunities to contribute in new ways, develop new products and processes, and generate constructive change that strengthens the company and benefits customers and colleagues.

As in Jordan Edelstein's career, success requires more than talent; you also have to be willing to work hard. Research has found that the world-class performers in many fields reach the top tier only after ten years or more of hard work.[86] The key is to engage in consistent practice, looking at the results and identifying where to improve. It's easy to see how this works for violinists or basketball players, but what about business managers? The answer is to focus on getting better results each time you try

any business task, whether writing a report, chairing a meeting, or interpreting a financial statement. To know whether you're getting better, ask for feedback from customers, colleagues, and supervisors.

To develop your full potential, assess yourself, including your interests, aptitudes, and personal character strengths. Think about it, ask others who know you well, conduct a formal exercise in which you learn what others consider to be your "best self,"[87] and use the resources of recent advances in psychology to identify your signature strengths.[88] Consider the professional image and reputation you would like to develop,[89] and continue building your capabilities. In elaborating on these objectives, consider the suggestions found throughout this book and your courses.

Be connected

Being *connected* means having many good working relationships and interpersonal contacts and being a team player with strong interpersonal skills. For example, those who want to become partners in professional service organizations like accounting, advertising, and consulting firms strive constantly to build a network of contacts. Their "connectedness" goal is to work not only with lots of clients but also with a half dozen or more senior partners, including several from outside their home offices and some from outside their country. A study of new auditors showed that social relationships improved newcomers' knowledge of the organization and their jobs, their social integration into the firm, and their commitment to the organization.[90]

Social capital is the goodwill stemming from your social relationships, and it can be mobilized on your behalf. It aids career success, compensation, employment, team effectiveness, successful entrepreneurship, and relationships with suppliers and other outsiders.[91] Today much of that social capital can be tapped online, at social networking Web sites. Besides the purely social sites like MySpace and Facebook, some of these sites are aimed at helping people tap business networks. For example, LinkedIn has more than 8 million registered users, with membership growing rapidly as currently registered members invite colleagues, family members, and friends to sign up. Even busy executives are willing to give LinkedIn a try because it allows sharing only among people who agree to be connected; acquaintances can introduce others only with permission. Keith Taylor, chief financial officer of Corfino, which provides finance and accounting services, became a member of another company's board of directors as a result of a LinkedIn connection. Carl Taibl, an accountant in San Ramon, California, uses LinkedIn to research prospective client firms. If he doesn't already know someone in one of those firms, he looks for someone who can introduce him to a manager there.[92]

Look at this another way: all business is a function of human relationships.[93] Building competitive advantage depends not only on you but on other people. Management is personal. Commercial dealings are personal. Purchase decisions, repurchase decisions, and contracts all hinge on relationships. Even the biggest business deals—takeovers—are intensely personal and emotional. Without good work relationships, you are an outsider, not a good manager and leader.

Actively manage your relationship with your organization

Many of the previous comments suggest the importance of taking responsibility for your own actions and your own career. Unless you are self-employed and your own boss, one way to do this is to think about the nature of the relationship between you and your employer. Figure 1.1 shows two possible relationships—and you have some control over which relationship you will be in.

Relationship #1 is one in which you view yourself as an employee and passively expect your employer to tell you what to do and give you pay and benefits. Your employer is in charge, and you are a passive recipient of its actions. Your contributions are likely to be adequate but minimal—you won't make the added contributions that strengthen your organization, and if all organizational members take this perspective, the organization is not likely to be strong for the long run. Personally, you may lose your job, or keep your job in a declining organization, or receive few positive benefits from working there and either quit or become cynical and unhappy in your work.

In contrast, relationship #2 is a two-way relationship in which you and your organization both benefit from one another. The mind-set is different: instead of doing what you are told, you think about how you can contribute—and you act accordingly. To the extent that your organization values your contributions, you are likely to benefit in return by receiving full and fair rewards, support for further personal development, and a more gratifying work environment. If you think in broad terms about how you can help your company, and if others think like this as well, there is likely to be continuous improvement in the company's ability to innovate, cut costs, and deliver quality products quickly to an expanding customer base. As the company's bottom line strengthens, benefits accrue to shareholders as well as to you and other employees.

What contributions can you make? You can do your basic work. But you can, and should, go further. You can also figure out new ways to add value—by thinking of and implementing new ideas that improve processes and results. You can do this by using your technical knowledge and skills, as in developing a better information system, accounting technique, or sales technique.

You also can contribute with your conceptual and human skills and your managerial actions (see Figure 1.2). You can execute the essential management functions and deliver competitive advantage. You can deliver strategic value—the *planning* function. You can take actions that help build a more dynamic organization—the *organizing* function. You can mobilize people to contribute to their fullest potential—the *leading* function. And you can learn and change—and help your colleagues and company learn and change—to adapt to changing realities and forge a successful future—the *controlling* function.

Survive and thrive

Figure 1.3 shows a résumé that might help a person not just survive, but thrive in the 21st century. Don't be discouraged if your résumé doesn't match this idealized résumé—it's tough to match, especially early in life! But do think about the messages. It indicates the kinds of skills that companies need now more than ever—and therefore the skills you should consider working to develop and the experiences you might want to accumulate.

Now—far more than ever—you will be accountable for your actions and for results. In the past, people at many companies could show up, do an OK job, get a decent evaluation, and get a raise equal to the cost of living and maybe higher. Today managers must do more, better. Management scholar Peter Drucker, in

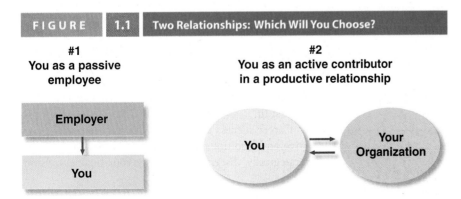

| FIGURE | 1.1 | Two Relationships: Which Will You Choose? |

#1
You as a passive employee

Employer
↓
You

#2
You as an active contributor in a productive relationship

You ⇄ **Your Organization**

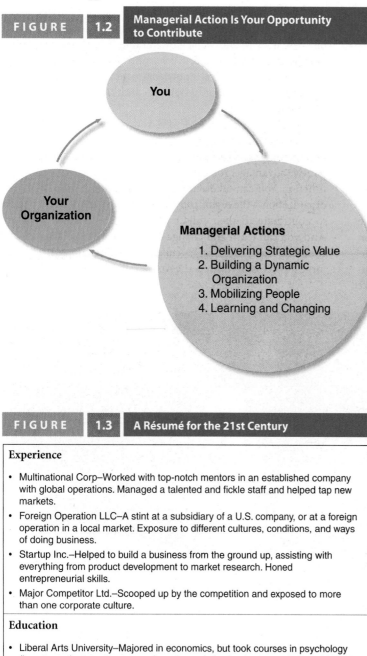

You

Your Organization

Managerial Actions

1. Delivering Strategic Value
2. Building a Dynamic Organization
3. Mobilizing People
4. Learning and Changing

Experience

- Multinational Corp–Worked with top-notch mentors in an established company with global operations. Managed a talented and fickle staff and helped tap new markets.
- Foreign Operation LLC–A stint at a subsidiary of a U.S. company, or at a foreign operation in a local market. Exposure to different cultures, conditions, and ways of doing business.
- Startup Inc.–Helped to build a business from the ground up, assisting with everything from product development to market research. Honed entrepreneurial skills.
- Major Competitor Ltd.–Scooped up by the competition and exposed to more than one corporate culture.

Education

- Liberal Arts University–Majored in economics, but took courses in psychology (how to motivate customers and employees), foreign language (the world is a lot bigger than the 50 states), and philosophy (to seek vision and meaning in your work).
- Graduate Studies–The subject almost didn't matter, so long as you developed your thinking and analytical skills.

Extracurricular

- Debating (where you learned to market ideas and think on your feet).
- Sports (where you learned discipline and teamwork).
- Volunteer work (where you learned to step outside your own narrow world to help others).
- Travel (where you learned about different cultures).

SOURCE: D. Brady, "Wanted: Eclectic Visionary with a Sense of Humor," *BusinessWeek*, August 28, 2000, p. 144. © 2009 Time Inc. All rights reserved.

considering what makes managers effective, notes that some are charismatic while some are not, and some are visionary while others are more numbers-oriented.[94] But successful executives do share some common practices:

- They ask "What needs to be done?" rather than "What do I want to do?"

- They write an action plan. They don't just think, they do, based on a sound, ethical plan.

- They take responsibility for decisions. This requires checking up, revisiting, and changing if necessary.

- They focus on opportunities rather than problems. Problems have to be solved, and problem solving prevents more damage. But exploiting opportunities is what creates great results.

This creative approach can help each employee stand out in some unique way. Career adviser Rachelle Canter advises identifying where you deliver superior results and thinking of that as your "brand." For instance, an executive might develop a track record of consistently improving productivity in various organizations, and an entry-level customer service worker might become the company's go-to employee for handling the toughest customers.[95]

Consider the different paths taken by three companies' information technology executives.[96] Dick Daniels, chief information officer for Capital One Auto Finance, enjoyed the various applications of data processing and took on every job he could in the field, rather than seeking out promotions. The experiences gave him an opportunity to communicate with people in various functions, making him valuable to the company overall when he was ready to move up to the executive level. Mark Hopkins, chief information officer (CIO) at Academic and Community Hospitals at the University of Pittsburgh Medical Center, started out on the computer side as a systems analyst; later he landed a job in administrative management of a hospital. The combined experience positioned him as an executive who could understand both business and IT issues. Finally, like Hopkins, Janice Malaszenko, vice president and CIO for Xerox Information Management, started out as a systems analyst. As she continued to take IT jobs with greater responsibility, she realized that she particularly enjoyed working for multinational companies, where she could be part of a "global perspective." When Xerox was preparing to develop a new IT strategy, she saw a perfect fit.

Career success is most likely if you are flexible, creative, and ambitious. You will need to learn how to think strategically, discern and convey your business vision,

make decisions, and work in teams. You will need to deliver competitive advantage and thrive on change. These and other topics, essential to your successful career, provide the focus for the following chapters.

DIY

Build Your Skills

Practice and apply your knowledge by going online at

www.mhhe.com/ BatemanM2e

WHAT YOU NEED TO KNOW

•• learning OBJECTIVES

After studying Chapter 2,
you will be able to:

L01 Describe how environmental forces influence
organizations and how organizations can
influence their environments.

L02 Distinguish between the macroenvironment
and the competitive environment.

L03 Explain why managers and organizations
should attend to economic and social
developments.

L04 Identify elements of the competitive
environment.

L05 Summarize how organizations respond to
environmental uncertainty.

L06 Define elements of an organization's culture.

L07 Discuss how an organization's culture affects
its response to its external environment.

2

The Environment of Business

Bob Stiller, founder and chairman of Green Mountain Coffee Roasters (GMCR), has brought his company a long way since its beginnings in a small Vermont café. He expanded his business by surveying the competition and choosing avenues that looked most promising. With the retail coffee market crowded by Starbucks, Seattle's Best Coffee, Caribou Coffee, and others, Stiller chose to focus on the quality of his coffee—offering more than 100 gourmet varieties—and to sell through retail stores, wholesale outlets, direct-mail catalogs, and on the Web. Recognizing consumers' growing interest in organic foods, GMCR also began offering organically grown coffees that were produced through fair trade practices—ensuring that farmers receive a fair price for their crops.[1] Executives such as Stiller must keep a sharp watch on developments outside their organizations, such as new competitors and changes in technology. These factors influence a variety of important decisions managers make. In this chapter, we discuss in detail how pressures from outside the organization help create the context in which managers and their companies must operate.

Learn the Inside Story

of how today's managers keep up with what's happening in the world around them. Listen to what Ed and Katie have to say about their experiences on the book Web site.

Coaching and Counseling is vital to staff morale. Address the situation, correct the situation, and let them know how big an asset they are. Always end on a positive note.
—Ed Hammer, Restaurant Manager

I believe that learning about the internal and external environment of business is helpful for decision-making. When changes occur in business, there is usually some motivation attributed to factors in its internal and external environment. Taking the time to learn about the internal and external environment of business not only benefits employees' knowledge and understanding, rather it helps the employees and their own decision-making process by making conclusions to the business' strengths, weaknesses, opportunities, and threats.
—Katie Storey, Student Life Coordinator

Glossary (margin)

OPEN SYSTEMS Organizations that are affected by, and that affect, their environment.

INPUTS Goods and services organizations take in and use to create products or services.

OUTPUTS The products and services organizations create.

EXTERNAL ENVIRONMENT All relevant forces outside a firm's boundaries, such as competitors, customers, the government, and the economy.

COMPETITIVE ENVIRONMENT The immediate environment surrounding a firm; includes suppliers, customers, rivals, and the like.

MACROENVIRONMENT The general environment; includes governments, economic conditions, and other fundamental factors that generally affect all organizations.

"The essence of a business is outside itself."

— Peter Drucker

LO 1 WHAT YOU NEED TO KNOW . . .

How do environmental forces influence organizations, and how can organizations influence their environments?

As we suggested in the first chapter, organizations are **open systems**—that is, they are affected by and in turn affect their external environments. They take in **inputs** like goods or services from their environment and use them to create products and services that are **outputs** to their environment, as shown in Figure 2.1. But when we use the term **external environment** here, we mean more than an organization's clients or customers; the external environment includes all relevant forces outside the organization's boundaries.

Many of these factors are uncontrollable. Companies large and small are buffeted or battered by recession, government interference, and competitors' actions. But their lack of control does not mean that managers can ignore such forces, use them as excuses for poor performance, and try to just get by. Managers must stay abreast of external developments and react effectively. In addition, as we will discuss later in this chapter, sometimes managers can influence components of the external environment.

Figure 2.2 shows the external environment of a business organization. The organization exists in its **competitive environment**, which is composed of the firm and its rivals, suppliers, customers (buyers), new entrants, and substitute or complementary products. At the more general level is the **macroenvironment**, which includes legal, political, economic, technological, demographic, and social and natural factors that generally affect all organizations.

This chapter discusses the basic characteristics of an organization's environment and the importance of that environment for strategic management. We also examine the *internal environment*, or *culture*, of the organization and the way that culture may influence the organization's response to its environment. Later chapters elaborate on many of the basic environmental forces introduced here. For example, technology will be discussed again in Chapters 4 and 14. Other chapters focus on ethics, social responsibility, and the natural environment. And Chapter 14 reiterates the theme that recurs throughout this text: organizations must change continually because environments change continually.

LO 2 WHAT YOU NEED TO KNOW . . .

Can you distinguish between the macroenvironment and the competitive environment?

THE MACROENVIRONMENT

All organizations operate in a macroenvironment, which is defined by the most general elements in the external environment that potentially can influence strategic decisions. Although a top executive team may have unique internal strengths and ideas about its goals, it must consider external factors before taking action.

Laws and regulations both protect and restrain organizations

U.S. government policies impose strategic constraints on organizations but may also provide opportunities. For example, the Library of Congress's Copyright Royalty Board recently alarmed Internet radio companies when it changed its regulations setting the royalty payments these companies owe recording companies and artists. Webcasters had been paying a percentage of their earnings, and because companies like AccuRadio are relatively young and have only

FIGURE 2.1	Organization Inputs and Outputs

Inputs
- Raw materials
- Services
- Equipment
- Capital
- Information

→ **Organization** →

Outputs
- Products
- Services

FIGURE 2.2 The External Environment

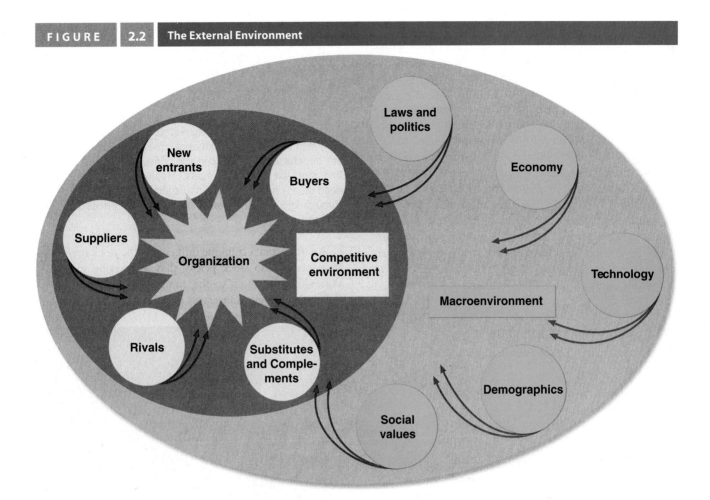

begun turning a profit, that arrangement limited costs. The new regulations would impose a flat fee each time a song is played, possibly raising AccuRadio's annual royalty cost from less than $50,000 to about $600,000 a year—far more than its profits and nearly equal to its entire revenue. Even big Webcasters like RealNetworks and AOL Radio said if the ruling stands, the fees would force them to substantially cut back their offerings. Still, some companies would benefit. Broadcast radio stations pay royalties only to the composers of the songs they play, so they would have an advantage relative to fast-growing but smaller online radio stations. And recording companies would receive more revenue from the new arrangement.[2]

The government can affect business opportunities through tax laws, economic policies, and international trade rulings. In some countries, for example, bribes and kickbacks are common and expected ways of doing business, but for U.S. firms they are illegal. Some U.S. businesses have been fined for using bribery when competing internationally. But laws can also assist organizations. Because U.S. federal and state governments protect property rights, including copyrights, trademarks, and patents, it is economically more attractive to start businesses in the United States than in countries where laws and law enforcement offer less protection.

Regulators are specific government organizations in a firm's more immediate task environment. Regulatory agencies such as the Occupational Safety and Health Administration (OSHA), the Interstate Commerce Commission (ICC), the Federal Aviation Administration (FAA), the Food and Drug Administration (FDA), the Equal Employment Opportunity Commission (EEOC), the National Labor Relations Board (NLRB), the Office of Federal Contract Compliance Programs (OFCCP), and the Environmental Protection Agency (EPA) have the power to investigate company practices and take legal action to ensure compliance with laws.

The Securities and Exchange Commission (SEC) regulates U.S. financial markets to protect investors. For instance, the SEC recently proposed regulations requiring companies to disclose more details about

?

DID YOU KNOW?

The U.S. Department of Commerce's Trade Advocacy Center, at www.export.gov/ advocacy/, was established to help U.S. businesses overcome hurdles that make it difficult for them to export goods or compete against foreign firms.

the total compensation paid to executives, including deferred compensation (pensions, severance pay) and perks (such as free housing and personal use of a corporate jet). The regulations are meant to help investors evaluate whether executives are being compensated at an appropriate level.[3]

Often the corporate community sees government as an adversary. However, many organizations realize that government can be a source of competitive advantages for an individual company or an entire industry. Public policy may prevent or limit new foreign or domestic competitors from entering an industry. Government may subsidize failing companies or provide tax breaks to some. Federal patents protect innovative products or production technologies. Legislation may be passed to support industry prices, thereby guaranteeing profits or survival. The government may even intervene to ensure the survival of certain key industries or companies, as it has done to help auto companies, airlines, and agricultural businesses.

(L)(O) 3   WHAT YOU NEED TO KNOW . . .

Why should managers and organizations attend to economic and social developments?

The economy affects a company's value

Although most Americans think in terms of the U.S. economy, the economic environment for organizations is much larger— created by complex interconnections among the economies of different countries. Growth and recessions occur worldwide as well as domestically.

The economic environment dramatically affects managers' ability to function effectively and influences their strategic choices. Interest and inflation rates affect the availability and cost of capital, growth opportunities, prices, costs, and consumer demand for products. Unemployment rates affect labor availability and the wages the firm must pay, as well as product demand. Steeply rising energy and health care costs have limited companies' ability to hire and raised the cost of doing business. Changes in the value of the dollar on world exchanges may make American products cheaper or more expensive than their foreign competitors.

▶ Economic forces have caused the fortunes of corn-based ethanol producers to swing wildly. For a time, soaring gasoline prices intensified the demand for alternative fuel sources for automobiles. That fact, coupled with a belief that ethanol fuel would reduce emissions of greenhouse gases, inspired the U.S. government to mandate the use of ethanol. Farmers responded by planting more corn, and energy companies built ethanol refineries.

But soon other forces pummeled the ethanol producers. First, flooding in the Midwest led to forecasts of high corn prices, and many ethanol producers tried to protect themselves by signing contracts for a generous $7 and more per bushel. Then fields dried and prospects for a good harvest improved, so corn prices started falling, leaving producers with contracts for overpriced corn.

More recently, the economy swung downward. A "bubble" of inflated real estate prices burst, contributing to problems for mortgage lenders that quickly spread to the entire financial industry. As credit dried up, the overall pace of business slowed dramatically, and oil prices fell, erasing some of ethanol's competitive advantage in the marketplace for fuel. But prices for corn also fell, keeping production costs down. Ethanol producers are hopeful that in the long run, drivers will need to rely more and more on alternative fuels. Meanwhile, ethanol companies need steady and farsighted management to guide them through the ups and downs of commodity prices and demand.[4] ◀

An important economic influence is the stock market. When investors bid up stock prices, they are paying more to own shares in companies, so the companies have more capital to fuel their strategies. Observers of the stock market watch trends

The recent economic woes in America have spurred the government to enact new laws to help lift the financial burden off of the shoulders of individuals and small businesses that are struggling. Shown here is President Barack Obama signing the economic stimulus bill, as Vice President Joe Biden looks on. What affect do you think this bill will have on the economy?

in major indexes such as the Dow Jones Industrial Average, Standard & Poor's 500, and NASDAQ Composite, which combine many companies' performance into a single measurement. In recent years, the indexes had risen to great heights, but then they dropped rapidly. The falling prices reflected an economy in which demand for homes and cars had shriveled, credit was difficult to obtain, exports tumbled, and unemployment rates soared.[5] Governments launched a variety of stimulus efforts to help companies get financing and to encourage consumers to start spending again. Stock markets have always rebounded eventually, even after a steep decline such as this one, as investors see hope for renewed business growth.

The stock market may also affect the behavior of individual managers. In publicly held companies, managers throughout the organization may feel required to meet Wall Street's earnings expectations. It is quite likely that you, too, at some point in your career, will be asked to improve a budget or estimate because your company does not want to disappoint "the Street." Such external pressures usually have a very positive effect—they help make many firms more efficient and profitable. But failure to meet those expectations can cause a company's stock price to drop, making it more difficult for the firm to raise additional capital for investment. The compensation of managers may also be affected, particularly if they have been issued stock options. These pressures sometimes lead managers to focus on short-term results at the expense of the long-term success of their organizations. Even worse, a few managers may be tempted to engage in unethical or unlawful behavior that misleads investors.[6]

Technology is changing every business function

Today a company cannot succeed without incorporating into its strategy the astonishing technologies that exist and are under development. As technology evolves, new industries, markets, and competitive niches develop. Advances in technology also permit companies to enter markets that would otherwise be unavailable to them, such as when cable TV companies adapted their technology to enter the market for Internet services.

New technologies also provide new production techniques. In manufacturing, sophisticated robots perform jobs without suffering fatigue, requiring vacations or weekends off, or demanding wage increases. New methods, such as injecting steam into oil fields at high pressure, are enabling Shell, Exxon-Mobil, and other oil companies to extract that valuable resource

?

DID YOU KNOW?

Researchers found that teens studying at their computers are also doing something else 65% of the time, and 26% of teens use several media at once. According to a study of multitasking and brain activity, we use different parts of the brain when we multitask while learning. Multitaskers used the part of the brain involved in repetitive skills, while those engaged only in learning used the area associated with memory.[10] Will this influence future managers' ability to think deeply about problems?

from locations that had once been considered depleted. In this case, technological and economic forces overlap: the rising price of oil has made it worthwhile for companies to develop and try the new technology.[7]

In addition, new technologies provide new ways to manage and communicate. Computerized management information systems (MISs) make information available when needed, and networking via the Internet makes it available where it is needed. Computers monitor productivity and note performance deficiencies. Telecommunications allow conferences to take place without requiring people to travel to the same location. As we will discuss in Chapter 4, strategies developed around the cutting edge of technological advances can create a competitive advantage; strategies that ignore competitors' technology lead to obsolescence and extinction.

Demographics describe your employees and customers

Demographics are measures of various characteristics of the people who make up groups or other social units. Work groups, organizations, countries, markets, and societies can be described statistically by referring to demographic measures such as their members' age, gender, family size, income, education, occupation, and so forth.

Managers must consider workforce demographics in formulating their human resources strategies. Population growth influences the size and composition of the labor force. In the decade from 2004 to 2014, the U.S. civilian labor force is expected to grow at a rate of 10 percent, reaching 162.1 million.[8] This growth is slower than during the previous decade, partly because young workers—those between the ages of 16 and 24—are declining in numbers. The fastest-growing age group will be workers who are 55 and older, who are expected to represent more than one-fifth of the labor force in 2014. What does this mean for employers? They will need to find ways to retain and fully use the talents of their experienced workers while competing for relatively scarce entry-level workers. Perhaps their older employees will be willing to work past the traditional retirement age of 65; research suggests that a lack of pensions and adequate savings will make retirement unaffordable for many of today's baby boomers.[9] Eventually, however, declining participation in work by older persons will force managers to find replacements for these highly experienced workers.

The education and skill levels of the workforce are another demographic factor managers must consider. The share of the U.S. labor force with at least some college education has been increasing steadily over the past several decades, from less than one-fourth of the workforce in 1970 to more than half today.[11] Even so, many companies invest heavily in training their entry-level workers, who may not have been adequately prepared for some of the more complex tasks the modern workplace requires. Also, as college has become a more popular option, employers are having difficulty recruiting employees for jobs that require knowledge of a skilled trade, such as machinists and toolmakers, especially in areas where the cost of living is so high that most residents are professionals.[12] However, as education levels improve around the globe, more organizations may send more technical tasks to lower-priced but highly trained workers overseas.

Another factor that significantly influences the U.S. population and labor force is immigration. Immigrants accounted for approximately 40 percent of the U.S. population growth recently.[13] Immigrants are frequently of working age but have different educational and occupational backgrounds from the rest of the labor force. The demographic importance of immigration intersects with legal issues governing who is permitted to work in the United States. For example, the federal government has recently cracked down not only on undocumented workers but also on the managers who hired them. Some companies have asked the government to admit more foreign workers with technical expertise that may be hard to find in the United States.

Immigration is one reason the labor force in the future will be more ethnically diverse than it is today. The biggest percentage of employment increases will be by Asian Americans and Hispanic populations, followed by African Americans.

In the last quarter of the 20th century, women joined the U.S. labor force in record numbers. Throughout the 1970s and 1980s, they became much more likely to take paying jobs. In the 1970s, only about one-third of women were in the labor force, but 60 percent had jobs in 1999. Since then, women's labor force participation rate has stayed near that level, declining slightly.[14]

A more diverse workforce has many advantages, but managers have to ensure they provide equality for women and minorities with respect to employment, advancement opportunities, and compensation. They must recruit, retain, train, motivate, and effectively utilize people of diverse demographic backgrounds who have the skills to achieve the company's mission.

Social issues shape attitudes toward your company and its products

Societal trends regarding how people think and behave have major implications for management of the labor force, corporate social actions, and strategic decisions about products and

High Design with a Conscience

The global economic recession affected every market—even luxury goods. Earlier, the demand for high-end designer merchandise had been exploding around the world. Now, consumers want to know where a garment's materials come from and how the garment is made. Concern for the environment and ethical business practices have moved onto high fashion's radar screen.

Leading the way is Stella McCartney—a British-born fashion designer who, unlike most of her competitors, uses no fur or leather in her creations and is fiercely committed to preserving the planet. If her name rings a bell, that is because she is the daughter of legendary Beatle Paul McCartney and his late wife, American photographer-turned-musician Linda Eastman. Stella and her siblings were raised as vegetarians on an organic farm in the English countryside.

Barely two years after her 1995 graduation in fashion design from Central St. Martin's College, McCartney became lead designer at haute couture House of Chloe in Paris. She worked there until 2001 before moving to Gucci, which now owns 50 percent of the Stella McCartney brand. Colleagues describe McCartney as gracious, kind, and fiercely true to her principles. Since her career's early days, McCartney has designed without leather or fur, saying she cannot condone the killing of animals "for the sake of fashion." Pointing to the connection between fur and leather and the environment, she asserts that the chemicals and water used in tanneries have a significant environmental impact. McCartney strives to operate a carbon-neutral business. Her London headquarters and most of her 11 retail outlets worldwide are powered by wind. Stella McCartney retail stores use biodegradable shopping bags made from corn.

McCartney doesn't design only for the elite. Since 2003, she has fashioned sportswear for Adidas, each year adding a collection for a different sport. Also, the one-time collection she created in 2005 for Sweden-based "fast-fashion" retailer H&M sold out rapidly. McCartney also markets a lingerie line, organic skin-care products, and a signature fragrance.

McCartney has a reputation for the imaginative use of fabrics, even in shoes and handbags: canvas, linen, Lucite, and a variety of faux leathers. Think it's impossible to command big bucks for a pair of nonleather shoes? Think again. A pair of ballerina flats on StellaMcCartney.com is markets. For example, during the 1980s and 1990s, women in the workforce often chose to delay having children as they focused on their careers, but today more women are having children and then returning to the workforce. As a result, companies have introduced more supportive policies, including family leave, flexible working hours, and child care assistance. Firms provide these benefits as a way of increasing a source of competitive advantage: an experienced workforce.

A prominent issue today pertains to natural resources: drilling for oil in formerly protected areas in the United States. Firms in the oil industry face considerable public opinion both in favor of preserving the natural environment and against the country's dependence on other countries for fuel. The protection of the natural environment will factor into social concerns and many types of management decisions.

How companies respond to these and other social issues may affect their reputation in the marketplace, which in turn may help or hinder their competitiveness. The public health issue of childhood obesity has given videogames a bad name among those who advocate for children to get off the couch and move. But two games have generated favorable publicity: Konami's Dance Dance Revolution (DDR), where players compete with dance moves, and Nintendo's Wii Sports, where players swing a remote control containing motion sensors to move a virtual tennis racket, bowling ball, baseball bat, or boxing gloves. The games have also been praised as an alternative to games with violent themes. Dean Bender, the public relations agent for DDR, said of his client, "With all the bad PR about violence, we became the white knights."[15] And Wii Sports players have reported breaking into a sweat and even straining muscles.[16]

L O 4 WHAT YOU NEED TO KNOW . . .
Can you identify elements of the competitive environment?

THE COMPETITIVE ENVIRONMENT

All managers are affected by the components of the macroenvironment we just discussed. But each organization also functions in a closer, more immediate competitive environment, consisting of the organizations with which the organization directly interacts. As shown in Figure 2.3, the competitive environment includes rivalry among current competitors and the impact of new entrants, substitute and complementary products, suppliers, and customers. This model was originally developed by Michael Porter, a Harvard professor and a noted authority on strategic management. According to Porter, successful managers do more than simply react to the environment; they act in ways that actually shape or change the organization's environment. Porter's model is an excellent method for analyzing the competitive environment and adapting to or influencing the nature of the competition.

Competitors come from all over the world

Among the various components of the competitive environment, competitors within the industry must first deal with one another. When organizations compete for the same customers and try to win market share at the others' expense, all must react to and anticipate their competitors' actions.

priced at $500; stiletto-heel boots go for $1,000 and up.

In addition to numerous design awards, McCartney has been praised by the Natural Resources Defense Council for creating environmentally responsible products. In 2009, *Fast Company* named McCartney to its "100 Most Creative People in Business" list, calling her "the new face of responsible luxury."

Q: Discussion Questions

- High fashion is known for its extravagance and luxury materials. Yet, Stella McCartney has achieved success without compromising her beliefs about not using animal products. How has McCartney benefited from the shift in societal attitudes? Do you think they will be sustained? Why or why not?
- How might the fashion industry leverage the current economic crisis to benefit consumers and the environment?

SOURCES: Corporate Web site, accessed June 4, 2009, http://www.stellamccartney.com; "The 100 Most Creative People in Business 2009," *Fast Company,* June 2009, p. 65; "Designer Stella McCartney and Discovery CEO David Zaslav Honored for Pioneering Environmental Work in Fashion and the Media Industries," Natural Resources Defense Council press release, March 30, 2009, http://www.nrdc.org; Suzy Menkes, "Making a World of Difference: Stella McCartney's Style Ethos," *New York Times,* March 25, 2009, http://www.mytimes.com; Suzy Menkes, "Sustainability Is Back in Fashion," *New York Times,* March 25, 2009, http://www.nytimes.com; Bridget Foley, "Stella Performance," *W Magazine,* October 2007, http://www.wmagazine.com; Ruth LaFerla, "Cruel Beauty," *New York Times,* January 11, 2007, http://www.nytimes.com.

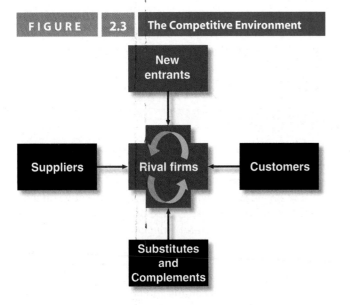

FIGURE 2.3 **The Competitive Environment**

New entrants

Suppliers   Rival firms   Customers

Substitutes and Complements

The first question to consider is: Who is the competition? Sometimes the answer is obvious. The major competitors in the market for videogame consoles are Sony (whose brand is the PlayStation), Microsoft (Xbox 360), and Nintendo (maker of the Wii). But if organizations focus exclusively on traditional rivalries, they miss the emerging ones. Coca-Cola and PepsiCo are obvious competitors, but consumer tastes have shifted away from soda to bottled water. The two companies have had to compete in introducing new products, not just in winning consumers over to their brand of cola.

As a first step in understanding their competitive environment, organizations must identify their competitors. Competitors may include many types of companies:

- Small domestic firms, especially their entry into tiny, premium markets
- Strong regional competitors
- Big new domestic companies exploring new markets
- Overseas firms, especially those that either try to solidify their position in small niches (a traditional Japanese tactic) or can draw on an inexpensive labor force on a large scale (as in China)
- Newer entries, such as firms offering their products on the Web

The growth in competition from other countries has been especially significant with worldwide reduction in international

A+

TIP

Even competitors sometimes collaborate when they have a common interest, such as research, public relations, or government policy. For example, companies join in financing promotional campaigns for their industry ("Got milk?"), agree on common product standards (as in DVDs), or engage in joint ventures. General Motors and Chrysler have collaborated to produce new hybrid technology for their cars. The collaboration was intended as a way to overcome Japanese firms' lead in hybrid vehicles. As a manager, you may identify a larger threat that causes you to collaborate with competitors in some areas, even as you continue competing in others.

trade barriers. For example, the North American Free Trade Agreement (NAFTA) sharply reduced tariffs on trade between the United States, Canada, and Mexico. Managers today confront a particular challenge from low-cost producers abroad.

Once competitors have been identified, the next step is to analyze how they compete. Competitors use tactics such as price reductions, new-product introductions, and advertising campaigns to gain advantage over their rivals. In the market for videogame consoles, Sony had been a leader and was expected to maintain its dominance when it launched its powerful PS3 model, choosing a technology-based strategy. The PS3 is a technological marvel that, by one account, combines "the [processing] speed of a low-end supercomputer with the [component] cooling techniques of a network server" (a high-end computer used to handle the needs of a network of personal computers).[17] Rather than using an existing processor, Sony tapped the expertise of suppliers to develop a new processor and interface. The system generates so much power that engineering teams had to bring in a special team of designers to simulate the air flow with various cooling designs and figure out how to arrange the microchips within the box to keep the whole system from melting down. In addition, Sony's engineers developed a high-definition display, with graphics so detailed that software engineers had to calculate the motions of the game's activities very precisely. If something in a game bounces or breaks, the software must show it moving as the laws of physics would in the real world. These advances generated a lot of excitement—and a high cost. By one estimate, making a top-of-the-line PS3 costs Sony about $840.

It's essential to understand what competitors are doing when you are honing your own strategy. When Sony launched its PS3, it couldn't charge a high enough price to cover its costs. It originally set the price at $599, still far above its competitors. The Xbox 360, which had been on the market for a year, was a less-advanced but comparable product selling for $399. But in the initial competition with PS3, Nintendo took a surprising lead by choosing an entirely different strategy for its Wii. Rather than competing on the basis of advanced graphics and powerful processing, the company offered something new and easy to use—its remote-control motion sensors instead of buttons and knobs. A Wii console costs just $249. While the PS3 and Wii both flew off store shelves in the early weeks of the

● **BARRIERS TO ENTRY** Conditions that prevent new companies from entering an industry.

greater. Several major barriers to entry are common:

- *Government policy*—For example, the FDA may forbid a new drug entrant, or the Patent and Trademark Office may grant a patent. When a patent expires, other companies can enter the market. The patents recently expired on several drugs made by Pfizer, including antidepressant Zoloft, allergy medicine Zyrtec, and blood pressure medicine Norvasc. At the same time, several research projects to introduce new, patented medicines failed, so Pfizer had to lay off employees and close some facilities to cut costs.[21] Some industries, such as liquor retailing, are regulated; more subtle government controls operate in mining and ski area development.

- *Capital requirements*—Getting started in some industries, such as building aircraft or operating a railroad, may cost so much that companies won't even try to raise such large amounts of money.

- *Brand identification*—When customers are loyal to a familiar brand, new entrants have to spend heavily. Imagine, for example, the costs involved in trying to launch a new cola against Coke or Pepsi. Similarly, Google's recent entry into the market for business software, with a package called Google Apps for Your Domain, surprised many people because Microsoft has dominated that segment for many years.[22]

- *Cost disadvantages*—Established companies may be able to keep their costs lower because they are larger, have more favorable locations, have existing assets, and so forth.

- *Distribution channels*—Existing competitors may have such tight distribution channels that new entrants struggle to get their goods or services to customers. For example, established food products have supermarket shelf space. New entrants must displace existing products with promotions, price breaks, intensive selling, and other tactics.

products' launch, PS3 sales over the next few years continually fell below expectations, while Wii became the top-selling game console in the United States. In fact, PS3 fell to *fourth* place in game console units sold, behind the older-generation PS2, which became Sony's lower-priced—and therefore more popular—alternative.[18]

Competition is most intense when there are many direct competitors (including foreign contenders), industry growth is slow, and the product or service cannot be differentiated. New, high-growth industries offer enormous opportunities for profits. When an industry matures and growth slows, profits drop. Then intense competition causes an industry shakeout: weaker companies are eliminated, and the strong companies survive.[19] We will discuss competitors and strategy further in Chapter 4.

New entrants arise when barriers to entry are low

New entrants into an industry compete with established companies. Phone companies have been challenged by cable and satellite services offering consumers attractive packages for broadband Internet services, instead of dial-up or DSL connections. More recently, the introduction of WiMax is poised to shake up cell phone and Internet carriers. WiMax, which can deliver citywide wireless Internet access and fast download speeds, lets cell phone and computer users go online without hunting for a Wi-Fi hotspot, much less a cord.[20]

If many factors prevent new companies from entering an industry, the threat to established firms is less serious. If there are few such **barriers to entry**, the threat of new entrants is

Some products are substitutes for or complements of yours

Besides products that directly compete, other products can affect a company's performance by being substitutes for or complements of the company's offerings. A *substitute* is a potential threat; customers use it as an alternative, buying less of one kind of product but more of another. For example, substitutes for coffee could be tea, cola, or water, and substitutes for movie theater tickets are DVD rentals from Blockbuster or Netflix.

A *complement* is a potential opportunity, because customers buy more of a given product if they also demand more of the complementary product. Examples include ink cartridges as a complement for printers and appliances as a complement for homes. When people buy more printers and homes, they buy more ink cartridges and appliances.

Technological advances and economic efficiencies are among the ways that firms can develop substitutes for existing products. The introduction of videogame systems created a substitute for television viewing that has drawn a large share of young men away from TV audiences. More recently, Internet offerings such as YouTube and MySpace have attracted videogame players away from their TV sets to interact with one another online. This example shows that substitute products or services can limit another industry's revenue potential. Companies in those industries are likely to suffer growth and earnings problems unless they improve quality or launch aggressive marketing campaigns. Nintendo's success with the Wii game console partly results from offering games such as Wii Sports that entice people who want to interact with the game, as well as by allowing them to create avatars to represent themselves in the various games, a feature that computer users enjoy in many online games and worlds. Sony's high-tech strategy for the PS3 aimed in part to make that console a substitute for buying a Blu-ray DVD player. However, prices of Blu-ray players have fallen dramatically, while the price of a PS3 remains high, so for many consumers, the combination of a Blu-ray player plus an Xbox 360 console has become a substitute for a PS3.[23]

In addition to current substitutes, companies need to think about potential substitutes that may be viable in the future. For example, possible alternatives to fossil fuels include nuclear fusion, solar power, and wind energy. The advantages promised by each of these technologies are many: inexhaustible fuel supplies, electricity "too cheap to meter," zero emissions, universal public acceptance, and so on. Yet each of these faces economic and technical hurdles.

Besides identifying and planning for substitutes, companies must consider complements for their products. Because game consoles and videogames are complementary products, console makers work closely with developers, giving them the information they need to create products to lure customers to their gaming systems. The complexity of the PS3 created another hurdle for Sony in this area. Because the system is so sophisticated, programming a game for PS3 costs roughly 30 percent more than creating a similar title for Microsoft's Xbox. That made game developers cautious about launching PS3 titles, which in turn made game players think twice about buying the new console. In the January following release of the PS3, only 2 of the top 20 games sold ("Resistance: Fall of Man" and "Madden NFL 07") were PS3 games.[24] To collaborate better with the game industry, Sony released programming tools for game developers.[25] The effort was especially important because developers such as Electronic Arts were quick to adjust their own product plans when sales of PS3 titles were lower than expected while sales of Wii titles were better than expected.[26]

As with substitutes, a company needs to watch for new complements that can change the competitive landscape. When the Wii became popular, some programmers saw an opportunity to offer a niche service: tweaking the software to offer customized avatars. Wii players can use Nintendo's software to select from a range of facial characteristics, height, and other features, but some users want a more customized look or perhaps a character modeled after a famous figure. An entrepreneur in Tokyo created Mii Station, which uses a customer-supplied photo to create a Mii look-alike for a $5 fee. A Web developer in Boston started Mii Plaza, a Web site where users can tap a database of more than 8,000 characters to collect and share Miis. Nintendo could have viewed these efforts as copyright infringement, but the company's initial response has been to treat Mii-related businesses as harmless.[27]

Suppliers provide your resources

Recall from our earlier mention of open systems that organizations must acquire resources (inputs) from their environment and convert those resources into products or services (outputs) to sell. Suppliers provide the resources needed for production, and those resources may come in several forms:

- *People*—supplied by trade schools and universities
- *Raw materials*—from producers, wholesalers, and distributors
- *Information*—supplied by researchers and consulting firms
- *Financial capital*—from banks and other sources

But suppliers are important to an organization for reasons beyond the resources they provide. Suppliers can raise their prices or provide poor-quality goods and services. Labor unions can go on strike or demand higher wages. Workers may produce defective work. Powerful suppliers, then, can reduce an organization's profits, particularly if the organization cannot pass on price increases to its customers.

In some industries, suppliers include labor unions. Although unionization in the United States has dropped below 10 percent of the private labor force, unions remain powerful in industries such as steel, autos, and transportation. Also, the Screen Actors Guild, the union representing workers in the entertainment industry, exerts considerable power on behalf of its members. Labor unions represent and protect the interests of their members on matters of hiring, wages, working conditions, job security, and due-process appeals. Historically, the relationship between management and labor unions has been adversarial, but today both sides realize that to improve productivity and competitiveness, management and labor must work together in collaborative relationships. Troubled labor relations can create higher costs, reduce productivity, and eventually lead to layoffs.[28]

Organizations are at a disadvantage if they become overly dependent on any powerful supplier. A supplier is powerful if the buyer has few other sources of supply or if the supplier has many other buyers. One of the problems plaguing the launch of the PS3 was a shortage of parts, and during the weeks leading up to the console's first Christmas, it was often out of stock in U.S. stores. Sony depended on Panasonic to provide disk drives and on IBM and ATI Technologies to deliver core processors and graphics chips.[29] For such a sophisticated product, the company couldn't go elsewhere for these components.

Switching costs are fixed costs buyers face if they change suppliers. For example, once a buyer learns how to operate a supplier's equipment, such as computer software, the buyer faces both economic and psychological costs in changing to a new supplier.

In recent years, more companies have improved their competitiveness and profitability through supply chain management, the management of the entire network of facilities and people that obtain raw materials from outside the organization, transform them into products, and distribute them to customers.[30] In the past, managers could pay less attention to supply chain management. Products tended to be standardized, overseas competition was rare, and the pace of change was slower. But increased competition has required managers to pay very close attention to their costs; they can no longer afford to hold large inventories, waiting for orders to come in. Also, once orders do come in, some products still sitting in inventory might well be out of date.

With the emergence of the Internet, customers look for products built to their specific needs and preferences—and they want them delivered quickly, at the lowest available price. This requires the supply chain to be not only efficient but also *flexible,* so that the organization's output can quickly respond to changes in demand.

Today, the goal of effective supply chain management is to have *the right product in the right quantity available at the right place at the right cost.* Boeing, the aircraft and defense systems company, provides a good example of effective supply chain management. Boeing forges partnerships with its suppliers to share knowledge that will help them learn how to operate more efficiently. At Boeing Integrated Defense Systems (IDS), Rick Behrens is senior manager of supplier development, charged with building close supplier relationships and helping them understand Boeing's commitment to "lean" operations, aimed at eliminating waste. Behrens tailors his approach to each supplier's familiarity with lean processes. He educates some suppliers in the basics of how to run lean operations; for others,

he sends a team to the organization to help them streamline certain activities. He also identifies Boeing specialists who can help suppliers with particularly challenging problems. Along the way, Behrens helps suppliers develop their abilities so that they can move from simply selling parts to providing complete subassemblies. In Behrens's words, "We need suppliers that can grow with us."[31]

In sum, choosing the right supplier is an important strategic decision. Suppliers can affect manufacturing time, product quality, costs, and inventory levels. The relationship between suppliers and the organization is changing in many companies. The close supplier relationship has become a new model for many organizations that are using a just-in-time manufacturing approach. And in some companies, innovative managers are forming strategic partnerships with their key suppliers in developing new products or new production techniques.

Customers ultimately determine your success

Customers purchase the goods or services an organization offers. Without customers, a company won't survive. You are a final consumer when you buy a McDonald's hamburger or a pair of jeans from Aéropostale. Intermediate consumers buy raw materials or wholesale products and then sell to final consumers, as when Sony buys components from IBM and ATI Technologies and uses them to make PS3 consoles. Types of intermediate customers include retailers, who buy from wholesalers and manufacturers' representatives and then sell to consumers, and industrial buyers, who buy raw materials (such as chemicals) to be converted into final products. Intermediate customers actually make more purchases than individual final consumers do.

Customers do much more than simply provide money for goods and services. They can demand lower prices, higher quality, unique product specifications, or better service. They also can play competitors against one another, as occurs when a car buyer (or a purchasing agent) collects different offers and negotiates for the best price. Often, today's customers want to be actively involved with their products, as when Wii

A+

TIP

Many U.S. manufacturers are concerned about the cost advantage that overseas manufacturers gain through their low-wage structure. They may even decide to send some jobs or even entire plants to less expensive workers overseas. However, in some situations, collaboration can help you remain competitive without relocating jobs. You may collaborate *externally,* with suppliers who work with you on improving quality, automation, and delivery and on lowering costs. You may also collaborate *internally,* working together with other managers and employees in every area to eliminate inefficiencies.

⊙ **ENVIRONMENTAL UNCERTAINTY**
Lack of information needed to
understand or predict the future.

users create a Mii avatar so that the characters in the game look like cartoon versions of themselves. Dell has taken customer input a step further by asking customers what they want the company to develop next. At Dell's IdeaStorm Web site (http://www. dellideastorm.com), visitors can post ideas for the next generation of computers and vote on the ideas they like best.[32]

The Internet has further empowered customers. It provides an easy source of information—both about product features and pricing. In addition, today's Internet users informally create and share messages about a product, which provide flattering free "advertising" at best or embarrassing and even erroneous bad publicity at worst. For example, enthusiastic gamers who favor one device or another have posted their homemade "commercials" pairing scenes from games with musical backgrounds on YouTube, as well as blunt point-by-point product comparisons about competing brands. Mocking Sony's claims that its PS3 is popular, fans of the Wii visited stores and filmed inventory sitting on shelves. One group of videos on YouTube even portrays an unofficial "brand," Wii60, to drive home the idea that consumers could purchase both a Wii and an Xbox 360 for the price of a PS3.[33] Today's companies may find it difficult to identify, much less respond to, these unofficial messages.

As we discussed in Chapter 1, customer service means giving customers what they want or need, the way they want it, the first time. This usually depends on the speed and dependability with which an organization can deliver its products. Actions and attitudes that provide excellent customer service include the following:

- Speed of filling and delivering normal orders.
- Willingness to meet emergency needs.
- Merchandise delivered in good condition.
- Readiness to take back defective goods and resupply quickly.
- Availability of installation and repair services and parts.
- Service charges (i.e., whether services are "free" or priced separately).[34]

An organization is at a disadvantage if it depends too heavily on powerful customers—those who make large purchases or can easily find alternative places to buy. If you are a firm's largest customer and can buy from others, you have power over that firm and probably can negotiate with it successfully. Your firm's biggest customers, especially if they can buy from other sources, will have the greatest negotiating power over you.

⃝⃝ 5 WHAT YOU NEED TO KNOW . . .

Can you summarize how organizations respond to environmental uncertainty?

ENVIRONMENTAL ANALYSIS

If managers do not understand how the environment affects their organization or cannot identify opportunities and threats that are likely to be important, their ability to make decisions and execute plans will be severely limited. For example, if little is known about customer likes and dislikes, organizations will have difficulty designing new products, scheduling production, or developing marketing plans. In short, timely and accurate environmental information is critical for running a business.

But information about the environment is not always readily available. For example, even economists have difficulty predicting whether an upturn or a downturn in the economy is likely. Moreover, managers find it difficult to forecast how well their own products will sell, let alone how a competitor might respond. In other words, managers often operate under conditions of uncertainty. Environmental uncertainty means that managers do not have enough information about the environment to understand or predict the future. Uncertainty arises from two related factors:

- *Complexity*—the number of issues to which a manager must attend, and the degree to which they are interconnected. Industries with many different firms that compete in vastly different ways tend to be more complex—and uncertain— than industries with only a few key competitors.

- *Dynamism*—the degree of discontinuous change that occurs within the industry. High-growth industries with products and technologies that change rapidly are more uncertain than stable industries where change is less dramatic and more predictable.[35]

As environmental uncertainty increases, managers need methods for collecting, sorting through, and interpreting information about the environment. We discuss some of these approaches in this section of the chapter. (In Chapter 4, we will also discuss how managers make decisions under conditions of uncertainty.) By analyzing forces in both the macroenvironment and the competitive environment, managers can identify opportunities and threats that might affect the organization.

"**Your most unhappy customers are your greatest source of learning.**"

—Bill Gates

● ENVIRONMENTAL SCANNING Searching for and sorting through information about the environment.

● COMPETITIVE INTELLIGENCE Information that helps managers determine how to compete better.

● SCENARIO A narrative that describes a particular set of future conditions.

● FORECASTING Method for predicting how variables will change the future.

Environmental scanning keeps you aware

The first step in coping with uncertainty in the environment is to pin down what might be important. Frequently, organizations and individuals act out of ignorance, only to regret those actions in the future. IBM, for example, had the opportunity to purchase the technology behind xerography but turned it down. Xerox saw the potential and took the lead in photocopying. Later, Xerox researchers developed the technology for the original computer mouse but failed to see its potential and missed an important opportunity.

To understand and predict changes, opportunities, and threats, organizations such as Shire Pharmaceuticals, T-Mobile, and Starbucks spend a good deal of time and money monitoring events in the environment. Environmental scanning includes searching out information that is unavailable to most people and sorting through that information to interpret what is important and what is not. Managers can ask questions such as these:

- Who are our current competitors?
- Are there few or many entry barriers to our industry?
- What substitutes exist for our product or service?
- Is the company too dependent on powerful suppliers?
- Is the company too dependent on powerful customers?[36]

Answers to these questions help managers develop **competitive intelligence**, the information necessary to decide how best to manage in the competitive environment they have identified. Porter's competitive analysis, discussed earlier, can guide environmental scanning and help managers evaluate the competitive potential of different environments. Table 2.1 describes two extreme environments: an attractive environment, which gives a firm a competitive advantage, and an unattractive environment, which puts a firm at a competitive disadvantage.[37]

Scenario development helps you analyze the environment

As managers try to determine the effect of environmental forces on their organizations, they often develop **scenarios** of the future—alternative combinations of different factors that form a total picture of the environment and the firm. For example, when Congress and the president must forecast the size of the federal budget deficit, they develop several scenarios about what the economy is likely to do over the next decade or so. Frequently, organizations develop a *best-case scenario* (the occurrence of events that are favorable to the firm), a *worst-case scenario* (the occurrence of unfavorable events), and some middle-ground alternatives. The value of scenarios is that they help managers develop contingency plans for what they might

do given different outcomes.[38] For example, as a manager, you will quite likely be involved in budgeting for your area. You will almost certainly be asked to list initiatives you would eliminate in case of an economic downturn and new investments you would make if your firm does better than expected.

Effective managers regard the scenarios they develop as living documents, not merely prepared once and put aside. They constantly update the scenarios to take into account relevant new factors that emerge, such as significant changes in the economy or actions by competitors.

Forecasting predicts your future environment

Whereas environmental scanning identifies important factors and scenario development develops alternative pictures of the future, **forecasting** predicts exactly how some variable or variables will change in the future. For example, in making capital investments, firms may forecast interest rates. In deciding to expand or downsize a business, firms may forecast the demand for goods and services or forecast the supply and demand of labor. Publications such as *Business Week's Business Outlook* provide forecasts to businesses both large and small.

The accuracy of forecasts varies from application to application. Because they extrapolate from the past to project the

TABLE 2.1	Attractive and Unattractive Environments		
Environmental Factor	**Unattractive**	**Attractive**
Competitors	Many; low industry growth; equal size; commodity	Few; high industry growth; unequal size differentiated
Threat of entry	High threat; few entry barriers	Low threat; many barriers
Substitutes	Many	Few
Suppliers	Few; high bargaining power	Many; low bargaining power
Customers	Few; high bargaining power	Many; low bargaining power

BENCHMARKING The process of comparing an organization's practices and technologies with those of other companies.

EMPOWERMENT The process of sharing power with employees, thereby enhancing their confidence in their ability to perform their jobs and their belief that they are influential contributors to the organization.

future, forecasts tend to be most accurate when the future ends up looking a lot like the past. Of course, we don't need sophisticated forecasts in those instances. Forecasts are most useful when the future will look radically different from the past. Unfortunately, that is when forecasts tend to be less accurate. The more things change, the less confidence we have in our forecasts. Here is some practical advice for using forecasts:

- Use multiple forecasts, and perhaps average their predictions.
- Remember that accuracy decreases as you go further into the future.
- Collect data carefully. Forecasts are no better than the data used to construct them.
- Use simple forecasts (rather than complicated ones) where possible.
- Keep in mind that important events often are surprises that depart from predictions.[39]

Benchmarking helps you become best in class

Besides trying to predict changes in the environment, firms can intensively study the best practices of various firms to understand their sources of competitive advantage. **Benchmarking** means identifying the best-in-class performance by a company in a given area—say, product development or customer service—and then comparing your processes with theirs. A benchmarking team collects information on its own company's operations and those of the other firm in order to determine gaps. These gaps serve as a point of entry to learn the underlying causes of performance differences. Ultimately, the team maps out a set of best practices that lead to world-class performance. We will discuss benchmarking further in Chapter 4.

RESPONDING TO THE ENVIRONMENT

For managers and organizations, responding effectively to their environments is almost always essential. Clothing retailers who pay no attention to changes in the public's style preferences, and manufacturers who fail to ensure they have steady sources of supply, are soon out of business. To respond to their environment, managers and companies have a number of options, which can be grouped into three categories:

1. Adapting to the environment
2. Influencing the environment
3. Selecting a new environment

Adapt to the environment

To cope with environmental uncertainty, organizations frequently adjust their structures and work processes. Figure 2.4 shows four different approaches that organizations can take in adapting to environmental uncertainty, depending on whether it arises from complexity, dynamism, or both.

When uncertainty arises from environmental complexity, organizations tend to adapt by *decentralizing* decision making. For example, if a company faces a growing number of competitors in various markets, if different customers want different things, if product features keep increasing, and if production facilities are being built in different regions of the world, executives probably cannot keep abreast of all activities and understand all the operational details of a business. In these cases, the top management team is likely to give lower-level managers authority to make decisions that benefit the firm. The term **empowerment** is used frequently today to talk about this type of decentralized authority.

To compete in volatile environments, organizations rely on knowledgeable and skilled workers. One way to develop such workers is to sponsor training programs. Alliances among employers, community colleges, universities, and nonprofit training programs are producing workers with much-needed skills in many industries. One program in New York, Per Scholas, trains computer repair technicians in one of the country's poorest areas—the Bronx. Funded by grants from private foundations and the New York City Council, the program gained momentum through its collaboration with Time Warner Cable and other companies looking for skilled employees.

Per Scholas boasts a job placement rate of 80 percent of its graduates, who earn about $12 per hour in the first year and $15 per hour in two years—often double what they would have earned without the training. One graduate, Cristina Rodriguez, works at Time Warner Cable as a broadband specialist. Her new skills have empowered her to become a high-performing employee. "What feels great is when I resolve someone's issue," she says. Rodriguez, fluent in both English and Spanish, is able to solve customers' problems in both languages.

FIGURE 2.4	Four Structural Approaches for Managing Uncertainty	
	Stable	**Dynamic**
Complex	Decentralized Bureaucratic (standardized skills)	Decentralized Organic (mutual adjustment)
Simple	Centralized Bureaucratic (standardized work processes)	Centralized Organic (direct supervision)

● **BUFFERING** Creating supplies of excess resources in case of unpredictable needs.

● **SMOOTHING** Leveling normal fluctuations at the boundaries of the environment.

● **FLEXIBLE PROCESSES** Methods for adapting the technical core to changes in the environment.

Training programs such as Per Scholas have grown more sophisticated in the last few years because of their close association with the companies that hire their graduates. These relationships give the programs insight into how the employers operate and what they need. Connie Ciliberti, vice president of human resources for Time Warner Cable, confirms the importance of this collaboration. "Per Scholas has spent time learning our business, understanding our measures of success," she says.[40]

In response to uncertainty arising from a dynamic environment, organizations tend to establish more flexible structures. Today the term *bureaucracy* generally has a bad connotation. While bureaucratic organizations may be efficient and controlled if the environment is stable, they tend to react slowly to changes in products, technologies, customers, or competitors. Because bureaucratic organizations tend to be formal and stable, they often cannot adjust to change or exceptional circumstances that "don't fit the rules." In these cases, more *organic* structures give organizations the flexibility to adapt. Organic structures are less formal than bureaucratic organizations; decisions are made through interaction and mutual adjustment among individuals rather than from a set of predefined rules.

adapting at the boundaries

Because they are open systems, organizations are exposed to uncertainties from both their inputs and outputs. In response, they can create buffers on both the input and output boundaries with the environment. Buffering creates supplies of excess resources to meet unpredictable needs. On the input side, organizations establish relationships with employment agencies to hire part-time and temporary help during rush periods when labor demand is difficult to predict. In the U.S. labor force, these workers, known as *contingent workers,* include 2.5 million on-call workers, 1.2 million temporary-help agency workers, and more than 800,000 workers provided by contract firms, suggesting widespread use of this approach to buffering labor input uncertainties.[41] On the output side of the system, most organizations use some type of ending inventories, keeping merchandise on hand in case a rush of customers decides to buy their products. Auto dealers are a common example of this practice; other companies that use buffer inventories include fast-food restaurants, bookstores, and even real estate agencies.[42]

In addition to buffering, organizations may try smoothing or leveling normal fluctuations at the boundaries of the environment. For example, during winter months in the north, when automobile sales drop off, dealers commonly cut the price of their in-stock vehicles to increase demand. At the end of each clothing season, retailers discount their merchandise to clear it out and make room for incoming inventories. These are examples of smoothing environmental cycles to level off fluctuations in demand.

adapting at the core

While buffering and smoothing manage uncertainties at the boundaries of the organization, firms also can establish flexible processes that allow for adaptation in their technical core. For example, firms increasingly try to customize their goods and services to meet customers' varied and changing demands. Even in manufacturing, where it is difficult to change basic core processes, firms are creating flexible factories. Instead of mass-producing large quantities of a "one-size-fits-all" product, organizations can use mass customization to produce customized products at an equally low cost. Whereas Henry Ford used to claim that "you could have a Model T in any color you wanted, as long as it was black," auto companies now offer a wide array of colors and trim lines, with different options and accessories. The process of mass customization involves the use of a network of independent operating units in which each performs a specific process

Celebrities Bono and Oprah have supported the organizations who are participating in the Product Red Program to help end AIDS in Africa through the Global Fund. What other opportunities do companies have to participate in voluntary actions to change their environment?

or task such as making a dashboard assembly on an automobile. When an order comes in, different modules join forces to deliver the product or service as specified by the customer.[43]

Influence your environment

In addition to adapting or reacting to the environment, managers and organizations can develop proactive responses aimed at changing the environment. Two general types of proactive responses are independent action and cooperative action.

independent action

A company uses independent strategies when it acts on its own to change some aspect of its current environment. Several independent strategies are possible:[44]

- *Competitive aggression*—Exploiting a distinctive competence or improving internal efficiency for competitive advantage (e.g., aggressive pricing and comparative advertising). Southwest Airlines cuts fares when it enters a new market, and Sony positioned itself as the gaming industry's technological leader with the launch of the PS3.

- *Competitive pacification*—Independent action to improve relations with competitors (e.g., helping competitors find raw materials). Kellogg Company promotes the cereal industry as a whole, as well as advertising its various brands.

- *Public relations*—Establishing and maintaining favorable images in the minds of those making up the environment (e.g., sponsoring sporting events). Weyerhaeuser Company advertises its reforestation efforts.

- *Voluntary action*—Voluntary commitment to various interest groups, causes, and social problems (e.g., donating supplies to tsunami victims). The Gap, Motorola, Nike, American Express, Converse, and other companies have signed on to Product Red, a program in which they market special Red-themed products and donate a percentage of the profits to the Global Fund, a project to help end AIDS in Africa.

- *Legal action*—Engaging the company in a private legal battle (e.g., lawsuits against illegal music copying). Viacom sued Google for allowing users to post copyrighted video clips on the Google-owned YouTube Web site.

- *Political action*—Efforts to influence elected representatives to create a more favorable business environment or limit competition (e.g., issue advertising; lobbying at state and national levels). In a recent year, pharmaceutical companies spent $1.1 billion to lobby members of Congress; insurers, the second biggest spenders on lobbying, paid out almost $900 million.[45]

Each of these examples shows how organizations—on their own—can have an impact on the environment.

cooperative action

In some situations, two or more organizations work together using cooperative strategies to influence the environment.[46] Several types of cooperative strategies are common:[47]

- *Contraction*—Negotiating an agreement between the organization and another group to exchange goods, services, information, patents, and so on. Suppliers and customers, or managers and labor unions, may sign formal agreements about the terms and conditions of their future relationships. These contracts are explicit attempts to make their future relationship predictable.

- *Cooptation*—Absorbing new elements into the organization's leadership structure to avert threats to its stability or existence. Many universities invite wealthy alumni to join their boards of directors.

- *Coalition*—Groups that coalesce and act jointly with respect to a set of political initiatives for some period of time. Local businesses may band together to curb the rise of employee health care costs, and organizations in some industries have formed industry associations and special-interest groups. You may have seen cooperative advertising strategies, such as when dairy producers, beef producers, or orange growers jointly pay to advertise their products on television. Life Is Good, a New England–based T-shirt company, used the latest economic downturn to strengthen cooperative action with the retailers that stock its products. According to cofounder Bert Jacobs, employees at Life Is Good began calling retailers to ask how they could help them through the slow times. Based on the feedback, Jacobs identified a need to establish online networks that retailers—his company's customers—could use for sharing ideas.[48]

At the organizational level, firms establish strategic alliances, partnerships, joint ventures, and mergers with competitors to deal with environmental uncertainties. Cooperative strategies such as these make most sense when two conditions exist:

1. Taking joint action will reduce the organizations' costs and risks.

2. Cooperation will increase their power (their ability to successfully accomplish the changes they desire).

Change the boundaries of the environment you're in

Besides changing themselves (environmental adaptation) or their environment, organizations can redefine or change which environment they are in. We refer to this last category as **strategic maneuvering**. By making a conscious effort to change the boundaries of its competitive environment, a firm can maneuver around potential threats and capitalize on

Top four industry/labor sectors for PAC spending

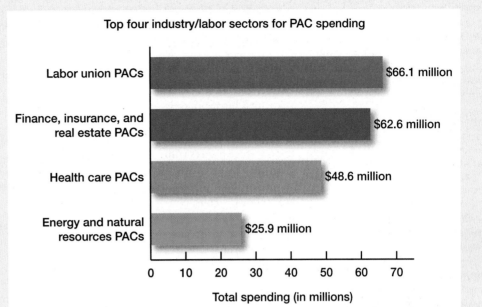

Labor union PACs	$66.1 million
Finance, insurance, and real estate PACs	$62.6 million
Health care PACs	$48.6 million
Energy and natural resources PACs	$25.9 million

Total spending (in millions)

DID YOU KNOW?

Companies or organizations within an industry sometimes form political action committees (PACs) to raise money to help elect lawmakers with favorable points of view. During the most recent presidential-election year, the biggest spenders were labor unions; the most PAC spending by businesses came from companies in finance, insurance, and real estate.[49]

That Was THEN . . .

Competition for business used to be strictly local. Often, a shopkeeper might be the only business in town, providing a multitude of products for customers.

This Is NOW . . .

Today's businesses compete on a global level. With their consumers' increasing incomes, Asian countries represent tremendous opportunities for growth. Shown here is a McDonald's advertisement in Japan.

opportunities.[50] Managers can use several strategic maneuvers, including domain selection, diversification, merger and acquisition, and divestiture.[51]

Domain selection is the entrance by a company into another suitable market or industry. For instance, the market may have limited competition or regulation, ample suppliers and customers, or high growth. An example is Nintendo's decision to create products such as the Wii that appeal to customer segments that have not been enthusiastic to purchase videogames, such as people intimidated by complicated game controllers and parents concerned about the violent content and sedentary play involved in videogames. By avoiding head-on competition to be the product with the best graphics or most advanced play, Nintendo was able to enjoy immediate profits from its new console. This approach builds on the company's earlier success with its DS, which lured not only young game players but also women and older-than-average players with its touch screens and games like Brain Age and Nintendogs.[52] Thus, Nintendo has used an existing expertise to broaden the goods and services it offers.

Diversification occurs when a firm invests in different types of businesses or products or when it expands geographically to reduce its dependence on a single market or technology. Apple's launch of the iPod is a good example of effective diversification. While Apple struggled in the highly competitive computer industry, where its Macintosh had only a 3 percent market share, the iPod has gobbled up three-quarters of the market for portable digital music players *and* for online music sales. More recently, its launch of the iPhone generated considerable buzz. The company's name change from "Apple Computer" to simply "Apple" makes sense in light of these diversification moves.[53]

A **merger** or **acquisition** takes place when two or more firms combine, or one firm buys another, to form a single company. Mergers and acquisitions can offer greater efficiency from combined operations or can give companies relatively quick access to new markets or industries. After Bayer acquired Schering, it announced plans to cut more than 6,000 jobs to "create an internationally successful pharmaceutical company with competitive cost structures," in the words of Werner Wenning, Bayer Schering Pharma's board chairman.[54] Electronic Arts, publisher of videogames, acquired Headgate Studios, a smaller game publisher whose titles include "Tiger Woods PGA Tour" and "Madden NFL." The acquisition helped Electronic Arts add quickly to its list of games for the Wii when sales of the console and its games exceeded expectations.[55]

Divestiture occurs when a company sells one or more businesses. At Ford Motor Company, recent operating losses and the costs of restructuring its workforce have brought about a cash shortage. To raise cash, Ford sold its Aston Martin sports-car brand and its Hertz rental-car unit.[56]

Organizations engage in strategic maneuvering when they move into different environments. Some companies, called **prospectors**, are more likely than others to engage in strategic maneuvering.[57] Aggressive companies continuously change the boundaries of their competitive environments by seeking new products and markets, diversifying, and merging or acquiring new enterprises. In these and other ways, corporations put their competitors on the defensive and force them to react. **Defenders**, in contrast, stay within a more limited, stable product domain.

Three criteria help you choose the best approach

Three general considerations help guide management's response to the environment:

1. Organizations should attempt to *change appropriate elements of the environment.* Environmental responses are most useful when aimed at elements of the environment that cause the company problems, provide opportunities, and allow the company to change successfully. Thus, Nintendo recognized that its game console would have difficulty competing on superior graphics, so it addressed underserved segments of the market, where customers and favorable publicity made the Wii successful.

2. Organizations should *choose responses that focus on pertinent elements of the environment.* If a company wants to better manage its competitive environment, competitive aggression and pacification are viable. Political action influences the legal environment, and contracting helps manage customers and suppliers.

▷ No business likes bad press, but if it occurs, managers must choose a response. They can ignore the negative publicity or address it in such a way that the incident is viewed as neutral, or even positive. When Washington, D.C., restaurateur Mark Sakuta discovered criticisms of his restaurant on the Web site for the *Washington Post,* he was at first puzzled. About 10 negative reviews appeared simultaneously, accusing the restaurant of using cookbook recipes instead of its own original concoctions, claiming that the floor was unstable, and more. A month later, another harsh review criticized the gratuity policy for large groups.

Sakuta knew that the first group of accusations was simply untrue. He suspected they were written by disgruntled former employees. So he called customer service at the Web site and asked to have the postings removed. The site manager agreed. But Sakuta did not ask to have the comment about the tipping policy removed because it was accurate. Instead, he decided to adjust the policy. He reasoned that if customers were uncomfortable with it, they might choose to dine elsewhere. Now Sakuta keeps closer tabs on food-related Web sites and blogs, looking for any comments about his business.[58]

3. Companies should *choose responses that offer the most benefit at the lowest cost.* Return-on-investment calculations should incorporate short-term financial considerations and long-term impact.

Strategic managers who consider these factors carefully will guide their organizations to competitive advantage more effectively.

 In the case of online critics, most responses cost little or nothing. Often, a person just wants to be heard. If it's a customer, "Maybe something they bought isn't working, and customer service says they can't do anything, so now they want to drag that business through the mud," says Joseph Fiore, vice president of CoreX Technology and Solutions. "They're hoping someone will come along and say that happened to me too." Fiore's firm investigates such blogs. Most such situations can be solved with an e-mail or a phone call. But a firm's managers must take action to correct any false information that has been posted so that it doesn't spread and ruin the company's reputation.

Taking a proactive stance can help as well. A company can set up its own site, providing a forum for customers to share feedback. "Some people just need to vent, and if you don't provide a place where you can monitor and do something about those complaints, then they often go elsewhere," warns Alysa Zeltzer, an associate attorney with a law firm in Washington, D.C. Either way, a firm should keep an eye on its Internet reputation.[59]

(L)(O) 6 WHAT YOU NEED TO KNOW . . .
Can you define elements of an organization's culture?

CULTURE AND THE INTERNAL ENVIRONMENT OF ORGANIZATIONS

One of the most important factors that influence an organization's response to its external environment is its culture. Organization culture is the set of important assumptions about the organization and its goals and practices that members of the company share. It is a system of shared values about what is important and beliefs about how the world works. It provides a framework that organizes and directs people's behavior on the job.[60] The culture of an organization may be difficult for an observer to define easily, yet like an individual's personality, it can often be sensed almost immediately. For example, the way people dress and behave, the way they interact with each other and with customers, and the qualities valued by their managers are usually quite different at a bank than they are at a rock-music company, and different again at a law firm or an advertising agency.

Cultures can be strong or weak; strong cultures can greatly influence the way people think and behave. A strong culture is one in which everyone understands and believes in the firm's goals, priorities, and practices. A strong culture can be a real advantage to the organization if the behaviors it encourages and facilitates are appropriate. The Walt Disney Company's culture encourages extraordinary devotion to customer service; the culture at Apple encourages innovation. Employees in these companies don't need rule books to dictate how they act, because these behaviors are conveyed as "the way we do things around here," rooted in their companies' cultures.

In contrast, a strong culture that encourages inappropriate behaviors can severely hinder an organization's ability to deal effectively with its external environment—particularly if the environment is undergoing change, as is almost always the case today. A culture that was suitable and even advantageous in a prior era may become counterproductive in a new environment. For instance, a small start-up may have an informal culture that becomes less suitable when the company grows, faces more competition, and requires decision making by a wide range of specialized employees spread out over many locations.

In its relatively short life as a company, Google quickly became a role model for its brainy culture of innovation. Software writers and engineers were attracted to Google not just for its famous perks such as free meals and laundry facilities but also for a climate in which they were encouraged to let their imaginations roam free, dreaming up ideas that could be crazy but just might be the next big thing on the Internet.

During a long-running business boom, that culture served Google well. The best engineers were thrilled to work for a company that let them spend one-fifth of their time on new projects of their own choosing. But when the economy slowed and the stock market nosedived, Google's managers had to cope with a new reality in which money was tight. Google could no longer afford its free-spending culture. Managers had to figure out how to maintain the best of the culture while innovating at a more prudent pace.

Google's modified culture now values setting priorities. New ideas are still welcome if they are focused on core businesses of search, advertising, and Web-based software applications. Managers are reassigning employees away from teams working on unrelated projects and using them to staff teams working on profitable ideas in the core areas. Employees who have an idea that can improve the computer user's experience are asked to consider also what impact that idea might have on Google's bottom line. Similarly, hiring has slowed, because managers must not only justify the talent of a candidate but also target hiring to particular business needs. The challenge will be to keep employees as excited about targeted innovation as they have been about freewheeling innovation.[61]

Similarly, when a merger or acquisition brings together organizations with strong cultures, cultural differences can encourage behaviors that are harmful to the combined organization. After Sprint acquired Nextel, conflicts arose because the two wireless carriers had different cultures. Sprint moved more cautiously, while Nextel's culture was more entrepreneurial. Such differences in style can be unsettling to employees on both sides and may help to explain why research has found much higher turnover rates among managers at companies that have been acquired.[62]

In contrast, at a company with a weak culture, different people hold different values, there is confusion about corporate goals, and it is not clear from one day to the next what principles should guide decisions. Some managers may pay lip service to

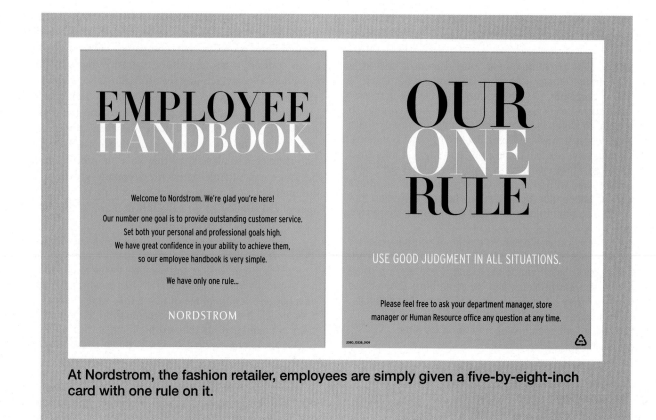

At Nordstrom, the fashion retailer, employees are simply given a five-by-eight-inch card with one rule on it.

some aspects of the culture ("we would never cheat a customer") but behave very differently ("don't tell him about the flaw"). As you can guess, such a culture fosters confusion, conflict, and poor performance. Most managers would agree that they want to create a strong culture that encourages and supports goals and useful behaviors that will make the company more effective. In other words, they want to create a culture that is appropriately aligned with the organization's competitive environment.[63]

Companies leave many clues to their culture

Let's say you want to understand a company's culture. Perhaps you are thinking about working there and you want a good "fit," or perhaps you are working there right now and want to deepen your understanding of the organization and determine whether its culture matches the challenges it faces. How would you go about making the diagnosis? A variety of things will give you useful clues about culture:

• *Corporate mission statements and official goals* are a starting point, because they will tell you the firm's desired public image. Most companies have a mission statement—even the CIA (you can find it at http://www.cia .gov). Your school has one, and you can probably find it online. But are these statements a

true expression of culture? A study of hospital employees and their managers found that managers rated their mission statement more positively than nonmanagers (even though employees had participated in developing it), and three out of ten employees were not even aware that the hospital had a mission statement (even though the hospital had processes for communicating about it).[64] So, even after reading statements of mission and goals, you still need to figure out whether the statements truly reflect how the firm conducts business.

• *Business practices* can be observed. How a company responds to problems, makes strategic decisions, and treats employees and customers tells a lot about what top management really values. After its acquisition of the *Los Angeles Times,* the Tribune Company's repeated efforts to cut costs at the *Times* and consolidate its Washington bureau with that of the chain's other newspapers told the acquired company's employees about the parent company's priorities.

• *Symbols, rites, and ceremonies* give further clues about culture. For instance, status symbols can give you a feel for how rigid the hierarchy is and for the nature of relationships between lower and higher levels. Who is hired and fired—and why—and the activities that are rewarded indicate the firm's real values.

• *The stories people tell* carry a lot of information about the company's culture. Every

TIP

Clues to a company's culture can be found by looking at what its corporate mission statement says, how employees behave and treat customers, who is rewarded and punished, and what stories employees tell and pass on.

company has its myths, legends, and true stories about important past decisions and actions that convey the company's main values. The stories often feature the company's heroes: people once or still active who possessed the qualities and characteristics that the culture especially values and who act as models for others about how to behave.

A strong culture combines these measures in a consistent way. The Ritz-Carlton hotel chain gives each employee a laminated card listing its 12 service values. Each day it carries out a type of ceremony: a 15-minute meeting during which employees from every department resolve problems and discuss areas of potential improvement. At these meetings, the focus is on the day's "wow story," which details an extraordinary way that a Ritz-Carlton employee lived up to one of the service values. For example, a family arrived at the Bali Ritz-Carlton with special eggs and milk because of their son's allergies, but the food had spoiled. The manager and dining staff couldn't find replacements in town, so the executive chef called his mother-in-law in Singapore and asked her to buy the necessary products and fly with them to Bali.[65]

(L)(O) 7 WHAT YOU NEED TO KNOW . . .

How does an organization's culture affect its response to its external environment?

In general, cultures can be categorized according to whether they emphasize flexibility versus control and whether their focus is internal or external to the organization. By juxtaposing these two dimensions, we can describe four types of organizational cultures, depicted in Figure 2.5:

- *Group culture.* A group culture is internally oriented and flexible. It tends to be based on the values and norms associated with affiliation. An organizational member's compliance with organizational directives flows from trust, tradition,

and long-term commitment. It tends to emphasize member development and values participation in decision making. The strategic orientation associated with this cultural type is one of implementation through consensus building. Leaders tend to act as mentors and facilitators.

- *Hierarchical culture.* The hierarchical culture is internally oriented by more focus on control and stability. It has the values and norms associated with a bureaucracy. It values stability and assumes that individuals will comply with organizational mandates when roles are stated formally and enforced through rules and procedures.

- *Rational culture.* The rational culture is externally oriented and focused on control. Its primary objectives are productivity, planning, and efficiency. Organizational members are motivated by the belief that performance that leads to the desired organizational objectives will be rewarded.

- *Adhocracy.* The adhocracy is externally oriented and flexible. This culture type emphasizes change in which growth, resource acquisition, and innovation are stressed. Organizational members are motivated by the importance or ideological appeal of the task. Leaders tend to be entrepreneurial and risk takers. Other members tend to have these characteristics as well.[66]

This type of diagnosis is important when two companies are considering combining operations, as in a merger, acquisition, or joint venture, because as we noted, cultural differences can sink these arrangements. In some cases, organizations investigating this type of change can benefit from setting up a "clean team" of third-party experts who investigate the details of each company's culture. For example, they might conduct employee focus groups, look for systems that empower employees to make independent decisions, and note how management talks about the company's founder, customers, and employees. In this way, the clean team can identify for the organizations' leaders the types of issues they will have to resolve and the values they must choose among as they try to establish a combined culture.[67]

Culture can be managed

We mentioned earlier in this chapter that one important way organizations have of responding to the environment is to *adapt* to it by changing the organization itself. One of the most important tools managers have for implementing such a change lies in their management of their organization's culture. For example, a strong focus on customer service will be difficult to establish in a culture that is inwardly instead of customer focused. Simple directives alone are often ineffective; the underlying values of the organization also have to be shifted in the desired direction. Most companies today know that making moves necessary to remain competitive is so essential that they require deep-rooted cultural changes. When that kind of change occurs, organization members may begin to internalize the new values and display the appropriate behaviors.

Top managers can take several approaches to managing culture. First, they should espouse lofty ideals and visions for the

FIGURE **2.5** **Competing-Values Model of Culture**

**Flexible
Processes**

Type: Group
Dominant Attribute:
Cohesiveness, participation,
teamwork, sense of family
Leadership Style: Mentor,
facilitator, parent figure
Bonding: Loyalty, tradition,
interpersonal cohesion
Strategic Emphasis: Toward
developing human resources,
commitment, and morale

Type: Adhocracy
Dominant Attribute:
Entrepreneurship, creativity,
adaptability, dynamism
Leadership Style: Innovator,
entrepreneur, risk taker
Bonding: Flexibility, risk,
entrepreneur
Strategic Emphasis: Toward
innovation, growth, new
resources

**Internal
Maintenance**

**External
Positioning**

Type: Hierarchy
Dominant Attribute: Order, rules
and regulations, uniformity,
efficiency
Leadership Style: Coordinator,
organizer, administrator
Bonding: Rules, policies and
procedures, clear expectations
Strategic Emphasis: Toward
stability, predictability, smooth

Type: Rational
Dominant Attribute: Goal
achievement, environment
exchange, competitiveness
Leadership Style: Production-
& achievement-oriented,
decisive
Bonding: Goal orientation,
production, competition
Strategic Emphasis: Toward
competitive advantage and
market superiority

**Control-Oriented
Processes**

SOURCE: Kim S. Cameron and Robert E. Quinn, *Diagnosing and Changing Organizational Culture* (Englewood Cliffs, NJ; Addison-Wesley, 1988). Used by permission of the author.

company that will inspire organization members. That vision should be articulated over and over until it becomes a tangible presence throughout the organization.

Second, executives must give constant attention to the mundane details of daily affairs such as communicating regularly, being visible and active throughout the company, and setting examples. The CEO not only should talk about the vision but also should embody it day in and day out. This makes the CEO's pronouncements credible, creates a personal example others can emulate, and builds trust that the organization's progress toward the vision will continue over the long run.

what type of company culture
is important to you
in your career?

one that emphasizes

teamwork ⟸ or ⟹ efficiency?
creativity ⟸ or ⟹ competitiveness?

Important here are the moments of truth requiring hard choices. Imagine top management trumpeting a culture that emphasizes quality and then discovering that a part used in a batch of assembled products is defective. Whether to replace the part at great expense in the interest of quality or to ship the defective part to save time and money is a decision that will reinforce or destroy a quality-oriented culture.

To reinforce the organization's culture, the CEO and other executives should routinely celebrate and reward those who exemplify the new values. Another key to managing culture involves hiring, socializing newcomers, and promoting employees on the basis of the

new corporate values. In this way, the new culture will begin to permeate the organization. While this may seem a time-consuming approach to building a new culture, effective managers recognize that replacing a long-term culture of traditional values with one that embodies the competitive values needed in the future can take years. But the rewards of that effort will be an organization much more effective and responsive to its environmental challenges and opportunities.

"Be the change you want to see in the world."

—Mahatma Gandhi

DIY

Build Your Skills

Practice and apply your knowledge by going online at

www.mhhe.com/ BatemanM2e

3

Ethics and Corporate Responsibility

Walmart, the world's largest retailer, has gone green. Since 2005 it has worked to plan and execute a sustainability strategy that includes using renewable energy sources, reducing its waste, and selling sustainable products. A packaging scorecard helps Walmart's 60,000 suppliers learn about Walmart's expectations and guides the firm in making its purchasing decisions. The company has built energy-efficient stores and retrofitted others, and it offers reusable shopping bags made of recycled materials. Although Walmart doesn't disclose financial details on the green initiative, it says the program is already saving money and resources, and it projects billions in savings over time.[1]

Hear the True Story

of how today's managers do the right thing. Listen to what Derrick and Elaine have to say.

"Ethics are crucial in the property management business. We are obligated to abide by fair housing laws in our day-to-day operations. Not only do we have an obligation as a company but also a social obligation to make sure our vendors and contractors are aware of these practices."
— *Derrick Hawthorne, Property Manager*

"The very nature and mission of my project is that of social responsibility. We are trying to do our part to help out developing countries in a way that an agricultural library is best equipped to do. Good workplace ethics translates into a better product for our subscribers. The better I and my employees perform, the better our product and the most useful it is to the end users, thus furthering the idea of social responsibility."
— *Elaine Guidero, Library Manager*

WHAT YOU NEED TO KNOW

●● learning **OBJECTIVES**

After studying Chapter 3,
you will be able to:

LO1 Describe how different ethical
perspectives guide decision
making.

LO2 Explain how companies influence
their ethics environment.

LO3 Outline a process for making
ethical decisions.

LO4 Summarize the important issues
surrounding corporate social
responsibility.

LO5 Discuss reasons for businesses'
growing interest in the natural
environment.

LO6 Identify actions managers can take
to manage with the environment in
mind.

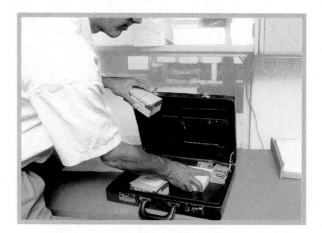

ETHICS The system of rules that governs the ordering of values.

This chapter addresses the values and manner of doing business adopted by managers as they carry out their corporate and business strategies. In particular, we will explore ways of applying ethics, the system of rules that governs the ordering of values. We do so based on the premise that managers, their organizations, and their communities thrive over the long term when the managers apply ethical standards that direct them to act with integrity. In addition, we consider the idea that organizations may have a responsibility to meet social obligations beyond earning profits within legal and ethical constraints. As you study this chapter, consider what kind of manager you want to be. What reputation do you hope to have? How would you like others to describe your behavior as a manager?

It's a big issue

Recent scandals engulfed company executives, independent auditors, politicians and regulators, and shareholders and employees. In some, executives at public companies made misleading statements to inflate stock prices, undermining the public's trust in the integrity of the financial markets. Often, the scandals were perpetrated by several people cooperating, and many of the guilty parties had been otherwise upstanding individuals.[2] Lobbyists have been accused—and some convicted—of buying influence with lavish gifts to politicians. Executives have admitted they received huge bonuses or stock options that were backdated to guarantee they would make money from investing in their company, regardless of whether their performance caused the stock's value to rise or fall. What other news disturbs you about managers' behavior? Tainted products in the food supply . . . damage to the environment . . . Internet scams . . . employees pressured to

employees, who had been encouraged to invest their retirement packages heavily in their company's stock, saw their savings disappear along with their company's reputation.

Still, simply talking about Enron and other famous cases as examples of lax company ethics doesn't get at the heart of the problem. Clearly, these cases involve "bad guys," and the ethical lapses are obvious. But saying "I would never do things like that" becomes too easy. The fact is that temptations exist in every organization. In a survey called the Spherion Workplace Snapshot, more than one-third of U.S. adults said they had observed unethical conduct at work. About one out of five reported seeing abuse or intimidation of employees; lying to employees, customers, vendors, or the public; or situations in which employees placed their own interests ahead of their company's interests.[4]

The motivations aren't always as obvious as greed. Another survey, conducted by the American Management Association and the Human Resource Institute, found that the top

> "It is truly enough said that a corporation has no conscience; but a corporation of conscientious men is a corporation with a conscience."
>
> —Henry David Thoreau

meet sales or production targets by any means? The list goes on, and the public becomes cynical. In a survey by public relations firm Edelman, barely more than half of American respondents said they trust business, and less than one-fourth said they trust CEOs. They're even suspicious of their own company's management; only 31 percent said they trust their own CEO.[3] Try to imagine the challenge of leading employees who don't trust you.

Sadly, when corporations behave badly, it's often not the top executives but the rank-and-file employees who suffer most. When companies such as energy trader Enron and insurance brokerage firm Marsh & McLennan saw their stocks tumble following scandals, executives were left with millions of dollars from their generous pay and bonus packages. In contrast,

justification given for unethical behavior was "pressure to meet unrealistic goals and deadlines."[5] Many of the decisions you will face as a manager will pose ethical dilemmas, and the right thing to do is not always clear.

It's a personal issue

"Answer true or false: 'I am an ethical manager.' If you answered 'true,' here's an uncomfortable fact: You're probably not."[6] These sentences are the first in a *Harvard Business Review* article called "How (Un)Ethical Are You?" The point is that most of us think we are good decision makers, ethical and unbiased. But the fact is, most people have unconscious biases that favor themselves and their own group. For example, managers often hire people who are like them, think they are immune to conflicts of interest, take more credit than they deserve, and blame others when they deserve some blame themselves.

To know that you have biases may help you try to overcome them, but usually that's not enough. Consider the basic ethical issue of telling a lie. Many people lie—some more than others, and in part depending on the situation, usually presuming that they will benefit from the lie. At a basic level, we all can make ethical arguments against lying and in favor of honesty. Yet it is useful to think thoroughly about the real consequences of lying.[7] Table 3.1 summarizes the possible outcomes of telling the truth or lying in different situations. People often lie or commit other ethical transgressions somewhat mindlessly, without realizing the full array of negative personal consequences.

Ethics issues are not easy, and they are not faced only by newsworthy corporate CEOs. You will face them; no doubt, you already have. You've got your own examples, but consider this one: more and more people at work use computers with Internet access. If the employer pays for the computer and the time you spend sitting in front of it, is it ethical for you to use the computer to do tasks unrelated to your work? Would you bend the rules for certain activities or certain amounts of time? Maybe you think it's OK to do a little online shopping during your lunch hour or to check scores during the World Series or March Madness. But what if you stream video of the games for your own and your coworkers' enjoyment or take a two-hour lunch to locate the best deal on a flat-panel TV?

Besides lost productivity, employers are most concerned about computer users introducing viruses, leaking confidential information, and creating a hostile work environment by downloading inappropriate Web content. Sometimes employees write blogs or post comments online about their company and its products. Obviously, companies do not want their employees to say bad things about them, but some companies are concerned about employees who are overly enthusiastic. When employees plug their companies and products on comments pages, this practice is considered spamming at best and deceptive if the employees don't disclose their relationship with their company. Another practice considered deceptive is when companies create fictional blogs as a marketing tactic without disclosing their sponsorship. And in a practice known as Astroturfing—because the "grassroots" interest it builds is fake—businesses pay bloggers to write positive comments about them. A Florida company known as PayPerPost will match advertisers with bloggers but now requires bloggers to disclose the relationship. Companies such as Coca-Cola, UPS, and IBM have established guidelines directing employees to identify themselves accurately in online communications so that they can participate in online conversations about their companies without being accused of deception.[8]

TABLE 3.1	Telling the Truth and Lying: Possible Outcomes	
Reason and Context of the Lie	**Results of Lying**	**Results of Truth-Telling**
Conflicting expectations	• Easier to lie than to address the underlying conflict. • Offers quick relief of the issue. • Leaves the underlying problem unresolved. • May have no meaningful consequences, good or bad. • Liar must rationalize the action in order to preserve positive self-concept.	• Emotionally more difficult than lying. • May correct underlying problem. • May provoke further conflict. • Sometimes difficult to have an impact on an impermeable structure. • Develops one's reputation as an "honest" person.
Negotiation	• Short-term gain. • Economically positive. • Harms long-term relationship. • Must rationalize to oneself.	• Supports high-quality long-term relationship. • Develops reputation of integrity. • Models behavior to others.
Keeping a confidence (that may require at least a lie of omission)	• Protects whatever good reason there is for the confidence. • Maintains a long-term relationship with the party for whom confidence is kept. • May project deceitfulness to the deceived party.	• Violates a trust to the confiding party. • Makes one appear deceitful to all parties in the long run. • Creates the impression of honesty beyond utility.
Reporting your own performance within an organization	• Might advance oneself or one's cause. • Develops dishonest reputation over time. • Must continue the sequence of lies to appear consistent.	• Creates reputation of integrity. • May not always be positive.

SOURCE: S. L. Grover, "The Truth, the Whole Truth, and Nothing but the Truth: The Causes and Management of Workplace Lying," *Academy of Management Executive* 19 (May 2005), pp. 148–57, table 1, p. 155.

Are these examples too small to worry about? What do you do that has potential ethical ramifications? This chapter will help you think through decisions with ethical ramifications.

L O 1 **WHAT YOU NEED TO KNOW . . .**

How do different ethical perspectives guide decision making?

ETHICS

The aim of ethics is to identify both the rules that should govern people's behavior and the "goods" that are worth seeking. Ethical decisions are guided by the underlying values of the individual. Values are principles of conduct such as caring, being honest, keeping promises, pursuing excellence, showing loyalty, being fair, acting with integrity, respecting others, and being a responsible citizen.[10]

Most people would agree that all of these values are admirable guidelines for behavior. However, ethics becomes a more complicated issue when a situation dictates that one value overrules others. An **ethical issue** is a situation, problem, or opportunity in which an individual must choose among several actions that must be evaluated as morally right or wrong.[11] Ethical issues arise in every facet of life; we concern ourselves here with business ethics in particular. **Business ethics** comprises the moral principles and standards that guide behavior in the world of business.[12]

Ethical systems shape how you apply ethics

Moral philosophy refers to the principles, rules, and values people use in deciding what is right or wrong. This seems to be a simple definition but often becomes terribly complex and difficult when facing real choices. How do you decide what is right and wrong? Do you know what criteria you apply and how you apply them?

Ethics scholars point to various major ethical systems as guides.[13] We will consider five of these:

1. Universalism
2. Egoism
3. Utilitarianism
4. Relativism
5. Virtue ethics

These major ethical systems underlie personal moral choices and ethical decisions in business.

A+

TIP

Here's a small but potentially powerful suggestion.[9] Change your vocabulary: The word "ethics" is too loaded, even trite. Substitute "responsibility" or "decency." And act accordingly.

universalism According to **universalism**, all people should uphold certain values, such as honesty and other values that society needs to function. Universal values are principles so fundamental to human existence that they are important in all societies—for example, rules against murder, deceit, torture, and oppression.

Some efforts have been made to establish global, universal ethical principles for business. The Caux Roundtable, a group of international executives based in Caux, Switzerland, worked with business leaders from Japan, Europe, and the United States to create the **Caux Principles for Business**.[14] Two basic ethical ideals underpin the Caux Principles: *kyosei* and human dignity. *Kyosei* means living and working together for the common good, allowing cooperation and mutual prosperity to coexist with healthy and fair competition. Human dignity concerns the value of each person as an end, not a means to the fulfillment of others' purposes.

?

DID YOU KNOW?

Are women more ethical than men? Studies have implied they are, at least by some measures. Surveys of business students found an increase in their interest in studying ethics, with a greater increase among women. Compared with their female counterparts, undergraduate male students in business and psychology showed stronger unethical attitudes and a tendency to behave unethically. When business students took an ethics curriculum, women made greater strides than men in improving their moral awareness and decision-making processes.[15]

Universal principles can be powerful and useful, but what people say, hope, or think they would do is often different from what they *really* do, faced with conflicting demands in real situations. Before we describe other ethical systems, consider the following example, and think about how you or others would resolve it.

 Suppose that Sam Colt, a sales representative, is preparing a sales presentation on behalf of his firm, Midwest Hardware, which manufactures nuts and bolts. Colt hopes to obtain a large sale from a construction firm that is building a bridge across the Missouri River near St. Louis. The bolts manufactured by Midwest Hardware have a 3 percent defect rate, which, although acceptable in the industry, makes them unsuitable for use in certain types of projects, such as those that might be subject to sudden, severe stress. The new bridge will be located near the New Madrid Fault line, the source of a major earthquake in 1811. The epicenter of that earthquake, which caused extensive damage and altered the flow of the Missouri, is about 190 miles from the new bridge site.

Bridge construction in the area is not regulated by earthquake codes. If Colt wins the sale, he will earn a commission of $25,000 on top of his regular salary. But if he tells the contractors about the defect rate, Midwest may lose the sale to a competitor whose bolts are slightly more reliable. Thus, Colt's ethical issue is whether to point out to the bridge contractor that in the event of an earthquake, some Midwest bolts could fail.[16]

egoism and utilitarianism

According to egoism, acceptable behavior is that which maximizes benefits for the individual. "Doing the right thing," the focus of moral philosophy, is defined by egoism as "do the act that promotes the greatest good for oneself." If everyone follows this system, according to its proponents, the well-being of society as a whole should increase. This notion is similar to Adam Smith's concept of the invisible hand in business. Smith argued that if every organization follows its own economic self-interest, the total wealth of society will be maximized.

Unlike egoism, utilitarianism directly seeks the greatest good for the greatest number of people. Consider whether utilitarianism would help guide ethical decision making with regard to student loan programs. Recently, New York's attorney general, Andrew Cuomo, investigated 100 colleges and half a dozen lenders for arrangements in which the lenders allegedly offered payments, stock grants, and perks to schools, and the schools listed the companies as "preferred lenders" in information given to students who wanted to borrow tuition money from private sources. For example, Citibank's student loan group had been paying schools a percentage of the loans resulting from referrals by the schools. Cuomo called the arrangements "kickbacks"; some schools replied that they were not being corrupted but used the money to add to the financial aid they could award to students. The investigation also looked into why at least one university's financial aid official owned stock in one of its "preferred" lenders, Student Loan Xpress—an arrangement that could be seen as a conflict of interest.[17]

Whereas ethics based on egoism would accept actions that allow the lenders to maximize their earnings and the financial aid officers to pursue whatever arrangements benefit themselves and their schools, utilitarianism requires a broader view. Most obviously, there is the question of what these arrangements cost students who make borrowing decisions on the assumption that "preferred" lenders will give students the best deals. But other students benefited if payments from lenders were used to augment the financial aid given to other students. The utilitarian approach might consider

- How many students benefited
- How much those students benefited
- How many students paid extra for loans
- How much more they paid

In fact, the companies involved may have preferred standards other than utilitarianism. Citibank responded to the allegations by agreeing to a code of conduct that forbids gifts in exchange for "preferred" status, and Student Loan Xpress's parent company, CIT Group, placed three executives on leave while it investigated the allegations.[18]

- **ETHICAL ISSUE** Situation, problem, or opportunity in which an individual must choose among several actions that must be evaluated as morally right or wrong.

- **BUSINESS ETHICS** The moral principles and standards that guide behavior in the world of business.

- **MORAL PHILOSOPHY** Principles, rules, and values people use in deciding what is right or wrong.

- **UNIVERSALISM** The ethical system stating that all people should uphold certain values that society needs to function.

- **CAUX PRINCIPLES** Ethical principles established by international executives based in Caux, Switzerland, in collaboration with business leaders from Japan, Europe, and the United States.

- **EGOISM** An ethical system defining acceptable behavior as that which maximizes consequences for the individual.

- **UTILITARIANISM** An ethical system stating that the greatest good for the greatest number should be the overriding concern of decision makers.

● **RELATIVISM** Philosophy that bases ethical behavior on the opinions and behaviors of relevant other people.

● **VIRTUE ETHICS** Perspective that what is moral comes from what a mature person with "good" moral character would deem right.

● **KOHLBERG'S MODEL OF COGNITIVE MORAL DEVELOPMENT** Classification of people based on their level of moral judgment.

● **SARBANES-OXLEY ACT** An act that established strict accounting and reporting rules to make senior managers more accountable and to improve and maintain investor confidence.

relativism It may seem that an individual makes ethical choices personally, applying personal perspectives. But this view is not necessarily true. Relativism defines ethical behavior based on the opinions and behaviors of relevant other people. In the previous example of student loans, U.S. business, government, and society largely agree that bribes, kickbacks, and conflicts of interest would not be acceptable behaviors for people in the lending industry—perhaps even less so for those charged with serving students. Those standards help to explain the rapid actions taken by the organizations when they found out about the situation.

Relativism acknowledges the existence of different ethical viewpoints. For example, *norms,* or standards of expected and acceptable behavior, vary from one culture to another. A study of Russian versus U.S. managers found that all followed norms of seeking informed consent about chemical hazards in work situations and paying wages on time. But in Russia more than in the United States, businesspeople were likely to consider the interests of a broader set of stakeholders (in this study, keeping factories open for the sake of local employment), to keep double books to hide information from tax inspectors and criminal organizations, and to make personal payments to government officials in charge of awarding contracts.[19] Relativism defines ethical behavior according to how others behave.

virtue ethics The moral philosophies just described apply different types of rules and reasoning. Virtue ethics is a perspective that goes beyond the conventional rules of society by suggesting that what is moral must also come from what a mature person with good "moral character" would deem right. Society's rules provide a moral minimum; moral individuals can transcend rules by applying their personal virtues such as faith, honesty, and integrity.

Yet, individuals differ in their moral development. Kohlberg's model of cognitive moral development classifies people into categories based on their level of moral judgment.[21] People in the *preconventional* stage make decisions based on concrete rewards and punishments and immediate self-interest. People in the *conventional* stage conform to the expectations of ethical behavior held by groups or institutions such as society, family, or peers. People in the *principled* stage see beyond authority, laws, and norms and follow their self-chosen ethical principles.[22] Some people forever reside in the preconventional stage, some move into the conventional stage, and some develop even further into the principled stage. Over time, and through education and experience, people may change their values and ethical behavior.

 Returning to the bolts-in-the-bridge example, *egoism* would result in keeping quiet about the bolts' defect rate. *Utilitarianism* would dictate a more thorough cost-benefit analysis and possibly the conclusion that the probability of a bridge collapse is so low compared to the utility of jobs, economic growth, and company growth that the defect rate is not worth mentioning. The *relativist* perspective might prompt the salesperson to look at company policy and general industry practice, and to seek opinions from colleagues and perhaps trade journals and ethics codes. Whatever is then perceived to be a consensus or normal practice would dictate action. Finally, *virtue ethics,* applied by people in the principled stage of moral development, would likely lead to full disclosure about the product and risks, and perhaps suggestions for alternatives that would reduce the risk.[23]

DID YOU KNOW?

In a recent survey ranking 180 nations from most to least honest, the United States came in 18th (tied with Japan and Belgium). The U.S. rating of 7.3 on a 10-point scale placed it among only 22 countries that scored at least a 7.0. The top ratings went to Denmark, Sweden, and New Zealand, each with 9.3. The bottom-ranked nations, including Somalia, Myanmar, and Iraq, tend to be among the poorest. Sadly, the combination of corruption and poverty in these nations can literally amount to a death sentence for many of their citizens.[20]

L O 2 WHAT YOU NEED TO KNOW . . .
How can companies influence their ethics environment?

Business ethics are valued but sometimes lacking

Insider trading, illegal campaign contributions, bribery and kickbacks, famous court cases, and other scandals have created a perception that business leaders use illegal means to gain competitive advantage, increase profits, or improve their personal positions. Neither young managers nor consumers believe top executives are doing a good job of establishing high ethical standards.[24] Some even joke that *business ethics* has become a contradiction in terms. Too often, these opinions are borne out by actual workplace experiences. In a recent survey of 700 employees holding a variety of jobs, 39 percent said their supervisor sometimes didn't keep promises, 24 percent said their supervisor had invaded their privacy, and

23 percent said their supervisor covered up his or her own mistakes by blaming someone else.[25]

Most business leaders believe they uphold ethical standards in business practices.[26] But many managers and their organizations must deal frequently with ethical dilemmas, and the issues are becoming increasingly complex. Here are just a few of the dilemmas challenging managers and employees today:[27]

- *Brands*—In-your-face marketing campaigns have sparked antibrand attitudes among people who see tactics as manipulative and deceptive.

- *CEO pay*—Nearly three-fourths of Americans say executives' pay packages are excessive.

- *Commercialism in schools*—Parent groups in hundreds of communities have battled advertising in the public schools.

- *Religion at work*—Many people seek spiritual renewal in the workplace, in part reflecting a broader religious awakening in America, while others argue that this trend violates religious freedom and the separation of church and boardroom.

- *Sweatshops*—At many colleges, students have formed anti-sweatshop groups, which picket clothing manufacturers, toymakers, and retailers.

- *Wages*—More than half of workers feel they are underpaid, especially as wages since 1992 have not grown as fast as productivity levels.

Two young men were arrested for hanging neon-lit boxes around Boston; the boxes were mistaken for explosives. But it turned out that the devices were nothing more than advertisements for an animated television show and movie produced by Cartoon Network, which is owned by Turner Broadcasting Systems. Parts of Boston were shut down for hours, police and other security resources were assigned to remove the boxes, and businesses and residents suffered from the incident. But who was responsible? Did the men display poor judgment by accepting the job? Or did responsibility ultimately lie with Cartoon Network and Turner Broadcasting?

Within several days, the head of Cartoon Network resigned, and Turner Broadcasting agreed to pay more than $1 million to the City of Boston as compensation for its emergency-response costs. Although similar boxes had been placed in nine other cities, none prompted the reaction that took place in Boston. "This is an irrational act," stated Kelly O'Keefe, director of executive education at the Virginia Commonwealth University Adcenter. "It is really guerrilla marketing gone awry, and it is inexcusable."[28]

Society demands an ethical climate

Responding to a series of corporate scandals—particularly the high-profile cases of Enron and WorldCom—Congress passed the **Sarbanes-Oxley Act** in 2002 to improve and maintain investor confidence. The law requires companies to do the following:

- Have more independent board directors, not just company insiders

- Adhere strictly to accounting rules

- Have senior managers personally sign off on financial results

Violations could result in heavy fines and criminal prosecution. One of the biggest impacts of the law is the requirement for companies and their auditors to provide reports to financial statement users about the effectiveness of internal controls over the financial reporting process.

Companies that make the effort to meet or exceed these requirements can reduce their risks by lowering the likelihood

Peter Berdovsky and Sean Stevens appeared in court for planting the boxes that were mistaken for bombs. Prosecutors agreed not to pursue criminal charges against them after the pair performed community service and gave a public apology in court.

of misdeeds and the consequences if an employee does break the law. Responding to a directive in the Sarbanes-Oxley Act, the U.S. Sentencing Commission modified the sentencing guidelines to say that organizations convicted of federal criminal laws may receive more lenient sentences if they are shown to have established an effective compliance and ethics program. To meet the requirements of these guidelines, organizations should establish written standards of ethical conduct and controls for enforcing them, assign responsibility to top managers to ensure that the program is working as intended, exclude anyone who violates the standards from holding management positions, provide training in ethics to all employees, monitor compliance, give employees incentives for complying and consequences for violating the standards, and respond with consequences and additional preventive measures if criminal conduct comes to light.[29]

Some executives say Sarbanes-Oxley distracts from their real work and makes them more risk averse. Some complain about the time and money needed to comply with the internal control reporting—reportedly spending millions of dollars for technology upgrades. Others point out that unethical behavior has negative consequences, especially when it includes illegal actions that later come to light. For example, companies that set up a hotline at which employees can report illegal or unethical conduct can find out when employees are engaged in fraud. Not only can fraud hurt customers, but it can also hurt the company itself when employees find ways to keep the company's cash or goods. The Association of Certified Fraud Examiners found that U.S. companies lose about 6 percent of their annual sales to fraud, but the losses are less than half that at organizations with a mechanism for reporting misconduct.[30] Regardless of managers' attitudes toward Sarbanes-Oxley, it creates legal requirements intended to improve ethical behavior.

Ethics are not shaped only by laws and by individual development and virtue. They also may be influenced by the company's work environment. The **ethical climate** of an organization refers to the processes by which decisions are evaluated and made on the basis of right and wrong.[31] For example, General Electric's top executives have demonstrated a commitment to promoting high levels of integrity without sacrificing the company's well-known commitment to business results. The measures taken by GE to maintain a positive ethical climate include establishing global standards for behavior to prevent ethical problems such as conflicts of interest and money laundering. As managers monitor the external environment, they are expected to consider legal and ethical developments, along with other concerns, so that the company can be prepared for new issues as they arise. Managers at all levels are rewarded for their performance in meeting both integrity and business standards, and when violations occur, even managers who were otherwise

successful are disciplined, sending a powerful message that ethical behavior is truly valued at GE.[32]

When people make decisions that are judged by ethical criteria, certain questions always seem to get asked: Why did she do it? Good motives or bad ones? His responsibility or someone else's? Who gets the credit, or the blame? So often, responsibility for unethical acts is placed squarely on the individual who commits them. But the work environment has a profound influence, as well. When employees feel pressured to meet unreasonable goals or deadlines, they may act individually, but managers are in part responsible for setting the right standards, selecting employees with the ability to meet standards, and providing employees with the resources required for success. Managers also need to keep the lines of communication open so that employees will discuss problems in meeting goals, rather than resorting to unethical and possibly illegal behavior.

Unethical corporate behavior may be the responsibility of an unethical individual, but it often also reveals a company culture that is ethically lax.[33] Maintaining a positive ethical climate is always challenging, but it is especially complex for organizations with international activities. Different cultures and countries may have different standards of behavior, and managers have to decide when relativism is appropriate, rather than adherence to firm standards. For example, consider the following real situations where ethics-related decisions have arisen in an international context. What would you do in each situation?

• You are a sales representative for a construction company in the Middle East. Your company wants very much to land a particular project. The cousin of the minister who will award

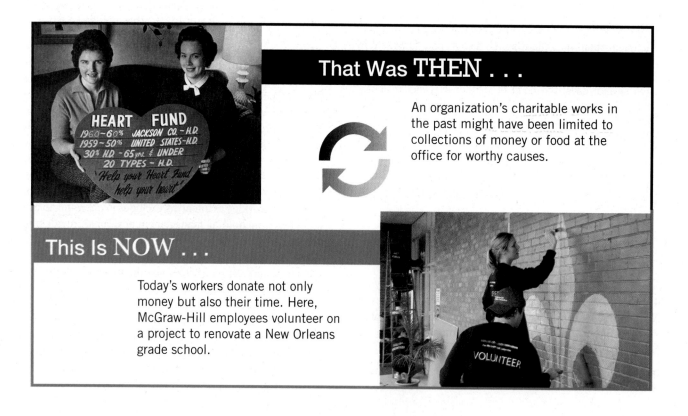

That Was THEN . . .

An organization's charitable works in the past might have been limited to collections of money or food at the office for worthy causes.

This Is NOW . . .

Today's workers donate not only money but also their time. Here, McGraw-Hill employees volunteer on a project to renovate a New Orleans grade school.

the contract informs you that the minister wants $20,000 in addition to the standard fees. If you do not make this payment, your competition certainly will—and will get the contract.

- You are international vice president of a multinational chemical corporation. Your company is the sole producer of an insecticide that will effectively combat a recent infestation of West African crops. The minister of agriculture in a small, developing African country has put in a large order for your product. Your insecticide is highly toxic and is banned in the United States. You inform the minister of the risks of using your product, but he insists on using it and claims it will be used "intelligently." The president of your company believes you should fill the order, but the decision ultimately is yours.

- You are a new marketing manager for a large automobile tire manufacturer. Your company's advertising agency has just presented plans for introducing a new tire into the Southeast Asia market. Your tire is a truly good product, but the proposed advertising is deceptive. For example, the "reduced price" was reduced from a hypothetical amount that was established only so it could be "reduced," and claims that the tire was tested under the "most adverse" conditions ignore the fact that it was not tested in prolonged tropical heat and humidity. Your superiors are not concerned about deceptive advertising, and they are counting on you to see that the tire does extremely well in the new market. Will you approve the ad plan?[34]

> "Associate with men of good quality, if you esteem your own reputation; for it is better to be alone than in bad company."
>
> —George Washington

danger signs In organizations, maintaining consistent ethical behavior by all employees is an ongoing challenge. What are some danger signs that an organization may be allowing or even encouraging unethical behavior? Many factors, including the following, create a climate conducive to unethical behavior:

- Excessive emphasis on short-term revenues over longer-term considerations
- Failure to establish a written code of ethics
- Desire for simple, "quick fix" solutions to ethical problems
- Unwillingness to take an ethical stand that may impose financial costs
- Consideration of ethics solely as a legal issue or a public relations tool
- Lack of clear procedures for handling ethical problems
- Responsiveness to the demands of shareholders at the expense of other constituencies[35]

To understand your organization's ethics climate, think about issues from the employees' perspective. What do people think is required to succeed? Do they think that ethical people "finish last" and that the "bad guys win"? Or vice versa, that the company rewards ethical behavior and won't tolerate unethical behavior?[36] Lynn Brewer, who brought to light the financial misdeeds of Enron, also heard Enron's management advocate values such as respect and integrity, but she later determined that these messages were just "window-dressing" and that people would undermine one another as they looked out for their self-interests. She eventually concluded that "no one cared" about unethical and illegal behavior in support of the company's stock price.[37]

Do you see danger signs in the judgment of AutoAdmit's founders? The small company operates a message board Web site targeting college and law school students. Some students have complained that participants on the site's law school message board have posted false and insulting messages about them that have humiliated them and may have interfered with their ability to find summer internships. Many employers use Internet searches as part of their background checks, and sites such as AutoAdmit might surface in search results. AutoAdmit founder Jarret Cohen told the *Washington Post* that he is reluctant to interfere with postings: "I want [the message board] to be a place where people can express themselves freely." He and his partner, Anthony Ciolli, define the matter in terms of free speech, insisting that "one finds overall a much deeper and much more mature level of insight in a community where the ugliest depths of human opinion are confronted, rather than ignored." Ciolli claims that only Cohen has the authority to remove offensive postings, and Cohen refuses to "selectively remove" comments. The site also does not keep information that would identify participants, using only screen names, because "people would not have as much fun" if employers could identify them. Ciolli and Cohen have so far avoided any accusation that their message boards are violating the law; AutoAdmit isn't liable for the content of messages written by visitors to the site.[38] But what do you think about the organization's ethical climate? Should it uphold values other than freedom of expression? What recourse do people have when anonymous posters can say anything they like?

corporate ethical standards People often give in to what they perceive to be the pressures or preferences of powerful others. In the workplace, that means managers influence their employees for good or for ill. As we'll see in the discussions of leadership and motivation later in the text, managers formally and informally shape employees' behavior with money, approval, good job assignments, a positive work environment, and in many other ways. That means managers are a powerful force for creating an ethical culture.

ETHICAL LEADER One who is both a moral person and a moral manager influencing others to behave ethically.

To create a culture that encourages ethical behavior, managers must be more than ethical people. They also should lead others to behave ethically.[39] At General Electric, chief executive Jeffrey Immelt demonstrates his concern for ethical leadership by beginning and ending each annual meeting with a statement of the company's integrity principles, emphasizing that "GE's business success is built on our reputation with all stakeholders for lawful and ethical behavior." These words are backed up with a reward system in which managers are evaluated for how well they meet ethics-related standards such as the use of audits, minimal customer complaints and lawsuits, avoidance of compliance actions by government regulators, and high ratings on employee surveys.[40]

It's been said that your reputation is your most precious asset. Here's a suggestion: set a goal for yourself to be seen by others as both a "moral person" and also as a "moral manager," someone who influences others to behave ethically. When you are both personally moral and a moral manager, you will truly be an ethical leader.[42] You can have strong personal character, but if you pay more attention to other things, and ethics is "managed" by "benign neglect," you won't have a reputation as an ethical leader.

IBM uses a guideline for business conduct that asks employees to determine whether under the full glare of examination by associates, friends, and family, they would remain comfortable with their decisions. One suggestion is to imagine how you would feel if you saw your decision and its consequences on the front page of the newspaper.[43] This "light of day" or "sunshine" ethical framework can be powerful.

Such fear of exposure compels people more strongly in some cultures than in others. In Asia, anxiety about losing face often makes executives resign immediately if they are caught in ethical transgressions or if their companies are embarrassed by revelations in the press. By contrast, in the United States, exposed executives might respond with indignation, intransigence, pleading the Fifth Amendment, stonewalling, an everyone-else-does-it self-defense, or by not admitting wrongdoing and giving no sign that resignation ever crossed their minds. Partly because of legal tradition, the attitude often is: never explain, never apologize, don't admit the mistake, do not resign, even if the entire world knows exactly what happened.[44]

Imagine a manager of a used-car dealership working hard to personify ethical business practices, for and with his customers and his employees.[41] This would create a powerful competitive advantage compared with the industry's reputation (or at least the common stereotype) for shady practices.

ethics codes The Sarbanes-Oxley Act, described earlier, requires that public companies periodically disclose whether they have adopted a code of ethics for senior financial officers—and if not, why not. Often, the statements are just for show, but when implemented well they can change a company's ethical climate for the better and truly encourage ethical behavior. Executives say they pay most attention to their company's code of ethics when they feel that stakeholders (customers, investors, lenders, and suppliers) try to influence them to do so, and their reasons for paying attention to the code are that doing so will help create a strong ethical culture and promote a positive image.[45]

Ethics codes must be carefully written and tailored to individual companies' philosophies. Aetna Life & Casualty believes that tending to the broader needs of society is essential to fulfilling its economic role. Johnson & Johnson has one of the most famous ethics codes; it is featured in Table 3.2. J&J consistently receives high rankings for community and social responsibility in *Fortune's* annual survey of corporate reputations.

Most ethics codes address subjects such as employee conduct, community and environment, shareholders, customers, suppliers and contractors, political activity, and technology. Often the codes are drawn up by the organizations' legal departments and begin with research into other companies' codes. The Ethics Resource Center in Washington assists companies interested in establishing a corporate code of ethics.[46]

TABLE	3.2	Johnson & Johnson's Ethics Code

We believe our first responsibility is to the doctors, nurses, and patients, to mothers and all others who use our products and services. In meeting their needs everything we do must be of high quality. We must constantly strive to reduce our costs in order to maintain reasonable prices. Customers' orders must be serviced promptly and accurately. Our suppliers and distributors must have an opportunity to make a fair profit.

We are responsible to our employees: the men and women who work with us throughout the world. Everyone must be considered as an individual. We must respect their dignity and recognize their merit. They must have a sense of security in their jobs. Compensation must be fair and adequate, and working conditions clean, orderly, and safe. Employees must feel free to make suggestions and complaints. There must be equal opportunity for employment, development, and advancement for those qualified. We must provide competent management, and their actions must be just and ethical.

We are responsible to the communities in which we live and work and to the world community as well.

We must be good citizens—support good works and charities and bear our fair share of taxes. We must encourage civic improvements and better health and education.

We must maintain in good order the property we are privileged to use, protecting the environment and natural resources.

Our final responsibility is to our stockholders. Business must make a sound profit. We must experiment with new ideas. Research must be carried on, innovative programs developed, and mistakes paid for. New equipment must be purchased, new facilities provided, and new products launched. Reserves must be created to provide for adverse times.

When we operate according to these principles, the stockholders should realize a fair return.

SOURCE: Reprinted with permission of Johnson & Johnson.

To make an ethics code effective, apply the following principles:

- Involve those who have to live with the code in writing it.
- Focus on real-life situations that employees can relate to.
- Keep it short and simple, so it is easy to understand and remember.
- Write about values and shared beliefs that are important and that people can really believe in.
- Set the tone at the top, having executives talk about and live up to the statement.[47]

When reality differs from the statement—as when a motto says people are our most precious asset or a product is the finest in the world, but in fact people are treated poorly or product quality is weak—the statement becomes a joke to employees rather than a guiding light.

ethics programs Corporate ethics programs commonly include formal ethics codes articulating the company's expectations regarding ethics; ethics committees that develop policies, evaluate actions, and investigate violations; ethics communication systems giving employees a means of reporting problems or getting guidance; ethics officers or ombudspersons

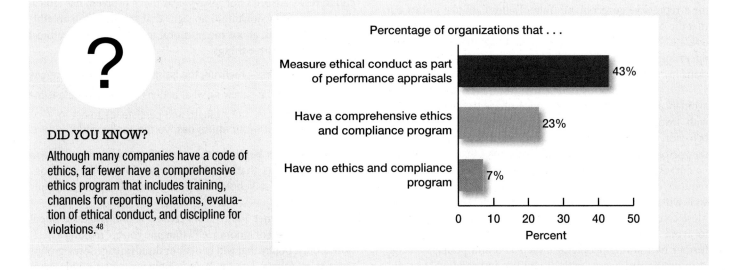

DID YOU KNOW?

Although many companies have a code of ethics, far fewer have a comprehensive ethics program that includes training, channels for reporting violations, evaluation of ethical conduct, and discipline for violations.[48]

Percentage of organizations that . . .

Measure ethical conduct as part of performance appraisals — 43%

Have a comprehensive ethics and compliance program — 23%

Have no ethics and compliance program — 7%

Percent

who investigate allegations and provide education; ethics training programs; and disciplinary processes for addressing unethical behavior.[49]

Ethics programs can range from compliance-based to integrity-based.[50] **Compliance-based ethics programs** are designed by corporate counsel to prevent, detect, and punish legal violations. Compliance-based programs increase surveillance and controls on people and impose punishments on wrongdoers. Program elements include establishing and communicating legal standards and procedures, assigning high-level managers to oversee compliance, auditing and monitoring compliance, reporting criminal misconduct, punishing wrongdoers, and taking steps to prevent offenses in the future.

Such programs should reduce illegal behavior and help a company stay out of court. But they do not create a moral commitment to ethical conduct; they merely ensure moral mediocrity. As Richard Breeden, former chairman of the Securities and Exchange Commission, said, "It is not an adequate ethical standard to aspire to get through the day without being indicted."[51]

Yahoo! is struggling with an ethical dilemma as it makes decisions about how to operate in China. The Chinese government arrested Wang Xiaoning for "inciting subversion" in his pro-democracy e-journal and sentenced him to 10 years in prison. According to the case filed against Yahoo! in the United States, the Chinese subsidiary of Yahoo! that Wang used provided the information that enabled officials to track him down. How can an Internet company that values free expression justify support for a repressive government? Yahoo!'s Jim Cullinan points out that the company has to obey the laws of the countries where it operates but adds that the company has been trying to develop operating principles that will help its people make ethical decisions in countries where governments have different values.[52]

Integrity-based ethics programs go beyond the mere avoidance of illegality; they are concerned with the law but also with instilling in people a personal responsibility for ethical behavior. With such a program, companies and people govern themselves through a set of guiding principles that they embrace.

For example, the Americans with Disabilities Act (ADA) requires companies to change the physical work environment so it will allow people with disabilities to function on the job. Mere compliance would involve making the changes necessary to avoid legal problems. Integrity-based programs would go further by training people to understand and perhaps change attitudes toward people with disabilities and sending clear signals that people with disabilities also have valued abilities. This

NovaCare believes strongly in integrity-based ethics programs.

effort goes far beyond taking action to stay out of trouble with the law.

When top management has a personal commitment to responsible ethical behavior, programs tend to be better integrated into operations, thinking, and behavior. For example, at a meeting of about 25 middle managers at a major financial services firm, every one of them told the company's general counsel that they had never seen or heard of the company's ethics policy document.[53] The policies existed but were not a part of the everyday thinking of managers. In contrast, a health care products company bases one-third of managers' annual pay raises on how well they carry out the company's ethical ideals. Their ethical behavior is assessed by superiors, peers, and subordinates—making ethics a thoroughly integrated aspect of the way the company and its people do business.

Companies with strong integrity-based programs include NovaCare (a provider of rehabilitation services to hospitals and nursing homes) and Wetherill Associates (a supplier of electrical parts to the automotive market). These companies believe that their programs contribute to competitiveness, higher morale, and sustainable relationships with key stakeholders.[54]

Ⓛ Ⓞ 3 WHAT YOU NEED TO KNOW . . .
Can you outline a process for making ethical decisions?

You can learn to make ethical decisions

We've said it's not easy to make ethical decisions. Such decisions are complex. For starters, you may face pressures that are difficult to resist. Also, it's not always clear that a problem has ethical dimensions; they don't hold up signs that say, "Hey, I'm an ethical issue, so think about me in moral terms!"[55] Making ethical decisions takes three things:

1. *Moral awareness*—realizing the issue has ethical implications
2. *Moral judgment*—knowing what actions are morally defensible
3. *Moral character*—the strength and persistence to act in accordance with your ethics despite the challenges[56]

Moral awareness begins with considering whether a decision has ramifications that disadvantage employees, the environment, or other stakeholders. Then the challenge is to apply moral judgment.

The philosopher John Rawls created a thought experiment based on the "veil of ignorance."[57] Imagine you are making a decision about a policy that will benefit or disadvantage some groups more than others. For example, a policy might provide extra vacation time for all employees but eliminate flex time, which

FIGURE 3.1 **A Process for Ethical Decision Making**

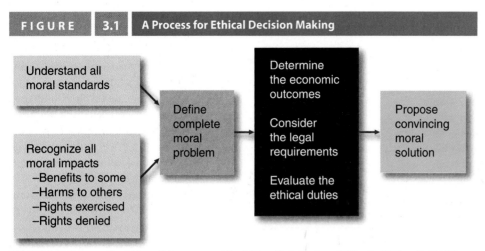

SOURCE: L. T. Hosmer, *The Ethics of Management,* 4th ed. (New York: McGraw-Hill/Irwin, 2003), p. 32. © 2003 The McGraw-Hill Companies.

allows parents of young children to balance their work and family responsibilities. Or you're a university president considering raising tuition or cutting financial support for study abroad.

Now pretend that you belong to one of the affected groups, but you don't know which one—for instance, those who can afford to study abroad or those who can't, or a young parent or a young single person. You won't find out until after the decision is made. How would you decide? Would you be willing to risk being in the disadvantaged group? Would your decision be different if you were in a group other than your own? Rawls maintained that only a person ignorant of his own identity can make a truly ethical decision. A decision maker can tactically apply the veil of ignorance to help minimize personal bias.

To resolve ethical problems, you can use the process illustrated in Figure 3.1. Understand the various moral standards (universalism, relativism, etc.), as described earlier in the chapter. Begin to follow a formal decision-making process. As we will discuss in more detail in Chapter 4, you identify and diagnose your problem, generate alternative solutions, and evaluate each alternative. Your evaluation should recognize the impacts of your alternatives: which people do they benefit and harm, which are able to exercise their rights, and whose rights are denied? You now know the full scope of the moral problem.

As you define the problem, it's easy to find excuses for unethical behavior. People can rationalize unethical behavior by denying responsibility ("What can I do? They're twisting my arm"), denying injury ("No one was badly hurt; it could have been worse"), denying the victim ("They deserved it"), social weighting ("Those people are worse than we are"), and appealing to higher loyalties ("It was for a higher purpose," or "I'm too loyal to my boss to report it").[58] Only days after the U.S. government had posted $85 billion to keep insurance giant American International Group from collapsing, AIG sent executives on a luxurious retreat. When asked to justify this, executives initially replied with excuses: the $440,000 spent was far, far less than the amount of the government bailout, and the executives who participated in the retreat did not work in the AIG division where the company's financial problems had originated.

Eventually, they had to concede that these responses did not really address the question of whether the retreat was an ethical use of company money at a time when the company—along with many of the taxpayers whose money was bailing out AIG—was undergoing an economic crisis.[59]

You must also consider legal requirements to ensure full compliance, and the economic outcomes of your options, including costs and potential profits. Figure 3.2 shows some of the costs associated with unethical behavior.[60] Some are obvious: fines and penalties. Others, like administrative costs and corrective actions, are less obvious. Ultimately, the effects on customers, employees, and government reactions can be huge. Being fully aware of the potential costs can help prevent people from straying into unethical terrain.

Ethical climate is heating up! Former Enron treasurer Ben Glisan, Jr. pleaded guilty to conspiracy and became the first ex-Enron executive to go to prison. Former Enron executives Jeff Skilling and Ken Lay were later arrested for their participation in the high-profile scandal case that led to the passage of the Sarbanes-Oxley Act in 2002. This case is considered to be one of the biggest business scandals in U.S. history.

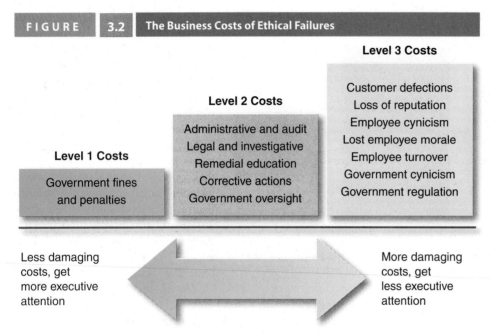

FIGURE 3.2 **The Business Costs of Ethical Failures**

Level 3 Costs

Customer defections
Loss of reputation
Employee cynicism
Lost employee morale
Employee turnover
Government cynicism
Government regulation

Level 2 Costs

Administrative and audit
Legal and investigative
Remedial education
Corrective actions
Government oversight

Level 1 Costs

Government fines
and penalties

Less damaging costs, get more executive attention

More damaging costs, get less executive attention

SOURCE: T. Thomas, J. Schermerhorn Jr., and J. Dienhart, "Strategic Leadership of Ethical Behavior in Business," *Academy of Management Executive* (May 2004), p. 58.

Evaluating your ethical duties requires looking for actions that meet the following criteria:

- You would be proud to see the action widely reported in newspapers.
- It would build a sense of community among those involved.
- It would generate the greatest social good.
- You would be willing to see others take the same action when you might be the victim.
- It doesn't harm the "least among us."
- It doesn't interfere with the right of all others to develop their skills to the fullest.[61]

As you can see, making ethical decisions is complex, but considering all these factors will help you develop the most convincing moral solution.

Ethics requires courage

Behaving ethically requires not just moral awareness and moral judgment but also moral character, including the courage to take actions consistent with your ethical decisions. Think about how hard it can be to do the right thing.[62] As you're growing up, you have plenty of peer pressure to conform to others' behavior, and it's not cool to be a snitch. On the job, how hard would it be to walk away from lots of money in order to "stick to your ethics"? To tell colleagues or your boss that you believe they've crossed an ethical line? To disobey a boss's order? To go over your boss's head to someone in senior management with your suspicions about accounting practices? To go outside the company to alert

others if someone is being hurt and management refuses to correct the problem?

PepsiCo managers faced a difficult choice when an executive secretary from Coca-Cola Company's headquarters contacted them to offer confidential documents and product samples for a price. Rather than seek an unethical (and illegal) advantage, Pepsi's managers notified Coca-Cola. There, management fired the secretary and contacted the FBI. Eventually, the secretary and two acquaintances were convicted of conspiring to steal trade secrets.[63] PepsiCo still doesn't have the secret recipe for Coke, but it did maintain its reputation as a competitor with integrity. Choosing integrity over short-term business gain took courage.

Many people lack the courage—or believe their company's management does. In a recent survey of employed adults, only about half of those who said they had witnessed unethical behavior at work said they would be likely to report it. A survey by the Society for Human Resource Management and Ethics Resource Center investigated the reasons behind this kind of reluctance. In that survey, employees who said they would not report the misdeeds they saw gave three main reasons for remaining silent: a belief that the company would not take corrective action, fear that management would retaliate against them for speaking up, and doubt that their report would be kept confidential.[64]

Behaving ethically in a strong ethical climate is complicated enough, but even more courage is necessary when you decide that the only ethical course of action is *whistleblowing*—telling others, inside or outside the organization, of wrongdoing. The road for whistleblowers is rocky. Many, perhaps most, whistleblowers suffer consequences such as being ostracized, treated rudely, or given undesirable assignments. At a Canadian manufacturing company, an employee reported a manager who had an arrangement with suppliers to inflate their invoices; the manager took the extra cash, costing the company more than $100,000. When the other employees found out what had happened, instead of blaming the manager, they began to distrust the whistleblower. Eventually, she quit.[65]

People decide whether to blow the whistle based on their perceptions of the wrongful act, their emotions (anger, resentment, fear), and a (usually informal) cost-benefit analysis.[66] Courage plays a role in the moral awareness involved in identifying an act as unethical, the moral judgment to fully consider the repercussions, and the moral character to take the ethical action.

From an organization's point of view, whistleblowing is either an asset or a threat, depending on the situation and management's perspective. In the example of the manager cheating the Canadian manufacturer, it was clearly to the company's advantage to know about the misdeeds so that management could stop the losses. But whistleblowing is a far different and more troubling matter when employees take their complaints to government agencies, report them to the media, or post them on blogs. When problems are resolved in public, the whistleblower is more often seen as acting against the company's interests.

For this reason, and in response to the revised sentencing guidelines under the Sarbanes-Oxley Act described earlier, some organizations set up channels for employees to report ethics problems so the organization can respond without the matter becoming a scandal. Ideally, the reporting method should keep the whistleblower's identity secret, management should investigate and respond quickly, and there should be no retaliation against whistleblowers who use proper channels. At Marvin Windows and Doors, which has thousands of employees working in a dozen facilities in the United States and Honduras, workers can go online to submit anonymous tips and suggestions in English or Spanish. The company's general counsel says

noneconomic concerns has been hotly debated for years. In the 1960s and 1970s, the political and social environment became more important to U.S. corporations as society focused on issues like equal opportunity, pollution control, energy and natural resource conservation, and consumer and worker protection.[70] Public debate addressed these issues and the ways business should respond. This controversy focused on the concept of corporate social responsibility—the obligation toward society assumed by business. A socially responsible business maximizes its positive effects on society and minimizes its negative effects.[71]

● CORPORATE SOCIAL RESPONSIBILITY Obligation toward society assumed by business.

● ECONOMIC RESPONSIBILITIES To produce goods and services that society wants at a price that perpetuates the business and satisfies its obligations to investors.

● LEGAL RESPONSIBILITIES To obey local, state, federal, and relevant international laws.

● ETHICAL RESPONSIBILITIES Meeting other social expectations, not written as law.

According to a study by the Association of Certified Fraud Examiners, companies that uncovered fraud most often learned about it from a coworker's tip, rather than from a formal audit.[67]

the system not only provides an early warning in case of problems as diverse as theft and safety concerns, but also maintains an overall culture of valuing ethics.[68]

Besides online reporting systems, such as e-mail and Web-based tools, companies can use drop boxes and telephone hotlines. Often, these channels of communication are administered by third-party organizations, whose employees protect whistleblowers' identity and have procedures to follow if the complaint involves higher-level executives who might be part of the usual group charged with responding to reports.[69]

(L)(O) 4   WHAT YOU NEED TO KNOW . . .

What are the important issues surrounding corporate social responsibility?

CORPORATE SOCIAL RESPONSIBILITY

Should business be responsible for social concerns beyond its own economic well-being? Do social concerns affect a corporation's financial performance? The extent of business's responsibility for

Social responsibilities can be categorized more specifically,[72] as shown in Figure 3.3. The economic responsibilities of business are to produce goods and services that society wants at a price that perpetuates the business and satisfies its obligations to investors. For Smithfield Foods, the largest pork producer in the United States, this means selling bacon, ham, and other products to customers at prices that maximize Smithfield's profits and keep the company growing over the long term. Economic responsibility may also extend to offering certain products to needy consumers at a reduced price.

Legal responsibilities are to obey local, state, federal, and relevant international laws. Laws affecting Smithfield cover a wide range of requirements, from filing tax returns to meeting worker safety standards. Ethical responsibilities include meeting other societal expectations, not written as law. Smithfield took on this level of responsibility when it responded to requests by major customers, including McDonald's and Walmart, that it discontinue the practice of using gestation crates to house its sows. The customers were reacting to pressure from animal rights advocates who consider it cruel for sows to live in the two-foot by seven-foot crates during their entire gestation period, which means they cannot walk, turn around, or stretch their legs for months at a time. The practice had been to move

Be a good global corporate citizen — Philanthropic Responsibility — **Do what is *desired* by global stakeholders**

Be ethical — Ethical Responsibility — **Do what is *expected* by global stakeholders**

Obey the law — Legal Responsibility — **Do what is *required* by global stakeholders**

Be profitable — Economic Responsibility — **Do what is *required* by global capitalism**

SOURCE: A. Carroll, "Managing Ethically with Global Stakeholders: A Present and Future Challenge," *Academy of Management Executive* (May 2004), pp. 116, 114–20.

3. *Mutuality*—viewing success not merely as personal gain, but a common victory

4. *Civil aspiration*—thinking not just in terms of "don'ts" (lie, cheat, steal, kill), but also in terms of positive contributions

5. *Intolerance of ineffective humanity*—speaking out against unethical actions

Do businesses really have a social responsibility?

Two basic and contrasting views describe principles that should guide managerial responsibility. The first holds that managers act as agents for shareholders and, as such, are obligated to maximize the present value of the firm. This tenet of capitalism is widely associated with the early writings of Adam Smith in *The Wealth of Nations,* and more recently with Milton Friedman, the Nobel Prize–winning economist of the University of Chicago. With his now-famous dictum "The social responsibility of business is to increase profits," Friedman contended that organizations may help improve the quality of life as long as such actions are directed at increasing profits.

Some considered Friedman to be "the enemy of business ethics," but his position was ethical: he believed it is unethical for unelected business leaders to decide what is best for society, and unethical for them to spend shareholders' money on projects unconnected to key business interests.[76] In addition, the context of Friedman's famous statement includes the qualifier that business should increase its profits while conforming to society's laws and ethical customs.

The alternative view is that managers should be motivated by principled moral reasoning. Followers of Friedman and *The Wealth of Nations* might sneer at such soft-headed propaganda. But Adam Smith wrote about a world different from the one we are in now, driven in the 18th century by the self-interest of small owner-operated farms and craft shops trying to generate a living income for themselves and their families. This self-interest was quite different from that of top executives of modern corporations.[77] It is noteworthy that Adam Smith also wrote *A Theory of Moral Sentiments,* in which he argued that "sympathy," defined as a proper regard for others, is the basis of a civilized society.[78]

Advocates of corporate social responsibility argue that, as members of society, organizations have a wider range of responsibilities beyond profitability. As members of society, organizations should actively and responsibly participate in the

the sows to a farrowing crate to give birth and then return them to the gestation crate soon after, when they became pregnant again. Smithfield plans to exchange the crates for "group housing," which allows the animals to socialize, even though group housing costs more.[73] Smithfield is not legally required to make the change (except in two states), and the arrangement may not maximize profits, but the company's actions help it maintain good customer relationships and a positive public image.

Finally, philanthropic responsibilities are additional behaviors and activities that society finds desirable and that the values of the business support. Examples include supporting community projects and making charitable contributions. Philanthropic activities can be more than mere altruism; managed properly, "strategic philanthropy" can become not an oxymoron but a way to build goodwill in a variety of stakeholders and even add to shareholder wealth.[74]

Robert Giacalone, who teaches business ethics at Temple University, believes that a 21st-century education must help students think beyond self-interest and profitability. A real education, he says, teaches students to leave a legacy that extends beyond the bottom line—a transcendent education.[75] A transcendent education has five higher goals that balance self-interest with responsibility to others:

1. *Empathy*—feeling your decisions as potential victims might feel them, to gain wisdom

2. *Generativity*—learning how to give as well as take, to others in the present as well as to future generations

● PHILANTHROPIC
RESPONSIBILITIES Additional
behaviors and activities that society finds desirable and that the
values of the business support.

● TRANSCENDENT EDUCATION An
education with five higher goals
that balance self-interest with
responsibility to others.

community and in the larger environment. From this perspective, many people criticized insurance companies after
Hurricanes Katrina and Rita devastated homes and businesses along the Gulf Coast. From a social responsibility

The Green Movement. David Best, president of Prism Software,
unloads a truck full of old computer equipment during an
e-cycling event near the Mall of America in Bloomington, Minnesota. Thousands of people lined up for blocks with carloads and
truckloads of old consumer appliances needing to be recycled.
The event is designed to help Minnesotans clean house and protect the environment against hazardous waste such as old monitors and televisions.

perspective, it was wrong for companies to watch out for their
bottom line and avoid paying claims where they could make a
case that the damage wasn't covered; the insurers should have
been more concerned about their devastated customers. Or consider how companies have responded to public criticism that
products manufactured in low-wage countries are produced
in "sweatshops," where employees work in conditions widely
viewed as unacceptable in developed nations such as the United
States. Do U.S. companies have a social responsibility to insist
on better working conditions? Walmart and other companies
that buy products made in China have written codes of conduct
and conducted onsite audits. Unfortunately, some enterprising Chinese consultants have set up services that help factories
hide violations instead of correcting them. Still, as demand for
Chinese-made products and pressure from multinational corporations have both intensified, observers say pay and working
conditions in China have generally improved.[79]

You can do good and do well

Profit maximization and corporate social responsibility used to
be regarded as leading to opposing policies. But in today's business climate, which emphasizes both doing good and doing well,
the two views can converge.[80] The Coca-Cola Company has set

up about 70 charitable projects to provide clean
water in 40 countries. These projects are helping some of the 1.2 billion people without access
to safe drinking water. The company is building
structures to "harvest" rainwater in India, expanding the municipal water supply in Mali, and delivering water purification systems and storage urns
to Kenya. These projects are aimed at burnishing
the company's image and targeting complaints
that the company is using too much of the world's
water supply to manufacture its beverages. From
a practical perspective, Coca-Cola's strategic planners have identified water shortages as a strategic
risk; from a values perspective, water is, in the
words of executive Neville Isdell, "at the very core
of our ethos," so "responsible use of that resource
is very important to us."[81]

Earlier attention to corporate social responsibility focused on alleged wrongdoing and how to
control it. More recently, attention has also been
centered on the possible competitive advantage
of socially responsible actions. DuPont has been
incorporating care for the environment into its
business in two ways it hopes will put it ahead
of the competition. First, the company has been
reducing its pollution, including a 72 percent cut in
greenhouse gas emissions since 1990. It hopes these
efforts will give it an advantage in a future where the government
regulates emissions, requiring competitors to play catch-up. In
addition, reducing emissions goes hand in hand with reducing waste and unnecessary use of energy, saving the company
money and directly benefiting the bottom line. Second, DuPont
has been developing products that are sustainable, meaning they
don't use up the earth's resources. Examples include corn-based
fabrics and new applications of its Tyvek material to make buildings more energy-efficient. DuPont expects these innovations
to give the company profitable access to the growing market for
environmentally friendly products.[82]

The real relationship between corporate social performance
and corporate financial performance is highly complex; socially
responsible organizations do not necessarily become more or
less successful in financial terms.[83] Some advantages are clear,
however. For example, socially responsible actions can have
long-term benefits. Companies can avoid unnecessary and
costly regulation if they are socially responsible. Honesty and
fairness may pay great dividends to the conscience, to the personal reputation, and to the public image of the company as
well as in the market response.[84] In addition, society's problems
can offer business opportunities, and profits can be made from
systematic and vigorous efforts to solve these problems. Firms
can perform a cost-benefit analysis to identify actions that will

maximize profits while satisfying the demand for corporate social responsibility from multiple stakeholders.[85] In other words, managers can treat corporate social responsibility as they would treat all investment decisions. This has been the case as firms attempt to reconcile their business practices with their effect on the natural environment.

 When William K. Reilly was planning a private takeover of the Texas utility TXU Corp, he teamed up with an unlikely ally—the not-for-profit organization Environmental Defense. By doing so, Reilly got the company he wanted, and Environmental Defense received important concessions from Reilly: to drop eight of the eleven proposed new power plants and to

Should pharmaceutical companies be allowed to advertise prescription medicines directly to the consumer? When patients request a product, doctors are more likely to prescribe it—even if the patients haven't reported the corresponding symptoms.

might not) lower its operating costs. For UPS, reducing carbon emissions would directly affect its day-to-day activities but still might not give the company a competitive advantage. For Toyota, reducing carbon emissions—say, by leading in the development and marketing of hybrid technology as well as by operating more efficiently—can be a significant part of its competitive advantage.

> ❝**The essential test that should guide corporate social responsibility is not whether a cause is worthy but whether it presents an opportunity to create shared value—that is, a meaningful benefit for society that is also valuable to the business.**❞
>
> —Michael E. Porter and Mark R. Kramer[88]

campaign for mandatory national emission controls. Why did this alliance work? "We all swim in the same culture—and the culture is going green," says Reilly.

As the tide of public opinion has begun to turn toward the preservation of the planet, companies must respect the wishes of their customers. "Companies have to be seen as responsible," warns Karen Van Bergen, vice president of McDonald's in Europe.[86]

For a clearer link between social and business goals, companies can benefit from integrating social responsibility with corporate strategy—and society can benefit as well. Applying the principles of strategic planning (described in Chapter 4), organizations can identify the specific areas in which they can capitalize on their strengths to neutralize threats and benefit from opportunities that result from serving the society of which they are a part.[87] For example, suppose a company is interested in exercising social responsibility for the environment by reducing its carbon emissions. The extent to which this choice is strategic varies from one company to another. Reducing carbon emissions would be a good deed for Bank of America but not directly related to its strategy, except to the extent it might (or

L O 5 WHAT YOU NEED TO KNOW . . .

What are the reasons for businesses' growing interest in the natural environment?

THE NATURAL ENVIRONMENT

Most large corporations developed in an era of abundant raw materials, cheap energy, and unconstrained waste disposal.[89] But many of the technologies developed during that era are contributing to the destruction of ecosystems. Industrial-age systems follow a linear flow of extract, produce, sell, use, and discard—what some call a "take-make-waste" approach.[90] But perhaps no time in history has offered greater possibilities for a change in business thinking than the 21st century.

Business used to look at environmental issues as a no-win situation: either you help the environment and hurt your business, or else you help your business at a cost to the environment. But now a shift is taking place as companies deliberately incorporate environmental values into competitive strategies and into the design and manufacturing of products.[91] Why? In addition to philosophical reasons, companies "go green" to satisfy consumer demand, react to a competitor's actions, meet requests from customers or suppliers, comply with guidelines, and create a competitive advantage.

General Electric CEO Jeff Immelt used to view environmental rules as a burden and a cost. Now he sees environmentally friendly technologies as one of the global economy's most significant business opportunities. Under a business initiative called Ecomagination, GE is looking for business opportunities from solving environmental problems. Ecomagination solutions already include wind turbines, materials for solar energy cells, and energy-efficient home appliances. Over a five-year period, GE's revenues from renewable-energy products have risen from $5 million to $7 *billion*.[92]

Economic activity has environmental consequences

We live in a risk society. That is, the creation and distribution of wealth generate by-products that can cause injury, loss, or danger to people and the environment. The fundamental sources of risk in modern society are the excessive production of hazards and ecologically unsustainable consumption of natural resources.[93] Risk has proliferated through population explosion, industrial pollution, and environmental degradation.[94]

Industrial pollution risks include air pollution, smog, global warming, ozone depletion, acid rain, toxic waste sites, nuclear hazards, obsolete weapons arsenals, industrial accidents, and hazardous products. More than 30,000 uncontrolled toxic waste sites have been documented in the United States alone, and the number is increasing by perhaps 2,500 per year. The situation is far worse in other parts of the world. The pattern, for toxic waste and many other risks, is one of accumulating risks and inadequate remedies.

The institutions that create environmental and technological risk (corporations and government agencies) also are responsible for controlling and managing the risks.[95] Lockheed Martin Corporation had to contain the spread of a chemical used in industrial degreasers when it leaked from a broken sump pump at an old facility in Florida. Even though Lockheed had sold the facility to another company, it had owned the property when the contamination was first discovered, so it was responsible. Lockheed's efforts included sealing off an old contaminated well at a cattle operation and providing a new well with clean water for the cattle.[96]

Sometimes the risks can be overwhelming. Regulators at the Environmental Protection Agency (EPA) determined that Asarco's metal-processing facility in Globeville, Colorado, had been polluting the community with lead and arsenic. The EPA declared 4.5 square miles a Superfund site, meaning it was a priority for a major cleanup, and Asarco was supposed to pay for the effort. Asarco, which faced more than $1 billion in cleanup costs for Globeville and more than 90 other contaminated sites in the United States, instead filed for bankruptcy and planned to shut down and sell the Globeville facility.[97]

Ⓛ Ⓞ **6** **WHAT YOU NEED TO KNOW . . .**
Can you identify actions managers can take to manage with the environment in mind?

Development can be sustainable

Ecocentric management has as its goal the creation of sustainable economic development and improvement of quality of life worldwide for all organizational stakeholders.[98] Sustainable growth is economic growth and development that meets the organization's present needs without harming the ability of future generations to meet their needs.[99] Sustainability is fully compatible with the natural ecosystems that generate and preserve life.

Some believe that the concept of sustainable growth can be applied in several ways:

- As a framework for organizations to use in communicating to all stakeholders

- As a planning and strategy guide

- As a tool for evaluating and improving the ability to compete.[100]

The principle can begin at the highest organizational levels and be made explicit in performance appraisals and reward systems.

▶ With two-thirds of the world's population expected to experience water scarcity by 2025 and shortages forecast for 36 U.S. states by 2013, businesses are becoming concerned about this essential natural resource. If you haven't experienced a water shortage, water usage might not seem to be an obvious area of concern, but it should be. For example, Levi Strauss & Company determined that making a pair of jeans requires about 500 gallons of water for growing, dying, and processing cotton.

Brewer SABMiller is a leader in making water conservation part of its strategy. Using an online computer application, the company submitted the GPS coordinates of factory and farm locations and learned where its operations are located in areas of water scarcity. About 30 SABMiller sites were in vulnerable areas. Executives decided to target one of those areas and develop a process they could apply elsewhere. They selected South Africa, whose breweries produce about one-sixth of the company's beer. Not only is South Africa facing water shortages, but its government has yet to provide access to safe drinking water for 5 million of its people.

To get hard information about its water consumption, the company measured water usage at each stage of its processes, from growing crops to rinsing out used bottles before recycling. SABMiller hired a consulting firm for this task. The most water was used in growing barley, maize (corn), and hops. Together with the water used in factories, 20 gallons of water are needed to produce each pint of beer. Based on the data, SABMiller's initial efforts are focusing on identifying and using more efficient irrigation technology, preventing waste from runoff and evaporation.[101]

Increasingly, firms are paying attention to the total environmental impact throughout the life cycle of their products.[102] **Life-cycle analysis (LCA)** is a process of analyzing all inputs and outputs, through the entire "cradle-to-grave" life of a product, to determine the total environmental impact of its production and use. LCA quantifies the total use of resources and the releases into the air, water, and land.

LCA considers the extraction of raw materials, product packaging, transportation, and disposal. Consider packaging alone. Goods make the journey from manufacturer to wholesaler to retailer to customer; then they are recycled back to the manufacturer. They may be packaged and repackaged several times, from bulk transport, to large crates, to cardboard boxes, to individual consumer sizes. Repackaging not only creates waste but also costs time. The design of initial packaging in sizes and formats adaptable to the final customer can minimize the need for repackaging, cut waste, and realize financial benefits.

Profitability need not suffer and may be increased by ecocentric philosophies and practices. Some, but not all, research

has shown a positive relationship between corporate environmental performance and profitability.[103] Of course, whether the relationship is positive, negative, or neutral depends on the strategies chosen and the effectiveness of implementation. And managers of profitable companies may feel more comfortable turning their attention to the environment than are managers of companies in financial difficulty.

Some organizations set environmental agendas

In the past, most companies were oblivious to their negative environmental impact. More recently, many began striving for low impact. Now, some strive for positive impact, eager to sell solutions to the world's problems. IBM has three decades of experience in lowering its environmental impact through efforts such as reducing waste in packaging and measuring carbon emissions. It has begun to use that experience as a strength, a basis for expertise it can sell to other organizations,

A New Meaning for "Greenhouses"

Since early Roman days, people have used greenhouses to grow plants—particularly to enjoy fruits and vegetables out of season. But not until the 1990s did greenhouses begin to gain popularity in the United States. The timing couldn't be better. The amount of farmable land per capita in the world continues to shrink, and over the next 50 years world population is expected to increase by 3 billion. At the same time, economists estimate, the demand for farm products will double.

As more regions suffer from drought from climate change and as power shortfalls increase, the notion of using glass houses to grow fruits and vegetables has become increasingly attractive. A leader in greenhouse-grown produce, Houweling Nurseries was founded in 1974 by

Cornelius Houweling, a Dutch immigrant to the United States and professional horticulturist. Today, the business includes farms in British Columbia and Oxnard, California.

In 2009, the company expanded its Oxnard site with a $53 billion, 40-acre greenhouse facility that uses sustainable practices to grow tomatoes year-round. Located in the center of California's $36 billion farming economy, the greenhouses stand as a triumph of 21st-century agricultural science. They are believed to be the world's first energy-neutral greenhouses. In fact, nothing goes to waste at Houweling Nurseries. Solar panels generate most of the electricity needed to power the greenhouse pumps and climate controls. Energy screens reduce heat loss. Should the temperature drop

during the night, the greenhouses are heated with waste heat collected from refrigeration exhaust. The 2.1 megawatts of electricity generated by the greenhouses could power 1,500 homes.

Fully enclosed, the greenhouses are nearly dust-free. Crops grow herbicide-free and nearly pesticide-free, using only about half the fertilizer of conventional crops. Colonies of bumblebees reside on-site and pollinate the crops. Houweling greenhouses use about 20 percent as much water as a field farm and only about a third as much as an ordinary greenhouse. Rainwater and irrigation runoff are captured in a man-made pond, filtered, and recirculated as needed. Watered individually through a complex computerized piping system, greenhouse-tended along with its computing power and other consulting services. Thus, one application might be to help clients measure and forecast the carbon emissions of their entire supply chain. By running calculations on its supercomputers, IBM consultants could help the clients find ways to lower their energy use.[104]

You don't have to be a manufacturer or a utility to jump on the green bandwagon. Web search giant Google is applying a three-pronged strategy aimed at reducing its "carbon footprint," that is, its output of carbon dioxide and other greenhouse gases. At Google, most greenhouse gas emissions are related to electricity consumption by its buildings and computers. So Google is first seeking ways to make buildings and computers more energy-efficient, such as by using high-efficiency lighting and installing power management software in its computers. Second, the company is developing ways to get more of its power from renewable sources, such as the solar power system at its facility in Mountain View, California. Finally, recognizing that its other efforts cannot yet eliminate Google's release of greenhouse gases, the company is purchasing "offsets"—funding projects that reduce greenhouse gas emissions elsewhere.[105]

Webs of companies with a common ecological vision can combine their efforts into high-leverage, impactful action.[106] In Kalundborg, Denmark, such a collaborative alliance exists among an electric power generating plant, an oil refiner, a biotech production plant, a plasterboard factory, cement producers, heating utilities, a sulfuric acid producer, and local agriculture and horticulture. Chemicals, energy (for heating and cooling), water, and organic materials flow among companies. Resources are conserved, "waste" materials generate revenues, and water, air, and ground pollution all are reduced.

Companies not only have the *ability* to solve environmental problems; they are coming to see and acquire the *motivation* as well. Some now believe that solving environmental problems is one of the biggest opportunities in the history of commerce.[107]

tomato plants live far longer than field crops. The plants grow to the ceiling; workers stand on ladders to harvest the fruit.

High-tech growing facilities like Houweling Nurseries yield as much as 20 times more tomatoes per acre than does a conventional farm. An estimated 5 million cartons of tomatoes are produced annually. In addition, at the Oxnard facility alone, Houweling has generated more than 450 full-time, year-round jobs in an industry that, like many in recessionary times, has been hard-hit by unemployment.

 Discussion Questions

- How does Houweling Nurseries serve as a forward-looking example for other agricultural businesses?
- Emerging environmental issues have created significant challenges for farming. Although costly, what could the construction of more greenhouses like the Houwelings mean for today's farmers? For the agricultural industry as a whole?

SOURCES: Company Web site, http://www.houwelings.com, accessed June 9, 2009; Oppenheimer Company Web site, "Casey Houweling: Growing with Oppenheimer," http://www.oppyproduce.com, accessed May 19, 2009; T. Burfield, "Opening of Houweling Nurseries Greenhouse Draws VIPs," *The Packer*, May 15, 2009, http://www.thepacker.com; S. Hoops, "Environmentally Friendly Greenhouses in Camarillo Impresses Experts," *Ventura County Star*, May 15, 2009, http://www.venturacountystar.com; J. Hirsch, "Greener Greenhouses Produce 21st Century Crops," *Los Angeles Times*, May 14, 2009, http://www.newsday.com; D. Babcock, "Grown under Glass: The Future of Greenhouse-Grown Products," *Produce Merchandising*, March 2009, http://producemerchandising.com.

●● learning **OBJECTIVES**

After studying Chapter 4,
you will be able to:

LO1 Summarize the basic steps in any
planning process.

LO2 Discuss how strategic planning
should be integrated with tactical
and operational planning.

LO3 Describe how strategy is based
on analysis of the external
environment and the firm's
strengths and weaknesses.

LO4 Discuss how companies can
achieve competitive advantage
through business strategy.

LO5 Identify the keys to effective
strategy implementation.

LO6 Explain how to make effective
decisions as a manager.

LO7 Summarize principles for group
decision making.

Strategic Planning

Nokia CEO Olli-Pekka Kallasvuo should have plenty of reasons to be happy. More than a billion reasons, you might say. Finland-based Nokia is the world's leading cell phone maker, and more than 1 billion people use its phones. Nokia leads the market in Europe, Asia, the Middle East, and Africa, selling more than its top three competitors combined. But Nokia doesn't have bragging rights in North America; Apple's iPhone and Research in Motion's BlackBerry eclipse Nokia there. In the wireless world no manufacturer can afford to be off its game. So Nokia has shifted its planning to become competitive in North America again. Along with new smart phones, Nokia has begun offering its Ovi online service, which allows users to download music, games, videos, and more. The firm also has introduced a mobile payment service for users to send and receive money via their cell phones.[1]

Master the Strategies

of setting a direction for your company. Listen to what Dara and Artemio have to say about planning strategically on the book Web site.

"I schedule out my day completely and keep a list of what needs to get done. I also make sure to follow up with staff daily and see if I can help with any tasks they need completed as well. In college, I would have cut back on the extracurricular activities and scheduled out my work better . . . less procrastination."

—Dara Johnson, Nonprofit Manager

"In my current position I'm 100 percent involved in setting goals and strategies that I do during the year. These goals and strategies help to continue to evolve the position that I have. At the same time, learning about new technologies helps me establish new goals."

—Artemio Ortiz, Digital Promotions Manager

It's almost impossible to imagine Nokia—or any organization—meeting significant challenges without developing a plan beforehand. Planning is a formal expression of managerial intent. It describes what managers decide to do and how they will do it. It provides the framework, focus, and direction required for a meaningful effort. Without planning, any improvements in an organization's innovation, speed, quality, service, and cost will be accidental, if they occur at all.

This chapter examines the most important concepts and processes involved in planning and strategic management. By learning these concepts and reviewing the steps outlined, you will be on your way to understanding the current approaches to strategically managing today's organizations. Also, whether or not managers are directly involved in strategic planning for their firms, they make key decisions that contribute to the successful implementation of that strategy. The chapter explores the types of decisions managers face, the ways they are made, and the ways they *should* be made.

L O 1 WHAT YOU NEED TO KNOW . . .

What are the basic steps in any planning process?

THE PLANNING PROCESS

Planning is the conscious, systematic process of making decisions about goals and activities that an individual, group, work unit, or organization will pursue in the future. Planning is not an informal or haphazard response to a crisis; it is a purposeful effort that is directed and controlled by managers and often draws on the knowledge and experience of employees at all levels. Figure 4.1 shows the steps in this process. Notice that planning moves in a *cycle*. The outcomes of plans are evaluated and, if necessary, revised.

Planning gives individuals and work units a clear map to follow in their future activities yet is flexible enough to allow for unique circumstances and changing conditions. We now describe the basic planning process in more detail. Later in this chapter, we will discuss how managerial decisions and plans fit into the larger purposes of the organization—its ultimate strategy, mission, vision, and goals.

Step 1: Analyze the situation

Planning begins with a situational analysis. Within their time and resource constraints, planners should gather, interpret, and summarize all information relevant to the planning issue in

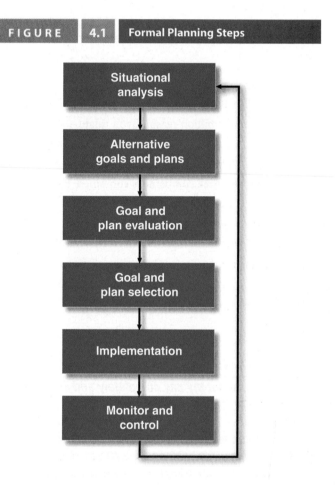

FIGURE 4.1 Formal Planning Steps

- Situational analysis
- Alternative goals and plans
- Goal and plan evaluation
- Goal and plan selection
- Implementation
- Monitor and control

question. They study past events, examine current conditions, and try to forecast future trends. The analysis focuses on the internal forces at work in the organization or work unit and, consistent with the open-systems approach (see Chapter 2), examines influences from the external environment. The outcome of this step is the identification and diagnosis of planning assumptions, issues, and problems.

A thorough situational analysis will provide information about the planning decisions you need to make. For example, if you are a manager in a magazine company considering the launch of a sports publication for the teen market, your analysis will include such factors as the number of teens who subscribe to magazines, the appeal of the teen market to advertisers, your firm's ability to serve this market effectively, current economic conditions, the level of teen interest in sports, and any sports magazines already serving this market and their current sales. Such an analysis will help you decide whether to proceed with the next step in your magazine launch.

Step 2: Generate alternative goals and plans

Based on the findings from situational analysis, the planning process should generate alternative goals that may be pursued and alternative plans for achieving those goals. This step should stress creativity and encourage managers and employees to think broadly. Once a range of alternatives has been developed, their merits and goals will be evaluated. Continuing with our magazine publishing example, the alternatives you might want to consider could include whether the magazine should be targeted at young men, young women, or both groups, and whether it should be sold mainly online, through subscriptions, or on newsstands.

Goals are the targets or ends the manager wants to reach. To be effective, goals should have certain qualities, which are easy to remember with the acronym SMART:

- *Specific*—When goals are precise, describing particular behaviors and outcomes, employees can more easily determine whether they are working toward the goals.

- *Measurable*—As much as possible, the goal should quantify the desired results, so that there is no doubt whether it has been achieved.

- *Attainable (but challenging)*—Employees need to recognize that they can attain the goals they are responsible for, so they won't become discouraged. However, they also should feel challenged to work hard and be creative.

- *Relevant*—Each goal should contribute to the organization's overall mission (discussed later in this chapter) and be consistent with its values, including ethical standards.

- *Time-bound*—Effective goals specify a target date for completion.

General Electric's goal of being first or second in all its markets is a well-known example of a goal that is specific, measurable, and challenging. SMART goals such as these not only point employees in the direction they should be going but also foster acceptance by those who are charged with achieving them. In other words, they both direct and motivate employees.

Plans are the actions or means the manager intends to use to achieve goals. At a minimum, planning should outline alternative actions that may lead to the attainment of each goal, the resources required to reach the goal, and the obstacles that may develop. IBM has goals to increase its profits, and the fastest-growing area of growth is in software. To meet profit goals, the software unit acquires existing software companies that have high-potential products but lack the means to promote them aggressively enough. IBM's software group plans how its gigantic sales force will sell the new products. Those plans include training the salespeople in what the new software does and how it can help IBM's clients. To improve the effectiveness of the sales force, the software group planned a selling system for categorizing and keeping track of each salesperson's leads.[2]

In this chapter we will talk about various types of plans:

- *Single-use plans* are designed to achieve a set of goals that are not likely to be repeated in the future. For example, city planners might prepare for an upcoming sesquicentennial celebration by putting in place a plan for parades, festivities, speeches, and food tents.

- *Standing plans* focus on ongoing activities designed to achieve an enduring set of goals. Many companies have standing plans for recruiting minority-group members and women. Standing plans may become more permanent policies and rules for running the organization.

- *Contingency plans* specify actions to take when a company's initial plans have not worked well or events in the external environment require a sudden change. Disasters, including the 2001 terrorist attacks and Gulf Coast hurricanes, have reminded many businesses how important contingency planning can be. But contingency plans are important for more-common situations as well. For example, many businesses are affected by snowstorms, increases in gasoline prices, computer breakdowns, or changes in customer tastes.

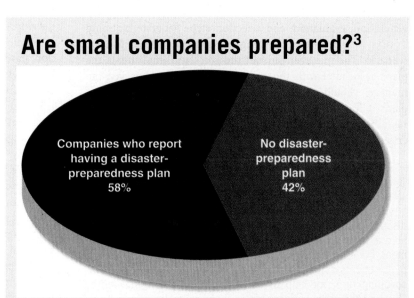

Are small companies prepared?[3]

Companies who report having a disaster-preparedness plan
58%

No disaster-preparedness plan
42%

Step 3: Evaluate goals and plans

Next, managers evaluate the advantages, disadvantages, and potential effects of each alternative goal and plan. They must prioritize the goals and even eliminate some of them. Also, managers consider how well alternative plans meet high-priority goals, considering the cost of each initiative and the likely investment return. In our magazine publishing example, your evaluation might determine that newsstand sales alone wouldn't be profitable enough to justify the launch. Perhaps you could improve profits with an online edition supplemented by Podcasts.

Step 4: Select goals and plans

Once managers have assessed the goals and plans, they select the most appropriate and feasible alternative. The evaluation process identifies the priorities and trade-offs among the goals

The partners brainstormed ideas for a new business plan. Looking over the prior year's results, they noticed that most of Cor Business's growth that year had come from small businesses, even though the partners had been directing most of their energy toward large companies like MasterCard and AT&T. As a matter of fact, as the economy had slowed, more and more nervous small-business owners had been looking for help from their firm.

Hull and the other partners drew up a new plan in which they would focus on serving small clients, helping them do what Cor Business's managers were doing—move beyond their fear of change to find new opportunities in challenging times. Hull counseled the owner of a real estate investment company to set aside his fears about the real estate downturn, reevaluate his data on the prospects for converting a warehouse into a restaurant, and go ahead with plans for what was in fact a well-researched, practical idea.[4]

> "Most discussions of decision making assume that only senior executives make decisions or that only senior executives' decisions matter. This is a dangerous mistake."
>
> —Peter Drucker

and plans. For example, if your plan is to launch a number of new publications and you're trying to choose among them, you might weigh the different up-front investment each requires, the size of each market, and which one fits best with your existing product line or company image. Experienced judgment plays an important role in this process. As you will discover later in the chapter, however, relying on judgment alone may not be the best way to proceed.

Typically, a formal planning process leads to a written set of goals and plans that are appropriate and feasible for a particular set of circumstances. In some organizations, the alternative generation, evaluation, and selection steps generate planning scenarios. A different contingency plan is attached to each scenario. The manager pursues the goals and implements the plans associated with the most likely scenario. However, the manager should also be prepared to switch to another set of plans if the situation changes and another scenario becomes relevant. This approach helps the firm anticipate and manage crises and allows greater flexibility and responsiveness.

If a company hasn't already considered possible scenarios, managers must be prepared to restart the planning process when an unexpected change brings disappointing results. This flexible approach to planning can help a company survive and even thrive in a turbulent environment. For example, when the economy recently took a downturn, major clients stopped calling on Cor Business, a management coaching firm, for help in developing their managers. Jeffrey Hull and the other partners of Cor Business realized their firm's survival required a new plan for bringing in business.

Step 5: Implement the goals and plans

Once managers have selected the goals and plans, they must implement them. Proper implementation is key to achieving goals. Managers and employees must understand the plan, have the resources to implement it, and be motivated to do so. Including employees in the previous steps of the planning process paves the way for the implementation phase. Employees usually are better informed, more committed, and more highly motivated when a goal or plan is one that they helped develop.

Finally, linking the plan to other systems in the organization, particularly the budget and reward systems, helps ensure its successful implementation. If the manager does not have or cannot find the financial resources to execute the plan, the plan is probably doomed. Similarly, linking goal achievement to the organization's reward system, such as bonuses or promotions, encourages employees to achieve goals and to implement plans properly.

Wells Fargo's top management saw the importance of linking its employees' pay to a new strategy. Chairman of the Board Dick Kovacevich saw that one of the nation's largest banks could stay competitive by excelling at "cross-selling," that is, encouraging the bank's existing customers to use more of its financial services. Bank customers typically go to different institutions for different services, but Wells Fargo beat the odds by getting employees at all levels to focus on customer needs, rather than product lines. Tellers and branch managers receive training aimed at this goal, and pay systems reward

● **SCENARIO** A narrative that describes a particular set of future conditions.

● **STRATEGIC PLANNING** A set of procedures for making decisions about the organization's long-term goals and strategies.

● **STRATEGIC GOALS** Major targets or end results relating to the organization's long-term survival, value, and growth.

● **STRATEGY** A pattern of actions and resource allocations designed to achieve the organization's goals.

The Hard Rock Café carries its strategy—to be identified with rock 'n' roll—through to its hotel signs.

employees for cross-selling. As a result, Wells Fargo customers use an average of 5.2 of the bank's products, roughly double the average for the industry. Selling to existing customers is much more profitable than winning new ones, so this strategy might seem obvious. Perhaps it is, but Wells Fargo board member Robert Joss says, "It's simple in concept but very hard in execution," adding that this successful implementation reflects Kovacevich's "great capacity to motivate people."[5]

Step 6: Monitor and control performance

Although it is sometimes ignored, the sixth step in the formal planning process—monitoring and controlling—is essential. Without it, you would never know whether your plan is succeeding. As we mentioned earlier, planning works in a cycle. Managers must continually monitor the actual performance of their work units against the unit's goals and plans. They also need to develop control systems to measure that performance and allow them to take corrective action when plans are implemented improperly or the situation changes. In our magazine publishing example,

newsstand and subscription sales reports let you know how well your new magazine launch is going. If subscription sales are below expectations, you may need to revise your marketing plan. We will discuss control systems in greater detail later.

⎝L⎠⎝0⎠ 2 WHAT YOU NEED TO KNOW . . .
How should strategic planning be integrated with tactical and operational planning?

LEVELS OF PLANNING

Planning is used by managers at all three levels described in Chapter 1: top-level (*strategic* managers), middle-level (*tactical* managers), and front-line (*operational* managers). However, the scope and activities of the planning process tend to differ at each level.

Strategic planning sets a long-term direction

Strategic planning involves making decisions about the organization's long-term goals and strategies. Strategic plans have a strong external orientation and cover major portions of the organization. Senior executives are responsible for the development and execution of the strategic plan, although they usually do not formulate or implement the entire plan personally.

Strategic goals are major targets or end results that relate to the long-term survival, value, and growth of the organization. Strategic managers—top-level managers—usually establish goals aimed at effectiveness (providing appropriate outputs) and efficiency (a high ratio of outputs to inputs). Typical strategic goals include growing, increasing market share, improving profitability, boosting return on investment, fostering quantity and quality of outputs, increasing productivity, improving customer service, and contributing to society.

A **strategy** is a pattern of actions and resource allocations designed to achieve the

FIGURE   4.2   **Hierarchy of Goals and Plans**

	Managerial Level	Level of Detail	Time Horizon
Strategic	Top	Low	Long (3–7 years)
Tactical	Middle	Medium	Medium (1–2 years)
Operational	Frontline	High	Short (<1 year)

organization's goals. An effective strategy provides a basis for answering five broad questions about how the organization will meet its objectives:

1. Where will we be active?
2. How will we get there (e.g., by increasing sales or acquiring another company)?
3. How will we win in the marketplace (e.g., by keeping prices low or offering the best service)?
4. How fast will we move, and in what sequence will we make changes?
5. How will we obtain financial returns (low costs or premium prices)?[6]

Later in this chapter, we discuss how managers try to craft a strategy by matching the organization's skills and resources to the opportunities found in the external environment.

Tactical and operational planning support the strategy

The organization's strategic goals and plans serve as the foundation for planning by middle-level and frontline managers. Figure 4.2 shows that as goals and plans move from the strategic

land a probe on Titan, Saturn's moon. Tactical plans may have a time horizon of a year or two, and operational plans may cover several months.

Tactical planning translates broad strategic goals and plans into specific goals and plans relevant to a particular portion of the organization, often a functional area such as marketing or human resources. Tactical plans focus on the major actions a unit must take to fulfill its part of the strategic plan. Suppose a strategy calls for the rollout of a new product line. The tactical plan for the manufacturing unit might involve the design, testing, and installation of the equipment needed to produce the new line.

Operational planning identifies the specific procedures and processes required at lower levels of the organization. Frontline managers usually focus on routine tasks such as production runs, delivery schedules, and human resource requirements.

The formal planning model is hierarchical, with top-level strategies flowing down through the levels of the organization into more specific goals and plans and an ever-more-limited timetable. But in today's complex organizations, planning is often less rigid. Managers throughout an organization may be involved in developing the strategic plan and contributing critical elements. Also, in practice, lower-level managers may make decisions that shape strategy, whether or not top executives realize it.

When Intel senior adviser Andy Grove suggested that the company exit the computer memory business, Intel was directing about one-third of its research dollars to memory-related projects. Yet, on a practical level, the company had already been exiting the business; only 4 percent of its total sales were for computer memory products. Why was this occurring, if it wasn't a defined strategy? Finance executives had directed manufacturing managers to set up factories in a way that would generate the biggest margins (revenues minus costs) per square inch of microchips produced. As computer memory became a money-losing commodity, manufacturing made fewer of those products. So, when Intel announced it would get out of the memory business, its strategy was catching up with its operational planning,

"We wanted Nike to be the world's best sports and fitness company. Once you say that, you have a focus. You don't end up making wing tips or sponsoring the next Rolling Stone world tour."

—Philip Knight, Nike Founder

level to the tactical level and then to the operational level, they become more specific and involve shorter time periods. A strategic plan typically has a time horizon of three to seven years, but sometimes it spans decades, as with the successful plan to

which had been driven by tactical plans.[7] The lesson for top managers is to make sure they are communicating strategy to all levels of the organization and paying attention to what is happening at all levels in the organization.

All levels of planning should be aligned

To be fully effective, the organization's strategic, tactical, and operational goals and plans must be *aligned*—that is, they must be consistent, mutually supportive, and focused on achieving the common purpose and direction. Whole Foods Market, for example, links its tactical and operational planning directly to its strategic planning. The strategic goal of Whole Foods is "to sell the highest-quality products that also offer high value for our customers." Its operational goals focus on ingredients, freshness, taste, nutritional value, safety, and appearance that meet or exceed its customers' expectations, including guaranteeing product satisfaction. Tactical goals include store environments that are "inviting, fun, unique, informal, comfortable, attractive, nurturing and educational" and safe and inviting work environments for its employees.

In the past, at one of Boeing's core businesses, Commercial Airplanes, a single-minded drive to achieve a strategy of maximum sales resulted in poor operational planning and disastrous relations with customers and suppliers. Salespeople wrote up orders for hundreds of aircraft by pricing many of them too low and promising rapid delivery. Production managers scrambled to hire tens of thousands of workers so that they could double production levels, and suppliers were pressed to ramp up production. Demand for components became so intense that some were delivered by helicopter and taxicab. Costs rose, and profits suffered.

Today, in contrast, the strategy for Boeing Commercial Airplanes is to grow at a sustainable pace. The unit now expands production capabilities only when it determines that the need will continue for at least two years. If a customer wants to place a major order, a committee that includes engineers and accountants must sign off on it after ensuring the company has the capacity to meet the contract's deadlines. Boeing also focuses more on collaborating with suppliers, sharing information to ensure that enough parts will be available without the expense of rush orders. Suppliers are relieved not to have to staff production lines for a surge and then lay off workers after a year or two. Production planning covers a time frame of several years, because the backlog can be that long. When some customers are uncertain about their needs, planners adjust the schedule to serve customers who are ready to buy and postpone orders from customers who don't mind waiting, keeping everyone satisfied without hiring extra workers for peak demand. Thanks to smoother staffing levels, Boeing can focus on training existing workers, rather than constantly hiring and laying off as orders surge and fall.[8]

STRATEGIC PLANNING PROCESS

Many organizations are changing the ways they develop and execute their strategic plans. Traditionally, strategic planning flowed from the top. Senior executives and specialized planning units developed goals and plans for the entire organization. Tactical and operational managers received those goals and plans, and then simply prepared procedures and budgets for their units. Today, however, senior executives increasingly are involving managers throughout the organization in strategy formulation.[9] In the current highly competitive and rapidly changing environment, executives need to look for ideas from all levels of the organization. Although top managers continue to furnish the organization's strategic direction, or "vision," tactical and operational managers provide valuable inputs to the organization's strategic plan. These managers also may formulate or change their own plans, making the organization more flexible and responsive.

Because of this trend, a new term for the strategic planning process has emerged: *strategic management. Strategic management* involves managers from all parts of the organization in the formulation and implementation of strategic goals and strategies. It integrates strategic planning and management into a single process. Strategic planning becomes an ongoing activity in which all managers are encouraged to think strategically and focus on long-term, externally oriented issues as well as short-term tactical and operational issues.

As shown in Figure 4.3, the strategic management process has six steps: (1) establishment of mission, vision, and goals; (2) analysis of external opportunities and threats; (3) analysis of internal strengths and weaknesses; (4) SWOT analysis and strategy formulation; (5) strategy implementation; and (6) strategic control. This planning and decision process resembles the planning framework discussed earlier.

First, establish a mission, vision, and goals

The first step in strategic planning is establishing a mission, a vision, and goals for the organization. The mission is a clear and concise expression of the organization's basic purpose. It describes what the organization does, who it does it for, its basic good or service, and its values. Here are some mission statements from firms you will recognize:[10]

> *McDonald's:* "To be our customers' favorite place and way to eat."

TACTICAL PLANNING A set of procedures for translating broad strategic goals and plans into specific goals and plans that are relevant to a particular portion of the organization, such as a functional area like marketing.

OPERATIONAL PLANNING The process of identifying the specific procedures and processes required at lower levels of the organization.

STRATEGIC MANAGEMENT A process that involves managers from all parts of the organization in the formulation and implementation of strategic goals and strategies.

MISSION An organization's basic purpose and scope of operations.

FIGURE 4.3 The Strategic Management Process

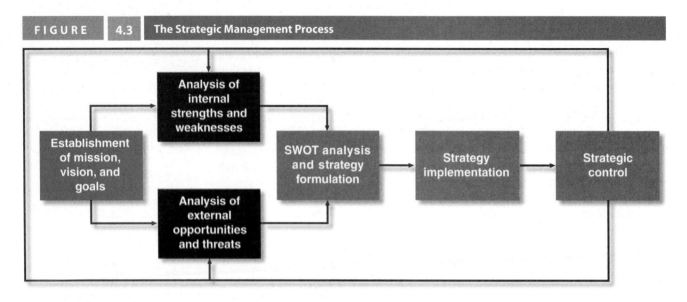

Microsoft: "We work to help people and businesses throughout the world to realize their full potential."

Allstate: "To be the best . . . serving our customers by providing peace of mind and enriching their quality of life through our partnership in the management of the risks they face."

The mission describes the organization as it currently operates. The strategic vision points to the future; it provides a perspective on where the organization is headed and what it can become. Here are some actual vision statements:[11]

DuPont: "To be the world's most dynamic science company, creating sustainable solutions essential to a better, safer and healthier life for people everywhere."

City of Redmond, Washington: "Together we create a community of good neighbors."

Great Lakes Naval Museum: "To enhance and become an integral part of the training mission of the Naval Service Training Command, Great Lakes, by instilling in our newest sailors a strong sense of tradition and heritage of Naval service in the United States."

The most effective vision statements inspire organization members. They offer a worthwhile target for the entire organization to work together to achieve. Often, these statements are not strictly financial, because financial targets alone may not motivate all organization members. Thus, DuPont's vision refers to being a "dynamic science company" that works toward a "better, safer and healthier life" for people. This vision inspires innovation aimed at making the world better—the type of work that is likely to motivate the scientists and other knowledge workers who can give the company an edge, ultimately improving DuPont's competitive position. Likewise,

"instilling . . . a strong sense of tradition and heritage" provides an inspirational and forward-looking perspective for operating the Great Lakes Naval Museum, in contrast to planning based only on budgets and historical displays.

Strategic goals evolve from the organization's mission and vision. For example, in support of its vision that "creating a community of good neighbors" is best done "together" with all sectors of the community, the City of Redmond has established goals such as these:

- Enhance citizen engagement in city issues
- Sustain the natural systems and beauty of the community
- Sustain a safe community with a coherent, comprehensive, cohesive approach to safety
- Maintain economic vitality

Different city departments would contribute to various aspects of this vision in the way they carry out their operational plans with an emphasis on collaborating with local businesses and residents.

Lofty words in a vision and mission statement cannot be meaningful without strong leadership support. At McDonald's, the commitment of past and present CEOs has played a large role in the success of the company's strategy implementation. Several years ago, the company was floundering as it lost sight of its commitment to quality, value, speed, and convenience. Under the leadership of James Cantalupo, the company created the mission statement quoted earlier, which placed the emphasis on the customer's experience. In the firm's "Plan to Win," strategic goals such as revamping restaurants for a better drive-through

The environmental analysis includes many elements:

- *Industry profile:* major product lines and significant market segments in the industry.

- *Industry growth:* growth rates for the entire industry, growth rates for key market segments, projected changes in patterns of growth, and the determinants of growth.

- *Industry forces:* threat of new industry entrants, threat of substitutes, economic power of buyers, economic power of suppliers, and internal industry rivalry.

> ## "There is no more powerful engine driving an organization toward excellence and long-term success than an attractive, worthwhile, and achievable vision of the future."
>
> —Burt Nanus[13]

experience and improving the quality of the menu supported the mission. When Jim Skinner took the job of chief executive, he enthusiastically backed the mission statement and its supporting Plan to Win, not hesitating to share credit for the company's continued success.[12]

Large firms generally provide public formal statements of their missions, visions, goals, and even values. The concepts and information within these statements should be communicated to everyone who has contact with the organization. Strong leadership provides statements of vision and goals to clarify the organization's purpose to key constituencies outside the organization. Clear vision and goals also help employees focus their talent, energy, and commitment. When you seek employment with a firm, review the firm's statements of mission, vision, and goals; they can help you determine whether the firm's purposes and values are compatible with your own.

ⓛⓞ 3 WHAT YOU NEED TO KNOW . . .

Can you describe how strategy is based on analysis of the external environment and the firm's strengths and weaknesses?

Second, analyze external opportunities and threats

The mission and vision drive the second component of the strategic management process: analysis of the external environment. Successful strategic management depends on an accurate and thorough evaluation of the competitive environment and macroenvironment, described in Chapter 2.

- *Competitor profile:* major competitors and their market shares.

- *Competitor analysis:* goals, strategies, strengths, and weaknesses of each major competitor.

- *Competitor advantages:* the degree to which industry competitors have differentiated their goods or services or achieved cost leadership.

- *Legislation and regulatory activities* and their effects on the industry.

- *Political activity:* the level of political activity undertaken by organizations and associations within the industry.

- *Social issues:* current and potential social issues and their effects on the industry.

- *Social interest groups:* consumer, environmental, and similar activist groups that try to influence the industry.

- *Labor issues:* key labor needs, shortages, opportunities, and problems confronting the industry.

- *Macroeconomic conditions:* economic factors that affect supply, demand, growth, competition, and profitability within the industry.

- *Technological factors:* scientific or technical methods that affect the industry, particularly recent and potential innovations.

The analysis begins with an examination of the industry. Next, organizational stakeholders are examined. Stakeholders are groups and individuals who affect and are affected by achievement of the organization's mission, goals, and strategies. They include buyers, suppliers, competitors, government and regulatory agencies, unions and employee groups, the financial community, owners and shareholders, and trade associations. The environmental analysis provides a map of these stakeholders and the ways they influence the organization.[14]

Collaborating with key stakeholders can help organizations successfully develop and implement their strategic plan. At software company Intuit, CEO Brad Smith launched strategy development by learning what was on the minds of some key stakeholders. He visited with his board of directors and investors and set up meetings with groups of employees who work directly with Intuit's customers.

Smith asked each group of stakeholders some key questions related to strategic analysis: "What is Intuit's biggest untapped opportunity? What is the biggest risk facing Intuit that keeps you up at night? What is the biggest mistake I can make as a CEO in my first year?" From the answers, Smith gained insights that helped him establish priorities for Intuit's strategy.

Smith learned that a sizable number of Intuit's business customers have international activities, so he determined that Intuit would have to become a more global company. Its QuickBooks financial software now handles multiple currencies for international transactions. In response to the competitive threat of a new release of financial software from Microsoft, Smith assembled managers to craft a marketing strategy that would convince customers to wait two more months for the next version of QuickBooks. That campaign caused QuickBooks sales to jump in spite of Microsoft's efforts.[15]

The environmental analysis also should examine other forces in the environment, such as economic conditions and technological factors. One critical task in environmental analysis is forecasting future trends. As noted in Chapter 2, forecasting techniques range from simple judgment to complex mathematical models that examine systematic relationships among many variables. Because of biases and limits on human thinking, even simple quantitative techniques can outperform the intuitive assessments of experts.

Frequently, the difference between an opportunity and a threat depends on how a company positions itself strategically. For example, some states have required that electric utilities get a certain share of their power from renewable sources such as wind and solar energy, rather than from fossil fuels, including coal, oil, and natural gas. This requirement poses an obvious threat to utilities, because the costs of fossil fuel energy are less, and customers demand low prices. However, some companies see strategic opportunities in renewable power. German conglomerate Schott has

developed a solar thermal technology in which sunlight heats oil in metal tubes enclosed in coated glass; the heated oil makes steam, which powers a turbine and generates electricity. Solar thermal energy, although it now costs more than fossil fuels, is more efficient than the solar panels installed on some buildings, and it can store extra power to be used on cloudy days.[16] Similarly, overflowing landfills are an expensive challenge for many municipalities, but a growing number are seeing an opportunity in the form of energy generation. As garbage decomposes, it produces methane gas, which is used as a fuel to power generators. In East Brunswick, New Jersey, for example, the Edgeboro landfill generates electricity that powers the county's wastewater treatment plant.[17]

Third, analyze internal strengths and weaknesses

As managers conduct an external analysis, they should also assess the strengths and weaknesses of major functional areas inside their organization. This internal resource analysis has several components:

- *Financial analysis*—Examines financial strengths and weaknesses through financial statements such as a balance sheet and an income statement and compares trends to historical and industry figures.

- *Human resources assessment*—Examines strengths and weaknesses of all levels of managers and employees and focuses on key human resources activities, including recruitment, selection, placement, training, labor (union) relationships, compensation, promotion, appraisal, quality of work life, and human resources planning.

- *Marketing audit*—Examines strengths and weaknesses of major marketing activities and identifies markets, key market segments, and the organization's competitive position (market share) within key markets.

- *Operations analysis*—Examines the strengths and weaknesses of the organization's manufacturing, production, or service delivery activities.

- *Other internal resource analyses*—Examine, as appropriate, the strengths and weaknesses of other organizational activities, such as research and development (product and process), management information systems, engineering, and purchasing.

TIP

Collaborating with key stakeholders often helps organizations execute their strategic plan. For example, working with potential buyers about product improvements often gives managers useful, profitable ideas they wouldn't otherwise have considered. Managers who develop nonadversarial relationships with unions may have an easier time achieving necessary work flow changes when a new product is launched. Cooperating with community organizations before a new plant is built will often speed up the approval process and may even produce other beneficial outcomes, such as improvements in local transportation.

● RESOURCES Inputs to a system that can enhance performance.

● CORE COMPETENCE A unique skill and/or knowledge an organization possesses that gives it an edge over competitors.

Is your firm strong enough financially to invest in new projects, and can your existing staff carry out its part of the plan? Is your firm's image compatible with its strategy, or will it have to persuade key stakeholders that a change in direction makes sense? This type of internal analysis provides an inventory of the organization's existing functions, skills, and resources as well as its overall performance level. Many of your other business courses will prepare you to conduct an internal analysis.

resources and core competencies

Without question, strategic planning has been strongly influenced in recent years by a focus on internal resources. Resources are inputs to production (recall systems theory) that can be accumulated over time to enhance the performance of a firm. Resources can take many forms, but they tend to fall into two broad categories:

1. *Tangible assets* such as real estate, production facilities, raw materials, and so on

2. *Intangible assets* such as company reputation, culture, technical knowledge, and patents, as well as accumulated learning and experience.

The Walt Disney Company, for example, has developed its strategic plan on combinations of tangible assets (including hotels and theme parks) and intangible assets (brand recognition, talented craftspeople, culture focused on customer service).[18]

Effective internal analysis provides a clearer understanding of how a company can compete through its resources. Resources are a source of competitive advantage only under all of the following circumstances:

- The resources are instrumental for creating customer *value*—that is, they increase the benefits customers derive from a good or service relative to the costs they incur.[19] For example, Amazon's powerful search technology, ability to track customer preferences and offer personalized recommendations, and quick product delivery are valuable resources.

- The resources are *rare* and not equally available to all competitors. At Merck, DuPont, and Dow Chemical, patented formulas represent rare resources. Amazon similarly sought a patent for its one-click shopping technique. If competitors have equal access to a resource, it can be valuable but cannot provide a competitive advantage.

- The resources are *difficult to imitate.* Earlier in this chapter, we saw that Wells Fargo has competed with much larger banks by developing expertise in cross-selling. Unlike, say, free checking accounts, this intangible resource is difficult to imitate because the bank has to train and motivate employees at all levels to adopt customer-oriented thinking and collaborate across divisions.[20] As in this example, where success relies on leadership and collaboration practices, resources tend to be harder to imitate if they are complex, with many interdependent variables and no obvious links between behaviors and desired outcomes.[21]

- The resources are well *organized.* For example, IBM, known primarily for computer hardware until it became more of a commodity than a source of competitive advantage, has organized its staff and systems to efficiently produce a consolidated technology product for its corporate clients—hardware, software, and service in one package. This spares its clients the cost of managing technology on their own.

Imagine how skilled Coca-Cola's global network of bottlers are to be able to deliver their product worldwide and more efficiently than any of their competitors. Shown here is a truck delivering Coke in India.

When resources are valuable, rare, inimitable, and organized, they can be viewed as a company's core competencies. Simply stated, a core competence is something a company does especially well relative to its competitors. Honda, for example, has a core competence in small-engine design and manufacturing, and Federal Express has a core competence in logistics and customer service. As in these examples, a core competence typically refers to a set of skills or expertise in some activity, rather than physical or financial assets.

▶ Kodak CEO Antonio Perez is trying to redefine his firm's core competencies. Once a film-based business, Kodak developed digital camera products that eventually became standard fare. Even though these new products generated huge sales, profits lagged. Perez wants Kodak to shift its focus, creating innovative products that will help people organize, classify, and manage their personal photo libraries, much as Apple products do for their music libraries. The strategy is for Kodak to concentrate on digital services instead of tangibles like cameras and film. The new digital services include online photo sharing and a rapid-fire scanning system called Scan the World, which takes those old shoe boxes filled with snapshots and transforms them into digital images, organized and catalogued by date.[22]

benchmarking To assess and improve performance, some companies use benchmarking, the process of assessing how well one company's basic functions and skills compare with those of another company or set of companies. The goal of benchmarking is to thoroughly understand the "best practices" of other firms and to undertake actions to achieve better performance and lower costs. Benchmarking programs have helped Ford, Corning, Hewlett-Packard, Xerox, and other companies make great strides in eliminating inefficiencies and improving competitiveness.

In London, doctors at Great Ormond Street Hospital for Children used benchmarking to improve their procedures for patient hand-offs, the times when patients are transferred from one hospital unit or doctor's care to another. A study by a Great Ormond surgeon found that poor outcomes often resulted from an accumulation of relatively minor mistakes, rather than large and obvious ones. So a team of doctors benchmarked their hand-off process against an organization that excels in complex procedures: the pit crew for Italy's Formula One Ferrari racing team. They learned, for example, that the pit crew carefully choreographs all their moves, based on information from a human factors engineer and a focus on minor mistakes. Unlike the surgical teams at Great Ormond, members of the pit crew know who is in charge, have clearly specified responsibilities, work in silence, and train for every imaginable contingency. The doctors developed ways to apply those procedures to their cardiac surgery team, with the result that technical errors declined by 42 percent and failures to share information dropped by half.[23]

Benchmarking against competitors only helps a company perform as well as they do, but strategic management aims to surpass those companies. Besides benchmarking against leading organizations in other industries, as Great Ormond Street Hospital did, companies may address this problem by engaging in internal benchmarking. That approach involves benchmarking internal operations and departments against one another to disseminate the company's best practices throughout the organization and thereby gain a competitive advantage.

Fourth, conduct a SWOT analysis and formulate strategy

Once managers have analyzed the external environment and the organization's internal resources, they have the information needed for a SWOT analysis: an assessment of the organization's strengths, weaknesses, opportunities, and threats. Strengths and weaknesses refer to internal resources. An organization's *strengths* might include skilled management, positive cash flow, and well-known and highly regarded brands. *Weaknesses* might be lack of spare production capacity and the absence of reliable suppliers. Opportunities and threats arise in the macroenvironment and competitive environment. Examples of *opportunities* are a new technology that could make the supply chain more

efficient and a market niche that is currently underserved. *Threats* might include the possibility that competitors will enter the underserved niche once it has been shown to be profitable. When Olli-Pekka Kallasvuo became CEO of Nokia, the firm was viewed as stodgy and slow to react to changes in the cellphone marketplace. Worse, critics characterized its product lineup as "tired." So Kallasvuo had to evaluate honestly where the company was strong and where it was weak, and where opportunities lay for improvement. He concluded that Nokia needed to evolve into a company whose management teams could embrace a diversity of opinions and create a management structure that better reflected the firm's global presence.[24]

SWOT analysis helps managers summarize the relevant, important facts from their external and internal analyses. Based on this summary, they can identify the primary and secondary strategic issues their organization faces. The managers then formulate a strategy that will build on the SWOT analysis to take advantage of available opportunities by capitalizing on the organization's strengths, neutralizing its weakness, and countering potential threats.

As an example, consider how SWOT analysis might be carried out at Microsoft. The company's size and earnings from its dominant operating system and Office suite of software are an obvious strength. The company has weaknesses as well. One of the fastest-growing areas of the computer business is Internet applications, especially profits from the sale of online advertising. Microsoft has struggled in this area, with its Internet search engine losing market share year after year, and online ad sales growing but only as a tiny segment of the market. The dominant threat to Microsoft in this area is widely considered to be Google, which not only dominates the search business—and its related advertising—but even has challenged Microsoft with free business applications. This analysis would explain Microsoft's recent efforts to buy DoubleClick, which arranges deals between advertisers and online publishers. DoubleClick, a big player in the online-advertising business, has expertise that Microsoft lacks.[25] By purchasing DoubleClick, Microsoft would use one of its strengths (its capital) to neutralize a weakness (inexperience and small market share in online advertising) and counter a threat (Google). Ironically, before the deal could close, Google emerged as another bidder for DoubleClick.[26]

corporate strategy A corporate strategy identifies the set of businesses, markets, or industries in which the organization competes and the distribution of resources among those businesses. The four basic alternatives for a corporate strategy range from very specialized to highly diverse:

1. Concentration—focusing on a single business competing in a single industry. In food retailing, Kroger and Safeway pursue concentration strategies. Frequently, companies pursue concentration strategies to gain entry into an industry when industry growth is good or when the company has a narrow range of competencies. C. F. Martin & Company pursues a concentration strategy by focusing on making the best possible guitars and guitar strings, a strategy that has

enabled the family-owned business to operate successfully for more than 150 years.

2. **Vertical integration**—expanding the organization's domain into supply channels or to distributors, generally to eliminate uncertainties and reduce costs associated with suppliers or distributors. At one time, Henry Ford had fully integrated his company from the ore mines needed to make steel all the way to the showrooms where his cars were sold.

General Electric's ownership of NBC is an example of conglomerate diversification. Shown from left to right during the giant merger announcement in 1986 are Grant Tinker, outgoing Chairman of NBC; Jack Welch, CEO of GE during the takeover; and Bob Wright, incoming Chairman of NBC.

3. **Concentric diversification**—moving into new businesses related to the company's original core business. William Marriott expanded his original restaurant business outside Washington, D.C., by moving into airline catering, hotels, and fast food. Each of these businesses within the hospitality industry is related in terms of the services it provides, the skills necessary for success, and the customers it attracts. Concentric diversification applies strengths in one business to gain advantage in another. Success in concentric diversification strategy requires adequate management and other resources for operating more than one business. Guitar maker C. F. Martin once tried expanding through purchases of other instrument companies, but management was stretched too thin to run them all well, so the company eventually divested the acquisitions and returned to its concentration strategy.[27]

4. **Conglomerate diversification**—expansion into unrelated businesses, typically to minimize risks due to market fluctuations in one industry. General Electric has diversified from its original base in electrical and home appliance products to such wide-ranging industries as health, finance, insurance, truck and air transportation, and even media, with its ownership of NBC.

The diversified businesses of an organization are sometimes called its business *portfolio*. A popular technique for analyzing

a corporation's strategy for managing its portfolio is the BCG matrix, developed by the Boston Consulting Group and shown in Figure 4.4. Each business in the corporation is plotted on the matrix on the basis of the growth rate of its market and the relative strength of its competitive position in that market (market share). The business is represented by a circle whose size depends on the business's contribution to corporate revenues.

There are four categories of businesses in the BCG matrix:

- *Question marks*—These high-growth, weak-competitive-position businesses require substantial investment to improve their position, or else they should be divested.

- *Stars*—Businesses with high growth and

SWOT ANALYSIS A comparison of strengths, weaknesses, opportunities, and threats that helps executives formulate strategy.

CORPORATE STRATEGY The set of businesses, markets, or industries in which an organization competes and the distribution of resources among those entities.

CONCENTRATION A strategy employed for an organization that operates a single business and competes in a single industry.

VERTICAL INTEGRATION The acquisition or development of new businesses that produce parts or components of the organization's product.

CONCENTRIC DIVERSIFICATION A strategy used to add new businesses that produce related products or are involved in related markets and activities.

CONGLOMERATE DIVERSIFICATION A strategy used to add new businesses that produce unrelated products or are involved in unrelated markets and activities.

FIGURE 4.4 The BCG Matrix

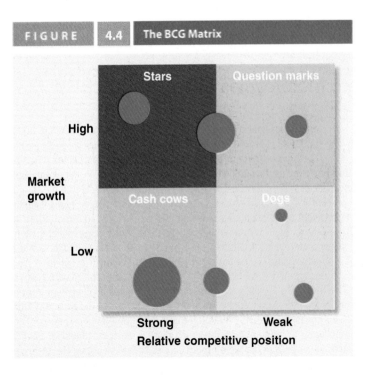

a strong competitive position require heavy investment, but their strong position lets them generate the needed revenues.

- *Cash cows*—These low-growth businesses with a strong competitive position generate revenues in excess of their investment needs, so they fund other businesses.

- *Dogs*—These low-growth, weak-competitive-position businesses should be divested after their remaining revenues are realized.

The BCG matrix is not a substitute for management judgment, creativity, insight, or leadership. But along with other techniques, it can help managers evaluate their strategy alternatives.[28] This type of thinking has recently helped Abbott Laboratories succeed. When Miles White took over as Abbott's CEO, he began restructuring the company's portfolio to emphasize growth. He sold off much of the company's diagnostics business, which was earning low returns, and purchased businesses with higher risks but potential to be stars. White says his goal is a portfolio of businesses that are innovative, growing, and delivering high returns.[29]

Ⓛ Ⓞ 4 **WHAT YOU NEED TO KNOW . . .**

How can companies achieve competitive advantage through business strategy?

business strategy After the top management team and board make the corporate strategic decisions, executives must determine how to compete in each business area. Business strategy defines the major actions by which an organization builds and strengthens its competitive position in the marketplace. A competitive advantage typically results from business strategies based on either keeping costs low or offering products that are unique and highly valued.[30]

Businesses using a **low-cost strategy** try to be efficient and offer a standard, no-frills product. Southwest Airlines' low-cost strategy is simply stated: "to be *the* low-fare airline." That strategy helps with operational planning; when someone suggested offering passengers chicken salad instead of peanuts on some flights, the chief executive asked whether chicken salad would help Southwest be "*the* low-fare airline."[31] Companies that succeed with a low-cost strategy often are large and take advantage of economies of scale—reductions in unit cost from large purchases or manufacturing runs—in production or distribution. Their scale may allow them to buy and sell goods and services at a lower price, which leads to higher market share, volume, and, ultimately, profits. To succeed, an organization using this strategy generally must be the cost leader in its industry or market segment. However, even a cost leader must offer a product that is acceptable to customers.

With a **differentiation strategy**, a company tries to be unique in its industry or market segment along dimensions that customers value. This unique or differentiated position within the industry often is based on high product quality, excellent marketing and distribution, or superior service. Nordstrom's commitment to quality and customer service is an excellent example of a differentiation strategy. Nordstrom's personal shoppers are available online, by phone, or in stores to select items for shoppers' consideration at no charge. Innovation is another ingredient of many differentiation strategies. In the market for toilet paper, Scott Paper Company once determined

Zero Motorcycles Leads the Pack

Motorcycles make noise, right? They did until Zero Motorcycles rolled out its new electric models, including one designed to revolutionize urban commuting. The Zero S is different from the other motorcycles you see on the road in the morning. It is lightweight at 225 pounds and accelerates quickly, with the high performance associated with larger motorcycles. But it has just a barely audible hum that is lost in the background noise of commuter traffic.

Since the Zero S relies on electricity for power instead of fossil fuels, its emissions are—you guessed it—zero. "Although there is some pollution associated with the production of electricity, a Zero motorcycle produces less than an eighth of the CO_2 pollution per mile [produced by a gasoline-powered] motorcycle," says the company. In addition, the Zero S has a nontoxic lithium ion battery, and most of the motorcycle body is completely recyclable. The power pack is approved for disposal in landfills and recharges in less than four hours when plugged into a standard household outlet, which means that owners can easily recharge overnight or while at work, if necessary. All of these features are vastly different from those of traditional gasoline-powered motorcycles.

How did Zero Motorcycles differentiate itself from its competitors? Through innovative management thinking. Founder Neal Saiki is also an inventor. He believes in his vision of an environmentally friendly, economical motorcycle. At just under $10,000—with no costs for fuel—the Zero S is about as inexpensive as transportation can get, except for a bicycle or walking shoes. In addition, the Zero S qualifies for a 10 percent federal plug-in tax credit, a sales tax deduction, and other incentives offered by different state governments. All of these features are attractive, but Saiki had to convince investors to back the Zero S venture. "We started building the motorcycle six years ago out of my own pocket," Saiki recalls. "My wife and I put all our savings into the company."

Yet Saiki didn't give up. Instead, he pressed ahead with what he knew was a good product that was different from anything else on the that it could not afford to compete for institutional sales based on price. Instead, the company began offering institutions a free dispenser that would hold larger rolls of paper, reducing the labor cost of replacing empty rolls. Scott initially was the only company selling the larger rolls, so it gained market share while competitors scrambled to catch up.[32]

New technology can support either of these strategies. It can give the business a cost advantage through pioneering lower-cost product designs and low-cost ways to perform needed operations, or it can support differentiation with unique goods or services that increase buyer value and thus command premium prices.

Industry leaders such as Xerox, 3M, Hewlett-Packard, and Merck built and now maintain their competitive positions through early development and application of new technologies. However, technology leadership also imposes costs and risks:[33]

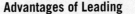

Advantages of Leading	Disadvantages of Leading
First-mover advantage	Greater risks
Little or no competition	Cost of technology development
Greater efficiency	Costs of market development and customer education
Higher profit margins	
Sustainable advantage	Infrastructure costs
Reputation for innovation	Costs of learning and eliminating defects
Establishment of entry barriers	Possible cannibalization of existing products
Occupation of best market niches	
Opportunities to learn	

For example, being a "first mover"—first to market with a new technology—may allow a company to charge a premium price because it faces no competition. Higher prices and greater profits can defray the costs of developing new technologies. This one-time advantage of being the technology leader can be turned into a sustainable advantage if competitors cannot duplicate the technology and the organization can keep building on the lead quickly enough to outpace competitors. Patents and scientific expertise can keep an organization in the lead for years. Japanese manufacturers use several small, incremental improvements to upgrade the quality of their products and processes continuously. All these minor improvements cannot be copied easily by competitors, and collectively they can provide a significant advantage.[34]

Being the first to develop or adopt a new technology does not always lead to immediate advantage and high profits, however. Technology

Nordstrom's differentiation strategy includes personal shoppers in the store, online, or over the phone.

market. "Our goal from the beginning was to engineer a high-performance electric urban street motorcycle that would change the face of the industry. The Zero S is a revolutionary motorcycle that is designed to tackle any city street, hill, or obstacle," Saiki says. "The innovation behind the Zero S is a high-performance motorcycle that also happens to be fully electric and green. The fact that it's electric means not having to get gas and reduced maintenance." That's something different.

Q: Discussion Questions

- The differentiation strategy of Zero S has its advantages. But what might be some of the disadvantages of being a "first mover" in this market?
- How does Neal Saiki's role as inventor and innovator affect the company's business strategy? How might the company's strategy be different if its founder's main area of expertise was finance or advertising instead?

SOURCES: Company Web site, http://www.zeromotorcycles.com, accessed May 26, 2009; Jonathan Welsh, "Motorcycle Review: The Zero S," *The Wall Street Journal*, May 25, 2009, http://online.wsj.com; Jorn Madslien, "Electric Bikemaker Woos Commuters," *BBC News*, May 12, 2009, http://news.bbc.co.uk; "Zero Motorcycles Zero S First Look," *Motorcycle USA*, April 7, 2009, http://www.motorcycle-usa.com; Ariel Schwartz, "The Zero S All-Electric Street Motorcycle Goes to Market," *Fast Company*, April 7, 2009, http://www.fastcompany.com; Chuck Squatriglia, "Zero Takes Electric Motorcycles to the Street," *Wired*, April 7, 2009, http://www.wired.com.

- **FUNCTIONAL STRATEGIES** Strategies implemented by each functional area of the organization to support the organization's business strategy.

- **STRATEGIC CONTROL SYSTEM** A system designed to support managers in evaluating the organization's progress regarding its strategy and, when discrepancies exist, taking corrective action.

leadership imposes high costs and risks that followers do not have to bear. Interestingly, technology followership also can be used to support both low-cost and differentiation strategies. If the follower learns from the leader's experience, it can avoid the costs and risks of technology leadership, thereby establishing a low-cost position. The makers of generic drugs use this type of strategy.

Followership can also support differentiation. By learning from the leader, the follower can adapt the products or delivery systems to fit buyers' needs more closely. Microsoft is famous for having built a successful company on this type of followership. The company's original operating system, MS-DOS, was purchased from Seattle Computer Works to compete with the industry's first desktop operating system, CP/M, sold by Digital Research. Marketing strength, combined with incremental product innovations, enabled Microsoft to steal the lead in software categories (for example, Excel's spreadsheet program beat Lotus 1-2-3, which had taken share from the first mover, VisiCalc).[35] Microsoft products, including music players, videogame consoles, and Web browsers, have been launched after technology leaders paved the way.

Whatever strategy managers adopt, *the most effective strategy is one that competitors are unwilling or unable to imitate.* If the organization's strategic plan is one that could easily be adopted by industry competitors, it may not be sufficiently distinctive or, in the long run, contribute significantly to the organization's competitiveness. For example, in some industries, such as computers, technology advances so fast that the first company to provide a new product is quickly challenged by later entrants offering superior products.[36]

functional strategy

The final step in strategy formulation is to establish the major functional strategies. **Functional strategies** are implemented by each functional area of the organization to support the business strategy. Major functional areas include production, human resources, marketing, research and development, finance, and distribution. For example, IBM's plan to grow by acquiring software companies requires functional strategies for training its sales force to understand the new products and for training the acquired company's employees to understand IBM's culture and procedures. Part of the functional strategy includes assigning each new employee to an experienced IBM mentor. At Wells Fargo, the strategy to grow through cross-selling requires functional strategies for advertising, training employees to cross-sell, and developing systems for sharing information across department boundaries.[37]

Functional strategies typically are developed by functional area executives with input of and approval from the executives responsible for business strategy. Senior strategic decision makers review the functional strategies to ensure that each major department is operating consistently with the organization's business strategies. For example, automated production techniques—even if they save money—would not be appropriate for a piano company like Steinway, whose products are strategically positioned (and priced) as high quality and handcrafted.

At companies that compete based on product innovation, strategies for research and development are especially critical. But in the recession that occurred at the beginning of this decade, General Electric cut back on research in lighting technology just as other companies were making advances in LED lighting. When the economy recovered, customers were looking for innovative lighting, but GE had fallen behind. Based on that experience, GE committed itself to an R&D strategy of maintaining budgets even when sales slow down. In the latest economic downturn, the company continued to fund a project involving the development of new aircraft engines with Honda Motor Company.[38]

Ⓛ Ⓞ **5** WHAT YOU NEED TO KNOW . . .

Can you identify the keys to effective strategy implementation?

Fifth, implement the strategy

As with any plan, simply formulating a good strategy is not enough. Strategic managers also must ensure that the new strategies are implemented effectively and efficiently. Recently, corporations and strategy consultants have been paying more attention to implementation. They realize that clever techniques and a good plan do not guarantee success.

Organizations are adopting a more comprehensive view of implementation. The organization structure, technology, human resources, employee reward systems, information systems, organization culture, and leadership style must all support the strategy. Just as an organization's strategy must be matched to the external environment, so must it also fit the multiple factors through which it is implemented. The remainder of this section discusses these factors and the ways they can be used to implement strategy.

Many organizations also are involving more employees in implementing strategies. Managers at all levels are formulating strategy and identifying and executing ways to implement it. Senior executives still may oversee the implementation process but are placing much greater responsibility and authority in the hands of others.

In general, strategy implementation involves four related steps:

1. *Define strategic tasks.* Articulate in simple language what a particular business must do to create or sustain a competitive advantage. Define strategic tasks to help employees understand how they contribute to the organization.

2. *Assess organization capabilities.* Evaluate the organization's ability to implement the strategic tasks. Typically, a task force interviews employees and managers to identify issues that help or hinder effective implementation, and then it summarizes the results for top management.

3. *Develop an implementation agenda.* Management decides how it will change its own activities and procedures, how critical interdependencies will be managed, what skills and individuals are needed in key roles, and what structures, measures, information, and rewards might ultimately support the needed behavior.

4. *Create an implementation plan.* The top management team, employee task force, and others develop the implementation plan. The top management team then monitors progress. The employee task force provides feedback about how others in the organization are responding to the changes.

This process, though straightforward, does not always go smoothly.[39] To prevent problems, top managers need to be actively involved, developing a statement of strategy and priorities that employees will accept. Communication is essential, including plenty of information shared by top management with all levels of the organization. Managers responsible for strategy implementation should ensure that the organization's various groups are coordinating their work rather than working at cross-purposes. Also, lower-level managers need coaching and training to help them lead their groups effectively. If strategy implementation lacks solid leadership, managers who cannot improve their skills will have to be replaced. Paying close attention to the processes by which strategies are implemented helps executives, managers, and employees ensure that strategic plans are actually carried out.[40]

Finally, control your progress

The final component of the strategic management process is strategic control. A **strategic control system** is designed to support managers in evaluating the organization's progress with its strategy and, when discrepancies exist, taking corrective action. The system must encourage efficient operations that are consistent with the plan while allowing flexibility to adapt to changing conditions. As with all control systems, the organization must develop performance indicators, an information system, and specific mechanisms to monitor progress. At Boeing, one obvious measure of its strategy to partner with suppliers is whether suppliers are keeping up with Boeing's need for components that meet its quality standards. In fact, as orders flowed in for the 787 Dreamliner, several suppliers began missing deadlines. Boeing dispatched teams of experts from various functions to visit the suppliers, diagnose the reasons for their difficulties, and help them catch up. It also has modified its strategy by having its own employees do more of the final assembly work in order to avoid falling further behind.[41]

Most strategic control systems include a budget to monitor and control major financial expenditures. In fact, as a first-time manager, you will most likely work with your work unit's budget—a key aspect of your organization's strategic plan. Your executive team may give you budget assumptions and targets for your area, reflecting your part in the overall plan, and you may be asked to revise your budget once all the budgets in your organization have been consolidated and reviewed.

The dual responsibilities of a control system—efficiency and flexibility—often seem contradictory with respect to budgets. The budget usually establishes spending limits, but changing conditions or the need for innovation may require different financial commitments during the period. To solve this dilemma, some companies have created two budgets: strategic and operational. For example, at Texas Instruments the strategic budget

● **CERTAINTY** The state that exists when decision makers have accurate and comprehensive information.

● **UNCERTAINTY** The state that exists when decision makers have insufficient information.

● **RISK** The state that exists when the probability of success is less than 100 percent and losses may occur.

● **READY-MADE SOLUTIONS** Ideas that have been seen or tried before.

is used to create and maintain long-term effectiveness, and the operational budget is tightly monitored to achieve short-term efficiency. The topic of control in general—and budgets in particular—is discussed in more detail in Chapter 13.

(L)(O) 6 WHAT YOU NEED TO KNOW . . .
How can you make effective decisions as a manager?

MANAGERIAL DECISION MAKING

Managers constantly face problems and opportunities, ranging from simple and routine decisions to problems requiring months of analysis. However, managers often ignore problems because they are unsure how much trouble will be involved in solving the problems, they are concerned about the consequences if they fail, and many management problems are so much more complex than routine tasks.[42] For these reasons, managers may lack the insight, courage, or will to act.

Why is decision making so challenging? Most managerial decisions lack structure and entail risk, uncertainty, and conflict.

Lack of structure is typical of managerial decisions.[43] Usually there is no automatic procedure to follow. Problems are novel and unstructured, leaving the decision maker uncertain about how to proceed. In other words, a manager's decisions most often have the characteristics of nonprogrammed decisions:[44]

Programmed Decisions	Nonprogrammed Decisions
Problem is frequent, repetitive, routine, with much certainty regarding cause-and-effect relationships.	Problem is novel, unstructured, with much uncertainty regarding cause-and-effect relationships.
Decision procedure depends on policies, rules, definite procedures.	Decision procedure needs creativity, intuition, tolerance for ambiguity, creative problem solving.
Examples: periodic reorders of inventory; procedure for admitting patients.	Examples: diversification into new products and markets; purchase of experimental equipment; reorganization of departments.

With nonprogrammed decisions, *risk and uncertainty* are the rule. If you have all the information you need, and can predict precisely the consequences of your actions, you are operating under a condition of certainty.[45] But perfect certainty is rare. More often, managers face uncertainty, meaning they have insufficient information to know the consequences of different actions. Decision makers may have strong opinions—they may feel sure of themselves—but they are still operating under uncertainty if they lack pertinent information and cannot estimate accurately the likelihood of different results.

When you can estimate the likelihood of various consequences but still do not know with certainty what will happen, you are facing risk. Risk exists when the probability of an action succeeding is less than 100 percent and losses may occur. If the decision is the wrong one, you may lose money, time, reputation, or other important assets. Risk as a quality of managerial decision making differs from *taking* a risk. Although it sometimes seems as though risk takers are admired and that entrepreneurs and investors thrive on taking risks, good decision makers prefer to *manage* risk. Knowing that their decisions entail risk, they anticipate the risk, minimize it, and control it.

For example, in new-product development, some companies have tapped into Web technology to help them reduce uncertainty about what customers will pay for. They learn about customer demand by including the customers in the design process, and they ask customers to commit to a purchase before they make a final production decision. A T-shirt company called Threadless reduces uncertainty and manages risk by basing its whole marketing model on this type of collaboration with customers. Professional and amateur graphic designers submit their ideas for T-shirt designs at the Threadless Web site, where customers vote on the designs they like. From hundreds of submissions, the company selects four to six of the top vote getters each week and pays their designers $1,000. But it makes and sells them only after a minimum number of customers have already ordered the shirt design.[46]

Formal decision making has six stages

Faced with these challenges, how can you make good decisions? The ideal decision-making process moves through six stages:

1. Identify and diagnose the problem.
2. Generate alternative solutions.
3. Evaluate alternatives.
4. Make the choice.
5. Implement the decision.
6. Evaluate the decision.

These stages are general and applicable to any decision. As Figure 4.5 shows, strategic planning is an application of this model; the steps are very similar.

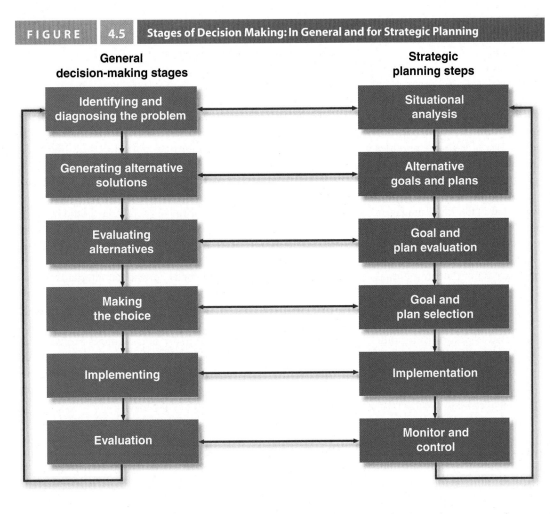

General decision-making stages

Identifying and diagnosing the problem

Generating alternative solutions

Evaluating alternatives

Making the choice

Implementing

Evaluation

Strategic planning steps

Situational analysis

Alternative goals and plans

Goal and plan evaluation

Goal and plan selection

Implementation

Monitor and control

identifying and diagnosing the problem

The decision-making process begins with recognition that a problem (or opportunity) exists and must be solved (or should be pursued). Typically, a manager realizes some discrepancy between the current state (the way things are) and a desired state (the way things ought to be). To detect such discrepancies, managers compare current performance against (1) *past* performance, (2) the *current* performance of other organizations or units, or (3) *future* expected performance as determined by plans and forecasts.[47] Larry Cohen, who founded Accurate Perforating with his father, knew his company was having difficulty making a profit, because costs at the metal company were rising while the prices customers were willing to pay remained unchanged. However, when the company's bank demanded immediate payment of its $1.5 million loan, Cohen realized the problem had to be solved, or the company would have to sell off all its assets and close.[48] You will learn more about how Cohen solved this problem as we look at the subsequent stages of the decision process.

The "problem" may actually be an opportunity that needs to be exploited: a gap between what the organization is doing now and what it can do to create a more positive future. In that case, decisions involve choosing how to seize the opportunity. To recognize important opportunities as a manager, you will need to understand your company's macro- and competitive environments (described in Chapter 2), including the opportunities offered by technological developments. According to Cisco Systems CEO John Chambers, managers who are ignorant about technology risk missing important transitions, dramatic shifts in the ways companies serve customers and work with their suppliers. Chambers advises managers to stay current by talking to people who challenge you and are willing to teach you.[49]

Recognizing that a problem or opportunity exists is only the beginning of this stage. The decision maker also must want to do something about it and must believe that the resources and abilities necessary for solving the problem exist.[50] Then the decision maker must dig in deeper and attempt to *diagnose* the true cause of the situation. Asking why, of yourself and others, is essential. Unfortunately, in the earlier example of Accurate Perforating, Larry Cohen did not ask why profits were declining; he simply assumed that the company's costs were too high.[51] A more thorough approach would include questions such as these:[52]

- Is there a difference between what is actually happening and what should be happening?
- How can you describe the deviation, as specifically as possible?
- What is/are the cause(s) of the deviation?
- What specific goals should be met?
- Which of these goals are absolutely critical to the success of the decision?

generating alternative solutions

The second stage of decision making links problem diagnosis to the development of alternative courses of action aimed at solving the problem. Managers generate at least some alternative solutions based on past experiences.[53]

Solutions range from ready made to custom made.[54] Decision makers who search for **ready-made solutions** use ideas they have tried before or follow the advice of others who have faced similar problems. Custom-made solutions, by contrast, must be designed for specific problems. This technique often combines ideas into new, creative solutions. For example, the earlier example of Threadless showed how a company's leaders solved the problem of competing in a fast-changing and fickle marketplace by combining the idea of Web communities with the already-popular product category of T-shirts printed with graphic designs. Potentially, custom-made solutions can be devised for any challenge.

Often, many more alternatives are available than managers realize. For example, what would you do if one of your competitors reduced prices? An obvious choice would be to reduce your own prices, but the only sure outcome of a price cut is lower profits. Fortunately, cutting prices is not the only alternative. If one of your competitors cuts prices, you should generate multiple options and thoroughly forecast the consequences of these different options. Options include emphasizing consumer risks to low-priced products, building awareness of your products' features and overall quality, and communicating your cost advantage to your competitors so they realize that they can't win a price war. If you do decide to cut your price as a last resort, do it fast—if you do it slowly, your competitors will gain sales in the meantime, which may embolden them to employ the same tactic again in the future.[55]

The example of Accurate Perforating shows the importance of looking for every alternative. The company had become successful by purchasing metal from steel mills, punching many holes in it to make screenlike sheets, and selling this material in bulk to distributors, who sold it to metal workshops, which used it to make custom products. Cohen admits, "We wound up in a very competitive situation where the only thing we were selling was price." Management cut costs wherever possible, avoiding investment in new machinery or processes. The result was an out-of-date factory managed by people accustomed to resisting change. Only after the bank called in its loan did Cohen begin to see alternatives. The bank offered one painful idea: liquidate the company. It also suggested a management consultant, who advised renegotiating payment schedules with the company's suppliers. Cohen also received advice from managers of a company Accurate had purchased a year before. That company, Semrow Perforated & Expanded Metals, sold more-sophisticated products directly to manufacturers, and Semrow's managers urged Cohen to invest more in finished metal products such as theirs.[56]

evaluating alternatives
The third stage of decision making involves determining the value or adequacy of the alternatives that were generated. In other words, which solution will be the best?

Too often, alternatives are evaluated with insufficient thought or logic. At Accurate Perforating, Cohen made changes to cut costs but dismissed the idea to invest in marketing finished metal products, even though these product lines were more profitable. Accurate's general manager, Aaron Kamins (also Cohen's nephew) counseled that money spent on finished metal products would be a distraction from Accurate's core business. That reasoning persuaded Cohen, even though it meant focusing on unprofitable product lines.[57]

Obviously, alternatives should be evaluated more carefully. Fundamental to this process is to predict the consequences that will occur if the various options are put into effect. Managers should consider several types of consequences. They include quantitative measures of success, such as lower costs, higher sales, lower employee turnover, and higher profits. Also, the decisions made at all levels of the organization should contribute to, and not interfere with, achieving the company's overall strategies. Business professors Joseph Bower and Clark Gilbert say that when it comes to decisions about investing in new projects, managers typically focus on whether alternatives generate the most sales or savings without asking the more basic question: In light of our strategy, is this investment an idea we should support at all?[58] When the recent downturn in the U.S. economy required cutbacks, many organizations as diverse as the State of California, Gulfstream Aerospace, and Gannett evaluated the alternatives of layoffs (permanent job cuts) versus furloughs (requiring employees to take some unpaid time off until demand picks up again). While layoffs save more money per employee, because the company doesn't have to continue paying for benefits, furloughs attempt to maintain relationships with talented employees, who are more likely than laid-off workers to return when the company needs them again. Furloughs may seem kinder to employees, who can hope to return to work eventually, but workers may not be eligible for unemployment compensation during the furlough period.[59]

The success or failure of the decision will go into the track records of those involved in making it. That means, as Cohen eventually learned, the decision maker needs to know when to call on others to provide expertise. The mistake of not fully evaluating alternatives and identifying consequences is not limited to small family businesses. When John Sculley was Apple's chief executive, he convinced himself that he was a technology expert and made some poor decisions related to Apple's pioneering launch of a personal digital assistant (PDA), the now-forgotten Newton. Under Sculley's direction, Apple packed the Newton with features, such as handwriting recognition, that customers didn't care about and didn't want to pay the Newton's high price to obtain. In contrast, Steve Jobs charged a hardware engineer, Tony Fadell, with the development of the iPod, and Fadell decided to collaborate with a firm that had already developed much of the technology that would be used in that successful portable music player.[60]

To evaluate alternatives, refer to your original goals, defined in the first stage. Which goals does each alternative meet and fail to meet? Which alternatives are most acceptable to you and to other important stakeholders? If several alternatives may solve the problem, which can be implemented at the lowest cost or greatest profit? If no alternative achieves all your goals, perhaps

How important is your assistant's opinion about the job candidates you interview for positions at all levels?

Don't Know
3%

No assistant
11%

Very unimportant
6%

Very important
37%

Somewhat unimportant
11%

Somewhat important
32%

DID YOU KNOW?

When managers make decisions, they often draw on other people's insights to help them evaluate alternatives. In a survey of Canadian executives, more than two-thirds said the opinion of their assistant was important in deciding which job candidate to hire—an important point to remember the next time you are job hunting.[61]

British entrepreneur Richard Branson shows a model of his proposed Spaceship Two, a vehicle he hopes will be developed by his company in the next few years, which would take private passengers on commercial space flights. To what degree do you think Branson's decision to move ahead with this idea was based on the maximizing strategy?

you can combine two or more of the best ones. Several more questions help:[62]

• Is our information about alternatives complete and current? If not, can we get more and better information?

• Does the alternative meet our primary objectives?

• What problems could we have if we implement the alternative?

Of course, results cannot be forecast with perfect accuracy. But sometimes decision makers can build in safeguards against an uncertain future by considering the potential consequences of several different scenarios. Then they generate contingency plans, described earlier in the discussion of strategic planning.

Some scenarios will seem more likely than others, and some may seem highly improbable. Ultimately, one of the scenarios will prove to be more accurate than the others. The process of considering multiple scenarios raises important "what if?" questions for decision makers and highlights the need for preparedness and contingency plans. As you read this, what economic scenario is unfolding? What are the important current events and trends? What scenarios could evolve six or eight years from now? How will *you* prepare?

making the choice Once you have considered the possible consequences of your options, it is time to make your decision. Some managers are more comfortable with the analysis stage. Especially with all the advanced technology that is available, quantitatively inclined people can easily tweak the assumptions behind every scenario in countless ways. But the temptation can lead to "paralysis by analysis"—that is, indecisiveness caused by too much analysis rather than the kind of active, assertive decision making that is essential for seizing new opportunities or thwarting challenges. The decision will differ according to the criteria and method used:[64]

• **Maximizing** is achieving the best possible outcome, the one that realizes the greatest positive consequences and the

SATISFICING Choosing an option that is acceptable, although not necessarily the best or perfect.

OPTIMIZING Achieving the best possible balance among several goals.

ILLUSION OF CONTROL People's belief that they can influence events, even when they have no control over what will happen.

FRAMING EFFECTS A decision bias influenced by the way in which a problem or decision alternative is phrased or presented.

MAXIMIZING A decision realizing the best possible outcome.

fewest negative consequences. In other words, maximizing results is the greatest benefit at the lowest cost, with the largest expected total return. Maximizing requires searching thoroughly for a complete range of alternatives, carefully assessing each alternative, comparing one to another, and then choosing or creating the very best. As a manager, you won't always have time to maximize; many decisions require quick responses, not exhaustive analysis. The necessary analysis requires money as well as time. But for decisions with large consequences, such as determining the company's strategy, maximizing is worthwhile—even essential.

- **Satisficing** is choosing the first option that is minimally acceptable or adequate; the choice appears to meet a targeted goal or criterion. When you satisfice, you compare your choice against your goal, not against other options, and you end your search for alternatives at the first one that is okay. If you are purchasing new equipment and your goal is to avoid spending too much money, you are satisficing if you buy the first adequate option that is within your budget. When the consequences are not huge, satisficing can actually be the ideal approach. But when managers satisfice, they may fail to consider important options. Returning to the earlier example of Accurate Perforating, when managers initially addressed declining profits, they were satisficing; they assumed they should focus on cutting costs and failed to identify alternatives that would boost profits by investing in new markets where they could charge more.

- **Optimizing** means achieving the best possible balance among several goals. Perhaps, in purchasing equipment, you are interested in quality and durability as well as price. Instead of buying the cheapest piece of equipment that works, you buy the one with the best combination of attributes, even though some options may be better on the price criterion and others may offer better quality and durability. Likewise, for achieving business goals, one marketing strategy could maximize sales while a different strategy maximizes profit. An optimizing strategy achieves the best balance among multiple goals.

?

DID YOU KNOW?

A scenario may use numbers that sound reasonable, but you should look at the data in different ways to check your assumptions. As Dean Kamen's company developed the Segway scooter, Kamen decided that each year Segway could capture 0.1 percent of the world's population. That percentage might sound conservative, but consider that 0.1 percent of 6 billion people is 6 million Segways a year! Kamen decided to build a factory that could produce 40,000 units a month; five years later, sales had reached fewer than 25,000.[63]

implementing the decision
The decision-making process does not end once a choice is made. The chosen alternative must be implemented. Sometimes the people involved in making the choice must put it into effect. At other times, they delegate the responsibility for implementation, as when a top management team changes a policy or operating procedure and has operational managers carry out the change.

Unfortunately, people sometimes make decisions but don't take action. Implementing may fail to occur when talking a lot is mistaken for doing a lot; if people just assume that a decision will "happen"; when people forget that merely making a decision changes nothing; when meetings, plans, and reports are seen as "actions," even if they don't affect what people actually do; and if managers don't check to ensure that what was decided was actually done.[65]

Those who implement the decision should *understand* the choice and why it was made. They also must be *committed* to its successful implementation. These needs can be met by involving those people in the early stages of the decision process. At Federal Warehouse Company, located in East Peoria, Illinois, executives decided to teach all the employees how to interpret the company's financial statements. Managers routinely review the company's performance in detail, and they invite all employees to participate in solving problems, including how to reduce costs by making the workplace safer. Employees—who had once assumed that if everyone was busy, the company must be profitable—have begun making many creative decisions that are helping profits climb.[66] By including all employees in the decision making, Federal fosters full understanding and total commitment.

Managers should plan implementation carefully by taking several steps:[67]

1. Determine how things will look when the decision is fully operational.

2. Chronologically order, perhaps with a flow diagram, the steps necessary to achieve a fully operational decision.

3. List the resources and activities required to implement each step.

4. Estimate the time needed for each step.

5. Assign responsibility for each step to specific individuals.

Decision makers should presume that implementation will *not* go smoothly. It is very useful to take a little extra time to *identify potential problems* and *identify potential opportunities* associated with implementation. Then you can take actions to prevent problems and also be ready to seize on unexpected opportunities. The following questions are useful:

- What problems could this action cause?
- What can we do to prevent the problems?
- What unintended benefits or opportunities could arise?
- How can we make sure they happen?
- How can we be ready to act when the opportunities come?

Many of the chapters in this book address implementation issues: how to allocate resources, organize for results, lead and motivate people, manage change, and so on. View the chapters from that perspective, and learn as much as you can about how to implement properly.

evaluating the decision The final stage in the decision-making process is evaluating the decision. It involves collecting information on how well the decision is working. If you set quantifiable goals—a 20 percent increase in sales, a 95 percent reduction in accidents, 100 percent on-time deliveries—before implementation of the solution, you can gather objective data for accurately determining the decision's success or failure.

Decision evaluation is useful whether the conclusion is positive or negative. Feedback that suggests the decision is working implies that the decision should be continued and perhaps applied elsewhere in the organization. Negative feedback means one of two things:

1. Implementation will require more time, resources, effort, or thought.
2. The decision was a bad one.

If the decision appears inappropriate, it's back to the drawing board. Then the process cycles back to the first stage: (re)definition of the problem. The decision-making process begins anew, preferably with more information, new suggestions, and an approach that attempts to eliminate the mistakes made the first time around. This is the stage where Accurate Perforating finally began to see hope. When cost-cutting efforts could not keep the company ahead of the competition or in favor with the bank, Larry Cohen turned the problem over to his general manager, Aaron Kamins. He gave Kamins 90 days to show that he could keep the business from going under. Kamins hired a consultant to help him identify more alternatives and make more professional decisions about investment and marketing. This stage of the implementation showed Kamins that the company needed better-educated management, and he began taking courses in an executive education program. With what he learned in school and from his consultant, Kamins realized that the advice he had received from the managers at the Semrow subsidiary—to invest in producing finished metal products—was wiser than he had realized. He arranged new financing to purchase modern equipment, hired salespeople, developed a Web site, and finally began to see profits from his improved decision making.[68]

Human nature erects barriers to good decisions

Vigilant and full execution of the six-stage decision-making process is the exception rather than the rule. But when managers use such rational processes, better decisions result.[69] Managers who make sure they engage in these processes are more effective.

Why don't people automatically invoke such rational processes? It is easy to neglect or improperly execute these processes, and decisions are influenced by subjective psychological biases, time pressures, and social realities.

psychological biases Decision makers are far from objective in the way they gather, evaluate, and apply information in making their choices. People have biases that interfere with objective rationality. Here are just a few of the many documented subjective biases:[70]

- **Illusion of control**—a belief that one can influence events even when one has no control over what will happen. Such overconfidence can lead to failure because decision makers ignore risks and fail to evaluate the odds of success objectively. In addition, they may believe they can do no wrong, or hold a general optimism about the future that can lead them to believe they are immune to risk and failure.[71] In addition, managers may overrate the value of their experience. They may believe that a previous project met its goals because of their decisions, so they can succeed by doing everything the same way on the next project. Rohit Girdhar admits that he held this type of bias until he tried a computer simulation that he assumed would confirm his skills as an experienced manager of software programmers. In the simulation, the workload increased, and he hired more workers, as he had in his prior jobs. But the added workers weren't as productive as his experience told him they would be, and his project fell behind. Girdhar learned to question his assumptions before making decisions.[72] Managers can correct for this problem by developing a realistic picture of their strengths and weaknesses and seeking out advisers who can point out consequences they may not have considered.

- **Framing effects**—phrasing or presenting problems or decision alternatives in a way that subjective influences override objective facts. In one example, managers indicated a desire to invest more money in a course of action that was reported to have a 70 percent chance of profit than in one said to have a 30 percent chance of loss.[73] The choices had equivalent chances of success; the way the options were expressed determined the managers' choices. Managers may also frame a problem as similar to problems they have already handled, so they don't search for new alternatives. When CEO Richard Fuld tackled financial problems at Lehman Brothers as the mortgage market tumbled, he assumed that the situation was much the same as a financial crisis in the late 1990s. Unfortunately for Lehman Brothers, the recent crisis was far worse. The firm declared bankruptcy—the largest in U.S. history—helping to send global financial markets into a tailspin. Similarly, when the head of the operations center of the Department of Homeland Security prepared for Hurricane Katrina as it headed for New Orleans, he assumed the storm would be like Florida hurricanes he had prepared for in the past. As information came in, he focused on the data that fit his expectations, but Katrina turned out to be far more devastating.[74]

- Discounting the future—in evaluating alternatives, weighing short-term costs and benefits more heavily than longer-term costs and benefits. This bias applies to students who don't study, workers who take the afternoon off to play golf when they really need to work, and managers who hesitate to invest funds in research and development programs that may not pay off until far into the future. In all these cases, avoiding short-term costs or seeking short-term rewards yields problems in the long term. Discounting the future partly explains government budget deficits, environmental destruction, and decaying urban infrastructure.[75]

time pressures In today's rapidly changing business environment, the premium is on acting quickly and keeping pace. The most conscientiously made business decisions can become irrelevant and even disastrous if managers take too long to make them.

To make decisions quickly, managers, at least North Americans, tend to skimp on analysis, suppress conflict, and make decisions alone without consulting other managers.[76] These strategies may speed up decision making, but they reduce decision *quality*. Carl Camden, CEO of Kelly Services, believed that rapid-fire decisions were the sign of a dynamic executive until he saw how this approach could hurt decision quality. After Camden joined Kelly, managers presented a proposal for expanding the temporary-services firm into the business of placing substitute teachers. Camden quickly came up with a half dozen reasons to say no. However, the managers kept returning with similar proposals until he gave in and launched the new division. It became one of the company's fastest-growing operations.[77]

Can managers under time pressure make decisions that are timely and high quality? A recent study of decision-making processes in microcomputer firms showed some important differences between fast-acting and slower firms.[78] The fast-acting firms realized significant competitive advantages without sacrificing the quality of their decisions. They used three important tactics:

1. Instead of relying on old data, long-range planning, and futuristic forecasts, they focus on *real-time information:* current information obtained with little or no time delay. For example, they constantly monitor daily operating measures like work in process rather than checking periodically the traditional accounting-based indicators such as profitability.

2. They *involve people more effectively and efficiently* in the decision-making process. They rely heavily on trusted experts, and this yields both good advice and the confidence to act quickly despite uncertainty.

3. They take a *realistic view of conflict:* they value differing opinions, but they know that if disagreements are not resolved, the top executive must make the final choice in the end. Slow-moving firms, in contrast, are stymied by conflict. Like the fast-moving firms, they seek consensus, but when disagreements persist, they fail to come to a decision.

social realities Many decisions are made by a group rather than by an individual manager. In slow-moving firms, interpersonal factors decrease decision-making effectiveness. Even the manager acting alone is accountable to the boss and to others and must consider the preferences and reactions of many people. Important managerial decisions are marked by conflict among interested parties. Therefore, many decisions are the result of intensive social interactions, bargaining, and politicking.

(L)(O) 7 **WHAT YOU NEED TO KNOW . . .**
What are the principles for group decision making?

Groups make many decisions

Sometimes a manager convenes a group of people to make an important decision. Some advise that in today's complex business environment, significant problems should *always* be tackled by groups.[79] As a result, managers must understand how groups operate and how to use them to improve decision making.

groups can help The basic philosophy behind using a group to make decisions is captured by the adage "Two heads are better than one." But is this statement really valid? Yes, it is—potentially. If enough time is available, groups usually make higher-quality decisions than most individuals acting alone. However, groups often are inferior to the *best* individual.[80]

How well the group performs depends on how effectively it capitalizes on the potential advantages and minimizes the

Are two heads really better than one?

● **DISCOUNTING THE FUTURE** A bias weighting short-term costs and benefits more heavily than longer-term costs and benefits.

● **GROUPTHINK** A phenomenon that occurs in decision making when group members avoid disagreement as they strive for consensus.

● **GOAL DISPLACEMENT** A condition that occurs when a decision-making group loses sight of its original goal and a new, less important goal emerges.

potential problems of using a group. Using groups to make a decision offers at least five potential advantages:[81]

1. More *information* is available when several people are making the decision. If one member doesn't have all the facts or the pertinent expertise, another member might.

2. A greater number of *perspectives* on the issues, or different *approaches* to solving the problem, are available. The problem may be new to one group member but familiar to another. Or the group may need to consider several viewpoints—financial, legal, marketing, human resources, and so on—to achieve an optimal solution.

3. Group discussion provides an opportunity for *intellectual stimulation.* It can get people thinking and unleash their creativity to a far greater extent than would be possible with individual decision making.

4. People who participate in a group discussion are more likely to *understand* why the decision was made. They will have heard the relevant arguments both for the chosen alternative and against the rejected alternatives.

5. Group discussion typically leads to a higher level of *commitment* to the decision. Buying into the proposed solution translates into high motivation to ensure that it is executed well.

The first three potential advantages of using a group suggest that better-informed, higher-quality decisions will result when managers involve people with different backgrounds, perspectives, and access to information. The last two advantages imply that decisions will be implemented more successfully when managers involve the people responsible for implementing the decision as early in the deliberations as possible.

groups can hurt
Things *can* go wrong when groups make decisions. Most of the potential problems concern the process through which group members interact with one another:[82]

• Sometimes one group member *dominates* the discussion. When this occurs—as when a strong leader makes his or her preferences clear—the result is the same as it would have been if the dominant individual had made the decision alone. However, the dominant person does not necessarily have the most valid opinions, and even if that person leads the group to a good decision, the process will have wasted everyone's time.

• *Satisficing* is more likely with groups. Most people don't like meetings and will do what they can to end them. This may include criticizing members who want to continue exploring new and better alternatives. The result is a satisficing, not an optimizing or maximizing, decision.

• *Pressure to avoid disagreement* can lead to a phenomenon called *groupthink.* Groupthink occurs when people choose not to disagree or raise objections because they don't want

to break up a positive team spirit. Some groups want to think as one, tolerate no dissension, and strive to remain cordial. Such groups are overconfident, complacent, and perhaps too willing to take risks. Pressure to go along with the group's preferred solution stifles creativity and other behaviors characteristic of vigilant decision making.

• *Goal displacement* often occurs in groups. Group members' goal should be to come up with the best possible solution. With **goal displacement**, new goals emerge to replace the original ones. When group members have different opinions, attempts at rational persuasion might become a heated disagreement, and then winning the argument becomes the new goal.

groups must be well led
Effective managers pay close attention to the group process; they manage it carefully. Effectively managing group decision making has three requirements:

1. *Appropriate leadership style*—The group leader must try to keep process-related problems to a minimum by ensuring that everyone has a chance to participate, not allowing the group to pressure individuals to conform, and keeping everyone focused on the decision-making objective.

2. *Constructive use of disagreement and conflict*—Total and consistent agreement among group members can be destructive, leading to groupthink, uncreative solutions, and a waste of the knowledge and diverse viewpoints that individuals bring to the group. A certain amount of *constructive* conflict should exist.[83] Conflict should be task related, involving

differences in ideas and viewpoints, rather than personal.[84] Still, even task-related conflict can hurt performance;[85] disagreement is good only when managed properly. Managers can increase the likelihood of constructive conflict by assembling teams of different types of people, creating frequent interactions and active debates, and encouraging multiple alternatives from a variety of perspectives.[86] Methods for encouraging different views include assigning someone the role of **devil's advocate**, someone who has the job of criticizing ideas. Or the leader may use a process called **dialectic**, a structured debate between two conflicting courses of action.[87] Structured debates between plans and counterplans can be useful before making a strategic decision—one team might present the case for acquiring a firm while another team advocates not making the acquisition.

3. *Enhancement of creativity*—To "get" creativity out of other people, give creative efforts the credit they are due, and don't punish creative failures.[88] Avoid extreme time pressure, if possible.[89] Support some innovative ideas without heeding projected returns. Stimulate and challenge people intellectually, and give people some creative freedom. Listen to employees' ideas, and allow enough time to explore different ideas. Put together groups of people with different styles of thinking and behaving. Get your people in touch with customers, and let them bounce ideas around. Protect your people from managers who demand immediate payoffs, don't understand the importance of creative contributions, or try to take credit for others' successes. People are likely to be more creative if they believe they are capable, know that their coworkers expect creativity, and believe that their employer values creativity.[90] A common technique for eliciting creative ideas is brainstorming. In **brainstorming**,

group members generate as many ideas about a problem as they can. As the ideas are presented, they are posted so everyone can read them and use the ideas as building blocks. The group is encouraged to say anything that comes to mind, except to criticize other people or their ideas.

 At Miron Construction Company, Theresa Lehman fosters creative thinking about sustainability—the effort to minimize the use of resources, especially those that are polluting and nonrenewable. Besides helping clients plan more sustainable buildings, Lehman, the director of sustainability at the building contractor—which is located in Neenah, Wisconsin—helps Miron itself operate in a greener way.

Lehman defines the problem—or opportunity—of running a sustainable construction company as one that extends beyond a building's features. Rather, all efforts to reduce waste contribute to sustainability. Says Lehman, "Everything needs to focus on doing things more effectively by reducing resources and eliminating waste." She seeks ideas from all employees and ensures that every idea receives careful consideration. For example, an employee suggested switching from paper paychecks to direct deposit for all workers. Besides saving paper, the change cuts printing and postage expenses. By taking ideas seriously and then communicating the practical benefits, Lehman reinforces the value of sustainability.

Lehman is ready with plenty of examples about the financial soundness of sustainability. As Miron adds to and renovates its own headquarters, it is installing geothermal heating and cooling, which will pay for itself in five years. It is replacing interior lights with LED bulbs that are expected to save about $12,000 in energy costs over the life of the bulbs. With benefits like these, it's no wonder that Lehman has been able to make sustainability a widely shared value at Miron.[91]

DIY

Build Your Skills

Practice and apply your knowledge by going online at

www.mhhe.com/
BatemanM2e

5

Entrepreneurship

Some extraordinary individuals were only in their 20s when they founded companies that became famously successful:[1]

- Bill Gates and Paul Allen started Microsoft.
- Michael Dell started Dell Computers.
- Steve Jobs and Steve Wozniak started Apple Computer.
- Fred Smith started Federal Express.
- Robert Swanson started Genentech.
- Phil Knight started Nike.
- Mark Zuckerberg started Facebook.

As they and countless others have demonstrated, great opportunity is available to talented people who are willing to work hard to achieve their dreams. **Entrepreneurship** occurs when an enterprising individual pursues a lucrative opportunity.[2] To be an entrepreneur is to initiate and build an organization, rather than being only a passive part of one.[3] It involves creating *new* systems, resources, or processes to produce *new* goods or services and/or serve *new* markets.[4]

Find Out More

about being entrepreneurs from J and Martha on the book Web site.

"*I understand what it takes to become an independent entrepreneur as my family has done this and I grew up in the business. Currently I do not have that desire. However, being an entrepreneur to get new ideas out there, programs, etc. within my organization is something I do and is encouraged in my organization.*"
—*Martha Zehnder Keller, Associate Director of Convention Services*

"*Being an entrepreneur is DEFINITELY something I strive to be each and every day. Whether it's in my current role at my firm or looking for outside opportunities, I hope to one day run my own business. Within my own role now, I have the ability to approach customers and prospects in my own way, choose to do as much or as little with what I have, and ultimately it has reflected upon the quality of work I put forward. I think that it is very encouraged and more often than not rewarded.*"
—*J John Maggio III, Sales Manager*

·· learning **OBJECTIVES**

After studying Chapter 5,
you will be able to:

LO1 Describe why people become
entrepreneurs and what it takes,
personally.

LO2 Summarize how to assess opportunities
to start new businesses.

LO3 Identify common causes of success
and failure.

LO4 Discuss common management
challenges.

LO5 Explain how to increase your chances
of success, including good business
planning.

LO6 Describe how managers of large
companies can foster entrepreneurship.

as its primary objectives. Entrepreneurs manage aggressively and develop innovative strategies, practices, and products. They and their financial backers usually seek rapid growth, immediate and high profits, and sometimes a quick sellout with large capital gains.

Richard Branson is a perfect example. He seems to have business in his blood. He was only a teen when he started his first company, a magazine called *Student,* in the mid-1960s. In 1970 Branson launched his next enterprise, the iconic Virgin Records, which generated his first fortune. Since then, Branson has built 200 other businesses, all under the Virgin umbrella: a global airline, a mobile-phone enterprise, and companies in financial services, publishing, and retailing. Today, the Virgin empire has nearly 50,000 employees in 29 countries, and Branson has a mind-boggling net worth of more than $5 billion. In 1999, he was knighted by Queen Elizabeth.[5]

Entrepreneurs differ from managers generally. An entrepreneur *is* a manager but engages in additional activities that not all managers do.[6] Traditionally, managers operate in a formal management hierarchy with well-defined authority and responsibility. In contrast, entrepreneurs use networks of contacts more than formal authority. And although managers usually prefer to own assets, entrepreneurs often rent or use assets on a temporary basis. Some say that managers often are slower to act and tend to avoid risk, whereas entrepreneurs are quicker to act and actively manage risk.

An entrepreneur's organization may be small, but it differs from a typical small business:[7]

- A **small business** has fewer than 100 employees, is independently owned and operated, is not dominant in its field, and is not characterized by many innovative practices. Small-business owners tend not to manage particularly aggressively, and they expect normal, moderate sales, profits, and growth.

- An **entrepreneurial venture** has growth and high profitability

"A man is known by the company he organizes."

—Ambrose Bierce

entrepreneurship excitement Consider these words from Jeffry Timmons, a leading entrepreneurship scholar and author: "During the past 30 years, America has unleashed the most revolutionary generation the nation has experienced since its founding in 1776. This new generation of entrepreneurs has altered permanently the economic and social structure of this nation and the world . . . It will determine more than any other single impetus how the nation

Ryan Clark (bottom) who recently won the 2009 Student Leadership Award from the Black Engineer of the Year Awards, poses with his twin brother, Ashton, at the Coordinated Science Laboratory in Urbana, Illinois. The Clark brothers are both juniors at the University of Illinois and in the past seven years have formed more than a dozen successful Web-based businesses, with products ranging from online music to sports apparel to parking-place reservations.

Myth 1: "Anyone can start a business." In fact, the easiest part is starting up. What is hardest is surviving, sustaining, and building a venture so its founders can realize a harvest.

Myth 2: "Entrepreneurs are gamblers." Actually, successful entrepreneurs take very careful, calculated risks. They do not deliberately seek to take more risk or to take unnecessary risk, nor do they shy away from unavoidable risk.

Myth 3: "Entrepreneurs want the whole show to themselves." Rather, it is extremely difficult to grow a higher-potential venture by working single-handedly. Higher-potential entrepreneurs build a team, an organization, and a company.

Myth 4: "Entrepreneurs are their own bosses and completely independent." Actually, entrepreneurs are far from independent. They have to serve many masters and stakeholders, including partners, investors, customers, suppliers, creditors, employees, and families, and honor social and community obligations.

Myth 5: "Entrepreneurs work longer and harder than managers in big companies." In reality, there is no such evidence. Some work more, some less.

Myth 6: "Entrepreneurs experience a great deal of stress and pay a high price." While there's no doubt that the entrepreneur's role is stressful and demanding, entrepreneurs find their jobs very satisfying. They are healthier and are much less likely to retire than those who work for others.

Myth 7: "Entrepreneurs are motivated solely by the quest for the almighty dollar." In fact, entrepreneurs seeking high-potential ventures are more driven by building enterprises and realizing long-term capital gains than by instant gratification through high salaries and perks.

Feeling in control of their own destinies and realizing their vision and dreams are also powerful motivators. Money is viewed as a tool and a way of keeping score.

Myth 8: "Entrepreneurs seek power and control over others." Actually, successful entrepreneurs are driven by the quest for responsibility, achievement, and results, rather than by power for its own sake. By virtue of their accomplishments, they may be powerful and influential, but these are more the by-products of the entrepreneurial process than a driving force behind it.

Myth 9: "If an entrepreneur is talented, success will happen in a year or two." An old maxim among venture capitalists says it all: the lemons ripen in two and a half years, but the pearls take seven or eight. Rarely is a new business established solidly in less than three or four years.

Myth 10: "Any entrepreneur with a good idea can raise venture capital." In practice, of the ventures of entrepreneurs with good ideas who seek out venture capital, only 1 to 3 out of 100 are funded.

Myth 11: "If an entrepreneur has enough start-up capital, he or she can't miss." Too much money at the outset often leads to lack of discipline and impulsive spending that usually result in serious problems and failure.

Myth 12: "Entrepreneurs are lone wolves and cannot work with others." The fact is, the most successful entrepreneurs are leaders who build great teams and effective relationships working with peers, directors, investors, key customers, key suppliers, and the like.

Myth 13: "Unless you attained 600 on your SATs or GMATs, you'll never be a successful entrepreneur." Entrepreneurial IQ actually is a unique combination of creativity, motivation, integrity, leadership, team building, analytical ability, and ability to deal with ambiguity and adversity.

and the world will live, work, learn, and lead in this century and beyond."[8]

Overhype? Sounds like it could be, but it's not. Entrepreneurship is transforming economies all over the world, and the global economy in general. In the United States since 1980, more than 95 percent of the wealth has been created by entrepreneurs.[9] It has been estimated that since World War II, small entrepreneurial firms have generated 95 percent of all radical innovation in the United States. The Small Business Administration has found that in states with more small-business start-ups, statewide economies tend to grow faster and employment levels tend to be higher than in states with less entrepreneurship.[10] An estimated 20 million Americans are running a young business or actively trying to start one.[11]

The self-employed love the entrepreneurial process, and they report the highest levels of pride, satisfaction, and income. Importantly, entrepreneurship is not about the privileged descendants of the Rockefellers and the Vanderbilts; instead, it provides opportunity and upward mobility for anyone who performs well.[12]

myths about entrepreneurship
Simply put, entrepreneurs generate new ideas and turn them into business ventures.[13] But entrepreneurship is not simple, and it is frequently misunderstood. Consider 13 myths about this important career option:[14]

Here is another myth: being an entrepreneur is great because you can "get rich quick" and enjoy a lot of leisure time while your employees run the company. But the reality is much more difficult. During the start-up period, you are likely to have a lot of bad days. It's exhausting. Even if you don't have employees, you should expect communications breakdowns and other "people problems" with agents, vendors, distributors, family, subcontractors, lenders, whomever. Dan Bricklin, the founder of VisiCalc, advises that the most important thing to remember is this: "You are not your business. On those darkest days when things aren't

ENTREPRENEUR An individual who establishes a new organization without the benefit of corporate sponsorship.

INTRAPRENEURS New-venture creators working inside big companies.

going so well—and trust me, you will have them—try to remember that your company's failures don't make you an awful person. Likewise, your company's successes don't make you a genius or superhuman."[15]

As you read this chapter, you will learn about two primary sources of new-venture creation:

1. Independent **entrepreneurs** are individuals who establish a new organization without the benefit of corporate support.

2. **Intrapreneurs** are new-venture creators working inside big companies; they are corporate entrepreneurs, using their company's resources to build a profitable line of business based on a fresh new idea.[16]

L O 1 WHAT YOU NEED TO KNOW . . .
Why do people become entrepreneurs, and what does it take, personally?

ENTREPRENEURSHIP

Two young entrepreneurs who recently founded a highly successful business are Tony Hsieh and Nick Swinmurn. In 1999, Swinmurn had the then-new idea to sell shoes online, but he needed money to get started. Hsieh, who at age 24 had already just sold his first start-up (LinkExchange, sold to Microsoft for $265 million), agreed to take a chance on the new venture. Swinmurn has moved on, but Hsieh remains at the helm of the company, called Zappos. In a recent year, Zappos enjoyed sales of $1 billion.[17]

Exceptional though their story may be, the real, more complete story of

Tony Hsieh is listed as an extraordinary entrepreneur. At the age of 24, he had already sold off his first venture and took on Zappos.com, where he continues to work today.

entrepreneurship is about people you've probably never heard of. They have built companies, thrived personally, created jobs, and contributed to their communities through their businesses. Or they're just starting out. Adnan Aziz, who earned degrees in bioengineering and political science at the University

of Pennsylvania, put his first degree to work when he got an idea from watching *Willie Wonka and the Chocolate Factory*. Impressed by the scene in which children lick fruit-flavored wallpaper, he developed and patented an invention: small soluble flavored strips of edible film he named Peel 'n Taste. He formed his company, First Flavor, and began negotiating deals with consumer products companies, hoping they would attach packets containing Peel 'n Taste strips to ads and packaging.[18]

Why become an entrepreneur?

Bill Gross has started dozens of companies. When he was a boy, he devised homemade electronic games and sold candy for a profit to friends. In college, he built and sold plans for a solar heating device, started a stereo equipment company, and sold a software product to Lotus. In 1996, he started Idealab, which hatched dozens of start-ups on the Internet. Recently launched Idealab companies include one that is making a three-dimensional printer, and another that sells robotics technology to supermarkets and toy companies. Through its Energy Innovations subsidiary, Idealab also has branched out into the now-hot market for alternative-energy technology.[19]

Why do Bill Gross and other entrepreneurs do what they do? Entrepreneurs start their own firms because of the challenge, profit potential, and enormous satisfaction they hope lies ahead. People starting their own businesses are seeking a better quality of life than they might have at big companies. They seek independence and a feeling they are part of the action. They get tremendous satisfaction from building something from nothing, seeing it succeed, and watching the market embrace their ideas and products.

People also start their own companies when they see their progress or ideas blocked at big corporations. When people are laid off, believe they will not receive a promotion, or are frustrated by bureaucracy or other features of corporate life, they may become entrepreneurs. Years ago, Philip Catron became disillusioned with his job as a manager at ChemLawn because he concluded that the lawn care company's reliance on pesticides contributed to illness in its employees, its customers' pets, and even the lawns themselves. Catron left to start NaturaLawn of America, based on the practice of integrated pest management (IPM), which uses natural and nontoxic products as much as possible, reducing pesticide use on lawns by 85 percent. Over two decades, Catron built NaturaLawn into 72 franchises in 25 states—and helped take IPM into the mainstream, as even his former employer has changed many of its practices.[20]

Immigrants may find conventional paths to economic success closed to them and turn to entrepreneurship.[21] The Cuban community in Miami has produced many successful entrepreneurs, as has the Vietnamese community throughout the United States. Sometimes the immigrant's experience gives him or her useful knowledge about foreign suppliers or markets that present an attractive business opportunity. Rakesh Kamdar immigrated to the United States from India to study computer science but noticed a way he could meet the huge U.S. demand for nursing talent. He set up DB Healthcare to recruit nurses from India to work in the United States. Unlike U.S. competitors that had failed, Kamdar set up meetings at DB's Indian offices, and he invited nurses to attend with their husbands, parents, and in-laws. His staff discussed family and individual questions related to the American jobs. Within a few years, DB Healthcare was earning millions of dollars.[22]

 Nearly 30 years ago, Chieu Le was a law student in Vietnam when he made his escape from the communist regime to Malaysia. After his wife joined him, they moved to New Mexico, where Le got several jobs in the food industry. Meanwhile, more of his family arrived, and eventually they all settled near San Jose, California. They started a small catering business, selling ethnic food from a truck parked outside various companies.

Today, Lee Bros. Foodservices operates 500 catering trucks that deliver prepared food to various locations and 22 Lee's Sandwiches shops throughout California, Arizona, and Texas. All of the shops are owned and run by extended-family members, and they serve traditional banh mi sandwiches along with American sandwiches made on baguettes or croissants. Many of the shops also have Internet access and have become a social gathering spot.

Le says their success is based on hard work: "We had to start from the very bottom and only through very hard, long days of work did we luckily become successful."[23]

What does it take to succeed?

What can we learn from the people who start their own companies and succeed? Let's start with the example of Ken Hendricks, founder of ABC Supply.[24] As he continues to acquire buildings and businesses, he sees opportunities where others see problems. Several years after the town's largest employer, Beloit Corporation, closed its doors, Hendricks bought its property, where he discovered almost a half million patterns (wooden molds) used to make a variety of machine parts. Although a bankruptcy court ordered that he be paid to move the patterns to the dump,

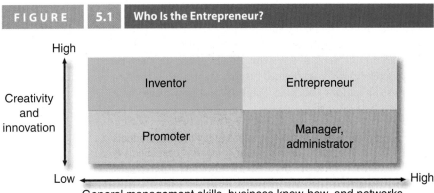

SOURCE: J. Timmons and S. Spinelli, *New Venture Creation,* 6th ed. (New York: McGraw-Hill/Irwin, 2004), p. 65. © 2004 The McGraw-Hill Companies.

Hendricks called on a friend, artist Jack De Munnik, and offered him the patterns as free material to create art. De Munnik fashioned them into tables, clocks, sculptures, and other pieces. Hendricks calculated, "Even if we only got $50 apiece for them, 50 times 500,000 is $25 million," and he noted that that amount could have "taken the Beloit Corporation out of bankruptcy."[25] This example shows how Hendricks thinks about business success: problems can be fixed. "It's how you look at something and how it's managed that make the difference."[26]

Ken Hendricks is a good example of what talents enable entrepreneurs to succeed. We express these characteristics in general terms with Figure 5.1. Successful entrepreneurs are innovators and also have good knowledge and skills in management, business, and networking.[27] In contrast, inventors may be highly creative but often lack the skills to turn their ideas into a successful business. Manager-administrators may be great at ensuring efficient operations but aren't necessarily innovators. Promoters have a different set of marketing and selling skills—useful for entrepreneurs, but those skills can be hired, whereas innovativeness and business management skills remain the essential combination for successful entrepreneurs.

L O 2 WHAT YOU NEED TO KNOW . . .

How do you assess opportunities to start new businesses?

What business should you start?

You need a good idea, and you need to find or create the right opportunity. The following discussion offers some general considerations for choosing a type of business. For guidance in matching your unique strengths and interests to a business type, another helpful resource is *What Business Should I Start? Seven Steps to Discovering the Ideal Business for You,* by Rhonda Abrams.

the idea Many entrepreneurs and observers say that in contemplating your business, you must start with a great idea.

A great product, a viable market, and good timing are essential ingredients in any recipe for success. For example, Tom Stemberg knew that the growing number of small businesses in the 1980s had no one dedicated to selling them office supplies. He saw his opportunity, so he opened his first Staples store, the first step toward a nationwide chain. Staples's sales now reach more than $18 billion annually.

▶ Some of the most exciting ideas today involve products that meet a very basic need at a very low cost. Socially responsible entrepreneurs are combining technological skills with concern for people who live without access to clean water and reliable electricity, creating high-tech projects that can improve lives in poor communities. For example, Nedjip Tozun and Sam Goldman founded D.light Design to develop and sell solar-powered lights, made with low-priced solar panels, efficient LEDs, and sophisticated power management software.

Tozun and Goldman see their market in developing countries, where many people rely on kerosene and diesel lamps, which not only provide a poor quality of lighting but also pollute the air and present a serious danger from fires and serious burns. Although the $25 price tag for a D.light lamp is high for many communities where people earn less than a dollar a day, when family members pool their resources, they find that the lamp allows them to work longer hours, save money previously spent on fuel, and skip long trips to buy fuel, so the purchase is a good investment in a cleaner, safer, life.

D.light Design is a business, not a charity. Tozun and Goldman see their buyers as "great customers" who recognize a "clear value proposition" in their product. They also see potential to expand into other solar-powered products, building their business as they meet basic needs.[28] ◀

Many great organizations have been built on a different kind of idea: the founder's desire to build a great organization, rather than offering a particular product or product line.[29] Examples abound. Bill Hewlett and David Packard decided to start a company and then figured out what to make. J. Willard Marriott knew he wanted to be in business for himself but didn't have a product in mind until he opened an A&W root beer stand. Masaru Ibuka had no specific product idea when he founded Sony in 1945. Sony's first product attempt, a rice cooker, didn't work, and its first product (a tape recorder) didn't sell. The company stayed alive by making and selling crude heating pads.

Darryl Hart and Robert Schummer founded Commodity Sourcing Group (CSG) in Detroit because of organizational challenges in the health care industry. Insurance companies and government agencies were limiting reimbursement levels, so the hospitals were trying to cut costs by outsourcing nonmedical activities such as printing, transportation, and laundry services.

CSG specializes in providing those services by arranging contracts with vendors. In addition, many hospitals have diversity programs to buy a share of their supplies and services from minority- and women-owned vendors. But these companies often are smaller and younger, so they may struggle with financing and management know-how. CSG mentors some of these companies. For example, to help a printing company fill a big contract, CSG bought the necessary equipment and let the company use it during the three years it reimbursed CSG. For a small distributor of janitorial products, CSG helped create marketing materials. Although in theory, these start-ups could eventually become competitors with CSG, Hart and Schummer see their mentoring as a way to strengthen Detroit's overall business environment.[31]

Many now-great companies had early failures. But the founders persisted; they believed in themselves and in their dreams of building great organizations. Although the conventional logic is to see the company as a vehicle for your products, the alternative perspective sees the products as a vehicle for your company. Be prepared to kill or revise an idea, but never give up on your company—this has been a prescription for success for many great entrepreneurs and business leaders. At organizations including Disney, Procter & Gamble, and Walmart, the founders' greatest achievements—their greatest ideas—were their organizations.[32]

A+

the opportunity Entrepreneurs spot, create, and exploit opportunities in a variety of ways.[33] Entrepreneurial companies can explore domains that big companies avoid and introduce goods or services that capture the market because they are simpler, cheaper, more accessible, or more convenient. While Shayne McQuade was touring Spain, he noticed that he had a problem figuring out how to recharge his cell phone. After his trip, McQuade developed a way to make backpacks and messenger bags containing solar panels. His company, Voltaic Systems, contracts to have the bags manufactured in China from material made out of recycled plastic. The products are sold in sporting goods stores, and McQuade is trying to get them stocked by Sam's Club. Eventually he hopes to offer briefcases with the solar power to recharge a laptop.[34]

To spot opportunities, think carefully about events and trends as they unfold. Consider, for example, the following possibilities:[35]

- *Technological discoveries.* Start-ups in biotechnology, microcomputers, and nanotechnology followed technological advances. Howard Berke, who has two Nobel Prize winners on his payroll, established Konarka Technologies to offer products based on advances in solar cells. In contrast to the older technology of solar panels, solar cells are based on organic chemicals, so they are more flexible and can be installed in a variety of products (see the previous example of Voltaic Systems).[36]

- *Demographic changes.* As the population ages, many organizations have sprung up to serve the older demographic, from Fit After Fifty exercise studios to assisted-living facilities. A business that targets both the aging population and the growth in single-parent and dual-career households is Errands Done Right. The service, launched by Donna Barber and Dawn Carter, targets those who are pressed for time or have difficulty getting around.[37]

- *Lifestyle and taste changes.* Start-ups have capitalized on clothing and music trends, desire for fast food, and growing interest in sports. In recent years, more consumers want to help take care of the environment, and more businesses are concerned about showing consumers that they care, too. This trend has opened a niche for Affordable Internet Services Online. The Web-hosting company, based in Romoland, California, is powered by 120 solar panels. Clients' Web sites can boast, "Site hosted with 100% solar energy."[38]

- *Economic dislocations,* such as booms or failures. Rising oil prices have spurred a variety of developments related to alternative energy or energy efficiency. Howard Berke, the entrepreneur behind Konarka Technolo-

gies' solar cells, says, "I don't come at this as an environmentalist. I come at this from good business sense. The cost of renewables . . . is more competitive when compared with fossil fuel."[39]

- *Calamities* such as wars and natural disasters. The terrorist attacks of September 2001 spurred concern about security, and entrepreneurs today are still pursuing ideas to help government agencies prevent future attacks. The devastating hurricanes on the Gulf Coast raised awareness of the importance of preparing for emergencies. Dennis Bertken and Nicholas Connor studied the market for emergency survival products and determined that few offerings were targeted to the most likely emergencies and related needs.

Harren Jhoti, Chief Executive and founder of a drug discovery and development company called Astex Therapeutics, receives the Chemistry World Entrepreneur of the Year Award at the annual Royal Society of Chemistry Innovations Awards in London. Mr. Jhoti built Astex over eight years, raising over £63 million. The annual award is presented to an individual who has established or contributed to the growth of a small or medium sized chemistry-related company.

They developed several products, such as a hand-cranked flashlight and a backpack filled with survival gear including food and water. Bertken and Connor founded Pacific Pathway, which sells these products in major stores under two brand names, Life+Gear and SafetyCross.[40]

- *Government initiatives and rule changes.* Deregulation spawned new airlines and trucking companies. Whenever the government tightens energy-efficiency requirements, opportunities become available for entrepreneurs developing ideas for cutting energy use.

 A decade ago, Ryan Black was surfing in Brazil where he noticed many Brazilians gulping huge bowls of frozen purple slush. He followed his curiosity and learned that the slush was made from acai berries, which grow in abundance in the area and can be turned into smoothie-like drinks when they are crushed, blended with water, and frozen. As Brazilians already know, the berries contain antioxidants and healthy omega fats. Reflecting on U.S. consumers' demand for more healthful foods, Ryan believed that he and his brother could deliver a new taste sensation that was also nutritious.

The brothers founded Sambazon to develop and market frozen acai drinks but had to educate the public, including restaurants, store owners, and other potential customers, about the product. "They'd put on quite a show, going from store to store and putting on this Barnum and Bailey act," recalls Larry Sidoti, vice president of development for Juice It Up! Franchise Corp., which agreed to

?

DID YOU KNOW?

In a recent three-year period, almost 900 new franchise concepts were launched in the United States. The categories with the most new concepts were food retailing, service businesses, and sports and recreation. The categories that added the most new franchise units were service businesses, building and construction, and child-related services.[44]

carry Sambazon. Sambazon now has 100 employees and sales of $12 million, with its products on the shelves at Whole Foods, Wild Oats, and Jamba Juice.[41]

franchises One important type of opportunity is the franchise. You may know intuitively what franchising is, or at least you can name some prominent franchises: McDonald's, Jiffy Lube, The Body Shop, Dunkin' Donuts. Franchising is an entrepreneurial alliance between two parties:[42]

1. The *franchisor*—an innovator who has created at least one successful store and seeks partners to operate the same concept in other local markets
2. The *franchisee*—the operator of one or more stores according to the terms of the alliance

For the franchisee, the opportunity is wealth creation via a proven (but not failureproof) business concept, with the added advantage of the franchisor's expertise. For the franchisor, the opportunity is wealth creation through growth. The partnership is manifest in a trademark or brand, and together the partners' mission is to maintain and build the brand. The Noodles & Company chain of fast-casual restaurants first grew by opening 79 company-owned locations. Management concluded that it could grow faster through franchising. Establishing standard menus and prices took a year, but franchising helped the company almost double its revenues in just two years.[43]

The Banatao Brothers Build Boards for the Green Wave

Y ou might think of surfers as living on the edge. They're involved in a sport that requires living near the edge of the ocean, gripping the edge of a surfboard with their toes. But there's another edge: the crest of the green wave. As consumers have become more aware of the importance of purchasing and using products that are environmentally friendly, entrepreneurs like Rey and Desi Banatao have begun to develop products from innovative green materials.

The Banatao brothers are lifelong, avid surfers. They know how particular surfers are about their surfboards. The boards must be just the right weight, have just the right flexibility and durability, and handle as expected under certain conditions. Surfers will respond well

to innovation as long as it benefits their performance. So when the Banatao brothers set out to shake up the surfboard industry by producing eco-friendly boards out of new materials replacing tried-and-true—but toxic—materials such as polyester and polyurethane foam, they knew they had to get it just right.

"We've spent time in the lab and in the water to understand how our combinations of materials and construction techniques behave," notes Rey Banatao. The result is the new Entropy surfboard, which is made of a sugar beet foam core that is wrapped in hemp cloth, instead of a polyurethane foam core encased in fiberglass. The next generation of Entropy surfboards will contain nontoxic, environmentally friendly materials developed by Bayer MaterialScience,

a division of Bayer Corporation. The new materials "increase durability by a factor of two or three," notes Rey Banatao.

As the Entropy surfboards hit the beach with surfers, the bio-friendly materials are getting the nod. The Banatao brothers believe that the Entropy boards are riding the waves—and the market—at a time when surfers are willing to try something new. "Now it's like the dot-com period for surfing," says Rey Banatao. He recognizes the importance of keeping ahead of the next wave of products to hit the market, understanding what his customers want and need. "At the end of the day, innovation is our only way to compete with the rest of the world," he notes. "Whether it's innovation in shape, material, or construction, we've got to keep progressing."

People often assume that buying a franchise is less risky than starting a business from scratch, but the evidence is mixed. A study that followed businesses for six years found the opposite of the popular assumption: 65 percent of the franchises studied were operating at the end of the period, while 72 percent of independent businesses were still operating. One reason may be that the franchises involved mostly a few, possibly riskier industries. A study that compared only restaurants over a three-year period found that 43 percent of the franchises and 39 percent of independent restaurants remained in business.[45]

If you are contemplating a franchise, consider its market presence (local, regional, or national), market share and profit margins, national programs for marketing and purchasing, the nature of the business, including required training and degree of field support, terms of the license agreement (e.g., 20 years with automatic renewal versus less than 10 years or no renewal), capital required, and franchise fees and royalties.[46] You can learn more from plenty of useful sources, including these:

- International Franchise Association (http://www.franchise.org)
- The Small Business Administration (http://www.sba.gov)
- Franchise Chat (http://www.franchise-chat.com)
- The Business Franchise Directory (http://www.businessfranchisedirectory.com)

In addition, the Federal Trade Commission investigates complaints of deceptive claims by franchisors and publishes information about those cases. Dale Cantone, who heads the Franchise and Business Opportunities unit for Maryland's attorney general, advises people to take their time in investigating business opportunities, consulting with an accountant or lawyer who has experience in franchising.[47]

the next frontiers

The next frontiers for entrepreneurship—where do they lie? When a business magazine asked prominent investors in new businesses to name the best ideas for a new start-up, their responses included next-generation batteries with enough juice to power cars after a seconds-long charge, longer-lasting tiny batteries to keep cell phones and cameras running for more hours, implantable wireless devices that can monitor heartbeats or blood sugar levels, and online social networking sites that allow artists and musicians to share and promote their work.[48]

One fascinating opportunity for entrepreneurs is outer space. Historically, the space market was driven by the government and was dominated by big defense contractors like Boeing and Lockheed Martin. But now, with demand for satellite launches and potential profits skyrocketing, smaller entrepreneurs are entering the field. Some of the most dramatic headlines involve space tourism. Zero Gravity already operates flights in converted Boeing 727 jets that simulate the experience of weightlessness by flying up and down like a roller-coaster 10,000 feet above the earth. Famous passengers who signed up for the $3,500 flights included business owner Martha Stewart and physicist Stephen Hawking.[49]

Virgin Galactic's first craft, the mother ship *White Knight Two*, was unveiled in 2008. Although the spacecraft itself is still under construction, the first passengers have already plunked down $200,000 each for the ride. Two hundred others are on a waiting list.[50] Other recent ventures in space have included using satellites for automobile navigation, tracking trucking fleets, and monitoring flow rates and leaks in pipelines; testing designer drugs in the near-zero-gravity environment; and using remote sensing to monitor global warming, spot fish concentrations, and detect crop stress for precision farming.

Homeland security is another newly burgeoning industry, including companies in a wide range of industries—baggage

The Banatao brothers enjoy coming up with new ideas for better surfboards. They also like the edgy world of surfing. "Surfing has always been about going against the grain," observes Rey Banatao. "When a surfer buys a custom board, there is a connection to the . . . crew of guys building [the] board. In today's global economy, that way of doing business doesn't happen any more, and is one of the last great things about surfing." Except, maybe, for the next big wave.

 **Discussion Questions**

- What lifestyle changes represent an opportunity for the Banatao brothers? How might the brothers further capitalize on this opportunity in order to expand their business?
- Discuss how demographic changes or economic fluctuations might affect the way the Banataos market their Entropy surfboards to consumers.

SOURCES: Company Web site, http://www.entropysurfboards.com, accessed June 3, 2009; Sarah Mosko, "Catch the Green Wave," *Santa Monica Daily Press,* May 15, 2009, http://www.smdp.com; "Entropy Sports and Bayer Team Up to Make Surfboard," *Surf News Daily,* May 14, 2009, http://www.surfnewsdaily.com; "Rey Banatao," *Craftsman Chronicle,* October 11–12, 2008, accessed at http://www.ice-ninefoamworks.com; and Andy Stone, "Green Wave," *Forbes,* September 1, 2008, http://www.forbes.com.

● **TRANSACTION FEE MODEL** Charging fees for goods and services.

● **ADVERTISING SUPPORT MODEL** Charging fees to advertise on a site.

● **INTERMEDIARY MODEL** Charging fees to bring buyers and sellers together.

● **AFFILIATE MODEL** Charging fees to direct site visitors to other companies' sites.

● **SUBSCRIPTION MODEL** Charging fees for site visits.

● **SIDE STREET EFFECT** As you head down a road, unexpected opportunities begin to appear.

screening, smallpox vaccines, capturing arrival and departure information on travelers, explosives detection systems, sensors for airborne pathogens. Some of the growth is supported by government investment in security-related technology. For example, the state of Illinois recently awarded grants to SSS Research, which develops database software that helps terrorism analysts, and RiverGlass, which develops software that connects databases to find patterns describing high-risk people. In Michigan, the state-funded Venture Michigan I Fund supports investment in Michigan-based start-ups in the security and other growth industries.[51]

the Internet The Internet is a business frontier that continues to expand. With Internet commerce, as with any start-up, entrepreneurs need sound business models and practices. You need to watch costs carefully, and you want to achieve profitability as soon as possible.[52]

At least five successful business models have proven successful for e-commerce:[53]

1. **Transaction fee model**— Companies charge a fee for goods or services. Amazon.com and online travel agents are prime examples.

2. **Advertising support model**— Advertisers pay the site operator to gain access to the demographic group that visits the operator's site. More than one-third of online ads are for financial services, and another 22 percent are for Web media. More than half of the ads appear on e-mail pages.[54]

3. **Intermediary model**—A Web site brings buyers and sellers together and charges a commission for each sale. The premier example is eBay.

4. **Affiliate model**—Sites pay commissions to other sites to drive business to their own sites. Zazzle.com, Spreadshirt.com, and CafePress.com are variations on this model. They sell custom-decorated gift items such as mugs and T-shirts. Designers are the affiliates; they choose basic, undecorated products (such as a plain shirt) and add their own designs. Visitors to a designer's Web site can link to, say, Zazzle and place an order, or they can go directly to Zazzle to shop. Either way, Zazzle sets the basic price, and the designer gets about 10 percent. Spreadshirt and CafePress let designers choose how much above the base price they want to charge consumers for the decorated product.[55]

5. **Subscription model**—The Web site charges a monthly or annual fee for site visits or access to site content. Newspapers and magazines are good examples.

A flight into space might become as easy as booking a flight to Florida thanks to Burt Rutan. His idea to launch people into space may have opened the door for an entire space tourism industry.

As the costs of computing continue to drop and more free software tools are being disseminated, setting up shop online costs less than it ever did. Munjal Shah's company, Riya, has set up an online shopping service called Like.com, which uses visual recognition software to help shoppers find products that look similar to one another. The search software, Shah says, was based on open-source programs and cost about $50,000; five years ago, it would have been unaffordable. In addition, because current computer chips work more efficiently, the cost to run Riya's Web servers is about one-tenth of what he would have paid a few years ago.[56]

side streets Trial and error can also be useful in starting new businesses. Some entrepreneurs start their enterprises and then let the market decide whether it likes their ideas. This method is risky, of course, and should be done only if you can afford the risks. But even if the original idea doesn't work, you may be able to capitalize on the **side street effect**.[57] As you head down a road, you come to unknown places, and unexpected opportunities begin to appear. And, while you are looking, *prepare* so you can act quickly and effectively on any opportunity that presents itself.

L O 3 WHAT YOU NEED TO KNOW...
Can you identify common causes of success and failure?

What does it take, personally?

Many people assume that there is an "entrepreneurial personality." No single personality type predicts entrepreneurial

That Was THEN . . .

Thomas Edison was one of the most pro-lific U.S. inventors and entrepreneurs. Among his 1,093 patents: the electric light bulb, phonograph, and motion picture camera.

This Is NOW . . .

Philip Rosedale finds his entrepreneurial inspiration inside a computer. His Second Life Web site—a virtual world filled with computer-generated characters, landscapes, stores, and much more—allows others to create and sell products, conduct meetings, advertise, or simply have fun.

success, but you are more likely to succeed as an entrepreneur if you have certain characteristics:[58]

highly adaptable, creative, skilled at conceptualizing, and attentive to details.

> "Even if you think you know it all, there's a lot of life lessons you're going to learn in school. Develop your network while you're there with peers and professors."
>
> —Sam Uisprapassorn, cofounder, Crimson Skateboards[60]

1. *Commitment and determination:* Successful entrepreneurs are decisive, tenacious, disciplined, willing to sacrifice, and able to immerse themselves totally in their enterprises.

2. *Leadership:* They are self-starters, team builders, superior learners, and teachers. Communicating a vision for the future of the company—an essential component of leadership—has a direct impact on venture growth.[59]

3. *Opportunity obsession:* They have an intimate knowledge of customers' needs, are market driven, and are obsessed with value creation and enhancement.

4. *Tolerance of risk, ambiguity, and uncertainty:* They are calculated risk takers and risk managers, tolerant of stress, and able to resolve problems.

5. *Creativity, self-reliance, and ability to adapt:* They are open-minded, restless with the status quo, able to learn quickly,

6. *Motivation to excel:* They have a clear results orientation, set high but realistic goals, have a strong drive to achieve, know their own weaknesses and strengths, and focus on what can be done rather than on the reasons things can't be done.

Bill Gross—whom you met in our earlier discussion of "Why become an entrepreneur?" exemplifies many of these characteristics. He persevered even after his brainchild, Idealab, apparently crashed and burned. The company was launched in the mid-1990s to nurture Internet start-ups as they were being formed left and right. Companies that Idealab invested in included eToys, Eve.com, and PetSmart.com. If you haven't heard of them, it's probably because they went out of business because sales couldn't keep up with the hype and the hopes. Today Gross explains that he hadn't intended for Idealab to help exclusively dot-com businesses, but that's what entrepreneurs were all starting in the 1990s. When the Internet boom crashed several years ago, Gross laid off employees and shuttered offices, but he

Customized products are just a click away. Zazzle .com produces customized T-shirts, posters, and postage stamps. It has built a library of over 500,000 digital images, including more than 3,500 items of copyrighted material licensed from Walt Disney's legendary characters such as Mickey Mouse and Goofy. Shown here is a sample of customized postage stamps provided by Zazzle.

maintained his vision of helping entrepreneurs. Instead of giving up, Gross established stricter criteria for funding companies in the future— and determined that he would choose companies whose activities make a difference. Of the company's near failure, Gross says, "We have a lot more wisdom now."[61]

making good choices Success is a
function not only of personal characteristics but also of making good choices about the business you start. Figure 5.2 presents a model for conceptualizing entrepreneurial ventures and making the best choices. According to this model, a new venture may involve high or low levels of *innovation,* or the creation of something new and different. It can also be characterized by low or high *risk,* including the probability of major financial loss, as well as psychological risk perceived by the entrepreneur, including risk to reputation and ego.[62] Combining these two variables, we can identify four kinds of new ventures:

1. In the upper-left quadrant, innovation is high (ventures are truly novel ideas), and there is

little risk. As examples, the inventors of Lego building blocks and Velcro fasteners could build their products by hand, at little expense. A pioneering product idea from Procter & Gamble might fit here if there are no current competitors and because, for a company of that size, the financial risks of new-product investments can seem relatively small.

2. In the upper-right quadrant, novel product ideas (high innovation) are accompanied by high risk because the financial investments and competition are great. A new drug or a new automobile would likely fall into this category.

3. Most small business ventures are in the lower right, where innovation is low and risk is high. They are fairly conventional entries in well-established fields. New restaurants, retail shops, and commercial outfits involve a sizable investment by the entrepreneur and face direct competition from similar businesses.

4. Finally, the low-innovation/low-risk category includes ventures that require minimal investment and/or face minimal competition for strong market demand. Examples are some service businesses having low start-up costs and those involving entry into small towns if there is no competitor and demand is adequate.

This matrix helps entrepreneurs think about their venture and decide whether it suits their particular objectives. It also helps identify effective and ineffective strategies. You might find one cell more appealing than others. The lower-left cell is likely to have relatively low payoffs but to provide more security. The possible risks and returns are higher in other cells, especially the upper right. So you might place your new-venture idea in the appropriate cell and pursue it only if it is in a cell where you would prefer to operate. If it is not, you can reject the idea or look for a way to move it toward a different cell.

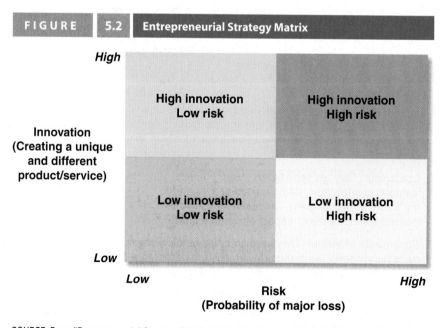

FIGURE 5.2 Entrepreneurial Strategy Matrix

SOURCE: From "Entrepreneurial Strategy Matrix: A Model of New and Ongoing Ventures," by Sonfield and Lussier. Reprinted from *Business Horizons,* May–June 1997. Copyright © 1997 by the Trustees at Indiana University, Kelley School of Business.

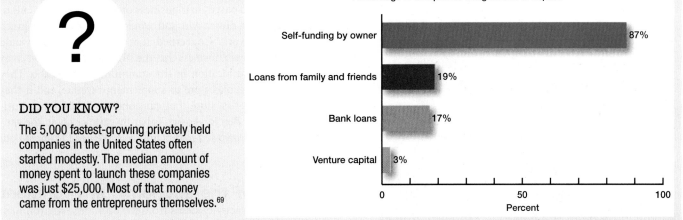

Percentage of companies using source of capital

Self-funding by owner — 87%
Loans from family and friends — 19%
Bank loans — 17%
Venture capital — 3%

Percent

The matrix also can help entrepreneurs remember a useful point: successful companies do not always require a cutting-edge technology or an exciting new product. Even companies offering the most mundane products—the type that might reside in the lower-left cell—can gain competitive advantage by doing basic things better than competitors.

Real estate is not usually considered a pioneering industry, but it does entail risk. Argentina-born developer Jorge Perez, a businessman familiar with risk, has been credited with revitalizing much of Miami, beginning with the building and renovation of affordable housing and garden apartment rentals. While most developers spread to the suburbs of Miami, believing that no one really wanted to live downtown, Perez took the opposite course: he focused entirely on the city itself. He began with a pair of condo towers that he built on the Miami River.

Today, Perez's company, The Related Group, is responsible for the three towers of the $1.6 billion Icon Brickell hotel and condominiums, another condo development called 500 Brickell, and the Loft 2—all overlooking Biscayne Bay. In all, The Related Group has constructed or renovated 11 major buildings downtown, giving Miami a fresh look and life. Not content to rest on past accomplishments, Perez has recently turned his sights toward projects in Atlanta and other cities overseas.[63]

Failure happens, but you can improve the odds of success

Success or failure lies ahead for entrepreneurs starting their own companies, as well as for those starting new businesses within bigger corporations. Entrepreneurs succeed or fail in private, public, and not-for-profit sectors, as well as in nations at all stages of development and of all political types.[64]

Estimated failure rates for start-ups vary. Most indicate that failure is more the rule than the exception. The failure rate is high for certain businesses like restaurants, and lower for successful franchises. Start-ups have at least two major liabilities: newness and smallness.[65] New companies are relatively unknown and must learn how to beat established competitors at doing something customers value. The odds of survival improve if the venture grows to at least 10 or 20 people, has revenues of $2 million or $3 million, and is pursuing opportunities with growth potential.[66]

Acquiring venture capital is not essential to the success of most start-up businesses; in fact, it is rare. Recent numbers from the Census Bureau say that more than three-fourths of start-up companies with employees were financed by entrepreneurs' own assets or assets of their families. Approximately one-tenth of businesses were financed with the owners' credit cards.[67] Still, in a recent quarter, venture capital firms invested more than $6 billion in almost 800 deals;[68] that's a sizable amount of money, even if the fraction of total new companies is small. And venture capital firms often provide expert advice that helps entrepreneurs improve the odds for success.

Further factors that influence success and failure include risk, the economic environment, various management-related hazards, and initial public stock offerings (IPOs).

risk It's a given: Starting a new business is risky. Entrepreneurs with plenty of business experience are especially aware of this. When Chris McGill was evaluating his idea for Mixx.com, a news Web site that could be personalized based on recommendations by users, he was *USA Today*'s vice president of strategy. To make Mixx succeed, McGill knew he would be leaving a well-paying job for an uncertain future in

you can find a lot of useful hyperlinks at the MIT Enterprise Forum, http://enterpriseforum.mit.edu/.

Richard Foos (left), Bob Emmer (center), and Garson Foos are successful entrepreneurs due to their creativity, innovation, and knowledge of their target customers' desires. They are shown here with a circa 1966-67 Batmobile children's arcade ride in their Shout! Factory headquarters in Los Angeles. As CEO of the Shout! Factory, Richard Foos runs an emporium filled with nostalgia-type collectibles.

which he had to line up financing and hire talented people in a turbulent business environment. But McGill also concluded that his experience at *USA Today* and prior management experience with *Yahoo News* gave him knowledge and connections for a successful Internet business.[70]

Successful entrepreneurs are realistic about risk. They anticipate difficulties and cushion their business to help it weather setbacks. In downtown Seattle, entrepreneurs Ben and Cindi Raykovich saw a risk when a major construction project began disrupting traffic around their store, Sound Sports. The Raykoviches had based their business on serving running enthusiasts who work downtown and would stop by on their lunch hour or after work. Concerned that the construction would drive away so much business that the store couldn't survive, they opened a second location in the community of Poulsbo. They intend for the second store to supplement revenue, and if they need to close the first store, they can continue to build their business in Poulsbo. Ben Raykovich is hardly cavalier about the situation: "My life is invested in this business. We need to spread out the risk."[71]

the role of the economic environment

Entrepreneurial activity stems from the economic environment as well as the behavior of individuals. For example, money is a critical resource for all new businesses. Increases in the money supply and the supply of bank loans, real economic growth, and improved stock market performance lead to both improved prospects and increased sources of capital. In turn, the prospects and the capital increase the rate of business formation. Under favorable conditions, many aspiring entrepreneurs find early success. But economic cycles soon change favorable conditions into downturns. To succeed, entrepreneurs must have the foresight and talent to survive when the environment becomes more hostile.

Although good economic times may make it easier to start a company and to survive, bad times can offer a chance to expand. Ken Hendricks of ABC Supply found a business opportunity in a grim economic situation: a serious downturn in the manufacturing economy of the Midwest contributed to the shutdown of his town's largest employer, the Beloit Corporation. Hendricks purchased the company's buildings and lured a diverse group of new employers to town, despite the economic challenges. In fact, Hendricks has a track record of turning around the struggling suppliers that ABC acquires.[72] Another silver lining in difficult economic times is that it's easier to recruit talent.

business incubators

The need to provide a nurturing environment for fledgling enterprises has led to the creation of business incubators. Business incubators, often located in industrial parks or abandoned factories, are protected environments for new, small businesses. Incubators offer benefits such as low rents and shared costs. Shared staff costs, such as for receptionists and secretaries, avoid the expense of a full-time employee but still provide convenient access to services. The staff manager is usually an experienced businessperson or consultant who advises the new business owners. Incubators often are associated with universities, which provide technical and business services for the new companies.

The heyday of business incubators came in the 1990s, when around 700 of them were financing start-ups, mainly emphasizing technology. Eight out of 10 shut down following the collapse of the Internet bubble, but the idea of nurturing new businesses persists. Naval Ravikant is developing a company tentatively named Hit Forge, which resembles the dot-com incubators. Hit Forge hired four engineers with experience in launching successful Internet concepts. The engineers have wide latitude to

You might not enjoy it Big-company managers and employees can specialize in what they love, whether it's selling or strategic planning. But entrepreneurs usually have to do it all, at least in the beginning. If you love product design, you also have to sell what you invent. If you love marketing, get ready to

The National Business Incubator Network estimates that 87 percent of companies that got started in an incubator are still in business five years later.[73]

try ideas, but they work under strict deadlines. They must go from concept to product within 90 days, and any enterprises that aren't growing after a year will be terminated. Unlike the older-style incubator, Hit Forge lets engineers work from the location of their choice, and the engineers retain half ownership in the ventures they develop. Also, whereas incubators in the 1990s might have spent $2 million developing an idea, today's launches might cost just $50,000.[74]

 One business incubator is thriving in Lebanon, New Hampshire. The Dartmouth Regional Technology Center (DRTC) offers young technology companies the business development support and services they need to grow. Funding for the incubator originally came from state and federal agencies, and nearby Dartmouth College sent some of the first businesses to the $8 million facility, which provides lab and office space, as well as shared conference areas.

When creative people gather, sparks fly, producing ideas for new solutions, goods and services, or processes. The DRTC is no exception. Some of the businesses that got their start there include Mascoma Corp, which has since patented a genetically engineered organism that can produce ethanol fuel efficiently, and Wellman Medical Solutions, whose founder invented a stabilizer for an ultrasound probe that can be used in a variety of medical situations. "I think that in the years to come you'll see that research which originated at Dartmouth has become the basis for companies that are nurtured through their early years at DRTC," predicts Roy Duddy, director of the New Hampshire Business Resource Center.[75]

L O 4 WHAT YOU NEED TO KNOW . . .
What are the common management challenges?

common management challenges As an entrepreneur, you are likely to face several common challenges that you should understand before you face them, and then manage effectively when the time comes.

manage the money too. This last challenge was almost a stumbling block for Elizabeth Busch, Anne Frey-Mott, and Beckie Jankewicz when they launched The Event Studio to run business conferences for their clients. All three women had experience with some aspect of running conferences, but when they started their company, they didn't fully think out all the accounting decisions they would need for measuring their income and cash flow. With some practical advice, they learned the basic accounting lessons that helped them avoid tax troubles later on. If they hadn't been willing to learn, entrepreneurship might not have been the right career path for them.[76]

Survival is difficult Zappos cofounder Tony Hsieh says, "We thought about going under every day—until we got a $6 million credit line from Wells Fargo."[77] Companies without much of a track record tend to have trouble lining up lenders, investors, and even customers. When economic conditions cool or competition heats up, a small start-up serving a niche market may have limited options for survival. Gary Gottenbusch worried when orders slowed at his Servatii Pastry Shop and Deli, located in Cincinnati. As a recession hit Ohio hard, customers were deciding that fancy breads and cakes were a luxury they could go without. Servatii might have closed, but Gottenbusch was willing to change his vision. He kept afloat and even added to sales by cultivating new distribution channels (sales in hospitals), new products (distinctive pretzel sticks), and cost-cutting measures (a purchasing association with other bakers in the area).[78]

Failure can be devastating. When Mary Garrison wanted to own a business, she chose the women's fitness industry and decided to buy a franchise from Lady of America Franchise Corporation. But when she held her grand opening, not a single person stopped by. Three months later, she closed. Garrison blames the franchisor for not providing the necessary promotional support, a complaint that Lady of America denies.[79]

 While still a student at the University of Missouri, Brian Laoruangroch started Green Mobile to buy, refurbish, and resell used cell phones. Originally, Laoruangroch's business was just a profitable hobby. Looking at phone prices on eBay, he concluded that he could earn money by buying and reselling phones. He recruited his brother Brett (another University of Missouri student), and they learned how to repair the phones. Then he launched a Web site to sell the phones. While the "Green" in Green Mobile implies the environmental value of recycling phones, the company's advertising emphasizes its low prices—$30 and up.

As sales grew, keeping up with the business plus school got complicated. First Green Mobile began operating a kiosk in a mall. That required employees. Then the company opened a store. That required borrowing. As revenues rose past $500,000, Laoruangroch faced decisions about opening a second store and borrowing from the Small Business Administration. He discovered that managing 30 employees was difficult and not necessarily a profitable scale for his business. He laid off some employees, concluding, "You can get a lot more done with a staff of 14 who care than with 25 or 30 people who don't."

With two stores and all the associated challenges, Laoruangroch finds himself working 60 to 80 hours a week—and wondering how he will ever find the time to finish earning his college degree.[80]

Growth creates new challenges   Just one in three *Inc.* 500 companies keeps growing fast enough to make this list of fastest-growing companies two years running. The reason: they are facing bigger challenges, competing with bigger firms, stretching the founders' capacities, and probably burning cash.[81] It's a difficult transition.

The transition is particularly complex for entrepreneurs who quickly face the possibility of expanding internationally. Whether a firm should expand internationally soon after it is created or wait until it is better established is an open question. Entering international markets should help a firm grow, but going global creates challenges that can make survival more difficult, especially when the company is young.

For instance, when Lou Hoffman decided to expand his public relations (PR) firm to Japan, to grow alongside existing clients, he was prepared for language and cultural differences but not for the high cost of doing business in that country. He first tried partnering with a translation service, figuring they could share expertise and help each other expand. But the translators really weren't interested in the PR business, so a year later, he was staffing the enterprise from scratch. Then Hoffman decided to open a Chinese office, and in that country, he couldn't find anyone familiar with both Chinese business and the creative business culture that had served his agency well. So he hired a Chinese PR staffer who was willing to spend a year at his California headquarters, just absorbing the business culture. That method worked for the Chinese market but flopped when Hoffman tried it for opening a London office;

the British employee didn't want to leave the California lifestyle and return home.[82] Of course, the risks tend to be lower when entrepreneurs (or their company's managers) have experience in serving foreign markets.[83]

In the beginning, the start-up mentality tends to be "we try harder."[84] Entrepreneurs work long hours at low pay, deliver great service, get good word-of-mouth, and their business grows. At first, it's "high performance, cheap labor." But with growth comes the need to pay higher wages to hire more people who are less dedicated than the founders. Then it's time to raise prices, establish efficient systems, or accept lower profits. The founder's talents may not spread to everyone else. You need a unique value proposition that will work as well with 100 employees, because hard work or instincts alone no longer will get the job done. Complicating matters is the continuing growth in customers' needs and expectations.[85]

Growth seems to be a consuming goal for most entrepreneurs. But some company founders reach the size where they're happy and don't want to grow any further. Reaching a golden mean is possible.[86] Also, sometimes growth needs to be restrained until the company is ready. Only a year after Gregory Wynn, Komichel Johnson, and Robert A. Jones III set up their homebuilding business, JLW Homes and Communities, they had an opportunity to build a 70-unit condominium project called Heritage Pointe. They determined that getting the job done would require a master builder, two assistants, and at least 100 workers. JLW had two master builders, who were already assigned to projects, and too few workers, so the partners reluctantly decided not to take the job. Jones recalls, "It was way too early for us to do this type of deal, . . . and I'm glad we did [turn it down] because if we didn't, we may have lost our shirts."[87] By carefully planning growth at a sustainable pace, JLW has become a successful Atlanta firm.

It's hard to delegate   As the business grows, entrepreneurs often hesitate to delegate work they are used to doing. Leadership deteriorates into micromanagement. For example, during the Internet craze, many company founders with great technical knowledge but little experience became "instant experts" in every phase of business, including branding and advertising.[88] Turns out, they didn't know as much as they thought, and their companies crashed. In contrast, Darren Herman kept his focus on what he knows. While still in his early 20s, Herman took his passion for videogames and his knowledge of marketing and came up with a business idea: IGA Worldwide, which works with advertisers and game developers to place advertising within videogames. Shortly after he launched IGA, Herman turned over the job of CEO to a more experienced person and named himself "senior business development director," which means he focuses on spotting new ideas and promoting the company to investors.[89]

> the *Inc.* 500 companies on the 2006 list started with a median of $75,000 in capital. One company reported starting with just a dollar.[90]

Misuse of funds Many unsuccessful entrepreneurs blame their failure on inadequate financial resources. Yet failure due to a lack of financial resources doesn't necessarily indicate a real lack of money; it could mean a failure to use the available money properly. A lot of start-up capital may be wasted—on expensive locations, great furniture, fancy stationery. Entrepreneurs who fail to use their resources wisely usually make one of two mistakes: they apply financial resources to the wrong uses, or they maintain inadequate control over their resources.

This problem may be more likely when a lucky entrepreneur gets a big infusion of cash from a venture capital firm or an initial offering of stock. For most start-ups, where the money on the line comes from the entrepreneur's own assets, he or she has more incentive to be careful. Tripp Micou, founder of Practical Computer Applications, says, "If all the money you spend is based on what you're bringing in [through sales], you very quickly focus on the right things to spend it on."[91] Micou, an experienced entrepreneur who expects the company's revenues to double each year for the next few years, believes that this financial limitation is actually a management advantage.

Poor controls Entrepreneurs, in part because they are very busy, often fail to use formal control systems. One common entrepreneurial malady is an aversion to record keeping. Expenses mount, but records do not keep pace. Pricing decisions are based on intuition without adequate reference to costs. As a result, the company earns inadequate margins to support growth.

Sometimes an economic slowdown provides a necessary alarm, warning business owners to pay attention to controls. When Servatii Pastry Shop and Deli's sales deteriorated while the prices of ingredients were rising, owner Gary Gottenbusch pushed himself to go "a little out of [his] comfort zone" and consulted with advisers at the Manufacturing Extension Partnership. Besides encouraging him to innovate, the advisers helped him set goals and monitor progress. One problem Gottenbusch tackled was the price of baking commodities, such as shortening and flour. He partnered with other local bakeries to form a purchasing association that buys in bulk and passes along the savings. Keeping costs down helped Servatii stay profitable when customers were trimming their budgets for baked goods.[92]

Even in high-growth companies, great numbers can mask brewing problems. Blinded by the light of growing sales, many entrepreneurs fail to maintain vigilance over other aspects of the business. In the absence of controls, the business veers out of control. So don't get overconfident; keep asking critical questions. Is our success based on just one big customer? Is our product just a fad that can fade away? Can other companies easily enter our domain and hurt our business? Are we losing a technology lead? Do we really understand the numbers, know where they come from, and have any hidden causes for concern?

Mortality One long-term measure of an entrepreneur's success is the fate of the venture after the founder's death. Founding entrepreneurs often fail to plan for succession. When death occurs, the lack of a skilled replacement for the founder can lead to business failure.

Management guru Peter Drucker offered the following advice to help family-managed businesses survive and prosper:[93]

- Family members working in the business must be at least as capable and hard-working as other employees.
- At least one key position should be filled by a nonfamily member.
- Someone outside the family and the business should help plan succession.

Family members who are mediocre performers are resented by others; outsiders can be more objective and contribute expertise the family might not have. Issues of management succession are often the most difficult of all, causing serious conflict and possible breakup of the firm.

Going public Sometimes companies reach a point at which the owners want to "go public." **Initial public stock offerings (IPOs)** offer a way to raise capital through federally registered and underwritten sales of shares in the company.[94] You need lawyers and accountants who know current regulations. The reasons for going public include raising more capital, reducing debt or improving the balance sheet and enhancing net worth, pursuing otherwise unaffordable opportunities, and improving credibility with customers and other stakeholders—"you're in the big leagues now." Disadvantages include the expense, time, and effort involved; the tendency to become more interested in the stock price and capital gains than in running the company properly; and the creation of a long-term relationship with an investment banking firm that won't necessarily always be a good one.[95]

Many entrepreneurs prefer to avoid going public, feeling they'll lose control if they do. States Yvon Chouinard of sports and apparel firm Patagonia: "There's a certain formula in business where you grow the thing and go public. I don't think it has to be that way. Being a closely held company means being able to take risks and try new things—the creative part of business. If I were owned by a bunch of retired teachers, I wouldn't be able to do what I do; I'd have to be solely concerned with the bottom line."[96]

Executing IPOs and other approaches to acquiring capital is complex and beyond the scope of this chapter. Sources for more information include *The Ernst & Young Guide to Raising Capital,* the National Venture Capital Association (http://www.nvca.org), VentureOne (http://www.ventureone.com), and *VentureWire* (link to this publication from http://www.venturecapital.dowjones.com/).

L O 5 WHAT YOU NEED TO KNOW . . .
How can you increase your chances of success, including good business planning?

Planning and resources help you succeed

Aside from financial resources, entrepreneurs need to think through their business idea carefully to help ensure its success.

This calls for good planning and nonfinancial resources.

planning

So you think you have identified a business opportunity and have the potential to make it succeed. Now what? Should you act on your idea? Where should you begin?

The business plan

Your excitement and intuition may convince you that you are on to something. But they might not convince anyone else. You need more thorough planning and analysis. This effort will help convince others to get on board and help you avoid costly mistakes.

The first formal planning step is to do an **opportunity analysis.** This analysis includes a description of the good or service, an assessment of the opportunity, an assessment of the entrepreneur (you), a specification of activities and resources needed to translate your idea into a viable business, and your source(s) of capital.[97] Your opportunity analysis should include the following questions:[98]

- What market need does my idea fill?
- What personal observations have I experienced or recorded with regard to that market need?
- What social condition underlies this market need?
- What market research data can be marshaled to describe this market need?
- What patents might be available to fulfill this need?
- What competition exists in this market? How would I describe the behavior of this competition?
- What does the international market look like?
- What does the international competition look like?
- Where is the money to be made in this activity?

The opportunity analysis, or opportunity assessment plan, focuses on the opportunity, not the entire venture. It provides the basis for deciding whether to act. Then the **business plan** describes all the elements involved in starting the new venture.[99] The business plan describes the venture and its market, strategies, and future directions. It often has functional plans for marketing, finance, manufacturing, and human resources. Table 5.1 outlines a typical business plan.

The business plan serves several purposes:

- It helps determine the viability of your enterprise.
- It guides you as you plan and organize.
- It helps you obtain financing.

It is read by potential investors, suppliers, customers, and others. Get help in writing a sound plan!

Key planning elements   Most business plans devote so much attention to financial projections that they neglect other important information—information that matters greatly to astute investors. In fact, financial projections tend to be overly optimistic. Investors know this and discount the figures.[100] In addition to the numbers, the best plans convey—and make certain that the entrepreneurs have carefully thought through—five key factors:[101]

1. *The people:* The new organization's people should be energetic and have skills and expertise directly relevant to the venture. For many astute investors, the people are the most important element, more important even than the idea. Venture capital firms often receive 2,000 business plans per year; many believe that ideas are a dime a dozen and what counts is the ability to execute. Arthur Rock, a legendary venture capitalist who helped start Intel, Teledyne, and Apple, stated, "I invest in people, not ideas. If you can find good people, if they're wrong about the product, they'll make a switch."[102]

2. *The opportunity:* You need a competitive advantage that can be defended. The focus should be on customers. Who is the customer? How does the customer make decisions?

The three founders of Amie Street, an online music retailer, have created competitive advantage by implementing a novel pricing system. At Amie Street, visitors rate songs from independent artists. As the rating goes up, so does the price. The musicians get 70% of the price.

TABLE 5.1 Outline of a Business Plan

I. **EXECUTIVE SUMMARY**
   A. Description of the Business Concept and the Business.
   B. The Opportunity and Strategy.
   C. The Target Market and Projections.
   D. The Competitive Advantages.
   E. The Economics, Profitability, and Harvest Potential.
   F. The Team.
   G. The Offering.

II. **THE INDUSTRY AND THE COMPANY AND ITS PRODUCT(S) OR SERVICE(S)**
   A. The Industry.
   B. The Company and the Concept.
   C. The Product(s) or Service(s).
   D. Entry and Growth Strategy.

III. **MARKET RESEARCH AND ANALYSIS**
   A. Customers.
   B. Market Size and Trends.
   C. Competition and Competitive Edges.
   D. Estimated Market Share and Sales.
   E. Ongoing Market Evaluation.

IV. **THE ECONOMICS OF THE BUSINESS**
   A. Gross and Operating Margins.
   B. Profit Potential and Durability.
   C. Fixed, Variable, and Semivariable Costs.
   D. Months to Breakeven.
   E. Months to Reach Positive Cash Flow.

V. **MARKETING PLAN**
   A. Overall Marketing Strategy.
   B. Pricing.
   C. Sales Tactics.
   D. Service and Warranty Policies.
   E. Advertising and Promotion.
   F. Distribution.

VI. **DESIGN AND DEVELOPMENT PLANS**
   A. Development Status and Tasks.
   B. Difficulties and Risks.
   C. Product Improvement and New Products.
   D. Costs.
   E. Proprietary Issues.

VII. **MANUFACTURING AND OPERATIONS PLAN**
   A. Operating Cycle.
   B. Geographical Location.
   C. Facilities and Improvements.
   D. Strategy and Plans.
   E. Regulatory and Legal Issues.

VIII. **MANAGEMENT TEAM**
   A. Organization.
   B. Key Management Personnel.
   C. Management Compensation and Ownership.
   D. Other Investors.
   E. Employment and Other Agreements and Stock Option and Bonus Plans.
   F. Board of Directors.
   G. Other Shareholders, Rights, and Restrictions.
   H. Supporting Professional Advisors and Services.

IX. **OVERALL SCHEDULE**

X. **CRITICAL RISKS, PROBLEMS, AND ASSUMPTIONS**

XI. **THE FINANCIAL PLAN**
   A. Actual Income Statements and Balance Sheets.
   B. Pro Forma Income Statements.
   C. Pro Forma Balance Sheets.
   D. Pro Forma Cash Flow Analysis.
   E. Breakeven Chart and Calculation.
   F. Cost Control.
   G. Highlights.

XII. **PROPOSED COMPANY OFFERING**
   A. Desired Financing.
   B. Offering.
   C. Capitalization.
   D. Use of Funds.
   E. Investor's Return.

XIII. **APPENDIXES**

SOURCE: J. A. Timmons, *New Venture Creation,* 5th ed., p. 374. Copyright © 1999 by Jeffry A. Timmons. Reproduced with permission of the author. © 1999 The McGraw-Hill Companies.

What price will the customer pay? How will the venture reach all customer segments? How much does it cost to acquire and support a customer, and to produce and deliver the product? How easy or difficult is it to retain a customer?

3. *The competition:* The plan must identify current competitors and their strengths and weaknesses, predict how they will respond to the new venture, indicate how the new venture will respond to the competitors' responses, identify future potential competitors, and consider how to collaborate with or face off against actual or potential competitors. The original plan for Zappos was for its Web site to compete with other online shoe retailers by offering a wider selection than they did. However, most people buy shoes in stores, so Zappos cofounders Nick Swinmurn and Tony Hsieh soon realized that they needed a broader view of the competition. They began focusing more on service and planning a distribution method that would make online shopping as successful as visiting a store.[103]

4. *The context:* The environment should be favorable from regulatory and economic perspectives. Such factors as tax policies, rules about raising capital, interest rates, inflation, and exchange rates will affect the viability of the new venture. The context can make it easier or harder to get backing. Importantly, the plan should make clear that you know that the context inevitably will change, forecast how the changes

will affect the business, and describe how you will deal with the changes.

5. *Risk and reward:* The risk must be understood and addressed as fully as possible. The future is uncertain, and the elements described in the plan will change. Although you cannot predict the future, you must contemplate head-on the possibilities of key people resigning, interest rates changing, a key customer leaving, or a powerful competitor responding ferociously. Then describe what you will do to prevent, avoid, or cope with such possibilities. You should also speak to the end of the process: how to get money out of the business eventually. Will you go public? Will you sell or liquidate? What are the various possibilities for investors to realize their ultimate gains?[105]

Selling the plan

Your goal is to get investors to support the plan. The elements of a great plan, as just described, are essential. Also important is who you decide to try to convince to back your plan.

Many entrepreneurs want passive investors who will give them money and let them do what they want. Doctors and dentists generally fit this image. Professional venture capitalists do not, as they demand more control and more of the returns. But when a business goes wrong—and chances are, it will—nonprofessional investors are less helpful and less likely to advance more (needed) money. Sophisticated investors have seen sinking ships before and know how to help. They are more likely to solve problems, provide more money, and also navigate financial and legal waters such as going public.[106]

View the plan as a way for you to figure out how to reduce risk and maximize reward, and to convince others that you understand the entire new-venture process. Don't put together a plan built on naïveté or overconfidence or one that cleverly hides major flaws. You might not fool others, and you certainly would be fooling yourself.

nonfinancial resources

Also crucial to the success of a new business are nonfinancial resources, including legitimacy in the minds of the public and the ways other people can help.

Legitimacy

An important resource for the new venture is legitimacy—people's judgment of a company's acceptance, appropriateness, and desirability.[107] When the market confers legitimacy, it helps overcome the "liability of newness" that creates a high percentage of new-venture failure.[108] Legitimacy helps a firm acquire other resources such as top managers, good employees, financial resources, and government support. In a

?

DID YOU KNOW?

According to the State New Economy Index, the most hospitable states for starting an innovative, new-economy business are Massachusetts, New Jersey, Maryland, Washington, and California.[104]

three-year study tracking business start-ups, the likelihood that a company would succeed at selling products, hiring employees, and attracting investors depended most on how skillfully entrepreneurs demonstrated that their business was legitimate.[109]

A business is legitimate if its goals and methods are consistent with societal values. You can generate legitimacy by visibly conforming to rules and expectations created by governments, credentialing associations, and professional organizations; by visibly endorsing widely held values; and by visibly practicing widely held beliefs.[110]

Networks

The entrepreneur is aided greatly by having a strong network of people. Social capital—being part of a social network and having a good reputation—helps entrepreneurs gain access to useful information, win trust and cooperation from others, recruit employees, form successful business alliances, receive funding from venture capitalists, and become more successful.[111] Social capital provides a lasting source of competitive advantage.[112]

To see just some of the ways social capital can help entrepreneurs, consider a pair of examples. Brian Ko, an engineer who founded Integrant Technologies, got useful advice from his investors, including private investors, a bank, and venture capital firms. One adviser taught Ko that acquiring patents during the start-up phase would help the company stay competitive during the long term, so Integrant spent the money to file applications for 150 patents in six years, positioning the company to protect its ideas as it gains market share and competitors' attention.[113]

Tim Litle has developed several successful innovations and businesses as a result of relationships with business school classmates and customers. Early in his career, a friend in politics wanted to target letters to different groups of citizens, and Litle worked with him to figure out how to do that now-common application with computers. He, the politician, and two other partners eventually built a business to provide the same service to marketers.[114]

Top-management teams

The top-management team is another crucial resource. Consider one of Sudhin Shahani's two start-ups, MyMPO, whose digital media services include Musicane, which lets musicians sell audio and video files and ringtones online at storefronts they create for themselves. The company's head of marketing was a singer.[115] Having a musician in that top spot may help Musicane build client relationships with other artists. Also, in companies that have incorporated, a board of directors improves the company's image, develops longer-term plans for expansion, supports day-to-day activities, and develops a network of information sources.

Advisory boards Whether or not the company has a formal board of directors, entrepreneurs can assemble a group of people willing to serve as an advisory board. Board members with business experience can help an entrepreneur learn basics like how to do cash-flow analysis, identify needed strategic changes, and build relationships with bankers, accountants, and attorneys. Musicane has an advisory board whose members include Bob Jamieson, the head of BMG Canada.[116] Jamieson can contribute inside knowledge of the music industry to complement Shahani's business training and give the organization credibility to investors and to musicians who might be interested in selling online.

Partners Often, two people go into business together as partners. Partners can help one another access capital, spread the workload, share the risk, and share expertise. One of the strengths of JLW Homes and Communities, the Atlanta construction business described earlier in this chapter, is that the three founding partners bring different areas of expertise to the business. Gregory Wynn was a master homebuilder, Komichel Johnson was a financial expert, and Robert A. Jones III was a successful salesperson. Johnson explains the advantage this way: "We don't all agree on the same issues, and we've had some heated arguments. . . . But we realize that through communication and laying out the facts, . . . we can overcome any issues that may arise within our organization."[117]

Despite the potential advantages of finding a compatible partner, partnerships are not always marriages made in heaven. "Mark" talked three of his friends into joining him in starting his own telecommunications company because he didn't want to try it alone. He learned quickly that while he wanted to put money into growing the business, his three partners wanted the company to pay for their cars and meetings in the Bahamas. The company collapsed. "I never thought a business relationship could overpower friendship, but this one did. Where money's involved, people change."

To be successful, partners need to acknowledge one another's talents, let each other do what they do best, communicate honestly, and listen to one another. That's what the partners in JLW Homes did when they turned down a chance to build a project they were understaffed for completing. Johnson, the financial expert, believed the company would make a good return, and Jones, the salesperson, was eager to move ahead, but homebuilder Wynn said the company was unprepared for a project of that size. Johnson and Jones bowed to Wynn's experience and were later glad they did.[118] Partners also must learn to trust each other by making and keeping agreements. If they must break an agreement, it is crucial that they give early notice and clean up after their mistakes.

A+

L O 6 WHAT YOU NEED TO KNOW . . .
How can managers of large companies foster intrapreneurship and an entrepreneurship?

CORPORATE ENTREPRENEURSHIP

Large corporations are more than passive bystanders in the entrepreneurial explosion. Consider Microsoft. Every spring, the company hosts Techfest, essentially a three-day science fair that spotlights innovations the company may pursue. About half of Microsoft's researchers come from around the world to be inspired and energized by the glimpse at their colleagues' creative projects.[119]

Even established companies try to find and pursue profitable new ideas—and they need in-house entrepreneurs (often called intrapreneurs) to do so. If you work in a company and are considering launching a new business venture, Table 5.2 can help you decide whether the new idea is worth pursuing.

Build support for your ideas

A manager with an idea to capitalize on a market opportunity will need to get others in the organization to buy in or sign on. In other words, you need to build a network of allies who support and will help implement the idea.

If you need to build support for a project idea, the first step involves *clearing the investment* with your immediate boss or bosses.[120] At this stage, you explain the idea and seek approval to look for wider support.

Higher executives often want evidence that the project is backed by your peers before committing to it. This involves *making cheerleaders*—people who will support the manager before formal approval from higher levels. Managers at General Electric refer to this strategy as "loading the gun"—lining up ammunition in support of your idea.

Next, *horse trading* begins. You can offer promises of payoffs from the project in return for support, time, money, and other resources that peers and others contribute.

Finally, you should *get the blessing* of relevant higher-level officials. This usually involves a formal presentation. You will need to guarantee the project's technical and political feasibility. Higher management's endorsement of the project and promises of resources help convert potential supporters into an enthusiastic team. At this point, you can go back to your boss and make specific plans for going ahead with the project.

Along the way, expect resistance and frustration—and use passion and persistence, as well as business logic, to persuade others to get on board.

| TABLE | 5.2 | Checklist for Choosing Ideas |

Fit with Your Skills and Expertise
Do you believe in the product or service?
Does the need it fits mean something to you personally?
Do you like and understand the potential customers?
Do you have experience in this type of business?
Do the basic success factors of this business fit your skills?
Are the tasks of the enterprise ones you could enjoy doing yourself?
Are the people the enterprise will employ ones you will enjoy working with and
   supervising?
Has the idea begun to take over your imagination and spare time?

Fit with the Market
Is there a real customer need?
Can you get a price that gives you good margins?
Would customers believe in the product coming from your company?
Does the product or service you propose produce a clearly perceivable customer
   benefit that is significantly better than that offered by competing ways to
   satisfy the same basic need?
Is there a cost-effective way to get the message and the product to the
   customers?

Fit with the Company
Is there a reason to believe your company could be very good at the business?
Does it fit the company culture?
Does it look profitable?
Will it lead to larger markets and growth?

What to Do When Your Idea Is Rejected
As an intrapreneur, you will frequently find that your idea has been rejected.
   There are a few things you can do.
1. Give up and select a new idea.
2. Listen carefully, understand what is wrong, improve your idea and your
   presentation, and try again.
3. Find someone else to whom you can present your idea by considering:
   a. Who will benefit most if it works? Can they be a sponsor?
   b. Who are potential customers? Will they demand the product?
   c. How can you get to the people who really care about intrapreneurial ideas?

SOURCE: G. Pinchot III, *Intrapreneuring,* Copyright © 1985 by John Wiley & Sons, Inc. Reprinted by permission of the author, http://www.pinchot.com.

Build intrapreneurship in your organization

Building an entrepreneurial culture is the heart of the corporate strategy at Acordia, a successful insurance company that recently changed its name to Wells Fargo TPA.[121] Its success in fostering a culture in which intrapreneurs flourish came from an intentional decision to foster entrepreneurial thinking and behavior, create new-venture teams, and change the compensation system so that it encourages, supports, and rewards creative and innovative behaviors. In other words, building intrapreneurship derives from careful and deliberate strategy.

Two common approaches used to stimulate intrapreneurial activity are skunkworks and bootlegging. Skunkworks are project teams designated to produce a new product. A team is formed with a specific goal within a specified time frame. A respected person is chosen to be manager of the skunkworks. In this approach to corporate innovation, risk takers are not punished for taking risks and failing—their former jobs are held for them. The risk takers also have the opportunity to earn large rewards.

Bootlegging refers to informal efforts—as opposed to official job assignments—in which employees work to create new products and processes of their own choosing and initiative. Informal can mean secretive, such as when a bootlegger believes the company or the boss will frown on those activities. But companies should tolerate some bootlegging, and some even encourage it. To a limited extent, they allow people freedom to pursue pet projects without asking what they are or monitoring progress, figuring bootlegging will lead to some lost time but also to learning and to some profitable innovations.

Merck, desiring entrepreneurial thinking and behavior in research and development, explicitly rejects budgets for planning and control. New-product teams don't *get* a budget. They must persuade people to join the team and commit *their* resources. This creates a survival-of-the-fittest process, mirroring the competition in the real world.[122] At Merck, as at Wells Fargo TPA, intrapreneurship derives from deliberate strategic thinking and execution.

Managing intrapreneurship is risky

Organizations that encourage intrapreneurship face an obvious risk: The effort can fail.[123] However, this risk can be managed. In fact, failing to foster intrapreneurship may represent a subtler but greater risk than encouraging it. The organization that resists entrepreneurial initiative may lose its ability to adapt when conditions dictate change.

The most dangerous risk in intrapreneurship is the risk of overrelying on a single project. Many companies fail while awaiting the completion of one large, innovative project.[124] The successful intrapreneurial organization avoids overcommitment to a single project and relies on its entrepreneurial spirit to produce at least one winner from among several projects.

Organizations also court failure when they spread their entrepreneurial efforts over too many projects.[125] If there are many projects, each effort may be too small in scale. Managers will consider the projects unattractive because of their small size. Or those recruited to manage the projects may have difficulty building power and status within the organization.

An entrepreneurial orientation encourages new ideas

Not only can we distinguish characteristics of individual entrepreneurs, but we can do the same for companies. Companies

SKUNKWORKS A project team designated to produce a new, innovative product.

BOOTLEGGING Informal work on projects, other than those officially assigned, of employees' own choosing and initiative.

ENTREPRENEURIAL ORIENTATION The tendency of an organization to identify and capitalize successfully on opportunities to launch new ventures by entering new or established markets with new or existing goods or services.

that are highly entrepreneurial differ from those that are not. CEOs play a crucial role in promoting entrepreneurship within large corporations.[126]

Entrepreneurial orientation is the tendency of an organization to engage in activities designed to identify and capitalize successfully on opportunities to launch new ventures by entering new or established markets with new or existing goods or services.[127] Entrepreneurial orientation is determined by five tendencies:

1. *Independent action*—The organization grants individuals and teams the freedom to exercise their creativity, champion promising ideas, and carry them through to completion.

2. *Innovativeness*—The firm supports new ideas, experimentation, and creative processes that can lead to new products or processes; it is willing to depart from existing practices and venture beyond the status quo.

3. *Risk taking*—The organization is willing to commit significant resources and perhaps borrow heavily, to venture into the unknown. The tendency to take risks can be assessed by considering whether people are bold or cautious, whether they require high levels of certainty before taking or allowing action, and whether they tend to follow tried-and-true paths.

4. *Proactiveness*—The organization acts in anticipation of future problems and opportunities. A proactive firm changes the competitive landscape; other firms merely react. Proactive firms, like proactive individuals, are forward thinking and fast to act, and

are leaders rather than followers.[129] Proactive firms encourage and allow individuals and teams to *be* proactive.

5. *Competitive aggressiveness*—The firm tends to challenge competitors directly and intensely to achieve entry or improve its position. In other words, it has a competitive tendency to outperform its rivals in the marketplace. This might involve striking fast to beat competitors to the punch, tackle them head-to-head, and analyze and target competitors' weaknesses.

Entrepreneurial orientation should enhance the likelihood of success and may be particularly important for conducting business internationally.[130]

Thus, an "entrepreneurial" firm engages in an effective combination of independent action, innovativeness, risk taking, proactiveness, and competitive aggressiveness.[131] The relationship between these factors and the performance of the firm is complicated and depends on many things. Still, you can imagine how the opposite profile—too many constraints on action, business as usual, extreme caution, passivity, and a lack of competitive fire—will undermine entrepreneurial activities. And without entrepreneurship, how would firms survive and thrive in a constantly changing competitive environment?

With four decades of entrepreneurship behind him, Richard Branson has turned his attention—and his wealth—to preserving the environment. In 2006 he pledged his transportation businesses' profits for 10 years (an estimated $3 billion) to fight global

> "I believe that we are all born with the ability to be an entrepreneur, but we have to unlearn the risk-averse behavior that became part of our culture in the developed world over the past 500 years. As information and communication technologies tear down these barriers, we will see a full circle as billions of people will be empowered to express their entrepreneurial genes."
>
> —Frank Moss, director, Media Lab, Massachusetts Institute of Technology; former CEO, Tivoli Systems; and cofounder, Stellar Computer and Infinity Pharmaceuticals[128]

warming. Branson is also funding research on renewable energy sources. These projects also led to additional entrepreneurial ventures. Virgin Group partnered with NTR, an Ireland-based developer of renewable energy, in a joint venture to build ethanol production plants. And Branson's financial arm, Virgin Money, established the Climate Change Fund, a green fund investing only in companies committed to high environmental standards.[132]

Thus, management can create environments that foster more entrepreneurship. If your bosses are not doing this, consider trying some entrepreneurial experiments on your own.[133] Seek out others with an entrepreneurial bent. What can you learn from them, and what can you teach others? Sometimes it takes individuals and teams of experimenters to show the possibilities to those at the top. Ask yourself, and ask others: between the bureaucrats and the entrepreneurs, who is having a more positive impact? And who is having more fun?

DIY

Build Your Skills

Practice and apply your knowledge by going online at www.mhhe.com/ BatemanM2e

•• learning **OBJECTIVES**

After studying Chapter 6,
you will be able to:

LO1 Define the characteristics of organization structure: organic or mechanistic, differentiation, and integration.

LO2 Summarize how authority operates and who generally holds top authority in a company.

LO3 Discuss how span of control affects structure and managerial effectiveness.

LO4 Explain how to delegate effectively.

LO5 Distinguish between centralized and decentralized organizations.

LO6 Define basic types of organization structures, and summarize their strengths.

LO7 Describe important mechanisms used to coordinate work.

LO8 Discuss how organizations can improve their agility through their strategy, commitment to customers, and use of technology.

6

Organizing for Action

For decades, the name Whirlpool has been synonymous with top-quality, high-performing appliances such as refrigerators and washing machines. But by the late 1990s, Whirlpool's sales growth had plateaued, and its profits were falling. Cost cutting was only a way to stop the bleeding, not a prescription for long-term health. So CEO David R. Whitwam revised the way his company was organized. Instead of isolating the generation of ideas in product divisions' engineering and marketing groups, he made it a responsibility of all employees. He assigned Nancy R. Snyder to be Whirlpool's Chief Innovation Officer. Snyder launched innovation training for all salaried employees and created a process for carrying the best ideas through to development. Under the new system, revenues from new products began pouring in.[1]

As Whitwam recognized, an organization's success often depends on the way work and responsibilities are organized. Ideally, managers make decisions that align their company's

Keep It Together

like Sheryl and Alicia by learning how managers organize and delegate authority.

"Learning more about delegation in school would definitely have benefited in understanding the advantages of being able to have others assist you with work-related tasks and helping to manage workload."
—Sheryl Freeman, Program Manager

"I believe formal planning is necessary for a long-term project. You need to stay on track to get the end result you are looking for. It is not a good idea to do formal planning for matters that are not as pressing as others because you lose sight of what is really important. You also do not want to spend too much time on doing something that will not help you get to where you want to be."
—Alicia Catalano, Sales Team Leader

structure with its strategy, so employees have the authority, skills, resources, and motivation to focus on the activities where they can contribute most to the company's success.

This chapter focuses on the vertical and horizontal dimensions of organization structure. We begin by covering basic

management scholars (Burns and Stalker) described this type of structure as a **mechanistic organization**, a formal structure intended to promote internal efficiency.[2] But they went on to suggest the modern corporation has another option: the **organic structure**, which is much less rigid and, in fact,

> ## "Take my assets—but leave me my organization and in five years I'll have it all back."
>
> —Alfred P. Sloan Jr.

principles of *differentiation* and *integration*. Next, we discuss the vertical structure, which includes issues of authority, hierarchy, delegation, and decentralization. Then we describe various forms of horizontal structure, including functional, divisional, and matrix forms. We illustrate the ways in which organizations can integrate their structures: achieving coordination by standardization, by plan, and by mutual adjustment. Finally, we focus on the importance of organizational flexibility and responsiveness—that is, the organization's ability to change its form and adapt to new strategies, technology innovations, changes in the environment, and other challenges.

(L)(0) 1 WHAT YOU NEED TO KNOW . . .
What are the characteristics of organization structure?

FUNDAMENTALS OF ORGANIZING

We often begin to describe a firm's structure by looking at its organization chart. The **organization chart** depicts the positions in the firm and the way they are arranged. The chart provides a picture of the reporting structure (who reports to whom) and the various activities that are carried out by different individuals. Most companies have official organization charts drawn up to give people this information.

Figure 6.1 shows a traditional organization chart. Note the various types of information that are conveyed in a simple way:

- The boxes represent different work.
- The titles in the boxes show the work performed by each unit.
- Reporting and authority relationships are indicated by solid lines showing superior–subordinate connections.
- Levels of management are indicated by the number of horizontal layers in the chart. All persons or units that are at the same rank and report to the same person are on one level.

The organization chart in Figure 6.1 resembles the structure of organizations that German sociologist Max Weber addressed when he wrote about the concept of bureaucracy at the beginning of the 20th century. Many years later, two British

emphasizes flexibility. The organic structure can be described as follows:

- Jobholders have broader responsibilities that change as the need arises.
- Communication occurs through advice and information, rather than through orders and instructions.
- Decision making and influence are more decentralized and informal.
- Expertise is highly valued.
- Jobholders rely more heavily on judgment than on rules.
- Obedience to authority is less important than commitment to the organization's goals.
- Employees depend more on one another and relate more informally and personally.

An organic organization depends heavily on an informal structure of employee networks. Astute managers are keenly aware of these interactions, and they encourage employees to work more as teammates than as subordinates who take orders from the boss.[3] As we will discuss later in this chapter, the more organic a firm is, the more responsive it is to changing competitive demands and market realities.

Besides differing in their reliance on informal networks and formal organization charts, company structures can vary in terms of their differentiation and integration.

- **Differentiation** means the organization is composed of many different units that work on different kinds of tasks, using different skills and work methods.
- **Integration** means these differentiated units are put back together so that work is coordinated into an overall product.[4]

Differentiation creates specialized jobs

Within an organization's structure, differentiation is created through division of labor and job specialization. **Division of labor** means the work of the organization is subdivided into smaller tasks to be performed by individuals and units throughout the organization. **Specialization** means different people or groups perform specific parts of the larger task. The two

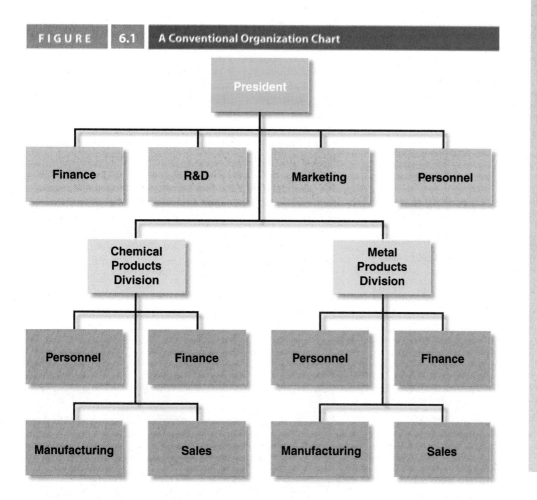

FIGURE 6.1 A Conventional Organization Chart

President

Finance | R&D | Marketing | Personnel

Chemical Products Division

Personnel | Finance

Manufacturing | Sales

Metal Products Division

Personnel | Finance

Manufacturing | Sales

● **ORGANIZATION CHART** The reporting structure and division of labor in an organization.

● **MECHANISTIC ORGANIZATION** A form of organization that seeks to maximize internal efficiency.

● **ORGANIC STRUCTURE** An organizational form that emphasizes flexibility.

● **DIFFERENTIATION** An aspect of the organization's internal environment created by job specialization and the division of labor.

● **INTEGRATION** The degree to which differentiated work units work together and coordinate their efforts.

● **DIVISION OF LABOR** The assignment of different tasks to different people or groups.

● **SPECIALIZATION** A process in which different individuals and units perform different tasks.

● **COORDINATION** The procedures that link the various parts of an organization to achieve the organization's overall mission.

concepts are, of course, closely related. Administrative assistants and accountants specialize in, and perform, different jobs; similarly, marketing, finance, and human resources tasks are divided among their respective departments. Specialization and division of labor are necessary because of the many tasks that must be carried out in an organization. The overall work of the organization would be too complex for any individual.[5]

Differentiation is high when an organization has many subunits and many specialists who think differently. Harvard professors Lawrence and Lorsch found that organizations in a complex, dynamic environment developed a high degree of differentiation to cope with the challenges. Companies in a simple, stable environment had low levels of differentiation. Companies in an intermediate environment had intermediate differentiation.[6]

Integration coordinates employees' efforts

As organizations differentiate their structures, managers must simultaneously consider issues of integration. The specialized tasks in an organization cannot be performed completely independently; they require some degree of communication and cooperation. Integration and its related concept, coordination,

refer to the procedures that link the various parts of the organization to achieve the organization's overall mission.

Integration is accomplished through structural mechanisms that enhance collaboration and coordination. Any job activity that links work units performs an integrative function. The more highly differentiated the firm, the greater the need for integration among its units. Lawrence and Lorsch found that highly differentiated firms were successful if they also had high levels of integration and were more likely to fail if they existed in complex environments but failed to integrate their activities adequately.[7] However, focusing on integration may slow innovation, at least for a while. In a study tracking the outcomes at information technology companies that acquired other firms, companies with more structural integration were less likely to introduce new products soon after the acquisition, but integration had less of an impact on product launches involving more-experienced target companies.[8]

These concepts permeate the rest of the chapter. First, we discuss *vertical differentiation* within organization structure—authority within an organization, the board of directors, the chief executive officer, and hierarchical levels, as well as issues pertaining to delegation and decentralization. Next, we turn to *horizontal differentiation* in an organization's structure, exploring issues of departmentalization that create functional, divisional, and matrix organizations. Then we cover issues relating to structural integration, including coordination, organizational roles, interdependence, and boundary spanning. Finally, we look at how these issues apply to organizations seeking greater agility.

(L)(O) 2 **WHAT YOU NEED TO KNOW . . .**

Can you summarize how authority operates and who generally holds top authority in a company?

THE VERTICAL STRUCTURE

The vertical dimension of a firm's structure shapes the company's reporting relationships, authority, and responsibility and accountability.

Authority is granted formally and informally

At the most fundamental level, the functioning of every organization depends on the use of authority, the legitimate right to make decisions and to tell other people what to do. For example, a boss has the authority to give an order to a subordinate. Traditionally, authority resides in *positions* rather than in people. The job of vice president of a particular division has authority over that division, regardless of how many people come and go in that position and who currently holds it.

In private business enterprises, the owners have ultimate authority. In most small, simply structured companies, the owner also acts as manager. Sometimes the owner hires another person to manage the business and its employees. The owner gives this manager some authority to oversee the operations, but the manager is accountable to—that is, reports and defers to—the owner, who retains the ultimate authority. In larger

companies, the principle is the same, but the structure of top management has several components:

- *Board of directors*—In corporations, the owners are the stockholders. But because there are numerous stockholders and these individuals generally lack timely information, few are directly involved in managing the organization. Stockholders elect a board of directors to oversee the organization. The board, led by the chairperson, makes major decisions affecting the organization, subject to corporate charter and bylaw provisions. Boards select, assess, reward, and perhaps replace the CEO; determine the firm's strategic direction and review financial performance; and assure ethical, socially responsible, and legal conduct.[9] The board's membership usually includes some top executives—called *inside directors.* Outside members of the board typically are executives at other companies. Successful boards tend to be those who are active, critical participants in determining company strategies.

- *Chief executive officer*—The authority officially vested in the board of directors is assigned to a chief executive officer

DID YOU KNOW?

In large corporations, most boards of directors have 9 to 13 directors. Boards are relying more on outside directors, including retired chief executive and chief financial officers.[10]

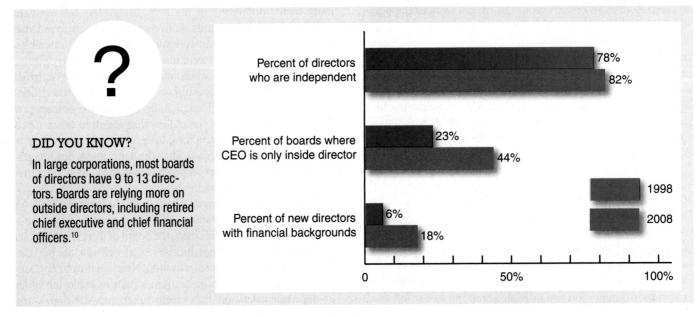

Percent of directors who are independent	78% / 82%
Percent of boards where CEO is only inside director	23% / 44%
Percent of new directors with financial backgrounds	6% / 18%

1998
2008

0   50%   100%

(CEO), who occupies the top of the organizational pyramid. The CEO is personally accountable to the board and to the owners for the organization's performance. In some corporations, one person holds the three positions of CEO, chair of the board of directors, and president.[11] More commonly, however, the CEO holds two of those positions, serving as either the chair of the board or the president of the organization. When the CEO is president, the chair may be honorary and do little more than conduct meetings. If the chair is the CEO, the president is second in command.

- *Top management team*—CEOs may share their authority with other key members of the top management team. Top management teams typically consist of the CEO, president, chief operating officer, chief financial officer, and other key executives. Rather than make critical decisions on their own, CEOs at companies such as Shell, Honeywell, and Merck regularly meet with their top management teams to make decisions as a unit.[12]

Formal position authority is generally the primary means of running an organization. An order that a boss gives to a lower-level employee is usually carried out. As this occurs throughout the organization day after day, the organization can move forward and achieve its goals.[13] However, authority in an organization is not always position-dependent. People with particular expertise, experience, or personal qualities may have considerable *informal* authority—scientists in research companies, for example, or employees who are computer-savvy.

report directly to them. This level is also called the *operational level* of the organization.

An authority structure is the glue that holds these levels together. Generally, but not always, people at higher levels have the authority to make decisions and tell lower-level people what to do. For example, middle managers can give orders to

Two respected top executives, Bill Gates (left) of Microsoft and Brad Anderson (right) of Best Buy, discuss the popularity of the Xbox 360 at the grand opening of the store in Bellevue, Washington.

"Authority without wisdom is like a heavy axe without an edge, fitter to bruise than polish."

—Anne Bradstreet

Hierarchy defines levels of authority

In Chapter 1, we discussed the three broad levels of the organizational pyramid, commonly called the *hierarchy*. The CEO occupies the top position as the senior member of top management. The top managerial level also includes presidents and vice presidents—the strategic managers in charge of the entire organization. The second broad level of the organization is middle management. At this level, managers are in charge of facilities or departments. The lowest level, made up of lower management and workers, includes office managers, sales managers, supervisors, and other first-line managers, as well as the employees who

first-line supervisors; first-line supervisors, in turn, direct operative-level workers.

A powerful trend for U.S. businesses over the past few decades has been to reduce the number of hierarchical layers. General Electric used to have 29 levels; today it has only a handful of layers, and its hierarchical structure is basically flat. Most executives today believe that fewer layers create a more efficient, fast-acting, and cost-effective organization. This also holds true for the subunits of major corporations. A study of 234 branches of a financial services company found that branches with fewer layers tended to have higher operating efficiency than did branches with more layers.[14]

This trend and research might seem to suggest that hierarchy is a bad thing, but entrepreneur Joel Spolsky learned that a completely flat structure is not necessarily ideal. When Spolsky and Michael Pryor started Fog Creek Software, they decided they would empower employees by having everyone report to the

○ SPAN OF CONTROL The number of subordinates who report directly to an executive or supervisor.

○ DELEGATION The assignment of new or additional responsibilities to a subordinate.

○ RESPONSIBILITY The assignment of a task that an employee is supposed to carry out.

○ ACCOUNTABILITY The expectation that employees will perform a job, take corrective action when necessary, and report upward on the status and quality of their performance.

two owners. The system worked fine for a few years until Fog Creek grew to 17 full-time employees. At that size, the company was no longer one small, happy family; employees had concerns and were finding it difficult to approach the partners and set up three-way meetings with them. So Spolsky and Pryor tapped two of the employees to serve as leaders of programming teams. Employees found it easier to talk to their team leader, and Spolsky concluded that this layer of "middle management" helps his company run more smoothly.[15]

L○ 3 WHAT YOU NEED TO KNOW . . .

How does span of control affect structure and managerial effectiveness?

Span of control determines a manager's authority

The number of people under a manager is an important feature of an organization's structure. The number of subordinates who report directly to an executive or supervisor is called the span of control. Differences in the span of control affect the shape of an organization. Holding size constant, narrow spans build a *tall* organization with many reporting levels. Wide spans create a *flat* organization with fewer reporting levels. The span of control can be too narrow or too wide. The optimal span of control maximizes effectiveness by balancing two considerations:

1. It must be narrow enough to permit managers to maintain control over subordinates.

2. It must not be so narrow that it leads to overcontrol and an excessive number of managers overseeing a few subordinates.

The optimal span of control depends on a number of factors. The span should be wide under the following conditions:

• The work is clearly defined and unambiguous.

• Subordinates are highly trained and have access to information.

• The manager is highly capable and supportive.

• Jobs are similar, and performance measures are comparable.

• Subordinates prefer autonomy to close supervisory control.

If the opposite conditions exist, a narrow span of control may be more appropriate.[16]

L○ 4 WHAT YOU NEED TO KNOW . . .

Can you explain how to delegate effectively?

Delegation is how managers use others' talents

As we recognize that authority in organizations is spread out over various levels and spans of control, we see the importance of delegation, the assignment of authority and responsibility to a subordinate at a lower level. Delegation often requires a subordinate to report back to his or her boss about how effectively the assignment was carried out. Delegation is perhaps the most fundamental feature of management at all levels, because it entails getting work done through others. The process can occur between any two individuals in any type of structure with regard to any task.

Some managers are comfortable fully delegating an assignment to subordinates; others are not. In the following example, consider the differences between these two office managers and the ways they gave out the same assignment. Are both managers using delegation?

▶ **Manager A:** "Call Tom Burton at Nittany Office Equipment. Ask him to give you the price list on an upgrade for our personal computers. I want to move up to a Core 2 Duo processor with 4 gigs of RAM and at least a 500-gigabyte hard drive. Ask them to give you a demonstration of the Vista operating system and Microsoft Office. I want to be able to establish a LAN for the entire group. Invite Cochran and Snow to the demonstration, and let them try it out. Have them write up a summary of their needs and the potential applications they see for the new systems. Then prepare me a report with the costs and specifications of the upgrade for the entire department. Oh, yes, be sure to ask for information on service costs."

Manager B: "I'd like to do something about our personal computer system. I've been getting some complaints that the current systems are too slow, can't run current software, and don't allow for networking. Could you evaluate our options and give me a recommendation on what we should do? Our budget is around $2,500 per person, but I'd like to stay under that if we can. Feel free to talk to some of the managers to get their input, but we need to have this done as soon as possible."

responsibility, authority, and accountability

When delegating work, it is helpful to distinguish among the concepts of authority, responsibility, and accountability. Responsibility means that a person is assigned a task that he or she is supposed to carry out. When delegating work responsibilities, the manager also should delegate to the subordinate enough authority to get the job done. *Authority,* recall, means that the person has the power and the right to make decisions, give orders, draw on resources, and do whatever else is necessary to fulfill the responsibility. Ironically, people often have more responsibility than authority; they must perform as well as they can through informal influence tactics instead of relying purely on authority.

As the manager delegates responsibilities, subordinates are held accountable for achieving results. Accountability means the subordinate's manager has the right to expect the subordinate to perform the job, and the right to take corrective action if the subordinate fails to do so. The subordinate must report upward on the status and quality of his or her performance.

However, the ultimate responsibility—accountability to higher-ups—lies with the manager doing the delegating. Managers remain responsible and accountable not only for their own actions but also for the actions of their subordinates. Managers should not use delegation to escape their own responsibilities; however, sometimes managers refuse to accept responsibility for subordinates' actions. They "pass the buck" or take other evasive action to ensure they are not held accountable for mistakes.[17] Ideally, empowering employees to make decisions or take action results in an increase in employee responsibility.

advantages of delegation

Delegating work offers important advantages, particularly when it is done effectively. Effective delegation leverages the manager's energy and talent and those of his or her subordinates. It lets managers accomplish much more than they could do on their own. Conversely, lack of or ineffective delegation sharply reduces what a manager can achieve. Delegation also conserves one of the manager's most valuable assets—his or her time. It frees the manager to devote energy to important, higher-level activities such as planning, setting objectives, and monitoring performance.

Another significant advantage of delegation is that it develops effective subordinates. Looking again at the different ways the two office managers gave out the same assignment, it is obvious that Manager B's approach is more likely to empower subordinates and help them develop. Delegation essentially gives the subordinate a more important job. The subordinate gains an opportunity to develop new skills and demonstrate potential for additional responsibilities and perhaps promotion—in effect, a vital form of on-the-job training that may pay off in the future. In addition, at least for some employees, delegation promotes a sense of being an important, contributing member of the organization, so these employees tend to feel a stronger commitment, perform their tasks better, and engage in more innovation.[18]

 An unusually broad example of delegation occurs at Illinois Tool Works, which allows managers to institute takeovers of other companies. ITW has built a reputation on its ability to acquire smaller firms quickly and efficiently. Now a conglomerate with 750 business units worldwide, ITW was originally a toolmaker. Its products still tend to be small and industrial—screws, auto parts, the plastic rings that hold a six-pack of soda, and the like. But ITW makes much of its money by buying and selling smaller firms. That's where managers like John Stevens, a mechanical engineer, come in.

Stevens and many others like him are being trained in the art of acquisition. CEO David Speer believes employees like Stevens are the perfect choice for the task because they know and understand the business. So ITW executives give two-day acquisition workshops for business-unit managers and then send them out to buy.[19]

Through delegation, the organization also receives payoffs. When managers can devote more time to important managerial functions while lower-level employees carry out assignments, jobs are done more efficiently and cost effectively. In addition, as subordinates develop and grow in their own jobs, their ability to contribute to the organization increases as well.

how should managers delegate?

In order to achieve the advantages we have just discussed, managers must delegate properly. As Figure 6.2 shows, effective delegation follows several steps.[20]

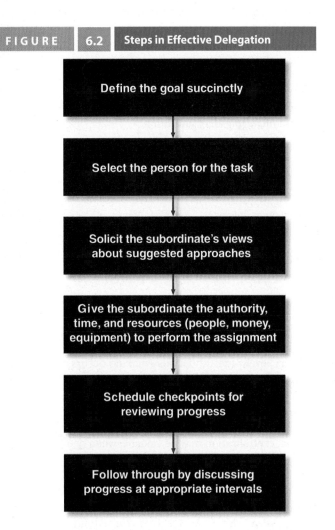

FIGURE 6.2 Steps in Effective Delegation

- Define the goal succinctly
- Select the person for the task
- Solicit the subordinate's views about suggested approaches
- Give the subordinate the authority, time, and resources (people, money, equipment) to perform the assignment
- Schedule checkpoints for reviewing progress
- Follow through by discussing progress at appropriate intervals

The first step in the delegation process, defining the goal, requires a manager to clearly understand the outcome he or she wants. Then the manager should select a person who is capable of performing the task. Delegation is especially beneficial when you can identify an employee who would benefit from developing skills through the experience of taking on the additional responsibility.

The person who gets the assignment should be given the authority, time, and resources to carry out the task successfully. The required resources usually involve people, money, and equipment, but they may also involve critical information that will put the assignment in context. ("Review every cost item carefully, because if we're the low bidder, we'll get the account.") Throughout the delegation process, the manager and the subordinate must work together and communicate about the project. The manager should seek the subordinate's ideas at the beginning and inquire about progress or problems at periodic meetings and review sessions. Even though the subordinate performs the assignment, the manager needs to be available and aware of its current status. These checkups also provide an important opportunity to offer encouragement and praise.

Some tasks, such as disciplining subordinates and conducting performance reviews, should not be delegated. But when managers err, it usually is because they delegated too little rather than too much. The manager who wants to learn how to delegate more effectively should remember this distinction: If you are not delegating, you are merely *doing* things; but the more you delegate, the more you are truly *building* and *managing* an organization.[21]

L O 5 WHAT YOU NEED TO KNOW . . .

Can you distinguish between centralized and decentralized organizations?

Decentralization spreads decision-making power

The delegation of responsibility and authority *decentralizes* decision making. In a **centralized organization**, important decisions usually are made at the top. In **decentralized organizations**, more decisions are made at lower levels. Ideally, decision making occurs at the level of the people who are most directly affected and have the most intimate knowledge about the problem. This is particularly important when the business environment is fast changing and decisions must be made quickly and well. Balanced against these criteria, centralization may be valuable when departments have different priorities or conflicting goals, which need to be mediated by top management. For example, when researchers modeled the search for new ideas in organizations, they found that the worst performance occurred in decentralized organizations where the search for new ideas was carried out at lower levels,

because ideas were presented for approval only if they benefited the particular department doing the search.[22]

Sometimes organizations change their degree of centralization, depending on the particular challenges they face. Tougher times often cause senior management to take charge, whereas in times of rapid growth, decisions are pushed farther down the chain of command. In the 1980s Harley-Davidson was in great financial difficulty and faced tough competition from Honda, Suzuki, and Yamaha. It needed strong, centralized leadership that could react quickly and decisively to survive. But once the crisis was past, this approach wasn't as effective in gaining the commitment and energy of employees, who were building the products and the relationships with customers. So, Harley-Davidson changed to a flatter, more empowered organization that decentralizes decision making. Today, the traditional hierarchy at the company has been replaced with collaborative leadership, based on the assumption that all employees can make decisions and take responsibility for meeting the organization's goals.[23]

Most executives today understand the advantages of pushing decision-making authority down to the point of the action. The level that deals directly with problems and opportunities has the most relevant information and can best foresee the consequences of decisions. Executives also see how the decentralized approach allows people to take timelier action.[24]

According to Raj Gupta, president of Environmental Systems Design (ESD), the engineering design firm decentralized as a necessary response to growth. A traditional "command-and-control" approach to management worked fine when the company was starting out, but now with 240 engineering and design professionals designing for diverse clients working on commercial, transportation, residential, manufacturing, energy, and other projects, it would be impossible for a few people at the top to dictate solutions. In fact, it wouldn't even be desirable, given the diverse expertise of its employees. So instead of grouping staff into functional departments such as sustainable design or electrical work, ESD has a structure in which studios of professionals serve particular clients, making decisions to meet their specialized needs.[25]

(L)(O) 6 WHAT YOU NEED TO KNOW . . .

What are the basic types of organization structures, and what are their strengths?

THE HORIZONTAL STRUCTURE

As the tasks of organizations become increasingly complex, the organization inevitably must be subdivided—that is, *departmentalized*. **Line departments** are those that have responsibility for the principal activities of the firm. Line units deal directly with the organization's primary goods or services; they make things, sell things, or provide customer service. At General Motors, line departments include product design, fabrication, assembly, distribution, and the like. Line managers typically have much authority and power in the organization, and they have the ultimate responsibility for making major operating decisions. They also are accountable for the "bottom-line" results of their decisions.

Staff departments are those that provide specialized or professional skills that support line departments. They include research, legal, accounting, public relations, and human resources departments. In large companies, each of these specialized units may have its own vice president, some of whom are vested with a great deal of authority, as when accounting or finance groups approve and monitor budgetary activities.

In traditionally structured organizations, conflicts often arose between line and staff departments. One reason was that career paths and success in many staff functions has depended on being an expert in that particular functional area, while success in line functions is based more on knowing the organization's industry. So, while line managers might be eager to pursue new products and customers, staff managers might seem to stifle these ideas with a focus on requirements and procedures. Line managers might seem more willing to take risks for the sake of growth, while staff managers seem more focused on protecting the company from risks. But in today's organizations, staff units tend to be less focused on monitoring and controlling performance and more interested in providing strategic support and expert advice.[26] For example, human resource managers have broadened their focus from merely creating procedures that meet legal requirements to helping organizations plan for, recruit, develop, and keep the kinds of employees who will give the organization a long-term competitive advantage. This type of strategic thinking not only makes staff managers more valuable to their organizations but also can reduce the conflict between line and staff departments.

As organizations divide work into different units, we can detect patterns in the way departments are clustered and arranged. The three basic approaches to departmentalization are functional, divisional, and matrix.

Functional organizations foster efficient experts

In a **functional organization**, jobs (and departments) are specialized and grouped according to *business functions* and the skills they require: production, marketing, human resources, research and development, finance, accounting, and so forth. Figure 6.3 is a basic functional organization chart.

- **CENTRALIZED ORGANIZATION** An organization in which high-level executives make most decisions and pass them to lower levels for implementation.

- **DECENTRALIZED ORGANIZATION** An organization in which lower-level managers make important decisions.

- **LINE DEPARTMENTS** Units that deal directly with the organization's primary goods and services.

- **STAFF DEPARTMENTS** Units that support line departments.

- **DEPARTMENTALIZATION** Subdividing an organization into smaller subunits.

- **FUNCTIONAL ORGANIZATION** Departmentalization around specialized activities such as production, marketing, and human resources.

| FIGURE | 6.3 | The Functional Organization |

The traditional functional approach to departmentalization has a number of potential advantages:[27]

1. *Economies of scale can be realized.* When people with similar skills are grouped, the company can buy more efficient equipment and obtain discounts for large purchases.

2. *Monitoring of the environment* is more effective. Each functional group is more closely attuned to developments in its own field, so it can adapt more readily.

3. *Performance standards* are better maintained. People with similar training and interests may develop a shared concern for performance in their jobs.

4. People have greater opportunity for *specialized training* and *in-depth skill development*.

5. Technical specialists are relatively *free of administrative work.*

6. *Decision making* and *lines of communication* are simple and clearly understood.

The functional form does have disadvantages, however. People may care more about their own function than about the company as a whole, and their attention to functional tasks may reduce their focus on overall product quality and customer satisfaction. Managers develop functional expertise but lack knowledge of the other areas of the business; they become specialists, not generalists. Between functions, conflicts arise, and communication and coordination fall off. In short, this structure may promote functional differentiation but not *functional integration.*

As a consequence, the functional structure may be most appropriate in rather simple, stable environments. If the organization becomes fragmented (or *dis*integrated), it may have difficulty developing and bringing new products to market and responding quickly to customer demands and other changes. Particularly when companies are growing and business environments are changing, organizations need to integrate work areas more effectively for flexibility and responsiveness. Other forms of departmentalization can be more flexible and responsive than the functional structure.

Demands for total quality, customer service, innovation, and speed have highlighted the shortcomings of the functional form. Functional organizations, being highly differentiated, create barriers to coordination across functions. Yet, the functional organization will not disappear, in part because functional specialists will always be needed, but functional managers will make fewer decisions. The more important units will be cross-functional teams with integrative responsibilities for products, processes, or customers.[28]

Divisional organizations develop a customer focus

As organizations grow and become increasingly diversified, their functional departments have difficulty managing a wide variety of products, customers, and geographic regions. In this case, organizations may restructure by creating a **divisional organization**, which groups all functions into a single division and duplicates functions across all the divisions. In the divisional organization chart in Figure 6.4, each division has

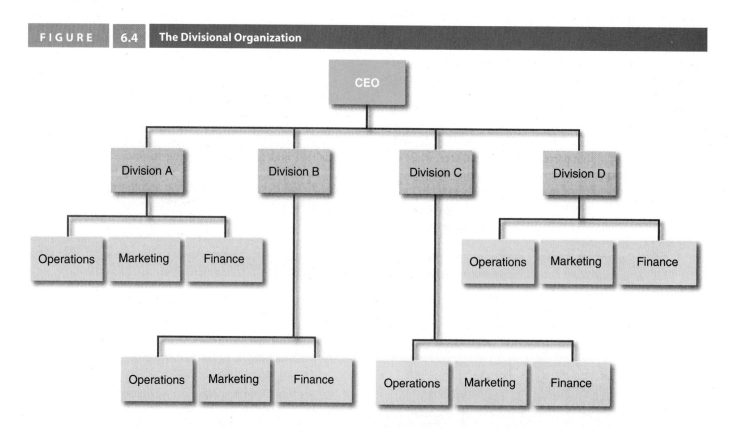

FIGURE 6.4 **The Divisional Organization**

its own operations, marketing, and finance department. Separate divisions may act almost as separate businesses or profit centers and work autonomously to accomplish the goals of the entire enterprise. Here are some examples of how the same tasks would be organized under functional and divisional structures:[29]

Functional Organization	Divisional Organization
A central purchasing department	A purchasing unit for each division
Separate companywide marketing, production, design, and engineering departments	Each product group's own experts in marketing, design, production, and engineering
A central city health department	Separate health units for the school district and the prison
Plantwide inspection, maintenance, and supply departments	Inspection, maintenance, and supply conducted by each production team

Organizations can create a divisional structure in several ways:

- *Product divisions*—All functions that contribute to a given product are organized under one product manager. Johnson & Johnson is an example of this form. It has more than 250 independent company divisions, many of which are responsible for particular product lines. Its subsidiary Cordis Corporation has divisions that develop and sell products for treating vascular diseases, while McNeil-PPC's products include Listerine and Plax mouthwashes.

  The product approach to departmentalization offers advantages and disadvantages.[30] Information needs are managed more easily, because people work closely on only one product. People are committed full-time to a particular product line, so they are aware of how their jobs fit into the broader scheme. Task responsibilities are clear, and managers are more independent and accountable. Also, managers receive broader training. Because the product structure is more flexible than the functional structure, it is best suited for unstable environments, when an ability to adapt rapidly to change is important. On the down side, coordination across product lines and divisions is difficult. And although managers learn to become generalists, they may not acquire the depth of expertise that develops in the functional structure. Functions are not centralized at headquarters, and the duplication of effort is expensive. And because decision making is decentralized, top management can lose control over decisions made in the divisions. Proper management of all the issues surrounding decentralization and delegation, as discussed earlier, is essential for this structure to be effective.[31]

- *Customer divisions*—Divisions are built around groups of customers. Pfizer recently replaced divisions based on location with three based on customer groups: primary care,

● DIVISIONAL ORGANIZATION
Departmentalization that groups units around products, customers, or geographic regions.

specialty care, and emerging markets. The pharmaceutical company hopes that this structure will make the company more responsive to the needs of doctors and their patients in each group.[32] Similarly, a hospital may organize its services around child, adult, psychiatric, and emergency cases. Bank loan departments commonly have separate groups handling consumer and business needs.

- *Geographic divisions*—Divisions are structured around geographic regions. Geographic distinctions include district, territory, region, and country. Macy's Group, formerly Federated Department Stores, has geographic divisions for its operations serving particular states or regions of the United States: Macy's East, Macy's Florida, Macy's Midwest, Macy's North, Macy's Northwest, Macy's South, and Macy's West, as well as Macys.com for online shoppers. Executives at Ford Motor Company include the CEO of Ford of Europe, the CEO of Ford of Mexico, and the president of Ford Motor (China) Ltd.

The primary advantage of the product, customer, and regional approaches to departmentalization is the ability to focus on customer needs and provide faster, better service. But again, duplication of activities across many customer groups and geographic areas is expensive.

Establishing customer divisions improved strategic decisions at Det Norske Veritas (DNV), a Norwegian firm that provides services related to risk management. Initially, the company's management assumed that any collaboration across divisions would build sales and profits, but the first effort flopped. Management tried combining the efforts of two business units: its consulting group and a unit that inspects food companies' production chains. The idea was that the combined groups could help food companies reduce risks in their supply chains. However, the group members were slow to share information about customers, thought time spent on the joint project undermined the work of their own division (which was how their performance was measured), and engaged in conflicts that caused project delays and cost overruns.

Disappointed with these early results, DNV's executives evaluated their decision making and realized they were assembling a collaboration project without first prioritizing the market opportunities, identifying the impact on each division's profits, and rewarding employees for collaborating. To improve future decisions, they restructured the company into business units serving particular markets. Based on market knowledge, each unit then investigated where collaboration would make sense for serving the needs of its market. Because the whole unit would benefit, it became easier to tie rewards to collaboration. One success came from the business unit serving the maritime industry. Managers determined that the IT specialists in this unit could collaborate with the risk management group to help shipping companies manage the risk of their computer systems malfunctioning. This time, customers *and* employees were enthusiastic.[33]

Matrix organizations try to be the best of both worlds

A **matrix organization** is a hybrid form of organization in which functional and divisional forms overlap. Managers and staff personnel report to two bosses—a functional manager and a divisional manager—creating a dual line of command. In Figure 6.5, for example, each project manager draws employees from each functional area to form a group for the project. The employees working on those projects report to the individual project manager as well as to the manager of their functional area.

A good example of the matrix structure can be found at Time Inc., the top magazine publisher in the United States and United Kingdom. At major Time Inc. titles like *Time, Sports Illustrated,* and *People,* production managers who are responsible for getting the magazines printed report both to the individual publishers and editors of each title *and* to a senior corporate executive in charge of production. At the corporate level, Time Inc. achieves enormous economies of scale by buying paper and printing in bulk and by coordinating production activities for the company as a whole. At the same time, production managers working at each title ensure the different needs and schedules of their individual magazines are met. Similar matrix arrangements are in place for other key managers, like circulation and finance. In this way, the company attempts to benefit from both the divisional and functional organization structures.

Like other organization structures, the matrix has both strengths and weaknesses:[34]

Advantages

- Decision making is decentralized to a level where information is processed properly and relevant knowledge is applied.

- Extensive communications networks help process large amounts of information.

- With decisions delegated to appropriate levels, higher management levels are not overloaded with operational decisions.

- Resource utilization is efficient because key resources are shared across several important programs or products at the same time.

- Employees learn the collaborative skills needed to function in an environment characterized by frequent meetings and more informal interactions.

- Dual career ladders are elaborated as more career options become available on both sides of the organization.

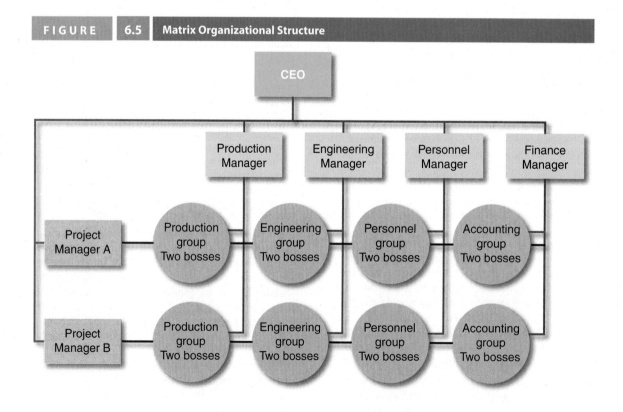

FIGURE 6.5 Matrix Organizational Structure

Disadvantages

- Confusion can arise because people do not have a single superior to whom they feel primary responsibility.

- The design encourages managers who share subordinates to jockey for power.

- The mistaken belief can arise that matrix management is the same thing as group decision making—in other words, everyone must be consulted for every decision.

- Too much democracy can lead to not enough action.

Many of the disadvantages stem from the matrix's inherent violation of the unity-of-command principle, which states that a person should have only one boss. Reporting to two superiors can create confusion and a difficult interpersonal situation, unless steps are taken to prevent these problems.

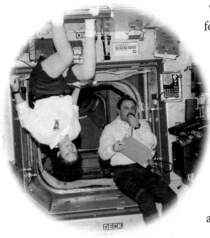

Organizations with highly specialized staff, such as NASA, typically use a matrix structure. Astronaut Susan J. Helms (left) is shown here with Russian cosmonaut Yury V. Usachev in the International Space Station.

matrix survival skills To a large degree, problems can be avoided if the key managers in the matrix learn the behavioral skills demanded in the matrix structure.[35] These skills vary depending on the manager's job. The *top executive* must learn to balance power and emphasis between the product and functional orientations. The middle managers, who are *product* or *division managers* and *functional managers,* must learn to collaborate and manage their conflicts constructively. Finally, the *two-boss managers,* who report to a product or division manager and to a functional manager, must learn how to be responsible to two superiors. This means prioritizing multiple demands and sometimes even reconciling conflicting orders. Some people function poorly under this ambiguous circumstance, which signals the end of their careers with the company. Others learn to be proactive, communicate effectively with both superiors, rise above the difficulties, and manage these work relationships constructively.

the matrix form today The popularity of the matrix form waned during the late 1980s, when many companies had difficulty implementing it. But lately, it has come back. Reasons for this resurgence include pressures to consolidate costs and be faster to market, creating a need for better coordination across functions in the business units, and a need for coordination across countries for firms with global business strategies. Many of the challenges created by the matrix are particularly acute in an international context, mainly because of the distances involved and the differences in local markets.[36]

The key to managing today's matrix is not the formal structure itself but the realization that the matrix is a *process.* Among managers who have adopted the matrix structure because of the complexity of the challenges they confront, many who had trouble implementing it failed to change the employee and managerial relationships within their organizations. Flexible organizations cannot be created merely by changing their structure. To allow information to flow freely throughout an organization, managers must also attend to the norms, values, and attitudes that shape people's behavior.[37]

Network organizations are built on collaboration

So far, we have been discussing variations of the traditional, hierarchical organization, within which all the business functions of the firm are performed. In contrast, a network organization is a collection of independent, mostly single-function firms that collaborate to produce a good or service. As depicted in

A+

TIP

The value of collaboration is particularly pronounced in a matrix organization. In the kind of structure illustrated in Figure 6.5, project group members may not be permanently assigned to the project manager. They may return to their functional area once the project has been completed. For this group to work effectively, the traditional command-and-control management style may not be the most appropriate. It might gain *compliance* from group members, but not their full *commitment,* making it harder to achieve the project's goals. Also, as the matrix organization draws on members of functional groups to tap their expertise, it is very important to get their full contribution. A collaborative process, in which the manager and participants develop a shared sense of ownership for the work they are doing, will generate better ideas, participation, and commitment to the project and its outcomes.

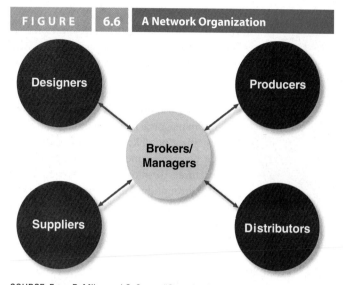

FIGURE 6.6 **A Network Organization**

Designers

Producers

Brokers/Managers

Suppliers

Distributors

SOURCE: From R. Miles and C. Snow, "Organizations: New Concepts for New Forms," *California Management Review*, Spring 1986, p. 65. Copyright © 1986 by The Regents of the University of California. Reprinted from the *California Management Review*, vol. 28, no. 3.

Figure 6.6, the network organization describes not one organization but a web of relationships among many firms. Network organizations are flexible arrangements among designers, suppliers, producers, distributors, and customers in which each firm is able to pursue its own distinctive core competence yet work effectively with other members of the network. Often members of the network share information electronically to respond quickly to customer demands. The normal boundary of the organization becomes blurred or porous, as managers within the organization interact closely with network members outside it. The network as a whole, then, can display the technical specialization of the functional structure, the market responsiveness of the product structure, and the balance and flexibility of the matrix.[38]

A very flexible version of the network organization is the **dynamic network**—also called the *modular* or *virtual* corporation. It is composed of temporary arrangements among members that can be assembled and reassembled to meet a changing competitive environment. The members of the network are held together by contracts that stipulate results expected (market mechanisms), rather than by hierarchy and authority. Poorly performing firms can be removed and replaced.

Such arrangements are common in the electronics, toy, and apparel industries, each of which creates and sells trendy products at a fast pace. Dynamic networks also are suited to organizations in which much of the work can be done independently by experts. For example, the more than 200 graphic designers affiliated with Logoworks provide design services to small-business customers looking for professional work without the overhead expense of an advertising agency. A popular Logoworks product is a $399 set of logo design ideas from three designers; the client picks his or her favorite, all the designers are paid a set fee, and the designer whose idea is chosen earns a bonus. Logoworks conducts marketing online, hires some designers, and negotiates freelance contracts with the rest.[39]

Successful networks potentially offer flexibility, innovation, quick responses to threats and opportunities, and reduced costs

Kiva's Network Reaches across the Globe

Imagine a not-for-profit network that invites strangers to lend money to other strangers—entrepreneurs scrambling to survive in developing countries. The loans are repaid 99 percent of the time. Aside from the likely repayment, the lender realizes no return on the investment—just the satisfaction of helping another individual succeed.

Pie in the sky? That's what venture capitalists told Matt and Jessica Flannery when the pair outlined their idea for a person-to-person microlending organization. Yet today Kiva is making a difference in the lives of hundreds of thousands of Third World entrepreneurs.

Here's how this network organization works. Would-be lenders visit Kiva's Web site (www.kiva.org), review the pictures and stories of the entrepreneurs profiled there, select one or more to support (lending $25 to $150 per individual entrepreneur), and wire the money. PayPal forwards the cash to a microfinance institution (MFI) in the entrepreneur's country. The MFI processes the loan, delivering the money in local currency to the individual's home. These "bankers on bikes" charge, on average, 20 percent interest—a far cry from the going rate of 100 to 200 percent in developing countries.

Since its launch in 2005, Kiva has raised loans totaling over $27 million from more than 270,000 people. Most are repaid within a year; only about 1 percent go into default. Kiva's operations are transparent. While Kiva scrutinizes MFIs carefully before affiliating with them (and the MFIs, in turn, vet the borrowers), some relationships don't pan out. The details of bad alliances and deadbeat borrowers are posted matter-of-factly for all to peruse.

The first recipient of Kiva funding was a Ugandan woman who operated a fish market. A $550 loan enabled her to expand her business and hire extra help. She repaid the loan within months.

Premal Shah (left) and Matt Flannery are the co-founders of Kiva.org, which they started in 2005. They appear here outside the office of Kiva.org in San Francisco, California.

Who provides the loans? Contributors are evenly distributed from ages 25 to 60. Slightly more than half are male; two-thirds earn more

and risk. But for these arrangements to be successful, several things must occur:

- The firm must choose the right specialty. It must be something (good or service) that the market needs and that the firm is better at providing than other firms—its core competence.
- The firm must choose collaborators that also are excellent at what they do and that provide complementary strengths.
- The firm must make certain that all parties fully understand the strategic goals of the partnership.
- Each party must be able to trust all the others with strategic information and also trust that each collaborator will deliver quality products even if the business grows quickly and makes heavy demands.

The role of managers shifts in a network from that of command and control to more like that of a **broker**. Broker/managers serve several important boundary roles that aid network integration and coordination:[40]

- *Designer role.* The broker serves as a network architect who envisions a set of groups or firms whose collective expertise could be focused on a particular good or service.
- *Process engineering role.* The broker serves as a *network cooperator* who takes the initiative to lay out the flow of resources and relationships and makes certain that everyone shares the same goals, standards, payments, and the like.
- *Nurturing role.* The broker serves as a network developer who nurtures and enhances the network (like team building) to make certain the relationships are healthy and mutually beneficial.

LO 7 WHAT YOU NEED TO KNOW . . .
Can you describe important mechanisms used to coordinate work?

ORGANIZATIONAL INTEGRATION

Besides structuring their organization around *differentiation*—the way the organization is composed of different jobs and tasks, and the way they fit on an organization chart—managers also need to consider *integration* and *coordination*—the way all parts of the organization work together. Often, the more differentiated the organization, the more difficult integration may be. Because of specialization and the division of labor, different groups of managers and employees develop different orientations. Employees think and act differently depending on whether they are in a functional department or a divisional group, are line or staff, and so on. When they focus on their particular units, it is difficult for managers to integrate all their activities.

Managers can use a variety of approaches to foster coordination among interdependent units and individuals. In some situations, managers might see that employees need to work closely together to achieve joint objectives, so they build mutual trust, train employees in a common set of skills, and reward teamwork. In other situations, organizations might rely more on

than $50,000 a year. By contrast, more women than men receive Kiva loans (women also have a higher repayment rate). While most not-for-profit organizations siphon off as much as 50 percent of contributions for administrative expenses, 100 percent of the monies donated to Kiva goes for loans.

Kiva president Premal Shah became interested in microfinance while studying economics at Stanford and received a grant to research the subject in India. Later, Shah joined PayPal as a product manager; today, PayPal waives all transaction fees in moving the cash to the recipient. Shah remarks, "The concept of getting a little bit of credit and someone taking a bet on you so you can pull yourself up by your bootstraps is very American." Maybe so, but its impact has been felt in dozens of countries.

Q: Discussion Questions

- How might the flexibility of a network organization enable Kiva to meet a need more effectively than traditional lenders can?
- Who are the collaborators in Kiva? How does the organization cultivate trust among these participants?

SOURCES: "When Small Loans Make a Big Difference," *Forbes,* June 3, 2008, http://www.forbes.com; Jeffrey M. O'Brien, "The Only Nonprofit That Matters," *Fortune,* February 26, 2008, http://money.cnn.com; Lee Rickwood, "Next Gen Giving: Charity and Social Networks," *PC World,* February 20, 2008, http://www.pcworld.ca; and Elinor Mills, "Kiva Humanizes Microlending to Third-World Entrepreneurs," *CNET News,* February 8, 2008.

individuals with unique talents and ideas, so they set up flexible work arrangements and reward individual achievements, while encouraging employees to share knowledge and develop respect for one another's contributions.[41] In general, however, coordination methods include standardization, plans, and mutual adjustment.[42]

Standardization coordinates work through rules and routines

When organizations coordinate activities by establishing routines and standard operating procedures that remain in place over time, we say that work has been standardized. **Standardization** constrains actions and integrates various units by regulating what people do. People often know how to act—and how to interact—because standard operating procedures spell out what they should do. For example, managers may establish standards for which types of computer equipment the organization will use. This simplifies the purchasing and training processes (everyone is on a common platform) and helps the different parts of the organization communicate.

To improve coordination, organizations may also rely on **formalization**—the presence of rules and regulations governing how people in the organization interact. Simple, often written, policies regarding attendance, dress, and decorum, for example, may help eliminate a good deal of uncertainty at work.

An important assumption underlying both standardization and formalization is that the rules and procedures should apply to most (if not all) situations. These approaches, therefore, are most appropriate in situations that are relatively stable and unchanging. In some cases, when the work environment requires flexibility, coordination by standardization may not be very effective. Who hasn't experienced a time when rules and procedures—frequently associated with a slow bureaucracy—prevented timely action to address a problem? In these instances, we often refer to rules and regulations as "red tape."[43]

Plans set a common direction

If laying out the exact rules and procedures by which work should be integrated is difficult, organizations may provide more latitude by establishing goals and schedules for interdependent units. **Coordination by plan** does not require the same high degree of stability and routinization required for coordination by standardization. Interdependent units are free to modify and adapt their actions as long as they meet the deadlines and targets required for working with others.

In writing this textbook, for example, we (the authors) sat down with a publication team that included the editors, the marketing staff, the production group, and support staff. Together we ironed out a schedule for developing this book that covered approximately a two-year period. That development plan included dates and "deliverables" that specified what was to be accomplished and forwarded to the others in the organization. The plan gave each subunit enough flexibility, and the overall approach allowed us to work together effectively.

Mutual adjustment allows flexible coordination

Ironically, the simplest and most flexible approach to coordination may just be to have interdependent parties talk to one another. **Coordination by mutual adjustment** involves feedback and discussions to jointly figure out how to approach problems and devise solutions that are agreeable to everyone. The popularity of teams today is in part due to the fact that they allow for flexible coordination; teams can operate under the principle of mutual adjustment.

> The Chinese motorcycle industry has figured out how to coordinate hundreds of suppliers in the design and manufacturing of motorcycles. Together, these small firms collaborate by working from rough blueprints to design, construct, and assemble related components, and then deliver them to another plant for final assembly. Because design and assembly are decentralized, suppliers can move quickly to make adjustments, try out new components, and make more changes if necessary before delivering a product for final assembly.
>
> Using this approach, the Chinese motorcycle industry is now designing and building new motorcycles faster and less expensively than any other country in the world. In fact, production has quadrupled from 5 million motorcycles a year to 20 million—which gives China about 50 percent of the worldwide motorcycle market.[44]

But the flexibility of mutual adjustment as a coordination device carries some cost. Hashing out every issue takes time and may not be the most expedient approach for organizing work. Imagine how long it would take to accomplish even the most basic tasks if subunits had to talk through every situation. Still, mutual adjustment can be very effective when problems are novel and cannot be programmed in advance with rules, procedures, or plans. Particularly during crises, in which rules and

STANDARDIZATION Establishing common routines and procedures that apply uniformly to everyone.

FORMALIZATION The presence of rules and regulations governing how people in the organization interact.

COORDINATION BY PLAN Interdependent units are required to meet deadlines and objectives that contribute to a common goal.

COORDINATION BY MUTUAL ADJUSTMENT Units interact with one another to make accommodations in order to achieve flexible coordination.

That Was THEN . . .

The automobile production line was a revolutionary way to organize manufacturing work. Its efficient assembly lines turned out identical copies of models at record pace. Before, parts for products had to be individually handcrafted and fitted together.

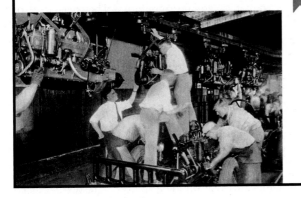

This Is NOW . . .

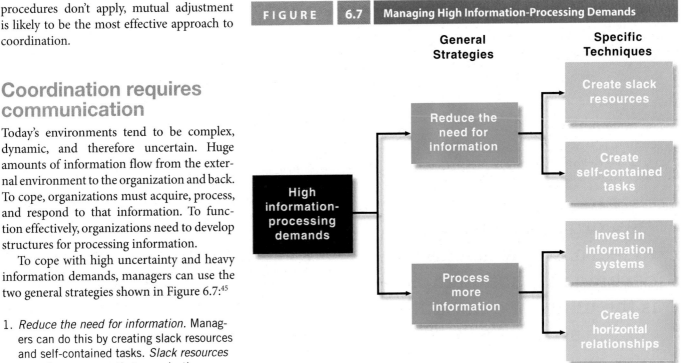

Some companies today have moved beyond mass production. Massachusetts-based Seven Cycles uses both high-tech computer programs and precision handcrafting to produce custom-built bikes tailored to each cyclist's specific needs and wants.

---

procedures don't apply, mutual adjustment is likely to be the most effective approach to coordination.

Coordination requires communication

Today's environments tend to be complex, dynamic, and therefore uncertain. Huge amounts of information flow from the external environment to the organization and back. To cope, organizations must acquire, process, and respond to that information. To function effectively, organizations need to develop structures for processing information.

To cope with high uncertainty and heavy information demands, managers can use the two general strategies shown in Figure 6.7:[45]

1. *Reduce the need for information.* Managers can do this by creating slack resources and self-contained tasks. *Slack resources* are extra resources that organizations

| FIGURE | 6.7 | Managing High Information-Processing Demands |

General Strategies → **Specific Techniques**

High information-processing demands →
- Reduce the need for information →
  - Create slack resources
  - Create self-contained tasks
- Process more information →
  - Invest in information systems
  - Create horizontal relationships

● ● **CHAPTER 6** Organizing for Action **143**

Information sharing is vital at the National Counterterrorism Center. Technology is used to enable the efficient and safe execution of information sharing.

can rely on in a pinch. For example, a company that carries inventory does not need as much information about sales demand or lead time. Part-time and temporary employees are another type of slack resource, because using them helps employers get around perfectly forecasting sales peaks. *Creating self-contained tasks* refers to changing from a functional organization to a product or project organization and giving each unit the resources it needs to perform its task. Information-processing problems are reduced because each unit has its own full complement of specialties, and communications flow within each team, rather than among a complex array of interdependent groups.

experience of the organization's human assets to increase collaboration and effectiveness. Managers may foster knowledge management by creating horizontal relationships. These may be as simple as assigning someone to serve as a *liaison* between groups, or they may be more complex, such as an interdepartmental task force or team.[46]

L O 8 WHAT YOU NEED TO KNOW . . .
How can organizations improve their agility?

ORGANIZATIONAL AGILITY

Managers today place a premium on *agility*—being able to act, and act fast, to meet customer needs and respond to other outside pressures. They want to correct past mistakes quickly and also to prepare for an uncertain future. They need to respond to threats and capitalize on opportunities when they come along. The particular structure the organization adopts to accomplish agility will depend on its *strategy,* its *customers,* and its *technology.*

Strategies promote organizational agility

Certain strategies, and the structures, processes, and relationships that accompany them, seem particularly well suited to improving an organization's ability to respond quickly and effectively to the challenges it faces. They reflect managers'

> "When I got [to Intuit], . . . I changed only one word in the operating values: I changed 'Think fast, move fast' to 'Think smart, move fast.' Because doing dumb things faster doesn't get you anywhere."
>
> —Steve Bennett, Intuit CEO[47]

2. *Increase information-processing capability.* An organization may do this by *investing in information systems* or engaging in *knowledge management*—capitalizing on the intellect and

> "An organization's ability to learn, and translate that learning into action rapidly, is the ultimate competitive advantage."
>
> —Jack Welch

determination to fully leverage people and assets to make the firm more agile and competitive. These strategies and structures are based on the firm's core competencies, strategic alliances, and abilities to learn, to engage all its people in achieving its objectives, and to adapt its structure to its size.

organizing around core competencies
A recent and important perspective on strategy and organization hinges on the concept of *core competence.*[48] As you learned in Chapter 4, a core competence is the capability—knowledge, expertise, skill—that underlies a company's ability to be a leader in providing a range of goods or services. It allows the company to compete on the basis of its core strengths and expertise, not just on what it produces.

Successfully developing a world-class core competence opens the door to a variety of opportunities; failure means being foreclosed from many markets. Thus, a well-understood, well-developed core competence can enhance a company's responsiveness and competitiveness. Strategically, companies must commit to excellence and leadership in competencies and strengthen them before they can win market share for specific products. Organizationally, the corporation should be viewed as a portfolio of competencies, not just of specific businesses.

Music and Coffee—A Harmonious Strategic Alliance! Apple and Starbucks created a partnership that allows Apple customers to sync to the Starbucks wireless internet network instantly from their iPod Touch, Macs, and iPhones to download music.

Managers who want to strengthen their firms' competitiveness need to focus on several related issues:

- Identify existing core competencies.
- Acquire or build core competencies that will be important for the future.
- Keep investing in competencies, so the firm remains world-class and better than competitors.
- Extend competencies to find new applications and opportunities for the markets of tomorrow.[49]

Keep in mind that it's not enough for an organization to *have* valuable resources that provide competencies; those resources have to be *managed* in a way that gives the organization an advantage.[50] That means managers have to do three things:

1. *Accumulate the right resources (such as talented people)*—Managers must determine what resources they need, acquire and develop those resources, and eliminate resources that don't provide value.

2. *Combine the resources in ways that give the organization capabilities,* such as researching new products or resolving problems for customers—These combinations may involve knowledge sharing and alliances between departments or with other organizations.

3. *Leverage or exploit their resources*—Managers must identify the opportunities where their competencies deliver value to customers (say, by creating new products or delivering existing products better than competitors) and then coordinate and deploy the employees and other resources needed to respond to those opportunities.

strategic alliances The modern organization has a variety of links with other organizations that are more complex than traditional stakeholder relationships. Today even fierce competitors are working together at unprecedented levels to achieve their strategic goals. For example, Federal Express has drop-off boxes at U.S. Postal Service facilities. The New York Times Company and Monster Worldwide formed an alliance in which job advertisements for 19 newspapers will carry the Monster.com brand. The arrangement gives the newspaper company, whose papers include the *New York Times* and *Boston Globe,* a stronger online presence and gives Monster better visibility in local job markets, which have traditionally been dominated by local papers.[51]

A strategic alliance is a formal relationship created with the purpose of joint pursuit of mutual goals. In a strategic alliance, individual organizations share administrative authority, form social links, and accept joint ownership. Such alliances are blurring firms' boundaries. They occur between companies and their competitors, governments, and universities. Such partnering often crosses national and cultural boundaries. Companies form strategic alliances to develop new technologies, enter new markets, and reduce manufacturing costs through outsourcing. Not only can alliances enable companies to move ahead faster and more efficiently, but they also are sometimes the only practical way to bring together the variety of specialists needed for operating in today's complex and fast-changing environment. Rather than hiring the experts who understand the technology and market segments for each new product, companies can form alliances with partners that already have those experts on board.[52]

Managers typically devote plenty of time to screening potential partners in financial terms. But for the alliance to work, the partners also must consider one another's areas of expertise and the incentives involved in the structure of the alliance. A comparison of research and development alliances found that the most innovation occurred when the partners were experts in moderately different types of research. If the partners were very different, they shared ideas and innovated more when the alliance was set up through equity (stock) ownership; for similar partners, they innovated more under a contract to do the research.[53]

Managers also must develop the human relationships in the partnership. The best alliances are true partnerships that meet the following criteria:[54]

• *Individual excellence:* Both partners add value, and their motives are positive (pursue opportunity) rather than negative (mask weaknesses).

• *Importance:* Both partners want the relationship to work because it helps them meet long-term strategic objectives.

• *Interdependence:* The partners need each other; each helps the other reach its goal.

• *Investment:* The partners devote financial and other resources to the relationship.

• *Information:* The partners communicate openly about goals, technical data, problems, and changing situations.

• *Integration:* The partners develop shared ways of operating; they teach each other and learn from each other.

• *Institutionalization:* The relationship has formal status with clear responsibilities.

• *Integrity:* Both partners are trustworthy and honorable.

Most of these ideas apply not only to strategic alliances but to any type of relationship.[55]

learning organizations

Being responsive requires continually changing and learning new ways to act. Some experts say the only sustainable advantage is learning faster than the competition. This has led to interest in an idea called the learning organization.[56] A **learning organization** is an organization skilled at creating, acquiring, and transferring knowledge, and at modifying its behavior to reflect new knowledge and insights.[57] GE, Corning, and Honda are good examples of learning organizations. Such organizations are skilled at solving problems, experimenting with new approaches, learning from their own experiences, learning from other organizations, and spreading knowledge quickly and efficiently.

How do firms become true learning organizations? There are a few important ingredients:[58]

• Their people engage in disciplined thinking and attention to details, making decisions based on data and evidence rather than guesswork and assumptions.

• They search constantly for new knowledge and ways to apply it, looking for expanding horizons and opportunities, not just quick fixes to current problems. The organization values and rewards individuals who expand their knowledge and skill in areas that benefit the organization.

• They carefully review successes and failures, looking for lessons and deeper understanding.

• They benchmark, that is, identify and implement the best practices of other organizations, stealing ideas shamelessly.

• They share ideas throughout the organization via reports, information systems, informal discussions, site visits, education, and training. Employees work with and are mentored by more-experienced employees.

high-involvement organizations

Another increasingly popular way to create a competitive advantage is participative management. Particularly in high-technology companies facing stiff international competition, the aim is to generate high levels of commitment and involvement as employees and managers work together to achieve organizational goals.

In a **high-involvement organization**, top management ensures that there is a consensus about the direction in which the business is heading. The leader seeks input from his or her top management team and from lower levels of the company. Task forces, study groups, and other techniques foster participation in decisions that affect the entire organization. Participants receive continual feedback regarding how they are doing compared with the competition and how effectively they are meeting the strategic agenda.

Structurally, this usually means that even lower-level employees have a direct relationship with a customer or supplier and thus receive feedback and are held accountable for delivering a good or service. The organization has a flat, decentralized structure built around a customer, good, or service. Employee involvement is particularly powerful when the environment changes rapidly, work is creative, complex activities require coordination, and firms need major breakthroughs in innovation and speed—in other words, when companies need to be more responsive.[59]

impact of organizational size

Large organizations are typically less organic and more bureaucratic. Jobs become more specialized, and distinct groups of specialists are created because large organizations can add a new specialty at lower proportional expense. The resulting complexity makes the organization harder to control, so management adds more levels to keep spans of control from becoming too large. Rules, procedures, and paperwork are also introduced.

But a huge, complex organization can find it hard to manage relationships with customers and among its own units. Larger companies also are more difficult to coordinate and control. While size may enhance efficiency, it also may create administrative difficulties that inhibit efficiency. Unilever, a giant consumer products company with more than 200,000 employees worldwide, not only has three organizations selling different product lines in each country it serves but until recently was run by two chairmen-CEOs, an artifact of a merger that took place decades ago. This cumbersome structure held back Unilever's efficiency and agility, making competition more difficult.[60] In contrast, smaller companies can move fast, provide quality goods and services to targeted market niches, and inspire greater involvement from their people.

Nimble, small firms frequently outmaneuver big bureaucracies, but size offers market power in buying and selling. The challenge, then, is to be both big and small to capitalize on the advantages of each. Solutions include decentralized decision making and the use of teams empowered to respond quickly to a changing environment.

 To stay flexible as it grew, Dur-A-Flex became a learning organization. As the company expanded from installing commercial and industrial flooring into also manufacturing the flooring systems and related products, its structure became too rigid. With separate manufacturing systems operating on three shifts, maintaining quality and speed across departments and shifts was awkward. Dur-A-Flex embarked on a program known as "lean" (described later in this chapter), which involves studying and improving every process. Every employee was trained in the methods and philosophy behind the lean approach.

According to Bill Greider, who led the lean initiative, "Once our focus turned to learning, everything changed." As employees began interacting in classes, divisions among groups slipped away. Employees learn about all aspects of Dur-A-Flex's business, from financial matters to flooring installation methods, as well as a variety of fun "electives" such as beer making. The learning approach not only helps employees cut costs and boost sales, but also builds their enthusiasm and empowers them.[61]

As large companies try to regain the responsiveness of small companies, they often consider *downsizing*, the planned elimination of positions, for example, by eliminating functions, hierarchical levels, or even whole units.[62] Recognizing that people will be unemployed and frightened, managers usually opt for downsizing only in response to pressure. Traditionally, companies have downsized when demand falls and seems unlikely to rebound soon. These layoffs save money so that the company can remain profitable—or at least viable—until the next upturn. More recently, however, global competition has forced companies to cut costs even when sales are strong and when, through technological advances, the same output can be produced by fewer employees. As a result, many companies have used downsizing to become more efficient. Whereas downsizing in response to a slowdown in demand has tended to have the most impact on operating-level jobs in manufacturing firms, downsizing to improve efficiency has focused on eliminating layers of management, so those layoffs target "white-collar" middle managers.

The recent recession has forced widespread downsizing across a variety of industries, not just manufacturing. For example, in response to a severe downturn in demand, Microsoft announced that, for the first time in its history, it would have to downsize, laying off about 5,000 employees (about 5 percent of its workforce). In a memo to employees, CEO Steve Ballmer acknowledged the risks of such an approach: "Our success at Microsoft has always been the direct result of the talent, hard work, and commitment of our people."[63] In effect, downsizing risks eliminating the very source of a company's success.

Done appropriately, downsizing can in fact make firms more agile. But even under the best circumstances, downsizing can be traumatic for an organization and its employees. Interestingly, the people who lose their jobs because of downsizing are not the only ones deeply affected. Those who keep their jobs tend to exhibit what has become known as *survivor's syndrome*.[64] They struggle with heavier workloads, wonder who will be next to go, try to figure out how to survive, lose commitment to the company and faith in their bosses, and become narrow-minded, self-absorbed, and risk-averse. Managers can engage in a number of positive practices to ease the pain and increase the effectiveness of downsizing:[65]

- Use downsizing only as a last resort, when other methods of improving performance by innovating or changing procedures have been exhausted.

- In choosing positions to eliminate, engage in careful analysis and strategic thinking.

- Train people to cope with the new situation.

- Identify and protect talented people.

- Give special attention and help to those who have lost their jobs.

- Communicate constantly with people about the process, and invite ideas for alternative ways to operate more efficiently.

- Identify how the organization will operate more effectively in the future, and emphasize this positive future and the remaining employees' new roles in attaining it.

Agile organizations focus on customers

In the end, the point of structuring a responsive, agile organization lies in enabling it to meet and exceed the expectations of its customers. Customers are vital to organizations because they purchase goods and services, and their continued relationships with the firm constitute the fundamental driver of sustained, long-term competitiveness and success. To meet customer needs, organizations focus on quality improvement.

organizing for quality improvement Managers may embed quality programs within any organizational structure. Total quality management (TQM) is a way of managing in which everyone is committed to continuous improvement of his or her part of the operation. TQM is a comprehensive approach to improving product quality and thereby customer satisfaction. It is characterized by a strong orientation toward customers (external and internal) and has become a theme for organizing work. TQM reorients managers toward involving people across departments in improving all aspects of the business. Continuous improvement requires mechanisms that facilitate group problem solving, information sharing, and cooperation across business functions. The walls that separate stages and functions of work tend to come down, and the organization operates in a team-oriented manner.[66]

One of the founders of the quality management movement was W. Edwards Deming. Deming's "14 points" of quality emphasize a holistic approach to management:

1. Create constancy of purpose—strive for long-term improvement rather than short-term profit.

2. Adopt the new philosophy—don't tolerate delays and mistakes.

3. Cease dependence on mass inspection—build quality into the process on the front end.

4. End the practice of awarding business on price tag alone—build long-term relationships.

5. Improve constantly and forever the system of production and service—at each stage.

6. Institute training and retraining—continually update methods and thinking.

7. Institute leadership—provide the resources needed for effectiveness.

8. Drive out fear—people must believe it is safe to report problems or ask for help.

9. Break down barriers among departments—promote teamwork.

10. Eliminate slogans, exhortations, and arbitrary targets—supply methods, not buzzwords.

11. Eliminate numerical quotas—they are contrary to the idea of continuous improvement.

12. Remove barriers to pride in workmanship—allow autonomy and spontaneity.

13. Institute a vigorous program of education and retraining—people are assets, not commodities.

14. Take action to accomplish the transformation—provide a structure that enables quality.

One of the most important contributors to total quality management has been the introduction of statistical tools to analyze the causes of product defects, in an approach called *Six Sigma Quality.* Sigma is the Greek letter used to designate the estimated standard deviation or variation in a process. (The higher the "sigma level," the lower the amount of variation.) The product defects analyzed may include anything that results in customer dissatisfaction—for example, late delivery, wrong shipment, or poor customer service, as well as problems with the product itself. When the defect has been identified, managers then engage the organization in a comprehensive effort to eliminate its causes and reduce it to the lowest practicable level. At Six Sigma, a product or process is defect-free 99.99966 percent of the time. Reaching that goal almost always requires managers to restructure their internal processes and relationships with suppliers and customers in fundamental ways. For example, managers may have to create teams from all parts of the organization to implement the process improvements that will prevent defects from arising.

The influence of TQM on the organizing process has become even more acute with the emergence of ISO standards. ISO 9001 is a series of voluntary quality standards developed by a committee working under the International Organization for Standardization (known as ISO), a network of national standards institutions in more than 150 countries. In contrast to most ISO standards, which describe a particular material, product, or process, the ISO 9001 standards apply to management systems at any organization and address eight principles:[67]

1. Customer focus—learning and addressing customer needs and expectations.

2. Leadership—establishing a vision and goals, establishing trust, and providing employees with the resources and inspiration to meet goals.

3. Involvement of people—establishing an environment in which employees understand their contribution, engage in problem solving, and acquire and share knowledge.

4. Process approach—defining the tasks needed to successfully carry out each process and assigning responsibility for them.

● SMALL BATCH Technologies that produce goods and services in low volume.

● LARGE BATCH Technologies that produce goods and services in high volume.

● CONTINUOUS PROCESS A process that is highly automated and has a continuous production flow.

● MASS CUSTOMIZATION The production of varied, individually customized products at the low cost of standardized, mass-produced products.

5. System approach to management—putting processes together into efficient systems that work together effectively.

6. Continual improvement—teaching people how to identify areas for improvement and rewarding them for making improvements.

7. Factual approach to decision making—gathering accurate performance data, sharing the data with employees, and using the data to make decisions.

8. Mutually beneficial supplier relationships—working in a cooperative way with suppliers.

U.S. companies first became interested in ISO 9001 because overseas customers, particularly those in the European Union, embraced it. Now some U.S. customers are making the same demand. As a result, hundreds of thousands of companies in manufacturing and service industries around the world are ISO certified. For example, UniFirst Corporation, a Massachusetts-based provider of workplace uniforms and protective work clothing, obtained ISO certification for its two Mexican plants through a process that included documenting all the facilities' processes and training employees in quality control.[68]

Technology can support agility

Another critical factor affecting an organization's structure and responsiveness is its *technology*. Broadly speaking, technology can be viewed as the methods, processes, systems, and skills used to transform resources (inputs) into products (outputs). Although we will discuss technology—and innovation—more fully later, in this chapter we want to highlight some of the important influences technology has on organizational design.

PMF Industries, a small custom metalworking company in Williamsport, Pennsylvania, produces stainless steel assemblies for medical and other uses. In the service industry, restaurants and doctors' offices provide a variety of low-volume, customized services. In a small batch organization, structure tends to be organic, with few rules and formal procedures, and decision making tends to be decentralized. The emphasis is on mutual adjustment among people.

- *Large batch technologies*—Companies with higher volumes and lower varieties than a job shop tend to be characterized as large batch, or mass production technologies. Examples include the auto assembly operations of General Motors and Ford, and in the service sector, McDonald's and Burger King. Their production runs tend to be standardized, and customers receive similar (if not identical) products. Machines may replace people in the physical execution of work. Structure tends to be more mechanistic. There are more rules and formal procedures, and decision making is more centralized with higher spans of control. Communication tends to be more formal, and hierarchical authority more prominent.

- *Continuous process technologies*—At the high-volume end of the scale are companies that use continuous process technologies, technologies that do not stop and start. Domino Sugar and Shell Chemical, for example, use continuous process technologies to produce a very limited number of products. People are completely removed from the work itself, which is done by machines and computers. People may run the computers that run the machines. Structure can return to a more organic form because less supervision is needed. Communication tends to be more informal, and fewer rules and regulations are established.

"Information technology and business are becoming inextricably interwoven. I don't think anyone can talk meaningfully about one without talking about the other."

—Bill Gates

technology configurations Research by Joan Woodward laid the foundation for understanding technology and structure. According to Woodward, three basic technologies characterize how work is done in service as well as manufacturing companies:[69]

- *Small batch technologies*—When goods or services are provided in very low volume or small batches, a company that does such work is called a *job shop*. For example,

organizing for flexible manufacturing Although issues of volume and variety are often seen as trade-offs in a technological sense, today organizations are trying to produce both high-volume and high-variety products at the same time. This is referred to as mass customization.[70] Automobiles, clothes, computers, and other products are increasingly being manufactured to match each customer's taste, specifications, and budget. You can now buy clothes cut to your proportions, supplements with the exact blend of the vitamins and

minerals you like, CDs with the music tracks you choose, and textbooks whose chapters are picked by your professor.

How do companies manage this type of customization at such low cost? As shown in Table 6.1, they organize around a dynamic network of relatively independent operating units.[71] Each unit performs a specific process or task—called a *module*—such as making a component, performing a credit check, or performing a particular welding method. Some modules may be performed by outside suppliers or vendors.

Different modules join forces to make the good or provide a service. How and when the various modules interact with one another are dictated by the unique requests of each customer. The manager's responsibility is to make it easier and less costly for modules to come together, complete their tasks, and then recombine to meet the next customer demand. The ultimate goal of mass customization is a never-ending campaign to expand the number of ways a company can satisfy customers.

One technological advance that has helped make mass customization possible is *computer-integrated manufacturing (CIM)*, which encompasses a host of computerized production efforts, including computer-aided design and computer-aided manufacturing. These systems can produce high-variety and high-volume products at the same time.[72] They may also offer greater control and predictability of production processes, reduced waste, faster throughput times, and higher quality. But managers cannot "buy" their way out of competitive trouble simply by investing in superior technology alone. They must also ensure that their organization has the necessary strategic and people strengths and a well-designed plan for integrating the new technology within the organization.

As the name implies, *flexible factories* provide more production options and a greater variety of products. They differ from traditional factories in three primary ways:[73]

1. The traditional factory has long production runs, generating high volumes of a standardized product. Flexible factories have much shorter production runs, with many different products.

2. Traditional factories move parts down the line from one location in the production sequence to the next. Flexible factories are organized around products, in work cells or teams, so that people work closely together and parts move shorter distances with shorter or no delays.

TABLE 6.1	Key Features in Mass Customization
Products	High variety and customization
Product design	Collaborative design; significant input from customers Short product development cycles Constant innovation
Operations and processes	Flexible processes Business process reengineering (BPR) Use of modules Continuous improvement (CI) Reduced setup and changeover times Reduced lead times JIT delivery and processing of materials and components Production to order Shorter cycle times Use of information technology (IT)
Quality management	Quality measured in customer delight Defects treated as capability failures
Organizational structure	Dynamic network of relatively autonomous operating units Learning relationships Integration of the value chain Team-based structure
Workforce management	Empowerment of employees High value on knowledge, information, and diversity of employee capabilities New product teams Broad job descriptions
Emphasis	Low-cost production of high-quality, customized products

SOURCE: Reprinted with permission of APICS—The Educational Society for Resource Management, *Production and Inventory Management* 41, no. 1 (2000), pp. 56–65.

3. Traditional factories use centralized scheduling, which is time-consuming, inaccurate, and slow to adapt to changes. Flexible factories use local or decentralized scheduling, in which decisions are made on the shop floor by the people doing the work.

Another organizing approach is **lean manufacturing**, based on a commitment to making an operation both efficient and effective; it strives to achieve the highest possible productivity and total quality, cost-effectively, by eliminating unnecessary steps in the production process and continually striving for improvement. Rejects are unacceptable, and staff, overhead, and inventory are considered wasteful. In a lean operation, the emphasis is on quality, speed, and flexibility more than on cost, efficiency, and hierarchy. If an employee spots a problem, the employee is authorized to halt the operation and signal for help to correct the problem at its source, so processes can be improved and future problems avoided. With a well-managed lean production process, a company can develop, produce, and distribute products with half or less of the human effort, space, tools, time, and overall cost.[74]

Toyota receives much of the credit for modeling and teaching a commitment to "think lean." Many manufacturing companies have tried to adopt a similar lean approach, but Toyota and others have also applied lean methods to nonmanufacturing processes. Toyota's product development, for example, also uses lean principles. The process begins with identifying what customers define as valuable so that employees don't waste time and money on things that customers don't care about. Early in the design process, teams bring together experts from various functions to identify potential problems and identify as many solutions as they can, to avoid the need to make design changes later in the process. Managers use their experience with past product development efforts to predict staffing requirements, and employees and technicians working for suppliers are assigned to projects only as they are needed. Further adding to efficiency and quality, the company uses standard parts, procedures, and skill sets wherever possible; detailed checklists help engineers ensure they are using best practices. With methods such as these, Toyota has been able to develop top-quality products faster and more consistently than its competitors. Similar approaches have also been used to improve services, such as operations at hospitals. St. Agnes Hospital in Baltimore has used lean principles to reduce costs and patient waiting times while improving safety, and the ThedaCare health system in Wisconsin saved more than $3 million in one year of using lean methods.[75]

For the lean approach to result in more effective operations, the following conditions must be met:[76]

- People are broadly trained rather than specialized.

● **LEAN MANUFACTURING** An operation that strives to achieve the highest possible productivity and total quality, cost-effectively, by eliminating unnecessary steps in the production process and continually striving for improvement.

● **JUST-IN-TIME (JIT)** A system that calls for subassemblies and components to be manufactured in very small lots and delivered to the next stage of the production process just as they are needed.

- Communication is informal and horizontal among line workers.

- Equipment is general purpose.

- Work is organized in teams, or cells, that produce a group of similar products.

- Supplier relationships are long-term and cooperative.

- Product development is concurrent, not sequential, and is done by cross-functional teams.

organizing for speed: time-based competition

Companies worldwide have devoted so much energy to improving product quality that high quality is now the standard attained by all top competitors. Competition has driven quality to such heights that quality products no longer are enough to distinguish one company from another. Time has emerged as the key competitive advantage that can separate market leaders from also-rans.[77]

One way to compete based on time is to set up **just-in-time (JIT)** operations. JIT calls for subassemblies and components to be manufactured in very small lots and delivered to the next stage in the process precisely at the time needed, or "just in time." A customer order triggers a factory order and the production process. The supplying work centers do not produce the next lot of product until the consuming work center requires it. Even external suppliers deliver to the company just in time.

"Big will not beat small any more. It will be the fast beating the slow."

—Rupert Murdoch

Just-in-time is a companywide philosophy oriented toward eliminating waste and improving materials throughout all operations. In this way, excess inventory is eliminated and costs are reduced. The ultimate goal of JIT is to serve the customer better by providing higher levels of quality and service. For example, by making products perfectly, companies eliminate the need for costly and time-consuming inspections. Likewise, production processes are shortened when they are streamlined so that parts are actually being worked on

Saturn has earned a reputation for superior customer satisfaction. Some of that reputation can be credited to Saturn's world-class distribution system.

every minute they are in production, rather than sitting on a table, waiting for an operator.

Many believe that only a fraction of JIT's potential has been realized and that its impact will grow as it is applied to other processes, such as service, distribution, and new-product development.[78] However, it's important to keep in mind that JIT offers efficiency only when the costs of storing items are greater than the costs of frequent delivery.[79]

While JIT concentrates on reducing time in manufacturing, companies are speeding up research and product development through the use of *simultaneous engineering*. Traditionally, when R&D completed its part of the project, the work was "passed over the wall" to engineering, which completed its task and passed it over the wall to manufacturing, and so on. In contrast, simultaneous engineering incorporates the issues and perspectives of all the functions—and customers and suppliers—from the beginning of the process.

This team-based approach results in a higher-quality product that is designed for efficient manufacturing *and* customer needs.[80] In the automobile industry, tools such as computer-aided design and computer-aided manufacturing (CAD/CAM) support simultaneous engineering by letting various engineers submit elements and showing how these submissions affect the overall design and the manufacturing process. With a modern CAD system, automobile engineers can enter performance requirements into a spreadsheet, and the system will identify a design that meets cost and manufacturing requirements. This technology has helped automakers slash product development time.[81] In the realm of computing, some organizations have taken this idea much further, making the programming code for their products available to the public so that anyone at any time can develop new ideas to use with their product, and the organization can decide to license any ideas that seem to have market potential.

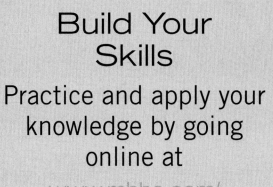

Build Your Skills

Practice and apply your knowledge by going online at

www.mhhe.com/ BatemanM2e

7

Managing Human Resources

In 1981, Pam Nicholson was a senior in college, and graduation was looming. So when recruiters from Enterprise Rent-A-Car appeared on campus, she jumped at the chance to interview. For Nicholson, who hoped to manage a small business someday, getting an offer to work behind the counter at an Enterprise rental location seemed ideal. Today, Nicholson is president and chief operating officer of the entire company. Industry observers might say that Nicholson's career success has something to do with the firm's formula for running a business: hire recent college grads looking for management experience, provide training and mentoring, promote from within, and put customers and employees first.[1]

Enterprise's approach to business is based on the expectation that success will follow from effective human resources management. **Human resources management (HRM)** deals with formal systems for managing people at work—one of the fundamental aspects of organizational and managerial life. Your first formal interaction with an

Stay in Touch

with the book's Web site for strategies today's managers use to find and keep valuable employees.

"Only when I had seen the mistrust and the passing of fault in a different service unit did I realize how essential the trust between service personnel and their managers is. If confidence is lacking from either side, then there is a good chance the accountability for mistakes and success will not be recognized, which in turn will create confusion and uncertainty."
—Ryan Kersten, Construction Manager

"Learning more about delegation would have been a great thing to learn in school as a manager. While you are in school you are the only one that can get assignments done, but when you are a manager you need to be able to give work to other people. It is hard at times because you want to be in control all the time, but it is a great way to build trust with people if you give them a task that needs to be done."
—Alicia Catalano, Sales Team Leader

WHAT YOU NEED TO KNOW

•• learning **OBJECTIVES**

After studying Chapter 7,
you should be able to:

LO1 Discuss how companies use human
resources management to gain competitive
advantage.

LO2 Give reasons why companies recruit both
internally and externally for new hires.

LO3 Identify various methods for selecting new
employees.

LO4 Evaluate the importance of spending on
training and development.

LO5 Explain alternatives for who appraises an
employee's performance.

LO6 Describe the fundamental aspects of a
reward system.

LO7 Summarize how unions and labor laws
influence human resources management.

● **HUMAN RESOURCES MANAGEMENT**
(HRM) Formal systems for the management of people within an organization.

> **"You can get capital and erect buildings, but it takes people to build a business."**
>
> —Thomas J. Watson, Founder, IBM

organization you wish to join will likely involve some aspect of its human resource function, and throughout your career as a manager you will be a part of, as well as be affected by, your organization's human resource management.

We begin this chapter by describing HRM as it relates to strategic management. Then we discuss the "nuts and bolts" of HRM: staffing, training, performance appraisal, rewards, and labor relations. Throughout the chapter, we discuss legal issues that affect each aspect of HRM.

(L)(O) **1 WHAT YOU NEED TO KNOW . . .**

How do companies use human resources management to gain competitive advantage?

STRATEGIC HUMAN RESOURCES MANAGEMENT

Human resources management plays a vital strategic role as organizations attempt to compete through people. You already know that firms can create a competitive advantage when they

possess or develop resources that are valuable, rare, inimitable, and organized. The same criteria apply to the strategic impact of human resources:

1. *People create value.* People can increase value by helping lower costs, provide something unique to customers, or both. Through empowerment, total quality initiatives, and continuous improvement, people at Corning, Xerox, and other companies add to the bottom line.

2. *Talent is rare.* People are a source of competitive advantage when their skills, knowledge, and abilities are not equally available to all competitors. Top companies invest in hiring and training the best and the brightest employees to gain a competitive advantage.

3. *A group of well-chosen, motivated people is difficult to imitate.* Competitors have difficulty matching the unique cultures of Disney, Southwest Airlines, and Mirage Resorts, which get the most from their employees.

4. *People can be organized for success.* People can deliver a competitive advantage when their talents are combined and deployed rapidly to work on new assignments at a moment's notice, as in the effective use of teamwork and collaboration.

These four criteria highlight the importance of people and show the close link between HRM and strategic management. Evidence is mounting that this focus brings positive business results. For example, a study by Deloitte & Touche associated the use of effective human resources practices with higher valuation of a company in the stock market.[2] Because employee skills, knowledge, and abilities are among an organization's most distinctive

Southwest Airlines is known for creating a unique culture that gets the most from employees. Southwest rewards its employees for excellent performance and maintains loyalty by offering free airfare, profit sharing, and other incentives. What benefits would you need to stay motivated?

and renewable resources, strategic management of people is more important than ever.

As more executives realize that their employees can be their organization's most valuable resources, human resources managers have played a greater role in strategic planning. HR specialists are challenged to know their organization's business, and line managers are challenged to excel at selecting and motivating the best people. As contributors to the organization's strategy, HR managers also face greater ethical challenges. When they were merely a specialized staff function, they could focus on, say, legal requirements for hiring decisions. But strategy decisions require them to be able to link decisions about staffing, benefits, and other HR matters to the organization's business success. For example, as members of the top management team, HR managers may need to implement drastic downsizing while still retaining top executives through generous salaries or bonuses, or they may hesitate to risk aggressively investigating and challenging corrupt management practices. In the long run, however, organizations are best served when HR leaders strongly advocate at least four sets of values: strategic, ethical, legal, and financial.[3]

Tough economic times deliver exciting HR opportunities as well as tough HR challenges. For example, companies that can hire during a recession gain access to a huge pool of talented people. Well-managed firms seize the opportunities and meet the challenges.

The four co-owners of PriceSpective, a consulting firm, meet monthly with senior managers to discuss whether their current staffing levels are appropriate for their coming needs. When sales are slow, PriceSpective institutes a temporary hiring freeze. Because these actions are part of a regular planning process, employees accept that managers are simply making course adjustments to keep the company efficient.

Family Dollar Stores is one of the companies that found opportunities during the recent recession. As shoppers switched to dollar stores from higher-priced retailers, Family Dollar opened more stores, receiving applications from workers with better-than-usual credentials. To meet a need for specialists for its information technology department, the company found experienced IT workers who had left Circuit City when that chain went out of business. Companies that, like Family Dollar, build up their staff when talented people are hungry for work can boost sales, improve efficiency, and gain an advantage over competitors—if they can keep and motivate these employees.[4]

Managing human capital to sustain a competitive advantage may be the most important part of an organization's HR function. But on a day-to-day basis, HR managers have many other concerns regarding their workers and the entire personnel puzzle: attracting talent; maintaining a well-trained, highly motivated, and loyal workforce; managing diversity; devising effective compensation systems; managing layoffs; and containing health care and pension costs. The best approaches depend on the circumstances of the organization, such as whether it is growing, declining, or standing still.

HR planning involves three stages

"Get me the right kind and the right number of people at the right time." It sounds simple enough, but meeting an organization's staffing needs requires strategic human resources planning—an activity with a strategic purpose derived from the organization's plans. The HR planning process occurs in three stages, shown in Figure 7.1:

1. *Planning*—To ensure that the right number and types of people are available, HR managers must know the organization's business plans—where the company is headed, in what businesses it plans to be, what future growth is expected, and so forth. Few actions are more damaging to morale than having to lay off recently hired employees because of inadequate planning for future needs.

2. *Programming*—The organization implements specific human resources activities, such as recruitment, training, and pay systems.

3. *Evaluating*—Human resources activities are evaluated to determine whether they are producing the results needed to contribute to the organization's business plans.

In this chapter, we focus on human resources planning and programming. Many of the other factors listed in Figure 7.1 are discussed in later chapters.

demand forecasts Perhaps the most difficult part of HR planning is conducting *demand* forecasts, that is, determining how many and what type of people are needed. Demand forecasts are derived from organizational plans. To develop the iPhone, Apple had to determine how many engineers and designers it needed to ensure such a complex product was ready to launch. Managers also needed to estimate how many iPhones the company would sell. Based on their forecast, they had to determine how many production employees would be required, along with the staff to market the phone, handle publicity for the product launch, and answer inquiries from customers learning how to use the new product. Similarly, companies selling

"Hire the best. Pay them fairly. Communicate freely. Provide challenges and rewards. Get out of their way. They'll knock your socks off."

—Mary Ann Allison

FIGURE 7.1 HR Planning Process

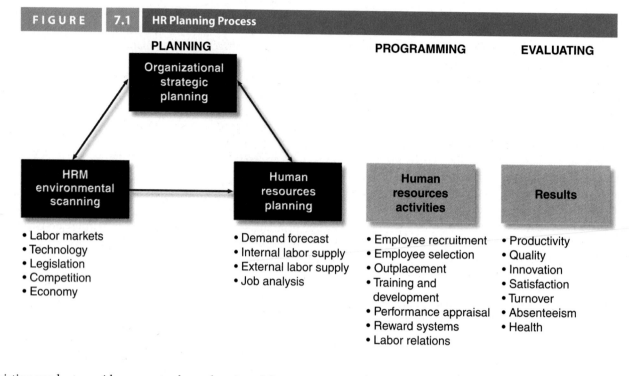

an existing product consider current sales and projected future sales growth as they estimate the plant capacity for future demand, the sales force required, the support staff needed, and so forth. They calculate the number of labor-hours required and then use those estimates to determine the demand for specific types of workers.

labor supply forecasts

Along with forecasting demand, managers must forecast the *supply of labor*—how many and what types of employees the organization actually will have. In performing a supply analysis, the organization estimates the number and quality of its current employees and the available external supply of workers. To estimate internal supply, the company typically relies on its experiences with turnover, terminations, retirements, promotions, and transfers. A computerized human resources information system can help considerably.

Externally, organizations look at workforce trends to make projections. Worldwide, the highly skilled, higher-paid jobs have been generated mostly in the cities of the industrialized world, where companies have scrambled to find enough qualified workers. At the same time, companies in industrialized

Hiring College Hunks to Haul Junk

It takes brains to manage brawn. And that's exactly what the cofounders of College Hunks Hauling Junk do daily. College Hunks Hauling Junk was established by high school friends Omar Soliman and Nick Friedman over summer vacation from college— they needed work, so they created a company. The young men borrowed a delivery truck from Soliman's mother's furniture store and offered to haul away people's unwanted junk. When they graduated, Soliman and Friedman decided to turn their project into something bigger, and College Hunks Hauling Junk hit the road.

For a fee, crew members will pick up unwanted furniture and other household, construction, or office debris from individuals or businesses. The College Hunks then recycle or donate whatever items they can, transporting to the dump only what cannot possibly be recycled or reused. Although some skeptics point out that many towns will collect large items left curbside as part of regular trash pickup (for an added cost), so demand for College Hunks will fall off, that doesn't seem to be happening. Homeowners and small-business owners seem to appreciate the convenience of the service as well as the knowledge that many of their items will be recycled or reused. Friedman identifies an additional reason: "We recognized that people placed a premium on having young, friendly, personable, and courteous teams coming in to do the work."

From the beginning, Soliman and Friedman envisioned a business that would expand through franchising. This requires forecasts of labor demand and supply in more than one location. It also requires the ability to select the right franchise owners to manage these franchises, including the junk-hauling hunks themselves. New franchise owners are put through a five-day training program at "Junk University." They learn every facet of the business, ranging from recruiting and hiring a workforce to management, sales, and marketing. Franchisees tend to recruit their junk haulers from nearby colleges. And while employees don't need to look like male runway models, they are required to be well groomed, with no visible piercings or tattoos. Female "hunkettes" are beginning to make their way from the corporate offices onto the trucks as well.

nations have used offshoring to move much of their routine and less-skilled work to nations with a large population willing to work for lower pay. However, the resulting demand for overseas talent has made it difficult to fill a variety of jobs throughout the world, from factory workers in China to engineering positions in India.[5]

In the United States, demographic trends have contributed to a shortage of skilled and highly educated workers. Traditional labor-intensive jobs in agriculture, mining, and assembly-line manufacturing have made way for jobs in technical, financial, and customized goods and service industries. These jobs often require much more training and schooling than the jobs they replace. Other trends may worsen this situation. For example, the upcoming retirement of the baby-boomer generation will remove many educated and trained employees from the workforce. And in math, science, and engineering graduate schools, fewer than half the students receiving graduate degrees are American-born. To fill U.S. jobs, companies must hire U.S. citizens or immigrants with permission to work in the United States.

Some managers have responded to this skills shortage by significantly increasing their remedial and training budgets.[6] Many companies have increased the labor supply by recruiting workers from other countries. However, this strategy is limited by the number of visas issued by the U.S. government. Retraining downsized workers is yet another approach to increasing the workforce labor pool.

 As the health care industry expands and manufacturing moves jobs overseas, some companies and not-for-profit organizations have begun collaborating to meet the needs of both industries by retraining laid-off manufacturing workers to enter the health care field. For example, the Manufacturers Association of Central New York teamed up with the Northern Area Health Education Center and Syracuse University to evaluate and retrain displaced workers for health care jobs.

Applicants take aptitude tests to determine what skills they already possess, such as teamwork or the ability to interpret graphics. Those who already show proficiency in certain areas can obtain a certificate of competency for those skills. A Web site hosted by the Northern Area Health Education Center posts the credential information so that interested employers such as hospitals or nursing homes can find potential job candidates; the site also shows candidates what types of jobs they would qualify for. The program focuses on jobs that do not require degrees or licenses, such as nursing assistants, pharmacy technicians, and paramedics.[7]

In contrast, earlier forecasts of an increasingly diverse workforce have become fact, adding greatly to the pool of available talent. Minorities, women, immigrants, older and disabled workers, and other groups have made the management of diversity a fundamental activity of today's manager. Because managing the "new workforce" is so essential, the next chapter is devoted to this topic.

reconciling supply and demand Once managers can estimate the supply of and demand for various types of employees, they develop approaches for reconciling the two. If organizations need more people than they currently have (a labor deficit), they can hire new employees, promote current employees to new positions, or outsource work to contractors. When organizations have more people than they need (a labor surplus), they can use attrition—the normal turnover of employees—to reduce the surplus if they have planned far enough in advance. The organization also may lay off employees or transfer them to other areas.

When managers need to hire, they can use their organization's compensation policy to attract talent. Large companies spend a lot of time gathering information about pay scales for the jobs

To date, the company has sold nearly 40 franchises that operate bright green and orange trucks in towns across the United States. What's next? "We grew super, super fast," notes CEO Omar Soliman. "Now we're playing catch up, getting all the systems in place so everything works smoother."

Q: Discussion Questions

- What factors might affect the demand for the services provided by College Hunks Hauling Junk? How might individual franchise owners deal with fluctuations in labor demand?
- The labor supply for College Hunks Hauling Junk is mainly college students. What are some risks and benefits of relying on college students as a workforce? How should this source of labor affect the ways that franchise owners recruit, select, and train workers?

SOURCES: Company Web site, http://www.1800junkusa.com, accessed June 5, 2009; Lindsey Gerdes, "Creative Career of the Week: College Hunks Hauling Junk," *BusinessWeek*, May 11, 2009, http://www.businessweek.com; Lynn Rosellini, "Dreamers: Hunks of Junk," *Reader's Digest*, April 2009, http://www.rd.com; Dee Gill, "Hauling Junk (with a Touch of Class)," *New York Times*, October 1, 2008, http://www.nytimes.com; and Janet Leiser, "College Hunks Hauling Junk Relocates to Tampa Bay," *Tampa Bay Business Journal*, March 21, 2008, http://tampabay.bizjournals.com.

they have available and making sure their compensation system is fair and competitive. We discuss pay issues later in this chapter.

job analysis Although issues of supply and demand are conducted at an organizational level, HR planning also focuses on individual jobs, using *job analysis*. **Job analysis** does two things:[8]

1. A *job description* tells about the job itself—the essential tasks, duties, and responsibilities involved in performing the job. The job description for an accounting manager might specify that the position will be responsible for monthly, quarterly, and annual financial reports, getting bills issued and paid, preparing budgets, ensuring the company's compliance with laws and regulations, working closely with line managers on financial issues, and supervising an accounting department of 12 people.

2. A *job specification* describes the skills, knowledge, abilities, and other characteristics needed to perform the job. For the accounting manager, the job requirements might include a degree in accounting or business, knowledge of computerized accounting systems, managerial experience, and excellent communication skills.

Job analysis provides the information required by virtually every human resources activity. It assists with the essential HR programs: recruitment, training, selection, appraisal, and reward systems. It may also help organizations defend themselves in lawsuits involving employment practices—for example, by clearly specifying what a job requires if someone claims unfair dismissal.[9] Ultimately, job analysis helps increase the value added by employees to the organization because it clarifies what is required to perform effectively.

(L)(O) 2 **WHAT YOU NEED TO KNOW . . .**
Why do companies recruit both internally and externally for new hires?

STAFFING THE ORGANIZATION

Once HR planning is completed, managers can focus on staffing the organization. The staffing function consists of three related activities: recruitment, selection, and outplacement.

Recruitment helps find job candidates

Recruitment activities increase the pool of candidates that might be selected for a job. Recruitment may be internal to the organization (considering current employees for promotions and transfers) or external. Each approach has advantages and disadvantages.[10]

internal recruiting The advantages of internal recruiting are that employers know their employees, and employees know their organization. External candidates who are unfamiliar with the organization may find they don't like working there. Also, the opportunity to move up within the organization may encourage employees to remain with the company, work hard, and succeed. Recruiting from outside the company can be demoralizing to employees. Many companies, such as Sears and Eli Lilly, prefer internal to external recruiting for these reasons.

Internal staffing has some drawbacks. If employees lack skills or talent, it yields a limited applicant pool, leading to poor selection decisions. Also, an internal recruitment policy can inhibit a company that wants to change the nature or goals of the business by bringing in outside candidates. In changing from a rapidly growing, entrepreneurial organization to a mature business with more stable growth, Dell went outside the organization to hire managers who better fit those needs.

Many companies that rely heavily on internal recruiting use a *job-posting system,* advertising open positions, typically on a bulletin board. Texas Instruments uses job posting. Employees complete a request form indicating interest in a posted job. The posted job description includes a list of duties and the minimum skills and experience required.

external recruiting External recruiting brings in "new blood" and can inspire innovation. Among the most frequently used sources of outside applicants are Internet job boards, company Web sites, employee referrals, newspaper advertisements, and college campus recruiting.

Recent surveys suggest that employers place the greatest emphasis on referrals by current employees and online job boards.[11] Some companies actively encourage employees to refer their friends by offering cash rewards. In fact, surveys show word-of-mouth recommendations are the way most job positions get filled. Not only is this method relatively inexpensive, but employees also tend to know who will be a good fit with the company.

Web job boards such as CareerBuilder, Monster, and Yahoo! HotJobs have exploded in popularity as a job-recruitment tool because they easily reach a large pool of job seekers. They have largely supplanted newspaper want ads, although print recruiting has grown somewhat, partly as a result of forming alliances with the job boards. Most companies also let people apply for jobs at their corporate Web

● JOB ANALYSIS A tool for determining what is done on a given job and what should be done on that job.

● RECRUITMENT The development of a pool of applicants for jobs in an organization.

● SELECTION Choosing from among qualified applicants to hire into an organization.

site, and many even list open positions. Some companies also are buying search engine ads to display next to the results for relevant terms such as *nurse*. Another online tool is to obtain leads through networking sites such as LinkedIn and Craigslist.

Employment agencies are another common recruitment tool, and for important management positions, companies often use specialized executive-search firms. Campus recruiting can be helpful for companies looking for applicants who have up-to-date training and innovative ideas. However, companies that rely heavily on campus recruiting and employee referrals must take extra care to ensure that these methods do not discriminate by generating pools of applicants who are, say, mostly women or primarily white.[12]

Wendy Kopp founded her not-for-profit organization, Teach for America (TFA), 20 years ago with the idea that some of the nation's best and brightest college graduates could—and would—make a real difference to students attending inner city and rural schools where resources are slim or nonexistent. The idea has resonated so greatly among graduating seniors and young professionals that Teach for America has become the largest hiring employer of college seniors in the nation. During a single year, nearly 20,000 students and graduates apply for roughly 2,400 positions. Applicants endure rigorous interviews, testing, and training before they are placed in a school, and they are asked to give a two-year commitment to the project.

All of this activity has not been lost on some of the biggest U.S. companies. In fact, investment bank J. P. Morgan found itself competing with Teach for America for a number of job candidates. So the bank and TFA teamed up to hold joint recruiting events at various colleges. J. P. Morgan has committed to deferring job offers to seniors who are accepted by both its training program and TFA, giving those graduates a chance to fulfill their TFA assignment. Why would the bank make this concession? "We want employees who are committed to serving the community as well as serving shareholders," explains David Puth, Morgan's head of global currency and commodities.[14]

Most companies use some combination of the methods we have been discussing, depending on the particular job or situation. For example, they might use internal recruiting for existing jobs that need replacements, and external

recruiting when the firm is expanding or needs to acquire some new skill.

Ⓛ Ⓞ 3 **WHAT YOU NEED TO KNOW . . .**
What are the various methods for selecting new employees?

Selection chooses applicants to hire

Selection builds on recruiting and involves decisions about whom to hire. As important as these decisions are, they are at times made carelessly or quickly. To help you in your own career, we describe a number of selection instruments you may encounter.

applications and résumés Application blanks and résumés provide basic information that help prospective employers make a first cut through candidates. Applications and résumés typically include the applicant's name, educational background, citizenship, work experiences, certifications, and the like. Their appearance and accuracy also say something about the applicant—spelling mistakes, for example, almost always disqualify you immediately. While providing important information, applications and résumés tend not to be useful as a basis for final selection decisions.

interviews The most popular selection tool is interviewing, and every company uses some type of interview. Employment interviewers must be careful about what they ask and how they ask it. As we will explain later, federal law requires employers to avoid discriminating on criteria such as sex and race; questions that distinguish candidates according to protected categories may be seen as evidence of discrimination.

In an *unstructured* (or nondirective) interview, the interviewer asks different interviewees different

what recruiting methods are most valuable?[13]

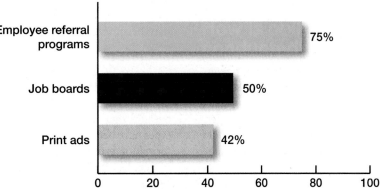

Percentage of respondents who say the method is effective or very effective:

Employee referral programs — 75%
Job boards — 50%
Print ads — 42%

0 20 40 60 80 100

STRUCTURED INTERVIEW Selection technique that involves asking all applicants the same questions and comparing their responses to a standardized set of answers.

questions. The interviewer may also use probes, that is, ask follow-up questions to learn more about the candidate.[15]

In a **structured interview**, the interviewer conducts the same interview with each applicant. There are two basic types of structured interview:

1. The *situational interview* focuses on hypothetical situations. Zale Corporation, a major jewelry chain, uses this type of interview to select sales clerks. A sample question is: "A customer comes into the store to pick up a watch he had left for repair. The watch is not back yet from the repair shop, and the customer becomes angry. How would you handle the situation?" Answering "I would refer the customer to my supervisor" might suggest that the applicant felt incapable of handling the situation independently.

2. The *behavioral description interview* explores what candidates have actually done in the past. In selecting accountants, Bill Bufe of Plante & Moran asks candidates how they handled a difficult person they have worked with, and Art King asks how candidates have handled a stressful situation, because he believes this shows how candidates "think on their feet."[16] Because behavioral questions are based on real events, they often provide useful information about how the candidate will actually perform on the job.

Each of these interview techniques offers different advantages and disadvantages, and many interviewers use more than one technique during the same interview. Unstructured interviews can help establish rapport and provide a sense of the applicant's personality, but they may not generate specific information about the candidate's ability. Structured interviews tend to be more reliable predictors of job performance because they are based on the job analysis that has been done for the position. They are also more likely to be free of bias and stereotypes. And because the same questions are being asked of all candidates for the job, an interview that is at least partly structured allows the manager to compare responses across different candidates.[17]

reference checks

Résumés, applications, and interviews rely on the applicant's honesty. To make an accurate selection decision, employers have to be able to trust the words of each candidate. Unfortunately, some candidates may exaggerate their qualifications or hide criminal backgrounds that could pose a risk to the employer. In a highly publicized incident, the dean of admissions at the Massachusetts Institute of Technology resigned after nearly three decades on the job because the

school learned she had provided false information about her educational background.[18] She had demonstrated an ability to perform the job functions but could no longer claim the level of integrity required by that position. Once lost, a reputation is hard to regain.

Because these and more ambiguous ethical gray areas arise, employers supplement candidate-provided information with other screening devices, including *reference checks*. Virtually all organizations contact references or former employers and educational institutions listed by candidates. Although checking references makes sense, reference information is becoming increasingly difficult to obtain as a result of several highly publicized lawsuits. In one case, an applicant sued a former boss on the grounds that the boss told prospective employers the applicant was a "thief and a crook." The jury awarded the applicant $80,000.[19] Still, talking to an applicant's previous supervisor is a common practice and often does provide useful information, particularly if specific job-related questions are asked ("Can you give me an example of a project candidate X handled particularly well?").

background checks

For a higher level of scrutiny, background investigations also have become standard procedure at many companies. Some state courts have ruled that companies can be held liable for negligent hiring if they fail to do adequate background checks. Types of checks include Social Security verification, past employment and education verification, and a criminal records check. A number of other checks can be conducted if they pertain to the specific job, including a motor vehicle record check (for jobs involving driving) and a credit check (for money-handling jobs).

Internet tools have made basic background checks fast and easy. A recent survey of executive recruiters learned that more than three-quarters use search engines such as Google to find out about candidates.[20] Such searches can turn up a variety of information, including what people have written on blogs or posted under their name on MySpace or Facebook. Internet users are advised to remember that anything carrying their name online may become information for potential employers, even years down the road.

personality tests

Employers have been more hesitant to use personality tests for employee selection, largely because they are hard to defend in court.[21] Some personality types have been associated with greater job satisfaction and performance, especially where the organization can build groups of people with similar positive traits.[22] As a result, personality tests are regaining popularity, and at some point in your career you will probably complete some personality tests. A number of well-known paper-and-pencil inventories measure personality traits such as sociability, adjustment, and energy. Typical questions are "Do you like to socialize with people?" and "Do you enjoy working hard?" Some personality tests try to determine the type of working conditions that the candidate prefers, to see if he or she would be motivated and productive in the particular job. For example, if the candidate prefers making decisions on his or her own but the job requires gaining the cooperation of others, another candidate might be a better fit.

drug testing Drug testing is now a frequently used screening instrument. Since the passage of the Drug-Free Workplace Act of 1988, applicants and employees of federal contractors and Department of Defense contractors and those under Department of Transportation regulations have been subject to testing for illegal drugs. Well over half of all U.S. companies conduct preemployment drug tests.

cognitive ability tests Among the oldest employment selection devices are cognitive ability tests. These tests measure a range of intellectual abilities, including verbal comprehension (vocabulary, reading) and numerical aptitude (mathematical calculations). About 20 percent of U.S. companies use cognitive ability tests for selection purposes.[23] Figure 7.2 shows some examples of cognitive ability test questions.

performance tests In a performance test, the test taker performs a sample of the job. Most companies use some type of performance test, typically for administrative assistant

FIGURE	7.2	Sample Measures of Cognitive Ability

Verbal

1. What is the meaning of the word surreptitious?
   a. covert
   b. winding
   c. lively
   d. sweet

2. How is the noun clause used in the following sentence: "I hope that I can learn this game."
   a. subject
   b. predicate nominative
   c. direct object
   d. object of the preposition

Quantitative

3. Divide 50 by .5 and add 5. What is the result?
   a. 25
   b. 30
   c. 95
   d. 105

4. What is the value of 144^2?
   a. 12
   b. 72
   c. 288
   d. 20736

Reasoning

5. _____ is to boat as snow is to _____
   a. sail, ski
   b. water, winter
   c. water, ski
   d. engine, water

6. Two women played 5 games of chess. Each woman won the same number of games, yet there were no ties. How can this be so?
   a. There was a forfeit.
   b. One player cheated.
   c. They played different people.
   d. One game was still in progress.

Mechanical

7. If gear A and gear C are both turning counter-clockwise, what is happening to gear B?
   a. It is turning counter-clockwise.
   b. It is turning clockwise.
   c. It remains stationary.
   d. The whole system will jam.

A   B   C

Answers: 1a, 2c, 3d, 4d, 5c, 6c, 7b.

SOURCE: George Bohlander, Scott Snell, and Arthur Sherman, *Managing Human Resources,* 12th ed. © 2001. Reprinted with permission of South-Western, a division of Thomson Learning, www.thomsonrights.com. Fax 800 730-2215.

and clerical positions. The most widely used performance test is the typing test. However, performance tests have been developed for almost every occupation, including managerial positions.

Assessment centers are the most notable offshoot of the managerial performance test.[24] A typical **assessment center** consists of 10 to 12 candidates who participate in a variety of exercises or situations; some of the exercises involve group interactions, and others are performed individually. Each exercise taps a number of critical managerial dimensions, such as leadership, decision-making skills, and communication ability. Assessors, generally line managers from the organization, observe and record information about the candidates' performance in each exercise.

integrity tests To assess job candidates' honesty, employers may administer integrity tests. Polygraphs, or lie detector tests, have been banned for most employment purposes.[25] Paper-and-pencil honesty tests are more recent instruments for measuring integrity. The tests include questions such as whether a person has ever thought about stealing and whether he or she believes other people steal. Although companies including Payless ShoeSource reported that losses due to theft declined following the introduction of integrity tests, the accuracy of these tests is still debatable.[26]

reliability and validity Regardless of the method used to select employees, two crucial issues need to be addressed:

1. **Reliability** refers to the consistency of test scores over time and across alternative measurements. For example, if three different interviewers talked to the same job candidate but drew very different conclusions about the candidate's abilities, there could be problems with the reliability of one or more of the selection tests or interview procedures.

2. **Validity** moves beyond reliability to assess the accuracy of the selection test.

Criterion-related validity refers to the degree to which a test actually predicts or correlates with job performance. Such validity is usually established through studies comparing test performance and job performance for a large enough sample of employees to enable a fair conclusion to be reached. For example, if a high score on a cognitive ability test strongly predicts good job performance, then candidates who score well will tend to be preferred over those who do not. Still, no test by itself perfectly predicts performance. Managers usually consider other criteria before making a final selection.

Content validity concerns the degree to which selection tests measure a representative sample of the knowledge, skills, and abilities required for the job. The best-known example of a content-valid test is a keyboarding test for administrative assistants because keyboarding is a task a person in that position almost always performs. However, to be completely content-valid, the selection process also should measure other skills the assistant would likely perform, such as answering the telephone, duplicating and faxing documents, and dealing with the public. Content validity is more subjective (less statistical) than evaluations of criterion-related validity but is no less important, particularly when an organization is defending employment decisions in court.

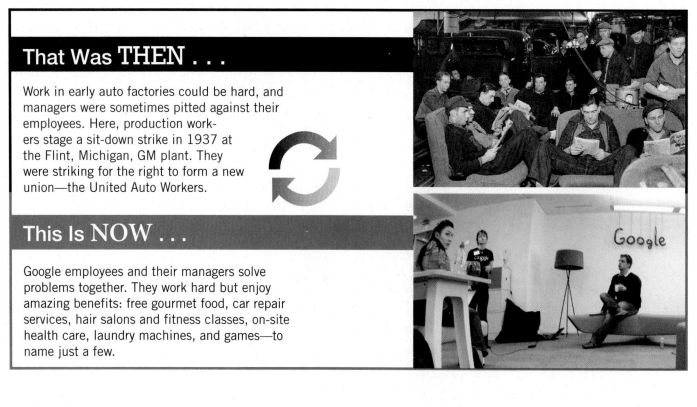

That Was THEN . . .

Work in early auto factories could be hard, and managers were sometimes pitted against their employees. Here, production workers stage a sit-down strike in 1937 at the Flint, Michigan, GM plant. They were striking for the right to form a new union—the United Auto Workers.

This Is NOW . . .

Google employees and their managers solve problems together. They work hard but enjoy amazing benefits: free gourmet food, car repair services, hair salons and fitness classes, on-site health care, laundry machines, and games—to name just a few.

Sometimes employees must be let go

Unfortunately, staffing decisions do not simply focus on hiring employees. As organizations evolve and markets change, the demand for certain employees rises and falls. Also, some employees simply do not perform at the level required. For these reasons, managers sometimes must make difficult decisions to terminate their employment.

layoffs As a result of the massive restructuring of American industry, many organizations have been *downsizing*—laying off large numbers of managerial and other employees. Dismissing any employee is tough, but when a company lays off a substantial portion of its workforce, the results can rock the foundations of the organization.[27] The victims of restructuring face all the difficulties of being let go—loss of self-esteem, demoralizing job searches, and the stigma of being out of work. Employers can help by offering outplacement, the process of helping people who have been dismissed from the company to regain employment elsewhere. Even then, the impact of layoffs goes further than the employees who leave. Many who remain will experience disenchantment, distrust, and lethargy. The way management deals with dismissals affects the productivity and satisfaction of those who remain. A well-thought-out dismissal process eases tensions and helps remaining employees adjust to the new work situation.

Organizations with strong performance evaluation systems benefit because the survivors are less likely to believe the decision was arbitrary. In addition, if laid-off workers are offered severance pay and help in finding a new job, remaining workers will be comforted. Companies also should avoid stringing out layoffs by dismissing a few workers at a time.

termination People sometimes "get fired" for poor performance or other reasons. Should an employer have the right to fire a worker? In 1884, a Tennessee court ruled: "All may dismiss their employee(s) at will for good cause, for no cause, or even for cause morally wrong." The concept that an employee may be fired for any reason is known as employment-at-will or *termination-at-will* and was upheld in a 1908 Supreme Court ruling.[28] The logic is that if the employee may quit at any time, the employer is free to dismiss at any time.

Since the mid-1970s, courts in most states have made exceptions to this doctrine based on public policy—a policy or ruling designed to protect the public from harm. Under the public policy exception, employees cannot be fired for such actions as refusing to break the law, taking time off for jury duty, or "whistle-blowing" to report illegal company behavior. So if a worker reports an environmental violation to the regulatory agency and the company fires him or her, the courts may argue that the firing was unfair because the employee acted for the good of the community. Another major exception is union contracts that limit an employer's ability to fire without cause.

Employers can avoid the pitfalls associated with dismissal by developing progressive and positive disciplinary procedures.[29]

Progressive means the manager takes graduated steps in trying to correct a workplace behavior. For example, an employee who has been absent receives a verbal reprimand for the first offense, and a written reprimand for the second offense. A third offense results in counseling and probation, and a fourth results in a paid-leave day to think over the consequences of future infractions. The employer is signaling to the employee that this is the "last straw." Arbitrators are more likely to side with an employer that fires someone when they believe the company has made sincere efforts to help the person correct his or her behavior.

The termination interview, in which the manager discusses the company's position with the employee, is stressful for both parties. Most experts believe that the immediate superior should be the one to deliver the bad news to employees. However, it is wise to have a third party, such as an HR manager, present for guidance and note-taking. Because announcing a termination is likely to upset the employee and occasionally leads to a lawsuit, the manager should prepare carefully. Preparation should include learning the facts of the situation and reviewing any documents to make sure they are consistent with the reason for the termination. During the termination interview, ethics and common sense dictate that the manager should be truthful but respectful, stating the facts and avoiding arguments. Here are some additional practical guidelines for conducting a termination interview:[30]

- **Do** give as much warning as possible for mass layoffs.
- **Do** sit down one on one with the individual, in a private office.
- **Do** complete a termination session within 15 minutes.
- **Do** provide written explanations of severance benefits.
- **Do** provide outplacement services away from company headquarters.
- **Do** be sure the employee hears about his or her termination from a manager, not a colleague.
- **Do** express appreciation for what the employee has contributed, if appropriate.
- **Don't** leave room for confusion when firing. Tell the individual in the first sentence that he or she is terminated.
- **Don't** allow time for debate during a termination session.

ASSESSMENT CENTER A managerial performance test in which candidates participate in a variety of exercises and situations.

RELIABILITY The consistency of test scores over time and across alternative measurements.

VALIDITY The degree to which a selection test predicts or correlates with job performance.

OUTPLACEMENT The process of helping people who have been dismissed from the company to regain employment elsewhere.

EMPLOYMENT-AT-WILL The legal concept that an employee may be terminated for any reason.

TERMINATION INTERVIEW A discussion between a manager and an employee about the employee's dismissal.

- **Don't** make personal comments when firing someone; keep the conversation professional.
- **Don't** rush a fired employee offsite unless security is an issue.
- **Don't** fire people on significant dates, like the 25th anniversary of their employment or the day their mother died.
- **Don't** fire employees when they are on vacation or have just returned.

legal issues and equal employment opportunity
Many laws have been passed governing employment decisions and practices. They will directly affect a good part of your day-to-day work as a manager, as well as the human resource function of your organization. Table 7.1 summarizes many of these major employment laws.

The 1938 *Fair Labor Standards Act* (FLSA), among other provisions, creates two employee categories: exempt and nonexempt. Employees are normally exempt from overtime pay if they have considerable discretion in how they carry out their jobs and if their jobs require them to exercise independent judgment. Managers usually fall in this category. Nonexempt employees are usually paid by the hour and must be paid

TABLE 7.1	U.S. Equal Employment Laws	
Act	**Major Provisions**	**Enforcement and Remedies**
Fair Labor Standards Act (1938)	Creates exempt (salaried) and nonexempt (hourly) employee categories, governing overtime and other rules; sets minimum wage, child-labor laws.	Enforced by Department of Labor, private action to recover lost wages; civil and criminal penalties also possible.
Equal Pay Act (1963)	Prohibits gender-based pay discrimination between two jobs substantially similar in skill, effort, responsibility, and working conditions.	Fines up to $10,000, imprisonment up to 6 months, or both; enforced by Equal Employment Opportunity Commission (EEOC); private actions for double damages up to 3 years' wages, liquidated damages, reinstatement, or promotion.
Title VII of Civil Rights Act (1964)	Prohibits discrimination based on race, sex, color, religion, or national origin in employment decisions: hiring, pay, working conditions, promotion, discipline, or discharge.	Enforced by EEOC; private actions, back pay, front pay, reinstatement, restoration of seniority and pension benefits, attorneys' fees and costs.
Executive Orders 11246 and 11375 (1965)	Requires equal opportunity clauses in federal contracts; prohibits employment discrimination by federal contractors based on race, color, religion, sex, or national origin.	Established Office of Federal Contract Compliance Programs (OFCCP) to investigate violations; empowered to terminate violator's federal contracts.
Age Discrimination in Employment Act (1967)	Prohibits employment discrimination based on age for persons over 40 years; restricts mandatory retirement.	EEOC enforcement; private actions for reinstatement, back pay, front pay, restoration of seniority and pension benefits; double unpaid wages for willful violations; attorneys' fees and costs.
Vocational Rehabilitation Act (1973)	Requires affirmative action by all federal contractors for persons with disabilities; defines disabilities as physical or mental impairments that substantially limit life activities.	Federal contractors must consider hiring disabled persons capable of performance after reasonable accommodations.
Americans with Disabilities Act (1990)	Extends affirmative action provisions of Vocational Rehabilitation Act to private employers; requires workplace modifications to facilitate disabled employees; prohibits discrimination against disabled.	EEOC enforcement; private actions for Title VII remedies.
Civil Rights Act (1991)	Clarifies Title VII requirements: disparate treatment impact suits, business necessity, job relatedness; shifts burden of proof to employer; permits punitive damages and jury trials.	Punitive damages limited to sliding scale only in intentional discrimination based on sex, religion, and disabilities.
Family and Medical Leave Act (1991)	Requires 12 weeks' unpaid leave for medical or family needs: paternity, family member illness.	Private actions for lost wages and other expenses, reinstatement.

overtime if they work more than 40 hours in a week. As a manager you will almost certainly need to specify the exempt or nonexempt status of anyone you hire.

Laws aimed at protecting employees from discrimination include the 1964 *Civil Rights Act,* which prohibits discrimination in employment based on race, sex, color, national origin, and religion. Title VII of the act specifically forbids discrimination in such employment practices as recruitment, hiring, discharge, promotion, compensation, and access to training.[31] The *Americans with Disabilities Act* prohibits employment discrimination against people with disabilities. Recovering alcoholics and drug abusers, cancer patients in remission, and AIDS patients are covered by this legislation. The 1991 *Civil Rights Act* strengthened all these protections and permitted punitive damages to be imposed on companies that violate them. The *Age Discrimination in Employment Act* of 1967 and its amendments in 1978 and 1986 prohibit discrimination against people age 40 and over. One reason for this legislation was the practice of dismissing older workers to replace them with younger workers earning lower pay.

One common reason employers are sued for discrimination is **adverse impact**—when a seemingly neutral employment practice has a disproportionately negative effect on a group protected by the Civil Rights Act.[32] For example, if equal numbers of qualified men and women apply for jobs but a particular employment test results in far fewer women being hired, the test may be considered to cause an adverse impact, making it subject to challenge on that basis.

Because of the importance of these issues, many companies have established procedures to ensure compliance with labor and equal-opportunity laws. For example, they may monitor and compare salaries by race, gender, length of service, and other categories to make sure employees across all groups are being fairly paid. Written policies can also help ensure fair and legal practices in the workplace, although the company may also have to demonstrate a record of actually following those procedures and making sure they are implemented. In this sense, effective management practices not only help managers motivate employees to do their best work but often help provide legal protection as well. For example, managers who give their employees regular, specific evaluations can prevent misunderstandings that lead to lawsuits. A written record of those evaluations is often useful in demonstrating fair and objective treatment.

Another law that affects staffing practices is the *Worker Adjustment and Retraining Notification Act* of 1989, commonly known as the *WARN Act* or *Plant Closing Bill.* It requires covered employers to give affected employees 60 days' written notice of plant closings or mass layoffs.

● **ADVERSE IMPACT** When a seemingly neutral employment practice has a disproportionately negative effect on a protected group.

(L)(O) **4** **WHAT YOU NEED TO KNOW . . .**
What is the importance of spending on training and development?

TRAINING AND DEVELOPMENT

Today's competitive environment requires managers to upgrade the skills and performance of employees—and themselves. Continual improvement increases both personal and organizational effectiveness. It makes organization members more useful in their current job and prepares them for new responsibilities. And it helps the entire organization handle new challenges and take advantage of new methods and technologies. These training and development activities are supported by appraising employees' performance and giving them effective feedback, as we will discuss in the next section.

U.S. businesses spend more than $55 billion to provide their employees with formal training annually. The greatest share of that spending goes to sales training, management and supervisory training, and training in information systems and information technology.[33] But competitive pressures require that companies consider the most efficient training methods. That means traditional classroom settings

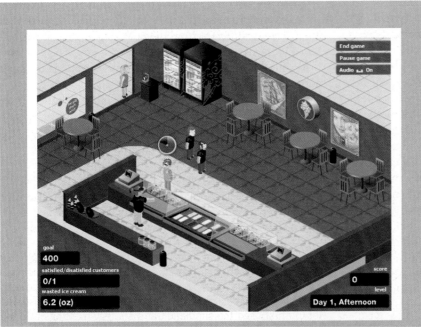

Cold Stone Creamery spends a portion of its training budget in developing computerized simulations to show how employee actions affect store performance. The company uses computer games because they are familiar and attractive to its young employees.

TRAINING Teaching lower-level employees how to perform their present jobs.

DEVELOPMENT Teaching managers and professional employees broad skills needed for their present and future jobs.

NEEDS ASSESSMENT An analysis identifying the jobs, people, and departments for which training is necessary.

ORIENTATION TRAINING Training designed to introduce new employees to the company and familiarize them with policies, procedures, culture, and the like.

TEAM TRAINING Training that provides employees with the skills and perspectives they need to collaborate with others.

DIVERSITY TRAINING Programs that focus on identifying and reducing hidden biases against people with differences and developing the skills needed to manage a diversified workforce.

PERFORMANCE APPRAISAL (PA) Assessment of an employee's job performance.

are often giving way to computerized methods.

Training programs include four phases

Although we use the general term *training* here, training sometimes is distinguished from development. **Training** usually refers to teaching lower-level employees how to perform their present jobs, while **development** involves teaching managers and professional employees broader skills needed for their present and future jobs.

Phase one of training usually starts with a **needs assessment**. Managers conduct an analysis to identify the jobs, people, and departments for which training is necessary. Job analysis and performance measurements are useful for this purpose.

Phase two involves the design of training programs. Training objectives and content are established from the needs assessment. For example, Recreational Equipment Inc. (REI) wants its sales associates to learn how to tell whether they are being approached by a "transactional customer," who simply wants to find and pay for a specific product, or a "consultative customer," who wants to spend some time discussing alternative features and benefits.[34]

Phase three involves decisions about the training methods and location—whether the training will be provided on or off the job. Common training methods are listed in Figure 7.3. The choices include lectures, role playing, business simulation, behavior modeling (watching a video and imitating what is observed), conferences, vestibule training (practicing in a simulated job environment), and apprenticeships. Another popular method is job rotation, or assigning employees to different jobs in the organization to broaden their experience and improve their skills. Smart managers often request assignment to jobs where they can be challenged and their skills broadened. The training method should be suited to the objectives defined in phase two. At REI, where the company wants sales associates to identify and respond to various interpersonal situations, much of the training involves role-playing, supplemented with video presentations. And Home Depot emphasizes mentoring for sales associates who work the

aisles but has a more efficient computer-based training program for the cashiers, whose jobs are more routine.[35]

Finally, *phase four* of training should evaluate the program's effectiveness. Measures of effectiveness include employee reactions (surveys), learning (tests), improved behavior on the job, and bottom-line results (e.g., an increase in sales or reduction in defect rates following the training program).

Training options achieve many objectives

Companies invest in training to enhance individual performance and organizational productivity. Programs to improve an employee's computer, technical, or communication skills are common, and some types of training have become standard across many organizations. **Orientation training** familiarizes new employees with their jobs, work units, and the organization in general. Done well, orientation training can increase morale and productivity and can lower employee turnover and the costs of recruiting and training.

Team training teaches employees the skills they need to work together and helps them interact. After General Mills acquired Pillsbury, it used a team training program called Brand Champions to combine the marketing expertise of the two companies and share knowledge among employees handling various functions such as sales and research and development. Most of the time, trainees engaged in team exercises to analyze brands, target customers, and develop marketing messages.[36]

Diversity training focuses on building awareness of diversity issues and providing the skills employees need to work with others who are different from them. Managing diversity is discussed in the next chapter.

As today's decentralized and leaner organizations have put more demands on managers, *management training programs* have become widespread. Such programs often seek to improve managers' *people skills*—their ability to delegate effectively, motivate their subordinates, and communicate and inspire others to achieve organization goals. *Coaching*—being trained by a superior—is usually the most effective and direct management-development tool. Managers may also participate in training programs that are used for all employees, such as job rotation, or attend seminars and courses specifically designed to help them improve supervisory skills or prepare for future promotion.

 NetApp, a data management company based in Sunnyvale, California, has an engaging approach to management training. The company hired BTS Group to develop a simulation game, modeled on NetApp's real-life business. NetApp first used the simulation at a strategy meeting of its top managers. The executives were so enthusiastic and creative about solving the simulation problem that the company invited middle managers to play the game as training for top posts, where strategic thinking is essential.

In the simulation, the managers were divided into five teams, bringing together managers from various functions. Each team was told to run an imaginary high-growth company named

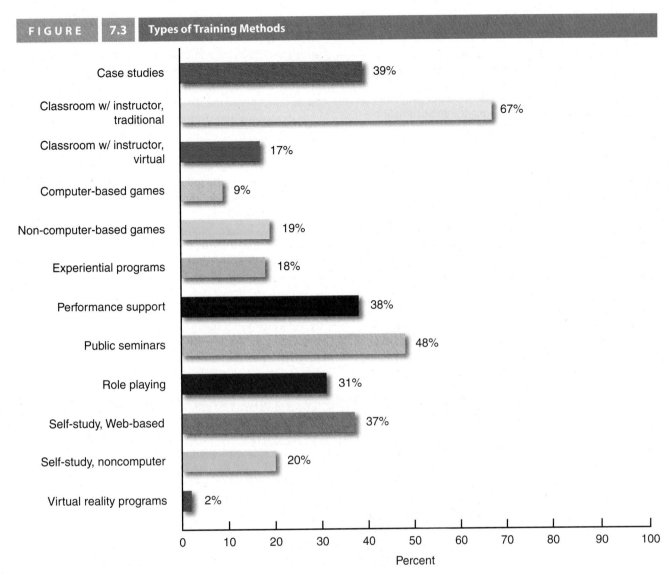

FIGURE 7.3 Types of Training Methods

Training Method	Percent
Case studies	39%
Classroom w/ instructor, traditional	67%
Classroom w/ instructor, virtual	17%
Computer-based games	9%
Non-computer-based games	19%
Experiential programs	18%
Performance support	38%
Public seminars	48%
Role playing	31%
Self-study, Web-based	37%
Self-study, noncomputer	20%
Virtual reality programs	2%

SOURCE: Holly Dolezalek, "Industry Report 2004," *Training,* October 2004, p. 32.

Pet-a-Toaster for three years, competing against the other teams. A year's worth of events were packed into each day of the training program. Each team received a booklet with details about Pet-a-Toaster, based on the market conditions actually facing NetApp. Teams allocated their resources, selected from among possible strategies, and reacted to events posed by the game (for example, a request from a big customer). BTS's simulation software analyzed the actions and provided feedback.

At the end of the simulation, BTS reported each team's results, including total sales and operating profits. Now NetApp's middle managers appreciate what it takes to run a company—and have greater respect for their leaders.[37]

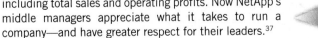

L O 5 WHAT YOU NEED TO KNOW . . .

Can you explain alternatives for who appraises an employee's performance?

PERFORMANCE APPRAISAL

One of the most important responsibilities you will have as a manager is performance appraisal (PA), the assessment of an employee's job performance. Done well, it can help employees improve their performance, pay, and chances for promotion; foster communication between managers and employees; and increase the employees' and the organization's effectiveness. Done poorly, it can cause resentment, reduce motivation, diminish performance, and even expose the organization to legal action.

Performance appraisal has two basic, equally important purposes:

1. *Administrative*—It provides managers with the information they need to make salary, promotion, and dismissal decisions; helps employees understand and accept the basis of

those decisions; and provides documentation that can justify those decisions in court.

2. *Developmental*—The information gathered can be used to identify and plan the additional training, experience, or other improvement that employees require. Also, the manager's feedback and coaching based on the appraisal help employees improve their day-to-day performance and can help prepare them for greater responsibilities.

What do you appraise?

Performance appraisals can assess three basic categories of employee performance: traits, behaviors, and results. *Trait appraisals* involve judgments about employee performance. The rater indicates the degree to which the employee possesses a trait such as initiative, leadership, and attitude. Usually the manager uses a numerical *ratings scale*. For example, if the measured trait is "attitude," the employee might be rated anywhere from 1 (very negative attitude) to 5 (very positive attitude). Trait scales are common, because they are simple to use and provide a standard measure for all employees. But they are often not valid as performance measures. Because they tend to be ambiguous as well as highly subjective—does the employee really have a bad attitude, or is he or she just shy?—they often lead to personal bias and may not be suitable for providing useful feedback.

Behavioral appraisals, while still subjective, focus on observable aspects of performance. They use scales describing specific, prescribed behaviors, which can help ensure that all parties understand what the ratings are really measuring. Because they are less ambiguous, they also can provide useful feedback. Figure 7.4 shows an example of a behaviorally anchored rating scale (BARS) for evaluating quality. Another common approach is the *critical incident* technique, in which the manager keeps a regular log by recording each significant employee behavior that reflects the quality of his or her performance ("Juanita impressed the client with her effective presentation today"; "Joe was late with his report"). This approach can be subjective and time consuming, and it may give some employees a sense that everything they do is being recorded. However, it reminds managers preparing a performance review what the employee actually did.

Results appraisals tend to be more objective and can focus on production data such as sales volume (for a salesperson), units produced (for a line worker), or profits (for a manager). One approach, **management by objectives (MBO)**, involves a subordinate and a supervisor agreeing in advance on specific performance goals (objectives). They develop a plan describing the time frame and criteria for determining whether the objectives have been reached. The aim is to agree on a set of objectives that are clear, specific, and reachable. An objective for a salesperson might be "Increase sales by 25 percent during the following year." An objective for a computer programmer might be "Complete two projects within the next six months."

MBO has several important advantages. First, it avoids the biases and measurement difficulties of trait and behavioral appraisals. At the end of the review period, the employee either has or has not achieved the specified objective. The employee is judged on actual job performance. Second, because the employee and manager have agreed on the objective at the outset, the employee is likely to be committed to the outcome, and misunderstanding is unlikely. Third, because the employee is directly responsible for achieving the objective, MBO supports empowerment of employees to adapt their behavior so they

| FIGURE | 7.4 | Example of BARS Used for Evaluating Quality |

Performance Dimension: Total Quality Management. This area of performance concerns the extent to which a person is aware of, endorses, and develops proactive procedures to enhance product quality, ensure early disclosure of discrepancies, and integrate quality assessments with cost and schedule performance measurement reports to maximize client's satisfaction with overall performance.

OUTSTANDING	7	Uses measures of quality and well-defined processes to achieve project goals. Defines quality from the client's perspective.
	6	Looks for/identifies ways to continually improve the process.
	5	Clearly communicates quality management to others. Develops a plan that defines how the team will participate in quality.
		Appreciates TQM as an investment.
AVERAGE	4	Has measures of quality that define tolerance levels.
	3	Views quality as costly. Legislates quality.
	2	Focuses his/her concerns only on outputs and deliverables, ignoring the underlying processes.
POOR	1	Blames others for absence of quality. Gives lip service only to quality concerns.

SOURCE: Landy, Jacobs, and Associates. Used with permission.

achieve the desired results. But the approach has disadvantages as well. Objectives may be unrealistic, frustrating the employee and the manager, or too rigid, leaving the employee without enough flexibility if circumstances change. Finally, MBO often focuses too much on short-term achievement at the expense of long-term goals.

None of these performance appraisal systems is easy to conduct properly, and all have drawbacks. In choosing an appraisal method, the following guidelines may prove helpful:

- Base performance standards on job analysis.
- Communicate performance standards to employees.
- Evaluate employees on specific performance-related behaviors rather than on a single global or overall measure.
- Document the performance appraisal process carefully.
- If possible, use more than one rater.
- Develop a formal appeal process.
- Always take legal considerations into account.[38]

Who should do the appraisal?

Just as multiple methods can be used to gather performance appraisal information, several different sources can provide that information:

- *Managers* and *supervisors* are the traditional source of appraisal information because they are often best positioned to observe an employee's performance.
- *Peers* and *team members* see different dimensions of performance and may be best at identifying leadership potential and interpersonal skills. Companies are therefore turning to peers and team members to provide input to the performance appraisal.
- *Subordinates* are becoming a more popular source of appraisal information, used by companies such as Xerox and IBM to give superiors feedback on how their employees view them. Often this information is given in confidence to the manager and not shared with superiors. Even so, this approach can make managers uncomfortable initially, but the feedback is often practical and can help them significantly improve their management style. Because this process gives employees power over their bosses, it is

generally used for development purposes only, not for salary or promotion decisions.

- *Internal and external customers* are relevant sources of performance appraisal information in companies, such as Ford and Honda, that are focused on total quality management. External customers have been used for some time to appraise restaurant employees. Internal customers can include anyone inside the organization who depends on an employee's work output.
- *Self-appraisals,* in which employees evaluate their own performance, usually are a good idea. Although they may be biased upward, the process of self-evaluation helps increase the employee's involvement in the review process and is a starting point for setting future goals.

Because each source of information has some limitations, and since different people may see different aspects of performance, Westinghouse, Eastman Kodak, and many other companies have involved more than one source for appraisal information. In a process known as 360-degree appraisal, feedback is obtained from subordinates, peers, and superiors—every level involved with the employee. Often the person being rated can select the appraisers, subject to a manager's approval, with the understanding that the individual appraisals are kept confidential; returned forms might not include the name of the appraiser, for example, and the results may be consolidated for each level.

The 360-degree appraisal delivers a fuller picture of the employee's strengths and weaknesses, and it often captures qualities other appraisal methods miss. For example, an employee may have a difficult relationship with his or her supervisor yet be highly regarded by peers and subordinates. The approach can lead to significant improvement, with employees often motivated to improve their ratings. On the downside, employees may be unwilling to rate colleagues harshly, so a certain uniformity of ratings may result. Also, the 360-degree appraisal is less useful than more objective criteria, like financial targets. It is usually aimed at employee development, rather than being a

A+

TIP

Appraisals are most effective when they are based on an ongoing relationship with employees and are not just a top-down formal judgment issued yearly. Managers of sports teams do not wait until the season is over to perform an appraisal. Instead, they work with team members throughout the season, and with the team as a whole, to improve the team's performance. Similarly, in high-functioning organizations, informal appraisal and feedback are constantly occurring. Managers discuss the organization's goals regularly to create a shared understanding of the required job performance. They try to create an atmosphere in which they and their employees are working together on a common agenda. And they communicate with their employees daily, praising or coaching as appropriate and together assessing progress toward goals. When managers and employees have open communication and employees feel fairly and effectively managed, the content of their appraisals should rarely surprise them.

tool for administrative decisions like raises. For those, results appraisals like MBO are more appropriate.[39]

How do you give employees feedback?

Giving performance feedback can be stressful for managers and subordinates because its purposes conflict to some degree. Providing growth and development requires understanding and support, but the manager must be impersonal and able to make tough decisions. Employees want to know how they are doing, but typically they are uncomfortable about getting feedback. Finally, the organization's need to make HR decisions conflicts with the individual employee's need to maintain a positive image.[40] These conflicts often make performance interviews difficult, so managers should conduct them thoughtfully.

In general, appraisal feedback works best when it is *specific* and *constructive*—related to clear goals or behaviors and clearly intended to help the employee rather than simply criticize. Managers have an interest not just in rating performance but in raising it, and effective appraisals take that into account. In addition, the appraisal is likely to be more meaningful and satisfying when the manager gives the employee a chance to discuss his or her performance and respond to the appraisal.

Interviews are most difficult with an employee who is performing poorly. Here is a useful interview format for when an employee is performing below acceptable standards:

If an employee has an addiction to drugs or alcohol, exhibits dangerous behavior, or is volatile, the manager must still give feedback. About 500 million workdays are lost each year due to alcoholism, and about 80 percent of alcoholics are employed either full- or part-time. But it is often difficult for a manager to point out the problem directly. "Managers can't identify the problem, even if they are sure, because that would mean they are making a diagnosis, and they aren't qualified to do that," explains Bill Arnold, corporate director of substance-abuse counseling services for Quad/Graphics. Human resource experts advise managers to treat the situation as a job performance issue instead, referring to lost productivity, missed meetings, and the like—and help the employee make plans for improvement.[41]

A potentially violent employee is another situation that needs feedback. Workers who shout threats or have angry outbursts "must be taken seriously," says Carmeline Procaccini, vice president of human resources at Pegasystems, a software company. "We've trained our managers not to take any chances," she continues. She advises supervisors to contact HR staff and executives immediately about any employee who seems overly upset or potentially violent. In the end, the firm must act in the best interests of its other employees.[42]

Here are some guidelines for giving feedback to an average employee:

1. Summarize the employee's performance, and be specific.
2. Explain why the employee's work is important to the organization.

> "Outstanding leaders go out of their way to boost the self-esteem of their personnel. If people believe in themselves, it's amazing what they can accomplish."
>
> —Sam Walton

1. Summarize the employee's specific performance. Describe the performance in behavioral or outcome terms, such as sales or absenteeism. Don't say the employee has a poor attitude; rather, explain which employee behaviors indicate a poor attitude.
2. Describe the expectations and standards, and be specific.
3. Determine the causes for the low performance; get the employee's input.
4. Discuss solutions to the problem, and have the employee play a major role in the process.
5. Agree to a solution. As a supervisor, you have input into the solution. Raise issues and questions, but also provide support.
6. Agree to a timetable for improvement.
7. Document the meeting.

Follow-up meetings may be needed.

3. Thank the employee for doing the job.
4. Raise any relevant issues, such as areas for improvement.
5. Express confidence in the employee's future good performance.

L O 6 WHAT YOU NEED TO KNOW . . .
Can you describe the fundamental aspects of a reward system?

DESIGNING REWARD SYSTEMS

Another major set of HRM activities involves reward systems. This section emphasizes monetary rewards such as pay and fringe benefits.

Pay decisions consider the company, position, and individual

Reward systems can serve the strategic purposes of attracting, motivating, and retaining people. The wages paid to employees are based on a complex set of forces. Beyond the body of laws governing compensation, a number of basic decisions must be made in choosing the appropriate pay plan. The wage mix is influenced by a variety of factors:[43]

- *Internal factors* include the organization's compensation policy, the worth of each job, the employee's relative worth, and the employer's ability to pay.

- *External factors* include conditions of the labor market, area wage rates, the cost of living, the use of collective bargaining (union negotiations), and legal requirements.

Three types of decisions are crucial for designing an effective pay plan:

1. *Pay level*—the choice of whether to be a high-, average-, or low-paying company. Compensation is a major cost for any organization, so low wages can be justified on a short-term financial basis. But being the high-wage employer—the highest-paying company in the region—ensures that the company will attract many applicants. Being a wage leader may be important during times of low unemployment or intense competition.

2. *Pay structure*—the choice of how to price different jobs within the organization. Jobs that are similar in worth usually are grouped together into job families. A pay grade, with a floor and a ceiling, is established for each job family. Figure 7.5 illustrates a hypothetical pay structure.

3. *Individual pay decisions*—different pay rates for jobs of similar worth within the same family. Differences in pay within job families are decided in two ways. First, some jobs are occupied by individuals with more seniority than others. Second, some people may perform better and therefore deserve higher pay. Setting an individual's pay below that of coworkers—like choosing an overall low pay level—may become more difficult for employers to sustain in the future, as more employees use online resources such as Salary.com and PayScale.com to check whether their pay is above or below the average amount for similar job titles.[44]

Unlike many other types of decisions in organizations, decisions about pay, especially at the individual level, often are kept confidential. Is that practice advantageous for organizations? Surprisingly, there is little evidence about this practice, even though it affects almost every private-sector employee.[45] Keeping pay decisions secret may help the organization by avoiding conflicts, protecting individuals' privacy, and reducing the likelihood that employees will leave to seek better pay if they are earning less than the average for their position. However, if decisions about pay are kept secret, employees may worry that decisions are unfair and may be less motivated because the link between performance and pay is unclear. Also, in an economic sense, labor markets are less efficient when information is unavailable, which can reduce organizations' ability to get the best workers at the optimum rate of pay. Given these possible pros and cons of pay secrecy, do you think this practice is wise? Is it ethical? And what about you—do you want to know how much your coworkers earn?

Incentive pay encourages employees to do their best

Various incentive systems have been devised to motivate employees to be more productive.[46] The most common are *individual incentive plans*, which compare a worker's performance

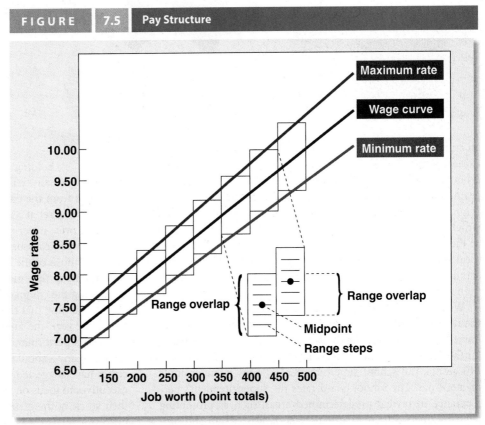

FIGURE 7.5 Pay Structure

SOURCE: From *Managing Human Resources,* 11th ed., by Bohlander/Snell/Sherman. © 1998. Reprinted with permission of South-Western, a division of Thomson Learning, www.thomsonrights.com. Fax 800 730-2215.

against an objective standard, with pay determined by the employee's performance. Examples include paying a salesperson extra for exceeding a sales target or awarding managers a bonus when their group meets a target. If effectively designed, individual incentive plans can be highly motivating. Some companies, including Walmart, are even beginning to use them for non-managers. Walmart hopes that using bonuses to reward hourly employees for meeting sales, profit, and inventory targets at their stores each quarter will build employees' job satisfaction and reduce turnover.[47]

Several types of group incentive plans, in which pay is based on group performance, are increasingly used today. The plans aim to give employees a sense of participation and ownership in the firm's performance. *Gainsharing plans* reward employees for increasing productivity or saving money in areas under their direct control.[48] For example, if the usual waste allowance in a production line has been 5 percent and the company wants production employees to reduce that number, the company may offer to split any savings gained with the employees. *Profit-sharing plans* are usually implemented in the division or organization as a whole, although some incentives may still be tailored to unit performance. In most companies, the profit-sharing plan is based on a formula for allocating

These chefs from Tersiguel's French Country Restaurant in Maryland have a reason to be smiling: their employer offers reward systems that include employer-matched 401(k), profit sharing, and health benefits.

an annual amount to each employee if the company exceeds a specified profit target. Although profit-sharing plans do not reward individual performance, they do give all employees a stake in the company's success and motivate efforts to improve the company's profitability. Enterprise Rent-A-Car, which gives branch managers great latitude to address the needs of their local markets, uses an incentive pay system that allows local offices to share in the profits they have generated. The arrangement is especially attractive to employees with an entrepreneurial streak.[49]

When objective performance measures are unavailable but the company still wants to base pay on performance, it uses a *merit pay system.* Individuals' pay raises and bonuses are based on the merit rating they receive from their boss. In Rochester, Minnesota, the school superintendent's bonus is an example of merit pay. The school board rates the superintendent's performance in several predetermined areas, such as promoting teamwork between the board and school district staff and supporting the board in developing a strategic plan. In a recent year, the superintendent received an average score of 3 on a four-point scale, so the board awarded him three-quarters of the maximum bonus.[50]

Executive pay has generated controversy

In recent years the issue of executive pay has stirred controversy. One reason is that the gap between the pay of top executives and the average pay of employees has widened considerably. In the 1980s CEOs made less than 40 times the average worker's pay, and the multiple has now reached 500 times the average worker's pay. This gap is considerably wider in the United States than it is abroad.[51] Besides the difference between executive and average-worker pay, the sheer size of CEO compensation also has been criticized. Top-earning CEOs can make tens of millions of dollars a year. Still, it's important to keep in mind that the huge awards that make headlines are not necessarily typical. In a recent year, CEOs of companies in the Standard & Poor's stock index earned on average $4.5 million, but the median was $2.5 million, because a few executives with far higher earnings pushed the average higher.[52]

The fastest-growing part of executive compensation comes from stock grants and *stock options.* Such options give the holder the right to purchase shares of stock at a specified price. For example, if the company's stock price is $8 a share, the company may award a manager the right to purchase a specific number of shares of company stock at that price. If the price of the stock rises to, say, $10 a share after a specified holding period—usually three years or more—the manager can *exercise* the option. He or she can purchase the shares from the company at $8 per share, sell the shares on the stock market at $10, and keep the difference. (Of course, if the stock price never rises above $8, the options will be worthless.) Companies issue options to managers to align their interests with those of the company's owners, the shareholders. The assumption is that managers will become even more focused on making the company successful, leading to a rise in its stock price. Assuming that the executives continue to own their stock year after year, the amount of their wealth that is tied to the company's performance—and their incentive to work hard for the company—should continually increase.[53] However, many critics have suggested that excessive use of options encouraged executives to focus on short-term results to drive up the price of their stock, at the expense of their firm's long-run competitiveness. More recently, a plunging stock market highlighted another problem with stock options: many options became essentially worthless, so they failed to reward employees.[54] In the future, employees may be wary about accepting stock options in lieu of less risky forms of pay.

Employees get benefits, too

Although pay has traditionally been employees' primary monetary reward, benefits have been receiving increased attention. Benefits currently make up a far greater percentage of the total payroll than they did in past decades.[55] The typical employer today pays about 30 percent of payroll costs in benefits. Throughout most of the past two decades, benefits costs have risen faster than wages and salaries, fueled by the rapidly rising cost of medical care. Accordingly, employers are attempting to reduce benefits costs, even as their value to employees is rising. Benefits are also receiving more management attention because of their increased complexity. Many new types of benefits are now available, and tax laws affect myriad fringe benefits, such as health insurance and pension plans.

Like pay systems, employee benefit plans are subject to regulation. Employee benefits are divided into those required by law and those optional for an employer. Three basic benefits are required by law:

1. *Workers' compensation* provides financial support to employees suffering a work-related injury or illness.

2. *Social Security,* as established in the Social Security Act of 1935, provides financial support to retirees; in subsequent amendments, the act was expanded to cover disabled employees. The funds come from payments made by employers, employees, and self-employed workers.

3. *Unemployment insurance* provides financial support to employees laid off for reasons they cannot control. Companies that have terminated fewer employees pay less into the unemployment insurance fund, so organizations have an incentive to minimize terminations.

Many employers also offer benefits that are not required. The most common are pension plans and medical and hospital insurance. Both of these programs are undergoing significant change, partly because, in a global economy, they have put U.S. firms at a competitive disadvantage. For example, U.S. employers spend an average of $9,000 for each employee with health insurance.[56] Overseas firms generally do not bear these costs, which are usually government funded, so they can compete more effectively on price. With U.S. medical costs rising rapidly, companies have reduced health benefits or asked employees to share more of their cost. A growing share of U.S. companies (more than one-third) offer no medical benefits at all, or they staff more positions with part-time workers and offer coverage only to full-time employees. At the same time, retirement benefits have been shifting away from guaranteed pensions. While a promised monthly pension used to be the norm, almost no company offers it to new employees today; most workers with such pensions are government employees.[57] More often, the employee, the employer, or both contribute to an individual retirement account or 401(k) plan, which is invested. Upon retirement, the employee gets the balance that has accumulated in the account.

Because of the wide variety of possible benefits and the considerable differences in employee preferences and needs, companies often use **cafeteria** or **flexible benefit programs**. In this type of program, employees are given credits, which they "spend" by selecting individualized packages of benefits, including medical and dental insurance, dependent care, life insurance, and so on.

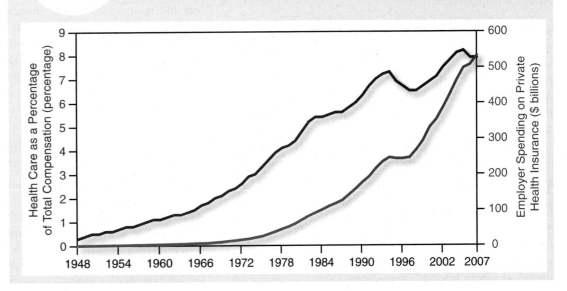

? Rapidly rising medical costs have made health care coverage an expensive part of employers' benefits packages.[58] Some employers—especially small ones—have coped by dropping health insurance altogether.

Pay and benefits must meet legal requirements

Several laws affect employee compensation and benefits. We have already mentioned the FLSA, which in addition to distinguishing between exempt and nonexempt employees also sets minimum wage, maximum hour, and child labor provisions.[59] The *Equal Pay Act (EPA)* of 1963 prohibits unequal pay for men and women who perform equal work. Equal work means jobs that require equal skill, effort, and responsibility and are performed under similar working conditions. The law does permit exceptions in which the difference in pay is due to a seniority system, merit system, incentive system based on quantity or quality of production, or any additional factor other than sex, such as market demand.

In contrast to the equal-pay-for-equal-work notion, comparable-worth doctrine implies that women who perform *different* jobs of *equal* worth as those performed by men should be paid the same wage.[60] For example, nurses (predominantly female) were found to be paid considerably less than skilled craftworkers (predominantly male), even though the two jobs were found to be of equal value or worth.[61] Under the Equal Pay Act, this would not constitute pay discrimination because the jobs are very different. But under the comparable-worth concept, these findings would indicate discrimination because the jobs are of equal worth. To date, no federal law requires comparable worth, and the Supreme Court has made no decisive rulings about it. However, some states have considered developing comparable-worth laws, and others have raised the wages of female-dominated jobs. For example, Minnesota passed a comparable-worth law for public-sector employees after finding that women on average were paid 25 percent less than men. Iowa, Idaho, New Mexico, Washington, and South Dakota also have comparable-worth laws for public-sector employees.[62]

Some laws influence benefit practices. The *Pregnancy Discrimination Act* of 1978 states that pregnancy is a disability and qualifies a woman to receive the same benefits that she would with any other disability. The *Employee Retirement Income Security Act (ERISA)* of 1974 protects private pension programs from mismanagement. ERISA requires retirement benefits to be paid to those who vest or earn a right to draw benefits and ensures retirement benefits for employees whose companies go bankrupt or who otherwise cannot meet their pension obligations.

Employers must protect health and safety

The *Occupational Safety and Health Act (OSHA)* of 1970 requires employers to pursue workplace safety. Employers must maintain records of injuries and deaths caused by workplace accidents and submit to on-site inspections. Large-scale industrial accidents and nuclear power plant disasters worldwide have focused attention on the importance of workplace safety.

Coal mining is one of many industries that benefit from safety laws. Mining is one of the five most dangerous jobs to perform, according to the U.S. Bureau of Labor Statistics. Nearly every coal miner can name a friend or family member who has been killed, maimed, or stricken with black lung disease. "You die quick or you die slow," reports one mine worker. Mine safety tragically returned to American consciousness in January 2006, when 12 miners died after being trapped by an explosion in the International Coal Group (ICG) mine in Sago, West Virginia. Critics of ICG's safety practices noted that more than 200 safety citations had been issued against the mine in the previous year, but fines totaled only $24,000.[63] However, according to the Mine Safety and Health Administration, mines have become safer. In the 1960s, hundreds of coal miners died in mine accidents every year; in 1986, 89 miners died (4.8 percent of coal miners), and even with the Sago tragedy in 2006, 47 miners (3.9 percent) died that year.[64]

Another area of concern is the safety of young workers, who may lack the confidence to speak up if they see health or safety problems. A recent study of teenage workers found that many were exposed to hazards and used equipment that should have been off-limits to teens under federal regulations. For example, almost half of teenaged grocery store employees said they had performed prohibited tasks such as using box crushers and dough mixers.[65]

L 0 7 WHAT YOU NEED TO KNOW . . .

How do unions and labor laws influence human resources management?

LABOR RELATIONS

Labor relations is the system of relations between workers and management. Labor unions recruit members, collect dues, and ensure that employees are treated fairly with respect to wages, working conditions, and other issues. When workers organize and negotiate with management, two processes are involved: unionization and collective bargaining. These processes have evolved since the 1930s in the United States to provide important employee rights.[66]

What labor laws exist?

Passed in 1935, the *National Labor Relations Act* (also called the *Wagner Act* after its legislative sponsor) ushered in an era of rapid unionization by declaring labor organizations legal, establishing five unfair employer labor practices, and creating the National Labor Relations Board (NLRB). Before the act, employers could fire workers who favored unions, and federal troops were often provided to put down strikes. Today the NLRB conducts unionization elections, hears complaints of

These protestors in Fontana, California accuse Walmart of paying low wages, offering no health care or benefits, and trying to prevent employees from forming unions. The protest resulted in seven arrests. How might the retail giant respond to these accusations?

authorization cards that permit workers to indicate whether they want an election to certify the union. The National Labor Relations Board will conduct an election if at least 30 percent of the employees sign authorization cards. Management has several choices at this stage: to recognize the union without an election, to consent to an election, or to contest the number of cards signed and resist an election.

If an election is warranted, an NLRB representative conducts the election by secret ballot. A simple majority of those voting determines the winner, so apathetic workers who do not vote in effect support the union. If the union wins the election, it is certified as the bargaining unit representative. Management and the union are then legally required to bargain in good faith to obtain a collective bargaining agreement or contract.

unfair labor practices, and issues injunctions against offending employers. The Wagner Act greatly assisted the growth of unions by enabling workers to use the law and the courts to organize and collectively bargain for better wages, hours, and working conditions. Minimum wages, health benefits, maternity leave, the 40-hour workweek, and other worker protections were largely the result of collective bargaining over many years by unions.

Public policy began on the side of organized labor in 1935, but over the next 25 years, the pendulum swung toward management. The *Labor-Management Relations Act,* or *Taft-Hartley Act* (1947), protected employers' free-speech rights, defined unfair labor practices by unions, and permitted workers to decertify (reject) a union as their representative.

Finally, the *Labor-Management Reporting and Disclosure Act,* or *Landrum-Griffin Act* (1959), swung the public policy pendulum midway between organized labor and management. By declaring a bill of rights for union members, establishing control over union dues increases, and imposing reporting requirements for unions, Landrum-Griffin was designed to curb abuses by union leadership and rid unions of corruption.

How do employees form unions?

The effort to form a union begins when a union organizer or local union representative describes to workers the benefits they may receive by joining.[67] The union representative distributes

Why do workers vote for a union? Four factors play a significant role:[68]

1. *Economic factors,* especially for workers in low-paying jobs—Unions attempt to raise the average wage rate for their members.

2. *Job dissatisfaction*—Poor supervisory practices, favoritism, lack of communication, and perceived unfair or arbitrary discipline and discharge are specific triggers of job dissatisfaction.

3. *Belief that the union has power* to obtain desired benefits can generate a pro-union vote.

4. The *image of the union*—Headline stories of union corruption and dishonesty can discourage workers from unionization.

How is collective bargaining conducted?

In the United States, management and unions engage in a periodic ritual (typically every three years) of negotiating an agreement over wages, benefits, hours, and working conditions. Disputes can arise during this process, and sometimes the workers go on strike to compel agreement on their terms. Such an action, known as an *economic strike,* is permitted by law, but strikes are rare today. Strikers are not paid while they are on strike, and few workers want to undertake this hardship unnecessarily. In addition, managers may legally hire replacement workers during a strike, offsetting some of the strike's effect. Finally, workers are as aware as managers of the tougher competition companies face today; if treated fairly, they will usually share management's interest in coming to an agreement.

Once an agreement is signed, management and the union sometimes disagree over *interpretation* of the agreement. Usually they settle their disputes through **arbitration**, the use of a neutral third party, typically jointly selected, to resolve the dispute. The United States uses arbitration while an agreement is in effect to avoid *wildcat strikes* (in which workers walk off the job in violation of the contract) or unplanned work stoppages.

Certain clauses are common in a collective bargaining agreement:

- *Security clause*—In a **union shop**, the contract requires workers to join the union after a set period of time. **Right-to-work** states, through restrictive laws, do not permit union shops; workers have the right to work without being forced to join a union. The southern United States has many right-to-work states.

- *Wage component*—The contract spells out rates of pay, including premium pay for overtime and paid holidays.

- *Individual rights*—These include the use of seniority to determine pay increases, job bidding, and the order of layoffs.

- *Grievance procedure*—This procedure gives workers a voice in what goes on during contract negotiations and administration.[69] In about 50 percent of discharge cases that go to arbitration, the arbitrator overturns management's decision and reinstates the worker.[70]

Unions have a legal duty of fair representation, which means they must represent all workers in the bargaining unit and ensure that workers' rights are protected.

What does the future hold?

In recent years union membership has declined to about 12 percent of the U.S. labor force—down from a peak of over 33 percent at the end of World War II. Increased automation eliminated many of the manufacturing jobs that used to be union strongholds. Employees in today's white-collar office jobs are less interested in joining unions and are also more difficult to organize. Tough global competition has made managers much less willing to give in to union demands, so the benefits of unionization are less clear to many workers—particularly young, skilled workers who no longer expect to stay with one company all their lives. In addition, elimination of inefficient work rules, the introduction of profit sharing, and a guarantee of no layoffs have been seen as steps toward a fundamentally different, cooperative long-term relationship.

When companies recognize that their success depends on the talents and energies of employees, the interests of unions and managers begin to converge. Rather than one side exploiting the other, unions and managers find common ground based on developing, valuing, and involving employees. Particularly in knowledge-based companies, the balance of power is shifting toward employees. Individuals, not companies, own their own human capital. This leaves poorly managed organizations in a particularly vulnerable position. To compete, organizations are searching for ways to obtain, retain, and engage their most valuable resources: human resources.

> "Endeavors succeed or fail because of the people involved. Only by attracting the best people will you accomplish great deeds."
>
> —Colin Powell

Build Your Skills

Practice and apply your knowledge by going online at

www.mhhe.com/BatemanM2e

WHAT YOU NEED TO KNOW

• • learning **OBJECTIVES**

After studying Chapter 8,
you will be able to:

LO1 Describe how changes in the U.S.
workforce make diversity a critical
organizational and managerial issue.

LO2 Distinguish between affirmative action
and managing diversity.

LO3 Explain how diversity, if well managed,
can give organizations a competitive edge.

LO4 Identify challenges associated with
managing a diverse workforce.

LO5 Define monolithic, pluralistic, and
multicultural organizations.

LO6 List steps managers and their organizations
can take to cultivate diversity.

LO7 Summarize the skills and knowledge
managers need to manage globally.

LO8 Identify ways in which cultural differences
across countries influence management.

In the previous chapter, we described the laws that require equal opportunity and fair treatment in the workplace. But a proactive approach—of seeking and capitalizing on the benefits of a diverse workforce—is fundamental to the success of many organizations today. For example, by hiring people from diverse backgrounds and emphasizing training and mentoring to help them contribute fully, Marriott International has created a competitive advantage in the hospitality industry.[1] In contrast, managers who lack the skills to lead men and women of different colors, cultures, ages, abilities, and backgrounds will be at a significant disadvantage in their careers.

In the United States, the number of racial and ethnic minorities is increasing far faster than the growth rate in the white, nonminority population, and women make up a sizable share of the workforce. American workers, customers, and markets are highly diverse and becoming even more so. In addition, businesses are increasingly global, so managers

Managing the Diverse Workforce

Learn the Key Ways

today's young managers are benefiting from employee diversity and a global perspective. Listen to what Joe and Angel have to say on the book Web site.

"It doesn't matter how old someone is, what gender they are or what race they are. Everyone can load boxes in a truck. The difficulty is relating to individuals on a personal level or resolving a conflict between different work groups".
—*Joe Kubinski, Operations Supervisor*

"Management is full of responsibility. Even though your rank may be higher in the company than others, treat everyone with respect and they will respect you as a manager. Talk with your coworkers and do not hand out orders. Remember that you want these people to want to be on your team."
—*Angel Chavez, Art Manager*

must be much more aware of, and sensitive to, cultural differences. Also, the creativity and innovation that are vital for organizational success are fostered in an atmosphere that celebrates different perspectives and bright people from all walks of life. Few societies have access to the range of talents available in the United States, with its immigrant tradition and racially and ethnically diverse population. Yet getting people from divergent backgrounds to work together effectively is not easy. For this reason, managing diversity is one of America's biggest challenges—and opportunities.

Managing diversity involves, first, such basic activities as recruiting, training, promoting, and utilizing to full advantage individuals with different backgrounds, beliefs, capabilities, and cultures. But it means more than just hiring women and minorities and making sure they are treated equally and encouraged to succeed. It also means understanding and deeply valuing employee differences to build a more effective and profitable organization. Organizations that strive to foster the richness that a diverse workforce brings also work to build bridges between those employees to tap their potential. Such inclusion moves beyond valuing the differences of employees to valuing the connections that arise and develop between them.

This chapter examines the meaning of diversity and the management skills and organizational processes involved in managing the diverse workforce effectively. We begin by identifying the changes in society and the workplace that are creating this more diverse U.S. workforce. Next, we consider challenges of diversity and ways to address those challenges. Then we explore the practices that support inclusion. Finally, because companies today have a global presence, we end by describing how to manage in environments with economic, cultural, and geographic differences.

"e pluribus unum"

Those people were considered outsiders because most did not speak English and had different customs and work styles. They struggled to gain acceptance in the steel, coal, automobile manufacturing, insurance, and finance industries. As late as the 1940s, and sometimes beyond, colleges routinely discriminated against immigrants, Catholics, and Jews, establishing strict quotas that limited their number, if any were admitted at all. This type of discrimination severely diminished the employment prospects of these groups until the 1960s.

Women's struggle for acceptance in the workplace was in some ways even more difficult. When the Women's Rights Movement was launched in Seneca Falls in 1848, most occupations were off-limits to women, and colleges and professional schools were closed to them. In the first part of the 20th century, when women began to be accepted into professional schools, they were subject to severe quotas. There was also a widespread assumption that certain jobs were done only by men, and other jobs only by women. As recently as the 1970s, classified-ad sections in newspapers listed jobs by sex, with sections headed "Help Wanted—Males" and "Help Wanted—Females." Women who wanted a bank loan needed a male cosigner, and married women were not issued credit cards in their own name.[2] This discrimination started to decline when the Civil Rights Act of 1964 and other legislation began to be enforced. Although women are still underrepresented at the most senior levels of corporate life, and their average pay rates still lag those of men, most jobs are now open to women.

The most difficult and wrenching struggle for equality involved America's nonwhite minorities. Rigid racial segregation of education, employment, and housing persisted for 100 years after the end of the Civil War. After years of courageous protest and struggle, the unanimous *Brown v. Board of Education* Supreme Court decision in 1954 declared segregation unconstitutional, setting the stage for laws we discussed in Chapter 7, including the Civil Rights Act of 1964. Although the struggle for equality is far from complete, many civil rights—equal

(L)(O) 1 **WHAT YOU NEED TO KNOW . . .**
How do changes in the U.S. workforce make diversity a critical organizational and managerial issue?

DIVERSITY: PAST, PRESENT, AND FUTURE

Diversity is far from a new challenge for managers in the United States. However, over time, U.S. businesses have changed their approach to managing diversity.

Diversity shaped America's past

From the late 1800s to the early 1900s, most of the immigrants to the United States came from Italy, Poland, Ireland, and Russia.

opportunity, fair treatment in housing, the illegality of religious, racial, and sex discrimination—received their greatest impetus from the Civil Rights movement.

With this background, the traditional American image of diversity emphasized assimilation. The United States was considered the "melting pot" of the world, a country where ethnic and racial differences were blended into an American purée. In real life, many ethnic and most racial groups retained their identities but did not express them at work. Deemphasizing their ethnic and cultural distinctions helped employees keep their jobs and get ahead.

Diversity is growing in today's workforce

Today, nearly half of the U.S. workforce consists of women, 14 percent of U.S. workers identify themselves as Hispanic or Latino, and 11 percent are black. One-third of all businesses in the United States are owned by women, employing about 20 percent of America's workers. Two-thirds of all global migration is into the United States.[3] U.S. businesses do not have a choice of whether to have a diverse workforce; if they want to survive, they must learn to manage a diverse workforce sooner or better than their competitors do.

Today's immigrants are willing to be part of an integrated team, but they no longer are willing to sacrifice their cultural identities to get ahead. Nor do they have to do so. Companies are recognizing that accommodating employees' differences pays off in business. Managers are also realizing that their customers are becoming increasingly diverse, so retaining a diversified workforce can provide a significant competitive advantage in the marketplace.

Diversity today refers to far more than skin color and gender. The term broadly refers to a variety of differences, summarized in Figure 8.1. These differences include religious affiliation, age, disability status, military experience, sexual orientation, economic class, educational level, and lifestyle, as well as gender, race, ethnicity, and nationality.

Although members of different groups (white males, people born during the Depression, homosexuals, Iraq war veterans, Hispanics, Asians, women, African Americans, etc.) share within their groups many common values, attitudes, and perceptions, much diversity also exists within each category. Every group consists of individuals who are unique in personality, education, and life experiences. There may be more differences among, say, three Asians from Thailand, Hong Kong, and Korea than among a white, an African American, and an Asian all born in Chicago. And white males differ in their personal or professional goals and values.

Thus, managing diversity may seem to be a contradiction. It means being acutely aware of characteristics *common* to a group of employees, while also managing these employees as *individuals*. Managing diversity means not just tolerating or accommodating all sorts of differences but supporting, nurturing, and utilizing these differences to the organization's advantage.

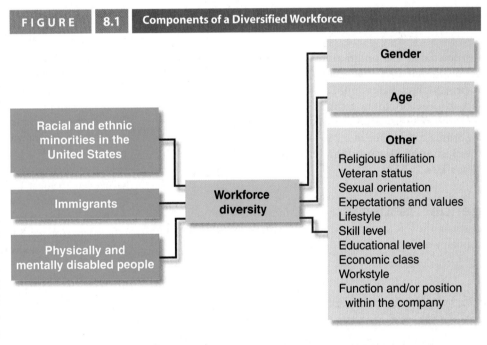

FIGURE 8.1 Components of a Diversified Workforce

Borders Books, for example, tries to match the demographics of its workforce with the demographics of the communities in which its stores operate. Top managers at the company say that sales are better as a result.

As Figure 8.2 shows, a sizable number of HR executives say their companies need to or plan to expand their diversity training programs. Although many companies initially

> "Human diversity makes tolerance more than a virtue; it makes it a requirement for survival."
>
> —Rene Dubos

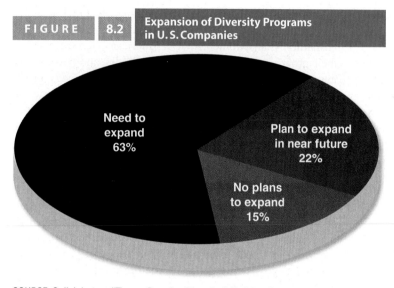

FIGURE 8.2 Expansion of Diversity Programs in U.S. Companies

Need to expand
63%

Plan to expand
in near future
22%

No plans
to expand
15%

SOURCE: Gail Johnson, "Time to Broaden Diversity," *Training*, September 2004, p. 16.

- Women make up about 47 percent of the workforce.
- The overall labor force participation rate of women rose throughout the 1970s through the 1990s and is now holding steady even as the participation rate of men gradually declines.
- Almost 60 percent of marriages are dual-earner marriages.
- One of every four married women in two-income households earns more than her husband does.[4]

Balancing work life with family responsibilities presents an enormous challenge. Although men's roles in our society have been changing, women still carry the bulk of family responsibilities. That puts women at a disadvantage in companies that expect employees, particularly at the managerial level, to put in long hours and sacrifice their personal lives for the sake of their jobs, organizations, and careers. It also may cause those companies to lose valuable talent. Some companies therefore offer their employees ways to balance work and family commitments with such benefits as onsite child care, in-home care for elderly family members, flexible work schedules, and the use of newer technologies that permit more work from home.

Still, as managers weigh employees' needs for flexibility against the organization's need for productivity, they have to make complex decisions weighing job requirements and each employee's contributions and motivation. Michele Coleman Mayes, senior vice president and general counsel of Pitney Bowes, agreed to let one attorney leave promptly at five o'clock each evening; the attorney works on her laptop at night as needed to meet her deadlines. But Mayes refused another employee's request to work part-time because the person in that position needed to be available each day to handle requests for other departments. Mayes tells her employees that scheduling decisions "may not always be equal, but I will try to be fair."[5]

institued diversity programs to prevent discrimination, more are beginning to see the programs as a crucial way to expand their customer bases both domestically and worldwide. In fact, two out of three companies said they had broadened their diversity programs because of increasing globalization, according to a survey of 1,780 HR and training executives by the Boston-based consulting firm Novations/J. Howard and Associates.

gender issues One of the most important developments in the U.S. labor market has been the growing number of women working outside the home. Consider this:

BNSF Taps the Strength of Veterans

In a recession economy, the people facing the toughest time landing a job may be America's returning veterans. In a recent year, unemployment for 18- to 24-year-old veterans stood at 14 percent, compared with 11.5 percent among nonveterans in the same age range.

Veterans acquire transferable skills in the military—such as communication, team building, problem solving, and critical thinking—yet many lack practical job experience and a college degree. As a result, prospective employers may overlook the military, which generates about 40,000 new civilian workers each year, as a viable source of job candidates.

But hiring from the military can make good sense. For most jobs in civilian life, a parallel

job is performed in the military. Also, in an all-volunteer military, service personnel tend to be older, more experienced, and better trained than in past years. Each branch of the military represents a diverse pool of talent, and some employers, like Fort Worth–based Burlington Northern Santa Fe Railway (BNSF), are paying attention.

BNSF's history of hiring veterans dates back to the Civil War. Since 2005, the company has hired more than 3,000 veterans, and its 39,000-employee workforce includes a significant number of National Guard and reservists. In 2008, more than one in five new hires were veterans. Nearly a thousand BNSF employees have been called to active duty since September 11, 2001.

Company chairman, president, and CEO Matt Rose says BNSF's veterans are "mission-focused, highly skilled, motivated and possess unique experiences and technical knowledge." Rose claims that military candidates mirror BNSF's core competencies: "leadership, teamwork, and the ability to perform safely in a fast-paced, dynamic environment."

Veterans who join BNSF undergo extensive "immersion" training in railroad industry operations. They may train for locomotive engineering positions or attend conductor training, learning operations roles and transportation techniques before continued field training.

Considered one of the nation's top military-friendly employers, BNSF includes in its careers Web site a page specifically geared to military

The desire for flexible scheduling is often cited as a reason why significant pay disparities remain between men and women. The average full-time working woman earns about 80 percent as much as men in the same job (recall the discussion in Chapter 7 about equal pay and comparable worth). Although the gap has narrowed most years since the 1970s, a recent study found that the gap between the earnings of college-educated men and women actually increased after they spent 10 years in the workforce. Some of the difference is explained by women tending to choose lower-paid occupations, work fewer hours, and devote time to bearing and raising children. But even when the researchers controlled for these and other known variables, one-quarter of the pay gap remained unexplained.[6]

Another concern involving female workers is the low representation of women in top jobs. As women—along with minorities—move up the corporate ladder, they encounter a glass ceiling, a metaphor for an invisible barrier that makes it difficult for women and minorities to move beyond a certain level in the corporate hierarchy. For example, just 12 women are chief executives of *Fortune* 500 companies—that's 12 out of 500. Looking at all corporate officers of those companies, 16 percent are women, and less than 2 percent are minority women.[7] Still, women's leadership is beginning to be seen at a broader range of companies. Today's well-known female CEOs include Indra Nooyi of PepsiCo, Ursula Burns of Xerox, Pat Woertz of Archer Daniels Midland, Brenda Barnes of Sara Lee, and Irene Rosenfeld of Kraft Foods.[8]

Some companies are helping women break through the glass ceiling. Accenture sponsors monthly networking events for its female employees and offers flexible schedules and part-time arrangements. The following 10 companies are among those the National Association of Female Executives recently identified as the "top 30" for executive women:[10]

Aetna	Marriott International
American Express	New York Times Co.
Bristol-Myers Squibb	Office Depot
Chubb & Son	Patagonia
Hewlett-Packard	Sallie Mae

DID YOU KNOW?

The percentage of female CEOs is expected to increase, but only slightly, reaching about 6 percent of *Fortune* 1000 CEOs by 2016.[9]

As women have gained more presence and power in the workforce, some have drawn attention to the problem of sexual harassment, which is unwelcome sexual conduct that is a term or condition of employment. Sexual harassment falls into two different categories:

1. *Quid pro quo harassment* occurs when "submission to or rejection of sexual conduct is used as a basis for employment decisions."

2. *Hostile environment* occurs when unwelcome sexual conduct "has the purpose or effect of unreasonably interfering with job performance or creating an intimidating, hostile, or offensive working environment." Behaviors that can cause a hostile work environment include persistent or pervasive displays of pornography, lewd or suggestive remarks, and demeaning taunts or jokes.

recruiting, helping returning veterans make the sometimes difficult transition to civilian life. The company offers enhanced benefits for employees called to active duty, including make-whole pay, continued health benefits, and care packages twice a year. Under some circumstances, employees' military service can even be credited as rail service. In 2008, *G.I. Jobs* ranked BNSF number two on its annual list of military-friendly organizations. BNSF is also a recent recipient of the U.S. Department of Defense Freedom Award.

 **Discussion Questions**

- How does hiring the nation's returning veterans make good business sense for BNSF?
- What attributes can make a veteran an attractive job candidate?

SOURCES: Company Web site, http://www.bnsf.com, accessed June 15, 2009; Heidi Russell Rafferty, "Choosing the Right Civilian Career," *VFW Magazine* [n.d.], http://www.vfw.org, accessed June 8, 2009; Jacob Carpenter, "Veterans Aim to Parlay Military Skills into Civilian Jobs during Job Fair at the Grand Valley Armory," *MLive.com*, May 15, 2009, http://www.mlive.com; Joshua Hudson, "Hiring America's Veterans," *G.I. Jobs,* December 2008, pp. 70–76; "Corporate America Competes Vehemently to Hire Military Veterans," *SmartBrief,* November 10, 2008, http://www.smartbrief.com; "Military Veterans Are Worth Hiring for Civilian Jobs," *New York Daily News,* June 29, 2008, http://www.nydailynews.com; Kurt Ronn, "Time to Call in the Military," *BusinessWeek,* April 23, 2007, http://www.businessweek.com.

Irene Rosenfeld has broken through the glass ceiling as CEO of Kraft Foods, overseeing the company with revenues upward of $30 billion.

sure their organization has an effective and comprehensive policy on harassment. Such a policy would have the following basic components:[12]

1. Develop a comprehensive organizationwide policy on sexual harassment and present it to all current and new employees. Stress that sexual harassment will not be tolerated under any circumstances. Emphasis is best achieved when the policy is publicized and supported by top management.

2. Hold training sessions with supervisors to explain Title VII requirements, their role in providing an environment free of sexual harassment, and proper investigative procedures when charges occur.

3. Establish a formal complaint procedure in which employees can discuss problems without fear of retaliation. The complaint procedure should spell out how charges will be investigated and resolved.

4. Act immediately when employees complain of sexual harassment. Communicate widely that investigations will be conducted objectively and with appreciation for the sensitivity of the issue.

5. When an investigation supports employee charges, discipline the offender at once. For extremely serious offenses, discipline should include penalties up to and including discharge. Discipline should be applied consistently across similar cases and among managers and hourly employees alike.

6. Follow up on all cases to ensure a satisfactory resolution of the problem.

Both categories of harassment violate Title VII of the Civil Rights Act of 1964, regardless of the sex of the harasser and the victim (in a recent year, more than 15 percent of complaints filed with the federal government came from males). If an employee files a complaint of sexual harassment with the Equal Employment Opportunity Commission, the commission may investigate and, if it finds evidence for the complaint, may request mediation, seek a settlement, or file a lawsuit with the potential for stiff fines—and negative publicity that may damage the company's ability to recruit the best employees in the future.

Harassment by creation of a hostile work environment is now more typical than quid pro quo harassment. Because it may involve more subjective standards of behavior, it puts an extra burden on managers to maintain an appropriate work environment by ensuring that all employees know what conduct is and is not appropriate and that there are serious consequences for this behavior. Even when managers do not themselves engage in harassment, if they fail to prevent it or to take appropriate action after receiving legitimate complaints about it, they may still be held liable, along with their companies, if a lawsuit is filed. Managers also need to know that the "hostile work environment" standard applies to same-sex harassment, as well as to non-gender-related cases, such as a pattern of racial or ethnic slurs. Teenaged workers are a particularly vulnerable population, since they are inexperienced, tend to hold lower-status jobs, and often feel hesitant or embarrassed to speak up. The federal Equal Employment Opportunity Commission has made this concern a priority and launched a teen-focused page called "Youth at Work" on its Web site (at http://www.youth.eeoc.gov).[11]

One way managers can help their companies prevent harassment, or avoid punitive damages if a lawsuit is filed, is to make

Companies such as Avon, Corning, and Metro-Goldwyn-Mayer have found that a strong commitment to diversity reduces problems with sexual harassment.[13]

Gender issues and the changing nature of work do not apply just to women. In some ways, the changing status of women has given men a chance to redefine their roles, expectations, and lifestyles. Some men are deciding that there is more to life than corporate success and are scaling back work hours and commitments to spend time with their families. Worker values are shifting toward personal time, quality of life, self-fulfillment, and family. Workers today, both men and women, are looking to achieve a balance between career and family.

minorities and immigrants Along with gender issues, the importance and scope of diversity are evident in the growth of racial minorities and immigrants in the workforce. Consider these facts:

• Black, Asian, and Hispanic workers hold more than one of every four U.S. jobs.

• Asian and Hispanic workforces are growing the fastest in the United States, followed by the African American workforce.

- Three in ten college enrollees are people of color.
- Foreign-born workers make up more than 15 percent of the U.S. civilian labor force. About half of these workers are Hispanic, and 22 percent are Asian.
- The younger Americans are, the more likely they are to be persons of color.
- One in 66 people in the United States identifies himself or herself as multiracial, and the number could soar to 1 in 5 by 2050.[14]

These numbers indicate that the term *minority*, as it is used typically, may soon become outdated.

Particularly in urban areas where white males do not predominate, managing diversity means more than eliminating discrimination; it means capitalizing on the wide variety of skills available in the labor market. Organizations that do not take full advantage of the skills and capabilities of minorities and immigrants are severely limiting their potential talent pool and their ability to understand and capture minority markets. Those markets are growing rapidly, along with their share of purchasing power. And if you sell to businesses, you are likely to deal with some minority-owned companies, because the number of businesses started by Asian American, African American, and Hispanic entrepreneurs is growing much faster than the overall growth in new companies in the United States. For example, more than half of the companies that started in California's high-tech Silicon Valley were founded by immigrants, and in a recent year, one-fourth of patent applications in the United States identified an immigrant as the inventor or a co-inventor.[15]

In a recent magazine ranking based on a company's representation of African Americans in four key areas (procurement, corporate board, senior management, and total workforce), Denny's stood out as making the most improvement following its discrimination lawsuits several years back.

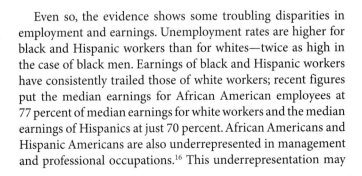

In many urban areas with large Asian, Hispanic, or African American populations, banks have deliberately increased the diversity of their managers and tellers to reflect the population mix in the community and attract additional business. If they did not, customers would readily notice and switch to other banks in the area where they would feel more welcome and comfortable. Such diversity permits better customer service, helping banks maintain their competitiveness. For example, tellers approached by new immigrants who do not yet speak English immediately call on their bilingual colleagues for help. The bilingual colleagues are also in a better position to assist the bank customers with special problems, such as income transfers from abroad.

Even so, the evidence shows some troubling disparities in employment and earnings. Unemployment rates are higher for black and Hispanic workers than for whites—twice as high in the case of black men. Earnings of black and Hispanic workers have consistently trailed those of white workers; recent figures put the median earnings for African American employees at 77 percent of median earnings for white workers and the median earnings of Hispanics at just 70 percent. African Americans and Hispanic Americans are also underrepresented in management and professional occupations.[16] This underrepresentation may itself help perpetuate the problem, because it can leave many aspiring young minorities with fewer role models or mentors.

There is considerable evidence that discrimination may account for at least some of the disparities in employment and earnings. For example, in one recent study, fictitious résumés were used to respond to help-wanted ads. Each résumé used either African American names like Lakisha and Jamal or white-sounding names like Emily and Greg. The résumés with white-sounding names were 50 percent more likely to get a callback for an interview than the same résumés with African American names. Despite equivalence in credentials, the often unconscious assumptions about different racial groups are very difficult to overcome.[17]

Nevertheless, significant progress has been made. Talented members of minority groups are among the executives running companies and their divisions in a wide variety of industries. Examples include Alvin Aviles, CEO of New York City Health and Hospitals Corporation; Harvey Brownlee, chief operating officer of KFC; Mei-Mei Chan, vice president of advertising for the Seattle Times Company; Carol Terakawa, a regional vice president at Yahoo!; and John Thompson, CEO of Symantec.[18]

Virtually every large organization today has policies and programs for increasing minority representation, including compensation systems that reward managers for increasing the diversity of their operations. FedEx, Xerox, Motorola, Shell, Sun Microsystems, and other companies have corporate diversity officers who help managers attract, retain, and promote minority and women executives. Many organizations, including Lockheed Martin and Dun and Bradstreet, are also supporting minority internships and MBA programs. The internship programs help students and organizations learn about one another and, ideally, turn into full-time employment opportunities. According to DiversityInc.com, the following companies recently ranked as the "top 10" companies for diversity:[19]

1. Johnson & Johnson
2. AT & T
3. Ernst & Young
4. Marriott International
5. Pricewaterhouse Coopers
6. Sodexo
7. Kaiser Permanente
8. Merck & Co.
9. The Coca-Cola Co.
10. IBM Corp.

For all these companies, developing, hiring, and retaining minority executives is critical for their ability to manage an ever-more-diverse workforce and to serve an increasing number of clients and customers with varied backgrounds.

mentally and physically disabled people

The largest unemployed minority population in the United States is people with disabilities. The share of the population with a disability is growing as the average worker gets older and heavier.[20] According to the U.S. Census Bureau, 18 percent of the population reports having some degree of disability, and 6 percent of the working-age population say they have a disability that makes it hard for them to get and keep a job.[21] Still, more than half of people with a disability held jobs during the year in which they were surveyed. And among those who are unemployed, many would like to find work.

The Americans with Disabilities Act (ADA), mentioned in Chapter 7, defines a disability as a physical or mental impairment that substantially limits one or more major life activities. Examples of such physical or mental impairments include those resulting from orthopedic, visual, speech, and hearing impairments; cerebral palsy; epilepsy; multiple sclerosis; HIV infections; cancer; heart disease; diabetes; mental retardation; psychological illness; specific learning disabilities; drug addiction; and alcoholism.[22]

New assistive technologies are making it easier for companies to comply with the ADA and for those with disabilities to be productive on the job. Making these accommodations can deliver unanticipated fringe benefits, too. The National Industries for the Blind (NIB), a Wisconsin company that markets products under the Skilcraft brand name, is a case in point. Seventy-five percent of NIB employees are visually impaired. Because the company's warehouse pickers have trouble reading instructions on paper, NIB installed a voice technology system that conveys instructions to workers through headsets. That technology has raised the productivity of the entire operation. Accuracy has improved, and workers—both blind and sighted—are able to pick and ship orders faster using the headsets.

For most businesses, mentally and physically disabled people represent an unexplored but fruitful labor market. Frequently, employers have found that disabled employees are more dependable than other employees, miss fewer days of work, and exhibit lower turnover. Tax credits are available to companies who hire disabled workers. In addition, managers who hire and support employees with disabilities are signaling to other employees and stakeholders their strong interest in creating an inclusive organization culture.

education levels

When the United States was primarily an industrial economy, many jobs required physical strength, stamina, and skill in a trade, rather than college and professional degrees. In today's service and technology economy, more positions require a college education, and even a graduate or professional degree. Today's prospective employees have responded by applying to college in record numbers. The proportion of the workforce with at least some college education has been growing steadily since the 1970s. The share of workers with a bachelor's degree has more than doubled since 1970. People with degrees in science and technology are in especially high demand. Employers often expand their search for scientists and computer professionals overseas, but visa requirements limit that supply.

At the other end of the spectrum, the share of workers with less than a high school diploma has tumbled from nearly 4 out of 10 in 1970 to below 1 out of 10 today. Among foreign-born workers, 28 percent have not completed high school.[23]

age groups

Today, almost 4 out of 10 workers are age 45 or older. As a result, entry-level workers for some positions are in short supply. Today's companies need to compete hard for a shrinking pool of young talent, preparing for applicants who know the job market and insist on the working conditions they value and the praise they were raised to expect. Bruce Tulgan, founder of Rainmaker Thinking, which specializes in researching generational differences, says Generation Y—today's young workers—tend to be "high-maintenance" but also "high-performing," having learned to process the flood of information that pours in over the Internet.[24] Many of these workers were raised by highly involved parents who filled their lives with "quality" experiences, so employers are designing work arrangements that are stimulating, involve teamwork, keep work hours reasonable to allow for outside activities, and provide for plenty of positive feedback. Employers are also updating their recruiting tactics to reach young workers where they are—online. Intermedia, which operates computer centers to host large-scale Web and e-mail software for small companies, says the social networking site LinkedIn helps the company reach well-qualified information technology workers. In the government sector, the Central Intelligence Agency and National Security Agency have set up pages on Facebook, where members who register for access can read information about job openings.[25]

 Pooling the knowledge of experienced workers with the energy and fresh ideas of younger workers can create a powerful workforce. Carolyn Martin of Rainmaker Thinking encourages her clients to develop mentoring programs so that important knowledge is passed from older to younger employees. "[Older workers] are walking out the door with a gold mine of experience, product knowledge, and historical perspective, and we're letting them go," she said at a recent economic conference. "Knowledge as power is out. Knowledge shared is in. Everyone, no matter what their age, is a teacher and a learner."

Martin suggests that employers hire older workers who can teach younger ones. Typically, she says, members of the baby boom generation—who are now beginning to retire—go on to start second careers anyway.[26]

Tomorrow's workers will be more varied than ever

Until recently, white American-born males dominated the U.S. workforce. This group still constitutes the largest percentage of workers—about 80 percent of U.S. workers are white, and more than half of them are male—but its share of the labor force is declining. Although the number of white male workers is expected to continue growing, the number of women and the numbers of Asian American, African American, and Hispanic workers are expected to grow faster.[27] This significant change in the workforce parallels trends in the overall U.S. population. Recently, the Census Bureau announced that, for the first time, about one in three residents of the United States is a racial or ethnic minority. The largest and fastest-growing minority group is Hispanics, closely followed by African Americans. In several states—California, Hawaii, New Mexico, and Texas—and the District of Columbia, these minority groups plus Asians, Native Americans, and Pacific Islanders combine to make a population that is "majority minority."[28]

During most of its history, the United States experienced a surplus of workers. But that is expected to change. Lower birth rates in the United States and other developed countries are resulting in a smaller labor force. An even more substantial slow-down in the pace of growth of the labor force is projected for the decade ending in 2016, as the baby-boom generation retires.[29]

Employers are likely to outsource some work to factories and firms in developing nations where birth rates are high and the labor supply is more plentiful. But they will have to compete for the best candidates from a relatively smaller and more diverse U.S. labor pool. Employers will need to know who these new workers are—and must be prepared to meet their needs.

In addition, the median age of America's workforce is rising, as the number of older workers swells while the number of young workers grows only slightly. Industries such as nursing and manufacturing are already facing a tremendous loss of expertise as a result of downsizing and a rapidly aging workforce. Other industries will soon be in similar straits.[30] On the plus side, almost 70 percent of workers between the ages of 45 and 74 told researchers with AARP (formerly the American Association of Retired Persons) that they intend to work in retirement. Retirees often return to the workforce at the behest of their employers, who can't afford to lose the knowledge accumulated by long-time employees, their willingness to work nontraditional shifts, and their reliable work habits, which have a positive effect on the entire work group.

To prevent an exodus of talent, employers need strategies to retain and attract skilled and knowledgeable older workers. Phased retirement plans that allow older employees to work fewer hours per week is one such strategy. Almost one-third of retiring faculty members at 16 University of North Carolina campuses take advantage of phased retirement, and the concept is catching on in many other public and private organizations. Other strategies include making workplace adaptations to help older workers cope with the physical problems they experience as they age, such as poorer vision, hearing, and mobility. Figure 8.3 shows how creative companies are rethinking their retirement policies and solving their skilled-labor shortage by attracting and retaining people over 55. These companies save on turnover and training costs and capitalize on the experience of their older employees.

L O 2 WHAT YOU NEED TO KNOW . . .

Can you distinguish between affirmative action and managing diversity?

MANAGING DIVERSITY VERSUS AFFIRMATIVE ACTION

Many organizations originally diversified their workforce out of concerns for social responsibility and legal necessity. To correct the past exclusion of women and minorities, companies introduced affirmative action—special efforts to recruit and hire qualified members of groups that have been discriminated against in the past. The intent is not to prefer these group members to the exclusion of others, but to correct for the history of discriminatory practices and exclusion. For example, in Portland, Oregon, about one-fifth of the city's population consists of various ethnic minorities, but only 12 percent of new construction employees are minorities. The city government, Portland Development Commission, Port of Portland, and regional and state transportation departments established affirmative action programs to increase minority group members' participation in public contracts.[32]

> for every young worker entering the workforce, two baby boomers are retiring.[31]

FIGURE | 8.3 | Top Five Approaches for More Fully Utilizing Older Employees

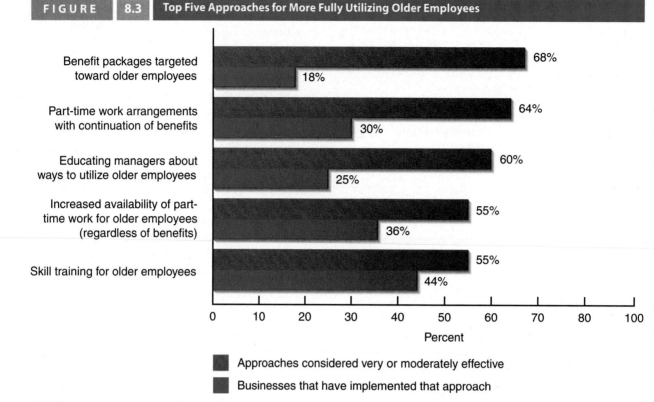

Approach		
Benefit packages targeted toward older employees	68%	18%
Part-time work arrangements with continuation of benefits	64%	30%
Educating managers about ways to utilize older employees	60%	25%
Increased availability of part-time work for older employees (regardless of benefits)	55%	36%
Skill training for older employees	55%	44%

Percent

■ Approaches considered very or moderately effective

■ Businesses that have implemented that approach

SOURCE: "American Business and Older Employees: A Survey of Findings," American Association of Retired Persons (AARP). Copyright © 2002 AARP (www.aarp.org). Reprinted with permission.

Such efforts, along with legal remedies to end discrimination, have had a powerful impact. Today the immigrant nature of American society is virtually taken for granted—even seen as a source of pride. And women, African Americans, Hispanics, and other minorities routinely occupy positions that in years past would have been totally closed to them.

Yet, employment discrimination persists, and in spite of upward mobility, some groups still lack full participation and opportunity in today's organizations. To move beyond correcting past wrongs and become truly inclusive requires a change in organization culture—one in which diversity is seen as contributing directly to the attainment of organization goals.

Seen in this way, affirmative action and diversity are complementary, not the same. In contrast to equal employment opportunity (EEO) and affirmative action programs, managing diversity means moving beyond legislated mandates to embrace a proactive business philosophy that sees differences as positive. In the end, *all* employees are different. These differences include the fundamental attributes of race, ethnicity, age, and gender, along with less obvious attributes like employees' place of origin, education, or life experience. All these elements add to the richness of talents and perspectives managers can draw on. In this broader sense, managing diversity involves making changes in organizations' systems, structures, and practices to eliminate barriers that may

Do you think that the election of our first African-American President will have an impact on affirmative action programs and the management of diversity in companies throughout the country?

keep people from reaching their full potential. It means treating people as individuals—*equally*, but not necessarily the *same*—recognizing that each employee will need different things to succeed. It asks managers to recognize and value the uniqueness of each employee and to see the different ideas and perspectives each brings to the organization as a source of competitive advantage. In short, managing diversity goes beyond getting more minorities and women into the organization. It creates an environment in which employees from *every* background listen to each other and work better together so that the organization as a whole will become more effective. This emphasis on coming together to benefit the whole has led many companies to begin referring to their objective as *diversity and inclusion*.

LO 3 WHAT YOU NEED TO KNOW . . .
How can diversity, if well managed, give organizations a competitive edge?

Well-managed diversity and inclusion can become a competitive advantage

Many organizations now view diversity from a more practical, business-oriented perspective, as a powerful tool for building competitive advantage. A study by the Department of Labor's Glass Ceiling Institute showed that the stock performance of firms that were high performers on diversity-related goals was over twice as high as that of other firms. In another recent study, companies with the highest percentage of women among senior managers had a significantly higher return to shareholders than companies with the lowest percentage. Conversely, announcements of damage awards from discrimination lawsuits frequently hurt stock returns.[33]

Managing a diverse workforce presents many advantages:

- *Ability to attract and retain motivated employees*—Companies with a reputation for providing opportunities for diverse employees will have a competitive advantage in the labor market. In addition, when employees believe their differences are not merely tolerated but valued, they may become more loyal, productive, and committed.

- *Better perspective on a differentiated market*—Just as women and minorities may prefer to work for an employer that values diversity, they may prefer to patronize such organizations. Similarly, each new generation has its own set of values and experiences, so diversity in ages can help the organization relate to more age groups of customers. A diverse workforce can give a company greater knowledge of the preferences and habits of this diversified marketplace, so it can design products and develop marketing campaigns to meet those consumers' needs, nationally and internationally.

- *Ability to leverage creativity and innovation in problem solving*—Work team diversity promotes creativity and innovation, because people from different backgrounds hold different perspectives. With a broader base of experience from which to approach a problem, diverse teams, when effectively managed, invent more options and create more solutions than homogeneous groups do. They also are freer to deviate from traditional approaches and practices, and are less likely to succumb to "groupthink."[35]

- *Enhancement of organizational flexibility*—A diverse workforce can make organizations more flexible, because successfully managing diversity requires a corporate culture that tolerates many different styles and approaches. Less restrictive policies and procedures and less standardized operating methods enable organizations to be more flexible and better able to respond quickly to environmental changes.

Executives at Aetna, Denny's, and FedEx are so convinced of the competitive potential of a diverse workforce that they tie a portion of management compensation to success in recruiting and promoting minorities and women.[36]

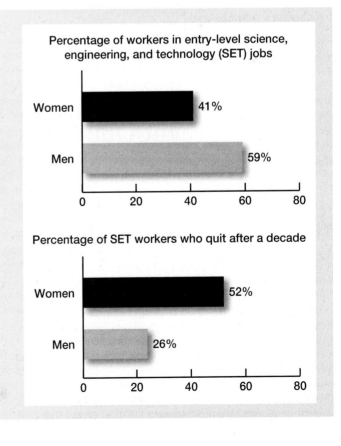

DID YOU KNOW?

Women are almost as likely as men to take jobs in science, engineering, and technology but are far more likely to quit, primarily because they feel isolated, lack mentors, find the work culture hostile, and are pressured to work long or rigid hours.[34]

Percentage of workers in entry-level science, engineering, and technology (SET) jobs

Women: 41%
Men: 59%

Percentage of SET workers who quit after a decade

Women: 52%
Men: 26%

Many law firms now routinely have diverse legal teams working together on a case. Complex cases often require fresh ideas, and a group of lawyers from the same background who all think the same way may not be able to be as innovative as a more diverse team. In addition, in jury trials, the impression that a legal team makes on a jury can help or badly hurt the client. Diverse jurors are more likely to be receptive to a visibly diverse team on which they see different kinds of lawyers participate. Recognizing the increased importance of legal-team diversity, some white-male-dominated law firms form alliances with minority-led firms, so they can collaborate on cases.

(L)(O) 4 WHAT YOU NEED TO KNOW . . .

What are the challenges associated with managing a diverse workforce?

A diverse and inclusive workforce is challenging to manage

In spite of the laws guaranteeing equal opportunity and the business advantages of diversity and inclusion, every year thousands of lawsuits are filed complaining of discrimination and unfair treatment, some involving large and well-respected firms.[37] Even in companies that are careful to avoid discrimination in hiring and pay, managing diversity can be difficult. Managers with all the goodwill in the world sometimes find it harder than they expected to get people from different backgrounds to work together for a common goal.[38]

some bore a male name and others a female name, and half implied that the person submitting the résumé was a parent. Employers were less likely to invite the supposed parents for an interview—but only if the name was female.[39] Since the résumés were otherwise identical, it appears that people make assumptions about mothers that do not apply to fathers or to childless women. In an organization that is oblivious to these different perspectives, managers may have more difficulty developing an enthusiastically shared sense of purpose.

- *Lower cohesiveness*—Diversity can create a lack of *cohesiveness,* defined as how tightly knit the group is and the degree to which group members perceive, interpret, and act on their environment in similar or mutually agreed-upon ways. Cohesiveness is lower because of differences in language, culture, and/or experience. When mistrust, miscommunication, stress, and attitudinal differences reduce cohesiveness, productivity may decline. This may explain the results of a study showing greater turnover among store employees who feel they are greatly outnumbered by coworkers from other racial or ethnic groups.[40] In a diverse group, managers are challenged to take the lead in building cohesiveness by establishing common goals and values.

- *Communication problems*—Perhaps the most common negative effect of diversity, communication problems include misunderstandings, inaccuracies, inefficiencies, and slowness. Speed is lost when not all group members are fluent in the same language or when additional time is required to explain things. Diversity can also lead to errors and misunderstandings. Group members may assume they interpret things similarly when they in fact do not, or they may disagree because of their different frames of reference.[41] For

> "Among CEOs of Fortune 500 companies, 58 percent are six feet or taller . . . Most of us, in ways we are not entirely aware of, automatically associate leadership with imposing physical stature."
>
> —Malcolm Gladwell

Becoming an effective manager of a diverse organization requires identifying and overcoming several challenges:

- *Unexamined assumptions*—Seeing the world from someone else's perspective can be difficult, because our own assumptions and viewpoints seem so normal and familiar. For example, heterosexuals may not even think before putting a picture of their loved ones on their desks, because the practice is so common and accepted, but for gay employees, displaying such a picture may cause considerable anxiety. Other unexamined assumptions involve the roles of men and women—for example, the assumption that women will shoulder the burden of caring for children, even if it conflicts with the demands of work. In a recent study, researchers sent employers résumés that were identical except that

example, if managers do not actively encourage and accept the expression of different points of view, some employees may be afraid to speak up at meetings, giving the manager a false impression that consensus has been reached.

- *Mistrust and tension*—People prefer to associate with others who are like themselves. This normal, understandable tendency can lead to misunderstanding, mistrust, and even fear of those who are different. For example, if women and minority-group members are routinely excluded from joining white male colleagues at business gatherings, they may feel isolated from their colleagues. Similarly, tension often develops between people of different ages—for example, what one generation might see as a tasteless tattoo may be a creative example of body art for a member of another generation. Such misunderstandings can cause stress, tension, and even resentment, making it harder to reach agreement.

- *Stereotyping*—We learn to interpret the world in a certain way based on our backgrounds and experiences. Our interests, values, and cultures filter, distort, block, and select what we perceive. We see and hear what we expect to see and hear. Group members often stereotype their "different" colleagues rather than accurately perceive and evaluate those persons' contributions, capabilities, aspirations, and motivations. Women may be stereotyped as not dedicated to their careers, older workers as unwilling to learn new skills, minority-group members as less educated or capable. Stereotypes may cost the organization dearly by stifling employees' ambition, so that they don't fully contribute. Research supports the idea that people perform better when they expect they can.[42] Unless managers are aware of their own and their employees' stereotypes, the stereotypes can shape important actions. For instance, employees labeled unmotivated or emotional will be given less stress-provoking (and perhaps less important) jobs than their coworkers, perhaps resulting in lower commitment, higher turnover, and underused skills.[43]

For all these reasons and more, managing diversity is not easy. Yet managers must confront these issues. They need to develop the skills and strategies diversity requires if they and their organizations are to succeed in our increasingly multicultural business environment.

(L)(O) 5 **WHAT YOU NEED TO KNOW . . .**
Can you define monolithic, pluralistic, and multicultural organizations?

● MONOLITHIC ORGANIZATION
An organization that has a low degree of structural integration—employing few women, minorities, or other groups that differ from the majority—and thus has a highly homogeneous employee population.

● PLURALISTIC ORGANIZATION
An organization that has a relatively diverse employee population and makes an effort to involve employees from different gender, racial, or cultural backgrounds.

MULTICULTURAL ORGANIZATIONS

To capitalize on the benefits and minimize the costs of a diverse workforce, managers can begin by examining their organization's prevailing assumptions about people and cultures. Table 8.1 shows some of the fundamental assumptions that may exist. Based on these assumptions, we can classify organizations as one of three types and describe their implications for managers:

1. A **monolithic organization** has very little *cultural integration;* its employee population is highly homogeneous. For example, in hiring, an organization might favor alumni of the same college, perhaps targeting members of fraternities who are enthusiastic about the school's football team. When a monolithic organization does employ people from groups other than the norm, they primarily hold low-status jobs. Minority group members must adopt the norms of the majority to survive. This fact, coupled with small numbers, keeps conflicts among groups low. Discrimination and prejudice typically prevail, informal integration is almost nonexistent, and minority group members do not identify strongly with the company.

2. **Pluralistic organizations** have a more diverse employee population and take steps to involve persons from different backgrounds. These organizations use an affirmative action

TABLE 8.1	Diversity Assumptions and Their Implications for Management		
Common and Misleading Assumptions		**Less Common and More Appropriate Assumptions**	
Homogeneity	*Melting pot myth:* We are all the same.	Heterogeneity	*Image of cultural pluralism:* We are not all the same; groups within society differ across cultures.
Similarity	*Similarity myth:* "They" are all just like me.	Similarity and difference	*They are not just like me:* Many people differ from me culturally. Most people exhibit both cultural similarities and differences when compared with me.
Parochialism	*Only-one-way myth:* Our way is the only way. We do not recognize any other way of living or working.	Equifinality	*Our way is not the only way:* There are many culturally distinct ways of reaching the same goal, of working, and of living one's life.
Ethnocentrism	*One-best-way myth:* Our way is the best way. All other approaches are inferior versions of our way.	Culture contingency	*Our way is one possible way:* There are many different and equally good ways to reach the same goal. The best way depends on the culture of the people involved.

SOURCE: From "Diversity Assumptions and Their Implications for Management" by Nancy J. Adler, *Handbook of Organization,* 1996. Reprinted courtesy of Marcel Dekker, Inc., New York.

approach, actively trying to hire and train a diverse workforce and to prevent any discrimination against minority group members. They typically have much more integration than do monolithic organizations, but as in monolithic organizations, minority group members tend to be clustered at certain levels or in particular functions. Because of greater cultural integration, affirmative action programs, and training programs, the pluralistic organization has some acceptance of minority group members into the informal network, much less discrimination, and less prejudice. With improved employment opportunities, minority group members feel greater identification with the organization. However, resentment of majority group members, coupled with the greater number of women and minorities, creates more conflict.

3. In **multicultural organizations,** diversity not only exists but is valued. In contrast to the pluralistic organization, which fails to address the cultural aspects of integration, these organizations fully integrate minority group members both formally and informally. But managers in such organizations do not focus primarily on employees' visible differences, like race or sex. Rather, managers value and draw on the *experience* and *knowledge* employees bring to the organization and help it achieve agreed-upon strategies and goals.[44] The multicultural organization is marked by an absence of prejudice and discrimination and by low levels of intergroup conflict. Such an organization creates a *synergistic* environment in which all members contribute to their maximum potential and the advantages of diversity can be fully realized.[45]

2. Assessing the organization's progress toward goals
3. Attracting employees
4. Training employees in diversity
5. Retaining employees

A recent study examining the performance of hundreds of companies over a 30-year period found that organizations in which responsibility for achieving diversity targets was assigned to particular individuals or groups made the most progress in increasing their share of female and black workers. Moderate change occurred in companies with mentoring and networking programs, but formal diversity training programs had little effect unless the organizations also used the other methods.[46] Thus, cultivating diversity needs to be a well-planned organizationwide effort in which each element is supported by the per-

Joe Dumars is one of the high percentage of minority NBA general managers.

sonal commitment of individual managers, who address this issue as seriously as they do other management challenges. These managers actively try to develop the skills, understanding, and practices that enable people of every background to do their best work in the common pursuit of the organization's goals.

▶ The National Basketball Association (NBA) has cultivated diversity throughout its history; in fact, it currently has the highest percentage of minority vice presidents and league office managers in the history of men's sports. Fifteen percent of NBA team vice presidents and 34 percent of the professionals who work in the league office are minorities. The NBA also has 12 African American head coaches, the highest number in pro sports. NBA spokesperson Brian McIntyre reports that this is business as usual for the organization. He says NBA commissioner David Stern "has long felt that a diverse workplace is the only workplace."[47] ◀

L O 6 WHAT YOU NEED TO KNOW . . .
What steps can managers and their organizations take to cultivate diversity?

HOW ORGANIZATIONS CAN CULTIVATE A DIVERSE WORKFORCE

An organization's plans for becoming multicultural and making the most of its diverse workforce should include five components:

1. Securing top management's leadership and commitment

Start by securing top managers' commitment

Obtaining top management's leadership and commitment is critical for diversity programs to succeed. Otherwise, the rest of the organization will not take the effort seriously. One way to communicate this commitment to all employees—and to the external environment—is to incorporate the organization's attitudes about diversity into the corporate mission statement and into strategic plans and objectives. Managers' compensation can be linked directly to accomplishing diversity goals. Adequate funding must be allocated to the diversity effort to ensure its success. Also, top management can set an example for other organization members by participating in diversity programs and making participation mandatory for all managers.

As we mentioned earlier, some organizations have established corporate offices or committees to coordinate the company-wide diversity effort and provide feedback to top management. Honeywell hired a "director of workforce diversity," and Avon a "director of multicultural planning and design." Other companies prefer to incorporate diversity management into the function of director of affirmative action or EEO.

The work of managing diversity cannot be done by top management or diversity directors alone. Many companies rely on minority advisory groups or task forces to monitor organizational policies, practices, and attitudes; assess their impact on the diverse groups within the organization; and provide feedback and suggestions to top management. At Equitable Life Assurance Society, employee groups meet regularly with the

> ## "Diversity: The art of thinking independently together."
>
> —Malcolm Forbes

CEO to discuss issues pertaining to women, African Americans, and Hispanics and make recommendations for improvement. At Honeywell, disabled employees formed a council to discuss their needs. They proposed and accepted an accessibility program that went beyond federal regulations for accommodations of disabilities.

As you can see, progressive companies are moving from asking managers what they think minority employees need and toward asking the employees themselves what they need.

Conduct an organizational assessment

The next step in managing diversity is routinely to assess the organization's workforce, culture, policies, and practices in areas such as recruitment, promotions, benefits, and compensation. Managers may evaluate whether they are attracting their share of diverse candidates from the labor pool and whether the needs of their customers are being addressed by the current composition of their workforce. The objective is to identify areas where there are problems or opportunities and to make recommendations when changes are needed. At Aetna, a measure is the percentage of employees who are multilingual; one way the company builds

this number is by offering noontime language lessons for interested employees.[48]

Attract a diverse group of qualified employees

Companies can attract a diverse, qualified workforce by using effective recruiting practices, accommodating employees' work and family needs, and offering alternative work arrangements.

recruitment A company's image can be a strong recruiting tool. Companies with reputations for hiring and promoting all types of people have a competitive advantage. Xerox gives prospective minority employees reprints of an article that rates the company as one of the best places for African Americans to work. Hewlett-Packard ensures that its female candidates are familiar with its high rating by *Working Woman* magazine.

Diversity is built into the origins of the Philadelphia law firm of Caesar Rivise. The firm's founder was Abraham Caesar, an attorney specializing in intellectual property (for example, patents and trademarks). In 1926, Caesar could not land a job at one of the local law firms because he was Jewish, so he founded his own firm, later adding partner Charles Rivise. The two attorneys wrote important reference books on patents, establishing a reputation as experts.

Given Caesar's early experiences, it's not surprising that his law firm committed itself to diversity in hiring. Stanley Cohen, now a partner, recalls that when he joined the firm in the 1960s, his secretary was a black man. Another Caesar Rivise employee since the 1960s, Bernice Mims, graduated at the top of her South Philadelphia High School class but lacked access to jobs because she was black and some employers stipulated "no Jews or Negroes." Caesar hired Mims as a law clerk, and she remained loyal to the firm, eventually working her way up to manager of human resources.

Today Caesar Rivise builds on its historical commitment to diversity by sponsoring diversity fellowships (tuition assistance and internships) at Drexel University's Earle Mack School of Law. Partnering with Drexel is a good strategic fit, because the university emphasizes technology and science—backgrounds that are important for working with corporate clients on technical matters.[49]

Many disabled persons and economically disadvantaged people are physically isolated from job opportunities. Companies can bring information about job opportunities to the source of labor, or they can transport the labor to the jobs. Polycast Technology in Stamford, Connecticut, contracts with a private van company to transport workers from the Bronx in New York City to jobs in Stamford. Days Inn recruits homeless workers in Atlanta and houses them in a motel within walking distance of their jobs.

accommodating work and family
needs More job seekers today are putting family needs first. Corporate work and family policies are now one of the most important recruiting tools. Employers that have adopted onsite child care report decreased turnover and absenteeism and improved morale. In addition to providing child care, many companies now assist with care for elderly dependents, offer time off to care for sick family members, provide parental leaves of absence, and offer various benefits that can be tailored to individual family needs. Some companies are accommodating the needs and concerns of dual-career couples by limiting relocation requirements or providing job search assistance to relocated spouses.

alternative work arrangements
Another way managers accommodate diversity is to offer flexible work schedules and arrangements. Stiff demand for engineering talent is motivating manufacturers to accommodate the needs of employees with family responsibilities. At Freescale Semiconductor, the focus is on meeting performance targets, not on working a set schedule. Section manager Amy Oesch says this approach has enabled her to juggle family responsibilities while moving up to positions of greater authority and earning a graduate degree.[50]

Other creative work arrangements include compressed workweeks (e.g., four 10-hour days) and job sharing, in which two part-time workers share one full-time job. Another option to accommodate working mothers and disabled employees is teleworking (working from home) or telecommuting (working from home via computer hookup to the main work site).

Train employees to understand and work with diversity

As you learned earlier, employees can be developed in several ways. Traditionally, most management training was based on the unstated assumption that "managing" means managing a homogeneous, often white-male, full-time workforce. But gender, race, culture, age, educational, and other differences create an additional layer of complexity.[51] Diversity training programs attempt to identify and reduce hidden biases and develop the skills needed to manage a diversified workforce effectively.

The majority of U.S. organizations sponsor some sort of diversity training. Typically, diversity training has two components: awareness building and skill building.

awareness building
Awareness building is designed to increase recognition of the meaning and importance of valuing diversity.[52] Its aim is not to teach specific skills but to sensitize employees to the assumptions they make about others and the way those assumptions affect their behaviors, decisions, and judgment. For example, male managers who have never reported to a female manager may feel awkward the first time they are required to do so. Awareness building can reveal this concern in advance and help the managers address it.

To build awareness, trainers teach people to become familiar with myths, stereotypes, and cultural differences as well as the organizational barriers that inhibit the full contributions of all employees. They develop a better understanding of corporate culture, requirements for success, and career choices that affect opportunities for advancement.

That Was THEN . . .

In the past, organizations didn't emphasize diversity in their hiring practices. As a result, the face of the workforce was typically white and male.

This Is NOW . . .

Today's managers work with employees from various backgrounds. Shown here is J. W. Marriott Jr., CEO of Marriott International, meeting with kitchen staff at the Boston Marriott Copley Place on one of his annual visits.

In most companies, the "rules" for success are ambiguous, unwritten, and perhaps inconsistent with written policy. A common problem for women, minorities, immigrants, and young employees is that they are unaware of many of the unofficial rules that are obvious to people in the mainstream. For example, organizations often have informal networks and power structures that may not be apparent or readily available to everyone. As a result, some employees may not know where to go when they need to get an idea approved or want to build support and alliances. For managers, valuing diversity means teaching the unwritten "rules" or cultural values to those who need to know them and changing the rules when necessary to benefit employees and hence the organization. It also requires inviting "outsiders" in and giving them access to information and meaningful relationships with people in power.

skill building

Skill building aims to develop the skills that employees and managers need to deal effectively with one another and with customers in a diverse environment. Most of the skills taught are interpersonal, such as active listening, coaching, and giving feedback. Ideally, the organizational assessment is used to identify which skills should be taught, tailoring the training to the specific business issues that were identified. For example, if too many women and minorities believe they lack helpful feedback, the skill-building program can address that issue. Likewise, training in flexible scheduling can help managers meet the company's needs while accommodating and valuing workers who want to set aside time to advance their education, participate in community projects, or look after elderly parents. Tying the training to specific, measurable business goals increases its usefulness and makes it easier to assess.

The Transportation Security Administration recently provided a combination of awareness training and skill building to prepare its airport security personnel to screen Muslim travelers without violating their civil rights. The TSA employees were taught that the religious customs of Islam include the hajj, an annual pilgrimage to Saudi Arabia. As a result, once a year air travelers include many groups of these pilgrims. The employees learned to recognize that, especially at the time of the hajj, women in head scarves traveling with men in beards may well be devoutly religious Muslims engaging in a deeply personal religious journey. Besides teaching about the customs and practices of Islam, the training prepared TSA employees to perform their jobs without discriminating; for example, they learned how to effectively screen passengers who were wearing head coverings and what to do if passengers were transporting holy water.[53]

Retain talented employees

As replacing qualified and experienced workers becomes more difficult and costly, retaining good workers is becoming much more important. Several policies and strategies can help managers increase retention of all employees, especially those who are "different" from the norm.[54]

support groups

Companies can form minority networks and other support groups to promote information exchange and social support. Support groups provide emotional and career support for members who traditionally have not been included in the majority's informal groups. They also can help diverse employees understand work norms and the corporate culture.

At Apple headquarters, support groups include a Jewish cultural group, a gay/lesbian group, an African American group, and a technical women's group. Avon encourages employees to organize into African American, Hispanic, and Asian networks by granting them official recognition and assigning a senior manager to provide advice. These groups help new employees adjust and give management feedback about problems that concern the groups.

Darden Restaurants started support groups, known as employee networks, at its Orlando, Florida, headquarters. Today there are five such groups: the Family Network, aimed at providing support to employees with families; Women's Network; Asian-American Network; African-American Network; and Hispanic Network. Each network sponsors social activities for the whole company, provides educational activities, and works with executives to develop mentoring relationships and share insights about groups served by Darden's various restaurant chains, including Red Lobster and Olive Garden.

Darden's employee networks are not meant only to help employees; they also must contribute to business goals. Each network prepared a three-year business plan that details how it expects to support Darden's growth. For instance, the Family Network sponsored a Take Your Child to Work Day at which children participated in focus groups that generated insights into children's menus.

About 40 percent of Darden's headquarters employees belong to at least one of the networks, which are open to any interested employee. Based on the success of the groups in Orlando, the company is rolling out network membership to its restaurant employees.[55]

mentoring

To help individuals enter the informal network that provides exposure to top management and access to information about organizational politics, many companies have implemented formal mentoring programs. Mentors are higher-level managers who help ensure that high-potential people are introduced to top management and socialized into the norms and values of the organization.

Aflac's efforts to develop a diverse workforce include programs aimed at retaining employees by offering them opportunities for development and advancement. The insurance company's mentoring program prepares agents from minority groups to move into management ranks. This program is part of a culture that demonstrates respect for all employees in a variety

MENTORS Higher-level managers who help ensure that high-potential people are introduced to top management and socialized into the norms and values of the organization.

Darden Restaurants' president and chief operating officer Drew Madsen (left) and chief executive officer Clarence Otis are shown in Darden's offices in Orlando, Florida. Improvement at Darden's Red Lobster, combined with continuing strong momentum from its Italian chain, Olive Garden, and the steady growth of its Smoky Bones barbecue chain, could lead Darden to its strongest stock performance in years. The company has 1,400 restaurants, making it the world's biggest casual dining operator.

of ways, including forums where employees can share information about their ethnic customs. Abbott Laboratories operates a mentoring program where employees can find mentors online. Employees interested in having or being a mentor submit profiles about themselves, and software suggests possible matches based on experiences, skills, and interests. The advantage of the online relationships is that employees aren't limited by their geographic location or their likelihood of meeting in the course of their daily work.[56]

career development and promotions To ensure that talented employees are not hitting a glass ceiling, companies such as Deloitte & Touche and Honeywell have established teams to evaluate the career progress of women, minorities, and employees with disabilities and to devise ways to move them up through the ranks. An extremely important step is to make sure deserving employees get a chance at line positions. Women in particular are often relegated to staff positions, like Human Resources, with less opportunity to demonstrate they can earn money for their employers. Career development programs that give exposure and experience in line jobs to a wide range of employees can make senior management positions more available to them.

systems accommodation Managers can support diversity by recognizing cultural and religious holidays, differing modes of dress, and dietary restrictions, as well as accommodating the needs of individuals with disabilities. Accommodations for disability may become more important in the future, as the median age of the workforce continues to rise. In addition, the rise in the *weight* of the average U.S. worker may raise disability concerns. Not only are the familiar health consequences such as heart disease, joint problems, and diabetes associated with increased weight, but one study found that obese workers had many more workplace injury claims and absences related to injuries.[57] This pattern suggests that managers of the future will be even more concerned than in the past with keeping their workers of all sizes on the job by maintaining safe workplaces and offering benefits that encourage healthy lifestyles (possibly through company-sponsored fitness programs).

accountability As we noted at the beginning of this section, one of the most effective ways to ensure that diversity efforts succeed is to hold managers accountable for hiring and developing a diverse workforce. Organizations must ensure that their performance appraisal and reward systems reinforce the importance of effective diversity management. At PepsiCo, each executive reporting to the CEO is assigned responsibility for employee development of a different group— for example, the company's women or Latinos or gay and lesbian employees. The executive responsible for that group must identify leadership talent, learn group members' concerns, identify areas where support is needed, and identify plans for addressing these issues.[58]

L O 7 WHAT YOU NEED TO KNOW . . .
Can you summarize the skills and knowledge managers need to manage globally?

MANAGING ACROSS BORDERS

Adding to the challenges and opportunities of diversity, today's managers are increasingly responsible for managing employees from other countries or managing operations in other countries. When establishing operations overseas, headquarters executives have a choice among sending **expatriates** (individuals from the parent country), using **host-country nationals** (natives of the host country), and deploying **third-country nationals**

● **EXPATRIATES** Parent-company nationals who are sent to work at a foreign subsidiary.

● **HOST-COUNTRY NATIONALS** Natives of the country where an overseas subsidiary is located.

● **THIRD-COUNTRY NATIONALS** Natives of a country other than the home country or the host country of an overseas subsidiary.

(natives of a country other than the home country or the host country).

While most corporations use some combination of all three types of employees, there are advantages and disadvantages of each. Colgate-Palmolive and Procter & Gamble use expatriates to get their products to market abroad more quickly. AT&T and Toyota have used expatriates to transfer their corporate cultures and best practices to other countries—in Toyota's case, to its U.S. plants. But sending employees abroad can cost three to four times as much as employing host-country nationals, and in many countries, the personal security of expatriates is an issue. As a result, firms may send their expatriates on shorter assignments and communicate internationally via telecommuting, teleconferencing, and other electronic means. Local employees are more available, tend to be familiar with the culture and language, and usually cost less because they need not be relocated. At Kraft Foods, a policy of letting local marketing experts make decisions about local markets freed Chinese marketers to redesign the Oreo cookie so it would be more palatable to Chinese consumers' tastes (and easier on their wallets).[59] In addition, local governments often provide incentives to companies that create good jobs for their citizens, or they may restrict the use of expatriates. The trend away from using expatriates in top management positions is especially apparent in companies that truly want to create a multinational culture. In Honeywell's European division, many of the top executive positions are held by non-Americans.[60]

Companies that engage in 24/7 manufacturing around the world generally benefit from hiring local workers and managers. RollEase, a Connecticut-based manufacturer of manual operating systems for hard and soft window coverings, has an engineer at its facility in China who can work on design changes while the U.S. workers are asleep at night. "We get stuff back from our engineer, and we check it during the day and give it back to him when we leave at night, which is the beginning of his workday," explains Joseph A. Cannaverde, a project manager. "We come in the next morning, and we have a finished drawing. When we walk out the door we are not stopping work."

But this type of management does not always go smoothly. Change orders might be misunderstood or not executed at all, resulting in lost time and productivity. So communication is vital. In the case of RollEase, the Chinese engineer has access to data from the

?

DID YOU KNOW?

Most of the growth in IBM's workforce is occurring in India, where employees handle software development, services, and customer support. IBM has more employees in India than in any other country outside the United States.[61]

firm's on-demand system so that he knows he has accurate information. He is also an employee of RollEase, not a subcontractor.[62]

Global managers need cross-cultural skills

Working internationally can be stressful, even for experienced "globalites." Table 8.2 identifies some of the primary stressors for expatriates at different stages of their assignments. It also shows ways for executives to cope with the stress, as well as some measures companies can take to ease the adjustment.

Given the challenges, many overseas assignments fail. The estimated *failure rate* among expatriates (defined as those who come home early) ranges from 20 to 70 percent, depending on the country of assignment. Each failed assignment may cost tens of thousands to hundreds of thousands of dollars.[63] Typically, the causes for failure extend beyond technical skills to include personal and social issues. In a recent survey of human resource managers around the globe, two-thirds said the main reason for failure is family issues, especially dissatisfaction of the employee's spouse or partner.[64] The problem may be compounded in this era of dual-career couples, in which one spouse may have to give up his or her job to accompany the expatriate manager to the new

Among the list of the greatest places to work in Mexico are several U.S.-based companies, including McDonald's, which ranked as the ninth-best company in 2007.

Stage	Primary Stressors	Executive Coping Response	Employer Coping Response
Expatriate selection	Cross-cultural unreadiness.	Engage in self-evaluation.	Encourage expatriate's self- and family evaluation. Perform an assessment of potential and interests.
Assignment acceptance	Unrealistic evaluation of stressors to come. Hurried time frame.	Think of assignment as a growth opportunity rather than an instrument to vertical promotion.	Do not make hard-to-keep promises. Clarify expectations.
Pre- and postarrival	Ignorance of cultural differences.	Do not make unwarranted assumptions of cultural competence and cultural rules.	Provide pre-, during, and postassignment training. Encourage support-seeking behavior.
Arrival	Cultural shock. Stressor reevaluation. Feelings of lack of fit and differential treatment.	Do not construe identification with the host and parent cultures as mutually exclusive. Seek social support.	Provide postarrival training. Facilitate integration in expatriate network.
Novice	Cultural blunders or inadequacy of coping responses. Ambiguity owing to inability to decipher meaning of situations.	Observe and study functional value of coping responses among locals. Do not simply replicate responses that worked at home.	Provide follow-up training. Seek advice from locals and expatriate network.
Transitional	Rejection of host or parent culture.	Form and maintain attachments with both cultures.	Promote culturally sensitive policies in host country. Provide Internet access to family and friends at home. Maintain constant communication and periodic visits to parent organization.
Mastery	Frustration with inability to perform boundary-spanning role. Bothered by living with a cultural paradox.	Internalize and enjoy identification with both cultures and walking between two cultures.	Reinforce rather than punish dual identification by defining common goals.
Repatriation	Disappointment with unfulfilled expectations. Sense of isolation. Loss of autonomy.	Realistically reevaluate assignment as a personal and professional growth opportunity.	Arrange prerepatriation briefings and interviews. Schedule postrepatriation support meetings.

SOURCE: From *Academy of Management Executive: The Thinking Manager's Source* by J. Sanchez et al. Copyright © 2000 by Academy of Management.

location. To ensure that an overseas posting will succeed, managers can encourage employees to talk to their spouse about what he or she will do in the foreign country.

For both the expatriate and the spouse, adjustment requires flexibility, emotional stability, empathy for the culture, communication skills, resourcefulness, initiative, and diplomatic skills.[65] When Kent Millington took the position of vice president of Asia operations for an Internet hosting company, his wife Linda quit her job to move with him to Japan. Especially for Linda Millington, the first three months were difficult, because she didn't speak Japanese, found the transit system confusing, and even struggled to buy food because she couldn't translate the labels. But she persevered and participated in classes and volunteer activities. Eventually, she and her husband learned to enjoy the experience and appreciated the chance to see just how well they could tackle a challenge.[66]

The following traits may be associated with candidates who are likely to succeed in a global environment:[67]

- *Sensitivity to cultural differences*—When working with people from other cultures, the candidate tries hard to understand their perspective.

- *Business knowledge*—The candidate has a solid understanding of the company's products and services.

- *Courage to take a stand*—The person is willing to take a stand on issues.

- *Bringing out the best in people*—He or she has a special talent for dealing with people.

- *Integrity*—The person can be depended on to tell the truth regardless of circumstances.
- *Insightfulness*—The candidate is good at identifying the most important part of a complex problem.
- *Commitment to success*—He or she clearly demonstrates commitment to seeing the organization succeed.
- *Risk taking*—The candidate takes personal as well as business risks.
- *Use of feedback*—The candidate has changed as a result of feedback.
- *Cultural adventurousness*—The person enjoys the challenge of working in countries other than his or her own.
- *Desire for opportunities to learn*—The candidate takes advantage of opportunities to do new things.
- *Openness to criticism*—The person does not appear brittle, as if criticism might cause him or her to break.
- *Desire for feedback*—He or she pursues feedback even when others are reluctant to give it.
- *Flexibility*—The candidate doesn't get so invested in things that he or she cannot change when something doesn't work.

Companies such as BP, Global Hyatt, and others with large international staffs have extensive training programs to prepare employees for international assignments. Other organizations, such as Coca-Cola, Motorola, Chevron, and Mattel, have extended this training to include employees located in the United States who deal in international markets. These programs focus on areas such as language, culture, and career development. The following measures also can help prevent global assignments from failing:

- Structure assignments clearly. Develop clear reporting relationships and job responsibilities.
- Create clear job objectives.
- Develop performance measurements based on objectives.
- Use effective, validated selection and screening criteria (both personal and technical attributes).
- Prepare expatriates and families for assignments (through briefings, training, support).
- Create a vehicle for ongoing communication with expatriates.
- Anticipate repatriation to facilitate reentry when they come back home.
- Consider developing a mentor program that will help monitor and intervene in case of trouble.

Managers who are sent on an overseas assignment usually wonder about the effect such an assignment will have on their careers. Selection for a post overseas is usually an indication that they are being groomed to become more effective managers in an era of globalization. Also, they often have more responsibility, challenge, and operating leeway than they might have at home. Yet they may be concerned that they will be "out of the loop" on key developments back home. Good companies and managers address that issue with effective communication between subsidiaries and headquarters and by a program of visitations to and from the home office. Communication technology makes it easy for expatriates to keep in touch with colleagues in their home country daily or even more often, through e-mail and phone calls. Alan Paul, an American journalist working in China, says Internet phone service, a Webcam, and podcasts of favorite radio programs also enable him to stay in touch with family and friends back home, even to the extent that he has to work hard to have "a fully engaged existence in China."[68]

Cross-cultural management extends beyond U.S. employees going abroad and includes effective management of inpatriates—foreign nationals who are brought in to work at the parent company. These employees bring their employer extensive knowledge about how to operate effectively in their home countries. They are also better prepared to communicate their organization's products and values when they return. But they often have the same types of problems as expatriates and may be even more neglected, because parent-company managers either are more focused on their expatriate program or unconsciously see the home country as normal—requiring no period of adjustment. Yet the language, customs, expense, and lack of local community support in the United States is at least as daunting to inpatriates as the experience of American nationals abroad.

L O 8 WHAT YOU NEED TO KNOW . . .

What are the ways in which cultural differences across countries influence management?

National cultures shape values and business practices

In many ways, cultural issues are the most elusive aspect of international business. In an era when modern transportation and

"If there is any great secret of success in life, it lies in the ability to put yourself in the other person's place and to see things from his point of view as well as your own."

—Henry Ford

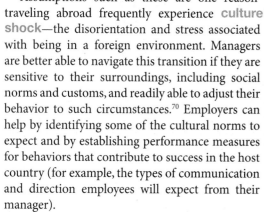

ETHNOCENTRISM The tendency to judge others by the standards of one's group or culture, which are seen as superior.

CULTURE SHOCK The disorientation and stress associated with being in a foreign environment.

communication technologies have created a "global village," it is easy to forget how deep and enduring the differences can be. Even though people everywhere drink Coke, wear blue jeans, and drive Toyotas, we are not all becoming alike. Each country is unique for reasons rooted in history, culture, language, geography, social conditions, race, and religion. These differences complicate any international activity and guide how a company should conduct business across borders. For example, while working in Hong Kong, Geoffrey Fowler discovered that his coworkers chose topics for small talk—people's weight, salary, and the size of their apartment— that would horrify Americans. At the same time, Chinese workers are put off by the American custom of combining lunch with a business meeting at which junior employees are chewing away while a superior in the company is talking.[69]

Ironically, while most of us would guess that the trick to working abroad is learning about a foreign culture, in reality our problems often stem from our being oblivious to our own cultural conditioning. Most of us pay no attention to how culture influences our everyday behavior, so we tend to adapt poorly to situations that are unique or foreign to us. Without realizing it, some managers may even act out of ethnocentrism— a tendency to judge foreign people or groups by the standards of one's own culture or group, and to see one's own standards as superior. Such tendencies may be totally unconscious—for example, the assumption that "in England they drive on the *wrong* side of the road," rather than merely on the left. Or they may reflect a lack of awareness of the values underlying a local culture—for example, an assumption that a culture does not air American television programming because it is backward, when it is actually committed to maintaining its traditional values and norms.

Assumptions such as these are one reason why people traveling abroad frequently experience culture shock—the disorientation and stress associated with being in a foreign environment. Managers are better able to navigate this transition if they are sensitive to their surroundings, including social norms and customs, and readily able to adjust their behavior to such circumstances.[70] Employers can help by identifying some of the cultural norms to expect and by establishing performance measures for behaviors that contribute to success in the host country (for example, the types of communication and direction employees will expect from their manager).

A wealth of cross-cultural research has been conducted on the differences and similarities among various countries. Geert Hofstede, for example, has identified four dimensions along which managers in multinational corporations tend to view cultural differences:

1. *Power distance*—the extent to which a society accepts the fact that power in organizations is distributed unequally.

2. *Individualism/collectivism*—the extent to which people act on their own or as a part of a group.

3. *Uncertainty avoidance*—the extent to which people in a society feel threatened by uncertain and ambiguous situations.

4. *Masculinity/femininity*—the extent to which a society values quantity of life (e.g., accomplishment, money) over quality of life (e.g., compassion, beauty).

Figure 8.4 graphs how 40 nations differ on the dimensions of individualism/collectivism and power distance. Of course, this depiction exaggerates the differences to some extent. Many Americans prefer to act as part of a group, just as many Taiwanese prefer to act individualistically. And globalization may have already begun to blur some of these distinctions. Still, to suggest no cultural differences exist is equally simplistic. Clearly, cultures such as the United States, which emphasize "rugged individualism," differ significantly from collectivistic cultures such as those of Pakistan, Taiwan, and Colombia. And to be effective in cultures that exhibit a greater power distance, managers often must behave more autocratically, perhaps inviting less participation in decision making.

In starting an insurance company in the United Arab Emirates, Texas native Michael Weinberg has learned a lot about that country's business culture. One surprise was the Arabs' far looser sense of time. On an early visit, Weinberg was doubtful when his partners—both Lebanese American and more familiar with the culture—assured him that showing up a few hours late for an appointment would be fine. As it turned out, their hosts were unruffled by their late arrival.

Traditionally, in Arabic culture, people's activities fit around the appointed times for prayer (related to the sun's position) and the climate's cycles of heating and cooling. In addition, partici-

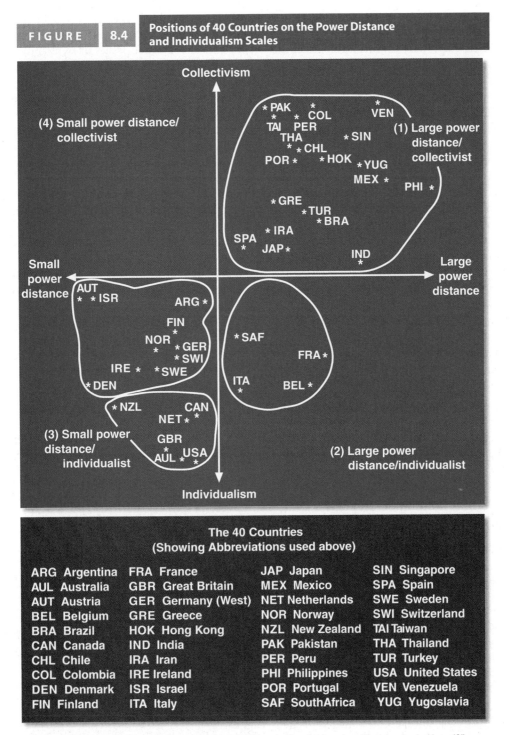

SOURCE: Geert Hofstede, "Motivation, Leadership, and Organization: Do American Theories Apply Abroad?" *Organizational Dynamics* 9, no. 1 (Summer 1980), pp. 42–63. Reprinted by permission.

pants in a meeting focus more on the relationships being built than on the next event on their calendar, so appointments often run longer than scheduled. These cultural norms result in a fluid understanding of time.

Still, visitors must be conscientious. They have to take into account the status of their host; a higher-status person expects visitors to be available as scheduled, even if that means a wait.

Weinberg has learned to use waiting time to catch up on his e-mail. He also calls ahead to confirm meeting times and to notify his host if he'll be late.

Acknowledging the challenges of learning a culture, Weinberg has also experienced the joys, noting the "hospitality, warmth, love, education, and charity" of the Arab people he has met.[71]

Effective managers are sensitive to these issues and consider them in dealing with people from other cultures. In contrast to people born in America, employees, coworkers, or customers from other countries might tend to communicate less directly, place more emphasis on hierarchy and authority, or make decisions more slowly. For example, an American manager working in Japan sent an e-mail to her American supervisor and Japanese colleagues in which she pointed out flaws in the process they were working on. The supervisor appreciated the alert, but her colleagues were embarrassed by behavior they considered rude; she should have inquired indirectly—say, by wondering what might happen if such a problem did exist. In another situation, a manager from Mexico showed respect for authority by phrasing ideas as questions during a meeting with superiors. Instead of seeing him as appropriately humble, his American colleagues concluded that he was indecisive. In general, managers of international groups can manage such misunderstandings by acknowledging cultural differences frankly and finding ways to work around them, by modifying the group (e.g., assigning tasks to subgroups), by setting rules to correct problems that are upsetting group members, or by removing group members who demonstrate they cannot work effectively within a particular situation.[72]

In addition, when working in the United States, foreign nationals will encounter a number of work-related differences:

- *Meetings*—Americans and workers from some other countries may have different views about the purpose of meetings and how much time can be spent. Managers should make sure foreign nationals are comfortable with the American approach.

- *Work(aholic) schedules*—Workers in countries with strong labor organizations often get many more weeks of vacation than American workers. Europeans in particular may balk at working on weekends. Matters such as these are most helpfully raised and addressed at the beginning of the work assignment.

- *E-mail*—Parts of the world have not yet embraced e-mail and voice mail the way U.S. workers have. Often, others prefer to communicate face to face. Particularly when language difficulties may exist, at the outset managers will probably want to avoid using e-mail for important matters.

- *Fast-trackers*—Although U.S. companies may take a young MBA graduate and put him or her on the fast track to management, most other cultures still see no substitute for the wisdom gained through experience. Experienced managers are often best for mentoring inpatriates.

- *Feedback*—Everyone likes praise, but other cultures tend to be less lavish in delivering positive feedback than the United States. U.S. managers should keep this point in mind when they give foreign nationals their performance reviews.[73]

International management introduces complex ethical challenges

If managers are to function effectively in a foreign setting, they must understand the ways culture influences how they are perceived and how others behave. One of the most sensitive issues in this regard is how culture plays out in terms of ethical behavior.[74] Issues of right and wrong get blurred as we move from one culture to another, and actions that may be customary in one setting may be unethical—even illegal—in another. The use of bribes, for example, is perceived as an accepted part of commercial transactions in many Asian, African, Latin American, and Middle Eastern cultures, and even in cultures that view bribery as a form of corruption, some companies offer bribes when they think bribery is part of the culture.[75]

What should a U.S. businessperson do? Failure to sweeten the deal with bribes can result in lost business. In the United States, the Foreign Corrupt Practices Act of 1977 prohibits U.S. employees from bribing foreign officials. (Small-business gifts or payments" to lower-level officials are permissible, if the dollar amount of the payments would not influence the outcome of the negotiations.) Likewise, countries of the Organization for Economic Cooperation and Development, including the United States, have prohibited bribes since 1977. Even so, a study found that less than half of U.S. managers said bribes were unacceptable, and 20 percent actually said they were always acceptable.[76]

Enforcement of the antibribery law—if only in the United States—became more vigorous following high-profile financial scandals at Enron, WorldCom, and other corporations. Still, even in companies with a solid reputation for ethical conduct, bribery can occur. Johnson & Johnson recently acknowledged that employees in certain subsidiaries were thought to have made bribes related to the sale of medical devices in "two small-market countries." The executive in charge of the subsidiaries accepted responsibility and retired, and the company voluntarily reported the problem to the U.S. Justice Department and the Securities and Exchange Commission, promising to cooperate in any government investigation.[77]

Without an understanding of local customs, ethical standards, and applicable laws, an expatriate may be woefully unprepared

> ## "Management is doing things right; leadership is doing the right things."
> — Peter F. Drucker

to work internationally. To safeguard against the problems and mitigate the punishment if an organization should be found guilty of bribery, the U.S. Sentencing Commission has deemed it essential for firms to establish effective ethics programs and see that they are enforced. To put teeth into the corporate ethics initiative, companies with global operations should be at least as engaged as domestic corporations in establishing and enforcing standards for ethical behavior. In Chapter 3, we identified a number of steps organizations should take. They include establishing and communicating the company's values, measuring performance in meeting ethical standards, rewarding employees at all levels for meeting those standards, and taking swift but fair action when violations occur. The primary difference in the international context is that these activities must be carried out with foreign business partners and employees in any subsidiary, franchise, or other company operation.

Interestingly, despite some obvious cultural differences, research suggests that regardless of nationality or religion, most people embrace a set of five core values:

1. Compassion
2. Fairness
3. Honesty
4. Responsibility
5. Respect for others

These values lie at the heart of human rights issues and seem to transcend more superficial differences among cultures. Finding

shared values allows companies to build more effective partnerships and alliances. As long as people understand that there is a set of core values, perhaps they can permit all kinds of differences in strategy and tactics.[78]

To a large extent, the challenge of managing across borders comes down to the philosophies and systems used to manage people. In moving from domestic to international management, managers need to develop a wide portfolio of behaviors and the capacity to adjust their behavior for a particular situation. This adjustment, however, should not compromise the values, integrity, and strengths of their home country. When managers can transcend national borders and move among different cultures, they can leverage the strategic capabilities of their organization and take advantage of the opportunities that our global economy has to offer.

DIY

Build Your Skills

Practice and apply your knowledge by going online at www.mhhe.com/BatemanM2e

9

Leadership

People get excited about the topic of leadership. They want to know: What makes a great leader? Executives at all levels in all industries are also interested in this question. They believe the answer will bring improved organizational performance and personal career success. They hope to acquire the skills that will transform an "average" manager into a true leader.

One such leader is Amory Lovins, a scientist, environmentalist, and entrepreneur who cofounded the Rocky Mountain Institute (RMI), a not-for-profit "think and do" tank in Colorado that conducts research and advises businesses, the government, and the military about strategies for using less energy and saving money. Lovins can't directly control the actions of his clients. Instead, he effectively uses patient persuasion built on his in-depth

Find Out What It Takes

to be a leader in today's organizations from Karianne and Joe.

"I've learned that there are two successful ways to manage people. Be a people person, where your employees want to work hard because they like working for you. Or be a process person, kind of rule with an iron fist and improve productivity by threatening job loss or cut hours. I find working with people in a relaxed, friendly environment helps the business and customers for the long term."
—Joe Kubinski, Operations Supervisor

"Personally, I have found that every time I have taken on a new professional challenge, a new level of leadership is required. In some cases, I think it is hard to know how to be best prepared until you find yourself in the situation. I always find that seeking the advice of a trusted and valued resource, whether it is a colleague or mentor, can help get me to the next place in my leadership ability. Even though I may rely on the advice of another person, ultimately by going through the process myself I learn from the situation and can apply the knowledge again in future situations."
—Karianne Wardell, Account Supervisor

●● learning **OBJECTIVES**

After studying Chapter 9,
you will be able to:

LO1 Summarize what people want and
organizations need from their leaders.

LO2 Explain how a good vision helps you be a
better leader.

LO3 Discuss the similarities and differences
between leading and managing.

LO4 Identify sources of power in organizations.

LO5 List personal traits and skills of effective
leaders.

LO6 Describe behaviors that will make you
a better leader, and identify when the
situation calls for them.

LO7 Distinguish between charismatic and
transformational leaders.

LO8 Describe types of opportunities to be a
leader in an organization.

LO9 Discuss how to further your own leadership
development.

knowledge of environmental matters and his ability to appreciate his clients' concern for economic well-being. This approach changes behavior by showing people possibilities they hadn't dreamed of.[1]

Of course, you don't have to form a think tank to acquire leadership skills. According to one source, "Leadership seems to be the marshaling of skills possessed by a majority but used by a minority. But it's something that can be learned by anyone, taught to everyone, denied to no one."[2]

"Every soldier has a right to competent command."

—Julius Caesar

What is leadership? To start, a leader is one who influences others to attain goals. The greater the number of followers, the greater the influence. And the more successful the attainment of worthy goals, the more evident the leadership. But we must explore beyond this bare definition to capture the excitement and intrigue that devoted followers and students of leadership feel when they see a great leader in action, to understand what organizational leaders really do, and to learn what it really takes to become an outstanding leader.

Outstanding leaders combine good strategic substance and effective interpersonal processes to formulate and implement strategies that produce results and sustainable competitive advantage.[3] They may launch enterprises, build organization cultures, win wars, or otherwise change the course of events.[4]

They are strategists who seize opportunities others overlook, but "they are also passionately concerned with detail—all the small, fundamental realities that can make or mar the grandest of plans."[5]

LO 1 WHAT YOU NEED TO KNOW . . .
What do people want and organizations need from their leaders?

WHAT DO WE WANT FROM OUR LEADERS?

What do people want from their leaders? Broadly speaking, they want help in achieving their goals.[6] Besides pay and promotions, these goals include support for personal development; clearing obstacles to high-level performance; and treatment that is respectful, fair, and ethical. Leaders serve people best by helping them develop their own initiative and good judgment, enabling them to grow, and helping them become better contributors. People want the kinds of things you will read about in this chapter and in other chapters of this book.

What do organizations need? Organizations need people at all levels to be leaders. Leaders throughout the organization are needed to do the things that their people want but also to help create and implement strategic direction. Organizations place people in formal leadership roles so that they will achieve the organization's goals. Marilyn Nelson, CEO of Carlson Companies, which operates Radisson Hotels, TGI Friday's, and Regent

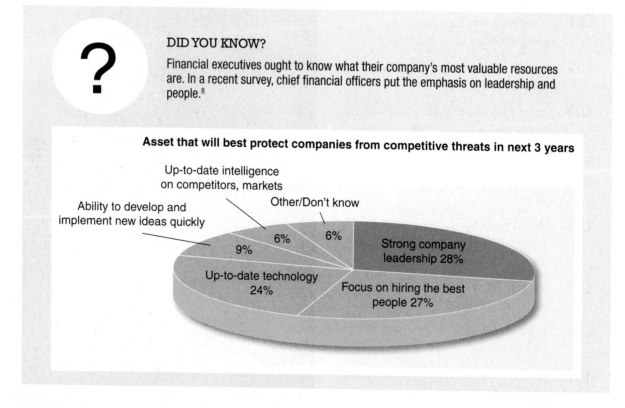

?

DID YOU KNOW?

Financial executives ought to know what their company's most valuable resources are. In a recent survey, chief financial officers put the emphasis on leadership and people.[8]

Asset that will best protect companies from competitive threats in next 3 years

Up-to-date intelligence on competitors, markets 6%

Other/Don't know 6%

Ability to develop and implement new ideas quickly 9%

Strong company leadership 28%

Up-to-date technology 24%

Focus on hiring the best people 27%

Seven Seas Cruises, recognizes that any chief executive's leadership role is to serve the company: "You actually have to subordinate your own emotions, your own desires, even make decisions on behalf of the whole that might conflict with what you would do on an individual basis."[7]

These two perspectives—what people want and what organizations need—are neatly combined in a set of five key behaviors identified by James Kouzes and Barry Posner, two well-known authors and consultants.[9] The best leaders, say Kouzes and Posner, do five things:

1. *Challenge the process*—They challenge conventional beliefs and practices, and they create change.

2. *Inspire a shared vision*—They appeal to people's values and motivate them to care about an important mission.

3. *Enable others to act*—They give people access to information and give them the power to perform to their full potential.

4. *Model the way*—They don't just tell people what to do; they are living examples of the ideals they believe in.

5. *Encourage the heart*—They show appreciation, provide rewards, and use various approaches to motivate people in positive ways.

You will read about these and other aspects of leadership in this chapter. The topics we discuss not only will help you become a better leader but also will give you benchmarks for assessing the competence and fairness with which your boss manages you.

(L)(O) 2 **WHAT YOU NEED TO KNOW . . .**
How does a good vision help you be a better leader?

VISION

"The leader's job is to create a vision," stated Robert L. Swiggett, former chair of Kollmorgen Corporation.[10] Until a few years ago, *vision* was not a word that managers uttered. But today, having a vision for the future and communicating that vision to others are known to be essential components of great leadership. "If there is no vision, there is no business," maintains entrepreneur Mark Leslie.[11] Joe Nevin, an MIS director, described leaders as "painters of the vision and architects of the journey."[12] Practicing businesspeople are not alone in this belief; academic research shows that a clear vision and communication of that vision lead to higher growth in entrepreneurial firms.[13]

A **vision** is a mental image of a possible and desirable future state of the organization. It expresses the leader's ambitions for the organization.[14] A leader can create a vision that describes high performance aspirations, the nature of corporate or business strategy, or even the kind of workplace worth building. The best visions are both ideal and unique.[15] If a vision conveys an *ideal,* it communicates a standard of excellence and a clear choice of positive values. If the vision is also *unique,* it communicates and inspires pride in being different from other

organizations. The choice of language is important; the words should express realism and optimism, an action orientation, and resolution and confidence that the vision will be attained.[16]

Visions can be small or large and can exist throughout all organizational levels. The important points are that (1) a vision is necessary for effective leadership; (2) a person or team can develop a vision for any job, work unit, or organization; and (3) many people, including managers who do not develop into strong leaders, fail to develop a clear vision—instead, they focus on performing or surviving day by day.

Put another way, leaders must know what they want.[17] And other people must understand what that is. The leader must be able to articulate the vision, clearly and often. Other people throughout the organization should understand the vision and be able to state it clearly themselves. That's a start. But the vision means nothing until the leader and followers take action to turn the vision into reality.[18]

One leader who articulates and models a clear vision is A. G. Lafley, board chairman and former CEO of Procter & Gamble. Lafley expresses his vision for the company with the slogan "The consumer is boss." According to this vision, every decision should be aimed at getting consumers to try P&G products and ensuring they like the products so much that they remember the experience as—at a minimum—satisfying. The vision guides major decisions such as restructuring research and development to bring in outside ideas and speed them to market, as well as Lafley's practice of visiting consumers in stores and homes, listening to their comments about using detergents and lotions. By following Lafley's vision, P&G has more than doubled the number of its brands with sales of at least $1 billion.[19]

A metaphor reinforces the important concept of vision.[20] Putting a jigsaw puzzle together is much easier if you have the picture on the box cover in front of you. Without the picture, or vision, the lack of direction is likely to result in frustration and failure. That is what communicating a vision is all about: making clear where you are heading.

Not just any vision will do. Visions can be inappropriate, and even fail, for a variety of reasons:[21]

- An inappropriate vision may reflect only the leader's personal needs. Such a vision may be unethical or may fail to gain acceptance by the market or by those who must implement it.

- Related to the first reason, an inappropriate vision may ignore stakeholder needs.

- Although effective leaders maintain confidence and persevere despite obstacles, the facts may dictate that the vision must change. You will learn more about change and how to manage it later.

Where do visions come from?[22] Leaders should be sensitive to emerging opportunities, develop the right capabilities or worldviews, and not be overly invested in the status quo. You also can capitalize on networks of insightful individuals who have ideas about the future. Some visions are accidental; a company may stumble into an opportunity, and the leader may get credit for foresight. Some leaders and companies launch many new initiatives and, through trial and error, hit occasional home runs. If the company learns from these successes, the "vision" emerges.

After a powerful tornado smashed through his town of Greensburg, Kansas, city administrator Steve Hewitt discovered that the storm had destroyed the homes of most of the town's 1,400 residents. It also wiped out Greensburg's hospital, fire station, elementary and high schools, water tower, and business district. Hewitt immediately contacted employees and assessed the extent of the damage. He found a safe place for

Georgetown head coach John Thompson III talks to his players during practice for the NCAA East Regional basketball tournament.

his family to stay and then turned his full attention to rescue and recovery.

First, Hewitt dealt with the emergency at hand, directing the search and rescue, and then the cleanup, by crews of city workers and volunteers operating out of tents. Even as these activities continued, Hewitt began making decisions about the future. Determined to rebuild, he saw an opportunity in the town's tragic circumstances.

Hewitt envisioned a town that would model an energy-efficient and sustainable lifestyle. He persuaded the city council to pass a resolution that all new municipal buildings meet the stiff LEED platinum certification for "green" buildings, awarded by the U.S. Green Building Council's Leadership in Energy and Environmental Design, for major energy savings. Hewitt communicated his vision in radio broadcasts and flyers handed out at emergency checkpoints. He educated the community about the practical advantages of rebuilding homes to meet LEED standards, persuading many homeowners and store owners to adopt the standards themselves. He developed plans for wind farms to supply electricity to the town. Besides inspiring the locals, these efforts drew publicity and donations, including an eco-friendly playground.[23]

L O 3 **WHAT YOU NEED TO KNOW . . .**
What are the similarities and differences between leading and managing?

LEADING AND MANAGING

Effective managers are not necessarily true leaders. Many administrators, supervisors, and even top executives perform their responsibilities successfully without being great leaders. But these positions afford an opportunity for leadership. The ability to lead effectively, then, sets the excellent managers apart from the average ones.

Management must deal with the ongoing, day-to-day complexities of organizations, but true leadership includes effectively orchestrating important change.[24] While managing requires planning and budgeting routines, leading includes setting the direction—creating a vision—for the firm. Management requires structuring the organization, staffing it with capable people, and monitoring activities; leadership goes beyond these functions by inspiring people to attain the vision. Great leaders keep people focused on moving the organization toward its ideal future, motivating them to overcome any obstacles.

Good leadership, unfortunately, is all too rare. Managers may focus on the activities that earn them praise and rewards, such as actions that cause a rise in the company's stock price, rather than making tough ethical decisions or investing in long-term results. Some new managers, learning that "quick wins" will help them establish their credibility as leaders, push a pet project while neglecting the impact on the very people they were assigned to lead. This approach backfires, because employees distrust this type of manager and lose any commitment they might have had to the team's long-term success. Successful leaders, in contrast, enlist the team in scoring *collective* quick wins that result from working together toward a shared vision.[25]

It is important to be clear that management and leadership are both vitally important. To highlight the need for more leadership is not to minimize the importance of management or managers. But leadership involves unique processes that are distinguishable from basic management processes.[26] Also, the requirement for different processes does not necessarily call for separate people. The same individual may manage and lead effectively—or may not.

Some people dislike the idea of distinguishing between management and leadership, maintaining that it is artificial or derogatory toward the managers and the management processes that make organizations run. Perhaps a more useful distinction is between supervisory and strategic leadership:[27]

- **Supervisory leadership** is behavior that provides guidance, support, and corrective feedback for day-to-day activities.
- **Strategic leadership** gives purpose and meaning to organizations by anticipating and envisioning a viable future for the organization and working with others to initiate changes that create such a future.[28]

Coach John Thompson III could be called a strategic leader. Formerly the head coach of the Princeton men's basketball team, Thompson was recently named head coach of Georgetown University's team. He was tapped to revitalize Georgetown's faltering program—ranked at the bottom of its conference—which had once been a powerhouse under the leadership of his father, John Thompson Jr. Thompson knows all about strategy. He knows how to develop discipline among his players and how to train them to choose their shots carefully and play a decisive game. And because he grew up on the Georgetown campus, watching his father coach, his sense of loyalty to the institution is ingrained. Georgetown University president John J. DeGioia credits Thompson for having successful experience plus "outstanding leadership and communication skills and . . . a deep commitment to the Georgetown tradition of academic excellence, integrity in competition, and basketball success." Proof of Thompson's leadership prowess came during his first two years of coaching at the school, when he led Georgetown into the NCAA tournament, restoring the program to national prominence.[29]

Good leaders need good followers

Organizations succeed or fail not only because of how well they are led but also because of how well followers follow. Just as managers are not necessarily good leaders, employees are not always good followers. As one leadership scholar puts it, "Executives are given subordinates; they have to earn followers."[30] But it's also true that good followers help produce good leaders.

As a manager, you will be asked to play the roles of both leader and follower. As you lead the people who report to you, you will report to your boss. You will be a member of some teams and committees, and you may head others. While the leadership roles get the glamour and therefore are the coveted roles, followers must perform their responsibilities conscientiously. Good followership is not merely obeying orders, although some bosses may view it that way. The most effective followers can think independently while remaining actively committed to organizational goals.[31] Robert Townsend, who led a legendary turnaround at Avis, says the most important characteristic of a follower may be the willingness to tell the truth.[32]

Effective followers also distinguish themselves by their enthusiasm and commitment to the organization and to a person or purpose—an idea, a product—other than themselves or their own interests. They master skills that are useful to their organizations, and they hold performance standards that are higher than required. Effective followers may not get the glory, but they know their contributions to the organization are valuable. And as they make those contributions, they study leaders in preparation for their own leadership roles.[33]

LO 4 WHAT YOU NEED TO KNOW . . .
Can you identify sources of power in organizations?

POWER AND LEADERSHIP

Central to effective leadership is **power**—the ability to influence other people. In organizations, this influence often means the ability to get things done or accomplish one's goals despite resistance from others.

Power can arise from five sources

One of the earliest and still most useful approaches to understanding power, offered by French and Raven, suggests that leaders have the five important potential sources of power shown in Figure 9.1:[34]

1. *Legitimate power*—A leader with legitimate power has the right, or the authority, to tell others what to do; employees are obligated to comply with legitimate orders. For example, a supervisor tells an employee to remove a safety hazard, and the employee removes the hazard because he has to obey the boss's authority. In contrast, when a staff person lacks the authority to give an order to a line manager, the staff person has no legitimate power over the manager. As you might guess, managers have more legitimate power over their direct reports than they do over their peers, bosses, and others inside or outside their organizations.[35]

FIGURE 9.1 Sources of Power

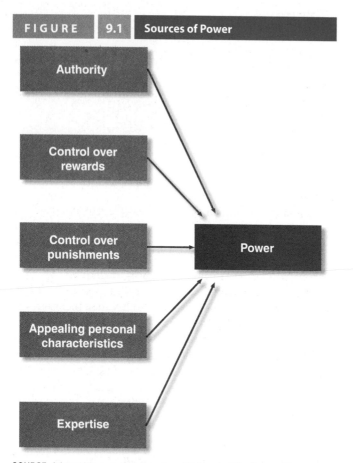

SOURCE: Adapted from J. R. P. French and B. Raven, "The Bases of Social Power," in *Studies in Social Power*, ed. D. Cartwright (Ann Arbor, MI: Institute for Social Research, 1959).

2. *Reward power*—The leader who has reward power influences others because she controls valued rewards; people comply with the leader's wishes to receive those rewards. For example, a manager works hard to achieve her performance goals and get a positive performance review and a big pay raise from her boss. In contrast, if company policy dictates that everyone receive the same salary increase, a leader's reward power decreases, because he or she is unable to give higher raises.

3. *Coercive power*—A leader with coercive power has control over punishments; people comply to avoid those punishments. For instance, a manager implements an absenteeism policy that administers disciplinary actions to offending employees. A manager has less coercive power if, say, a union contract limits her ability to punish.

4. *Referent power*—A leader with referent power has personal characteristics that appeal to others; people comply because of admiration, personal liking, a desire for approval, or a desire to be like the leader. For example, young, ambitious managers emulate the work habits and personal style of a successful, charismatic executive. An executive who is incompetent, disliked, and commands little respect has little referent power.

5. *Expert power*—A leader who has expert power has certain expertise or knowledge; people comply because they believe

in, can learn from, or can otherwise gain from that expertise. For example, a sales manager gives his salespeople some tips on how to close a deal. The salespeople then alter their sales techniques because they respect the manager's expertise. However, this manager may lack expert power in other areas, such as finance, so his salespeople may ignore his advice concerning financial matters.

People who are in a position that gives them the right to tell others what to do, who can reward and punish, who are well liked and admired, and who have expertise on which other people can draw will be powerful members of the organization. All of these sources of power are potentially important. In general, lower-level managers have less legitimate, coercive, and reward power than do middle- and higher-level managers.[36] But although it is easy to assume that the most powerful bosses are those who have high legitimate power and control major rewards and punishments, it is important not to underestimate the more "personal" sources like expert and referent power.[37]

Tim Cook is a true leader for Apple. He stepped into the leadership role as the interim CEO when Steve Jobs needed to take a medical leave of absence from the company. Cook's leadership style, as described by Fortune magazine, is that of "an intense workaholic, but cool, calm, and never, ever raises his voice."

L O 5 WHAT YOU NEED TO KNOW . . .

What are the personal traits and skills of effective leaders?

TRADITIONAL APPROACHES TO UNDERSTANDING LEADERSHIP

There are three traditional approaches to studying leadership:

1. The trait approach
2. The behavioral approach
3. The situational approach

Certain traits may set leaders apart

The trait approach is the oldest leadership perspective; it focuses on individual leaders and tries to determine the personal characteristics (traits) that great leaders share. What set Winston Churchill, Alexander the Great, Gandhi, and Martin Luther King Jr. apart from the crowd? The trait approach assumes the existence of a leadership personality and assumes that leaders are born, not made.

From 1904 to 1948, researchers conducted more than 100 leadership trait studies.[38] At the end of that period, management scholars concluded that no particular set of traits is necessary for a person to become a successful leader. Enthusiasm for the trait approach diminished, but some research on traits continued. By the mid-1970s, a more balanced view emerged: although no traits *ensure* leadership success, certain characteristics are potentially useful. The current perspective is that some personality characteristics—many of which a person need not be born with but can strive to acquire—do distinguish effective leaders from other people:[39]

1. *Drive.* Drive refers to a set of characteristics that reflect a high level of effort, including high need for achievement, constant striving for improvement, ambition, energy, tenacity (persistence in the face of obstacles), and initiative. In several countries, the achievement needs of top executives have been shown to be related to the growth rates of their organizations.[40] But the need to achieve can be a drawback if leaders focus on personal achievement and get so involved with the work that they do not delegate enough authority and responsibility. Also, while need for achievement predicts organizational effectiveness in entrepreneurial firms, it does not predict success for division heads in larger and more bureaucratic firms.[41]

2. *Leadership motivation.* Great leaders *want* to lead. So it helps to be *extraverted*—extraversion is consistently related to leadership emergence and leadership effectiveness.[42] Also important is a high need for power, a preference to be in leadership rather than follower positions.[43] A high power need induces people to try influencing others and sustains interest and satisfaction in the leadership process. When the power need is exercised in moral and socially constructive ways, leaders inspire more trust, respect, and commitment to their vision.

3. *Integrity.* Integrity is the correspondence between actions and words. Honesty and credibility, in addition to being desirable characteristics in their own right, are especially important for leaders, because these traits inspire trust in others.

4. *Self-confidence.* Self-confidence is important because the leadership role is challenging, and setbacks are inevitable. A self-confident leader overcomes obstacles, makes decisions despite uncertainty, and instills confidence in others. Of course, you don't want to overdo this; arrogance and cockiness have triggered more than one leader's downfall.

5. *Knowledge of the business.* Effective leaders have a high level of knowledge about their industries, companies, and technical matters. Leaders must have the intelligence to interpret vast quantities of information. Advanced degrees are useful in a career, but ultimately they are less important than acquired expertise in matters relevant to the organization.[45]

Percy Sutton has exhibited these leadership traits as the founder of Inner City Broadcasting and, more recently, cofounder of information technology company Synematics. A lawyer by training, Sutton represented civil rights activist Malcolm X until his death in 1965. Later he served in the New York State assembly, sold real estate, bought an oil well in Nigeria, and shipped heavy machinery.

Then Sutton and a partner bought a radio station and incorporated it into Inner City Broadcasting, which now includes 19 stations, run by Sutton's son Pierre. In 1980, Sutton bought

A senior partner in a law firm told his attorneys about the importance of trust. When a young, ambitious lawyer asked how one can gain trust, the senior partner replied, "Try being trustworthy."[44]

the failing Apollo Theater in New York City's Harlem and brought it out of bankruptcy. Although he lost $31 million on the project, he is proud of rescuing this landmark in African American history, which bolstered the local economy. "When I look out on the street I see all of the activity, and there is a great comfort in knowing that I started it," he says, adding, "For me it has never been about the money."

Sutton attributes his success to constant learning (he reads seven newspapers a day), skill, and a positive attitude. He told a reporter, "I'm a happy person. I'm a good lawyer. I challenge things. And in spite of the injuries that have been inflicted on me in my life, I manage to like people."[46]

Finally, there is one personal skill that may be the most important: the ability to perceive the needs and goals of others and to adjust one's personal leadership approach accordingly.[47] Effective leaders do not rely on one leadership style; rather, they are capable of using different styles as the situation warrants.[48] This quality is the cornerstone of the situational approaches to leadership, which we will discuss shortly.

Ⓛ Ⓞ **6** **WHAT YOU NEED TO KNOW . . .**

Can you describe behaviors that will make you a better leader and identify when the situation calls for them?

Certain behaviors may make leaders effective

The **behavioral approach** to leadership tries to identify what good leaders do. Should leaders focus on getting the job done or on keeping their followers happy? Should they make decisions autocratically or democratically? The behavioral approach downplays personal characteristics in favor of the actual behaviors that leaders exhibit. Studies of leadership behavior have considered the degree to which leaders emphasize task perfor-

mance versus group maintenance and the extent to which leaders invite employee participation in decision making.

task performance and group maintenance
Leadership requires getting the job done. **Task performance behaviors** are the leader's efforts to ensure that the work unit or organization reaches its goals. This dimension is variously referred to as *concern for production, directive leadership, initiating structure,* or *closeness of supervision.* It includes a focus on work speed, quality and accuracy, quantity of output, and following the rules.[49] This type of leader behavior improves leader job performance and group and organizational performance.[50]

In exhibiting **group maintenance behaviors**, leaders take action to ensure the satisfaction of group members, develop and maintain harmonious work relationships, and preserve the group's social stability. This dimension is sometimes referred to as *concern for people, supportive leadership,* or *consideration.* It includes a focus on people's feelings and comfort, appreciation of them, and stress reduction.[51] This type of leader behavior has a strong positive impact on follower satisfaction, motivation, and leader effectiveness.[52]

What *specific* behaviors do performance- and maintenance-oriented leadership imply? To help answer this question, assume you have been asked to rate your boss on these two dimensions. If a leadership study were conducted in your organization, you would be asked to fill out a questionnaire in which you answer questions such as the following:[53]

Questions to Identify Task Performance Leadership

1. Is your superior strict about observing regulations?
2. To what extent does your superior give you instructions and orders?
3. Is your superior strict about the amount of work you do?
4. Does your superior urge you to complete your work by a specified time?
5. Does your superior try to make you work to your maximum capacity?
6. When you do an inadequate job, does your superior focus on the inadequate way the job is done?
7. Does your superior ask you for reports about the progress of your work?
8. How precisely does your superior work out plans for goal achievement each month?

Questions to Identify Group Maintenance Leadership

1. Can you talk freely with your superior about your work?
2. Does your superior generally support you?
3. Is your superior concerned about your personal problems?
4. Do you think your superior trusts you?
5. Does your superior give you recognition when you do your job well?

6. When a problem arises in your workplace, does your superior ask your opinion about how to solve it?

7. Is your superior concerned about your future benefits, such as promotions and pay raises?

8. Does your superior treat you fairly?

Leader-Member Exchange (LMX) theory highlights the importance of leader behaviors not just toward the group as a whole but toward individuals on a personal basis.[54] The focus in the original formulation, which has since been expanded, is primarily on the leader behaviors historically considered group maintenance.[55] According to LMX theory, and as supported by research evidence, maintenance behaviors such as trust, open communication, mutual respect, mutual obligation, and mutual loyalty form the cornerstone of relationships that are satisfying and perhaps more productive.[56]

logical and probably represent the prevalent beliefs among managers about the general effects of these approaches.

Democratic styles, appealing though they may seem, are not always the most appropriate. When speed is of the essence, democratic decision making may be too slow, or people may want decisiveness from the leader.[61] Whether a decision should be made autocratically or democratically depends on the characteristics of the leader, the followers, and the situation.[62] Thus, a situational approach to leader decision styles, discussed later in the chapter, is appropriate.

Performance and Maintenance Behaviors The performance and maintenance dimensions of leadership are independent of each other. In other words, a leader can behave in ways that emphasize one, both, or neither of these dimensions. Some research indicates that the ideal combination is to engage in both types of leader behaviors.

> ❝ **"A leader's job is to see possibility in people."** ❞
>
> —Carly Fiorina, former CEO, Hewlett-Packard[57]

Remember, though, the potential for cross-cultural differences. Maintenance behaviors are important everywhere, but the specific behaviors can differ from one culture to another. For example, in the United States, maintenance behaviors include dealing with people face-to-face; in Japan, written memos are preferred over giving directions in person, thus avoiding confrontation and permitting face-saving in the event of disagreement.[58]

participation in decision making
How should a leader make decisions? More specifically, to what extent should leaders involve their people in making decisions?[59] As a dimension of leadership behavior, *participation in decision making* can range from autocratic to democratic:

- **Autocratic leadership** makes decisions and then announces them to the group.
- **Democratic leadership** solicits input from others. Democratic leadership seeks information, opinions, and preferences, sometimes to the point of meeting with the group, leading discussions, and using consensus or majority vote to make the final choice.

effects of leader behavior
How the leader behaves influences people's attitudes and performance. Studies of these effects focus on autocratic versus democratic decision styles or on performance- versus maintenance-oriented behaviors.

Decision Styles The classic study comparing autocratic and democratic styles found that a democratic approach resulted in the most positive attitudes, but an autocratic approach resulted in somewhat higher performance.[60] A **laissez-faire** style, in which the leader essentially made no decisions, led to more negative attitudes and lower performance. These results seem

A team of Ohio State University researchers investigated the effects of leader behaviors in a truck manufacturing plant of International Harvester.[63] Generally, supervisors scoring high on *maintenance behaviors* (which the researchers termed *consideration*) had fewer grievances and less turnover in their work units than supervisors who were low on this dimension. The opposite held for *task performance behaviors* (called *initiating structure*). Supervisors high on this dimension had more grievances and higher turnover rates.

When maintenance and performance leadership behaviors were considered together, the results were more complex. But one conclusion was clear: when a leader rates high on performance-oriented behaviors, he or she should also be maintenance oriented. Otherwise, the leader will face high levels of employee turnover and grievances.

At about the same time the Ohio State studies were being conducted, a research program at the University of Michigan was studying the impact of the same leader behaviors on groups' job performance.[64] Among other things, the researchers concluded that the most effective managers engaged in what they called *task-oriented behavior*: planning, scheduling, coordinating, providing resources, and setting performance goals. Effective managers also exhibited more *relationship-oriented behavior*: demonstrating trust and confidence, being friendly and considerate, showing appreciation, keeping people informed, and so on. As you can see, these dimensions of leader behavior are essentially the task performance and group maintenance dimensions.

After the Ohio State and Michigan findings were published, it became popular to talk about the ideal leader as one who is always both performance and maintenance oriented. The best-known leadership training model to follow this style is Blake and Mouton's Leadership Grid.[®65] In grid training, managers are

FIGURE | 9.2 | **The Leadership Grid®**

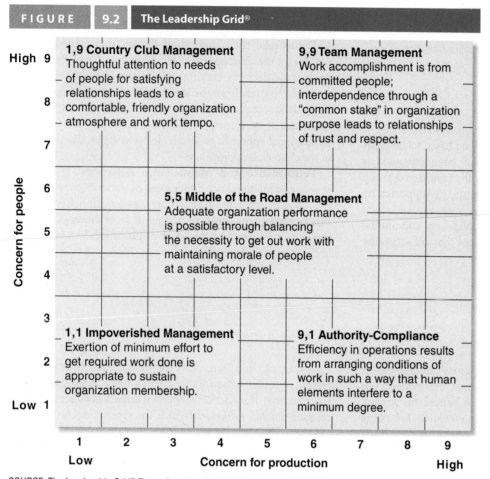

SOURCE: The Leadership Grid® Figure from *Leadership Dilemmas—Grid Solutions,* p. 29, by Robert R. Blake and Anne Adams McCanse. Copyright © 1991, by Robert R. Blake and the Estate of Jane S. Mouton. Used with permission. All rights reserved.

rated on their performance-oriented behavior (called *concern for production*) and maintenance-oriented behavior (*concern for people*). Then their scores are plotted on the grid shown in Figure 9.2. The highest score is a 9 on both dimensions. Managers who score less than a 9,9—for example, those who are high on concern for people but low on concern for production—would then receive training on how to become a 9,9 leader.

For a long time, grid training was warmly received by U.S. business and industry. Later, however, it was criticized for embracing a simplistic, one-best-way style of leadership and ignoring the possibility that 9,9 is not best under all circumstances. For example, even 1,1 leadership can be appropriate if employees know their jobs (so they don't need to receive directions). Also, they may enjoy their jobs and coworkers enough that they do not care whether the boss shows personal concern for them. Still, if the manager is uncertain how to behave, it probably is best to exhibit behaviors that are related to both task performance and group maintenance.[66]

In fact, a wide range of effective leadership styles exists. Organizations that understand the need for diverse leadership styles will have a competitive advantage in the modern business

environment over those in which managers believe there is only "one best way."

The best way to lead depends on the situation

According to proponents of the **situational approach** to leadership, universally important traits and behaviors don't exist. Rather, effective leader behaviors vary from situation to situation. *The leader should first analyze the situation and then decide what to do.* In other words, look before you lead.

A head nurse in a hospital described her situational approach to leadership this way: "My leadership style is a mix of all styles. In this environment I normally let people participate. But in a code blue situation where a patient is dying I automatically become very autocratic: 'You do this; you do that; you, out of the room; you all better be quiet; you, get Dr. Mansfield.' The staff tell me that's the only time they see me like that. In an emergency like that, you don't have time to vote, talk a lot, or yell at each other. It's time for someone to set up the order.

"I remember one time, one person saying, 'Wait a minute, I want to do this.' He wanted to do the mouth-to-mouth resuscitation. I knew the person behind him did it better, so I said, 'No, he does it.' This fellow told me later that I hurt him so badly to yell that in front of all the staff and doctors. It was like he wasn't good enough. So I explained it to him: that's the way it is. A life was on the line. I couldn't give you warm fuzzies. I couldn't make you look good because you didn't have the skills to give the very best to that patient who wasn't breathing anymore."[67] This nurse has her own intuitive situational approach to leadership. She knows the potential advantages of the participatory approach to decision making, but she also knows that in some circumstances she must make decisions herself.

The first situational model of leadership was proposed in 1958 by Tannenbaum and Schmidt. In their classic *Harvard Business Review* article, these authors described how managers should consider three factors before deciding how to lead:[68]

1. *Forces in the manager* include the manager's personal values, inclinations, feelings of security, and confidence in subordinates.

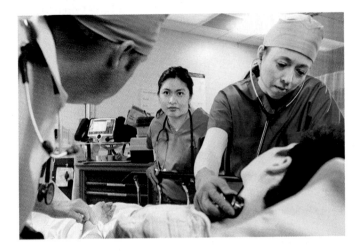

2. *Forces in the subordinate* include his or her knowledge and experience, readiness to assume responsibility for decision making, interest in the task or problem, and understanding and acceptance of the organization's goals.

3. *Forces in the situation* include the type of leadership style the organization values, the degree to which the group works effectively as a unit, the problem itself and the type of information needed to solve it, and the amount of time the leader has to make the decision.

Consider which of these forces makes an autocratic style most appropriate and which dictates a democratic, participative style. By engaging in this exercise, you are constructing a situational theory of leadership.

Although the Tannenbaum and Schmidt article was published a half century ago, most of its arguments remain valid. Since that time, other situational models have emerged. We will focus here on four: the Vroom model for decision making, Fiedler's contingency model, Hersey and Blanchard's situational theory, and path-goal theory.

the Vroom model of leadership In the tradition of Tannenbaum and Schmidt, the Vroom model emphasizes the participative dimension of leadership: how leaders go about making decisions. The model uses the basic situational approach of assessing the situation before determining the best leadership style.[69] The following situational factors are used to analyze problems:[70]

- *Decision significance*—The significance of the decision to the success of the project or organization.

- *Importance of commitment*—The importance of team members' commitment to the decision.

- *Leader's expertise*—Your knowledge or expertise in relation to this problem.

- *Likelihood of commitment*—The likelihood that the team would commit itself to a decision that you might make on your own.

- *Group support for objectives*—The degree to which the team supports the organization's objectives at stake in this problem.

- *Group expertise*—Team members' knowledge or expertise in relation to this problem.

- *Team competence*—The ability of team members to work together in solving problems.

- SITUATIONAL APPROACH Leadership perspective proposing that universally important traits and behaviors do not exist, and that effective leadership behavior varies from situation to situation.

- VROOM MODEL A situational model that focuses on the participative dimension of leadership.

Each of these factors is based on an important attribute of the problem the leader faces and should be assessed as either high or low.

The Vroom model, shown in Figure 9.3, operates like a funnel. You answer the questions one at a time, choosing high or

FIGURE 9.3 Vroom's Model of Leadership

Time-Driven Model

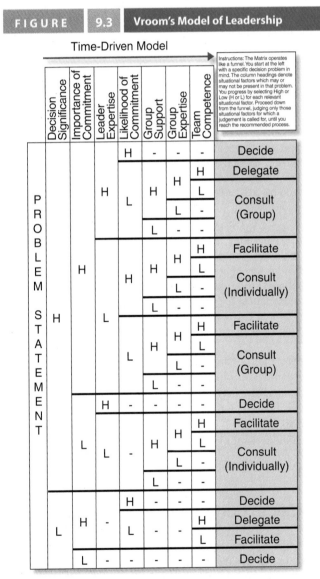

Instructions: The Matrix operates like a funnel. You start at the left with a specific decision problem in mind. The column headings denote situational factors which may or may not be present in that problem. You progress by selecting High or Low (H or L) for each relevant situational factor. Proceed down from the funnel, judging only those situational factors for which a judgement is called for, until you reach the recommended process.

Decision Significance	Importance of Commitment	Leader Expertise	Likelihood of Commitment	Group Support	Group Expertise	Team Competence	
H	H	H	H	-	-	-	Decide
H	H	H	L	H	H	H	Delegate
H	H	H	L	H	H	L	Consult (Group)
H	H	H	L	H	L	-	
H	H	H	L	L	-	-	
H	H	L	H	H	H	H	Facilitate
H	H	L	H	H	H	L	Consult (Individually)
H	H	L	H	H	L	-	
H	H	L	H	L	-	-	
H	H	L	L	H	H	H	Facilitate
H	H	L	L	H	H	L	Consult (Group)
H	H	L	L	H	L	-	
H	H	L	L	L	-	-	
H	L	H	-	-	-	-	Decide
H	L	L	-	H	H	H	Facilitate
H	L	L	-	H	H	L	Consult (Individually)
H	L	L	-	H	L	-	
H	L	L	-	L	-	-	
L	H	H	-	-	-	-	Decide
L	H	-	L	-	-	H	Delegate
L	H	-	L	-	-	L	Facilitate
L	L	-	-	-	-	-	Decide

SOURCE: V. Vroom, "Leadership and the Decision-Making Process," *Organizational Dynamics*, Spring 2000, pp. 82–94. Copyright © 2000 with permission from Elsevier Science.

● FIEDLER'S CONTINGENCY MODEL OF LEADERSHIP EFFECTIVENESS
A situational approach to leadership postulating that effectiveness depends on the personal style of the leader and the degree to which the situation gives the leader power, control, and influence over the situation.

● TASK-MOTIVATED LEADERSHIP
Leadership that places primary emphasis on completing a task.

● RELATIONSHIP-MOTIVATED LEADERSHIP
Leadership that places primary emphasis on maintaining good interpersonal relationships.

low for each, sometimes skipping questions as you follow the appropriate path. Eventually, you reach one of 14 possible endpoints. For each endpoint, the model states which of five decision styles is most appropriate. Several different decision styles may work, but the style recommended is the one that takes the least time.

The five leader decision styles have the following definitions:[71]

1. *Decide*—You make the decision alone and either announce or "sell" it to the group. You may use your expertise in collecting information that you deem relevant to the problem from the group or others.

2. *Consult individually*—You present the problem to the group members individually, get their suggestions, and then make the decision.

3. *Consult the group*—You present the problem to the group members in a meeting, get their suggestions, and then make the decision.

4. *Facilitate*—You present the problem to the group in a meeting. You act as a facilitator, defining the problem to be solved and the boundaries within which the decision must be made. Your objective is to get concurrence on a decision. Above all, you take care to ensure that your ideas are not given any greater weight than those of others simply because of your position.

5. *Delegate*—You permit the group to make the decision within prescribed limits. The group undertakes the identification and diagnosis of the problem, developing alternative procedures for solving it, and deciding on one or more alternative solutions. While you play no direct role in the group's deliberations unless explicitly asked, your role is an important one behind the scenes, providing needed resources and encouragement.

The styles indicate that there are several shades of participation, not just autocratic or democratic.

Of course, not every managerial decision warrants this complicated analysis. But the model becomes less complex after you work through it a couple of times. Also, using the model for major decisions ensures that you consider the important situational factors and alerts you to the most appropriate style to use.

Fiedler's contingency model
According to Fiedler's contingency model of leadership effectiveness, effectiveness depends on two factors: the personal style of the leader and the degree to which the situation gives the leader power, control, and influence over the situation.[72] Figure 9.4 illustrates this model. The upper half of the figure shows the situational analysis, and the lower half indicates the appropriate style. In the upper portion, three questions are used to analyze the situation:

1. Are leader–member relations good or poor? (To what extent is the leader accepted and supported by group members?)

2. Is the task structured or unstructured? (To what extent do group members know what their goals are and how to accomplish them?)

3. Is the leader's position power strong or weak (high or low)? (To what extent does the leader have the authority to reward and punish?)

These three sequential questions create a decision tree (from top to bottom, in the figure) in which a situation is classified into one of eight categories. The lower the category number, the more favorable the situation is for the leader; the higher the number, the less favorable the situation. Fiedler originally called this variable "situational favorableness" but now it is "situational control." Situation 1 is the best: relations are good, task structure is high, and power is high. In the least favorable situation (8), in which the leader has very little situational control, relations are poor, tasks lack structure, and the leader's power is weak.

Different situations dictate different leadership styles. Fiedler measured leadership styles with an instrument assessing the leader's *least preferred coworker* (LPC), that is, the attitude toward the follower the leader liked the least. This was considered an indication more generally of leaders' attitudes toward people. If a leader can single out the person she likes the least, but her attitude is not all that negative, she received a high score on the LPC scale. Leaders with more negative attitudes toward others would receive low LPC scores. Based on the LPC score, Fiedler considered two leadership styles:

1. Task-motivated leadership places primary emphasis on completing the task and is more likely exhibited by leaders with low LPC scores.

2. Relationship-motivated leadership emphasizes maintaining good interpersonal relationships and is more likely from high-LPC leaders.

These leadership styles correspond to task performance and group maintenance leader behaviors, respectively.

The lower part of Figure 9.4 indicates which style is situationally appropriate. For situations 1, 2, 3, and 8, a task-motivated leadership style is more effective. For situations 4 through 7, relationship-motivated leadership is more appropriate.

Fiedler's theory was not always supported by research. It is better supported if we replace the eight specific levels of situational control with three broad levels: low, medium, and high. The theory was controversial in academic circles, partly because it assumed leaders cannot change their styles but must be

● HERSEY AND BLANCHARD'S SITUATIONAL THEORY A life-cycle theory of leadership postulating that a manager should consider an employee's psychological and job maturity before deciding whether task performance or maintenance behaviors are more important.

● JOB MATURITY The level of the employee's skills and technical knowledge relative to the task being performed.

● PSYCHOLOGICAL MATURITY An employee's self-confidence and self-respect.

● PATH-GOAL THEORY A theory that concerns how leaders influence subordinates' perceptions of their work goals and the paths they follow toward attainment of those goals.

FIGURE	9.4	Fiedler's Analysis of Situations in Which the Task- or Relationship-Motivated Leader Is More Effective

Leader–member relations	Good				Poor			
Task structure	Structured		Unstructured		Structured		Unstructured	
Leader position power	High	Low	High	Low	High	Low	High	Low
	1	2	3	4	5	6	7	8

Favorable for leader → Unfavorable for leader

Type of leader most effective in the situation	Task-motivated	Task-motivated	Task-motivated	Relationship-motivated	Relationship-motivated	Relationship-motivated	Relationship-motivated	Task-motivated

SOURCE: D. Organ and T. Bateman, *Organizational Behavior,* 4th ed. McGraw-Hill, 1990. © 1990 The McGraw-Hill Companies.

assigned to situations that suit their styles. However, the model has withstood the test of time and still receives attention. Most important, it brought a focus on the significance of finding a fit between the situation and the leader's style.

Hersey and Blanchard's situational theory
Hersey and Blanchard developed a situational model that added another factor the leader should take into account before deciding whether task performance or maintenance behaviors are more important. In their situational theory, originally called the *life-cycle theory of leadership,* the key situational factor is the maturity of the followers.[73] Job maturity is the level of the followers' skills and technical knowledge relative to the task being performed; psychological maturity is the followers' self-confidence and self-respect. High-maturity followers have the ability and the confidence to do a good job.

The theory proposes that the more mature the followers, the less the leader needs to engage in task performance behaviors. Maintenance behaviors are not important with followers with low or high maturity but are important for followers of moderate maturity. For low-maturity followers, the emphasis should be on performance-related leadership; for moderate-maturity followers, performance leadership is somewhat less important and

maintenance behaviors become more important; and for high-maturity followers, neither dimension of leadership behavior is important.

Little academic research has been done on this situational theory, but the model is popular in management training seminars. Regardless of its scientific validity, Hersey and Blanchard's model provides a reminder that it is important to treat different people differently. Also, it suggests the importance of treating the same individual differently from time to time as he or she changes jobs or acquires more maturity in her or his particular job.[74]

path-goal theory
Perhaps the most comprehensive and generally useful situational model of leadership effectiveness is path-goal theory. Developed by Robert House, path-goal theory gets its name from its concern with how leaders influence followers' perceptions of their work goals and the paths they follow toward goal attainment.[75]

Path-goal theory has two key situational factors:

1. Personal characteristics of followers

2. Environmental pressures and demands with which followers must cope to attain their work goals

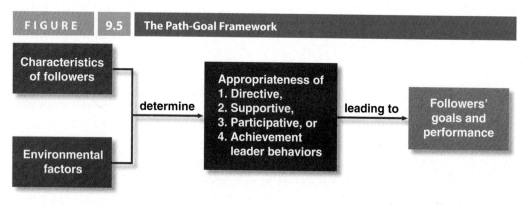

FIGURE 9.5 The Path-Goal Framework

These factors determine which leadership behaviors are most appropriate.

The theory identifies four pertinent leadership behaviors:

1. *Directive leadership,* a form of task performance-oriented behavior

2. *Supportive leadership,* a form of group maintenance-oriented behavior

3. *Participative leadership,* or decision style

4. *Achievement-oriented leadership,* or behaviors geared toward motivating people, such as setting challenging goals and rewarding good performance

These situational factors and leader behaviors are merged in Figure 9.5. As you can see, appropriate leader behaviors—as determined by characteristics of followers and the work environment—lead to effective performance.

The theory also specifies *which* follower and environmental characteristics are important. There are three key follower characteristics:

1. *Authoritarianism* is the degree to which individuals respect, admire, and defer to authority.

2. *Locus of control* is the extent to which individuals see the environment as responsive to their own behavior. People with an internal locus of control believe that what happens to them is their own doing; people with an external locus of control believe that it is just luck or fate.

3. *Ability* is people's beliefs about their own abilities to do their assigned jobs.

Path-goal theory states that these personal characteristics determine the appropriateness of various leadership styles. For example, the theory makes the following propositions:

- A directive leadership style is more appropriate for highly authoritarian people, because such people respect authority.

- A participative leadership style is more appropriate for people who have an internal locus of control, because these individuals prefer to have more influence over their own lives.

- A directive style is more appropriate when subordinates' ability is low. The directive style helps people understand what has to be done.

Appropriate leadership style is also determined by three important environmental factors:

- *Tasks*—Directive leadership is inappropriate if tasks already are well structured.

- *Formal authority system*—If the task and the authority or rule system are dissatisfying, directive leadership will create greater dissatisfaction. If the task or authority system is dissatisfying, supportive leadership is especially appropriate, because it offers one positive source of gratification in an otherwise negative situation.

- *Primary work group*—If the primary work group provides social support to its members, supportive leadership is less important.

Path-goal theory offers many more propositions. In general, the theory suggests that the functions of the leader are to (1) make the path to work goals easier to travel by providing coaching and direction, (2) reduce frustrating barriers to goal attainment, and (3) increase opportunities for personal satisfaction by increasing payoffs to people for achieving performance goals. The best way to do these things depends on your people and on the work situation. Again, analyze, and then adapt your style accordingly.

substitutes for leadership

Sometimes leaders don't have to lead, or situations constrain their ability to lead effectively. The situation may be one in which leadership is unnecessary or has little impact. Substitutes for leadership can provide the same influence on people as leaders otherwise would have.

Certain follower, task, and organizational factors are substitutes for task performance and group maintenance leader behaviors.[76] For example, group maintenance behaviors are less important and have less impact if people already have a closely knit group, they have a professional orientation, the job is inherently satisfying, or there is great physical distance between leader and followers. So, physicians who are strongly concerned with professional conduct, enjoy their work, and work independently do not need social support from hospital administrators.

Task performance leadership is less important and will have less of a positive effect if people have a lot of experience and ability, feedback is supplied to them directly from the task or by computer, or the rules and procedures are rigid. If these factors are operating, the leader does not have to tell people what to do or how well they are performing.

The concept of substitutes for leadership does more than indicate when a leader's attempts at influence will and will not work. It provides useful and practical prescriptions for how to manage more efficiently.[77] If the manager can develop the work situation to the point where a number of these substitutes for leadership are operating, the leader can spend less time attempting to influence people and will have more time for other important activities.

Research indicates that substitutes for leadership may be better predictors of commitment and satisfaction than of performance.[78] These substitutes are helpful, but you can't put substitutes in place and think you have completed your job as leader. And as a follower, consider this: If you're not getting good leadership, and if these substitutes are not in place, create your own "substitute" for leadership—self-leadership. Take the initiative to motivate yourself, lead yourself, create positive change, and lead others.

(L)(O) 7 WHAT YOU NEED TO KNOW . . .
What are the differences between charismatic and transformational leaders?

CONTEMPORARY PERSPECTIVES ON LEADERSHIP

So far, you have learned the major classic approaches to understanding leadership, all of which remain useful today. Several new developments are revolutionizing our understanding of this vital aspect of management.

Charismatic leaders inspire their followers

Like many great leaders, Ronald Reagan had charisma. So does Barack Obama. In industry, Thomas Watson, Alfred Sloan, Steve Jobs, and Richard Branson also have been charismatic leaders.

Charisma is an elusive concept—easy to spot but hard to define. What *is* charisma, and how does one acquire it? According to one definition, "Charisma packs an emotional wallop for followers above and beyond ordinary esteem, affection, admiration, and trust . . . The charismatic is an idolized hero, a messiah and a savior."[79] Many people, particularly North Americans, value charisma in their leaders. But some people don't like the term *charisma;* it can be associated with the negative charisma of evil leaders whom people follow blindly.[80] Yet, charismatic leaders who display appropriate values and use their charisma for appropriate purposes serve as ethical role models for others.[81]

Charismatic leaders are dominant, exceptionally self-confident, and have a strong conviction in the moral righteousness of their beliefs.[82] They strive to create an aura of competence and success and communicate high expectations for and confidence in followers. Ultimately, charismatic leaders satisfy other people's needs.[83]

The charismatic leader articulates ideological goals and makes sacrifices in pursuit of those goals.[84] Martin Luther King Jr.

had a dream for a better world, and John F. Kennedy spoke of landing a human on the moon. In other words, such leaders have a compelling vision. The charismatic leader also arouses a sense of excitement and adventure. He or she is an eloquent speaker who exhibits superior verbal skills, which helps communicate the vision and motivate followers. Walt Disney mesmerized people with his storytelling; had enormous creative talent; and instilled in his organization strong values of good taste, risk taking, and innovation.[85]

Martin Luther King Jr. was a charismatic leader with a compelling vision: a dream for a better world.

Leaders who possess these characteristics or do these things inspire in their followers trust, confidence, acceptance, obedience, emotional involvement, affection, admiration, and higher performance.[86] For example, having charisma not only helps CEOs inspire other employees in the organization but also may enable them to influence external stakeholders, including customers and investors.[87] Evidence for the positive effects of charismatic leadership has been found in a wide variety of groups, organizations, and management levels, and in countries including India, Singapore, the Netherlands, China, Japan, and Canada.[88]

Charisma has been shown to improve corporate financial performance, particularly under conditions of uncertainty—that is, in risky circumstances or when environments are changing and people have difficulty understanding what they should do.[89] Uncertainty is stressful, and it makes people more receptive to the ideas and actions of charismatic leaders. By the way, too, as an organization's (or team's) performance improves under a person's leadership, others see that person as increasingly charismatic as a result of the higher performance.[90]

Transformational leaders revitalize organizations

Charisma can contribute to transformational leadership. **Transformational leaders** get people to transcend their personal interests for the sake of the larger community.[91] They generate excitement and revitalize organizations. At Hewlett-Packard, the ability to generate excitement is an explicit criterion for selecting managers. In the United Kingdom, Richard Branson of Virgin Group is a transformational leader who built a global business empire.[92]

The transformational process moves beyond the more traditional *transactional* approach to leadership. **Transactional leaders** view management as a series of transactions in which they use their legitimate, reward, and coercive powers to give commands and exchange rewards for services rendered. Unlike transformational leadership, transactional leadership is dispassionate; it does not excite, transform, empower, or inspire people to focus on the interests of the group or organization. However, transactional approaches may be more effective for individualists than for collectivists.[93]

generating excitement Transformational leaders generate excitement in several ways:[94]

- They are *charismatic*, as described earlier.
- They give their followers *individualized attention*. They delegate challenging work to deserving people, keep lines of communication open, and provide one-on-one mentoring to develop their people. They do not treat everyone alike, because not everyone *is* alike.

- They are *intellectually stimulating*. They arouse in their followers an awareness of problems and potential solutions. They articulate the organization's opportunities, threats, strengths, and weaknesses. They stir the imagination and generate insights. As a result, problems are recognized, and high-quality solutions are identified and implemented with the followers' full commitment.

Jim McCluney, CEO of data storage firm Emulex, likes his employees to tease him a little. He believes it's good management to let people relax and poke fun at him, because it helps people come up with creative new ideas and solutions. "He's really a lot of fun to be around," says one colleague. McCluney is known for hosting pizza days and appearing in employees' offices or at their desks to chat.

McCluney explains the reason for his approach. "If you make your management team really on board, working and adding their unique skills and getting as much diversity of views and opinion on a given problem, the company really thrives." Without abdicating his responsibilities as a leader, he values the brainpower of his managers and employees. He jumps in when decisive action is needed, but he knows the pitfalls of trying to do everything himself instead of giving managers some free rein. McCluney sees leadership as "a balance between knowing when to be authoritative and when to be collaborative."[95]

skills and strategies At least four skills or strategies contribute to transformational leadership:[96]

1. *Having a vision*—Leaders have a goal, an agenda, or a results orientation that grabs attention.

2. *Communicating their vision*—Through words, manner, or symbolism, leaders relate a compelling image of the ultimate goal.

Majora Carter Leads the Fight for Environmental Justice

Majora Carter is an activist for two causes that at first glance might seem unrelated: the environment and unemployed workers. Nearly a decade ago, while working with several nonprofit organizations, Carter learned that New York City planned to build another waste-processing plant near the Bronx neighborhood where she had grown up. The trash and diesel fumes from the 60,000 garbage trucks that would pass through each week, along with pollution from two sewage treatment plants and four power plants already located in the Bronx, would further compromise an already unhealthy environment. The neighborhood's residents had high rates of asthma, diabetes, and obesity.

Carter swung into action. First, she created Sustainable South Bronx (SSBx) to defeat the new garbage plant. Next, she obtained a grant to establish a training program called Bronx Environmental Stewardship Training (BEST) in order to prepare the neighborhood's many unemployed residents for local jobs designed to improve the neighborhood.

Through BEST job training, Bronx residents learned such eco-friendly skills as green-roof installation and maintenance, urban forestry, brown-field cleanup, and the retrofitting of buildings to increase energy efficiency. When local jobs became available, BEST graduates were the first to be tapped. Carter believes that residents who are educated to improve their own environment will have a greater commitment to their jobs. So far, that has proven to be true.

Since then, Carter and SSBx have helped several green start-up companies. One such venture is SmartRoofs, which employs local workers to replace tar and blacktop roofs with a durable and lightweight layer of plant growth. The plants absorb less heat than blacktop, keeping buildings cooler in the summer, reducing reliance on fans and air conditioning. Plants also absorb water and provide oxygen, improving air quality.

Recently Carter formed the Majora Carter Group, which offers consulting services to other cities, towns, and organizations. One of her first clients was a town in North Carolina

3. *Building trust*—Being consistent, dependable, and persistent, leaders position themselves clearly by choosing a direction and staying with it, thus projecting integrity.

4. *Having positive self-regard*—Leaders do not feel self-important or complacent, but rather recognize their personal strengths, compensate for their weaknesses, nurture and continually develop their talents, and know how to learn from failure. They strive for success rather than merely try to avoid failure.

Transformational leadership has been identified in industry, the military, and politics.[97] Examples of transformational leaders in business include Henry Ford (founder of Ford Motor Company), Herb Kelleher (former CEO of Southwest Airlines), Jeff Bezos (founder of Amazon.com), David Neeleman (in his former role as leader of JetBlue), and Lee Iacocca (who led Chrysler's turnaround during the 1980s).[98] As with studies of charisma, transformational leadership and its positive impact on follower satisfaction and performance have been demonstrated in countries the world over, including Egypt, Germany, China, England, and Japan.[99] A study in Korean companies found that transformational leadership predicted employee motivation, which in turn predicted creativity.[100] Under transformational leadership, people view their jobs as more intrinsically motivating (see Chapter 13 for more on this) and are more strongly committed to work goals.[101] And top management teams agree more clearly about important organizational goals, which translates into higher organizational performance.[102]

transforming leaders Importantly, transformational leadership is not the exclusive domain of presidents and chief executives. In the military, leaders who received transformational leadership training had a positive impact on followers' personal development. They also were successful as *indirect* leaders: military recruits under the transformational leaders' direct reports were stronger performers.[103] Don't forget,

though: the best leaders are those who can display both transformational and transactional behaviors.[104]

Ford Motor Company, in collaboration with the University of Michigan School of Business, put thousands of middle managers through a program designed to stimulate transformational leadership.[105] The training included analysis of the changing business environment, company strategy, and personal reflection and discussion about the need to change. Participants assessed their own leadership styles and developed a specific change initiative to implement after the training—a change that would make a needed and lasting difference for the company.

Over the next six months, the managers implemented change on the job. Almost half of the initiatives resulted in transformational changes in the organization or work unit; the rest of the changes were smaller, more incremental, or more personal. Whether managers made small or transformational changes depended on their attitude going into the training, their level of self-esteem, and the amount of support they received from others on the job. Although some managers did not respond as hoped, almost half embraced the training, adopted a more transformational orientation, and tackled significant transformations for the company.

Level 5 leadership, a term well known among executives, is considered by some to be the ultimate leadership style. Level 5 leadership is a combination of strong professional will

that hired her to develop a comprehensive yet practical plan for adapting to climate change. Carter recommends the green-roof approach for soaking up flooding rainwater rather than building a huge new structure to catch floodwater. Carter is also helping Belfast, Northern Ireland, deal with problems similar to those of the Bronx: pollution, poverty, and joblessness. Her solutions, based on her Bronx experiences, apply the island's signature color—green.

Q: Discussion Questions

- Majora Carter can be described as a transformational leader. Why do you think she is described this way, and why is this particularly important to the success of her organizations?
- Discuss examples of the four skills and strategies of transformational leadership that Majora Carter exhibits.

SOURCES: SSBx Web site, http://www.ssbx.org, accessed June 15, 2009; Majora Carter Group Web site, http://www.majoracartergroup.com, accessed June 15, 2009; Maguerite Holloway, "The Green Power Broker," *New York Times*, December 14, 2008, http://www.nytimes.com; Adam Aston, "Majora Carter: Greener Neighborhoods, Sustainable Jobs," *BusinessWeek*, October 27, 2008, http://www.businessweek.com.

(determination) and personal humility that builds enduring greatness.[106] Thus, a Level 5 leader is relentlessly focused on the organization's long-term success while behaving with modesty, directing attention toward the organization rather than him- or herself. Examples include John Chambers, CEO of Cisco Systems, and IBM's former chief executive, Louis Gerstner. Gerstner is widely credited for turning around a stodgy IBM by shifting its focus from computer hardware to business solutions. Following his retirement, Gerstner wrote a memoir that details what happened at the company but says little about himself. Although Level 5 leadership is seen as a way to transform organizations to make them great, it requires first that the leader exhibit a combination of transactional and transformational styles.[107]

 Before his 30th birthday, Robert Chapman stepped into the job of chief executive of his family's business, Barry-Wehmiller Companies (B-W), following the sudden death of his father. Revenues at B-W, which makes packaging equipment and sells related services, grew rapidly during the early years of Chapman's leadership but then plunged as demand dried up.

Chapman reacted by assembling his management team to evaluate what had gone wrong. The group determined that the earlier growth had been "undisciplined," not directed to areas where long-term success would be most likely. The team developed a company vision aimed at balanced and sustainable growth. Since then, says Chapman, the company has "never varied" from "executing our vision with discipline and passion."

The passion comes from a commitment to "people-centric leadership." Under Chapman, B-W managers must care about their employees, give them authority to make important decisions, and clarify how their contributions enhance the company's vision. An Organizational Empowerment Team develops leaders and applies methods such as lean manufacturing through which employees contribute to improved operations.

Chapman believes companies can change the world through their impact on individual employees. Challenging employees to contribute to the corporate vision gives them a chance to feel that their efforts matter; recognition programs show them that they are appreciated. The result is what Chapman calls an "inspirational environment." The company is growing again, too.[108]

Authentic leadership adds an ethical dimension

In general, authentic leadership is rooted in the ancient Greek philosophy "To thine own self be true."[109] In your own leadership, you should strive for authenticity in the form of honesty, genuineness, reliability, integrity, and trustworthiness. Authentic transformational leaders care about public interests (community, organizational, or group), not just their own.[110] They are willing to sacrifice their own interests for others, and they can be trusted. They are ethically mature; people view leaders who exhibit moral reasoning as more transformational than leaders who do not.[111]

Pseudotransformational leaders are the opposite: they talk a good game, but they ignore followers' real needs as their own self-interests (power, prestige, control, wealth, fame) take precedence.[112]

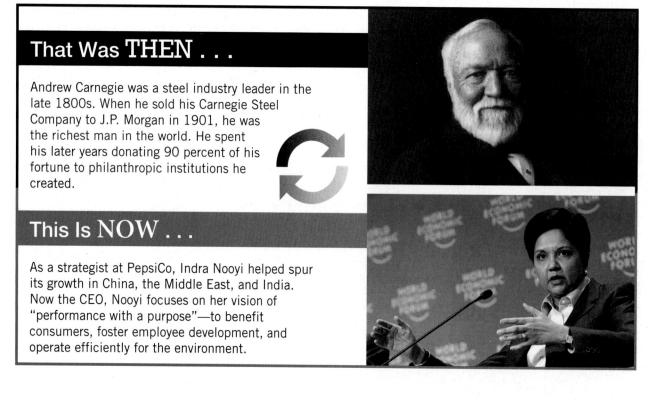

That Was THEN . . .

Andrew Carnegie was a steel industry leader in the late 1800s. When he sold his Carnegie Steel Company to J.P. Morgan in 1901, he was the richest man in the world. He spent his later years donating 90 percent of his fortune to philanthropic institutions he created.

This Is NOW . . .

As a strategist at PepsiCo, Indra Nooyi helped spur its growth in China, the Middle East, and India. Now the CEO, Nooyi focuses on her vision of "performance with a purpose"—to benefit consumers, foster employee development, and operate efficiently for the environment.

Can you describe types of opportunities to be a leader in an organization?

Today's organizations offer many opportunities to lead

A common view of leaders is that they are superheroes acting alone, swooping in to save the day. But especially in these complex times, leaders cannot and need not act alone. Business guru John Hersey advises today's leader to be a "SAGE." The letters in *sage* remind leaders to *seek out* other people, *ask* good questions that focus on the other person, *get involved* with other people, and *enrich* people's lives. That outward-looking approach helps leaders identify fresh solutions to vexing problems and invites followers to engage fully with the cause.[113]

Effective leadership must permeate the organization, not reside in one or two superstars at the top. The leader's job becomes one of spreading leadership abilities throughout the firm.[114] Make people responsible for their own performance. Create an environment in which each person can figure out what needs to be done and then do it well. Point the way and clear the path so that people can succeed. Give them the credit they deserve. Make heroes out of *them*. Thus, what is now required of leaders is less the efficient management of resources and more the effective unleashing of people and their intellectual capital.

This perspective uncovers a variety of nontraditional leadership roles that are emerging as vitally important.[115] The term **servant-leader** was coined by Robert Greenleaf, a retired AT&T executive. The term is paradoxical in the sense that "leader" and "servant" are usually opposites; the servant-leader's relationship with employees is more like that of serving customers. For the individual who wants to both lead and serve others, servant-leadership is a way of relating to others to serve their needs and enhance their personal growth while strengthening the organization. For example, when David Wolfskehl, founder of Action Fast Print, stopped telling his employees what to do and instead asked how he could help them solve their problems, productivity jumped 30 percent.[116]

A number of other nontraditional roles provide leadership opportunities. **Bridge leaders** are those who leave their cultures for a significant period of time.[117] They live, go to school, travel, or work in other cultures. Then they return home, become leaders, and through their expanded repertoire they serve as bridges between conflicting value systems within their own cultures or between their culture and other cultures.

With work often being team based, **shared leadership** occurs when leadership rotates to the person with the key knowledge, skills, and abilities for the issue facing the team at a particular time.[118] Shared leadership is most important when tasks are interdependent, are complex, and require creativity. High-performing teams engaged in such work exhibit more shared leadership than poor-performing teams. In consulting teams, the higher the shared leadership, the higher their clients rated the teams' performance.[119] The role of formal leader remains important—the formal leader still designs the team, manages its external boundaries, provides task direction, emphasizes the importance of the shared leadership approach, and engages in the transactional and transformational activities described here. But at the same time, the metaphor of geese in V-formation adds strength to the group: the lead goose periodically drops to the back, and another goose moves up and takes its place at the forefront.

Lateral leadership does not involve a hierarchical, superior–subordinate relationship but instead invites colleagues at the same level to solve problems together.[120] You alone can't provide a solution to every problem, but you can create processes through which people work collaboratively. If you can get people working to improve methods collaboratively, you can help create an endless stream of innovations. In other words, it's not about you providing solutions to problems; it's about creating better interpersonal processes for finding solutions. Strategies and tactics can be found throughout this book, including the chapters on decision making, organization structure, teams, communication, and change.

GE is famous for developing the leadership skills of employees with potential so that the organization will have strong leaders at many levels. Pictured here are Jack Welch (left) and Jeffrey Immelt (right).

● **AUTHENTIC LEADERSHIP** A style in which the leader is true to himself or herself while leading.

● **PSEUDOTRANSFORMATIONAL LEADERS** Leaders who talk about positive change but allow their self-interest to take precedence over followers' needs.

● **SERVANT-LEADER** A leader who serves others' needs while strengthening the organization.

● **BRIDGE LEADERS** Leaders who bridge conflicting value systems or different cultures.

● **SHARED LEADERSHIP** Rotating leadership, in which people rotate through the leadership role based on which person has the most relevant skills at a particular time.

● **LATERAL LEADERSHIP** Style in which colleagues at the same hierarchical level are invited to collaborate and facilitate joint problem solving.

Good leaders need courage

To be a good leader, you need the courage to create a vision of greatness for your unit; identify and manage allies, adversaries, and fence sitters; and execute your vision, often against opposition. This does not mean you should commit career suicide by alienating too many powerful people; it does mean taking reasonable risks, with the good of the firm at heart, in order to produce constructive change.

For example, Charles Elachi needed courage when he took the position of director of NASA's Jet Propulsion Laboratories (JPL) at the beginning of the decade, when a series of budget cuts and efforts to cut corners had resulted in two failed attempts to gather data from Mars exploration projects. In that environment, morale was poor, and public support for JPL was weak. But rather than looking for people to blame, Elachi, a physicist and JPL veteran, got everyone focused on the ambitious next project, the Mars Exploration Rover, which would involve sending two spacecraft to the Red Planet and landing rovers on the surface to conduct exploration—with the first launch just 27 months away. Undaunted by the two previous failures, Elachi clearly but politely communicated to everyone that another failure was out of the question. At the beginning of the project, he had team leaders list every test that would be necessary before the first spacecraft was sent into orbit. Two years later, he pulled out his "Incompressible Test List" and insisted that team members carry out every procedure—and that the agency fund them. In the end, the mission actually exceeded expectations.[121]

DEVELOPING YOUR LEADERSHIP SKILLS

As with other things, you must work at *developing* your leadership abilities. Great musicians and great athletes don't become great on natural gifts alone. They also pay their dues by practicing, learning, and sacrificing. Leaders in a variety of fields, when asked how they became the best leader possible, offered the following comments:[125]

- "I've observed methods and skills of my bosses that I respected."
- "By taking risks, trying, and learning from my mistakes."
- "Reading autobiographies of leaders I admire to try to understand how they think."
- "Lots of practice."
- "By making mistakes myself and trying a different approach."
- "By purposely engaging with others to get things done."
- "By being put in positions of responsibility that other people counted on."

> ❝ **When you connect with a purpose greater than yourself, you are fearless; you think big.** ❞
>
> —Nancy Barry, on leaving her executive position at the World Bank to become president of Women's World Banking, which makes microloans to impoverished women around the world[122]

Specifically, fulfilling your vision will require some of the following acts of courage:[123]

- Seeing things as they are and facing them head-on, making no excuses and harboring no wishful illusions
- Saying what needs to be said to those who need to hear it
- Persisting despite resistance, criticism, abuse, and setbacks

Courage includes stating the realities, even when they are harsh, and publicly stating what you will do to help and what you want from others. This means laying the cards on the table honestly: here is what I want from you . . . What do you want from me?[124]

How do I start?

How do you go about developing your leadership abilities? You don't have to wait until you land a management job or even finish your education. You can begin establishing credibility by practicing honesty, learning from your mistakes, and becoming competent in your chosen field. You also should learn to manage your time well so that you will set a good example for others and help them achieve your group's goals. Third, you should look for—and then seize—opportunities to take actions that will help the groups to which you already belong. Even before you are a supervisor, you can practice listening carefully when you are in a group and sharing what you know so that the whole group will be better informed. Finally, begin building a network of personal contacts by reaching out to others to offer help, not just to request it.[126]

(L)(O) 9 WHAT YOU NEED TO KNOW . . .

How can you further your own leadership development?

When you are searching for your next job, look for a position with an employer that is committed to developing leadership talent. Best practices include using self-assessments to identify specific areas for development and combining classroom training with individualized coaching. Ideally, leadership development is connected to opportunities to practice the skills you are learning about, so ask about chances to lead a project or a team, even for short periods of time.[127]

More specifically, here are some developmental experiences you should seek:[128]

- *Assignments*—Building something from nothing; fixing or turning around a failing operation; taking on project or task force responsibilities; accepting international assignments.
- *Other people*—Having exposure to positive role models; increasing visibility to others; working with people of diverse backgrounds.
- *Hardships*—Overcoming ideas that fail and deals that collapse; confronting others' performance problems; breaking out of a career rut.
- *Other events*—Formal courses; challenging job experiences; supervision of others; experiences outside work.

What are the keys?

The most effective developmental experiences have three components: assessment, challenge, and support.[129] *Assessment* includes information that helps you understand where you are now, what your strengths are, your current levels of performance and leadership effectiveness, and your primary development needs. You can think about your past feedback, previous successes and failures, people's reactions to your ideas and actions, your personal goals, and the strategies you should implement to make progress. You can seek answers from your peers at work, bosses, family, friends, customers, and anyone else who knows you and how you work. The information you collect will help clarify what you need to learn, improve, or change.

The most potent developmental experiences provide *challenge*—they stretch you. We all think and behave in habitual, comfortable ways. This is natural, and perhaps sufficient to survive. But you've probably heard people say how important it can be to get out of your comfort zone—to tackle situations that require new skills and abilities, that are confusing or ambiguous, or that you simply would rather not deal with. Sometimes the challenge comes from lack of experience; other times, it requires changing old habits. It may be

Build Your Skills

Practice and apply your knowledge by going online at

www.mhhe.com/
BatemanM2e

Julie Sajda, foodservice director at Hearst Tower in Manhattan, developed herself as a leader by seeking out challenging assignments and by tapping into expertise from mentors.

uncomfortable, but this is how great managers learn. Remember, some people don't bother to learn or refuse to learn. Make sure you think about your experiences along the way and reflect on them afterward, introspectively and in discussion with others.

You receive *support* when others send the message that your efforts to learn and grow are valued. Without support, challenging developmental experiences can be overwhelming. With support, it is easier to handle the struggle, stay on course, open up to learning, and actually learn from experiences. Support can come informally from other people, more formally through the procedures of the organization, and through learning resources such as training, constructive feedback, and conversations with mentors or colleagues.

What develops in leadership development? Through such experiences, you can acquire more self-awareness and self-confidence, a broader perspective on the organizational system, creative thinking, the ability to work more effectively in complex social systems, and the ability to learn from experience—not to mention leadership skills.

WHAT YOU NEED TO KNOW

•• learning OBJECTIVES

After studying Chapter 10,
you will be able to:

LO1 Identify the kinds of behaviors managers need to motivate in people.

LO2 List principles for setting goals that motivate employees.

LO3 Summarize how to reward good performance effectively.

LO4 Describe the key beliefs that affect people's motivation.

LO5 Discuss ways in which people's individual needs affect their behavior.

LO6 Define ways to create jobs that motivate.

LO7 Summarize how people assess fairness and how to achieve fairness.

LO8 Identify causes and consequences of a satisfied workforce.

10 Motivating People

This chapter tackles an age-old question: How can a manager motivate people to work hard and perform at their best levels? Tony Hsieh, CEO of online shoe seller Zappos (a subsidiary of Amazon), believes happy employees are the key to creating happy customers, because they are motivated to deliver excellent customer service. Zappos selects employees with a passion for service and then sets them free to be themselves and use their best judgment, rather than constraining them with scripted responses and time limits on customer calls. Other ways in which Zappos strengthens the commitment of its employees include time away from work for team building and the publication of an annual *Zappos Culture Book,* in which employees reflect, often earnestly, on the meaning of their work and the company's culture and values.[1]

A sales manager in one company had another unique approach to this question. Each month, the person with the worst sales performance took home a live goat for the weekend. The manager hoped the goat-of-the-month employee would be so embarrassed that

Gain Insight

on how today's managers motivate their people from Katie and Elaine.

"Yes, motivation is underlying in many ways while working. Whether you reflect on your own motivation or observing the motivation of others, people are motivated for different reasons: promotion, validation, reputation, or for family. Regardless of reason, managers can help to find ways to motivate employees so that they perform to the best of their ability."
—Katie Storey, Student Life Coordinator

"I try to manage people in the way that I would like to be managed. I am most motivated to do a particular task when I am allowed the 'hands off' approach, and the trust that is implicitly given when using that approach. I have noticed, though, that this style is not for everyone. It is crucial to understand when people need extra guidance—they won't always tell you—and when they can be let loose. Much of that understanding comes from observing and talking with employees."
—Elaine Guidero, Library Manager

he or she would work harder the next month to increase sales.[2] This sales manager may get high marks for creativity. But if he is graded by results, as he grades his salespeople, he will fail. He may succeed in motivating a few of his people to increase sales, but some good people will be motivated to quit the company.

> **"The reward of a thing well done is to have done it."**
>
> —Ralph Waldo Emerson

L O 1 WHAT YOU NEED TO KNOW . . .
What kinds of behaviors do managers need to motivate in people?

MOTIVATING FOR PERFORMANCE

Understanding why people do the things they do on the job is not an easy task for a manager. *Predicting* their response to management's latest productivity program is harder yet. Fortunately, enough is known about motivation to give the thoughtful manager practical, effective techniques for increasing people's effort and performance.

Motivation refers to forces that energize, direct, and sustain a person's efforts. All behavior, except involuntary reflexes like eye blinks (which have little to do with management), is motivated. A highly motivated person will work hard to achieve performance goals. With adequate ability, understanding of the job, and access to the necessary resources, such a person will be highly productive.

To be effective motivators, managers must know what behaviors they want to motivate people to exhibit. Although productive people do a seemingly limitless number of things, most of the important activities can be grouped into five general categories:[3]

1. Join the organization.
2. Remain in the organization.
3. Come to work regularly.
4. Perform—that is, work hard to achieve high *output* (productivity) and high *quality.*
5. Exhibit good citizenship by being committed and performing above and beyond the call of duty to help the company.

On the first three points, you should reject the common recent notion that loyalty is dead and accept the challenge of creating an environment that will attract and energize people so that they commit to the organization.[4] The importance of citizenship behaviors may be less obvious than productivity, but these behaviors help the organization function smoothly. They also make managers' lives easier.

Plante & Moran is an accounting and business advisory firm that sets a gold standard for loyal, happy employees. The firm, which employs 1,500 staff, has been on *Fortune*'s list of "100 Best Companies to Work For" for nine consecutive years. *Fortune* refers to Plante & Moran's organizational culture as "employee-centric," reporting that the firm's turnover is a mere 11 percent, one of the lowest rates in the entire accounting field. Plante & Moran also has the greatest percentage of women partners in the industry—19 percent. The reason for these positive statistics is the company's concern for its employees' families.

One of the firm's programs, the Personal Tightrope Action Committee, was originally developed to address needs of working parents and now focuses on work/life balance. Employees can take advantage of such family-oriented amenities as an onsite child care center and high chairs in the cafeteria. "We are exceedingly pleased with our staff and their commitment to the Golden Rule, which is the foundation for our winning culture," says managing partner Bill Hermann. He explains, "People perform better when they enjoy their environment and trust their colleagues."[5]

Many ideas have been proposed to help managers motivate people to engage in these constructive behaviors. The most useful of these ideas are described in the following pages. We start with the most fundamental *processes* that influence the motivation of all people. These processes—described by goal-setting, reinforcement, and expectancy theories—suggest actions for managers to take. Then we discuss the *content* of what people want and need from work, how individuals differ from one another, and how understanding people's needs leads to prescriptions for designing motivating jobs and empowering people to perform at the highest possible levels. Finally, we discuss the most important beliefs and perceptions about fairness that people hold toward their work, and the implications for motivation.

> **"Employee loyalty exists, but it depends upon what the company is willing to do for its employees."**
>
> —Vinnie, an employee at a New York investment bank, on why he turned down a job paying 30 percent more to stay with his current employer, who allows him to telecommute[6]

● MOTIVATION Forces that energize, direct, and sustain a person's efforts.

● GOAL-SETTING THEORY A motivation theory stating that people have conscious goals that energize them and direct their thoughts and behaviors toward a particular end.

LO 2 WHAT YOU NEED TO KNOW . . .

What are the principles for setting goals that motivate employees?

SETTING GOALS

Providing work-related goals is an extremely effective way to stimulate motivation. In fact, it is perhaps the most important, valid, and useful approach to motivating performance.

Goal-setting theory states that people have conscious goals that energize them and direct their thoughts and behaviors toward a particular end.[7] Keeping in mind the principle that goals matter, managers set goals for employees or collaborate with them on goal setting. For example, a satellite TV company might set goals for increasing the number of new subscribers, the number of current subscribers who pay for premium channels, or the timeliness of responses to customer inquiries.[8] Goal setting works for any job in which people have control over their performance.[9] You can set goals for performance quality and quantity, plus behavioral goals like cooperation or teamwork.[10] In fact, you can set goals for whatever is important.[11]

Well-crafted goals are highly motivating

The most powerful goals are *meaningful;* noble purposes that appeal to people's "higher" values add extra motivating power.[12] Johnson & Johnson pursues profit, but it's also about improving health care. ServiceMaster, the cleaning and maintenance company, has a religious commitment that appeals to its employees, and Huntsman Chemical has goals of paying off corporate debt but also relieving human suffering—it sponsors cancer research and a number of charities. Meaningful goals also may be based on data about competitors; exceeding competitors' performance can stoke people's competitive spirit and desire to succeed in the marketplace.[13] This point is not just about the values companies espouse and the lofty goals they pursue; it's also about leadership at a more personal level. Compared with followers of transactional leaders, followers of transformational leaders (recall Chapter 9) view their work as more important and as highly congruent with their personal goals.[14]

Goals also should be *acceptable* to employees. This means, among other things, that they should not conflict with people's personal values and that people should have reasons to pursue the goals. Allowing people to participate in setting their work goals—as opposed to having the boss set goals for them—tends to generate goals that people accept and pursue willingly.

Acceptable, maximally motivating goals are *challenging but attainable.* In other words, they should be high enough to inspire better performance but not so high that people can never reach them. One team of consultants to an international corporation created more than 40 programs aimed at increasing quality. The company announced it did not expect significant quality improvement until the *fourth year* of the program. Such a goal is not nearly demanding enough.[15] In contrast, Robert R. Ruffolo Jr. successfully remade Wyeth's research and development operation by setting quotas for the number of compounds the scientists have to move through each stage of the development process, as well as financial targets that each project must meet. Projects that do not meet these requirements are quickly dropped so that scientists can move to more promising ideas. Although researchers initially resisted the targets, they have seen that the goals help them focus their efforts where they matter most.[16]

Ideal goals do not merely exhort employees in general terms to improve performance and start doing their best. Instead, goals should be *specific and quantifiable,* more like Esco's target that by 2011 it will generate at least 5 percent of its revenue from selling products it has newly invented, or like Guitar Center's objective that whenever a phone rings in one of its stores, a salesperson will pick it up before the fourth ring.[17] Bringing

Ben & Jerry's is known for making some of the world's finest ice cream. But its social responsibility is also highly important to many employees and customers. Ben & Jerry are shown here with the rock band Daughtry to launch their latest ice cream flavor "ONE Cheesecake Brownie" with proceeds going to help fight global poverty.

these principles together, Microsoft uses the acronym SMART to create motivating goals: specific, measurable, achievable, results based, and time specific.[18]

Stretch goals help employees reach new heights

Some firms today set stretch goals—targets that are exceptionally demanding, and that some people would never even think of. There are two types of stretch goals:[19]

1. Vertical stretch goals are aligned with current activities, including productivity and financial results.

2. Horizontal stretch goals involve people's professional development, such as attempting and learning new, difficult things.

Impossible though stretch goals may seem to some, they often are in fact attainable.

Stretch goals can shift people away from mediocrity and toward major achievement. But if someone tries in good faith yet doesn't meet a stretch goal, don't punish—remember how difficult these goals are! Base your assessment on how much performance has improved, how the performance compares with that of others, and how much progress has been made.[20]

Goal setting must be paired with other management tools

Goal setting is an extraordinarily powerful management technique. But even specific, challenging, attainable goals work better under some conditions than others. For example, if people lack relevant ability and knowledge, managers might get better results from simply urging them to do their best or setting a goal to learn rather than a goal to achieve a specific performance

level.[21] Individual performance goals can be dysfunctional if people work in a group and cooperation among team members is essential to team performance.[22] Individualized goals can create competition and reduce cooperation. If cooperation is important, performance goals should be established *for the team.*

Goals can generate manipulative game playing and unethical behavior. People sometimes find ingenious ways to set easy goals and convince their bosses that they are difficult.[23] Or they may find ways to meet goals simply to receive a reward, without necessarily contributing to the company's success. For example, one measure of an instructor's success is high ratings from participants when they fill out questionnaires after a training program. To meet the goal of achieving a high score, some instructors hand out treats or prizes or end sessions early—practices that are unlikely to add to what trainees actually learn. Even more perversely, when Rockford Acromatic Products Company promoted employee health by offering bonuses to employees who quit smoking for several months, several workers first *started* smoking so they could quit and earn the bonus.[24] In addition, people who don't meet their goals are more likely to engage in unethical behavior than are people who are trying to do their best but have no specific performance goals. This is true regardless of whether they have financial incentives, and it is particularly true when people fall just short of reaching their goals.[25]

Another familiar example comes from the pages of financial reports. Some executives have mastered the art of "earnings management," precisely meeting Wall Street analysts' earnings estimates or beating them by a single penny.[26] The media trumpet, and investors reward, the company that meets or beats the estimates. People sometimes meet this goal by either manipulating the numbers or initiating whispering campaigns to persuade analysts to lower their estimates, making them more attainable. The marketplace wants short-term, quarterly performance, but

Stonyfield Farm Motivates through Its Mission

Stonyfield Farm, the world's leading maker of organic yogurt, is probably also one of the world's happiest accidents. It was founded in New Hampshire as a school for organic farming; teachers Samuel Kaymen and Gary Hirshberg made and sold yogurt as a sideline to pay the bills. When customers clamored for their products, the two founders decided to concentrate on yogurt instead of the school. Today, Stonyfield Farm generates $320 million a year selling all-organic smoothies, cultured soy, frozen yogurt, ice cream, and milk. Stonyfield buys milk only from family-owned organic dairy farms and pays farmers not to treat cows with synthetic bovine hormone.

Hirshberg, the company's "CE-Yo," says Stonyfield's aim is to try to make people feel

good inside. That begins with producing a high-quality, healthful product. On the premise that healthy food can come only from a healthy planet, Stonyfield prints pro-environment messages on its packaging and donates 10 percent of its profits to environmental causes. Practicing what it preaches, Stonyfield installed a solar plant to help power its operations.

Hirshberg also aims to make his employees feel good inside. With Stonyfield's high ideals, the most fundamental way to build that feeling is by showing employees that their work contributes to the company's success. Twice a year, all employees attend business update meetings, where management shares details of the company's finances. The meetings not only look at costs and sales but provide an

opportunity for Hirshberg to reinforce the company's values, including its commitment to quality, which is especially critical for a business that sells a premium brand. At these meetings, Hirshberg encourages open communication and invites questions, so employees "see what is going on," including all the risks and opportunities facing Stonyfield.

Volunteerism is encouraged—and rewarded. Stonyfield introduced a program called "Making a Difference," in which employees are paid for up to 16 hours per year of community service. Winners of the company's Yogurtarian Award receive cash prizes for work in the community. After five years with Stonyfield, employees are eligible for an eight-week paid sabbatical. The corporate newsletter reports on employees

long-term viability is ultimately more important to a company's success.

It is important *not* to establish a single productivity goal if there are other important dimensions of performance.[27] For instance, if the acquisition of knowledge and skills is important, you can also set a specific and challenging learning goal like "identify ten ways to develop relationships with users of our products." Productivity goals will likely enhance productivity, but they may also cause

Vickie Stringer set her goal to publish her life story and pursued that goal with determination, eventually selling 100,000 copies. Along the way, she developed relationships with book distributors and eventually founded her firm, Triple Crown Publications.

employees to neglect other areas, such as learning, tackling new projects, or developing creative solutions to job-related problems. A manager who wants to motivate creativity can establish creativity goals along with productivity goals for individuals or for brainstorming teams.[28]

Set your own goals, too

Goal setting works for yourself as well—it's a powerful tool for self-management. Set goals for yourself; don't just try hard or hope for the best. Create a statement of purpose for yourself comprising an inspiring distant vision, a mid-distant goal along the way, and near-term objectives to start working on immediately.[29] So, if you are going into business, you might articulate your goal for the type of businessperson you want to be in five years, the types of jobs that could create the opportunities and teach you what you need to know to become that businessperson, and the specific schoolwork and job search activities that can get you moving in those directions. And on the job, apply this chapter's goal-setting advice to yourself.

L O 3 **WHAT YOU NEED TO KNOW . . .**
How can you reward good performance effectively?

REINFORCING PERFORMANCE

Goals are universal motivators. So are the processes of reinforcement described in this section. In 1911, psychologist Edward Thorndike formulated the **law of effect**: behavior

---

who have used time off to serve communities as far afield as Israel and the Dominican Republic.

Employee well-being is such a fundamental part of how Stonyfield operates that it is part of the company's mission. Along with selling high-quality products, educating consumers, and practicing environmental responsibility, that mission includes the following commitment: "To provide a healthful, productive and enjoyable work place for all employees, with opportunities to gain new skills and advance personal career goals."

Q: Discussion Questions

- How do CE-Yo Gary Hirshberg and the Stonyfield Farm mission motivate employees?
- Hirshberg believes customer loyalty is the key to his company's success. How might motivating employees contribute to building customer loyalty?

SOURCES: Company Web site, http://www.stonyfield.com, accessed June 19, 2009; "Gary Hirshberg—Stonyfield Farm," *Starting Up Green* [n.d.], http://www.startingupgreen.com, accessed June 19, 2009; "Stonyfield Farm," *SuperEco,* October 27, 2008, http://www.supereco.com; Jackie Cook, "Best Green Companies for America's Children," *Working Mother Media,* April 17, 2008, http://www.workingmothermediainc.com; "Gary Hirshberg Argues That His Company Is Doing a Lot to Support Organic Farmers," *Grist,* March 7, 2008, http://www.grist.org; and Jacob Gordon, "The TH Interview: Gary Hirshberg, CE-Yo of Stonyfield Farm," March 6, 2008, http://www.treehugger.com.

that is followed by positive consequences probably will be repeated.[30] This powerful law of behavior laid the foundation for countless investigations into the effects of the positive consequences, called **reinforcers**, that motivate behavior. **Organizational behavior modification** attempts to influence people's behavior and improve performance[31] by systematically managing work conditions and the consequences of people's actions.

Four key consequences of behavior either encourage or discourage people's behavior (see Figure 10.1):

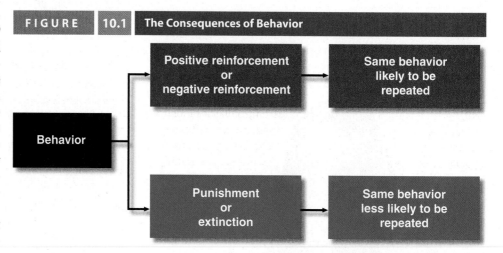

FIGURE 10.1 The Consequences of Behavior

- Behavior → Positive reinforcement or negative reinforcement → Same behavior likely to be repeated
- Behavior → Punishment or extinction → Same behavior less likely to be repeated

1. **Positive reinforcement**—applying a consequence that increases the likelihood that the person will repeat the behavior that led to it. Examples of positive reinforcers include compliments, letters of commendation, favorable performance evaluations, and pay raises. Chris Kinnersley, vice president of safety and organizational development at Staker & Parson Company (a construction materials and services company), has helped the company's managers learn to select rewards that are immediate and personal. For example, the loader operators who work most efficiently might be rewarded by being assigned to the equipment known to be most comfortable.[32]

2. **Negative reinforcement**—removing or withholding an undesirable consequence. For example, a manager takes an employee off probation because of improved performance. One way to understand the success of Capital One's Future of Work project is that it is a kind of negative reinforcement. This project recognizes that keeping a job can be a strain if you have family or personal obligations that conflict with the structured routine of a nine-to-five job in an office away from home. The Future of Work project alleviates some of this strain by letting employees use a company-provided laptop, iPod, and BlackBerry so they can avoid some of the schedule conflicts of full-time work by getting work done at home or on the road, as well as in Capital One's flexible facilities.[33]

3. **Punishment**—administering an aversive consequence. Examples include criticizing or shouting at an employee, assigning an unappealing task, and sending a worker home without pay. Negative reinforcement can involve the *threat* of punishment by not delivering punishment when employees perform satisfactorily. Punishment is the actual delivery of the aversive consequence. Managers use punishment when

they think it is warranted or when they believe others expect them to, and they usually concern themselves with following company policy and procedure.[34]

4. **Extinction**—withdrawing or failing to provide a reinforcing consequence. When this occurs, motivation is reduced, and the behavior is *extinguished,* or eliminated. Managers may unintentionally extinguish desired behaviors by not giving a compliment for a job well done, forgetting to say thanks for a favor, setting impossible performance goals so that the person never experiences success, and so on. Extinction may be used to end undesirable behaviors, too. The manager might ignore long-winded observations during a meeting or fail to acknowledge unimportant e-mail in the hope that the lack of feedback will discourage the employee from continuing.

The first two consequences, positive and negative reinforcement, are positive for the person receiving them—the person either gains something or avoids something negative. As a result, the person who experiences these consequences will be motivated to behave in the ways that led to the reinforcement. the last two consequences, punishment and extinction, are negative outcomes for the person receiving them: motivation to repeat the behavior that led to the undesirable results will be reduced.

Managers should be careful to match consequences to what employees will actually find desirable or undesirable. At Staker & Parson, a supervisor once made the mistake of "punishing" an employee for tardiness by suspending him for three days during fishing season. The employee was delighted.[35]

Be careful what you reinforce

You've learned about the positive effects of a transformational leadership style, but giving rewards to high-performing people is also essential.[36] Unfortunately, sometimes organizations and managers reinforce the wrong behaviors.[37] For example, compensation plans that include stock options are intended to

> **"The worst mistake a boss can make is not to say well done."**
>
> —John Ashcroft, business executive

reinforce behaviors that add to the company's value, but stock options also can reinforce decisions that artificially deliver short-term gains in stock prices, even if they hurt the company in the long run.

At some companies, employees are reinforced with admiration and positive performance evaluations for multitasking—say, typing e-mail while on the phone or checking text messages during meetings. This behavior may look efficient and send a signal that the employee is busy and valuable, but a growing body of research says multitasking actually slows the brain's efficiency and can contribute to mistakes.[38] Scans of brain activity show that the brain is not able to concentrate on two tasks at once; it needs time to switch among the multitasker's activities. So managers who praise the hard work of multitaskers may be unintentionally reinforcing inefficiency and failure to think deeply about problems.

To use reinforcement effectively, managers must identify which kinds of behaviors they reinforce and which they discourage. Michael LeBoeuf, a writer of popular business books, said the greatest management principle is "The things that get rewarded get done." LeBoeuf advises rewarding the following kinds of activity:[39]

- *Solid solutions* instead of quick fixes.
- *Risk taking* instead of risk avoiding.
- *Applied creativity* instead of mindless conformity.
- *Decisive action* instead of paralysis by analysis.
- *Smart work* instead of busywork.
- *Simplification* instead of needless complication.
- *Quietly effective behavior* instead of squeaky wheels.
- *Quality work* instead of fast work.
- *Loyalty* instead of turnover.
- *Working together* instead of working against.

Also, the reward system has to support the firm's strategy, defining people's performance in ways that pursue strategic objectives.[40] Organizations should reward employees for developing themselves in strategically important ways—for building new skills that are critical to strengthening core competencies and creating value.

Managers should use reinforcers creatively. Sprint, where many workers spend their day sitting in front of a computer, reinforces healthy behavior by providing onsite exercise facilities, where employees can enjoy workouts during their lunch hours.[41] For Steven T. Bigari, owner of 12 McDonald's restaurants, the basic challenge was how to motivate low-wage workers to stay on the job when faced with struggles to find affordable day care and transportation. Facing stiff competition from Taco Bell, Bigari concluded he couldn't afford higher wages, but he helped a local church set up a day care program, and he visited police auctions during his Saturday lunch breaks in order to purchase low-priced but reliable cars, which he resold to employees at cost.[42]

Innovative managers use nonmonetary rewards, including intellectual challenge, greater responsibility, autonomy, recognition, flexible benefits, and greater influence over decisions. Julian Duncan, an assistant brand manager at Nike, has felt valued and encouraged because top-level managers take time to listen to him and address his concerns. For example, a vice president spent half an hour with Duncan, discussing a question Duncan had e-mailed to him.[44] These and other rewards for high-performing employees, when creatively devised and applied, can continue to motivate when pay and promotions are scarce. Employees at Brown Flynn—a firm that provides services to help companies exercise social responsibility—receive practical benefits such as profit sharing and creative ones like jewelry and shopping sprees, but the intangibles may be what matter most. Employees describe Brown Flynn as offering challenges and rewards, mutual respect, recognition for hard work, and opportunities to exercise leadership.[45] And one of Steven Bigari's McDonald's employees said she preferred working for him to earning slightly more at a corporate-owned restaurant, because of the way Bigari treats employees: "He's not in it for himself; he's in it for the people."[46]

Methodist Hospital System, located in Houston, recently gave each of its employees a $250 gift card to buy gasoline.[43]

Should you punish mistakes?

How a manager reacts to people's mistakes has a big impact on motivation. Punishment is sometimes appropriate, as when people violate the law, ethical standards, important safety rules, or standards of interpersonal treatment, or when they fail to attend or perform like a slacker. But sometimes managers punish people when they shouldn't—when poor performance isn't the person's fault or when managers take out their frustrations on the wrong people.

Managers who overuse punishment or use it inappropriately create a climate of fear in the workplace.[47] Fear causes people to focus on the short term, sometimes creating problems in the longer run. Fear also creates a focus on oneself, rather than on the group and the organization. B. Joseph White, president of the University of Illinois, recalls consulting for a high-tech entrepreneur who heard a manager present a proposal and responded with brutal criticism: "That's the . . . stupidest idea I ever heard in my life. I'm disappointed in you." According to White, this talented manager was so upset she never again felt fully able to contribute.[48]

For managers to avoid such damage, the key is how to think about and handle mistakes. Recognize that everyone makes mistakes and that mistakes can be dealt with constructively by discussing and learning from them. Don't punish, but praise people who deliver bad news to their bosses. Treat failure to act as a failure but don't punish unsuccessful, good-faith efforts. If you're a leader, talk about your failures with your people, and show how you learned from them. Give people second chances, and maybe third chances. Encourage people to try new things, and don't punish them if what they try doesn't work out.

Feedback is essential reinforcement

Most managers don't provide enough useful feedback, and most people don't receive or ask for feedback enough.[49] As a manager, you should consider all potential causes of poor performance, pay full attention when employees ask for feedback or want to discuss performance issues, and give feedback according to the guidelines you read about in Chapter 7.

Feedback can be offered in many ways.[50] Customers sometimes give feedback directly; you also can request customer feedback and give it to the employee. You can provide statistics on work that the person has directly influenced. A manufacturing firm can put the phone number or Web site of the production team on the product so that customers can contact the team directly. Performance reviews should be conducted regularly. And bosses should give regular, ongoing feedback—it helps correct problems immediately, provides immediate reinforcement for good work, and prevents surprises when the formal review comes.

For yourself, try not to be afraid of receiving feedback; instead, you should actively seek it. And when you get feedback, don't ignore it. Try to avoid negative emotions like anger, hurt, defensiveness, or resignation. Think: it's up to me to get the feedback I need; I need to know these things about my performance and behavior; learning about myself will help me identify needs and create new opportunities; it serves my interest best to know rather than not know; taking initiative on this gives me more power and influence over my career.[51]

PERFORMANCE-RELATED BELIEFS

In contrast to reinforcement theory, which describes the processes by which factors in the work environment affect people's behavior, expectancy theory considers some of the cognitive processes that go on in people's heads. According to **expectancy theory**, the person's work *efforts* lead to some level of *performance*.[52] Then performance results in one or more *outcomes* for the person. This process is shown in Figure 10.2. People develop two important kinds of beliefs linking these three events:

1. Expectancy, which links effort to performance
2. Instrumentality, which links performance to outcomes

If you try hard, will you succeed?

The first belief, **expectancy**, is people's perceived likelihood that their efforts will enable them to attain their performance goals. An expectancy can be high (up to 100 percent), such as when a student is confident that if she studies hard, she can get a good grade on the final exam. An expectancy can also be low (down to a 0 percent likelihood), such as when a suitor is convinced that his dream date will never go out with him.

All else equal, high expectancies create higher motivation than do low expectancies. In the preceding examples, the student is more likely to study for the exam than the suitor is to pursue the dream date, even though both want their respective outcomes.

Expectancies can vary among individuals, even in the same situation. For example, a sales manager might initiate a competition in which the top salesperson wins a free trip to Hawaii. In such cases, the few top people, who have performed well in the past, will be more motivated by the contest than will the historically average and below-average performers. The top people will have higher expectancies—stronger beliefs that their efforts can help them turn in the top performance.

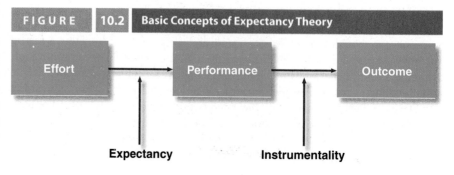

FIGURE 10.2 Basic Concepts of Expectancy Theory

Effort → Performance → Outcome

Expectancy   Instrumentality

If you succeed, will you be rewarded?

The example about the sales contest illustrates how performance results in some kind of outcome, or consequence, for the person. Actually, it often results in several outcomes. For example, turning in the best sales performance could lead to (1) a competitive victory, (2) the free trip to Hawaii, (3) feelings of achievement, (4) recognition from the boss, (5) prestige throughout the company, and (6) resentment from other salespeople.

But how certain is it that performance will result in all of those outcomes? Will winning the contest really generate resentment? Will it really lead to increased prestige?

These questions address the second key belief described by expectancy theory: instrumentality.[53] Instrumentality is the perceived likelihood that performance will be followed by a particular outcome. Like expectancies, instrumentalities can be high (up to 100 percent) or low (approaching 0 percent). For example, you can be fully confident that if you get favorable customer reviews, you'll get a promotion, or you can feel that no matter what your customers say, the promotion will go to someone else.

Also, each outcome has an associated valence. Valence is the value the person places on the outcome. Valences can be positive, as a Hawaiian vacation would be for most people, or negative, as in the case of the other salespeople's resentment.

All three beliefs must be high

For motivation to be high, expectancy, instrumentalities, and total valence of all outcomes must all be high. A person will *not* be highly motivated if any of the following conditions exist:

- He believes he can't perform well enough to achieve the positive outcomes that he knows the company provides to good performers (high valence and high instrumentality but low expectancy).

- He knows he can do the job and is fairly certain what the ultimate outcomes will be (say, a promotion and a transfer). However, he doesn't want those outcomes or believes other, negative outcomes outweigh the positive (high expectancy and high instrumentality but low valence).

- He knows he can do the job and wants several important outcomes (a favorable performance review, a raise, and a promotion). But he believes that no matter how well he performs, the outcomes will not be forthcoming (high expectancy and positive valences but low instrumentality).

Expectancy theory identifies leverage points

Expectancy theory helps the manager zero in on key leverage points for influencing motivation. Three implications are crucial:

1. *Increase expectancies.* Provide a work environment that facilitates good performance, and set realistically attainable performance goals. Provide training, support, required resources, and encouragement so that people are confident they can perform at the expected levels. Recall that charismatic leaders excel at boosting their followers' confidence.

2. *Identify positively valent outcomes.* Understand what people want to get out of work. Think about what their jobs do and do not (but could) provide them. Consider how people may differ in the valences they assign to outcomes. Know the need theories of motivation, described in the next section, and their implications for identifying important outcomes.

3. *Make performance instrumental toward positive outcomes.* Make sure that good performance is followed by personal recognition and praise, favorable performance reviews, pay increases, and other positive results. Also, ensure that working hard and performing well will have as few negative results as possible. The way you emphasize instrumentality may need to be tailored to employees' locus of control. For people who have an external locus of control, tending to attribute results to luck or fate, you may need to reinforce behaviors (more than outcomes) frequently so that they see a

connection between what they do and what you reward. It is useful to realize, too, that bosses usually provide (or withhold) rewards, but others do so as well[54] Peers, direct reports, customers, and others can offer compliments, help, and praise. Organizations may set up formal reward systems as well. Umpqua Bank in Roseburg, Oregon, set up a link called "Brag Box" on its intranet, where employees can post comments about good deeds by their coworkers. Umpqua's vice president for rewards and recognition regularly checks the Brag Box and notifies managers when their employees have received a compliment, so the managers can further reinforce compliments with praise.[55]

Companies have experimented to learn more about how managers can motivate. A billing and records firm called MED3000 wants to lower the health care costs of its employees, so it invites them to fill out assessments of their health risks; employees with certain risks are steered to programs aimed at managing those risks. But what valued outcomes can the company provide? The general chance to improve one's health is not sufficient. MED3000 divided its employees into three groups: one receives $25 for filling out the assessment; a second group receives the cash plus a $25 gift card to the supermarket; and a third group is enrolled in a weekly lottery with a chance to win up to $150 for completing the assessment. As it turns out, the lottery generated the best response rate.

Another company, Amica Mutual Insurance, offers a variety of wellness programs, including a fitness center, subsidies for participating in Weight Watchers, and stop-smoking programs. Still, a sizable share of employees had diabetes, a condition that can become serious—and expensive—if poorly managed. Amica began offering a program tailored to its employees with diabetes. Those who complete a series of preventive-health exams receive 100 percent coverage of the cost of their diabetes medications. The exams actually cut costs associated with complications, and for employees, visiting the doctor five times feels more doable than, say, a weight loss program. Also, the free medicine is a valued reward.[56]

Ⓛ Ⓞ **5** **WHAT YOU NEED TO KNOW . . .**

How do people's individual needs affect their behavior?

UNDERSTANDING PEOPLE'S NEEDS

So far we have focused on *processes* underlying motivation. The manager who appropriately applies goal-setting, reinforcement, and expectancy theories is creating essential motivating elements in the work environment. But motivation also is affected by characteristics of the person. The second type of motivation theory, *content theories,* indicates the kinds of needs that people want to satisfy. People have different needs energizing and motivating them toward different goals and reinforcers. The extent

to which and the ways in which a person's needs are met or not met at work affect his or her behavior on the job.

The most important theories describing the content of people's needs are Maslow's need hierarchy, Alderfer's ERG theory, and McClelland's needs.

Maslow arranged needs in a hierarchy

Abraham Maslow organized five major types of human needs into a hierarchy, as shown in Figure 10.3.[57] The **need hierarchy** illustrates Maslow's conception of people satisfying their needs in a specified order, from bottom to top. The needs, in ascending order, are as follows:

1. *Physiological*—food, water, sex, and shelter.
2. *Safety or security*—protection against threat and deprivation.
3. *Social*—friendship, affection, belonging, and love.
4. *Ego*—independence, achievement, freedom, status, recognition, and self-esteem.
5. *Self-actualization*—realizing one's full potential; becoming everything one is capable of being.

According to Maslow, people are motivated to satisfy the lower needs before they try to satisfy the higher needs. In today's workplace, physiological and safety needs generally are well satisfied, making social, ego, and self-actualization needs preeminent. But safety issues are still very important in manufacturing, mining, and other work environments. And for months after the terrorist attacks of September 2001, employees still felt fear, denial, and anger—especially women, people with children,

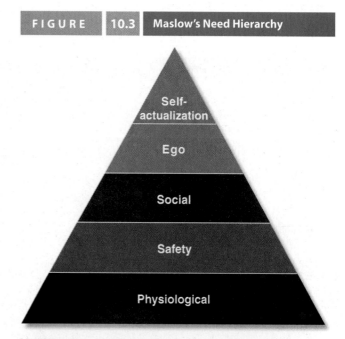

| FIGURE | 10.3 | Maslow's Need Hierarchy |

SOURCE: D. Organ and T. Bateman, *Organizational Behavior,* 4th ed. McGraw-Hill, 1990. © 1990 The McGraw-Hill Companies.

● **MASLOW'S NEED HIERARCHY**
A conception of human needs
organizing needs into a hierarchy
of five major types.

● **ALDERFER'S ERG THEORY** A human needs
theory developed by Alderfer postulating
that people have three basic sets of needs
that can operate simultaneously.

and those close to the events.[58] To deal with such safety issues, managers can show what the firm will do to improve security and manage employee risk, including crisis management plans.

Once a need is satisfied, it is no longer a powerful motivator. For example, labor unions negotiate for higher wages, benefits, safety standards, and job security. These bargaining issues relate directly to the satisfaction of Maslow's lower-level needs. Only after these needs are reasonably satisfied do the higher-level needs—social, ego, and self-actualization—become dominant concerns.

Maslow's hierarchy is a simplistic and not altogether accurate theory of human motivation.[59] For example, not everyone progresses through the five needs in hierarchical order. But Maslow made three important contributions. First, he identified important need categories, which can help managers create effective positive reinforcers. Second, it is helpful to think of two general levels of needs, in which lower-level needs must be satisfied before higher-level needs become important. Third, Maslow alerted managers to the importance of personal growth and self-actualization.

Self-actualization is the best-known concept arising from this theory. According to Maslow, the average person is only 10 percent self-actualized. In other words, most of us are living and working with a large untapped reservoir of potential. The implication is clear: managers should help create a work environment that provides training, resources, autonomy, responsibilities, and challenging assignments. This type of environment gives people a chance to use their skills and abilities creatively and allows them to achieve more of their full potential.

So treat people not merely as a cost to be controlled but as an asset to be developed. Many companies have embarked on programs that offer their people personal growth experiences. An employee at Federal Express said, "The best I can be is what I can be here. Federal Express … gave me the confidence and self-esteem to become the person I had the potential to become."[60]

Individual managers also can promote employee growth. Pete Wamsteeker's first supervisor, at a feed company, routinely invited him to discuss his career plans, and Wamsteeker does the same for his employees now that he has become general manager of Cargill Animal Nutrition. When Wamsteeker took that position, he started by learning about his employees so that he could

ensure each was in the job where he or she could contribute best. For example, he determined that an employee with a technical background and a quiet, analytical nature would thrive in a job that involves determining how pork producers can be more productive.[61]

Organizations gain by fully using their human resources. Employees gain by capitalizing on opportunities to meet their higher-order needs on the job. At Campbell Soup Company, managers are rewarded for developing their employees, and Lisa Walker, business director of Campbell USA's wellness team, rises to the challenge. She helped one employee learn to collaborate better so that he would be seen as a team player with promotion potential. Walker's employee appreciated that her coaching gave him an opportunity for greater achievement, status, and self-esteem.[62]

Alderfer identified three work-related needs

A theory of human needs that is more advanced than Maslow's is Alderfer's ERG theory.[63] Maslow's theory has general applicability, but Alderfer aims expressly at understanding people's needs at work. **ERG theory** postulates three sets of needs:

1. *Existence* needs are all material and physiological desires.

2. *Relatedness* needs involve relationships with other people and are satisfied through the process of mutually sharing thoughts and feelings.

3. *Growth* needs motivate people to productively or creatively change themselves or their environment. Satisfaction of the growth needs comes from fully utilizing personal capacities and developing new capacities.

What similarities do you see between Alderfer's and Maslow's needs? Roughly speaking, existence needs subsume physiological and security needs, relatedness needs are similar to social and esteem needs, and growth needs correspond to self-actualization.

ERG theory proposes that several different needs can be operating at once. So while Maslow would say that self-actualization is important to people only after other sets of needs are satisfied, Alderfer maintains that people—particularly working people in our postindustrial society—can be motivated to satisfy existence, relatedness, and growth needs at the same time.

 Companies can use this knowledge as they design compensation or benefits programs. Kahler Slater Architects, a 150-employee architecture and design firm, faced economic pressures, causing a rollback of employee benefits, including health care coverage. But to tailor the cutbacks to its staff, company principals found out from employees exactly which benefits meant the most to them. Then the managers came up with a package that worked for all.

Employees reported that one of their most-valued benefits was paid time off, but they gave up less-important perks like free pastries in the company office. They also contributed more to their health care coverage. To boost morale and help build camaraderie, the firm began hosting after-work social gatherings. It also offered employees more options for working from home to help them manage their schedules and conflicts.[64]

Consider which theory best explains the motives identified by Diane Schumaker-Krieg to describe her successful career in the financial services industry. Schumaker-Krieg says she was "driven . . . by fear" in October 1987, when she was working for investment firm Dillon Read at the time of the stock market crash. Layoffs were spreading throughout the industry, jobs were scarce, and she was supporting her son following a divorce. Out of determination to take care of her son, Schumaker-Krieg reacted to being laid off by writing a business plan to adapt research for sale to small customers. She persuaded Dillon Read to fund the idea for a year, began building the business, moved it to Credit Suisse, and within years

DID YOU KNOW?

Yarde Metals set up a "nap room" with couches, pillows, soft lighting, and an alarm clock at its headquarters in Southington, Connecticut. Why? Studies suggest that workers who nap may stay healthier—and that means fewer absences and lower costs for health insurance.[65]

was earning $150 million in profits for her employer. During that time she remarried and earned enough to retire, but she continues working, now as managing director of Credit Suisse's U.S. Equity Research. She sees her current motivation as enjoyment of her accomplishments, her business relationships, and opportunities to continue innovating.[66] Certainly, lower-level needs dominated the early years of Schumaker-Krieg's career, but did the basis for her motivation move one step at a time through all the levels of Maslow's hierarchy?

Maslow's theory is better known to American managers than Alderfer's, but ERG theory has more scientific support.[67] Both have practical value in that they remind managers of the types of reinforcers or rewards that can be used to motivate people. Regardless of whether the manager prefers the Maslow or the Alderfer theory of needs, he or she can motivate people by helping them satisfy their needs, particularly by offering opportunities for self-actualization and growth.

McClelland said managers seek achievement, affiliation, and power

David McClelland also identified a number of basic needs that guide people. According to McClelland, three needs are most important for managers:[68]

1. The need for *achievement*—a strong orientation toward accomplishment and an obsession with success and goal attainment. Most managers and entrepreneurs in the United States have high levels of this need and like to see it in their employees.

2. The need for *affiliation*—a strong desire to be liked by other people. Individuals who have high levels of this need are oriented toward getting along with others and may be less concerned with performing at high levels.

3. The need for *power*—a desire to influence or control other people. This need can be a negative force (termed *personalized power*) if it is expressed through the aggressive manipulation and exploitation of others. People high on the personalized-power need want power purely for the pursuit of their own goals. But the need for power also can be a positive motive, called *socialized power,* which is channeled toward the constructive improvement of organizations and societies.

Different needs predominate for different people. Now that you have read about these needs, think about yourself—which one(s) are most and least important to you?

> "The degree to which you will find the right recognition [of employees' successes] is equal to the degree to which you know the employee[s], you know their wants and needs."
>
> —Erika Anderson, organizational development consultant[69]

● EXTRINSIC REWARDS Rewards given to a person by the boss, the company, or some other person.

● INTRINSIC REWARD Reward a worker derives directly from performing the job itself.

Low need for affiliation and moderate to high need for power are associated with managerial success for both higher- and lower-level managers.[70] One reason the need for affiliation is not necessary for leadership success is that managers high on this need have difficulty making tough but necessary decisions that will upset some people.

Do need theories apply internationally?

How do the need theories apply abroad?[71] Although managers in the United States care most strongly about achievement, esteem, and self-actualization, managers in Greece and Japan are motivated more by security. Social needs are most important in Sweden, Norway, and Denmark. "Doing your own thing"— the phrase from the 1960s that describes an American culture oriented toward self-actualization—is not even translatable into Chinese. "Achievement," too, is difficult to translate into most other languages. Researchers in France, Japan, and Sweden would have been unlikely to even conceive of McClelland's achievement motive, because people of those countries are more group-oriented than individually oriented.

Clearly, achievement, growth, and self-actualization are profoundly important in the United States, Canada, and Great Britain. But these needs are not universally important. Every manager must remember that need importance varies from country to country and that people may not be motivated by the same needs. One study found that employees in many countries are highly engaged at companies that have strong leadership, work/life balance, a good reputation, and opportunities for employees to contribute, while another found variations from country to country:[72] employees in Canada were attracted by competitive pay, work/life balance, and opportunities for advancement; workers in Germany by autonomy; in Japan by high-quality coworkers; in the Netherlands by a collaborative work environment; and in the United States by competitive

health benefits. Generally, no single way is best, and managers can customize their approaches by considering how individuals differ.[73]

(L)(O) 6 **WHAT YOU NEED TO KNOW . . .**
How can you create jobs that motivate?

DESIGNING MOTIVATING JOBS

Here's an example of a company that gave a "reward" that didn't motivate. One of Mary Kay Ash's former employers gave her a sales award: a flounder fishing light. Unfortunately, she doesn't fish. Fortunately, she later was able to design her own organization, Mary Kay Cosmetics, around two kinds of motivators that *mattered* to her people:[74]

1. **Extrinsic rewards** are given to people by the boss, the company, or some other person.
2. An **intrinsic reward** is a reward the person derives directly from performing the job itself.

An interesting project, an intriguing subject that is fun to study, a completed sale, and the discovery of the perfect solution to a difficult problem all can give people the feeling that they have done something well. This is the essence of the motivation that comes from intrinsic rewards.

Intrinsic rewards are essential to the motivation underlying creativity.[75] A challenging problem, a chance to create something new, and work that is exciting can provide intrinsic motivation that inspires people to devote time and energy to the task. So do managers who allow people some freedom to pursue the tasks that interest them most. The opposite situations result in routine, habitual behaviors that interfere with creativity.[76] A study in manufacturing facilities found that employees initiated more applications for patents, made more novel and useful suggestions, and were rated by their managers as more creative when their jobs were challenging and their managers did not control their activities closely.[77]

Conversely, some jobs and organizations create environments that quash creativity and motivation.[79] The classic example of a demotivating job is the highly specialized assembly-line job; each worker performs one boring operation before passing the work along to the next worker. Such specialization, or the "mechanistic" approach to job design, was the prevailing practice through most of the 20th century.[80] But jobs that are too simple and routine result in employee dissatisfaction, absenteeism, and turnover.

Especially in industries that depend on highly motivated knowledge workers, keeping talented employees

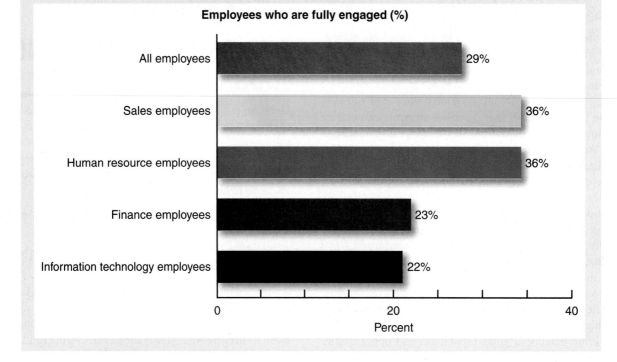

Employees who are fully engaged (%)

Category	Percent
All employees	29%
Sales employees	36%
Human resource employees	36%
Finance employees	23%
Information technology employees	22%

Percent

may require letting them design their own jobs so that their work is more interesting than it would be elsewhere.[81] Jobs can be designed in the following ways to increase intrinsic rewards and therefore motivation.

Managers can make work more varied and interesting

With **job rotation**, workers who spend all their time in one routine task can instead move from one task to another. Rather than dishing out the pasta in a cafeteria line all day, a person might work the pasta, then the salads, and then the vegetables or desserts. Job rotation is intended to alleviate boredom by giving people different things to do at different times.

As you may guess, job rotation may simply move the person from one boring job to another. But job rotation can benefit everyone when done properly, with people's input and career interests in mind. At Thomson, an international publishing company, new information technology (IT) employees can participate in a job rotation program that helps them learn about the company's diverse business units and identify the area that best fits their talents and interests. Harrah's

Entertainment also uses job rotation for its IT workers, which gives them a broad knowledge of the business that enhances their value to the company at the same time it opens up opportunities for career development. About one out of five IT employees at Harrah's chooses to participate in the job rotation program.[82]

Job enlargement is similar to job rotation in that people are given different tasks to do. But while job rotation involves doing one task at one time and changing to a different task at a different time, job enlargement assigns the worker multiple tasks at the same time. Thus, an assembly worker's job is enlarged if he or she is given two tasks to perform rather than one. In a study of job enlargement in a financial services organization, enlarged jobs led to higher job satisfaction, better error detection by clerks, and improved customer service.[83]

With job enlargement, the person's additional tasks are at the same level of responsibility. More profound changes occur when jobs are enriched. **Job enrichment** means that jobs are restructured or redesigned by adding higher levels of responsibility. This practice includes giving people not only more tasks but higher-level ones, such as when decisions are delegated downward and authority is decentralized. Efforts to redesign jobs by enriching them are now common in American industry.

● JOB ROTATION
Changing from
one routine task to
another to alleviate
boredom.

● JOB ENLARGEMENT
Giving people
additional tasks at
the same time to
alleviate boredom.

● JOB ENRICHMENT
Changing a task to
make it inherently
more rewarding,
motivating, and
satisfying.

● TWO-FACTOR
THEORY Herzberg's
theory describing
two factors affect-
ing people's work
motivation and
satisfaction.

● HYGIENE FACTORS
Characteristics of
the workplace, such
as company policies,
working conditions,
pay, and supervision,
that can make people
dissatisfied.

● MOTIVATORS Factors
that make a job more
motivating, such as
additional job respon-
sibilities, opportunities
for personal growth and
recognition, and feelings
of achievement.

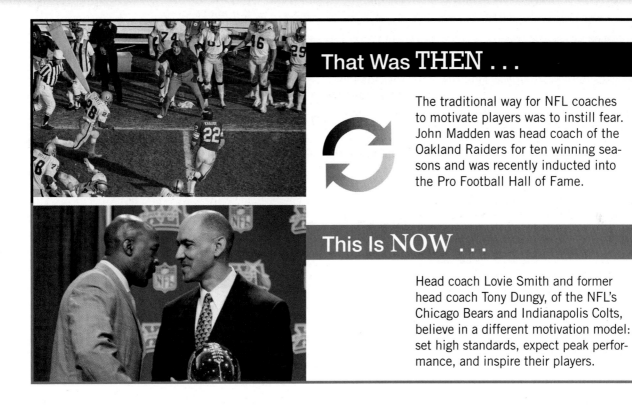

That Was THEN . . .

The traditional way for NFL coaches to motivate players was to instill fear. John Madden was head coach of the Oakland Raiders for ten winning seasons and was recently inducted into the Pro Football Hall of Fame.

This Is NOW . . .

Head coach Lovie Smith and former head coach Tony Dungy, of the NFL's Chicago Bears and Indianapolis Colts, believe in a different motivation model: set high standards, expect peak performance, and inspire their players.

The first approach to job enrichment was Herzberg's two-factor theory, followed by the Hackman and Oldham model.

Herzberg proposed two important job-related factors

Frederick Herzberg's two-factor theory distinguished between two broad categories of factors that affect people working on their jobs:[84]

1. **Hygiene factors** are *characteristics of the workplace:* company policies, working conditions, pay, coworkers, super-vision, and so forth. These factors can make people unhappy if they are poorly managed. If they are well managed, and viewed as positive by employees, the employees will no longer be dissatisfied. However, no matter how good these factors are, they will not make people truly satisfied or moti-vated to do a good job.

2. **Motivators** describe the *job itself,* that is, what people do at work. Motivators are the nature of the work itself, actual job responsibilities, opportunity for personal growth and rec-ognition, and the feelings of achievement the job provides. According to Herzberg, the key to true job satisfaction and motivation to perform lies in this category of factors. When

motivators are present, jobs are presumed to be satisfying and motivating for most people.

Herzberg's theory has been criticized by many scholars, so we will not go into more detail about his original theory. But Herzberg was a pioneer in the area of job design and still is a respected name among American managers. In addition, even if the specifics of his theory do not hold up to scientific scrutiny, he made several important contributions. Herzberg's theory highlights the important distinction between extrinsic rewards (from hygiene factors) and intrinsic rewards (from motiva-tors). It also reminds managers not to count solely on extrinsic rewards to motivate workers but to focus on intrinsic rewards as well. Finally, it set the stage for later theories, such as the Hack-man and Oldham model, that explain more precisely how man-agers can enrich people's jobs.

Hackman and Oldham: meaning, responsibility, and feedback provide motivation

Following Herzberg's work, Hackman and Oldham proposed a more complete model of job design.[85] Figure 10.4 illustrates their model. As you can see, well-designed jobs lead to high motivation, high-quality performance, high satisfaction, and low absenteeism and turnover. These outcomes occur when people experience three critical psychological states (noted in the middle column of the figure):

1. They believe they are doing something meaningful because their work is important to other people.

2. They feel personally responsible for how the work turns out.

3. They learn how well they performed their jobs.

These psychological states occur when people are working on enriched jobs, that is, jobs that offer the following five core job dimensions:

1. *Skill variety*—different job activities involving several skills and talents. For example, management trainees at Enterprise Rent-A-Car try their hands at every area of the business, including hiring employees, washing cars, waiting on customers, working with body shops, and ordering supplies. Assistant manager Sarah Ruddell defines the broad responsibilities as a plus: "You're not stuck doing the same thing over and over again."[86]

2. *Task identity*—the completion of a whole, identifiable piece of work. At State Farm Insurance, agents are independent contractors who sell and provide service for State Farm products exclusively. They have built and invested in their own businesses. As a result, agent retention and productivity are far better than industry norms.[87]

3. *Task significance*—an important, positive impact on the lives of others. According to Diane Castiglione, the director of recruitment for the U.S. State Department, people are drawn to careers in the Foreign Service because the work matters. Castiglione says Foreign Service employees are aware that they are serving the interests of their country, "whether that means helping an American citizen who has lost his passport or who has been arrested, or whether it means trying to figure out a way to help a U.S. business engage in business in another country, . . . whether it means trying to work on issues involving human rights."[88] Similarly, James Perry, an expert on motivation of government employees, says these workers generally have a strong commitment to serving the public good, including public welfare and stewardship of public resources.[89]

4. *Autonomy*—independence and discretion in making decisions. In a research hospital, a department administrator

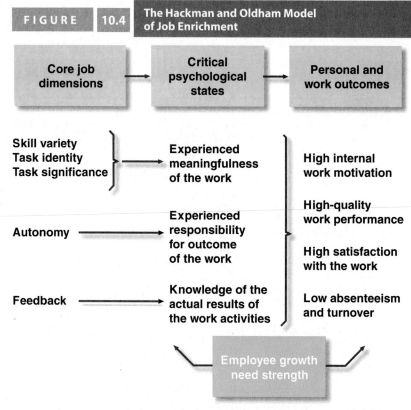

FIGURE 10.4 The Hackman and Oldham Model of Job Enrichment

SOURCE: From "A New Strategy for Job Enrichment" by J. Richard Hackman et al., *California Management Review*. Copyright © 1975 by the Regents of the University of California. Reprinted from the *California Management Review*, vol. 17, no. 4. By permission of The Regents.

told her people to do the kinds of research they wanted as long as it was within budget (and legal!). With no other guidelines—that is, complete autonomy—productivity increased sixfold in a year.[90]

DID YOU KNOW?

According a recent survey of 27,000 people, the workers most likely to be satisfied with their jobs were clergy members, firefighters, physical therapists, authors, and special-education teachers. Job satisfaction was least likely among laborers (except construction), clothing salespeople, hand packers and packagers, food preparers, and roofers.[92] Do the most satisfying jobs have more of Hackman and Oldham's job characteristics?

5. *Feedback*—information about job performance. Many companies post charts or provide computerized data indicating productivity, number of rejects, and other data. At Whole Foods Market, teams are responsible for hiring and scheduling in their area of the store. Team leaders get information about each month's payroll expense versus the budgeted amount. If the team comes in under budget, everyone knows, because everyone gets a share of the savings. This practical feedback inspires teams to hire carefully and work hard.[91]

The most effective job enrichment increases all five core dimensions.

A person's growth need strength will help determine just how effective a job enrichment program might be. **Growth need strength** is the degree to which individuals want personal and psychological development. Job enrichment would be more successful for people with high growth need strength. But very few people respond negatively to job enrichment.[93]

To motivate, empowerment must be done right

Today many managers talk about "empowering" their people. Individuals may—or may not—feel empowered, and groups can have a "culture" of empowerment that enhances work-unit performance.[94] **Empowerment** is the process of sharing power with employees, thereby enhancing their confidence in their ability to perform their jobs and their belief that they are influential contributors to the organization. Unfortunately, empowerment doesn't always live up to its hype. One problem is that managers undermine it by sending mixed messages like "Do your own thing—the way we tell you."[95] But empowerment can be profoundly motivating when done properly.[96]

Empowerment changes employees' beliefs—from feeling powerless to believing strongly in their own personal effectiveness.[97] As a result, people take more initiative and persevere in achieving their goals and their leader's vision even in the face of obstacles.[98] Specifically, empowerment encourages the following beliefs among employees:[99]

- They perceive *meaning* in their work; their job fits their values.
- They feel *competent,* or capable of performing their jobs with skill.
- They have a sense of *self-determination,* of having some choice in regard to the tasks, methods, and pace of their work.
- They have an *impact*—that is, they have some influence over important strategic, administrative, or operating decisions or outcomes on the job.

When speaking of times when they felt disempowered, people had the following comments:[100]

- I had no input into a hiring decision of someone who was to report directly to me. I didn't even get to speak to the candidate.
- I worked extremely hard—long hours and late nights—on an urgent project, and then my manager took full credit for it.
- My suggestions, whether good or bad, were either not solicited or, worse, ignored.
- The project was reassigned without my knowledge or input.

In contrast, people expressed empowerment in the following examples:

- I was able to make a large financial decision on my own. I got to write a large check without being questioned.
- After having received a memo that said, "Cut travel," I made my case about why it was necessary to travel for business

reasons, and I was told to go ahead.
- My president supported my idea without question.
- All the financial data were shared with me.

To foster empowerment, management must create an environment in which all the employees feel they have real influence over performance standards and business effectiveness within their areas of responsibility.[101] An empowering work environment provides people with *information* necessary for them to perform at their best, *knowledge* about how to use the information and how to do their work, *power* to make decisions that give them control over their work, and the *rewards* they deserve for the contributions they make.[102] Such an environment reduces costs because fewer people are needed to supervise, monitor, and coordinate. It improves quality and service because high performance is inspired at the source, the people who do the work. It also allows quick action because people on the spot see problems, solutions, and opportunities for innovation on which they are empowered to act.

It is essential to give people clear strategic direction but to leave some room for flexibility and calculated risk taking. For example, Southwest Airlines' strategic principle of "meet customers' short-haul travel needs at fares competitive with the cost of automobile travel" helps employees keep strategic objectives in mind and use their discretion in making complicated decisions about service offerings, route selection, cabin design, ticketing procedures, and pricing.[103] More specific actions include increasing signature authority at all levels; reducing the number of rules and approval steps; assigning nonroutine jobs; allowing independent judgment, flexibility, and creativity; defining jobs more broadly as projects rather than tasks; and providing more access to resources and people throughout the organization.[104]

Empowerment does not mean allowing people to decide trivial things like what color to paint the lunchroom. For empowerment to make a difference, people must have an impact on things they care about, such as quality and productivity.[105] Companies that have successfully used empowerment programs include Lord Corporation in Dayton, Ohio (which produces engine mounts for aircraft), and Herman Miller (the Michigan-based furniture manufacturer).[106]

 Empowerment seems to be at the heart of motivation for employees of Google. Rather than just guessing what employees want, Google has applied its commitment to careful analysis. The company developed a computer algorithm (mathematical procedure) to see where its challenges lie in retaining its best talent. The algorithm evaluates data from employee surveys, performance reviews, pay histories, and peer reviews to identify which employees are most at risk of leaving the company.

A key lesson has already emerged: employees are most likely to leave Google if they believe the company is not fully tapping into their expertise. Most likely, this issue will continue to be significant. In Google's early years, employees enjoyed the thrill of being part of something new and rapidly expanding. The growth offered seemingly limitless possibilities, and employees had exceptional leeway to work on projects of their own invention. After more than a decade, the company has almost 20,000 employees and a greater need to coordinate their work and set priorities for allocating resources. To motivate employees to stay, Google will have to figure out how it can continue offering flexibility for learning and experimentation, perhaps coupled with more formal structures such as career paths.[107]

You should not be surprised when empowerment causes some problems, at least in the short term. Problems accompany virtually any change, including changes for the better. It's important to remember that empowerment brings responsibility, and employees don't necessarily like the accountability at first.[108] People may make mistakes, especially until they have had adequate training. Because more training is needed, costs are higher. Because people acquire new skills and make greater contributions, they may demand higher wages. But if they are well trained and truly empowered, they will deserve the pay—and they and the company will benefit.

(L)(O) 7   **WHAT YOU NEED TO KNOW . . .**
How do people assess and achieve fairness?

ACHIEVING FAIRNESS

Ultimately, one of the most important issues in motivation surrounds people's view of what they contribute to the organization and what they receive from it. Ideally, they will view their relationship with their employer as a well-balanced, mutually beneficial exchange. As people work and realize the outcomes or consequences of their actions, they assess how fairly the organization treats them.

The starting point for understanding how people interpret their contributions and outcomes is equity theory.[109] **Equity theory** proposes that when people assess how fairly they are treated, they consider two key factors:

1. *Outcomes,* as in expectancy theory, refer to the various things the person receives on the job: recognition, pay, benefits, satisfaction, security, job assignments, punishments, and so forth.
2. *Inputs* refer to the contributions the person makes to the organization: effort, time, talent, performance, extra commitment, good citizenship, and so forth.

People generally expect that the outcomes they receive will reflect, or be proportionate to, the inputs they provide—a fair day's pay (and other outcomes) for a fair day's work (broadly defined by how people view all their contributions).

But this comparison of outcomes to inputs is not the whole story. People also pay attention to the outcomes and inputs others receive. At salary review time, for example, most people—from executives on down—try to pick up clues that will tell them who got the biggest raises. As described in the following section, they compare ratios, try to restore equity if necessary, and derive more or less satisfaction based on how fairly they believe they have been treated.

People assess equity by making comparisons

Equity theory suggests that people compare the ratio of their own outcomes to inputs against the outcome-to-input ratio of some comparison person. The comparison person can be a coworker, a boss, or an average industry pay scale. Stated more succinctly, people compare:

$$\text{Their own } \frac{\text{Outcomes}}{\text{Inputs}} \quad \text{versus} \quad \text{Others'} \frac{\text{Outcomes}}{\text{Inputs}}$$

If the ratios are equivalent, people believe the relationship is equitable, or fair. Equity causes people to be satisfied with their treatment. But the person who believes his or her ratio is lower than another's will feel inequitably treated. Inequity causes dissatisfaction and leads to an attempt to restore balance to the relationship.

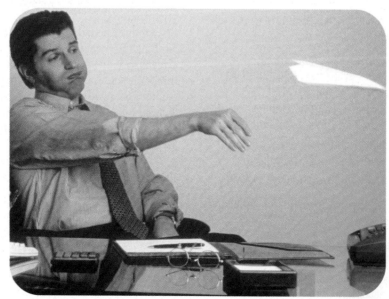

Inequity and the negative feelings it creates may appear anywhere. As a student, perhaps you have been in the following situation. You stay up all night and get a C on the exam. Meanwhile, another student studies a couple of hours, goes out for the rest of the evening, gets a good night's sleep, and gets a B. You perceive your inputs (time spent studying) as much greater than the other student's, but your outcomes are lower. You are displeased at the seeming unfairness. In business, the same thing sometimes happens with pay raises. One manager puts in 60-hour weeks, earned a degree from a prestigious university, and believes she is destined for the top. When her archrival—whom she perceives as less deserving ("she never comes into the office on weekends, and all she does when she is here is butter up the boss")—gets the higher raise or the promotion, she experiences severe feelings of inequity. In the world of sports, motivation problems resulting from perceived pay inequities may be the reason major league baseball teams that have great differences in their player salaries tend to win fewer games.[110]

Many people have felt inequity when they learn about large sums paid to high-profile CEOs. Ironically, one reason for rising CEO pay is an effort to set pay using a method that looks something like the equity comparison: the board of directors compares the CEO's pay with that of chief executives at organizations in a "peer group." Until 2006, companies did not have to disclose which companies were in the peer group, but one example exposed in the courtroom has suggested how inequity can arise. Richard A. Grasso received $140 million in compensation as chairman of the New York Stock Exchange. A compensation expert hired by New York's attorney general learned that the companies of the peer group used as a basis for setting Grasso's pay had median revenues more than 25 times that of the NYSE, media assets 125 times the NYSE's, and a median number of employees that was about 30 times that of the NYSE.[111] Even when a company chooses an appropriate peer group, many boards try to pay their executives in the top one-fourth of the group. The drive to keep everyone's pay above average means the average keeps climbing.

Assessments of equity are not made objectively. They are subjective perceptions or beliefs. In the preceding example of the two managers, the one who got the bigger raise probably felt she deserved it. Even if she admits to working fewer hours, she may convince herself she can because she is more efficient. In the example of the students, the one who scored higher may believe the outcome was equitable because (1) she worked harder over the course of the semester, and (2) she's smart (ability and experience, not just time and effort, can be seen as inputs).

People who feel inequitably treated try to even the balance

People who feel inequitably treated and dissatisfied are motivated to do something to restore equity. They have a number of options that they carry out to change the ratios or to reevaluate the situation and decide it is equitable after all.

The equity equation shown earlier indicates a person's options for restoring equity when they feel inequitably treated:

- *Reducing their inputs*—giving less effort, performing at lower levels, or quitting: "Well, if that's the way things work around here, there's no way I'm going to work that hard (or stick around)."

- *Increasing their outcomes:* "My boss is going to hear about this. I deserve more; there must be some way I can get more."

● EQUITY THEORY A theory stating that people assess how fairly they have been treated according to two key factors: outcomes and inputs.

● PROCEDURAL JUSTICE Using a fair process in decision making and making sure others know that the process was as fair as possible.

- *Decreasing others' outcomes:* For example, an employee may sabotage work to create problems for his company or boss.[112] People can change their perceptions of an outcome, not just the outcome itself: "That promotion isn't as great a deal as she thinks. The pay is not that much better, and the headaches will be unbelievable."

- *Increasing others' inputs*—Here, too, the change may be in perceptions: "The more I think about it, the more I see he deserved it. He's worked hard all year, he's competent, and it's about time he got a break."

Thus, a person can restore equity in a number of ways by behaviorally or perceptually changing inputs and outcomes. On the positive side, people may care about group equity and *may even increase their inputs* to keep a situation equitable for the group. In the first few months of each year, many accountants face a flood of work related to annual reports and tax preparation. At Gramkow, Carnevale, Seifert & Company, an accounting firm in Oradell, New Jersey, Kenneth Benkow works six days a week and many evenings during tax time. He explains, "What helps motivate me is that I look around the office and I see people who are working as hard or harder than I am. You feel guilty if you're not pulling your own weight."[113]

Procedures—not just outcomes—should be fair

Inevitably, managers make decisions that have outcomes more favorable for some than for others. Those with favorable outcomes will be pleased; those with worse outcomes, all else equal, will be more displeased. But managers desiring to put salve on the wounds—say, of people they like or respect or want to keep and motivate—still can reduce the dissatisfaction. They do this by demonstrating that they provide **procedural justice**—using a fair process in decision making and helping others know that the process was as fair as possible. When people perceive procedural fairness, they are more likely to support decisions and decision makers.[114] For example, one year after layoffs, managers' use of procedural justice (in the form of employee participation in decisions) still predicted survivors' organizational commitment, job satisfaction, and trust toward management.[115]

Even if people believe that their *outcome* was inequitable and unfair, they are more likely to view justice as having been served if the *process* was fair. You can increase people's beliefs that the process was fair by making the process open and visible, stating decision criteria in advance rather than after the fact, making sure that the most appropriate people—those who have valid information and are viewed as trustworthy—make the decisions, giving people a chance to participate in the process, and providing an appeal process that allows people to question decisions safely and receive complete answers.[116] This kind of treatment is expressed by Deere and Company's former chief executive, Bob Lane. Lane says that even when "we have to let people go" because the company is struggling, "each and every individual has inherent worth," so management must treat employees with dignity and help them understand the reasons behind the actions.[117]

In contrast, at an elevator plant in the United States, an army of consultants arrived one day, without explanation.[118] The rumor mill kicked in; employees guessed the plant would be shut down or some of them would be laid off. Three months later, management unveiled its new plan, involving a new method of manufacturing based on teams. But management did not adequately answer questions about the purpose of the changes, employees resisted, conflicts arose, and the formerly popular plant manager lost the trust of his people. Costs skyrocketed, and quality plummeted.

Concerned, management conducted an employee survey. Employees doubted that the survey results would lead to any positive changes and worried that their honesty would anger management. But management reacted by admitting its implementation mistakes and beginning to communicate critical business information, the limited options available, and the need for change. Employees came to view the business problem as theirs as well as management's, but they still worried about job losses. Although management retained the right to lay people off, it promised it would not lay off employees to institute teamwork and would provide training and development to keep employees when possible, as well as share performance data regularly. These efforts marked the beginning of the restoration of trust

Former John Deere CEO Bob Lane stands next to a riding lawn mower made by Deere & Company, the world's leading manufacturer of agricultural machinery. Lane believes in treating people with dignity, even when delivering bad news.

and commitment, followed by steady improvements in performance.

(L)(O) 8 WHAT YOU NEED TO KNOW . . .
Can you identify causes and consequences of a satisfied workforce?

JOB SATISFACTION

If people feel fairly treated from the outcomes they receive or the processes used, they will be satisfied. A satisfied worker is not necessarily more productive than a dissatisfied one; sometimes people are happy with their jobs because they don't have to work hard! But job dissatisfaction, aggregated across many individuals, creates a workforce that is more likely to exhibit the following characteristics:

- Higher turnover
- Higher absenteeism
- Less good citizenship among employees[119]
- More grievances and lawsuits
- Strikes
- Stealing, sabotage, and vandalism
- Poorer mental and physical health (which can mean higher job stress, higher insurance costs, and more lawsuits)[120]
- More injuries[121]
- Poor customer service[122]
- Lower productivity and profits[123]

All of these consequences of dissatisfaction, either directly or indirectly, are costly. Sadly, a survey of U.S. households found that a majority of workers are dissatisfied with their jobs, with the greatest amount of dissatisfaction among workers aged 25 and younger.[124]

Job satisfaction is especially important for relationship-oriented service employees such as real estate agents, hair stylists, and stockbrokers. Customers develop (or don't develop) a commitment to a specific service provider. Satisfied service providers are less likely to quit the company and more likely to provide an enjoyable customer experience.[125]

Companies are improving the quality of work life

Quality of work life (QWL) programs create a workplace that enhances employee well-being and satisfaction. The general goal of QWL programs is to satisfy the full range of employee needs. People's needs apparently are well met at First Horizon National, which offers a flexible benefits package including health and dental insurance, paid vacation, tuition reimbursement, discounts for child care and financial products, and reimbursement for adoption-related expenses. More unusually, First Horizon extends those benefits to workers who telecommute and work part-time. The company repeatedly appears on *Fortune*'s list of the 100 Best Companies to Work For, but more important is the impact on workers like Brenda Fung, a 13-year veteran and recently part-time designer of the company's intranet. Fung told a reporter, "This company has been so generous to me. There's no way I could even think of leaving."[126]

QWL addresses eight categories:[127]

1. Adequate and fair compensation.
2. A safe and healthy environment.
3. Jobs that develop human capacities.
4. A chance for personal growth and security.
5. A social environment that fosters personal identity, freedom from prejudice, a sense of community, and upward mobility.
6. Constitutionalism—the rights of personal privacy, dissent, and due process.
7. A work role that minimizes infringement on personal leisure and family needs.
8. Socially responsible organizational actions.

Organizations differ drastically in their attention to QWL. Critics claim that QWL programs don't necessarily inspire employees to work harder if the company does not tie rewards directly to individual performance. Advocates of QWL claim that it improves organizational effectiveness and productivity. The term *productivity,* as applied by QWL programs, means much more than each person's quantity of work output.[128] It also includes turnover, absenteeism, accidents, theft, sabotage, creativity, innovation, and especially the quality of work.

Psychological contracts are understandings of give-and-take

The relationship between individuals and employing organizations typically is formalized by a written contract. But in employees' minds there also exists a **psychological contract**—a set of perceptions of what they owe their employers and what their employers owe them.[129] This contract, whether it is seen as being upheld or violated—and whether the parties trust one another or not—has important implications for employee satisfaction and motivation and the effectiveness of the organization.

Historically, in many companies the employment relationship was stable and predictable. Now mergers, layoffs, and other disruptions have thrown asunder the "old deal."[130] In traditionally managed organizations, employees were expected to be loyal, and employers would provide secure employment. Today the implicit contract goes something like this:[131] if people stay, do their own job plus someone else's (who has been downsized), and do additional things like participating in task forces, the company will try to provide a job (if it can), provide gestures that it cares, and keep providing about the same pay (with periodic small increases). The likely result of this not-very-satisfying arrangement: uninspired people in a struggling business.

But a better deal is possible for both employers and employees.[132] Ideally, your employer will provide continuous skill updating and an invigorating work environment in which you can use your skills and are motivated to stay even though you may have other job options.[133] An example of such a modern psychological contract is Allstate's general employment contract, shown in Table 10.1. Thus, you could work for a company

● **QUALITY OF WORK LIFE (QWL) PROGRAMS** Programs designed to create a workplace that enhances employee well-being.

● **PSYCHOLOGICAL CONTRACT** A set of perceptions of what employees owe their employers, and what their employers owe them.

Wood & Grieve Website?

TABLE	10.1	Allstate Employability Contract

You should expect Allstate to:

1. Offer work that is meaningful and challenging.
2. Promote an environment that encourages open and constructive dialogue.
3. Recognize you for your accomplishments.
4. Provide competitive pay and rewards based on your performance.
5. Advise you on your performance through regular feedback.
6. Create learning opportunities through education and job assignments.
7. Support you in defining career goals.
8. Provide you with information and resources to perform successfully.
9. Promote an environment that is inclusive and free from bias.
10. Foster dignity and respect in all interactions.
11. Establish an environment that promotes a balance of work and personal life.

Allstate expects you to:

1. Perform at levels that significantly increase our ability to outperform the competition.
2. Take on assignments critical to meeting business objectives.
3. Continually develop needed skills.
4. Willingly listen to and act upon feedback.
5. Demonstrate a high level of commitment to achieving company goals.
6. Exhibit no bias in interactions with colleagues and customers.
7. Behave consistently with Allstate's ethical standards.
8. Take personal responsibility for each transaction with our customers and for fostering their trust.
9. Continually improve processes to address customers' needs.

SOURCE: Courtesy of Allstate Insurance Company. Cited in E. E. Lawler III, *Treat People Right!* (San Francisco: Jossey-Bass, 2003).

that provides the following deal: if you develop the skills we need, apply them in ways that help the company succeed, and behave consistently with our values, we will provide a challenging work environment, support for your development, and full, fair rewards for your contributions. Such a "contract" is likely to produce a mutually beneficial and satisfying relationship and a high-performing, successful organization.

Consider how business coach Ram Charan assumed this new psychological contract in advising a frustrated HR manager.[134] The manager had asked Charan for guidance in coping with bureaucratic red tape that frustrated the entire group, including the manager himself. Charan encouraged the manager to reframe the situation as a need for learning, creativity, and leadership. The manager, said Charan, should investigate what the managers in other departments need from HR, so that his people would truly be serving business needs and helping to solve business problems. Charan also encouraged the manager to learn about his employees' career goals and interests, so that he can focus on ways to develop his people's strengths through assignments and greater decision-making authority within the department. If the HR manager accepts Charan's guidance, he and his people will face more difficult yet more interesting challenges than they would by simply defining themselves as a static part of a bureaucracy.

Build Your Skills

Practice and apply your knowledge by going online at

www.mhhe.com/ BatemanM2e

11

Teamwork

As Cisco Systems has grown, the computer networking giant has stayed nimble by delegating work to teams whose membership crosses functional, departmental, and national lines.[1] Sometimes—as in Cisco's case—teams "work," but sometimes they don't. The goal of this chapter is to help make sure that your management and work teams succeed, rather than fail. Almost all companies now use teams to produce goods and services, to manage projects, and to make decisions and run the company.[2] For you, this has two vital implications:

1. You *will* be working in and perhaps managing teams.
2. The *ability* to work in and lead teams is valuable to your employer and important to your career.

Fortunately, coursework focusing on team training can enhance students' teamwork knowledge and skills.[3]

Explore the Ways

today's managers build and lead teams. Listen to what Sarah and Derrick have to say on the book Web site.

"Teamwork is what makes your team strong and happy. I find in my store all of the associates work together to wardrobe a client or even reach a common goal; there is no competition. Our team has gone through many changes but the teamwork has kept us strong."
—Sarah Albert, Clothing Retail Manager

"I think, as a manager, building a good team means that you can empower people to do tasks effectively around you. Then you have the opportunity to look at the bigger picture as opposed to just the day-to-day monotonous routine—those things are still important; however, if you have empowered other people to make decisions, then you can sit back and look at the overall picture, which may require bigger decisions that you wouldn't necessarily have the time for without the assistance of your team."
—Derrick Hawthorne, Property Manager

•• learning **OBJECTIVES**

After studying Chapter 11,
you should be able to:

LO1 Discuss how teams can contribute to
an organization's effectiveness.

LO2 Distinguish the new team environment
from that of traditional work groups.

LO3 Summarize how groups become
teams.

LO4 Explain why groups sometimes fail.

LO5 Describe how to build an effective
team.

LO6 List methods for managing a team's
relationships with other teams.

LO7 Identify ways to manage conflict.

THE CONTRIBUTIONS OF TEAMS

Team-based approaches to work have generated excitement. Used appropriately, teams can be powerfully effective as a *building block for organization structure*. Organizations like Semco, Whole Foods, and Kollmorgen (a manufacturer of printed circuits and electro-optic devices) are structured entirely around teams. 3M's breakthrough products emerge through the use of teams that are small entrepreneurial businesses within the larger corporation.

Teams also can increase *productivity,* improve *quality,* and reduce *costs.* By adopting a team structure and culture, Battle Creek, Michigan–based Summit Pointe, a mental health organization, has saved millions of dollars while improving patient care.[4] Honeywell's teams saved more than $11 million after

receive tangible organizational rewards that they could not have achieved working alone. After General Mills acquired Pillsbury, the managers of the meals division decided they needed to develop a common culture that would promote employee engagement, so they set up a Spirit Team of staff members to select activities. Realizing that just having fun together would not develop a deeper sense of purpose, the team decided to partner with a nonprofit organization, Perspectives Family Center, and support this organization with several events each year. Employees who participate feel great about what they do, and they connect the experience with a sense that their company cares about its local community.[10]

Team members can give one another feedback; identify opportunities for growth and development; and train, coach, and mentor.[11] A marketing representative can learn about financial modeling from a colleague on a new-product development team, and the financial expert can learn about consumer marketing. Experience working together in a team, and developing strong problem-solving capabilities, is a vital supplement to specific job skills or functional expertise. And the skills are transferable to new positions.

> **"No one can whistle a symphony. It takes an orchestra to play it."**
>
> —Halford E. Luccock

reducing production times and shipping more than 99 percent of orders on time.[5] At Nucor's steel plant in Decatur, Alabama, general manager Rex Query credits teamwork for high productivity and improved safety.[6]

Teams also can enhance *speed* and be powerful forces for *innovation* and *change.* 3M and many other companies are using teams to create new products faster. Lenders cut home mortgage approval times from weeks to hours, and life insurance companies cut time to issue new policies from six weeks to one day.[7] General Mills uses a team approach to make decisions about the packaging for its products. For product divisions such as Big G cereals, Yoplait yogurt, or Green Giant vegetables, Packaging Partners teams bring together employees from brand design, engineering, production, research and development, and other relevant functions to figure out how packaging can reduce waste, cut costs, and send a clearer marketing message. In addition, Strategy Map teams convene employees from various product divisions to study packaging using a particular material and determine ways to work more efficiently with suppliers.[8]

Teams also provide many *benefits for their members.*[9] The team is a useful learning mechanism. Members learn about the company and themselves, and they acquire new skills and performance strategies. The team can satisfy important personal needs, such as affiliation and esteem. Team members may

THE NEW TEAM ENVIRONMENT

The words *group* and *team* often are used interchangeably.[12] Modern managers sometimes use the word *teams* to the point that it has become cliché; they talk about teams while skeptics perceive no real teamwork. So, making a distinction between groups and teams can be useful:

- A *working group* is a collection of people who work in the same area or have been drawn together to undertake a task but do not necessarily come together as a unit and achieve significant performance improvements.

- A real **team** is formed of people (usually a small number) with complementary skills who trust one another and are committed to a common purpose, common performance goals, and a common approach for which they hold themselves mutually accountable.[13]

 Even writing can be a team activity. Evolved Media Network is a small firm whose entire mission is to produce documents collaboratively. In one recent project, two editors and five writers prepared a 450-page book on SAP's enterprise resource planning software. The team accomplished this feat by using a Web site called a *wiki* (from the Hawaiian phrase *wiki wiki,* which means "faster, faster"). A wiki allows users to compose, delete, and edit content. Everyone can keep track of what everyone else is working on. "The value of wikis comes from a group of people who are now working together in a different way," says company founder Dan Woods. "Content is shared, and everybody's progress is visible to each other." That process gives all participants a feeling of shared ownership, according to Woods.

Although collaboration is the main thrust of wiki participation, Woods does recommend choosing a team leader. The leader oversees the entering of information, motivates team members to contribute, and makes sure the information included is valuable to the project. The leader can train team members new to the technology and ensure that the wiki is functioning properly.[14]

Organizations have been using groups for a long time, but today's workplaces are different.[15] Teams are used in many different ways, and to far greater effect, than in the past. Table 11.1 highlights just a few of the differences between the traditional work environment and the way true teams work today. Ideally, people are far more involved, they are better trained, cooperation is higher, and the culture is one of learning as well as producing.

Organizations have different types of teams

Your organization may have hundreds of groups and teams, but they can be classified into just a few primary types.[16] **Work teams** make or do things such as manufacture,

assemble, sell, or provide service. They typically are well defined, a clear part of the formal organizational structure, and composed of a full-time, stable membership. Work teams are what most people think of when they think of teams in organizations.[17]

Project and development teams work on long-term projects, often over a period of years. They have specific assignments, such as research or new-product development, and members usually must contribute expert knowledge and judgment. These teams work toward a one-time product, disbanding once their work is completed. Then new teams are formed for new projects.

Parallel teams operate separately from the regular work structure of the firm on a temporary basis. Members often come from different units or jobs and are asked to do work that is not normally done by the standard structure. Their charge is to recommend solutions to specific problems. They

- **TEAM** A small number of people with complementary skills who are committed to a common purpose, set of performance goals, and approach for which they hold themselves mutually accountable.

- **WORK TEAMS** Teams that make or do things like manufacture, assemble, sell, or provide service.

- **PROJECT AND DEVELOPMENT TEAMS** Teams that work on long-term projects but disband once the work is completed.

- **PARALLEL TEAMS** Teams that operate separately from the regular work structure, and exist temporarily.

TABLE 11.1	The New Team Environment	
Traditional Environment	**Team Environment**
Managers determine and plan the work.	Managers and team members jointly determine and plan the work.
Jobs are narrowly defined.	Jobs require broad skills and knowledge.
Cross-training is viewed as inefficient.	Cross-training is the norm.
Most information is "management property."	Most information is freely shared at all levels.
Training for nonmanagers focuses on technical skills.	Continuous learning requires interpersonal, administrative, and technical training for all.
Risk taking is discouraged and punished.	Measured risk taking is encouraged and supported.
People work alone.	People work together.
Rewards are based on individual performance.	Rewards are based on individual performance and contributions to team performance.
Managers determine "best methods."	Everyone works to continuously improve methods and processes.

SOURCE: From *Leading Teams* by J. Zenger and Associates. Reprinted by permission.

- **MANAGEMENT TEAMS** Teams that coordinate and give direction to the subunits under their jurisdiction and integrate work among subunits.

- **TRANSNATIONAL TEAMS** Work groups composed of multinational members whose activities span multiple countries.

- **VIRTUAL TEAMS** Teams that are physically dispersed and communicate electronically more than face-to-face.

- **TRADITIONAL WORK GROUPS** Groups that have no managerial responsibilities.

deal to acquire deposits from American Bank, a team of employees from branch management, deposit services, and information technology studied American's products to make sure Bradford was ready to offer similar services to its new customers.[18]

Management teams coordinate and give direction to the subunits under their jurisdiction and integrate work among subunits.[19] The management team is based on authority stemming from hierarchical rank and is responsible for the overall performance of the business unit. Managers responsible for different subunits form a team together, and at the top of the organization resides the executive management team that

seldom have authority to act, however. Examples include task forces and quality or safety teams formed to study a particular problem. Whenever Baltimore's Bradford Bank acquires or starts up another operation, it assembles a team of employees drawn from various divisions to smooth the transition for customers. For example, when Bradford signed a

One example of a project and development team is the pictured Omnica product development team. The 28-person team is responsible for producing medical and high-tech products for their clients faster and more efficiently than they could by any other means.

establishes strategic direction and manages the firm's overall performance.

Transnational teams are work teams composed of multinational members whose activities span multiple countries.[20] Such teams differ from other work teams not only by being multicultural but also by often being geographically dispersed, being psychologically distant, and working on highly complex projects having considerable impact on company objectives.

Transnational teams tend to be virtual teams, communicating electronically more than face-to-face, although other types of teams may operate virtually as well. A virtual team encounters difficult challenges: building trust, cohesion, and team identity, and overcoming the isolation of virtual team members.[21] Ways that managers can overcome these challenges and improve the effectiveness of virtual teams include ensuring that team members understand how they are supposed to keep in touch, setting aside time at the beginning of virtual meetings to build relationships, ensuring that all participants in meetings and on message boards have a chance to communicate, sharing meeting minutes and progress reports, and recognizing and rewarding team members' contributions.[22]

Self-managed teams empower employees

Today many different types of work teams exist, with many different labels. The terms can be confusing and sometimes are used interchangeably out of a lack of awareness of actual differences.

Virtual Teams Find the Right Balance at Smart Balance

When Smart Balance margarine first appeared on supermarket shelves in 1997, it couldn't have launched at a more opportune time. The oldest members of the Baby Boom generation were hitting age 50. American consumers in general had started to show concern about obesity and healthful living. Many were taking an interest in healthful foods like Smart Balance, a heart-healthy alternative to butter and other spreads made from a patented blend of vegetable and fruit oils proven to raise the level of "good" cholesterol.

Smart Balance Inc. is headed by Stephen Hughes, a long-time food-industry marketer whose résumé includes launching Conagra's successful Healthy Choice product line,

revitalizing Tropicana, and moving niche brands like Celestial Seasonings tea and Silk soy milk to center stage. Hughes's growth strategy for Smart Balance includes extending the brand beyond margarine, to milk, cream cheese, yogurt, sour cream, and more.

Smart Balance employs a "virtual" business model—that is, only about 70 employees are on the company payroll; the rest are independent contractors. Product development, management, and marketing are handled in-house. Nearly every other organizational function is outsourced, including manufacturing, IT, sales, and distribution.

Hiring independent contractors is one way to keep an employer's costs down. For example,

the company requires less office space when contractors work off-site. It saves money by having fewer workers with expensive benefits like health and disability insurance, and it avoids payroll costs during slow periods. Yet, a workforce with a significant population of independent contractors could face a challenge in performing like a traditional team.

For this reason, Smart Balance takes deliberate steps to cultivate a team culture. Managers are careful to treat employees and contractors as players with an equal stake in the company's success, and management looks for ways to deepen contractor relationships. The company communicates frequently and inclusively, holding all-company meetings twice a year for both

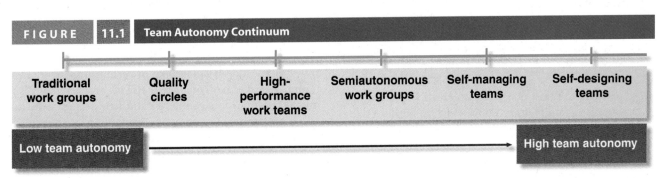

FIGURE 11.1 Team Autonomy Continuum

SOURCE: R. Banker, J. Field, R. Schroeder, and K. Sinha, "Impact of Work Teams on Manufacturing Performance: A Longitudinal Field Study," *Academy of Management Journal.* Copyright © 1996 by Academy of Management. Reproduced with permission of Academy of Management via Copyright Clearance Center.

Figure 11.1 shows the different types according to how much autonomy they have.[23] To the left, teams are more traditional with little decision-making authority, being under the control of direct supervision. To the right the teams have more autonomy, decision-making power, and self-direction. Let's define each category:

- **Traditional work groups** have no managerial responsibilities. The first-line manager plans, organizes, staffs, directs, and controls them, and other groups provide support activities, including quality control and maintenance.

- **Quality circles** are voluntary groups of people drawn from various production teams who make suggestions about quality but have no authority to make decisions or execute.

- **Semiautonomous work groups** make decisions about managing and carrying out major production activities but still get outside support for quality control and maintenance.

- **Autonomous work groups**, or *self-managing teams*, control decisions about and execution of a complete range of tasks—acquiring raw materials and performing operations, quality control, maintenance, and shipping. They are fully responsible for an entire product or an entire part of a production process.

- **Self-designing teams** do all of that and go one step further—they also have control over the design of the team. They decide themselves whom to hire, whom to fire, and what tasks the team will perform.

Movement from left to right on the continuum corresponds with more and more worker participation. Toward the right, the participation is not trivial and not merely advisory. It has real substance, going beyond suggestions to include action and impact.

permanent staff and contractors. To ensure that contractors feel a part of the culture, management shares business information and results with them, and includes them in celebrations of company accomplishments.

So far, these efforts seem to be working: Revenues in 2008 doubled to nearly $222 million, and the company expects to hit the $1 billion mark by 2014, chiefly through the introduction of new products.

 **Discussion Questions**

- Smart Balance's practice of staffing deeply through independent contractors may not work for all employers. Why do you think it has worked for Smart Balance?
- Suggest several ways that managers at Smart Balance can build cohesiveness in their "virtual" teams.

SOURCES: Company Web site, http://www.smartbalance.com, accessed June 19, 2009; Rebecca Reisner, "A Smart Balance of Staff and Contractors," *BusinessWeek*, June 16, 2009, http://www.businessweek.com; Joann S. Lublin, "Smart Balance Keeps Tight Focus on Creativity," *The Wall Street Journal*, June 8, 2009, http://online.wsj.com; Matthew Boyle, "Food's Next Billion-Dollar Brand?" *Fortune*, June 4, 2008, http://money.cnn.com; "CEO Hughes Lists 2007 Accomplishments and Reiterates Plans for Growth," *Bio-Medicine*, March 19, 2008, http://www.bio-medicine.org; and Neil A. Martin, "Next Stop: Fat City," *Barrons.com*, September 17, 2007, http://online.barrons.com.

● **SELF-MANAGED TEAMS** Autonomous work groups in which workers are trained to do all or most of the jobs in a unit, have no immediate supervisor, and make decisions previously made by first-line supervisors.

The trend today is toward **self-managed teams**, in which workers are trained to do all or most of the jobs in the unit, they have no immediate supervisor, and they make decisions previously made by first-line supervisors.[24] Self-managed teams are most often found in manufacturing. People may resist self-managed work teams, in part because they don't want so much responsibility and the change is difficult.[25] In addition, many people don't like to do performance evaluation of teammates or to fire people, and poorly managed conflict may be a particular problem in self-managed teams.[26] But when companies have introduced teams that reach the point of being truly self-managed, results have included lower costs and greater levels of team productivity, quality, and customer satisfaction.[27] Overall, semiautonomous and autonomous teams are known to improve the organization's financial and overall performance, at least in North America.[28]

Such results have inspired U.S.-based multinational firms to use self-managed teams in their foreign facilities. For example, Goodyear Tire & Rubber initiated self-managed work teams in Europe, Latin America, and Asia; Sara Lee in Puerto Rico and Mexico; and Texas Instruments in Malaysia. These companies are learning—and other companies should be forewarned—of the different ways different cultures might respond to self-managed teams, and to customize implementation according to cultural values.[29]

(L)(O) **3** WHAT YOU NEED TO KNOW . . .
How do groups become teams?

HOW GROUPS BECOME REAL TEAMS

As a manager, you will want your group to become an effective team. To accomplish this, you need to understand how groups can become true teams and why groups sometimes fail to become teams. Groups become true teams through basic group activities, the passage of time, and team development activities.

Group activities shift as the group matures

Assume you are the leader of a newly formed group—actually a bunch of people. What will you face as you attempt to develop your group into a high-performing team? If groups are to develop successfully, they will engage in various activities, including these broad categories:[30]

➤ *Forming*—Group members attempt to lay the ground rules for what types of behavior are acceptable.

- *Storming*—Hostilities and conflict arise, and people jockey for positions of power and status.
- *Norming*—Group members agree on their shared goals, and norms and closer relationships develop.
- *Performing*—The group channels its energies into performing its tasks.

Groups that deteriorate move to a *declining* stage, and temporary groups add an *adjourning* or terminating stage. Groups terminate when they complete their task or when they disband due to failure or loss of interest and new groups form, as the cycle continues.

Virtual teams also go through these stages of group development.[31] The forming stage is characterized by unbridled optimism: "I believe we have a great team and will work well together. We all understand the importance of the project and intend to take it seriously." Optimism turns into reality shock in the storming stage: "No one has taken a leadership role. We have not made the project the priority that it deserves." The norming stage comes at about the halfway point in the project life cycle, in which people refocus and recommit: "You must make firm commitments to a specific time schedule." The performing stage is the dash to the finish, as teammates show the discipline needed to meet the deadline.

Over time, groups enter critical periods

A key aspect of group development is the passage of time. Groups pass through critical periods, or times when they are particularly open to formative experiences.[32] The first such critical period is in the forming stage, at the first meeting, when rules and roles are established that set long-lasting precedents. A second critical period is the midway point between the initial meeting and a deadline (for instance, completing a project or making a presentation). At this point, the group has enough experience to understand its work; it comes to realize that time is becoming a scarce resource and the team must "get on with it"; and enough time remains to change its approach if necessary.

In the initial meeting, the group should establish desired norms, roles, and other determinants of effectiveness, which are discussed throughout this chapter. At the second critical period (the midpoint), groups should renew or open lines of communication with outside constituencies. The group can use fresh information from its external environment to revise its approach to performing its task and ensure that it meets the needs of customers and clients. Without these activities, groups may get off on the wrong foot from the beginning, and members may never revise their behavior in the appropriate direction.[33]

Some groups develop into teams

As a manager or group member, you should expect the group to engage in all the activities just discussed at various times. But groups are not always successful. They do not always engage in the developmental activities that turn them into effective, high-performing teams.

A useful developmental sequence is depicted in Figure 11.2. The figure shows the various activities as the leadership of the group moves from traditional supervision, through a more participative approach, to true team leadership.[34]

It is important to understand a couple of points about this model. Groups do not necessarily keep progressing from one "stage" to the next; they may remain permanently in the supervisory level or become more participative but never make it to true team leadership. As a result, progress on these dimensions must be a conscious goal of the leader and the members, and all should strive to meet these goals. Your group can meet these goals—and become a true team—by engaging in the activities in the figure.

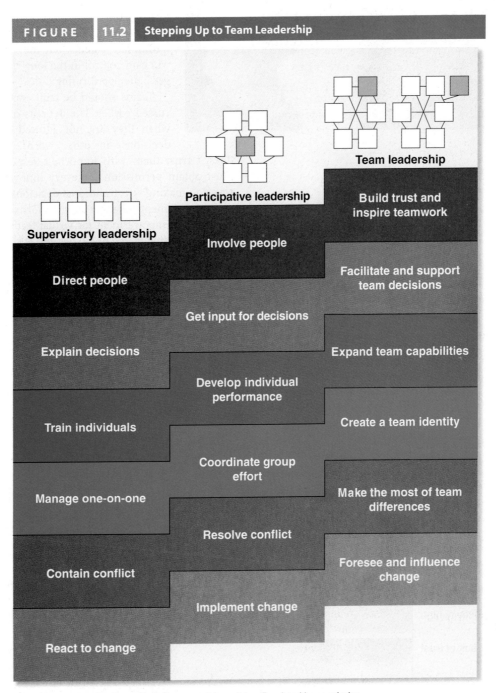

FIGURE 11.2 Stepping Up to Team Leadership

SOURCE: From *Leading Teams* by J. Zenger and Associates. Reprinted by permission.

It is not easy to build high-performance teams. *Teams* is often just a word used by management to describe merely putting people into groups. "Teams" sometimes are launched with little or no training or support systems. For example, both managers and group members need new skills to make a group work. These skills include learning the art of diplomacy, tackling "people issues" head on, and walking the fine line between encouraging autonomy and rewarding team innovations without letting the team get too independent and out of control.[37] Giving up some control is difficult for managers from traditional systems, but they have to realize they will gain control in the long run by creating stronger, better-performing units.

Teams should be truly empowered, as we discussed earlier. The benefits of teams are reduced when they are not allowed to make important decisions—in other words, when management doesn't trust them with important responsibilities. If teams must obtain permission for every innovative idea, they will revert to making safe, traditional decisions.[38]

Empowerment enhances team performance even among virtual teams. Empowerment for virtual teams includes thorough training in using the technologies and strong technical support from management. Some virtual teams have periodic face-to-face interactions, which help performance; empowerment is particularly helpful for virtual teams that don't often meet face-to-face.[39]

Failure lies in not knowing and doing what makes teams successful. To be successful, you must apply clear thinking and appropriate practices.[40] That is what the rest of the chapter is about.

(L)(O) 4 WHAT YOU NEED TO KNOW . . .
Why do groups sometimes fail?

Why do groups sometimes fail?

Team building does not necessarily progress smoothly through such a sequence, culminating in a well-oiled team and superb performance.[35] Some groups never do work out. Such groups can be frustrating for managers and members, who may feel teams are a waste of time and that the difficulties outweigh the benefits.

(L)(O) 5 WHAT YOU NEED TO KNOW . . .
How is an effective team built?

BUILDING EFFECTIVE TEAMS

All the considerations just described form the building blocks of an effective work team. But what does it really mean for a team to be effective? What, precisely, can a manager do to design a truly effective team? Team effectiveness is defined by three criteria:[41]

1. The *productive output* of the team meets or exceeds the standards of

Building a team can be challenging.[36]

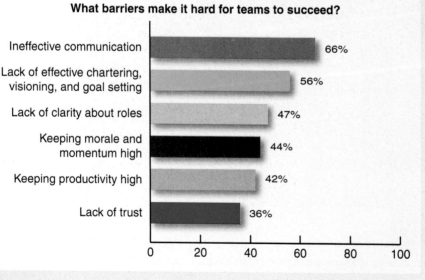

What barriers make it hard for teams to succeed?

Barrier	Percentage
Ineffective communication	66%
Lack of effective chartering, visioning, and goal setting	56%
Lack of clarity about roles	47%
Keeping morale and momentum high	44%
Keeping productivity high	42%
Lack of trust	36%

quantity and quality; the team's output is acceptable to the customers, inside or outside the organization, who receive the team's goods or services. At Lockheed Martin, Clarence L. "Kelly" Johnson's group designed, built, and flew the first U.S. tactical jet fighter, XP80, in 143 days.[42] A team of doctors, nurses, and administrators at the University of Texas's M. D. Anderson Cancer Center defined goals for improving patient care, identified changes that would meet the goals, and persuaded the center's physicians to adopt the changes. As a result, performance at the center exceeded the team's goals for increasing visits and decreasing the time that elapses between a patient's first visit and his or her surgery.[43]

2. Team members realize *satisfaction* of their personal needs. Johnson gave his Lockheed teams the freedom to innovate and stretch their skills. Team members were enthusiastic and realized great pride and satisfaction in their work.

3. Team members remain *committed* to working together again; that is, the group doesn't burn out and disintegrate after a grueling project. Looking back, the members are glad they were involved. In other words, effective teams remain viable and have good prospects for repeated success in the future.[44]

For help in developing these qualities, teams may use team-building activities or work with an outside coach. Team building usually involves activities focused on relationships among team members. Whether these activities are as simple as a group discussion or as elaborate as a weekend retreat with physical challenges, the team-building event should be followed by an opportunity for participants to evaluate what they learned and how they will apply those lessons at work.[45] Coaching a team should be different from coaching individual team members because it focuses on how the group as a whole operates and how it can improve interactions so that it will accomplish its goals.[46] The process doesn't have the confidentiality of one-on-one coaching, and the coach has to pace the process so that everyone is included. Team coaching addresses issues such as what the team is focused on, how it sets goals, and how it can improve communication and decision making. Ideally, the coaching helps a team develop enough that it can begin to coach itself.

Based on years of studying team performance, Harvard professor Richard Hackman has identified principles of team effectiveness, including this simple rule: teams need to properly define their membership. However, many don't, perhaps because people hate to exclude someone. When a team problem came to light at a financial services company, the chief executive determined that the chief financial officer was unable to collaborate effectively with others on the executive team. So the CEO asked the financial executive to skip the "boring" team meetings, keeping their communications one-on-one. Without the CFO, the executive team began to function much better.

Another barrier: People tend to focus too much on harmony, assuming that when team members feel good about their participation, the team is effective. Actually, effectiveness comes first: team members feel satisfied when their team works effectively.

In a study of symphony orchestras, satisfaction came from how the musicians felt *after* a performance.

A third mistake Hackman encounters is the assumption that team members can be together too long, to the point that the team runs out of ideas. But aside from research and development teams, which should periodically add new members, Hackman has found that a more frequent problem is the opposite: team members haven't been together long enough to learn to work well together. Airplane cockpit crews, for example, perform much better when they have flown together previously.[47]

Effective teams focus on performance

The key element of effective teamwork is commitment to a common purpose.[48] The best teams are those that have been given an important performance challenge by management and then have reached a common understanding and appreciation of their purpose. Without such understanding and commitment, a group will be just a bunch of individuals.

The best teams also work hard at developing a common understanding of how they will work together to achieve their purpose.[49] They discuss and agree on such details as how tasks and roles will be allocated and how team members will make decisions. The team should develop norms for examining its performance strategies and be amenable to changing them when appropriate. For example, work teams usually standardize at least some processes, but they should be willing to try creative new ideas if the situation calls for them.[50] With a clear, strong, motivating purpose and effective performance strategies, people will pull together into a powerful force that has a chance to achieve extraordinary things.

The team's general purpose should be translated into specific, measurable performance goals.[51] You already learned about how goals motivate individual performance. Performance can be defined by collective end products, instead of an accumulation of individual products.[52] Team-based performance goals help define and distinguish the team's product, encourage communication within the team, energize and motivate team members, provide feedback on progress, signal team victories (and defeats), and ensure that the team focuses clearly on results. Teams with both difficult goals and specific incentives to attain them achieve the highest performance levels.[53]

The best team-based measurement systems inform top management of the team's level of performance and help the team understand its own processes and gauge its own progress. Ideally, the team plays the lead role in designing its own measurement system. This responsibility is a great indicator of whether the team is truly empowered.[54]

Teams, like individuals, need feedback on their performance. Feedback from customers is especially crucial. Some customers for the team's products are inside the organization. Teams should be responsible for satisfying them and should be given or should seek performance feedback. Better yet, wherever possible, teams should interact directly with external customers who make the ultimate buying decisions about their goods and services. External customers typically provide the most honest, and most crucial and useful, performance feedback.[55]

To ensure the safety of themselves and each other, Boots & Coots firefighters need to maintain trust and communicate under some of the toughest circumstances.

Managers motivate effective teamwork

Sometimes individuals work less hard and are less productive when they are members of a group. Such social loafing occurs when individuals believe that their contributions are not important, others will do the work for them, their lack of effort will go undetected, or they will be the lone sucker if they work hard but others don't. Perhaps you have seen social loafing in some of your student teams.[56] Conversely, sometimes individuals work harder when they are members of a group than when they are working alone. This social facilitation effect occurs because individuals usually are more motivated in the presence of others, are concerned with what others think of them, and want to maintain a positive self-image.

A social facilitation effect is maintained—and a social loafing effect can be avoided—under the following conditions:[57]

- Group members know each other.
- They can observe and communicate with one another.
- Clear performance goals exist.
- The task is meaningful to the people working on it.
- Group members believe that their efforts matter and that others will not take advantage of them.
- The culture supports teamwork.

Under ideal circumstances, everyone works hard, contributes in concrete ways to the team's work, and is accountable to other team members. Accountability to one another, rather than just to "the boss," is an essential aspect of good teamwork. Accountability inspires mutual commitment and trust.[58] Trust in your teammates—and their trust in you—may be the ultimate key to effectiveness.

Team effort is also generated by designing the team's task to be motivating. Techniques for creating motivating tasks appear in the guidelines for job enrichment discussed in Chapter 10. Tasks are motivating when they use a variety of member skills and provide high task variety, identity, significance, autonomy, and performance feedback.

Ultimately, teamwork is motivated by tying rewards to team performance.[59] If team performance can be measured validly, team-based rewards can be given accordingly. It is not easy to move from a system of rewards based on individual performance to one based on team performance and cooperation. It also may not be appropriate, unless people are truly interdependent and must collaborate to attain true team goals.[60] Team-based rewards are often combined with regular salaries and rewards based on individual performance. At Nucor, where production employees work in teams of 12 to 20, team members earn bonuses based on the tons of steel shipped each week. To ensure high quality, the amount of any bad product is subtracted from total shipments—and if defective products reach the customer, the amount subtracted is multiplied by 3. On average, the amount of the team bonuses equals 170 to 180 percent of the team members' base salary. This type of motivation works because Nucor teams are empowered to make decisions aimed at improving their productivity, and the company actively shares performance data with its employees.[61]

If team performance is difficult to measure validly, then desired behaviors, activities, and processes that indicate good teamwork can be rewarded. Individuals within teams can be given differential rewards based on teamwork indicated by active participation, cooperation, leadership, and other contributions to the team.

If team members are to be rewarded differentially, such decisions are better *not* left only to the boss.[62] They should be made by the team itself, through peer ratings or multirater evaluation systems. Why? Team members are in a better position to observe, know, and make valid reward allocations. Finally, the more teams the organization has, and the more a full team orientation exists, the more valid and effective it will be to distribute rewards via gainsharing and other organizationwide incentives.

Effective teams have skilled members

Team members should be selected and trained so that they become effective contributors to the team. The teams themselves often hire their new members.[63] MillerCoors Brewing Company and Eastman Chemical teams select members based on the results of tests designed to predict how well they will contribute to team success in an empowered environment. At Texas

Instruments, Human Resources screens applicants, and then team members interview them and make selection decisions.

Generally, the skills required by teams include technical or functional expertise, problem-solving and decision-making skills, and interpersonal skills. Some managers and teams mistakenly overemphasize some skills, particularly technical or functional ones, and underemphasize the others. In fact, social skills can be critical to team functioning; one worker with a persistently negative attitude—for example, someone who bullies or constantly complains—can and often does put an entire team into a downward spiral.[64] It is vitally important that all three types of skills be represented, and developed, among team members.

practices, drug and alcohol abuse, and employee theft, or they may not care about these issues (or may even condone such practices). Health consciousness is the norm among executives at some companies, but smoking is the norm at tobacco companies. Some groups have norms of distrust and of being closed toward one another, but as you might guess,

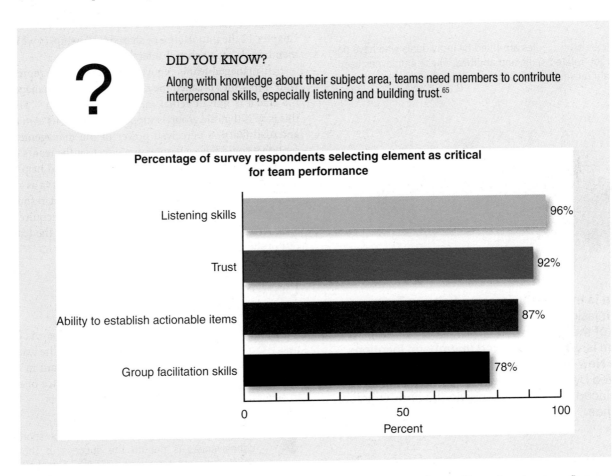

DID YOU KNOW?

Along with knowledge about their subject area, teams need members to contribute interpersonal skills, especially listening and building trust.[65]

Percentage of survey respondents selecting element as critical for team performance

Element	Percent
Listening skills	96%
Trust	92%
Ability to establish actionable items	87%
Group facilitation skills	78%

Norms shape team behavior

Norms are shared beliefs about how people should think and behave. For example, some people like to keep information and knowledge to themselves, but teams should try to establish a norm of knowledge sharing because it can improve team performance.[66] From the organization's standpoint, norms can be positive or negative. In some teams, everyone works hard; in other groups, employees are opposed to management and do as little work as possible. Some groups develop norms of taking risks, others of being conservative.[67] A norm could dictate that employees speak of the company either favorably or critically. Team members may show concern about poor safety

norms of trust and open discussion about conflict can improve group performance.[68]

A professor described his consulting experiences at two companies that exhibited different norms in their management teams.[69] At Federal Express Corporation, a young manager interrupted the professor's talk by proclaiming that a recent decision by top management ran counter to the professor's point about corporate planning. He was challenging top management to defend its decision. A hot debate ensued, and after an hour everyone went to lunch without a trace of hard feelings. But at another corporation, the professor opened a meeting by asking a group of top managers to describe the company's culture. There was silence. He asked again. More silence. Then someone passed him an unsigned note that read, "Dummy, can't you see that we can't speak our minds? Ask for the input anonymously, in writing." As you can see, norms are important, and can vary greatly from one group to another.

Team members must fill important roles

Roles are different sets of expectations for how different individuals should behave. Although norms apply generally to all team members, different roles exist for different members within the norm structure.

Two important sets of roles must be performed:[70]

1. Task specialist roles are filled by individuals who have particular job-related skills and abilities. These employees keep the team moving toward accomplishment of the objectives.

Pictured is the Cassini Imaging Science Team, whose mission is to guide the cameras that take photos of the outer reaches of space. Though the team is widely dispersed (members' locations include New York, California, and Belgium), they are united by a shared sense of purpose and a high value placed on scientific knowledge and technical excellence.

2. Team maintenance specialists develop and maintain harmony within the team. They boost morale, give support, provide humor, soothe hurt feelings, and generally exhibit a concern with members' well-being.

Note the similarity between these roles and the important task performance and group maintenance leadership behaviors you learned about in Chapter 9. As suggested there, some of these roles will be more important than others at different times and under different circumstances. But these behaviors need not be carried out only by one or two leaders; any member of the team can assume them at any time. Both types of roles can be performed by different individuals to maintain an effectively functioning work team.

What roles should leaders perform? Superior team leaders are better at several things:[71]

- *Relating*—exhibiting social and political awareness, caring for team members, and building trust
- *Scouting*—seeking information from managers, peers, and specialists, and investigating problems systematically
- *Persuading*—influencing team members, as well as obtaining external support for teams
- *Empowering*—delegating authority, being flexible regarding team decisions, and coaching

Leaders also should roll up their sleeves and do real work to accomplish team goals, not just supervise.[72] Finally, recall from Chapter 12 the importance of shared leadership, in which group members rotate or share leadership roles.[73]

Self-managed teams report to a management representative who sometimes is called the *coach*. In true self-managed teams, the coach is not an actual member of the team.[74] The reason this is so is that the group is supposed to make its own decisions and also that the perceived power of the management representative could have a dampening effect on the team's openness and autonomy. The role of the coach, then, is to help the team understand its role in the organization and to serve as a resource for the team. The coach can provide information, resources, and insight that team members do not or cannot acquire on their own. And the coach should be an advocate for the team in the rest of the organization.

Cohesiveness affects team performance

One of the most important properties of a team is cohesiveness.[75] Cohesiveness refers to how attractive the team is to its members, how motivated members are to remain in the team, and the degree to which team members influence one another. In general, it refers to how tightly knit the team is.

▶ Besides contributing to the success of sports teams, cohesiveness is behind the success of the team of sports commentators on ESPN's *Baseball Tonight*. Sports reporters and commentators don't just call games as they see them, on the fly. Instead, they do a lot of homework, planning the content of each show that viewers see. During pregame meetings, the *Baseball Tonight* analysts talk about the different games that will be played that day or evening, including the pitching matchups, player statistics, overall team performances, and interesting points they might discuss during the game. Then, as they watch the games unfold, the commentators together make note of events to pursue in more depth later. Making a broadcast look effortless and spontaneous takes a lot of give-and-take behind the scenes. And for members of this entertainment team, it's also highly satisfying. John Kruk, a former All-Star outfielder and first baseman, as well as an analyst with ESPN's show, says, "I get to manage every night, I get to be a

● **ROLES** Different sets of expectations for how different individuals should behave.

● **TASK SPECIALIST** An individual who has more advanced job-related skills and abilities than other group members possess.

● **TEAM MAINTENANCE SPECIALIST** Individual who develops and maintains team harmony.

● **COHESIVENESS** The degree to which a group is attractive to its members, members are motivated to remain in the group, and members influence one another.

pitching coach every night, I get to be a hitting coach every night. At the end of the day, I haven't lost one game. I'm undefeated."[76]

the importance of cohesiveness Cohesiveness is important for two primary reasons:

1. It contributes to *member satisfaction*. In a cohesive team, members communicate and get along well with one another. They feel good about being part of the team. Even if their jobs are unfulfilling or the organization is oppressive, people gain some satisfaction from enjoying their coworkers.

2. It has a major impact on *performance*.[77] A recent study of manufacturing teams led to a conclusion that performance improvements in both quality and productivity occurred in the most cohesive unit, whereas conflict within another team prevented any quality or productivity improvements.[78] Sports fans read about this all the time. When teams are winning, players talk about the team being close, getting along well, and knowing one another's games. In contrast, losing is attributed to infighting and divisiveness.

But this interpretation is simplistic; exceptions to this intuitive relationship occur. Tightly knit work groups can also be disruptive to the organization, such as when they sabotage the assembly line, get their boss fired, or enforce low performance norms. When does high cohesiveness lead to good performance, and when does it result in poor performance? The ultimate outcome depends on two things:

1. The task
2. Performance norms

the task If the task is to make a decision or solve a problem, cohesiveness can lead to poor performance. Groupthink occurs when a tightly knit group is so cooperative that agreeing with one another's opinions and refraining from criticizing others' ideas become norms. For a cohesive group to make good decisions, it should establish a norm of constructive disagreement. This type of debating is important for groups up to the level of boards of directors.[79] In top-management teams it has been shown to improve the financial performance of companies.[80]

The effect of cohesiveness on performance, in contrast, can be positive, particularly if the task is to produce some tangible output. In day-to-day work groups for which decision making is not the primary task,

cohesiveness can enhance performance. But that depends on the group's performance norms.[81]

performance norms Some groups are better than others at ensuring that their members behave the way the group prefers. Cohesive groups are more effective than noncohesive groups at norm enforcement. But the next question is: do they have norms of high or low performance?

As Figure 11.3 shows, the highest performance occurs when a cohesive team has high-performance norms. But if a highly cohesive group has low-performance norms, that group will have the worst performance. In the group's eyes, it will have succeeded in achieving its goal of poor performance. Noncohesive groups with high-performance norms can be effective from the company's standpoint. However, they won't be as productive as they would be if they were more cohesive. Noncohesive groups with low-performance norms perform poorly, but they will not ruin things for management as effectively as cohesive groups with low-performance norms.

Managers can build cohesiveness and high-performance norms

As Figure 11.3 suggests, managers should build teams that are cohesive and have high-performance norms. The following actions can help create such teams:[82]

- *Recruit members with similar attitudes, values, and backgrounds.* Similar individuals are more likely to get along with one another. Don't do this, though, if the team's task requires heterogeneous skills and inputs—a homogeneous committee or board might make poor decisions, because it will lack different information and viewpoints and may succumb to groupthink. Recent research has shown that educational

| FIGURE 11.3 | **Cohesiveness, Performance Norms, and Group Performance** |

Performance norms

		Low	High
Cohesiveness	**High**	High goal attainment (group's perspective) and lowest task performance (management's perspective)	High goal attainment and task performance
	Low	Poor goal attainment and task performance	Moderate goal attainment and task performance

diversity and national diversity provide more benefits than limitations to groups' use and application of information.[83]

- *Maintain high entrance and socialization standards.* Teams and organizations that are difficult to get into have more prestige. Individuals who survive a difficult interview, selection, or training process will be proud of their accomplishment and feel more attachment to the team.

- *Keep the team small* (but large enough to get the job done). The larger the group, the less important members may feel. Small teams make individuals feel like large contributors.

- *Help the team succeed, and publicize its successes.* You read about empowerment in the preceding chapter; you can empower teams as well as individuals.[84] Be a path-goal leader who facilitates success; the experience of winning brings teams closer together. Then, if you inform superiors of your team's successes, members will believe they are part of an important, prestigious unit. Teams that get into a good performance track continue to perform well as time goes on, but groups that don't often enter a downward spiral in which problems compound over time.[85]

Self-managed teams can have a positive impact on productivity. But people often resist self-managed teams, in part because they don't want to accept so much responsibility and it is difficult for them to adjust to the change in the decision-making process.

- *Be a participative leader.* Participation in decisions gets team members more involved with one another and striving toward goal accomplishment. Too much autocratic decision making from above can alienate the group from management.

- *Present a challenge from outside the team.* Competition with other groups makes team members band together to defeat the enemy (witness what happens to school spirit before the big game against an archrival). Some of the greatest teams in business and in science have been completely focused on winning a competition.[86] But don't *you* become the outside threat. If team members dislike you as a boss, they will become more cohesive—but their performance norms will be against you, not with you.

- *Tie rewards to team performance.* To a large degree, teams are motivated just as individuals are: they do the activities that are rewarded. Make sure that high-performing teams get the rewards they deserve and that poorly performing groups get fewer rewards. You read about this earlier. Bear in mind that not just monetary rewards but also recognition for good work are powerful motivators. Recognize and celebrate team accomplishments. The team will become more cohesive and perform better to reap more rewards. Performance goals will be high, the organization will benefit from higher team motivation and productivity, and team members' individual needs will be better satisfied. Ideally, membership on a high-performing team that is recognized as such throughout the organization will become a badge of honor.[87]

But keep in mind that strong cohesiveness encouraging "agreeableness" can be dysfunctional. For problem solving and decision making, the team should establish norms promoting an open, constructive atmosphere including honest disagreement over issues without personal conflict and animosity.[88]

L O 6 **WHAT YOU NEED TO KNOW . . .**
What are the methods for managing a team's relationships with other teams?

MANAGING LATERAL RELATIONSHIPS

Teams do not function in a vacuum; they are interdependent with other teams. For example, at Texas Instruments, teams are responsible for interfacing with other teams to eliminate production bottlenecks and implement new processes and also for working with suppliers on quality issues.[89] Thus, some activities crucial to the team are those that entail dealing with people *outside* the group.

Some team members should manage outward

Several vital roles link teams to their external environments, that is, to other individuals and groups inside and outside the organization. A specific type of role that spans team boundaries is the **gatekeeper**, a team member who stays abreast of current information in scientific and other fields and informs the group of important developments. Information useful to the group can also include information about resources, trends, and political support throughout the corporation or the industry.[90]

The team's strategy dictates the team's mix of internally versus externally focused roles and the ways the mix changes over time. There are several general team strategies:[91]

- The **informing** strategy entails making decisions with the team and then telling outsiders of the team's intentions.

- **Parading** means the team's strategy is to simultaneously emphasize internal team building and achieve external visibility.

GATEKEEPER A team member who keeps abreast of current developments and provides the team with relevant information.

INFORMING A team strategy that entails making decisions with the team and then informing outsiders of its intentions.

PARADING A team strategy that entails simultaneously emphasizing internal team building and achieving external visibility.

PROBING A team strategy that requires team members to interact frequently with outsiders, diagnose their needs, and experiment with solutions.

- **Probing** involves a focus on external relations. This strategy requires team members to interact frequently with outsiders; diagnose the needs of customers, clients, and higher-ups; and experiment with solutions before taking action.

The balance between an internal and external strategic focus and between internal and external roles depends on how much the team needs information, support, and resources from outside. When teams have a high degree of dependence on outsiders, probing is the best strategy. Parading teams perform at an intermediate level, and informing teams are likely to fail. They are too isolated from the outside groups on which they depend.

Informing or parading strategies may be more effective for teams that are less dependent on outside groups, for example, established teams working on routine tasks in stable external environments. But for most important work teams—task forces, new-product teams, and strategic decision-making teams tackling unstructured problems in a rapidly changing external environment—effective performance in roles that involve interfacing with the outside will be vital.

Some relationships help teams coordinate with others in the organization

Managing relationships with other groups and teams means engaging in a dynamic give-and-take that ensures proper coordination throughout the management system. To many managers, this process often seems like a free-for-all. To help understand the process and make it more productive, we can identify and examine the different types of lateral role relationships and take a strategic approach to building constructive relationships.

Different teams, like different individuals, have roles to perform. As teams carry out their roles, several distinct patterns of working relationships develop:[92]

- *Work-flow relationships* emerge as materials are passed from one group to another. A group commonly receives work from one unit, processes it, and sends it to the next unit in the process. Your group, then, will come before some groups and after others in the process.

- *Service relationships* exist when top management centralizes an activity to which a large number of other units must gain access. Common examples are technology services, libraries, and clerical staff. Such units must assist other people to help them accomplish their goals.

- *Advisory relationships* are created when teams with problems call on centralized sources of expert knowledge. For

TIP

Remember that teams don't produce results in a vacuum; they perform best by collaborating with other teams.

example, staff members in the human resources or legal department advise work teams.

- *Audit relationships* develop when people not directly in the chain of command evaluate the methods and performances of other teams. Financial auditors check the books, and technical auditors assess the methods and technical quality of the work.

- *Stabilization relationships* involve auditing before the fact. In other words, teams sometimes must obtain clearance from others—for example, for large purchases—before they act.

- *Liaison relationships* involve intermediaries between teams. Managers often are called on to mediate conflict between two organizational units. Public relations people, sales managers, purchasing agents, and others who work across organizational boundaries serve in liaison roles as they maintain communications between the organization and the outside world.

Teams should assess each working relationship with another unit by asking basic questions: "From whom do we receive, and to whom do we send work? What permissions do we control, and to whom must we go for authorizations?" In this way, teams can better understand whom to contact and when, where, why, and how to do so. Coordination throughout the working system improves, problems are avoided or short-circuited before they get too serious, and performance improves.[93]

L O 7 WHAT YOU NEED TO KNOW . . .
Can you identify ways to manage conflict?

Conflicts arise both within and among teams

The complex maze of interdependencies throughout organizations provides many opportunities for conflict to arise among groups and teams. Some conflict can be constructive for the organization. Typically, conflict can foster creativity when it is about ideas, rather than personalities. In contrast, at a nonprofit organization, team members were committed to maintaining harmony during meetings, but their unresolved differences spilled over into nasty remarks outside of the office.[94]

Many factors cause great potential for destructive conflict: the sheer number and variety of contacts, ambiguities in jurisdiction and responsibility, differences in goals, intergroup competition for scarce resources, different perspectives held by members of different units, varying time horizons in which some units attend to long-term considerations and others focus on short-term needs, and others. Tensions and anxieties are likely to arise in teams that are demographically diverse, include members from different parts of the organization, or are composed of contrasting personalities. Both demographic and cross-functional heterogeneity initially lead to problems such as stress, lower cooperation, and lower cohesiveness.[95]

 As chief executive of Global Adjustments, a firm specializing in relocations and cross-cultural issues, Ranjini Manian sees firsthand some of the challenges that arise in multicultural teams. One challenge that Manian has often observed involves how people from different cultures cope with uncertainty. She finds that Europeans and North Americans tend to try minimizing uncertainty through rules, plans, and schedules, while her Indian colleagues are more likely to focus on adapting to surprises as they occur. The apparently more relaxed approach of the latter group can frustrate Western colleagues, who may interpret that behavior as a lack of commitment to goals. And when an Indian-style belief that uncertainty is inevitable leads to vague or incomplete plans, Western businesspeople tend to view those plans as unprofessional.

The solution for such differences, in Manian's view, is to learn about, respect, and adapt to team members' cultural practices. In the case of coping with uncertainty, Manian appreciates the value of careful planning but sees virtue in balancing this skill with flexibility and calm in the face of unexpected problems or opportunities. When team members can do both, their team will be both forward-thinking and agile.[96]

Over time and with communication, diverse groups actually tend to become more cooperative and perform better than do homogeneous groups. Norms of cooperation can improve performance, as does the fact that cross-functional teams engage in more external communication with more areas of the organization.[97]

How should you react to conflict?

Teams inevitably face conflicts and must decide how to manage them. The aim should be to make the conflict productive, that is, to make those involved believe they have benefited rather than lost from the conflict.[98] People believe they have benefited from a conflict when they see the following outcomes:

- A new solution is implemented, the problem is solved, and it is unlikely to emerge again.

- Work relationships have been strengthened, and people believe they can work together productively in the future.

People handle conflict in different ways. You have your own style; others'

styles may be similar or may differ. Their styles depend in part on their country's cultural norms. For example, the Chinese are more concerned with collective than with individual interests, and they are more likely than managers in the United States to turn to higher authorities to make decisions rather than resolve conflicts themselves.[99] But culture aside, any team or individual has several options regarding how they deal with conflicts.[100] These personal styles of dealing with conflict, shown in Figure 11.4, are distinguished based on how much people strive to satisfy their own concerns (the assertiveness dimension) and how much they focus on satisfying the other party's concerns (the cooperation dimension).

For example, a common reaction to conflict is avoidance. In this situation, people do nothing to satisfy themselves or others. They either ignore the problem by doing nothing at all or address it by merely smoothing over or deemphasizing the disagreement. This, of course, fails to solve the problem or clear the air. When Paul Forti was a middle manager in a management consulting firm, he was passed over for a promotion, and the organization brought in an outsider who was at first too busy to discuss his disappointment and future role in the firm. He handled the situation with avoidance, and as a result, their working relationship suffered for weeks.[101]

Accommodation means cooperating on behalf of the other party but not being assertive about one's own interests. Compromise involves moderate attention to both parties' concerns, being neither highly cooperative nor highly assertive. This style results in satisficing but not optimizing solutions. Competing is a strong response in which people focus strictly on their own wishes and are unwilling to recognize the other person's concerns. Finally, collaboration emphasizes both cooperation and assertiveness. The goal is to maximize satisfaction for both parties. Collaboration changed Paul Forti's relationship with his boss at the consulting firm. The new approach literally started

FIGURE 11.4 Conflict Management Strategies

SOURCE: K. Thomas, "Conflict and Conflict Management." In *Handbook of Industrial and Organizational Psychology*, ed. M. D. Dunnette. Copyright © 1976. Reprinted by permission of the editor.

by accident, when the senior manager slipped on some ice, Forti came to her aid, and she commented that she would like to get to know him better. Over lunch, she expressed her respect for Forti, and they developed a better working relationship in which she gave him interesting assignments and made sure clients knew about his expertise. Thus, although Forti hadn't gotten the promotion, he did get many opportunities to develop his career.[102]

Imagine that you and a friend want to go to a movie together, and you have different movies in mind. If he insists that you go to his movie, he is showing the competing style. If you agree, even though you prefer another movie, you are accommodating. If one of you mentions a third movie that neither of you is excited about but both of you are willing to live with, you are compromising. If you realize you don't know all the options, do some research, and find another movie that you're both enthusiastic about, you are collaborating.

Different approaches are necessary at different times.[103] For example, competing can be necessary when cutting costs or dealing with other scarce resources. Compromise may be useful when people are under time pressure, when they need to achieve a temporary solution, or when collaboration fails. People should accommodate when they learn they are wrong or to minimize loss when they are outmatched. Even avoiding may be appropriate if the issue is trivial or resolving the conflict should be someone else's responsibility.

But when the conflict concerns important issues, when both sets of concerns are valid and important, when a creative solution is needed, and when commitment to the solution is vital to implementation, collaboration is the ideal approach. Collaboration can be achieved by airing feelings and opinions, addressing all concerns, and avoiding goal displacement by not letting personal attacks interfere with problem solving. An important technique is to invoke **superordinate goals**—higher-level organizational goals toward which everyone should be striving and that ultimately need to take precedence over personal or unit preferences.[104] Collaboration offers the best chance of reaching mutually satisfactory solutions based on the ideas and interests of all parties, and of maintaining and strengthening work relationships.

That Was THEN . . .

In days past, workers may not have been called on to collaborate for teamwork—except maybe at a company outing.

This Is NOW . . .

WHOLE FOODS MARKET

Teams are now the backbone of workplaces. Whole Foods Market operates through decentralized teamwork. Store departments, such as produce, prepared food, and bakery, have team leaders and set their own performance goals.

Mediating can help resolve a conflict

Managers spend a lot of time trying to resolve conflict between *other* people. You already may have served as a **mediator**, a "third party" intervening to help settle a conflict between other people. Third-party intervention, done well, can improve working relationships and help the parties improve their own conflict-management, communication, and problem-solving skills.[105]

Some insight comes from a study of human resource (HR) managers and the conflicts with which they deal.[106] HR managers encounter every type of conflict imaginable: interpersonal difficulties from minor irritations to jealousy to fights; operations issues, including union issues, work assignments, overtime, and sick leave; discipline over infractions ranging from drug use and theft to sleeping on the job; sexual harassment and racial bias; pay and promotion issues; and feuds or strategic conflicts among divisions or individuals at the highest organizational levels.

In the study, the HR managers successfully settled most of the disputes. These managers typically follow a four-stage strategy:

1. They *investigate* by interviewing the disputants and others and gathering more information. While talking with the disputants, they seek both parties' perspectives, remaining as neutral as possible. The discussion should stay issue-oriented, not personal.

2. They *decide* how to resolve the dispute, often in conjunction with the disputants' bosses. In preparing to decide what to do, blame should not be assigned prematurely; at this point they should be exploring solutions.

3. They *take action* by explaining their decisions and the reasoning, and advise or train the disputants to avoid future incidents.

4. They *follow up* by making sure everyone understands the solution, documenting the conflict and the resolution, and monitoring the results by checking back with the disputants and their bosses.

Throughout, the objectives of the HR people are to be fully informed so that they understand the conflict; to be active and assertive in trying to resolve it; to be as objective, neutral, and impartial as humanly possible; and to be flexible by modifying their approaches according to the situation.

Here are some other recommendations for more effective conflict management.[108] Don't allow dysfunctional conflict to build, or hope or assume that it will go away. Address it before it escalates. Try to resolve it, and if the first efforts don't work, try others. Even if disputants are not happy with your decisions, there are benefits to providing fair treatment, making a good-faith effort, and giving them a voice in the proceedings. Remember, too, that you may be able to ask HR specialists to help with difficult conflicts.

Conflicts can arise for any team—the trick is to make them productive. This ad promotes the American Arbitration Association's mission to train professionals on how to effectively minimize and manage conflict— "before the mud starts flying."

Conflict isn't always face-to-face

When teams are geographically dispersed, as is often the case for virtual teams, team members tend to experience more conflict and less trust.[109] Conflict management affects the success of virtual teams.[110] In a recent study, avoidance hurt performance.

Accommodation—conceding to others just to maintain harmony rather than assertively attempting to negotiate integrative solutions—had no effect on performance. Collaboration had a positive effect on performance. The researchers also uncovered two surprises: compromise hurt performance, and competition helped performance. Compromises hurt because they often are watered-down, middle-of-the-road, suboptimal solutions. Competitive behavior was useful because the virtual teams were temporary and under time pressure, so having some individuals behave dominantly and impose decisions to achieve efficiency was useful rather than detrimental.

When people have problems in business-to-business e-commerce (e.g., costly delays), they tend to behave competitively and defensively rather than collaboratively.[111] Technical problems and recurring problems test people's patience. The conflict will escalate unless people use more cooperative, collaborative styles. Try to prevent conflicts before they arise; for example, make sure your information system is running smoothly before linking with others. Monitor and reduce or eliminate problems as soon as possible. When problems arise, express your willingness to cooperate, and then *actually be* cooperative. Even technical problems require the social skills of good management.

WHAT YOU NEED TO KNOW

•• learning OBJECTIVES

After studying Chapter 12,
you will be able to:

LO1 Discuss important advantages of
two-way communication.

LO2 Identify communication problems
to avoid.

LO3 Describe when and how to use the
various communication channels.

LO4 Summarize ways to become a better
"sender" and "receiver" of information.

LO5 Explain how to improve downward,
upward, and horizontal communication.

LO6 Summarize how to work with the
company grapevine.

LO7 Describe the boundaryless organization
and its advantages.

12

Communicating

Effective communication is a fundamental aspect of job performance and managerial effectiveness.[1] It is a primary means by which managers carry out the responsibilities described throughout this book, such as making group decisions, sharing a vision, coordinating individuals and work groups within the organization's structure, hiring and motivating employees, and leading teams. In these and other areas of management, managers have to be able to share ideas clearly and convincingly, and they have to listen effectively to the ideas of others. In this chapter, we present important communication concepts and practical guidelines for improving your effectiveness. We also discuss communication at the interpersonal and organizational levels.

Get Practical Tips

on how today's managers communicate effectively with their employees from Angel and Martha.

"Clear communication is very important when dealing with people outside the U.S. We work with many overseas companies that do not speak our slang English. In order to get my instructions correct the first time, I need to read and reread my instructions making sure that an outsider can clearly follow the process that I am trying to explain. You cannot assume that one just knows what you're talking about no matter what country they are from. Minds other than your own can interpret instructions in thousands of different ways."
—Angel Chavez, Art Manager

"Flex Your Style! It is so important when communicating that you are able to flex your style of communication to that of the person you are dealing with. It doesn't matter if it is written, verbal, body language, etc. People relate and trust those they can connect with. By changing your style of communication to match theirs you are able to connect with them. We live in a very diverse world and it is important to be able to communicate with everyone."
—Martha Zehnder Keller, Associate Director of Convention Services

● **COMMUNICATION** The transmission of information and meaning from one party to another through the use of shared symbols.

● **ONE-WAY COMMUNICATION** A process in which information flows in only one direction—from the sender to the receiver, with no feedback loop.

● **TWO-WAY COMMUNICATION** A process in which information flows in two directions—the receiver provides feedback, and the sender is receptive to the feedback.

● **PERCEPTION** The process of receiving and interpreting information.

● **FILTERING** The process of withholding, ignoring, or distorting information.

(L)(O) 1 WHAT YOU NEED TO KNOW . . .
What are the important advantages of two-way communication?

INTERPERSONAL COMMUNICATION

When people in an organization conduct a meeting, share stories in the cafeteria, or deliver presentations, they are making efforts to communicate. To understand why communication efforts sometimes break down and find ways to improve your communication skills, it helps to identify the elements of the communication process. **Communication** is the transmission of information and meaning from one party to another through the use of shared symbols. Figure 12.1 shows a general model of how one person communicates with another.

The *sender* initiates the process by conveying information to the *receiver*—the person for whom the message is intended. The sender has a *meaning* he or she wishes to communicate and *encodes* the meaning into symbols (the words chosen for the message). Then the sender *transmits,* or sends, the message through some *channel,* such as a verbal or written medium.

The receiver *decodes* the message (e.g., reads it) and attempts to *interpret* the sender's meaning. The receiver may provide *feedback* to the sender by encoding a message in response to the sender's message.

The communication process often is hampered by *noise,* or interference in the system, that blocks perfect understanding. Noise could be anything that interferes with accurate communication: ringing telephones, thoughts about other things, or simple fatigue or stress.

The model in Figure 12.1 is more than a theoretical treatment of the communication process: it points out the key ways in which communications can break down. Mistakes can be made at each stage of the model. A manager who is alert to potential problems can perform each step carefully to ensure more effective communication. The model also helps explain

the topics discussed next: the differences between one-way and two-way communication, communication pitfalls, misperception, and the various communication channels.

Communication should flow in two directions

In **one-way communication**, information flows in only one direction—from the sender to the receiver, with no feedback loop. A manager sends an e-mail to a subordinate without asking for a response. An employee phones the information technology (IT) department and leaves a message requesting repairs for her computer. A supervisor scolds a production worker about defects and then storms away.

When receivers respond to senders—Person B becomes the sender and Person A the receiver—**two-way communication** has occurred. One-way communication in situations like those just described can become two-way if the manager's e-mail invites the receiver to reply with any questions, the IT department returns the employee's call and asks for details about the computer problem, and the supervisor calms down and listens to the production worker's explanation of why defects are occurring.

True two-way communication means not only that the receiver provides feedback but also that the sender is receptive to the feedback. In these constructive exchanges, information is shared between both parties rather than merely delivered from one person to the other.

Because one-way communication is faster and easier for the sender, it is much more common than it should be. A busy executive finds it easier to dash off an e-mail message than to discuss a nagging problem with a subordinate. Also, he doesn't have to deal with questions or be challenged by someone who disagrees.

Two-way communication is more difficult and time-consuming than one-way communication. However, it is more accurate; fewer mistakes occur, and fewer problems arise. When receivers have a chance to ask questions, share concerns, and make suggestions or modifications, they understand more precisely what is being communicated and what they should do with the information.[2]

Consider what happened to Dick Nicholson when he was a sales manager attending a company reception for the sales department. Out of Nicholson's earshot, his company's chairman asked the vice president why a particular employee—a chronic underperformer—was "still a salesman." The vice president then told Nicholson what he thought the chairman meant: the chairman

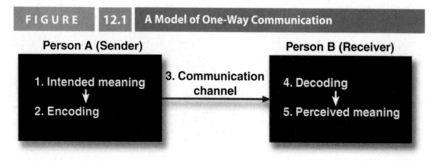

| FIGURE | 12.1 | A Model of One-Way Communication |

Person A (Sender)
1. Intended meaning
2. Encoding

3. Communication channel

Person B (Receiver)
4. Decoding
5. Perceived meaning

Two-way communication is more difficult and time-consuming than one-way communication. However, it is more accurate with fewer mistakes occurring and fewer problems arising.

wanted to promote the salesperson. If communication were limited to one way, Nicholson could have simply carried out the chairman's apparent order, but instead he visited the chairman later and asked for an explanation. He was relieved when the chairman explained that he was wondering why the ineffective salesperson was still working for the company at all.[3]

(L)(O) 2 WHAT YOU NEED TO KNOW . . .

Can you identify communication problems to avoid?

Watch out for communication pitfalls

As we know from personal experience, the sender's intended message does not always get across to the receiver. You are operating under an illusion if you think there is a perfect correlation between what you say and what people hear.[4] Errors can occur in all stages of the communication process. In the encoding stage, words can be misused, decimal points entered in the wrong places, facts left out, or ambiguous phrases inserted. In the transmission stage, a memo may get lost on a cluttered desk, the words on the screen may be too small to read from the back of the room, or words may be spoken with ambiguous inflections.

Decoding problems arise when the receiver doesn't listen carefully or reads too quickly and overlooks a key point. And, of course, receivers can misinterpret the message, as when a reader draws the wrong conclusion from an unclear text message, a listener takes a general statement by the boss too personally, or a sideways glance is taken the wrong way.

> When George Franks started a new job, his boss always seemed too busy to talk. A mentor suggested that Franks make a habit of asking his boss how he could help. But his boss interpreted the repeated questions as meaning the boss couldn't keep up with his job. Offended, he retaliated by "dumping all the projects no one else wanted" on Franks.[5]

More generally, people's perceptual and filtering processes create misinterpretations. **Perception** is the process of receiving and interpreting information. Such processes are not perfectly objective. They are subjective, as people's self-interested motives and attitudes toward the sender and the message bias their interpretations. People assume that others share their views, and naturally pay more attention to their own views than to the views of others.[6] But perceptual differences get in the way of consensus. To remedy this situation, it helps to remember that others' viewpoints are legitimate and to incorporate others' perspectives into your interpretation of issues.[7] Generally, adopting another person's viewpoint is fundamental to working collaboratively. And your ability to take others' perspectives—say, to really understand the viewpoints of customers or suppliers—can improve others' assessments of your performance.[8]

Filtering is the process of withholding, ignoring, or distorting information. Senders do this, for example, when they tell the boss what they think the boss wants to hear or give unwarranted compliments rather than honest criticism. Receivers also filter information; they may fail to recognize an important message or may attend to some aspects of the message but not others.

Filtering and subjective perception pervade one interesting aspect of the communications dynamic: how men and women differ in their communicating styles. A female manager at a magazine tended to phrase the assignments she gave her reporters as questions: "How would you like to do the X project with Y?" and

"The single biggest problem with communication is the illusion that it has taken place."

—G. B. Shaw

"I was thinking of putting you on the X project; is that okay?" She was criticized by her male boss, who told her she did not assume the proper demeanor with her staff.[9] The female owner of a retail operation told one of her store managers to do something by saying, "The bookkeeper needs help with the billing. How would you feel about helping her out?" He said fine but didn't do it. Although the boss thought he meant he would do it, the store manager said he meant to indicate how he would feel about helping. He decided he had better things to do.[10]

Because of such filtering and perceptual differences, you cannot assume the other person means what you think he means, or understands the meanings you intend. Managers need to excel at reading interactions and adjusting their communication styles and perceptions to the people with whom they interact.[11] The very human tendencies to filter and perceive subjectively underlie much of the ineffective communication, and the need for more effective communication practices, that you will read about in the rest of this chapter.

Mistaken perceptions cause misunderstandings

A common thread underlying the discussion so far is that people's perceptions can undermine attempts to communicate. People do not pay attention to everything going on around them. They inadvertently send mixed signals that can undermine the

A+

TIP

Being able to see the other person's viewpoint is one of the ultimate keys to effective collaboration.

intended messages. Different people attend to different things, and people interpret the same message in different ways.

If the communication is between people from different cultures, these problems are magnified.[12] Communication breakdowns often occur when business transactions take place between people from different countries. Nancy J. Adler, an expert in international management, suggests the following tactics for communicating effectively with someone who speaks a different language:[13]

Verbal Behavior

- *Clear, slow speech.* Enunciate each word. Do not use colloquial expressions.
- *Repetition.* Repeat each important idea using different words to explain the same concept.
- *Simple sentences.* Avoid compound, long sentences.
- *Active verbs.* Avoid passive verbs.

Nonverbal Behavior

- *Visual restatements.* Use as many visual restatements as possible, such as pictures, graphs, tables, and slides.
- *Gestures.* Use more facial and appropriate hand gestures to emphasize the meaning of words.
- *Demonstrations.* Act out as many themes as possible.
- *Pauses.* Pause more frequently.
  - *Summaries.* Hand out written summaries of your verbal presentation.

Accurate Interpretation

- *Silence.* When there is a silence, wait. Do not jump in to fill the silence. The other person is probably just thinking more slowly in the nonnative language or translating.
- *Intelligence.* Do not equate poor grammar and mispronunciation with lack of intelligence; it is usually a sign of nonnative-language use.
- *Differences.* If unsure, assume difference, not similarity.

Comprehension

- *Understanding.* Do not just assume that they understand; assume that they do not understand.
- *Checking comprehension.* Have colleagues repeat their understanding of the material back to you. Do not simply ask if they understand or not. Let them explain to you what they understand.

Design

- *Breaks.* Take more frequent breaks. Second-language comprehension is exhausting.

- *Small modules.* Divide the material to be presented into smaller modules.
- *Longer time frame.* Allocate more time for each module than you usually need for presenting the same material to native speakers of your language.

Motivation

- *Encouragement.* Verbally and nonverbally encourage and reinforce speaking by nonnative-language participants.
- *Drawing out.* Explicitly draw out marginal and passive participants.
- *Reinforcement.* Do not embarrass novice speakers.

An example highlights the operation of mixed signals and misperceptions. A bank CEO knew that he had to downsize his organization, and the employees who remained would have to commit to customer service, become more empowered, and really *earn* customer loyalty.[14] Knowing that his employees would have concerns about the coming reorganization, he decided to promise that he would do his best to guarantee employment to the survivors.

What signals did the CEO communicate to his people by his promises? One positive signal was that he cared about his people. But he also signaled that *he* would take care of *them,* thus undermining his goal of giving them more responsibility and empowering them. The employees wanted management to take responsibility for the market challenge that *they* needed to face by learning new ways of doing business. Inadvertently, the CEO spoke to their backward-looking desire for security, rather than conveying that the bank's future depended on *their* efforts. However, the CEO did avoid a common pitfall at companies that announce plans for downsizing or outsourcing: ignoring the emotional significance of their message.[15] Sometimes managers are so intent on delivering the business rationale for the changes that they fail to acknowledge the human cost of layoffs. When employees hear a message that neglects to address their feelings, they generally interpret the message to mean that managers don't care.

Consider how many problems can be avoided—and how much more effective communication can be—if people take the time to do four things:

1. Ensure that the receivers attend to the message they are sending.
2. Consider the other party's frame of reference and attempt to convey the message with that viewpoint in mind.
3. Take concrete steps to minimize perceptual errors and improper signals in sending and receiving.
4. Send consistent messages.

You should make an effort to predict people's interpretations of your messages and think in terms of how they could *misinterpret* your messages. It helps to say not only what you mean but also what you *don't* mean. Every time you say, "I am not saying *X,* I am saying *Y,*" you eliminate a possible misinterpretation.[16]

(L)(O) 3 WHAT YOU NEED TO KNOW . . .
When and how should you use the various communication channels?

Communications flow through different channels

Communication can be sent through a variety of channels (step 3 in Figure 12.1), including oral and written. Each channel has advantages and disadvantages.

Oral communication includes face-to-face discussion, telephone conversations, and formal presentations and speeches. Advantages are that questions can be asked and answered; feedback is immediate and direct; the receiver(s) can sense the sender's sincerity (or lack of it); and oral communication is more persuasive and sometimes less expensive than written. Yet, oral communication also has disadvantages: it can lead to spontaneous, ill-considered statements (and regret), and there is no permanent record of it (unless an effort is made to record it).

Written communication includes e-mail, memos, letters, reports, computer files, and other written documents. Advantages to using written messages are that the message can be revised several times, it is a permanent record that can be saved, the message stays the same even if relayed through many people, and the receiver has more time to analyze the message. Disadvantages are that the sender has no control over where, when, or if the message is read; the sender lacks immediate feedback; the receiver may not understand parts of the message; and the message must be longer to contain enough information to answer anticipated questions.[17]

You should weigh these considerations when deciding whether to communicate orally or in writing. Also, sometimes it is wise to use both channels, such as following up a meeting with a confirming memo or writing a letter to prepare someone for your phone call.

Electronic media offer flexible, efficient channels

More and more of today's oral and written communication takes place through electronic media. Managers use computers not only to gather and distribute quantitative data but also to "talk" with others electronically. In electronic decision rooms, software supports simultaneous access to shared files, and allows people to share views and do work collectively.[18] Other means of electronic communication include *teleconferencing,* in which groups of people in different locations interact over telephone lines and perhaps see one another on monitors as they participate in group discussions *(videoconferencing).* Also, you probably are intimately familiar with e-mail, instant messaging, text messaging, and blogging.

E-mail has become a fundamental tool of workplace communication, with the average corporate user handling 171 messages a day.[19] Instant messaging (IMing) is less widespread in business settings, but its use is growing. According to a recent survey, 35 percent of employees surveyed said they use IMing at work.[20] New versions of e-mail software may encourage workers to use a wider variety of electronic communication tools. IBM's recent update to Lotus Notes, called Notes 8, lets e-mail users use tabs to launch an IM session or open word-processing or spreadsheet files to create attachments. Users can also organize documents, messages, and calendars by project, letting all project participants review the information and receive notifications when it changes. The latest version of Microsoft's Outlook

e-mail program lets users make Internet phone calls, as well as write and review documents in a SharePoint collaborative workspace. The advantage of a collaborative workspace is that all participants can go directly to a central location and work directly on a project, without the intervening step of an e-mail.[21] These technology advances encourage collaboration along with communication.

Blogging—posting text to a Web site—also has arrived in the business world. Some companies use blogs to communicate with the external environment, for example, by sharing information about product uses or corporate social responsibility efforts. Blogs also may foster communication within the organization.[22] A project team might have a blog where the team leader posts frequent updates along with relevant presentations and spreadsheets. Searching the blog site can be an easy way for team members to find information about the project. They also can post ideas and comments in response to the blogger's entries. Similarly, blogs can be used to encourage collaboration among employees with a shared interest in particular products, functions, or customers.

The most recently developed tools for electronic communication generally fall into a category called **Web 2.0**, a set of Internet-based applications that encourage user-provided

Twitter as a Lifeline during Disasters

"**W**hat are you doing?" It's a familiar question—particularly to legions of Twitter users worldwide. Social networking site Twitter provides a fast, easy way to stay close to friends, offering up the minutiae of life in real-time "bytes"—for example, "washing my sister's car," "catching a movie with friends," or "thinking about studying for econ midterm but need pizza first." With each tweet limited to 140 characters, Twitterers quickly learn to get their message across succinctly.

When Gen-Xers Jack Dorsey, Biz Stone, and Evan Williams founded Twitter in 2006, their idea was to enable users to access a communication network at what they called "the lowest common denominator." To access Twitter, users need nothing more than a cell phone with instant-messaging capability. As a result, the site has grown exponentially. By mid-2009, Twitter users numbered more than 24 million, with more than 17 million in the United States alone.

Twitter co-founders Biz Stone (left) and Evan Williams are shown here in their office in San Francisco.

Twitter quickly became something more than a casual conduit for staying in touch. The site is a valuable medium for reporting and tracking information during disasters and world events. When wildfires struck Southern California in

2007, for example, Twitterers began reporting details within seconds, helping residents get up-to-the-minute news and evaluate their safety.

After earthquakes devastated China in May 2008, Twitter became the primary source of eyewitness accounts. It reported information even faster than the U.S. Geological Survey, the agency responsible for tracking quake readings worldwide. Just weeks later, when earthquakes hit Los Angeles, cell-phone-delivered tweets flooded the Twitter network within seconds. In contrast, it was nine minutes before the Associated Press reported the story.

When a US Airways jet made an emergency landing on the Hudson River in 2009, it was a Twitter user who, with his cell phone, snapped a photo of the plane gliding into the river and posted it on a Twitter photo-sharing

● WEB 2.0 A set of Internet-based applications that encourage user-provided content and collaboration.

content and collaboration. The most widely used Web 2.0 applications include social networking, podcasts, RSS (really simple syndication, where users subscribe to receive news, blogs, or other information they select), and wikis (online publications created with contributions from many authors/users). These tools became popular at such sites as Facebook, YouTube, and Wikipedia, but users have brought the experience to work, applying online collaboration to business needs. Unlike the first generation of Internet applications, introduced to organizations when information technology (IT) departments evaluated an application and made a purchase, employees typically begin using Web 2.0 tools on their own to meet a need. Rod Smith, IBM's vice president for emerging Internet technologies, recalls a meeting at which he told Royal Bank of Scotland's IT head about wikis. The IT chief said the bank didn't use them, but when Smith asked the other participants, more than two dozen said *they* did.[23]

advantages

The advantages of electronic communication are numerous and dramatic. Within firms, advantages include the sharing of more information and the speed and efficiency in delivering routine messages to large numbers of people across vast geographic areas. Business-related wikis such as Socialtext let project teams post their ideas in one forum for others to add contributions. Socialtext allows project leaders to grant users access based on their need to know and participate. Web Crossing uses wikis for product development. Michael Krieg, vice president of marketing, says the wikis save the company "untold amounts of paper, postage, meetings, travel budgets, conference calls, and the time required to coordinate it all."[24]

Communicating electronically can reduce time and expenses devoted to traveling, photocopying, and mailing. When a fire caused by a truck accident closed a major freeway route in the San Francisco Bay area, Valerie Williamson skipped the traffic mess by visiting with her colleague Brian Friedlander at her company's virtual office in Second Life, an online virtual world. Williamson and Friedlander used avatars (animated images of themselves) to navigate their meeting in the online conference room of their real-world business, Electric Sheep Company.[25] Second Life participants can use their avatars to conduct business communications such as giving PowerPoint presentations, streaming audio and video, and asking questions.

Some companies, including Boeing, use brainstorming software that allows anonymous contributions, presuming it will add more honesty to internal discussions. Research indicates more data sharing and critical argumentation, and higher-quality decisions, with a group decision support system than is found in face-to-face meetings.[26] But anonymity also offers potential for lies, gossip, insults, threats, harassment, and the release of confidential information.[27]

disadvantages

The disadvantages of electronic communication include the difficulty of solving complex problems that require more extended, face-to-face interaction and the inability to pick up subtle, nonverbal, or inflectional clues about what the communicator is thinking or conveying. In online bargaining—even before it begins—negotiators distrust one another more than in face-to-face negotiations. After the

site. The surreal image appeared worldwide in minutes. Today, the Federal Emergency Management Agency (FEMA) hosts a Twitter page and uses it to provide real-time information on disasters like the 2009 flooding in West Virginia.

Twitter played a central role in covering the 2008 U.S. presidential election, with both the Obama and McCain campaigns twittering and the Web site setting up special election pages. After 2009's hotly contested elections in Iran and a government-imposed news blackout, activists used Twitter to keep the rest of the world informed.

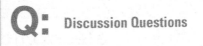
Q: Discussion Questions

- What are Twitter's advantages as an electronic communication medium? Its disadvantages?
- When might a manager find Twitter an appropriate communication channel? When might a manager want to discourage employees from using Twitter?

SOURCES: Federal Emergency Management Agency, "Twitter FEMA Now: We Want to Hear from You," FEMA Web site, http://www.fema.gov, accessed June 19, 2009; Lev Grossman, "Iran Protests: Twitter, the Medium of the Movement," *Time*, June 17, 2009, http://www.time.com; Jamie Diamond, "The Twitter Guys," *New York Times*, May 8, 2009, http://nytimes.com; United Press International,

"Don't Fight Twitter, Disaster Expert Says," UPI Web site, March 6, 2009, http://www.upi.com; Claudine Beaumont, "New York Plane Crash: Twitter Breaks the News, Again," *London Telegraph*, January 16, 2009, http://www.telegraph.co.uk; Shira Ovide, "Twittering the USAirways Plane Crash," *The Wall Street Journal*, January 15, 2009, http://blogs.wsj.com; Erica Noonan, "Life Is Tweet," *Boston Globe*, January 4, 2009, http://www.boston.com; John Cox, "Tweets, Twits, and the California Earthquake," *Network World*, July 30, 2008, http://www.networkworld.com; Mathew Ingram, "Twitter Breaks Chinese Earthquake News," *Toronto Globe and Mail*, May 12, 2008, http://www.theglobeandmail.com; and Mitch Wagner, "Google Maps and Twitter Are Essential Information Resources for California Fires," *InformationWeek*, October 24, 2007, http://www.informationweek.com.

negotiation (compared with face-to-face negotiators), people usually are less satisfied with their outcomes, even when the outcomes are economically equivalent.[28]

Although organizations rely heavily on computer-aided communication for group decision making, face-to-face groups generally take less time, make higher-quality decisions, and are more satisfying for members.[29] E-mail is most appropriate for routine messages that do not require the exchange of large quantities of complex information. It is less suitable for confidential information, resolving conflicts, or negotiating.[30] Employees have reported being laid off via e-mail and even text messages.[31] These more impersonal forms of communication can hurt feelings, and an upset employee can easily forward messages, which often has a snowball effect that can embarrass everyone involved. Like e-mail, IMs can help people work together productively, but they can also leak sensitive information.

Companies are worried about leaks and negative portrayals, and they may require employees to agree to specific guidelines before starting blogs. Some general guidelines should guide corporate bloggers:[32]

- Remember that blogs posted on a company's Web site should avoid any content that could embarrass the company or disclose confidential information.
- Stick to the designated topic of any company-sponsored blog.
- If members of the media contact you about reporting on a blog you have written, get official approval before proceeding.

Most electronic communications are quick and easy, and some are anonymous. As a result, one inevitable consequence of electronic communication is "flaming": hurling insults, sending "nastygrams," venting frustration, snitching on coworkers to the boss, and otherwise breaching protocol. E-mail, blogs, and IMing liberate people to send messages they would not say to a person's face. Without nonverbal cues, "kidding" remarks may be taken seriously, causing resentment and regret. Some people try to clear up confusion with emoticons such as smiley faces, but those efforts can further muddy the intent.[33] Also, confidential messages, including details about people's personal lives and insulting, embarrassing remarks, occasionally become public knowledge through electronic leaks.

Other downsides to electronic communication are important.[34] Different people and sometimes different working units latch onto different channels as their medium of choice. For example, an engineering division might use e-mail most, but a design group might rely primarily on instant messaging and neglect e-mail. Another disadvantage is that electronic messages sometimes are monitored or seen inadvertently by those for whom they are not intended. Be careful with your IMs: Make sure you don't accidentally send them to the wrong person and that they don't pop up on the screen during a PowerPoint presentation.[35] One way to avoid sending to the wrong person is to close all IM windows except those you're currently using for active conversations. Deleting electronic messages—whether e-mail, IMs, or cell phone text messages—does not destroy them; they are saved elsewhere. Recipients can forward them to others, without the original sender knowing it. Many companies use software to monitor e-mail and IMs. And the messages can be used in court cases to indict individuals or companies. Electronic messages sent from work and on company-provided devices are private property—but they are private property of the system's owner, not of the sender.

An e-mail golden rule (like the sunshine rule in the ethics chapter): don't hit "send" unless you'd be comfortable having the contents on the front page of a newspaper, being read by your mother or a competitor. And it's not a bad idea to have a colleague read nonroutine e-mails before you send them.

managing the electronic load Electronic communication media seem essential these days, and people wonder how they ever worked without them. But the sheer volume of communication can be overwhelming, especially when it doesn't let up during meetings, breaks, or after work.[36]

Fortunately, a few rules of thumb can help you manage your electronic communications.[38] For the problem of information overload, the challenge is to separate the truly important from the routine. Effective managers find time to think about bigger business issues and don't get too bogged down

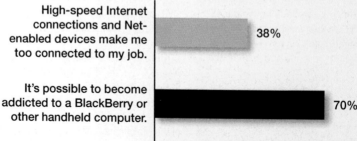

Americans are cautious about electronic overload.[37]

Percent of American adults who said . . .

High-speed Internet connections and Net-enabled devices make me too connected to my job. — 38%

It's possible to become addicted to a BlackBerry or other handheld computer. — 70%

0   20   40   60   80   100

in responding to every message that seems urgent but may be trivial. Essential here is to think strategically about your goals, identify the items that are most important, and prioritize your time around those goals. This is easier said than done, of course, but it is essential, and it helps. Most communication software has tools that can help. For example, with instant messaging, set your "away" message when you want to concentrate on something else. And Lotus is developing a feature that lets e-mail users see immediately whether messages in their in box are addressed only to them or to a group of recipients. Often a group e-mail is a lower priority. Of course, management also has a role to play. Some employees check messages constantly because they believe (perhaps correctly) that this is what their bosses expect of them. Managers can help employees by limiting and communicating the times during which they expect a prompt response.[39]

A few more specific suggestions: With e-mail, don't hit "reply to all" when you should hit just "reply." Get organized by creating folders sorted by subject, priority, or sender, and flag messages that require follow-up. If you receive a copy, you don't need to respond; it's just for your information.

Some companies are recognizing the downsides of electronic media overuse. At U.S. Cellular, executive vice president Jay Ellison took the radical step of banning e-mail altogether on Fridays. After some resistance, employees found that they were building deeper working relationships through phone calls and face-to-face visits.[40] And at PBD Worldwide Fulfillment Services, Fridays without e-mail have taught new (or old) communication habits that are spilling over into the rest of the week. E-mail volume at PBD dropped 75 percent and translated into greater efficiency.[41]

As overwhelming as electronic communications can be, you can take steps to simplify them. For example, a global customer-account-management team established two ground rules:

1. Whenever a member communicated with a customer, the member was to send a briefing to all team members.

2. They designated a primary contact on the team for each customer, with no one else on the team authorized to discuss or decide strategies or policies with the customer.

If contacted by a customer, team members would direct the customer to the appropriate contact person. These steps simplified communication channels and greatly reduced contradictory and confusing messages.[42]

the virtual office
Many entrepreneurs conduct business via open "offices" on the Internet, working off their computers from wherever they happen to be. Similarly, major companies like IBM, GE, and Prudential California Realty are slashing office space and giving people laptop or notebook computers, telecommunications software, voice mail, and other communications technologies so that they can work virtually anywhere, anytime.[43] Based on the philosophy that management's focus should be on what people do, not where they are, the **virtual office** is a mobile office in which people can work anywhere— home, car, airport, customers' offices—as long as they have the tools to communicate with customers and colleagues.

As computer processing power has increased, some companies have begun taking the virtual office to a new, more

That Was THEN . . .

Me, type? Dictating memos and letters to secretaries used to occupy hours of a manager's communication time.

This Is NOW . . .

Communications networks now are high-tech and global, allowing an instantaneous flow of messages. Shown here is a TelePresence system, which allows virtual face-to-face meetings with far-flung employees.

interactive level. As mentioned earlier, Electric Sheep Company set up a virtual office on the Second Life Web site, where people can use avatars to watch themselves interact in a virtual world. Another organization with a virtual office in Second Life is the American Library Association's Washington office. The ALA's virtual office is in Second Life's Cybrary City, near several libraries. Visitors can seek library services such as help in building a collection or consulting references.[44]

In the short run at least, the benefits of virtual offices appear substantial. Saving money on rent and utilities is an obvious advantage. In Merced, California, Prudential California Realty's 10 agents stay connected with each other and their clients via the Internet, sharing information on individual Web sites and through e-mail.[45] A virtual office also gives employees access to whatever information they need from the company, whether they are in a meeting, visiting a client, or working from home.[46] Hiring and retaining talented people is easier because virtual offices support scheduling flexibility and even may make it possible to keep an employee who wants to relocate—for example, with a spouse taking a new job in another city.

But what will be the longer-term impact on productivity and morale? We may be in danger of losing too many "human moments"—those authentic encounters that happen only when two people are physically together.[47] Some people hate working at home. Some send faxes, e-mail, and voice mail in the middle of the night—and others receive them. Some work around the

clock yet feel they are not doing enough. Long hours of being constantly close to the technical tools of work can cause burnout. And in some companies, direct supervision at the office is necessary to maintain the quality of work, especially when employees are inexperienced and need guidance. The virtual office requires changes in human beings and presents technical challenges, so although it is much hyped and useful, it will not completely replace real offices and face-to-face work.

Consulting giant Accenture has offices in 150 cities, but its employees spend most of their time at clients' workplaces. Under those conditions, cultivating teamwork is difficult for managers, and developing a career is challenging for consultants, who may have a client on one continent, a supervisor on another, and support staff in a third country.

To foster communication and maintain strong working relationships, Accenture assigns each new consultant to a career counselor, a senior employee in the same specialty who helps the employee develop his or her career. For example, consultant Keyur Patel is a retailing consultant with Accenture. Whether at a client's location in San Francisco or at home in Atlanta, Patel checks in with his career counselor about once a month. The counselor advised Patel to spend Fridays at the Atlanta office, making face-to-face connections with his colleagues there.

Patel also has to keep in touch with his manager, based in Detroit. They check in by phone monthly. Accenture trains its managers in how to lead virtual teams. They learn to schedule conference calls that respect time differences and to allow plenty

TABLE 12.1	Suggested Media Choices for Sample Situations		
Situation	**Poor Choice**		**Better Choice**
1	Memo		Small group meetings
Rationale: The memo does not offer the feedback potential necessary to explain what may be seen as obscure information. Moreover, with these employees there is a possibility of literacy problems. A group meeting will allow for an oral explanation after which participants can more easily ask questions about any of the complex materials.			
2	Phone		Voice mail or e-mail
Rationale: For a simple message like this, there is no need to use a rich medium when a lean one will do the job.			
3	E-mail, voice mail		Face-to-face, telephone
Rationale: In situations requiring persuasion the sender must be able to quickly adapt the message to the receiver in order to counter objections. This is not a feature of either e-mail or voice mail. Face-to-face communication offers the sender the greatest flexibility. The phone is the next best alternative.			
4	Teleconference		Fax, computer conference
Rationale: A teleconference is apt to overly accentuate the status and personality differences among the engineers. Fax or computer conferencing would allow the quality of the ideas to be the central focus of interaction. Moreover, quick feedback is still possible with these media.			
5	Newsletter		Video
Rationale: If employees are already persuaded of the updated system's merit, you can probably use the newsletter. But a videotape graphically conveys information that requires demonstration, and will educate people about procedures.			

SOURCE: From *Communicating for Managerial Effectiveness* by P. G. Clampitt. Copyright © 1991 by Sage Publications, Inc. Reprinted by permission of Sage Publications, Inc.

of opportunity for casual conversation that maintains a sense of belonging to the team. Accenture also uses a Web conferencing system for online meetings, as well as a company networking site called People Pages, where employees can read each other's profiles and send messages.[48]

Use "richer" media for complex or critical messages

Some communication channels convey more information than others. The amount of information a medium conveys is called **media richness**.[49] The more information or cues a medium sends to the receiver, the "richer" the medium is.[50] The richest media are more personal than technological, provide quick feedback, allow lots of descriptive language, and send different types of cues. Face-to-face communication is the richest medium because it offers a variety of cues in addition to words: tone of voice, facial expression, body language, and other nonverbal signals. It also allows more descriptive language than, say, a memo does. In addition, it affords more opportunity for the receiver to give feedback to and ask questions of the sender, turning one-way into two-way communication.

The telephone is less rich than face-to-face communication, electronic mail is less rich yet, and memos are the least rich medium. In general, you should send difficult and unusual messages through richer media, transmit simple and routine messages through less rich media, and use multiple media for important messages that you want to ensure people attend to and understand.[51] You should also consider factors such as cost, which medium your receiver prefers, and the preferred communication style in your organization.[52] In the following situations, based on the message and the audience, which channel would you select?[53]

1. A midsize construction firm wants to announce a new employee benefit program.

2. A manager wishes to confirm a meeting time with 10 employees.

3. Increase enthusiasm in a midsize insurance company for a program that asks employees from different departments to work on the same project team.

4. A group of engineers who are geographically dispersed want to exchange design ideas with one another.

5. Describe a straightforward but somewhat detailed and updated version of a voice mail system to 1,000 employees who are geographically dispersed.

Compare your ideas with the recommendations in Table 12.1.

Financial guru Suze Orman has been ranked as one of the best presenters by *BusinessWeek* magazine for her ability to relay information in easy-to-understand ways. She delivers financial information using clear, concise, and direct language. Great business communicators use simple language to discuss complex issues.

L O 4 **WHAT YOU NEED TO KNOW . . .**
How can you become a better "sender" and "receiver" of information?

IMPROVING COMMUNICATION SKILLS

In recent years, employers have been dismayed by college graduates' poor communication skills. A demonstrated ability to communicate effectively makes a job candidate more attractive and distinguishes him or her from others. You can do many things to improve your communication skills, both as a sender and as a receiver.

Senders can improve their presentations, writing, word choice, and body language

To start, be aware that honest, direct, straight talk is important but all too rare. CEOs are often coached on how to slant their messages for different audiences—the investment community, employees, or the board. That's not likely to be straight talk. The focus of the messages can differ, but they can't be inconsistent. People should be able to identify your perspective, your reasoning, and your intentions.[54] Beyond this basic point, senders can improve their skills in making persuasive presentations, writing, language use, and sending nonverbal messages.

presentation and persuasion skills Throughout your career, you will be called on to state your case on a variety of issues. You will have information and perhaps an opinion or proposal to present to others. Typically, your goal will be to "sell" your idea. In other words, your challenge will be to persuade others to go along with your recommendation. As a leader, you will find that some of your toughest challenges arise when people do not want to do what has to be done. Leaders have to be persuasive to get people on board.[55]

Your attitude in presenting ideas and persuading others is very important. Persuasion is not what many people think: merely selling an idea or convincing others to see things your way. Don't assume that it takes a "my way or the highway" approach, with a one-shot effort to make a hard sell and resisting compromise.[56] It usually is more constructive to consider persuasion a process of learning from each other and negotiating a shared solution. Persuasive speakers are seen as authentic, which happens when speakers are open with the audience, make a connection, demonstrate passion, and show they are listening as well as speaking. Practice this kind of authenticity by noticing and adopting the type of body language you use when you're around people you're comfortable with, planning how to engage directly with your listeners, identifying the reasons why you care about your topic, and watching for nonverbal cues as well as fully engaging when you listen to audience comments and questions.[57]

The most powerful and persuasive messages are simple and informative, are told with stories and anecdotes, and convey excitement.[58] People are more likely to remember and buy into your message if you can express it as a story that is simple, unexpected, concrete, credible, and includes emotional content. For example, Nordstrom motivates employees by passing along stories of times when its people have provided extraordinary service, such as warming up customers' cars while they shopped or ironing a shirt so that a customer could wear it to a meeting. Rubal Jain sold a customer on his India-based express-delivery service Safexpress by recounting how the company had delivered 69,000 copies of the latest Harry Potter release to bookstores around the country all at the precise release time—a far more dramatic case than data about on-time deliveries.[59] To be credible, a communicator backs up the message with actions consistent with the words.

Our colleague Lynn Hamilton offers 10 useful tips for making formal presentations more powerful:[60]

1. *Spend adequate time on the **content** of your presentation.* It's easy to get so distracted with PowerPoint slides or concern about delivery skills that the actual content of a presentation is neglected. Know your content inside and out; you'll be able to discuss it conversationally and won't be tempted to memorize. If you believe in what you're saying

Writing down your objective will help you focus on your *bottom line*. Everything else in a presentation—the structure, the words, the visuals—should support your objective.

3. ***Tell** the audience the **purpose** of the presentation.* As the saying goes, "Tell them what you're going to tell them, then tell them, then tell them what you've told them." Use a clear preview statement early on to help the audience know where you're taking them.

4. *Provide **meaning**, not just data.* Today, information is widely available; you won't impress people by overloading them with data. People have limited attention spans and want presenters to help *clarify the meaning* of data.

5. ***Practice, practice, practice**.* Appearing polished and relaxed during a presentation requires rehearsal time. Practice making your points in a variety of ways. Above all, don't memorize a presentation's content.

6. *Remember that a presentation is more like a **conversation** than a speech.* Keep your tone conversational yet professional. Audience members will be much more engaged if they feel you are talking *with* them rather than *at* them. Rely on PowerPoint slides or a broad outline to jog your memory.

7. *Remember the incredible power of **eye contact**.* Look at individual people in the audience. Try to have a series of one-on-one conversations with people in the room. This will calm you and help you connect with your audience.

8. ***Allow imperfection**.* If you forget what you were going to say, simply pause, look at your notes, and go on. Don't "break character" and effusively apologize or giggle or look mortified. Remember that an audience doesn't know your material nearly as well as you do and won't notice many mistakes.

9. *Be prepared to **answer tough questions**.* Try to anticipate the toughest questions you might receive. Plan your answers in advance. If you don't have an answer, acknowledge the fact and offer to get the information later.

10. *Provide a **crisp wrap-up** to a question-and-answer session.* Whenever possible, follow the Q&A period with a brief summary statement. Set up the Q&A session by saying,

> "When [cultivated people] look, they see clearly. When they listen, they think of how to hear keenly . . . In their demeanor, they think of how to be respectful. In their speech, they think of how to be truthful . . . When in doubt, they think of how to pose questions."
>
> —Confucius

and *own* the material, you will convey enthusiasm and will be more relaxed.

2. *Clearly understand the **objective** of your presentation.* Answer this question with one sentence: "What do I want the audience to believe following this presentation?"

"We'll take questions for 10 minutes and then have a few closing remarks." This prevents your presentation from just winding down to a weak ending. Also, if you receive hostile or hard-to-answer questions, you'll have a chance to have the final word.

writing skills Effective writing is more than correct spelling, punctuation, and grammar (although these help!). Good writing above all requires clear, logical thinking.[61] The act of writing can be a powerful aid to thinking, because you have to think about what you really want to say and what the logic is behind your message.[62]

You want people to find your memos and reports readable and interesting. Strive for clarity, organization, readability, and brevity.[63] Brevity is much appreciated by readers who are overloaded with documents, including wordy memos. Use a dictionary and a thesaurus, and avoid fancy words.

Your first draft rarely is as good as it could be. If you have time, revise it. Take the reader into consideration. Go through your entire document, and delete all unnecessary words, sentences, and paragraphs. Use specific, concrete words rather than abstract phrases. Instead of saying, "A period of unfavorable weather set in," say, "It rained every day for a week."

Be critical of your own writing. If you want to improve, start by reading *The Elements of Style* by William Strunk and E. B. White and the most recent edition of *The Little, Brown Handbook*.[64]

The principles of effective writing apply to online communications, including Web sites. The key is to focus on the audience's viewpoint. This avoids common pitfalls, such as planning a site based on what online marketing expert Seth Rosenblatt calls the "highest-paid person's opinion"—for example, featuring a photo of the chief executive officer on the home page. Simple, positive language also is important, especially online, where visitors are likely to skim the page for answers.

One company that has revamped its Web site to communicate more effectively with customers is A. C. Moore, which sells products for arts and crafts. The original Web site offered only corporate information and instructional materials for using its products, and the company hoped that site visitors would make purchases online, if it were easy enough. For example, A. C. Moore simplified the process of requesting e-mail about products. Now, instead of registering to get on a mailing list, Web site visitors can just click a link on the bottom of every page.

Most important, A. C. Moore listens. Its Web site includes a customer forum, where participants can trade craft ideas and comment about their experiences with the company and its products. Once, when customers began complaining about shipping costs, employees developed an alternative. They posted the idea of switching to a low flat rate for all orders; the forum participants reacted positively, so the company made the change. Such customer-oriented changes have increased A. C. Moore's Web site traffic and sales.[65]

language Word choice can enhance or interfere with communication effectiveness. For example, jargon is actually a form of shorthand and can make communication more effective when both the sender and the receiver know the buzzwords. But when the receiver is unfamiliar with the jargon, misunderstandings result. When people from different functional areas or disciplines communicate with one another, misunderstandings often occur because of "language" barriers. As in writing, simplicity usually helps.

Whether speaking or writing, you should consider the receiver's background—cultural as well as technical—and adjust your language accordingly. When you are receiving, don't assume that your understanding is the same as the speaker's intentions. Cisco CEO John Chambers, whose background is in business, simply asks the engineering managers in his high-tech company to explain any jargon. He says, "They do it remarkably well."[66] At the same time, Chambers shows respect and enhances his credibility by being truly interested in their work. Whenever Chambers travels with or reviews engineers, he asks them to teach him a topic—and he listens.

The meaning of word choices also can vary by culture. Japanese people use the simple word *hai* (yes) to convey that they understand what is being said; it does not necessarily mean they agree. Asian businesspeople rarely use the direct "no," using more subtle ways of disagreeing.[67] Global teams fail when members have difficulties communicating because of language, cultural, and geographic barriers. Heterogeneity harms team functioning at first. But when they develop ways to interact and communicate, teams develop a common identity and perform well.[68]

When conducting business overseas, try to learn something about the other country's language and customs. Americans are less likely to do this than people from some other cultures; few Americans consider a foreign language necessary for doing business abroad, and a significant majority of U.S. firms do not require employees sent abroad to know the local language.[69] But those who do will have a big edge over competitors who do not.[70] Making the effort to learn the local language builds rapport, sets a proper tone for doing business, aids in adjustment to culture shock, and especially can help you "get inside" the other culture.[71] You will learn more about how people think, feel, and behave in their personal and business dealings.

Nonverbal signals convey meaning, too

People send and interpret signals other than those that are spoken or written. These nonverbal messages can support or undermine the stated message. Often, nonverbal cues make a greater impact than other signals. In employees' eyes, managers' actions often speak louder than the words managers choose. Project manager Steve Bailey had already given many presentations when he attended a presentation skills workshop. There, a facilitator pointed out Bailey's habit of clasping and unclasping his hands as he spoke. The behavior was distracting and conveyed a lack of authority. When Bailey stopped making that gesture, he discovered that his audiences tended to be more convinced by his presentations.[72]

In conversation, except when you intend to convey a negative message, you should give nonverbal signals that express warmth, respect, concern, a feeling of equality, and a willingness to listen. Negative nonverbal signals show coolness, disrespect, lack of interest, and a feeling of superiority.[73] The following suggestions can help you send positive nonverbal signals:

- Use *time* appropriately. Avoid keeping your employees waiting to see you. Devote enough time to your meetings with them, and communicate frequently, which signals your interest in their concerns.

- Make your *office arrangement* conducive to open communication. A seating arrangement that avoids separating people helps establish a warm, cooperative atmosphere. In contrast, when you sit behind your desk and your subordinate sits before you, the environment is more intimidating and authoritative.[74]

- Remember your *body language*. Research indicates that facial expression and tone of voice can account for 90 percent of the communication between two people.[75] Several nonverbal body signals convey a positive attitude toward the other person: assuming a position close to the person; gesturing frequently; maintaining eye contact; smiling; having an open body orientation, such as facing the other person directly; uncrossing the arms; and leaning forward to convey interest in what the other person is saying.

Silence is an interesting nonverbal situation. The average American is said to spend about twice as many hours per day in conversation as the average Japanese.[76] North Americans tend to talk to fill silences. Japanese allow long silences to develop, believing they can get to know people better. Japanese believe that two people with good rapport will know each other's thoughts. The need to use words implies a lack of understanding.

nonverbal signals in different countries

Here are just a few nonverbal mistakes that Americans might make in other countries.[77] Nodding the head up and down in Bulgaria means no. The American thumb-and-first-finger circular A-OK gesture is vulgar in Brazil, Singapore, Russia, and Paraguay. The head is sacred in Buddhist cultures, so you must never touch someone's head. In Muslim cultures, never touch or eat with the left hand, which is thought unclean. Crossing your ankle over your knee is rude in Indonesia, Thailand, and Syria. Don't point your finger toward yourself in Germany or Switzerland—it insults the other person.

You also must correctly interpret the nonverbal signals of others. Chinese scratch their ears and cheeks to show happiness. Greeks puff air after they receive a compliment. Hondurans touch their fingers below their eyes to show disbelief or caution. Japanese indicate embarrassment or "no" by sucking in air and hissing through their teeth. Vietnamese look to the ground with their heads down to show respect. Compared with Americans, Russians use fewer facial expressions, and Scandinavians fewer hand gestures, whereas people in Mediterranean and Latin cultures may gesture and touch more. Brazilians are more likely than Americans to interrupt, Arabs to speak loudly, and Asians to respect silence.

Use these examples not to stereotype but to remember that people in other cultures have different styles and to aid in communication accuracy.

Receivers can improve their listening, reading, and observational skills

Once you become effective at sending oral, written, and nonverbal messages, you are halfway toward becoming a complete communicator. However, you must also develop adequate receiving capabilities. Receivers need good listening, reading, and observational skills.

listening In today's demanding work environment, managers need excellent listening skills. Although it is easy to assume that good listening is easy and natural, in fact it is difficult and far less common than needed. Catherine Coughlin practiced her listening skills as a customer service representative for Union Electric Company during the summers of the years she was earning her college degree. Whether an individual was calling about an unpaid bill, a power outage, or just looking for an excuse to talk to somebody, Coughlin found that "you've got to respect everyone and their story" and then decide how to respond. Over the following decades, Coughlin used that experience to build a successful career with Southwestern Bell Telephone and its successor companies. She is now president and chief executive officer of AT&T Midwest and is still committed to careful listening.[78]

A basic technique called *reflection* will help a manager listen effectively.[80] **Reflection** is a process by which a person states what he or she believes the other person is saying. This technique places greater emphasis on listening than on talking. When both parties actively engage in reflection, they get into each other's frame of reference rather than listening and responding from their own. The result is more accurate two-way communication.

> **"You never learn anything while you're talking."**
>
> —Catherine Coughlin, CEO, AT&T Midwest[79]

● REFLECTION Process by
which a person states
what he or she believes
the other person is saying.

Besides using reflection, you can improve how well you listen by practicing the following techniques:[81]

1. *Find an area of interest.* Even if you decide the topic is dull, ask yourself, "What is the speaker saying that I can use?"

2. *Judge content, not delivery.* Don't get caught up in the speaker's personality, mannerisms, speaking voice, or clothing. Instead, try to learn what the speaker knows.

3. *Hold your fire.* Rather than getting immediately excited by what the speaker seems to be saying, withhold evaluation until you understand the speaker's message.

4. *Listen for ideas.* Don't get bogged down in all the facts and details; focus on central ideas.

5. *Be flexible.* Have several systems for note taking, and use the system best suited to the speaker's style. Don't take too many notes or try to force everything said by a disorganized speaker into a formal outline.

6. *Resist distraction.* Close the door, shut off the radio, move closer to the person talking, or ask him or her to speak louder. Don't look out the window or at papers on your desk.

7. *Exercise your mind.* Some people tune out when the material gets difficult. Develop an appetite for a good mental challenge.

8. *Keep your mind open.* Many people get overly emotional when they hear words referring to their most deeply held convictions, for example, *union, subsidy, import, Republican* or *Democrat,* and *big business.* Try not to let your emotions interfere with comprehension.

9. *Capitalize on thought speed.* Take advantage of the fact that most people talk at a rate of about 125 words per minute, but most of us think at about four times that rate. Use those extra 400 words per minute to think about what the speaker is saying rather than turning your thoughts to something else.

10. *Work at listening.* Spend some energy. Don't just pretend you're paying attention. Show interest. Good listening is hard work, but the benefits outweigh the costs.

For managers, the stakes are high; failure to listen causes managers to miss good ideas and can even drive employees away. When Ben Berry was a senior systems analyst at a hospital, he was assigned to help lead a team charged with developing computer applications. The other team leader, a doctor, had little interest in hearing ideas from Berry and the team members. He was more focused on issuing directions. The team members and Berry felt discouraged from participating. Berry tried discussing the issue with his supervisor and with the doctor, but the doctor never saw a need to listen, so Berry left the organization to take another job.[82]

Listening begins with personal contact. Staying in the office, keeping the door closed, and eating lunch at your desk are sometimes necessary to get pressing work done, but that is no way

TIP

Can you really be an effective collaborator if you don't know how to listen?

to stay on top of what's going on. Better to walk the halls, initiate conversations and go to lunch even with people outside your area, have coffee in a popular gathering place, and maybe even move your desk onto the factory floor.[83]

When a manager takes time to really listen to and get to know people, they think, "She's showing an interest in me" or "He's letting me know that I matter" or "She values my ideas and contributions." Trust develops. Listening and learning from others are even more important for innovation than for routine work. Successful change and innovation come through lots of human contact.

reading Illiteracy is a significant problem in the United States. Even if illiteracy is not a problem in your organization, reading mistakes are common and costly. As a receiver, for your own benefit, read memos and e-mail as soon as possible, before it's too late to respond. You may skim most of your reading materials, but read important messages, documents, and passages slowly and carefully. Note important points for later referral. Consider taking courses to increase your reading speed and comprehension skills. Finally, don't limit your reading to items about your particular job skill or technical expertise; read materials that fall outside your immediate concerns. You never know when a creative and useful idea will be inspired by a novel, a biography, a sports story, or an article about a problem in another business or industry.

observing Effective communicators are also capable of observing and interpreting nonverbal communications. For example, by reading nonverbal cues, a presenter can determine how her talk is going and adjust her approach if necessary. Some companies train their sales force to interpret the nonverbal signals of potential customers. People can also decode nonverbal signals to determine whether a sender is being truthful or deceitful. In the United States, deceitful communicators tend to maintain less eye contact, make either more or fewer body movements than usual, and smile either too much or too little. Verbally, they offer fewer specifics than do truthful senders.[84]

A vital source of useful observations comes from visiting people, plants, and other locations to get a firsthand view.[85] Many corporate executives rely heavily on reports from the field

"You can observe a lot by watching."

— Yogi Berra

and don't travel to remote locations to observe what is going on. Reports are no substitute for actually seeing things happen in practice. Frequent visits to the field and careful observation can help a manager develop deep understanding of current operations, future prospects, and ideas for how to fully exploit capabilities.[86]

Of course, you must *accurately interpret* what you observe. A Canadian conducting business with a high-ranking official in Kuwait was surprised that the meeting was held in an open office and was interrupted constantly.[87] He interpreted the lack of a big, private office and secretary to mean that the Kuwaiti was of low rank and uninterested in doing business, so he lost interest in the deal. The Canadian observed the facts accurately, but his perceptual biases and limited awareness of cultural differences in norms caused him to misinterpret what he saw.

The Japanese are particularly skilled at interpreting every nuance of voice and gesture, putting most Westerners at a disadvantage.[88] When one is conducting business in Asian or other countries, local guides can be invaluable not only to interpret language but to "decode" behavior at meetings, what subtle hints and nonverbal cues mean, who the key people are, and how the decision-making process operates.

(L)(O) 5 **WHAT YOU NEED TO KNOW . . .**
How can you improve downward, upward, and horizontal communication?

ORGANIZATIONAL COMMUNICATION

Being a skilled communicator is essential to being a good manager and team leader. But communication must also be managed throughout the organization. Every minute of every day, countless bits of information are transmitted through an organization. The flow of information affects how well people perform. When a group's success depends on discovering new information, individuals who independently tap information from a variety of sources help achieve that success. For evaluating information and arriving at decisions, people in the most effective groups communicate extensively with their team members (a richly connected network). The most productive teams switch back and forth between using centralized networks and richly connected networks.[89] These patterns of communication may include communications traveling downward, upward, horizontally, and informally within the organization.

Downward communication directs, motivates, coaches, and informs

Downward communication refers to the flow of information from higher to lower levels in the organization's hierarchy.

Examples include a manager giving an assignment to an assistant, a supervisor making an announcement to his subordinates, and a company president delivering a talk to her management team. Downward communication that provides relevant information helps create employee identification with the company, supportive attitudes, and decisions consistent with the organization's objectives.[90]

People must receive the information they need to perform their jobs and become—and remain—loyal members of the organization. But they often lack adequate information.[91] Several problems underlie the lack of information:

- *Information overload*—Managers and employees are bombarded with so much information that they fail to absorb everything. Much of the information is not very important, but its volume causes a lot of relevant information to be lost.

- *Lack of openness between managers and employees*—Managers may believe, "No news is good news," "I don't have time to keep them informed of everything they want to know," or "It's none of their business, anyway." Some managers withhold information even if sharing it would be useful.

- *Filtering*—As we discussed earlier in the chapter, when messages are passed from one person to another, some information is left out. When a message passes through many people, more information may be lost during each transmission. The message also can be distorted as people add words or interpretations. Filtering poses serious problems in organizations when messages are communicated downward through many organizational levels and much information is lost.

The data in Figure 12.2 suggest that by the time messages reach the people for whom they are intended, the receivers may get very little useful information. The fewer authority levels through which communications must pass, the less information will be lost or distorted. As a result, in flatter organizations, filtering is less of a problem with downward communication.

Managers can address some of these issues by fostering a culture that values communication. At a large telecommunications company, employees consistently rated the human resource (HR) division best at communicating with them. The divisional president sent out monthly e-mail messages about new accounts, products in development, hiring trends, and individual employees' accomplishments. Employees and managers were also kept up-to-date through face-to-face communications at quarterly town hall meetings, monthly meetings of line managers, and weekly senior-management meetings. And the president invited about 10 employees at a time to communicate informally at monthly breakfasts and lunches.[92]

coaching Some of the most important downward communications occur when managers give performance feedback to their direct reports. We discussed earlier the importance of giving feedback and positive reinforcement when it is deserved. It is also important to explicitly discuss poor performance and areas that can be improved.

Coaching is dialogue with a goal of helping another be more effective and achieve his or her full potential on the job.[93] Done properly, coaching develops executives and enhances performance.[94] When people have performance problems or exhibit behaviors that need to be changed, coaching is often the best way to help them change and succeed. And coaching is not just for poor performers; as the greatest athletes know, it is for anyone who is good and aspires to excellence. Coaches for executives sometimes are hired from the outside, but a coach from outside your organization may not fully understand the context in which you work.[95] So don't take advice automatically. The best use of a coach is as a sounding board, helping you think through the potential impact of your ideas, generate new options, and learn from experience.

Companies including Coca-Cola use coaching as an essential part of their executive development process. When done well, coaching is true dialogue between two committed people engaged in joint problem solving. It is far more than an occasion for highlighting poor performance, delivering reprimands, or giving advice. Good coaching requires achieving real understanding of the problem, the person, and the situation; jointly generating ideas for what to do; and encouraging the person to improve. Good coaches ask a lot of questions, listen well, provide input, and encourage others to think for themselves. Effective coaching requires honesty, calmness, and supportiveness, all aided by a sincere desire to help. The ultimate and longest-lasting form of help is enabling people to think through and solve their own problems.

downward communication in difficult times

Adequate downward communication can be particularly valuable during difficult times. During corporate mergers and acquisitions, employees feel anxious and wonder how the changes will affect them. Ideally (and ethically), top management should communicate with employees about the change as early as possible.

But some argue against that approach, on the grounds that informing employees about the reorganization might cause them to quit too early. Then too, top management often cloisters itself, prompting rumors and anxiety. CEOs and other senior execs are surrounded by lawyers, investment bankers, and so on—people who are paid merely to make the deal happen, not to make it work. Yet with the people who are affected by the deal, you must increase, not decrease, communication.[96]

In a merger of two *Fortune* 500 companies, two plants received very different information.[97] All employees at both plants received the initial letter from the CEO announcing the merger. But after that, one plant was kept in the dark while the other was continually filled in on what was happening. Top management gave employees information about layoffs, transfers, promotions and demotions, and changes in pay, jobs, and benefits.

Which plant do you think fared better as the difficult transitional months unfolded? In both plants, the merger decreased employees' job satisfaction and commitment to the organization and increased their belief that the company was untrustworthy, dishonest, and uncaring. In the plant whose employees got little information, these problems persisted for a long time. But in the plant where employees received complete information, the situation stabilized, and attitudes improved toward their normal levels. Full communication not only helped employees survive an anxious period but also served a symbolic value by signaling care and concern for employees. Without such communications, employee reactions to a merger or acquisition may be so negative as to undermine the corporate strategy.

open-book management

Executives often are proud of their newsletters, staff meetings, videos, and other vehicles of downward communication. More often than not, the information provided concerns company sports teams, birthdays, and new copy machines. But today a more unconventional philosophy is gathering steam. Open-book management is the practice of sharing with employees at all levels of the organization vital information previously meant for management's eyes only. This information includes financial goals, income statements, budgets, sales, forecasts, and other relevant data about company performance and prospects. This practice is dramatically different from the traditional closed-book approach in which people may or may not have a clue about how the company is doing, may or may not believe the things that management tells them, and

FIGURE 12.2 Information Loss in Downward Communication

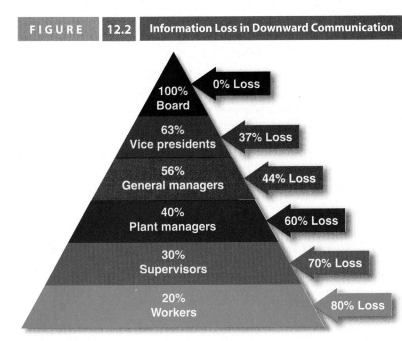

100% Board — 0% Loss
63% Vice presidents — 37% Loss
56% General managers — 44% Loss
40% Plant managers — 60% Loss
30% Supervisors — 70% Loss
20% Workers — 80% Loss

may or may not believe that their personal performance makes a difference. Open-book management is controversial, as many managers prefer to keep such information to themselves. Sharing strategic plans and financial information with employees could lead to leaks to competitors or to employee dissatisfaction with compensation. But the companies that share this information claim a favorable impact on motivation and productivity. Cecil Ursprung, president and CEO of Reflexite Corporation in New Britain, Connecticut, said, "Why would you tell 5 percent of the team what the score was and not the other 95 percent?"[98]

Father of scientific management Frederick Taylor early in the 20th century would have considered opening the books to all employees "idiotic."[99] But then Jack Stack tried it at Springfield ReManufacturing Corporation, which was on the brink of collapse.[100] The results? A reporter called Jack Stack's SRC "the most highly motivated and business-savvy work force I ever encountered." In addition, "I met fuel-injection-pump rebuilders who knew the gross margins of every nozzle and pump they produced. I met crankshaft grinders and engine assemblers who could discuss the ROI of their machine tools." The rewards they deserve are part of the picture, too: "I met a guy who worked on turbochargers and ran his area as if it were his own small business. Then again, why shouldn't he? Like the other employees, he was an owner of SRC."[101]

Other small companies joined the movement. Then bigger companies, including BP Canada, R. H. Donnelley, Wabash National, and Baxter Healthcare, began to use open-book management.

Opening the books, done properly, is a complete communications system that makes sense to people on the shop floor just as it does to the top executives. Moving toward open-book management includes these basic steps:[102]

1. Provide the information.
2. Teach basic finance and the basics of the business.
3. Empower people to make decisions based on what they know.
4. Make sure everyone shares directly in the company's success (and risks), such as through stock ownership and bonuses.

Upward communication is invaluable to management

Upward communication travels from lower to higher ranks in the hierarchy. Adequate upward communication is important for several reasons:[103]

- Managers learn what's going on. Management gains a more accurate picture of subordinates' work, accomplishments, problems, plans, attitudes, and ideas.
- Employees gain from the opportunity to communicate upward. People can relieve some of their frustrations, achieve a stronger sense of participation in the enterprise, and improve morale.
- Effective upward communication facilitates downward communication as good listening becomes a two-way street.

A manufacturing company relied on upward communication as it prepared to operate shifts around the clock. Managers expected that the change would be challenging for some employees, so it assembled a focus group of factory workers to inform management about how the new work shifts would affect workers' families and other commitments, including night school. Discussing possibilities with the focus group members before the change had been formally announced posed the risk that employees would spread rumors, but management determined that this risk was less important than the risk of proceeding with ignorance of employees' concerns. The change to the new shifts took employees' concerns into account and proceeded smoothly.[105]

The problems common in upward communication resemble those for downward communication. Managers, like their subordinates, are bombarded with information and may neglect or miss information from below. In addition, some employees are not always open with their bosses; filtering occurs upward as well as downward. People tend to share only good news with their bosses and suppress bad news for several reasons:

- They want to appear competent.
- They mistrust their boss and fear that if he or she finds out about something they have done, they will be punished.
- They fear the boss will punish the messenger, even if the reported problem is not that person's fault.
- They believe they are helping their boss if they shield him or her from problems.

For these and other reasons, managers may not learn about important problems. As one leadership expert put it, "If the messages from below say you are doing a flawless job, send back for a more candid assessment."[106]

When Howard Stringer became Sony Corporation's first foreign CEO, he was plagued by several upward—and downward—communication problems with his Japanese

> ## "Many people believe that if you are doing a good job and accomplishing something, your bosses necessarily know this, but they don't."
>
> —Jeffrey Pfeffer, professor of organizational behavior, Stanford[104]

● **UPWARD COMMUNICATION** Information that flows from lower to higher levels in the organization's hierarchy.

● **HORIZONTAL COMMUNICATION** Information shared among people on the same hierarchical level.

coworkers. The management team that he inherited preferred to deal with problems in the company's traditional Japanese manner—quietly, without informing him that anything was happening. While this method might be effective in handling a small personal disagreement, it unraveled into trouble for Sony, resulting in the delayed launch of the PlayStation 3 gaming system and a battery recall. Stringer had tried to encourage his top managers to cooperate with one another and consider new ways of developing products, but they had resisted. So when PlayStation was delayed and the battery recall occurred, Stringer decided it was time to reorganize his team.

Stringer replaced the head of the videogame division (who had been particularly uncommunicative) and began to receive every report dealing with manufacturing problems, including what he calls "more e-mails than I care to read." He notes that although "you can't go through a Japanese company with a sledgehammer," he has asserted his authority in more decisions recently. Stringer also maintains that Sony has begun experiencing far more communication among managers at the same level. Stringer says, "We can tell you in any given day, every single incidence that happens in any of our manufacturing, so I think we've learned quite a lot from this experience." Sony's CEO hopes never again to have a day when he doesn't know exactly what's going on inside his company.[107]

managing upward communication Generating useful information from below requires managers to both *facilitate* and *motivate* upward communication. For example, they can have an open-door policy and encourage people to use it, have lunch or coffee with employees, use surveys, institute a productivity program for suggestions, or have town-hall meetings. They can ask for employee advice, make informal visits to plants, really think about and respond to employee suggestions, and distribute summaries of new ideas and practices inspired by employee suggestions and actions.[108]

Some executives practice MBWA (management by wandering around). That term, coined by Ed Carlson of United Airlines, refers simply to getting out of the office, walking around, and talking frequently and informally with employees.[109] At the headquarters of Secura Insurance in Appleton, Wisconsin, CEO John Bykowski makes a habit of walking through the building to talk with and listen to employees.[110] In the offices of the *South Florida Sun-Sentinel*, editor Earl Maucker is known for dropping in to employees' offices and cubicles. Maucker is known among his editorial staff for being accessible and frank, so they trust what he says.[111]

At an aerospace company, management brought in consultants because trust and communications between management and employees were poor. The consultants assembled a team of employees to study the problem, and their top-priority recommendation was for managers to conduct informal walk-arounds, visiting employees in their work areas. The members of the problem-solving team told management they wanted these visits as a signal that managers cared to get to know them, spend time with them, and listen to them.[112]

Useful upward communication must be reinforced and not punished. Someone who tries to talk to a manager about a

problem must not be consistently brushed off. An announced open-door policy must truly be open-door. Also, people must trust their supervisor and know that he or she will not hold a grudge if they deliver negative information. To get honesty, managers must truly listen, not punish the messenger for being honest, and act on valid comments.

Horizontal communication fosters collaboration

Much information needs to be shared among people on the same hierarchical level. Such horizontal communication can take place among people in the same work team or in different departments. For example, a purchasing agent discusses a problem with a production engineer, and a task force of department heads meets to discuss a particular concern. Horizontal communication also occurs with people outside the firm, including potential investors.[113]

Horizontal communication has several important functions:[114]

- It allows units to share information, coordinate work, and solve mutual problems.
- It helps resolve conflicts.
- By allowing interaction among peers, it provides social and emotional support.

All these factors contribute to morale and effectiveness. David Carere, vice president, finance–credit and account settlement for Rich Products, emphasizes that his staff must collaborate with employees in other functions, especially sales and customer service. This horizontal collaboration helps the frozen-dessert company ensure that its sales are profitable and that bad debt is kept to a minimum. To foster communication between his employees and those in other departments, Carere sets up meetings where the credit department explains its role to employees of other departments and learns more about what they do.[115]

managing horizontal communication In complex environments, in which decisions in one unit affect another, information must be shared horizontally. An example of good horizontal communication is Motorola's annual conference for sharing best practices across functional and business groups throughout the company. NASA co-locates scientists from different disciplines. And Hewlett-Packard uses common databases for different product groups to share information and ideas.[117]

General Electric offers a great example of how to use productive horizontal communication as a competitive weapon.[118] GE's businesses could operate independently, but each is supposed to help the others. They transfer technical resources, people, information, ideas, and money among themselves. GE accomplishes this high level of communication and cooperation through easy

?

DID YOU KNOW?

Today's office workers engage in four modes of work: *focus* work (concentrating on a task that may involve thinking, writing, and reflecting), *collaborating* (working with others to generate and evaluate ideas), *learning* (acquiring new knowledge), and *socializing* (developing relationships). Employees of top-performing companies devote more time to the work modes requiring more horizontal communication—including 16 percent more time socializing.[116]

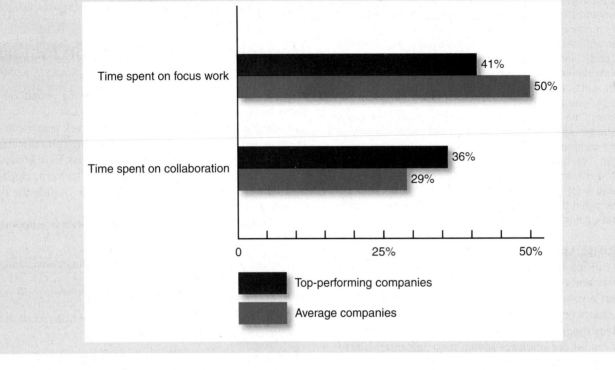

- Time spent on focus work: 41% (Top-performing companies), 50% (Average companies)
- Time spent on collaboration: 36% (Top-performing companies), 29% (Average companies)

0   25%   50%

■ Top-performing companies
■ Average companies

access between divisions and to the CEO; a culture of openness, honesty, trust, and mutual obligation; and quarterly meetings in which all the top executives get together to share information and ideas. Similar activities take place at lower levels as well.

(L)(O) 6   WHAT YOU NEED TO KNOW . . .

How can you work with the company grapevine?

Informal communication needs attention

Organizational communications differ in formality:

- *Formal communications* are official, organization-sanctioned episodes of information transmission. They can move upward, downward, or horizontally and often are prearranged and necessary for performing some task.

- *Informal communication* is more unofficial. People gossip; employees complain about their boss; people talk about their favorite sports teams; work teams tell newcomers how to get by.[119]

The **grapevine** is the social network of informal communications. Informal networks provide people with information, help them solve problems, and teach them how to do their work successfully. You should develop a good network of people willing and able to help.[120] However, the grapevine can be destructive when irrelevant or erroneous gossip and rumors proliferate and harm operations.[121]

What does this mean for you personally? Don't engage in e-gossip. Embarrassing episodes become public, and lawsuits based on defamation of character and invasion of privacy have used e-mail evidence. But don't avoid the grapevine, either.[122]

Listen, but evaluate before believing what you hear. Who is the source? How credible is he or she? Does the rumor make sense? Is it consistent or inconsistent with other things you know or have heard? Seek more information. Don't stir the pot.

managing informal communication   Rumors start over any number of topics, including salaries, job security, costly mistakes, and the identity of people who are leaving or being promoted. Rumors can destroy people's faith and trust in the company—and in each

● **GRAPEVINE** Informal communication network.

● **BOUNDARYLESS ORGANIZATION** Organization in which there are no barriers to information flow.

other. But the grapevine cannot be eliminated. So, managers need to *work with* the grapevine. The grapevine can be managed in several ways:[123]

- If a manager hears a story that could get out of hand, he or she should *talk to the key people* involved to get the facts and their perspectives. Don't allow malicious gossip.

- To *prevent* rumors from starting, managers can explain events that are important but have not been explained; dispel uncertainties by providing facts; and establish open communications and trust over time.[124] These efforts are especially important during times of uncertainty, such as after a merger or layoff or when sales slow down, because rumors increase along with anxiety. For example, when advertising revenues fell at R. H. Donnelley, which publishes yellow-pages directories, management stepped up efforts to make sure employees heard any company news straight from management, rather than on the news. Donnelley also encouraged its managers to make regular visits to salespeople to answer their questions.[125]

- The manager should *neutralize* rumors once they have started. Disregard the rumor if it is ridiculous; openly confirm any parts that are true; make public comments (no comment is seen as a confirmation of the rumor); deny the rumor, if the denial is based in truth (don't make false denials); make sure communications about the issue are consistent; select a spokesperson of appropriate rank and knowledge; and hold town meetings if needed.[126]

L O 7 WHAT YOU NEED TO KNOW . . .

Can you describe the boundaryless organization and its advantages?

Boundaryless organizations have no barriers to information flow

Many executives and management scholars today believe organizations need to ensure free access to information in all directions. Jack Welch, when he was CEO of General Electric, coined the term *boundarylessness*. A **boundaryless organization** is one without any barriers to information flow. If no boundaries separate people, jobs, processes, and places, then ideas, information, decisions, and actions can move to where they are most needed.[127] This free flow does not imply a random free-for-all of unlimited communication and information overload. It implies information available *as needed,* moving quickly and easily enough that the organization functions far better as a whole than as separate parts.

GE's chief learning officer uses the metaphor of the organization as a house with three kinds of boundaries: the floors and ceilings, the walls separating the rooms, and the outside walls. In organizations, these barriers correspond to the boundaries between different organizational levels, between different units and departments, and between the organization and its external stakeholders, such as suppliers and customers. GE also

identifies a fourth wall: global boundaries separating domestic from global operations.[128]

A method of breaking down boundaries is GE's famous Workout program, a series of meetings for business members across multiple hierarchical levels, characterized by extremely frank, tough discussions that break down vertical boundaries. Workout has involved over hundreds of thousands of GE people; in any given week, thousands may be participating in a Workout program.[129] Workout is also done with customers and suppliers, breaking down outside boundaries. GE has reached out to the community by sharing this expertise with nonprofits, such as CommonBond Communities, a provider of affordable housing. A GE employee led a Workout session in which CommonBond employees identified how to improve processes and horizontal communication.[130]

GE uses plenty of other techniques to break down boundaries, too. It relentlessly benchmarks competitors and companies in other industries to learn best practices all over the world. GE places different functions together physically, such as engineering and manufacturing. It shares services across units. And it sometimes shares physical locations with its customers.

Boundaryless organizations intentionally create dialogue across boundaries, turning barriers into permeable membranes. As the GE people put it, people from different parts of the organization need to learn "how to talk."[131] They must also learn "how to walk." That is, dialogue is essential, but it must be followed by commensurate action.

13

Managerial Control

Legal Sea Foods started out as a tiny fish market that George Berkowitz opened in 1950 next to his father's grocery store in Cambridge, Massachusetts. Today, it is a seafood empire, running more than 30 restaurants from Boston to Boca Raton and generating $200 million in annual revenues. How could a restaurant success story like Legal Sea Foods occur in an industry loaded with competitors and subject to the whims of the economy and Mother Nature? One reason is that Legal Sea Foods is fanatical about quality and employs formal systems to control quality in its supply chain, financial activities, information technology, and human resources.[1]

Dig Deeper

into how today's managers make sure employees and systems are meeting important goals. Listen to what Sheryl and J have to say on the book Web site.

> *"Effective managers need to make certain that their verbal message and actions are in sync. They need to be clear, concise, direct, and in a manner that your audience understands what is being communicated."*
> —Sheryl Freeman, Program Manager

> *"I have seen where one person makes all the decisions and that it ultimately cripples the ability of a company to grow beyond its current scope. If a manager has no real power or authority, then they feel useless and ultimately will become unhappy."*
> —J John Maggio III, Sales Manager

WHAT YOU NEED TO KNOW

•• learning OBJECTIVES

After studying Chapter 13, you should be able to:

LO1 Explain why companies develop control systems for employees.

LO2 Summarize how to design a basic bureaucratic control system.

LO3 Describe the purposes for using budgets as a control device.

LO4 Define basic types of financial statements and financial ratios used as controls.

LO5 List procedures for implementing effective control systems.

LO6 Identify ways in which organizations use market control mechanisms.

LO7 Discuss the use of clan control in an empowered organization.

● **CONTROL** Any process that directs the activities of individuals toward the achievement of organizational goals.

● **BUREAUCRATIC CONTROL** The use of rules, regulations, and authority to guide performance.

● **MARKET CONTROL** Control based on the use of pricing mechanisms and economic information to regulate activities within organizations.

● **CLAN CONTROL** Control based on the norms, values, shared goals, and trust among group members.

● **STANDARD** Expected performance for a given goal: a target that establishes a desired performance level, motivates performance, and serves as a benchmark against which actual performance is assessed.

Ⓛ Ⓞ **1 WHAT YOU NEED TO KNOW . . .**

Why do companies develop control systems for employees?

SPINNING OUT OF CONTROL?

Control is one of the fundamental forces that keep the organization together and heading in the right direction. Control is any process that directs the activities of individuals toward the achievement of organizational goals. It is how effective managers make sure that activities are going as planned. Some managers don't want to admit it, but control problems—the lack of controls or the wrong kinds of controls—frequently cause irreparable damage to organizations. Here are some signs that a company lacks controls:

- *Lax top management*—Senior managers do not emphasize or value the need for controls, or they set a bad example.

- *Absence of policies*—The firm's expectations are not established in writing.

- *Lack of agreed-upon standards*—Organization members are unclear about what needs to be achieved.

- *"Shoot the messenger" management*—Employees feel their careers would be at risk if they reported bad news.

- *Lack of periodic reviews*—Managers do not assess performance on a regular, timely basis.

- *Bad information systems*—Key data are not measured and reported in a timely and easily accessible way.

- *Lack of ethics in the culture*—Organization members have not internalized a commitment to integrity.

Ineffective control systems result in problems ranging from employee theft to lead in the paint of children's toys. Research in Motion was publicly embarrassed when failure to fully test a "noncritical system routine" for updating its computer servers caused the e-mail service on its BlackBerry devices to crash for hours throughout North America.[2] Employees simply wasting time cost U.S. employers billions of dollars each year![3]

Control has been called one of the Siamese twins of management. The other twin is planning. Some means of control are necessary because once managers form plans and strategies, they must ensure that the plans are carried out. They must make sure that other people are doing what needs to be done and not doing inappropriate things. If plans are not carried out properly, management must take steps to correct the problem. This process is the primary control function of management. By ensuring creativity, enhancing quality, and reducing cost, managers must figure out ways to control the activities in their organizations.

Not surprisingly, effective planning facilitates control, and control facilitates planning. Planning lays out a framework for the future and, in this sense, provides a blueprint for control. Control systems, in turn, regulate the allocation and use of resources and, in so doing, facilitate the process of the next phases of planning. In today's complex organizational environment, both functions have become more difficult to implement while they have become more important in every department of the organization. Managers today must control their people, inventories, quality, and costs, to mention just a few of their responsibilities.

According to William Ouchi of the University of California at Los Angeles, managers can apply three broad strategies for achieving organizational control:[5]

1. **Bureaucratic control** is the use of rules, standards, regulations, hierarchy, and legitimate authority to guide performance. It includes such items as budgets, statistical reports, and performance appraisals to regulate behavior and results. It works best where tasks are certain and workers are independent.

2. **Market control** involves the use of prices, competition, and exchange relationships to regulate activities in organizations as though they were economic transactions. Business units may be treated as profit centers and trade resources (services or goods) with one another via such mechanisms. Managers who run these units may be evaluated on the basis of profit and loss. Market control is most effective

❝ **"More than at any time in the past, companies will not be able to hold themselves together with the traditional methods of control: hierarchy, systems, budgets, and the like . . . The bonding glue will increasingly become ideological."** ❞

—Collins & Porras[4]

where tangible output can be identified and a market can be established between the parties to be controlled.

3. **Clan control**, unlike the first two types, does not assume that the interests of the organization and individuals naturally diverge. Instead, it is based on the idea that employees may share the values, expectations, and goals of the organization and act in accordance with them. When members of an organization have common values and goals—and trust one another—formal controls may be less necessary. Clan control is based on interpersonal processes of organization culture, leadership, and groups and teams. It works best where there is no "one best way" to do a job and employees are empowered to make decisions.

(L)(O) 2 WHAT YOU NEED TO KNOW . . .
Can you summarize how to design a basic bureaucratic control system?

BUREAUCRATIC CONTROL SYSTEMS

Bureaucratic (or formal) control systems are designed to measure progress toward set performance goals and, if necessary, to apply corrective measures to ensure that performance achieves managers' objectives. Control systems detect and correct significant variations, or discrepancies, in the results of planned activities.

Control systems have four steps

As Figure 13.1 shows, a typical control system has four major steps:

1. Setting performance standards
2. Measuring performance
3. Comparing performance against the standards and determining deviations
4. Taking action to correct problems and reinforce successes

step 1 : setting performance standards

Every organization has goals: profitability, innovation, satisfaction of customers and employees, and so on. A **standard** is the level of expected performance for a given goal. Standards are targets that establish desired performance levels, motivate performance, and serve as benchmarks against which to assess actual performance. Standards can be set for any activity—financial activities, operating activities, legal compliance, charitable contributions, and so on.[6]

We have discussed principles of setting performance standards in other chapters. For example, employees tend to be motivated by specific, measurable performance standards that are challenging and aim for improvement over past performance. Typically, performance standards are derived from job requirements, such as increasing market share by 10 percent, reducing costs 20 percent, and answering customer complaints within 24 hours. But performance standards don't apply just to people in isolation; they frequently integrate human and system performance. HealthPartners, a Bloomington, Minnesota, nonprofit organization that operates clinics and a hospital and offers health insurance plans, sets ambitious standards for patient care. To achieve a goal of reducing diabetes complications by 30 percent, HealthPartners measured existing practices and results, and then set up a standard protocol for exams and treatments, including the requirement that any abnormal results receive an immediate response. To encourage its physicians to follow the protocol, HealthPartners offers financial incentives for compliance. In little more than a decade, HealthPartners exceeded its goal for improved diabetes care. A local eye doctor commented that it was easy to tell which diabetic patients have coverage through HealthPartners because so few of them suffer diabetes-related damage to their retinas. HealthPartners has similar programs for treatment of cardiovascular disease and depression and for improving the health status of patients who are obese or smoke.[7]

Government Motors? General Motors former Chairman and CEO Rick Wagoner is shown here talking about the company's restructuring plans during a news conference in February 2009. He later resigned under pressure from the White House, as Fritz Henderson took over as the new CEO. Two months later a historic restructuring plan was implemented that would give the majority ownership of the ailing automaker to the federal government to help them fight off bankruptcy. What type of control is exemplified by this action?

FIGURE 13.1 The Control Process

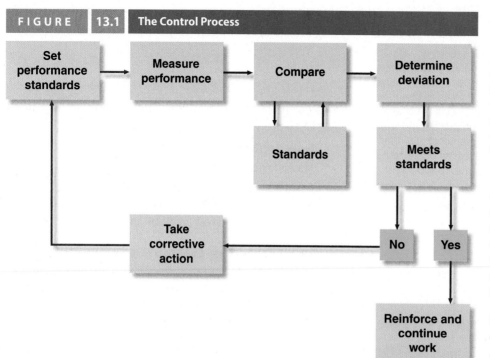

Performance standards can be set with respect to various measures of success:

- Quantity
- Quality
- Time used
- Cost

For example, production activities include volume of output (quantity), defects (quality), on-time availability of finished goods (time use), and dollar expenditures for raw materials and direct labor (cost). Many important aspects of performance, such as customer service, can be measured by the same standards—adequate supply and availability of products, quality of service, speed of delivery, and so forth.

Sometimes quality standards involve meeting or exceeding standards set by government agencies. Recently, the Food and Drug Administration proposed loosening its standards for the ingredients in products labeled "chocolate" to allow the use of vegetable fats other than cocoa butter. If the rule change takes effect, candies like Whoppers malted milk balls and PayDay Chocolatey Avalanche could put "chocolate" in their names.

Some true chocolate lovers are horrified, but Nick Malgieri, director of

At the Baccarat factory in France, the workers in the quality control area are responsible for the quality and selection of these fine cut crystal glasses.

the baking program at the Institute of Culinary Education in New York, says, "No one is going to force a high-class chocolate maker to add vegetable fat to chocolate."[8] At companies that seek a reputation for premium quality, the recipe standards can remain as strict as ever, and chocolate aficionados will be on the alert.

One word of caution: the downside of establishing performance targets and standards is that they may not be supported by other elements of the control system. Each piece of the system is important and depends on the others. Otherwise, the system can get terribly out of balance.

step 2: measuring performance

The second step in the control process is to measure performance levels. For example, managers can count units produced, days absent, papers filed, samples distributed, and dollars earned. Performance data commonly are obtained from three sources:

1. *Written reports* include computer printouts and on-screen reports. Thanks to computers' data-gathering and analysis capabilities and decreasing costs, companies of any size can gather huge amounts of performance data.

2. *Oral reports* allow for two-way communication. When a salesperson contacts his or her supervisor each evening to report the day's accomplishments, problems, and customer reactions, the manager can ask questions to gain additional information or clear up any misunderstandings. When necessary, tentative corrective actions can be worked out during the discussion.

3. *Personal observation* involves going to the area where activities take place and watching what is occurring. The manager can directly observe work methods, employees' nonverbal signals, and the general operation. Personal observation gives a detailed picture of what is going on, but it also has some disadvantages. It does not provide accurate quantitative data; the information usually is general and subjective. Also, employees can misunderstand the purpose of personal observation as mistrust or lack of confidence. Still, many managers believe in the value of firsthand observation. As you learned in earlier chapters,

personal contact can increase leadership visibility and upward communication. It also provides valuable information about performance to supplement written and oral reports.

Regardless of the performance measure used, the information must be provided to managers on a timely basis. For example, consumer-goods companies like General Foods carefully track new-product sales in selected local markets first so that they can make any necessary adjustments well before a national rollout. Information that is not available is of little or no use to managers.

step 3: comparing performance with the standard

The third step in the control process is comparing performance with the standard. In this process, the manager evaluates the performance. For some activities, relatively small deviations from the standard are acceptable, while in others a slight deviation may be serious. In many manufacturing processes, a significant deviation in either direction (e.g., drilling a hole that is too small or too large) is unacceptable. In other cases, a deviation in one direction, such as sales or customer satisfaction below the target level, is a problem, but a deviation in the other—exceeding the sales target or customer expectations—is a sign employees are getting better-than-expected results. Therefore, managers who perform the oversight must analyze and evaluate the results carefully.

The managerial principle of exception states that control is enhanced by concentrating on the exceptions to, or significant deviations from, the expected result or standard. In other words, in comparing performance with the standard, managers need to direct their attention to the exception—for example, a handful of defective components produced on an assembly line or the feedback from customers who are upset or delighted with a service. Atlanta-based US Security Associates uses information technology to gather performance data on its uniformed security guards and dispatches supervisors to investigate any variances from performance norms, such as a failure of a guard to sign in at a client's location on time.[9]

With the principle of exception, only exceptional cases require corrective action. This principle is important in controlling. The manager is not concerned with performance that equals or closely approximates the expected results. Managers can save much time and effort if they apply the principle of exception.

The accounting and consulting firm of Moody, Famiglietti & Andronico (MFA) uses a formal control process to ensure that it provides exceptional service tailored to each client's needs and preferences. The Tewksbury, Massachusetts, firm adopted the U.S. Army's practice of conducting before-action reviews and after-action reviews to learn from experience and apply those lessons in the future.

When employees are preparing to handle an assignment, they call a short meeting with everyone who has worked with that client during the previous year, as well as employees who have handled similar assignments for other clients. During this before-action review, participants trade experiences with and knowledge about the client—say, questions that are likely to arise or existing tools for handling common problems. The input from this meeting helps the team establish goals.

During the assignment, team members meet periodically to assess progress and identify any adjustments needed. Soon after the project's completion, the team reassembles to compare outcomes with goals. Participants identify successful actions to recommend in the future, as well as mistakes to avoid next time. Besides noting whether they helped the client meet goals, they also record what they learned about serving the client. Because lessons they learn will come up at future before-action reviews, MFA employees are motivated to fix mistakes and improve methods.[10]

step 4: taking action to correct problems and reinforce successes

The last step in the control process is to take appropriate action when there are significant deviations. This step ensures that operations are adjusted to achieve the planned results—or to continue exceeding the plan if the manager determines that is possible. If significant variances are discovered, the manager usually takes immediate and vigorous action.

An alternative approach is for the corrective action to be taken, not by higher-ups, but by the operator at the point of the problem. In computer-controlled production technology, two basic types of control are feasible:

1. *Specialist control*—Operators of computer-numerical-control (CNC) machines must notify engineering specialists of malfunctions. With this traditional division of labor, the specialist takes corrective action.

> ❝ **"Mistakes and problems are inevitable in complex enterprises. . . . We shouldn't expect heads of established organizations to be perfect, but we should expect them to catch and correct their mistakes quickly."** ❞
>
> —Rosabeth Moss Kanter, professor, Harvard Business School[11]

2. *Operator control*—Multiskilled operators can rectify their own problems as they occur. This strategy is more efficient because deviations are controlled closer to their source. It is also more satisfying, because operators benefit by having a more enriched job.

At Microscan System, which makes bar-code scanners, every employee is responsible for ensuring the quality of his or her work, resulting in efficient operations. Engineers are responsible for preventing and correcting problems in product and process design, and production workers are responsible for preventing and correcting defects in the processes they carry out.[12]

The selection of the corrective action depends on the nature of the problem. The corrective action may involve a shift in marketing strategy (if, say, the problem is lower-than-expected sales), a disciplinary action, a new way to check the accuracy of manufactured parts, or a major modification to a process or system. Sometimes managers learn they can get better results if they adjust their own practices. Yum Brands, whose franchise restaurants include KFC, Taco Bell, Pizza Hut, and Long John Silver's, conducts regular surveys to learn whether employees feel strong commitment to their jobs. These data are shared with managers to help them measure their performance as leaders and motivators. Jonathan McDaniel, a Houston KFC manager, once learned that his employees were unhappy with their work hours. He began asking them ahead of time whether they wanted particular days off each month—information that

?

DID YOU KNOW?

When corrective action is needed to solve a systemic problem, such as major delays in work flow, often a team approach is most effective. A corrective action is more likely to gain wider acceptance if it is based on a common effort and takes into account multiple points of view. As we discussed earlier, teams may bring a greater diversity of resources, ideas, and perspectives to problem solving.

Knowledgeable team members can steer the team away from implementing simplistic solutions that ignore the problem's underlying causes. They are more likely to consider the effects of any solution on other parts of the organization, preventing new problems from arising later. And they may develop solutions that managers might not have considered on their own. As a result, any corrective action that is finally adopted will probably be more effective. Team-based problem solving also helps managers build and reinforce a culture of high standards.

helped him create better schedules and end a cause of employee dissatisfaction.[13]

Bureaucratic control occurs before, during, and after operations

Bureaucratic control combines three approaches, defined according to their timing:

1. **Feedforward control** takes place before operations begin and includes policies, procedures, and rules designed to ensure that planned activities are carried out properly. Examples include inspection of raw materials and proper selection and training of employees.

2. **Concurrent control** takes place while plans are being carried out. It includes directing, monitoring, and fine-tuning activities as they occur.

3. **Feedback control** focuses on the use of information about results to correct deviations from the acceptable standard after they arise.

feedforward control
Feedforward control (sometimes called *preliminary control*) is future oriented; its aim is to prevent problems before they arise. Instead of waiting for results and comparing them with goals, a manager can exert control by limiting activities in advance. For example, companies have policies defining the scope within which decisions are made. A company may dictate that managers must adhere to clear ethical and legal guidelines when making decisions. Formal rules and procedures also prescribe people's actions before they occur. For example, legal experts advise companies to establish policies forbidding disclosure of proprietary information or making clear that employees are not speaking for the company when they post messages on blogs, microblogging sites such as Twitter, or social-networking sites such as Facebook. Human resource policies defining what forms of body art are acceptable to display at work can avoid awkward case-by-case conversations about a tattoo that offends coworkers or piercings that are incompatible with the company's image.[14]

Recently, more managers have grown concerned about the organizational pitfalls of workplace romances, and some have sought a solution in feedforward controls. As wonderful as it is to find love, problems can arise if romantic activities between a supervisor and subordinate create a conflict of interest or charges of sexual harassment. Other employees might interpret the relationship wrongly—that the company sanctions personal relationships as a path to advancement. In addition, romantic ups-and-downs can spill over into the workplace and affect everyone's mood and motivation. Controls aimed at preventing such problems in an organization include training in appropriate behavior (including how to avoid sexual harassment) and even requiring executives and their romantic interests to sign "love contracts" in which they indicate that the relationship is voluntary and welcome. A copy of the contract goes into the

● **FEEDFORWARD CONTROL** The control process used before operations begin, including policies, procedures, and rules designed to ensure that planned activities are carried out properly.

● **CONCURRENT CONTROL** The control process used while plans are being carried out, including directing, monitoring, and fine-tuning activities as they are performed.

● **FEEDBACK CONTROL** Control that focuses on the use of information about previous results to correct deviations from the acceptable standard.

company's personnel files in case the attachment disintegrates and an unhappy employee wants to blame the company for having allowed it in the first place.[15]

concurrent control

Concurrent control, which takes place while plans are carried out, is the heart of any control system. On a manufacturing floor, all efforts are directed toward producing the correct quantity and quality of the right products in the specified amount of time. In an airline terminal, the baggage must get to the right airplanes before flights depart. And in many settings, supervisors watch employees to ensure they work efficiently and avoid mistakes.

Advances in information technology have created powerful concurrent controls. Computerized systems give managers immediate access to data from the remotest corners of their companies. For example, managers can update budgets instantly from a continuous flow of performance data. In production facilities, monitoring systems that track errors per hour, machine speeds, and other measures let managers correct small production problems before they become disasters. Point-of-sale terminals in store checkout lines send sales data back to a retailer's headquarters to show which products are selling in which locations.

For James Skinner, CEO of McDonald's, paying attention to what is happening in the restaurants is critical. McDonald's launches of new menu items such as its McCafé premium coffee drinks, breakfast burritos, and McGriddle sandwiches have been hits with customers looking for value in their food purchases. Skinner and his staff check sales monthly in all stores to assess what is selling well throughout the global chain and to make adjustments. Monitoring these details as they occur has allowed McDonald's to grow even during the recent recession.[16]

feedback control

Feedback control is involved when performance data have been gathered and analyzed and the results have been returned to someone (or something) in the process to make corrections. When supervisors monitor behavior, they are exercising concurrent control. When they point out and correct improper performance, they are using feedback as a means of control.

Timing is an important aspect of feedback control. Long time lags often occur between performance and feedback, such as when actual spending is compared with the quarterly budget, instead of weekly or monthly, or when some aspect of performance is compared with the projection made a year earlier. Yet, if feedback on performance is not timely, managers cannot quickly identify and eliminate the problem and prevent more serious harm.[17]

Some feedback processes are under real-time (concurrent) control, such as a computer-controlled robot on an assembly line. Such units have sensors that continually determine whether they are in the correct position to perform their functions. If they are not, a built-in control device makes immediate corrections.

In other situations, feedback processes require more time. Some companies that value innovation are applying social network analysis, which uses data from surveys to create diagrams showing which employees collaborate with which colleagues. Employees who are at a hub of information sharing are the organization's "innovation catalysts"—people who actively participate in information sharing. Managers can use the social network analysis to reward innovation catalysts; give them important assignments; and, in areas where not enough collaboration is occurring, train and motivate employees to share knowledge.[18]

the role of six sigma

One of the most important quality-control tools to emerge is Six Sigma, which we mentioned in Chapter 6. It is a particularly robust and powerful application of feedback control. Six Sigma is designed to reduce defects in all organization processes—not just product defects but anything that may result in customer dissatisfaction, such as inadequate service, delayed delivery, and excessively high prices due to high costs or inefficiency. The system was developed at Motorola in the late 1980s, when the company found it was being beaten consistently in the competitive marketplace by foreign firms that were able to produce higher-quality products at a lower cost. Since then, the technique has been widely adopted and even improved on by many companies, such as GE, Allied Signal, Ford, and Xerox.

Sigma is the Greek letter used in statistics to designate the estimated standard deviation, or variation in a process. It indicates how often defects in a process are likely to occur. The lower the sigma number, the higher the level of variation or defects; the higher the sigma number, the lower the level of variation or defects. For example, a two-sigma-level process has more than 300,000 defects per million opportunities (DPMO)—not a very well-controlled process. A three-sigma-level process has 66,807 DPMO, which is roughly a 93 percent level of accuracy. Many organizations operate at this level, which on its face does not sound too bad, until we consider its implications—for example, 7 items of airline baggage lost for every 100 processed. The additional costs to organizations of such inaccuracy are enormous. Even at just above a 99 percent defect-free rate, or 6,210 DPMO, the accuracy level is often unacceptable—the statistical equivalent of about 50 dropped newborn babies a day.[19]

At six-sigma-level, a process is producing fewer than 3.4 defects per million, which means it is operating at a 99.99966 percent level of accuracy. Six Sigma companies have not only close to zero product or service defects but also substantially lower production costs and cycle times and much higher levels of customer satisfaction. The methodology isn't just for the factory floor, either. Accountants have used Six Sigma to improve the quality of their audits investigating risks faced by their clients.[20]

The Six Sigma approach is based on an intense statistical analysis of business processes that contribute to customer satisfaction. For example, a process GE measured when it began using the method was product delivery time. Once the defects or variations are measured, their causes are analyzed. Teams of employees work on designing and testing new processes that will reduce the causes of the variations. For example, if the team finds that delivery delays are caused by production bottlenecks, it will work on eliminating those. When an improved process is installed, it is analyzed again for remaining defects, and employees then work on reducing those. This cycle continues until the desired quality level is achieved. In this way, the Six Sigma process leads to continuous improvement in an organization's operations.

Six Sigma has come under some criticism for not always delivering business results.[21] One likely reason Six Sigma doesn't always improve the bottom line is that it focuses only on how to eliminate defects in a process, not whether the process is the best one for the organization. So, for example, at 3M, a drive to improve efficiency through Six Sigma has been blamed for slowing the flow of innovative ideas. At Home Depot, Six Sigma has been credited with improving such processes as customer checkout and deciding where to place products in stores, but some say the effort took store workers away from customers. One way managers can apply the strengths of Six Sigma and minimize the drawbacks is by setting different goals and control processes for the company's mature products than for its areas of innovation.

The Columbus Metropolitan Library used Six Sigma to the benefit of its workers, customers, and overall processes. The library, a not-for-profit organization, faced a freeze on budget increases, squeezing staff and services, so the library's managers had to figure out how to perform better without added resources. To accomplish this, they turned to the Lean Six Sigma (LSS) approach, which combines Six Sigma quality improvement methods with efforts to eliminate waste in time, materials, and complex processes. Library managers settled on areas needing improvement, formed teams, and began to identify and define the library's specific problems.

One of the narrower projects involved reviewing how long a customer had to wait to speak to a staff member after dialing the library's information line. The line is a crucial link to the public, handling nearly 400,000 calls a year. Despite its importance, customers sometimes had to wait as much as 5 minutes to speak with someone—creating general dissatisfaction with the library. At first glance, it seemed that more staff would be needed to alleviate the problem. But when the project team dug deeper and applied statistical analysis, they discovered that the wait time was really caused by the length of the recorded menu and the way staff was trained to handle it. With reprogramming of the menu and retraining of the current staff, most calls to the information line are now answered in fewer than 15 seconds.

The library has also undertaken projects involving community relations and development, requests for printed documents, human resources, and finance. "Of course, true systemwide quality improvement will require more than a handful of successful projects," writes library executive Shaunessy Everett. But the Columbus Metropolitan Library is now a true devotee of the Six Sigma approach.[22]

Management audits control various systems

Over the years, management audits have developed as a means of evaluating the effectiveness and efficiency of various systems within an organization, from social responsibility programs to accounting control. Management audits may be external or internal. Managers conduct external audits of other companies and internal audits of their own companies. Some of the same tools and approaches are used for both types of audit.[23]

external audits An external audit occurs when one organization evaluates another organization. Typically an external body such as a certified public accountant (CPA) firm conducts financial audits of an organization (discussed later in the chapter). But any company can conduct external audits of competitors or other companies for its own strategic decision-making purposes. This type of analysis investigates other organizations for possible merger or acquisition, determines the soundness of a company that will be used as a major supplier, or discovers the strengths and weaknesses of a competitor to maintain or better exploit the competitive advantage of the investigating organization. Publicly available data usually are used for these evaluations.[24]

External audits provide essential feedback control when they identify legal and ethical lapses that could harm the organization and its reputation. They also are useful for preliminary control because they can prevent problems from occurring. If a company seeking to acquire other businesses gathers adequate, accurate information about possible candidates, it is more likely to acquire the most appropriate companies and avoid unsound acquisitions.

internal audits An organization may assign a group to conduct an internal audit to assess what the company has done for itself and what it has done for its customers or other recipients of its goods or services. The company can be evaluated on a number of factors, including financial stability, production efficiency, sales effectiveness, human resources development, earnings growth, energy use, public relations, civic responsibility, and other criteria of organizational effectiveness. The audit reviews the company's past, present, and future, including any risks the organization should be prepared to face.[25] A recent study found that the stock prices of companies with highly rated audit committees tended to rise faster than shares of companies with lower-rated internal auditors. The higher-rated audit committees probably do a better job of finding and eliminating undesirable practices.[26]

To perform a management audit, auditors list desired qualifications and assign a weight to each qualification. Among

● MANAGEMENT AUDIT An evaluation of the effectiveness and efficiency of various systems within an organization.

● EXTERNAL AUDIT An evaluation conducted by one organization, such as a CPA firm, on another.

● INTERNAL AUDIT A periodic assessment of a company's own planning, organizing, leading, and controlling processes.

● BUDGETING The process of investigating what is being done and comparing the results with the corresponding budget data to verify accomplishments or remedy differences; also called *budgetary controlling.*

the most common undesirable practices uncovered by a management audit are the performance of unnecessary work, duplication of work, poor inventory control, uneconomical use of equipment and machines, procedures that are more costly than necessary, and wasted resources. At Capital One Financial Corporation, the human resource (HR) department performed an audit of facilities usage. Over several months, staff members walked through headquarters, noting which desks were occupied. The audit determined that more than 4 out of 10 desks were unused each day, and another 3 out of 10 were unused at least part of the day. Employees were away at meetings, visiting clients, or working flexible schedules. The HR staff developed a plan for Capital One to operate more efficiently in one-third of its space. Now most employees keep their work items in a cart, which they take to a desk when they need one. The change saves the company $3 million a year.[27]

(L)(O) 3 WHAT YOU NEED TO KNOW . . .
What are the purposes for using budgets as a control device?

Budgetary controls compare results with a plan

Budgetary control is one of the most widely recognized and commonly used methods of managerial control. It ties together feedforward control, concurrent control, and feedback control, depending on the point at which it is applied. *Budgetary control is the process of finding out what's being done and comparing the results with the corresponding budget data to verify

accomplishments or remedy differences. Budgetary control commonly is called budgeting.

fundamental budgetary considerations
In private industry, budgetary control begins with an estimate of sales and expected income. Table 13.1 shows a budget with a forecast of expected sales (the *sales budget*) on the

TABLE 13.1	A Sales-Expense Budget						
	January		**February**		**March**	
	Estimate	Actual	Estimate	Actual	Estimate	Actual
Sales	$1,200,000		$1,350,000		$1,400,000	
Expenses						
General overhead	$ 310,000		$ 310,000		$ 310,000	
Selling	242,000		275,000		288,000	
Producing	327,000		430,500		456,800	
Research	118,400		118,400		115,000	
Office	90,000		91,200		91,500	
Advertising	32,500		27,000		25,800	
Estimated gross profit	$ 80,100		$ 97,900		$ 112,900	

top row, followed by several categories of estimated expenses for the first three months of the year. In the bottom row, the profit estimate is determined by subtracting each month's budgeted expenses from the sales in that month's sales budget. Columns next to each month's budget provide space to enter the actual accomplishments so that managers can readily compare expected amounts and actual results.

Although this discussion of budgeting focuses on the flow of money into and out of the organization, budgeting information is not confined to finances. The entire enterprise and any of its units can create budgets for their activities, using units other than dollars, if appropriate. For example, many organizations use production budgets forecasting physical units produced and shipped, and labor can be budgeted in skill levels or hours of work required.

A primary consideration of budgeting is the length of the budget period. All budgets are prepared for a specific time period. Many budgets cover one, three, or six months or one year. The length of time selected depends on the primary purpose of the budgeting. The period should include the enterprise's complete normal cycle of activity. For example, seasonal variations should be included for production and for sales. The budget period commonly coincides with other control devices, such as managerial reports, balance sheets, and statements of profit and loss. Selection of the budget period also should consider the extent to which reasonable forecasts can be made.

Budgetary control proceeds through three stages:

1. *Establishing expectancies* starts with the broad plan for the company and the estimate of sales, and it ends with budget approval and publication.

2. The *budgetary operations* stage deals with finding out what is being accomplished and comparing the results with expectancies.

3. The last stage, as in any control process, involves *responding appropriately* with some combination of reinforcing successes and correcting problems.

Although practices differ widely, a member of top management often serves as the chief coordinator for formulating and using the budget. Usually the chief financial officer (CFO) has these duties. He or she needs to be less concerned with the details than with resolving conflicting interests, recommending adjustments when needed, and giving official sanction to the budgetary procedures. In a small company, budgeting responsibility generally rests with the owner.

types of budgets
There are many types of budgets. Several are frequently used:

- *Sales budget.* Usually data for the sales budget include forecasts of sales by month, sales area, and product.

- *Production budget.* The production budget commonly is expressed in physical units. Required information for preparing this budget includes types and capacities of machines, economic quantities to produce, and availability of materials.

- *Cost budget.* The cost budget is used for areas of the organization that incur expenses but no revenue, such as human resources and other support departments. Cost budgets may also be included in the production budget. Costs may be fixed (independent of the immediate level of activity), like rent, or variable (rising or falling with the level of activity), like raw materials.

- *Cash budget.* The cash budget is essential to every business. It should be prepared after all other budget estimates are completed. The cash budget shows the anticipated receipts and expenditures, the amount of working capital available, the extent to which outside financing may be required, and the periods and amounts of cash available.

TerraCycle's Cost-Control Formula Is Garbage

Many products today are made from various types of waste—old tires, scrap metal, plastic bottles. Companies look for ways to recycle and reuse just about every material imaginable. But the founder of one company looked to the ground for his business inspiration and came up with a unique idea for plant fertilizer: worm poop. Tom Szaky was a student when he entered his university's annual business plan competition. He used an old high school science project as its basis. Using the worms to generate fertilizer was cheap, simple, and organic. Best of all, his business idea won the prize. In fact, the company he eventually started—TerraCycle—was largely funded by various business competition winnings.

Szaky is still under the age of 30. Despite the fact that his organic plant food, TerraCycle, is now sold in such stores as Home Depot and Walmart, Szaky still thinks the way a student does when it comes to budgets. That means cheap. The company is located not far from his alma mater, Princeton. He hosts college interns each summer in a rambling old house furnished with cast-off dorm furniture and used computers that have been discarded by larger companies but still have more than enough computing power for TerraCycle. The furnishings are eclectic, but free. "No entrepreneur should ever buy furniture or mediocre computer equipment," advises Szaky. "Everything here is garbage. Princeton renovates one dorm a year, so we get all that." Gesturing toward a huge fan and

a 52-inch TV, he says, "That's all student waste. You find it in dumpsters on move-out day." The interns work for peanuts, but they love the job.

One reason TerraCycle is so successful is that its product is inexpensive to produce. TerraCycle is made from the waste of red worms that eat garbage. The worms don't incur labor costs and never stop producing waste. The compost of waste is brewed into a kind of tea on which plants seem to thrive. It is packed in reused soda bottles outfitted with spray tops that have been discarded by manufacturers of other spray products. And the boxes in which all the bottles are shipped are the misprinted cast-offs from other companies. Because everything that Szaky uses has already been used before, the whole operation is a bargain.

- *Capital budget.* The capital budget is used for the cost of fixed assets like plant and equipment. Such costs are usually treated, not as regular expenses, but as investments because of their long-term nature and importance to the organization's productivity.

- *Master budget.* The master budget includes all the major activities of the business. It brings together and coordinates all the activities of the other budgets and can be thought of as a "budget of budgets."

Traditionally, budgets were imposed *top-down,* with senior management setting specific targets for the entire organization at the beginning of the budget process. In today's more complex organizations, the budget process is more likely to be *bottom-up,* with top management setting the general direction, while lower-level and midlevel managers actually develop the budgets and submit them for approval. When the budgets are consolidated, senior managers can determine whether the organization's budget objectives are being met. Then the budget is either approved or sent back down the hierarchy for additional refinement.

Accounting records must be inspected periodically to ensure they were properly prepared and are correct. **Accounting audits,** which are designed to verify accounting reports and statements, are essential to the control process. This audit is performed by members of an outside firm of public accountants. Knowing that accounting records are accurate, true, and in keeping with generally accepted accounting practices (GAAP) creates confidence that a reliable base exists for sound overall controlling purposes.

activity-based costing

Traditional methods of cost accounting may be inappropriate in today's business environment because they are based on outdated methods of rigid hierarchical organization. Instead of assuming that organizations are bureaucratic "machines" that can be separated into component functions such as human resources, purchasing, and maintenance, companies such as Hewlett-Packard and GE have used **activity-based costing (ABC)** to allocate costs across business processes.

ABC starts with the assumption that organizations are collections of people performing many different but related activities to satisfy customer needs. The ABC system is designed to identify those streams of activity and then allocate costs across particular business processes. The basic procedure, outlined in Figure 13.2, works as follows: First, employees are asked to break down what they do each day in order to define their *basic activities.* For example, employees in Dana Corporation's material control department engage in a number of activities that range from processing sales orders and sourcing parts to requesting engineering changes and solving problems. These activities form the basis for ABC. Second, managers look at total expenses computed by traditional accounting—fixed costs, supplies, salaries, fringe benefits, and so on—and spread total amounts over the activities according to the amount of time spent on each activity. At Dana, customer service employees spend nearly 25 percent of their time processing sales orders and only about 3 percent scheduling parts. Thus, 25 percent of the total cost ($144,846) goes to order processing, and 3 percent ($15,390) goes to scheduling parts. As can be seen in Figure 13.2, both the traditional and ABC systems reach the same bottom line. However, because the ABC method allocates costs across business processes, it provides a more accurate picture of how costs should be charged to products and services.[28]

● **ACCOUNTING AUDITS** Procedures used to verify accounting reports and statements.

● **ACTIVITY-BASED COSTING (ABC)** A method of cost accounting designed to identify streams of activity and then to allocate costs across particular business processes according to the amount of time employees devote to particular activities.

This means that he can offer the same bargain to retailers—who can earn gross margins that are double or triple what they'd earn on the more familiar chemically produced fertilizers.

Szaky observes that one day, his company could even show a negative cost for materials if it is equipped and paid to haul the garbage that the worms eat, but TerraCycle hasn't reached that stage yet. Right now the firm is concentrating on producing its inexpensive organic product and making sure that consumers know about it and are able to buy it. "If you buy an organic banana," notes Szaky, "you're going to pay twice as much for it. We have an organic product that's both better and cheaper than the conventional product." His product may be garbage, but he's not talking trash.

Q: Discussion Questions

- Identify some criteria that you think Szaky would use in establishing performance standards for TerraCycle. What methods might he use to measure performance?
- What elements of budgetary control does Szaky use to help his business develop and grow?

SOURCES: David Flaum, "Here's the Real Poop on Recycling," *Memphis Commercial Appeal,* August 7, 2007, http://www.terracycle.net; "Waste, Worms, and Wealth: The Story of TerraCycle," U.S. Environmental Protection Agency, May 15, 2007, http://www.epa.gov; Katherine Walsh, "How TerraCycle Built a Corporate Network with Discarded Hardware and Open Source Software," *CIO,* April 5, 2007, http://www.cio.com; "Worm Poo in Plastic Bottles: Get Rich and Save the World," *CNN,* January 26, 2007, http://www.cnn.com; and Bo Burlingham, "The Coolest Little Start-Up in America," *Inc.,* July 2006, http://www.inc.com.

- **BALANCE SHEET** A report that shows the financial picture of a company at a given time and itemizes assets, liabilities, and stockholders' equity.
- **ASSETS** The values of the various items the corporation owns.
- **LIABILITIES** The amounts a corporation owes to various creditors.
- **STOCKHOLDERS' EQUITY** The amount accruing to the corporation's owners.
- **PROFIT AND LOSS STATEMENT** An itemized financial statement of the income and expenses of a company's operations.

FIGURE	13.2	How Dana Discovers What Its True Costs Are

Old way

Old-style accounting identifies costs according to the category of expense. The new math tells you that your real costs are what you pay for the different tasks your employees perform. Find that out and you will manage better.

Salaries
$371,917

Fringes
$118,069

Supplies
$76,745

Fixed Costs
$23,614

Total $590,345

New way

Activity-based costing

	Salaries	Fringes	Supplies	Fixed costs
Process sales order				$144,846
Source parts				$136,320
Expedite supplier orders				$ 72,143
Expedite internal processing				$ 49,945
Receive supplier quality				$ 47,599
Reissue purchase orders				$ 45,235
Expedite customer orders				$ 27,747
Schedule intracompany sales				$ 17,768
Request engineering change				$ 16,704
Resolve problems				$ 16,648
Schedule parts				$ 15,390
Total $590,345				

SOURCE: Courtesy Dana Corporation.

This heightened accuracy can give managers a more realistic picture of how the organization is actually allocating its resources. It can highlight where wasted activities are occurring or whether activities cost too much relative to the benefits provided. Managers can then act to correct the problem. For example, Dana's most expensive activity is sales-order processing. Its managers might try to find ways to lower that cost, freeing up resources for other tasks. By providing this type of information, ABC has become a valuable method for streamlining business processes.

(L) (O) 4 WHAT YOU NEED TO KNOW . . .

Can you define basic types of financial statements and financial ratios used as controls?

Financial controls include balance sheets and profit and loss statements

In addition to budgets, businesses commonly use other statements for financial control. Two financial statements that help control overall organizational performance are the balance sheet and the profit and loss statement.

balance sheet

The balance sheet shows the financial picture of a company at a given time. This statement itemizes three elements:

1. **Assets** are the values of the various items the corporation owns.

2. **Liabilities** are the amounts the corporation owes to various creditors.

3. **Stockholders' equity** is the amount accruing to the corporation's owners.

The relationship among these three elements is as follows:

Assets = Liabilities + Stockholders' equity

Table 13.2 shows an example of a balance sheet. During the year, the company grew because it enlarged its building and acquired more machinery and equipment by means of long-term debt in the form of a first mortgage. Additional stock was sold to help finance the expansion. At the same time, accounts receivable were increased, and work in process was reduced. Observe that Total assets ($3,053,367) = Total liabilities ($677,204 + $618,600) + Stockholders' equity ($700,000 + $981,943 + $75,620).

Summarizing balance sheet items over a long period of time uncovers important trends and gives a manager further insight into overall performance and areas in which adjustments are needed. For example, at some point, the company might decide that it would be prudent to slow down its expansion plans.

profit and loss statement

The profit and loss statement is an itemized financial statement of the income and expenses of a company's operations. Table 13.3 shows a comparative statement of profit and loss for two consecutive years. In this illustration, the enterprise's operating revenue has increased. Expense also has increased, but at a lower rate, resulting in a higher net income. Some managers draw up tentative profit and loss statements and use them as goals. Then they measure performance against these goals or standards. From comparative statements of this type, a manager can identify trouble areas and correct them.

Controlling by profit and loss is most commonly used for the entire enterprise and, in the case of a diversified corporation, its divisions. However, controlling can be by departments, as in a decentralized organization in which department managers have control over both revenue and expense. In that case, each department has its own profit and loss statement. Each department's output is measured, and a cost, including overhead, is charged to each department's operation. Expected net income is the standard for measuring a department's performance.

TABLE 13.2 A Comparative Balance Sheet

Comparative Balance Sheet for the Years Ending December 31	This Year	Last Year
Assets		
Current assets:		
Cash	$161,870	$119,200
U.S. Treasury bills	250,400	30,760
Accounts receivable	825,595	458,762
Inventories:		
Work in process and finished products	429,250	770,800
Raw materials and supplies	251,340	231,010
Total current assets	1,918,455	1,610,532
Other assets:		
Land	157,570	155,250
Building	740,135	91,784
Machinery and equipment	172,688	63,673
Furniture and fixtures	132,494	57,110
Total other assets before depreciation	1,202,887	367,817
Less: Accumulated depreciation and amortization	67,975	63,786
Total other assets	1,134,912	304,031
Total assets	$3,053,367	$1,914,563
Liabilities and stockholders' equity		
Current liabilities:		
Accounts payable	$287,564	$441,685
Payrolls and withholdings from employees	44,055	49,580
Commissions and sundry accruals	83,260	41,362
Federal taxes on income	176,340	50,770
Current installment on long-term debt	85,985	38,624
Total current liabilities	667,204	622,021
Long-term liabilities:		
15-year, 9 percent loan, payable in each of the years 2002–2015	210,000	225,000
5 percent first mortgage	408,600	
Registered 9 percent notes payable		275,000
Total long-term liabilities	618,600	500,000
Stockholders' equity:		
Common stock: authorized 1,000,000 shares, outstanding last year 492,000 shares, outstanding this year 700,000 shares at $1 par value	700,000	492,000
Capital surplus	981,943	248,836
Earned surplus	75,620	51,706
Total stockholders' equity	1,757,563	792,542
Total liabilities and stockholders' equity	$3,053,367	$1,914,563

TABLE 13.3	A Comparative Statement of Profit and Loss		

Comparative Statement of Profit and Loss for the Years Ending June 30			
	This Year	Last Year	Increase or Decrease
Income:			
Net sales	$253,218	$257,636	$4,418*
Dividends from investments	480	430	50
Other	1,741	1,773	32
Total	255,439	259,839	4,400*
Deductions:			
Cost of goods sold	180,481	178,866	1,615
Selling and administrative expenses	39,218	34,019	5,199
Interest expense	2,483	2,604	121*
Other	1,941	1,139	802
Total	224,123	216,628	7,495
Income before taxes	31,316	43,211	11,895*
Provision for taxes	3,300	9,500	6,200*
Net income	$ 28,016	$ 33,711	$5,695*

*Decrease.

financial ratios An effective approach for checking an enterprise's overall performance is to use key financial ratios, which suggest strengths and weaknesses. Key ratios are calculated from selected items on the profit and loss statement and the balance sheet.

1. *Liquidity ratios* indicate a company's ability to pay short-term debts. The most common liquidity ratio is *current assets to current liabilities,* called the **current ratio** or *net working capital ratio.* This ratio indicates the extent to which current assets can decline and still be adequate to pay current liabilities. Some analysts set a ratio of 2 to 1, or 2.00, as the desirable minimum. For example, if you refer back to Table 13.2, the liquidity ratio there is about 2.86 ($1,918,455/$667,204). The company's current assets are more than capable of supporting its current liabilities.

2. *Leverage ratios* show the relative amount of funds in the business supplied by creditors and shareholders. An important example is the **debt-equity ratio**, which indicates the company's ability to meet its long-term financial obligations. If this ratio is less than 1.5, the amount of debt is not considered excessive. In Table 13.2, the debt-equity ratio is only 0.35 ($618,600/$1,757,563). The company has financed its expansion almost entirely by issuing stock rather than by incurring significant long-term debt.

3. *Profitability ratios* indicate management's ability to generate a financial return on sales or investment. For example, **return on investment (ROI)** is a ratio of profit to capital used, or a rate of return from capital (equity plus long-term debt). This ratio lets managers and shareholders assess how well the firm is doing compared with other investments. For example, in Table 13.2, if the company's net income were $300,000 this year, its return on capital would be 12.6 percent ($300,000/($1,757,563 + $618,600)), normally a reasonable rate of return.

using financial ratios Although ratios provide performance standards and indicators of what has occurred, exclusive reliance on financial ratios can have negative consequences. Ratios usually are expressed in limited time horizons (monthly, quarterly, or yearly), so they often cause **management myopia**—managers focus on short-term earnings and profits at the expense of their longer-term strategic obligations.[29] To reduce management myopia and focus attention further into the future, control systems can use long-term (say, three- to six-year) targets.

A second negative outcome of ratios is that they relegate other important considerations to a secondary position. Managers focused on ratios may not pay enough attention to research and development, management development, progressive human resource practices, and other considerations. As a result, the use of ratios should be supplemented with other control measures. Organizations can hold managers accountable for market share, number of patents granted, sales of new products, human resource development, and other performance indicators.

Bureaucratic control has a downside

So far you have learned about control from a mechanical viewpoint. But organizations are not strictly mechanical; they are composed of people. While control systems are used to constrain people's behavior and make their future behavior predictable, people are not machines that automatically fall into line as the designers of control systems intend. In fact, control systems can lead to dysfunctional behavior. To set up an effective control system, managers need to consider how people will react to it, including three potential negative responses:[30]

1. Rigid bureaucratic behavior
2. Tactical behavior
3. Resistance

rigid bureaucratic behavior

Often people act in ways that will look good on the control system's measures. This tendency is useful when it focuses people on required behaviors. But it can result in rigid, inflexible behavior geared toward doing *only* what the system requires. For example, in the earlier discussion of the Six Sigma control process, we noted that it emphasizes efficiency over innovation. After 3M began using Six Sigma extensively, it slipped from its goal of having at least one-third of sales come from newly released products. When George Buckley took the CEO post, only one-fourth of sales were coming from new products. Buckley began relying less extensively on efficiency controls, because, as he explained to a reporter, "Invention is by its very nature a disorderly process."[31] The control challenge, of course, is for 3M to be both efficient and creative.

Rigid bureaucratic behavior occurs when control systems prompt employees to stay out of trouble by following the rules. Unfortunately, such systems often lead to poor customer service and make the entire organization slow to act. Some companies, including General Motors and UPS, enforce rules that employees must keep their desks neat. Of course, a chaotic workplace has its problems, but one survey found that people who said their desks were "very neat" spent more of their day looking for items than people who said their desks were "fairly messy."[32] By that measure, controlling neatness actually makes employees less efficient. Likewise, trying to control your own productivity by limiting phone calls and e-mail to certain times of day is beneficial only if ignoring the phone or e-mail won't cause you to annoy customers or miss important problems.

We have all been victimized at some time by rigid bureaucratic behavior. Reflect for a moment on this now classic story of a "nightmare" at a hospital:

> At midnight, a patient with eye pains enters an emergency room at a hospital. At the reception area, he is classified as a nonemergency case and referred to the hospital's eye clinic. Trouble is, the eye clinic doesn't open until the next morning. When he arrives at the clinic, the nurse asks for his referral slip, but the emergency room doctor had forgotten to give it to him. The patient has to return to the emergency room and wait for another physician to screen him. The physician refers him back to the eye clinic and to a social worker to arrange payment. Finally, a third doctor looks into his eye, sees a small piece of metal, and removes it—a 30-second procedure.[33]

Stories such as these have, of course, given bureaucracy a bad name. Some managers will not even use the term *bureaucratic control* because of its potentially negative connotation. However, the control system itself is not the problem. The problems occur when the systems are no longer viewed as tools for running the business but instead as rules for dictating rigid behavior.

tactical behavior

Control systems will be ineffective if employees engage in tactics aimed at "beating the system." The most common type of tactical behavior is to manipulate information or report false performance data. People may produce invalid data about what *has* been done and about what *can* be done. False reporting about the past is less common because it is easier to identify someone who misreports what happened than someone who incorrectly predicts or estimates what might happen. Still, managers sometimes change their accounting systems to "smooth out" the numbers. Also, people may intentionally feed false information into a management information system to cover up errors or poor performance. Recently, several customs inspectors at Orlando Sanford International Airport said their supervisors had pressured them to speed up the processing of passengers by entering "generic" data instead of actually questioning the passengers. According to the inspectors, when the system flagged passengers for additional screening during busy periods, they were told to guess the information, such as race and length of stay, rather than asking the passengers to provide the information. The justification for this behavior was that time pressure gave them only a minute to screen each passenger, so they could keep the line moving and keep the public satisfied with their agency's work.[34]

More commonly, people falsify predictions or requests for the future. When asked to give budgetary estimates, employees usually ask for more than they need. Or if they believe a low estimate will help them get a budget or a project approved, they may submit unrealistically *low* estimates. Budget-setting sessions can become tugs-of-war between subordinates trying to get slack in the budget and superiors attempting to minimize slack. Similar tactics are exhibited when managers negotiate unrealistically low performance standards so that subordinates will have little trouble meeting them, when salespeople project low forecasts so they will look good by exceeding them, and when workers slow down the work pace while time-study analysts are setting work pace standards. The people in these examples are concerned only with their own performance figures, not with the overall performance of their department or company.

resistance to control

Often people strongly resist control systems. They do so for several reasons:

- Comprehensive control systems increase the accuracy of performance data and make employees more accountable for their actions. Control systems uncover mistakes, threaten people's job security and status, and decrease people's autonomy.

- Control systems can change expertise and power structures. For example, management information systems can speed up the costing, purchasing, and production decisions previously made by managers. Those individuals may fear a loss of expertise, power, and decision-making authority as a result.

- Control systems can change an organization's social structure. They can create competition and disrupt social groups and friendships. People may end up competing against those with whom they formerly had comfortable, cooperative relationships. People's social needs are important, so they

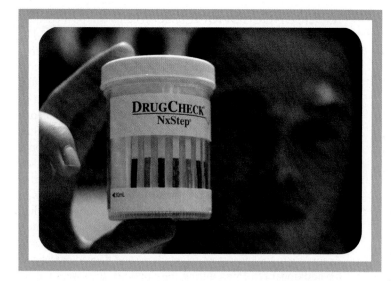

will resist control systems that reduce satisfaction of those needs.

- Control systems may be seen as an invasion of privacy, lead to lawsuits, and cause low morale.

 When Ford CEO Alan Mulally toured the automobile-testing facility at product-rating organization Consumer Reports, he and two senior engineers heard a lot of criticism from the Consumer Reports team about the inefficient design of the new Ford Edge crossover SUV. For example, the Ford Edge lacks an electronic door opener found in many of its rivals. That feature can be a big deal to a shopper who arrives at the vehicle with arms full of groceries on a rainy day and has to drop the packages to open the door or rear hatch. But as the engineers received this criticism, they became more and more defensive about their design. Mulally identified this behavior as one of his company's biggest problems: employees' tendency to explain away mistakes instead of tackling them.

Back at headquarters, Mulally examined the history of Ford compacts and learned that every time a Ford dealer sells a compact instead of a truck or SUV, the company loses $3,000. He was told that Ford needed to sell many of these cars anyway, to reach the firm's required target for corporate average fuel economy. But Mulally wasn't satisfied with the answer and asked, "Why haven't you figured out a way to make a profit [on these cars]?" Managers admitted that, for years, Ford has accepted the inevitability of losing money.[35]

(L)(O) 5 **WHAT YOU NEED TO KNOW . . .**

What are the procedures for implementing effective control systems?

Managers can make control systems more effective

Effective control systems maximize potential benefits and minimize dysfunctional behaviors. To achieve this, management needs to design control systems that meet several criteria:

- The systems are based on valid performance standards.
- They communicate adequate information to employees.
- They are acceptable to employees.
- They use multiple approaches.
- They recognize the relationship between empowerment and control.

establish valid performance standards An effective control system must be based on valid and accurate performance standards. The most effective standards, as discussed earlier, tend to be expressed in quantitative terms; they are objective rather than subjective. Also, the measures should be difficult to sabotage or fake. Moreover, the system must incorporate all important aspects of performance. For example, a company that focused only on sales volume without also looking at profitability might soon go out of business. As you learned earlier, unmeasured behaviors are neglected. Consider performance standards for delivering training and other HR programs, which often emphasize trainee satisfaction as reported on surveys. In contrast, the Philadelphia Department of Licenses and Inspections verified that its training improved employee performance. The department, notorious for long lines and rude workers, sought help from the Philadelphia Ritz-Carlton Hotel (the chain is known for its superb customer service). The hotel's area general manager trained 40 department workers in how to improve their service skills. Afterward, the department checked wait times for license applicants, which dropped from 82 minutes to 14 minutes. The department is continuing its partnership with Ritz-Carlton through additional employee training.[36]

Management also must defend against another problem: too many measures that create overcontrol and employee resistance. To make many controls tolerable, managers can emphasize a few key areas while setting "satisfactory" performance standards in others. Or they can set simple priorities, such as directing a purchasing agent to meet targets in the following order: quality, availability, cost, inventory level. Finally, managers can set tolerance ranges, as when financial budgets include optimistic, expected, and minimum levels.

Many companies' budgets set cost targets only. This causes managers to control spending but also to neglect earnings. At Emerson Electric, profit and growth are key measures. If an unanticipated opportunity to increase market share arises, managers can spend what they need to go after it. The phrase "it's not in the budget" is less likely to stifle people at Emerson than it is at most other companies.

This principle applies to nonfinancial aspects of performance as well. At many customer service call centers, control aims to maximize efficiency by focusing on the average amount of time each agent spends handling each phone call. But the business objectives of call centers should also include other measures such as cross-selling products or improving customer satisfaction and repeat business. Carlson Leisure Travel Services is one of a

Executives say their companies are better at financial controlling than controlling nonfinancial performance. [37]

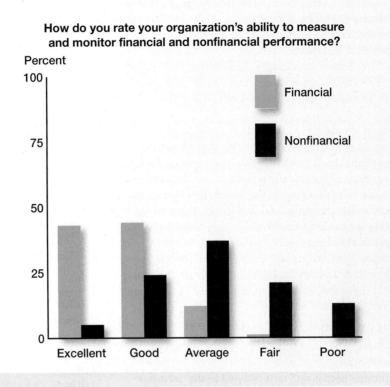

How do you rate your organization's ability to measure and monitor financial and nonfinancial performance?

Percent

- Financial
- Nonfinancial

Excellent | Good | Average | Fair | Poor

growing number of companies using new technology to analyze the content—not just the duration—of each call and capture information about the amount sold by call center agents.[38]

Business consultant Michael Hammer summarizes these points in terms of what he calls seven "deadly sins" of performance measurement to avoid:[39]

1. *Vanity*—using measures that are sure to make managers and the organization look good. For example, a company might measure order fulfillment in terms of whether products are delivered by the latest date promised by the organization, rather than by the tougher and more meaningful measure of when the customers request to receive the products.

2. *Provincialism*—limiting measures to functional or departmental responsibilities, rather than the organization's overall objectives. If a company's transportation department measures only shipping costs, it won't have an incentive to consider that shipping reliability (delivery on a given date) will affect performance at the company's stores or distribution centers.

3. *Narcissism*—measuring from the employee's, manager's, or company's point of view, rather than the customer's. For example, a maker of computer systems measured on-time shipping of each component; if 90 percent of the system's components arrived at the customer on time, it was 90 percent on time. But from the customer's point of view, the system wasn't on time at all, because the customer needed *all* the components to use the system.

4. *Laziness*—not expending the effort to analyze what is important to measure. An electric power company simply assumed customers cared about installation speed, but in fact, customers really cared more about receiving an accurate installation schedule.

5. *Pettiness*—measuring just one component of what affects business performance. An example would be clothing manufacturers that assume they should just consider manufacturing cost, rather than the overall costs of making exactly the right products available in stores when customers demand them.

6. *Inanity*—failing to consider the way standards will affect real-world human behavior and company performance. A fast-food restaurant targeted waste reduction and was surprised when restaurant managers began slowing down operations by directing their employees to hold off on cooking anything until orders were placed.

7. *Frivolity*—making excuses for poor performance rather than taking performance standards seriously. In some organizations, more effort goes to blaming others than to correcting problems.

According to Hammer, the basic correction to these "sins" is to carefully select standards that look at entire business processes, such as product development or order fulfillment, and identify which actions make those processes succeed. Then managers should measure performance against these standards precisely, accurately, and practically, making individuals responsible for their achievement and rewarding success.

provide adequate information

Management must communicate to employees the importance and nature of the control system. Then people must receive feedback about their performance. Feedback motivates people and provides information that enables them to correct their own deviations from performance standards. Allowing people to initiate their own corrective action encourages self-control and reduces the need for outside supervision. *Open-book management,* described in an earlier chapter, is a powerful use of this control principle.

Information should be as accessible as possible, particularly when people must make decisions quickly and frequently. For example, a national food company with its own truck fleet had a difficult problem. The company wanted drivers to go through customer sales records every night, insert new prices from headquarters every morning, and still make their rounds—an impossible set of demands. To solve this control problem, the company installed personal computers in more than 1,000 delivery trucks. Now drivers use their PCs for constant communication with headquarters. Each night drivers send information about the stores, and each morning headquarters sends prices and recommended stock mixes.

In general, a manager designing a control system should evaluate the information system in terms of the following questions:[40]

- Does it provide people with data relevant to the decisions they need to make?

- Does it provide the right amount of information to decision makers throughout the organization?

- Does it provide enough information to each part of the organization about how other, related parts of the organization are functioning?

Ritz-Carlton sets performance measures for maintaining its impressive reputation and ensures that employees see how they contribute. The measures are based on the key factors behind the hotel chain's success: its mystique, employee engagement, customer engagement, product service excellence, community involvement, and financial performance. For each success factor, cross-functional teams identify targets as detailed as the number of scuff marks on elevator doors or the percentage of satisfied employees at a location. Because these teams include frontline employees, employees believe that their input matters.

At each location, at the beginning of every shift, all employees meet to discuss activities, issues, and Ritz-Carlton's business philosophy. They compare recent performance against the targets in each area. These conversations reinforce the key performance factors and help employees appreciate the importance of what they do.

Each business unit focuses on up to three priorities, with each employee working to improve customer, employee, or financial results. Employees appreciate their role in giving guests a special experience. When Joanne Hanna checked into a Ritz-Carlton after a grueling series of airport delays, a hotel employee carried her bags and listened to her frustration. After learning she didn't have time for a spa visit or a masseuse, he brought her a scented candle—and had the information entered into Ritz-Carlton's database. Now, on every visit, a candle in Hanna's room reminds her of the employee's empathy.[41]

ensure acceptability to employees

Employees are less likely to resist a control system and exhibit dysfunctional behaviors if they accept the system. They are more likely to accept systems that have useful performance standards but are not overcontrolling. Employees also will find systems more acceptable if they believe the standards are possible to achieve.

The control system should emphasize positive behavior rather than focusing on simply controlling negative behavior. McBride Electric, an electrical contracting company, uses an electronic monitoring system called DriveCam to encourage its drivers to behave responsibly in terms of safety and fuel consumption. A DriveCam video monitor in each truck records activity inside and outside the cab; it saves that recording only if the truck is involved in a specified "trigger event" such as braking hard or swerving. Management explained the system to the drivers, emphasizing that it would help the company improve profits (a relevant message in a company that practices open-book management) and would protect the workers if they were ever accused falsely of unsafe practices. Not only did McBride immediately begin seeing improvements in safety and vehicle wear and tear, but it was also able to make good on its promise to defend employees. An anonymous phone caller complained that poor driving by a McBride driver had caused him to wreck his car. The McBride manager who took the call explained that he would be able to review a video taken from the truck that day—and the caller quickly hung up.[42] This approach exhibits the motivational quality of "procedural justice," described in Chapter 10. It gave employees the feeling that they were being evaluated by a fair process, so they were more likely to accept it.

DID YOU KNOW?

One of the best ways to establish reasonable standards and thus gain employee acceptance of the control system is to involve employees in setting the standards. Participation in decision making secures people's understanding and cooperation and results in better decisions. Collaborating with employees in control-system decisions that affect their jobs will help overcome resistance and foster acceptance of the system. In addition, employees on the front line are more likely to know which standards are most important and practical. Finally, if standards are established in collaboration with employees, employees will more readily cooperate to solve the problem when results deviate from standards.

maintain open communication When deviations from standards occur, it is important that employees feel able to report the deviations so that the problem can be addressed. If employees believe their managers want to hear only good news or, worse, if they fear reprisal for reporting bad news, even if it is not their fault, then any controls in place are much less likely to be effective. Problems may go unreported or even reach the point where solutions are much more expensive or difficult. But if managers create an environment of openness and honesty, where employees feel comfortable sharing even negative information and are appreciated for doing so in a timely fashion, then the control system is much more likely to work effectively.

> ## "I've learned that mistakes can often be as good a teacher as success."
>
> —Jack Welch, former CEO, General Electric

Still, managers sometimes need to discipline employees who are failing to meet important standards. In such cases, an approach called *progressive discipline* is usually most effective. In this approach, clear standards are established, but failure to meet them is dealt with in a progressive, or step-by-step, process. The first time an employee's sales performance has been worse than it should have been, the supervising manager may offer verbal counseling or coaching. If problems persist, the next step might be a written reprimand. This type of reasonable and considered approach signals to all employees that the manager is interested in improving their performance, not in punishing them.

use multiple approaches Multiple controls are necessary. For example, banks need controls on risk so that they don't lose a lot of money from defaulting borrowers, as well as profit controls including sales budgets that aim for growth in accounts and customers.

As you learned earlier in this chapter, control systems generally should include both financial and nonfinancial performance targets and incorporate aspects of preliminary, concurrent, and feedback control. In recent years, a growing number of companies have combined targets for managers into a balanced scorecard, a combination of four sets of performance measures:[43]

1. Financial
2. Customer satisfaction
3. Business processes (quality and efficiency)
4. Learning and growth

The goal is generally to broaden management's horizon beyond short-term financial results so that the company's long-term success is more likely. For example, Hyde Park Electronics had been using a variety of financial controls when it adopted a business scorecard that added metrics such as on-time delivery, employee satisfaction, and sales impact of marketing activities. Profits under the balanced scorecard reached record levels.[44] The balanced scorecard also is adaptable to nonprofit settings. Ocean-Monmouth Legal Services, which provides legal services to poor people in New Jersey, uses a balanced scorecard to track progress in meeting strategic, operational, financial, and client satisfaction goals. The organization's executive director, Harold E. Creacy, credits the approach with helping to cope with the rising costs and tight resources that so often plague nonprofits.[45]

Effective control also requires managers and organizations to use many of the other techniques and practices of good management. For example, compensation systems grant rewards for meeting standards and impose consequences if they are not met. And to gain employee acceptance, managers may rely on many of the other communication and motivational tools that we discussed in earlier chapters, such as persuasion and positive reinforcement.

Ⓛ Ⓞ **6** **WHAT YOU NEED TO KNOW . . .**

Can you identify ways in which organizations use market control mechanisms?

THE OTHER CONTROLS: MARKETS AND CLANS

Although the concept of control has always been a central feature of organizations, the principles and philosophies underlying its use are changing. In the past, control was focused almost exclusively on bureaucratic (and market) mechanisms. Generations of managers were taught that they could maximize productivity by regulating what employees did on the job—through standard operating procedures, rules, regulations, and close supervision. To increase output on an assembly line, for example, managers in the past tried to identify the "one best way" to approach the work and then to monitor employees' activities to make certain that they followed standard operating procedures. In short, they controlled work by dividing and simplifying tasks, a process referred to as *scientific management*.

Although formal bureaucratic control systems are perhaps the most pervasive in organizations (and the most talked about in management textbooks), they are not always the most effective. *Market controls* and *clan controls* may represent more flexible, though no less potent, approaches to regulating performance.

Market controls let supply and demand determine prices and profits

Market controls involve the use of economic forces—and the pricing mechanisms that accompany them—to regulate performance. The system works like this: When output from an individual, department, or business unit has value to other people, a price can be negotiated for its exchange. As a market for these transactions becomes established, two effects occur:

- Price becomes an indicator of the value of the good or service.

- Price competition has the effect of controlling productivity and performance.

The basic principles that underlie market controls can operate at the level of the corporation, the business unit (or department), and the individual. Figure 13.3 shows a few ways in which market controls are used in an organization.

market controls at the corporate level

In large, diversified companies, market controls often are used to regulate independent business units. Particularly in large conglomerate firms that act as holding companies, business units typically are treated as profit centers that compete with one another. Top executives may place few bureaucratic controls on business unit managers but evaluate performance in terms of profit and loss data. While decision making and power are decentralized to the business units, market controls ensure that business unit performance is in line with corporate objectives.

This use of market control mechanisms has been criticized by those who insist that economic measures do not adequately reflect the complete value of an organization. Employees often suffer as diversified companies are repeatedly bought and sold based on market controls.

market controls at the business unit level

Market control also can be used within business units to regulate exchanges among departments and functions. One way organizations try to apply market forces to internal transactions is through transfer pricing. A **transfer price** is the charge by one unit in the organization for a good or service that it supplies to another unit of the same organization. For example, in automobile manufacturing, transfer prices may be affixed to components and subassemblies before they are shipped to subsequent business units for final assembly. Ideally, the transfer price reflects what the receiving business unit would have to pay for that good or service in the marketplace.

As organizations have more options to outsource goods and services to external partners, market controls such as transfer prices provide natural incentives to keep costs down and quality up. Managers stay in close touch with prices in the marketplace to make sure their own costs are in line, and they try to improve the service they provide to increase their department's value to the organization. Consider the situation in which training and development activities can be done internally by the human resources department or outsourced to a consulting firm. If the human resources department cannot supply quality training at a reasonable price, there may be no reason for that department to exist inside the firm. Similarly, Penske Truck Leasing Company began outsourcing many of its finance processes to a company called Genpact, not only for lower prices but also for the expertise developed by that specialized firm to compete in the marketplace. Penske's senior vice president of finance, Frank Cocuzza, says the department spends $20 million less per year than it did to perform the same functions in-house. At the same time, it has improved its rate of collections

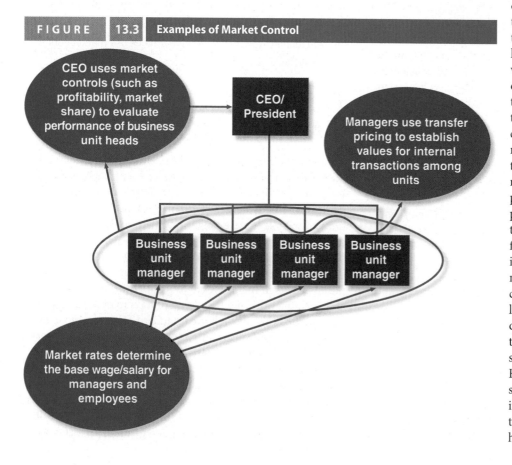

FIGURE 13.3 Examples of Market Control

CEO uses market controls (such as profitability, market share) to evaluate performance of business unit heads

CEO/President

Managers use transfer pricing to establish values for internal transactions among units

Business unit manager

Business unit manager

Business unit manager

Business unit manager

Market rates determine the base wage/salary for managers and employees and learned thousands of ways to make his own operation more efficient, modeled after Genpact's lean practices.[46]

market controls at the individual level

Market controls also are used at the individual level. For example, in situations where organizations are trying to hire employees, the supply and demand for particular skills influence the wages employees can expect to receive and the rate organizations are likely to pay. Employees or job candidates who have more valuable skills tend to be paid a higher wage. Of course, wages don't always reflect market rates—sometimes they are based (perhaps arbitrarily) on internal resource considerations—but the market rate is often the best indicator of an employee's potential worth to a firm.

Market-based controls such as these are important in that they provide a natural incentive for employees to enhance their

A+

TIP
Outsourcing can keep managers in touch with market prices and provide expertise not available within an organization.

skills and offer them to potential employers. Even after individuals gain employment, market-based wages are important as controls in that persons with higher economic value may be promoted faster to higher positions in the organization.

Market controls often are used by boards of directors to manage CEOs of major corporations. Although many people think of CEOs as the people controlling everyone else in the company, a CEO is accountable to the board of directors, and the board must ensure that the CEO acts in its interest. Absent board control, CEOs may act in ways that make them look good personally (such as making the company bigger or more diversified) but that do not lead to higher profits for the firm. And as recent corporate scandals have shown, without board control, CEOs may also artificially inflate the firm's earnings or not fully declare expenses, making the firm look much more successful than it really is.

Traditionally, boards have tried to control CEO performance mainly through the use of incentive pay, including bonuses tied to short-term profit targets. In large U.S. companies, most CEO compensation is tied to the company's performance. In addition to short-term incentives, boards use long-term incentives linked to the firm's share price, usually through stock options, which we discussed earlier. Also, balanced scorecards are intended to keep CEOs focused on the company's longer-term health. And under the Sarbanes-Oxley Act, board members are expected to exercise careful control over the company's financial performance, including oversight of the CEO's compensation package.

L O 7 WHAT YOU NEED TO KNOW . . .
How is clan control used in an empowered organization?

Clan control relies on empowerment and culture

Managers are discovering that control systems based solely on bureaucratic and market mechanisms are insufficient for directing today's workforce. There are several reasons:

- *Employees' jobs have changed.* Employees working with computers, for example, have more variable jobs, and much of their work is intellectual and therefore invisible. Because of this, there is no one best way to perform a task, and programming or standardizing jobs is extremely difficult. Close supervision also is unrealistic because it is nearly impossible to supervise activities such as reasoning and problem solving.

- *The nature of management has changed.* Managers used to know more about the job than employees did. Today, with the shift to knowledge work, employees typically know more

Are the sometimes ridiculously high salaries that today's professional athletes are paid truly indicative of the players' skills?

> # "As a manager the important thing is not what happens when you are there, but what happens when you are not there."
>
> —Ken Blanchard

about their jobs than anyone else does. When real expertise in organizations exists at the very lowest levels, hierarchical control becomes impractical.[47]

- *The employment relationship has changed.* The social contract at work is being renegotiated. Employees once were most concerned about pay, job security, and the hours of work. Today, however, more and more employees want to be more fully engaged in their work, taking part in decision making, devising solutions to unique problems, and receiving assignments that are challenging and involving. They want to use their brains.

For these three reasons, the concept of *empowerment* not only has become more popular in organizations but also has become a necessary aspect of a manager's

> ## "Use good judgment in all situations. There will be no additional rules."
>
> —Nordstrom's employee manual

repertoire of control. With no "one best way" to approach a job and no way to scrutinize what employees do every day, managers must empower employees to make decisions and trust that they will act in the firm's best interests. But this does not mean giving up control. It means creating a strong culture of high standards and integrity so that employees will exercise effective control on their own.

Recall our discussion of organization culture in Chapter 2. An organization culture that encourages the wrong behaviors will severely hinder an effort to impose effective controls. But if managers create and reinforce a strong culture that encourages correct behavior, one in which everyone understands management's values and expectations and is motivated to act in accordance with them, then clan control can be

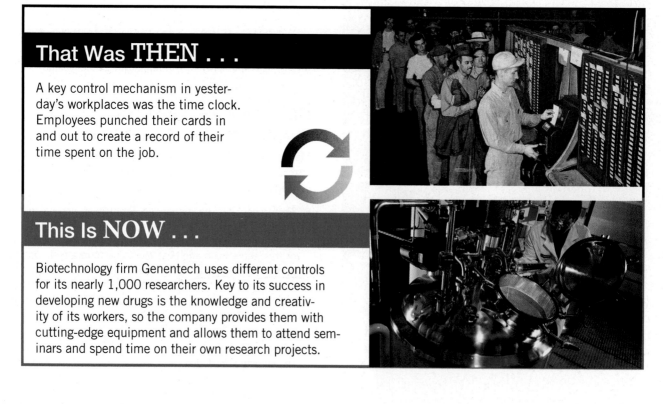

That Was THEN . . .

A key control mechanism in yesterday's workplaces was the time clock. Employees punched their cards in and out to create a record of their time spent on the job.

This Is NOW . . .

Biotechnology firm Genentech uses different controls for its nearly 1,000 researchers. Key to its success in developing new drugs is the knowledge and creativity of its workers, so the company provides them with cutting-edge equipment and allows them to attend seminars and spend time on their own research projects.

very effective.[48] As we noted at the beginning of this chapter, *clan control* involves creating relationships built on mutual respect and encouraging each individual to take responsibility for his or her actions. Employees work within a guiding framework of values, and they are expected to use good judgment. For example, at NetApp, an IT company specializing in data storage and protection, a commitment to employee empowerment prompted the switch from a 12-page travel policy to some simple guidelines for employees who need to go on a business trip: "We are a frugal company. But don't show up dog-tired to save a few bucks. Use your common sense."[49] An empowered organization emphasizes satisfying customers, rather than pleasing the boss. Mistakes are tolerated as the unavoidable by-product of dealing with change and uncertainty and are viewed as opportunities to learn. And team members learn together.

Here are a few practical guidelines for managing in an empowered world:[50]

- *Put control where the operation is.* Layers of hierarchy, close supervision, and checks and balances are quickly

disappearing and being replaced with self-guided teams. For centuries even the British Empire—as large as it was—never had more than six levels of management including the Queen.

- *Use "real time" rather than after-the-fact controls.* Issues and problems must be solved at the source by the people doing the actual work. Managers become a resource to help out the team.

- *Rebuild the assumptions underlying management control to build on trust rather than distrust.* Today's "high-flex" organizations are based on empowerment, not obedience. Information must facilitate decision making, not police it.

- *Move to control based on peer norms.* Clan control is a powerful thing. Workers in Japan, for example, have been known to commit suicide rather than disappoint or lose face within their team. Although this is extreme, it underlines the power of peer influence. The Japanese have a far more homogeneous culture and set of values than we do. In North America, we must build peer norms systematically and put much less emphasis on managing by the numbers.

- *Rebuild the incentive systems to reinforce responsiveness and teamwork.* The twin goals of adding value to the customer and team performance must become the dominant raison d'être of the measurement systems.

The resiliency and time investment of clan control are a double-edged sword. Clan control takes a long time to develop and an even longer time to change. This gives an organization stability and direction during periods of upheaval in the environment or the organization (e.g., during changes in top management). Yet if managers want to establish a new culture—a new form of clan control—they must help employees unlearn the old values and embrace the new. We will talk more about this transition process in the next chapter of this book.

Build Your Skills

Practice and apply your knowledge by going online at

www.mhhe.com/ BatemanM2e

WHAT YOU NEED TO KNOW

•• learning OBJECTIVES

After studying Chapter 14, you should be able to:

LO1 Summarize how to assess technology needs.

LO2 Identify the critieria on which to base technology decisions.

LO3 Evaluate key ways of acquiring new technologies.

LO4 Describe the elements of an innovative organization.

LO5 List characteristics of successful development projects.

LO6 Discuss what it takes to be world class.

LO7 Describe how to manage change effectively.

LO8 List tactics for creating a successful future.

14

Innovating and Changing

Technological innovation is complex, moving fast—and vital for a firm's competitive advantage. Today's organizations depend on their managers' ability to capitalize on new technologies and other changes not only to carry out their basic tasks more efficiently and effectively but also to retain an edge on their competitors. Because technology and rapid innovation are critical for success, managers must understand how technologies can change the ways organizations compete and the ways people work.

Earlier in the text, we defined *technology* as the methods, processes, systems, and skills used to transform resources into products. More generally, we can think of technology as the commercialization of science: the systematic application of scientific knowledge to a new product, process, or service. In this sense, technology is embedded in every product, service, and procedure used or produced.[1] But if we find a better way to accomplish our task, we have an innovation. *Innovation* is a change in method or technology—a positive, useful departure from previous ways of doing things.

Look to the Future

with today's managers to see how Karianne and Artemio they innovate and manage change.

"The largest challenge is simply put; people do not like change. Regardless if the change will provide a more positive outcome than originally envisioned, people do not like change. With this fact in mind, I have found that providing new or updated information as soon as possible will help other people process a change. Additionally, completing the due diligence to be able to explain in detail why a change was necessary and how it will better affect the outcome is important."
—Karianne Wardell, Account Supervisor

"Some keys that I've learned about dealing with change in the workplace is that change can have a positive effect on your work environment and at the same time it can help you understand your work much better. I would suggest to people about change, to learn how to embrace it and at the same time adapt with it; that way once you understand it, you can use that change to help you in the future."
—Artemio Ortiz, Digital Promotions Manager

There are two fundamental types of innovation:

1. *Process innovations* are changes that affect the way outputs are produced. Examples from Chapter 6 include flexible manufacturing practices such as just-in-time, mass customization, and simultaneous engineering.

2. *Product innovations* are changes in the actual outputs (goods and services) produced.[2]

These two categories cover a multitude of creative new ideas. They can change product offerings, the basic "platforms" or features and processes used to create products, the customer problems the organization can solve, the types of customers the organization serves, the nature of the experience provided by the organization, the way the organization earns money from what it does, the efficiency and effectiveness of its processes, the structure of the organization, the supply chain through which it delivers goods and services, the physical or virtual points at which it interacts with customers, the ways the organization communicates, and the brand associated with the organization and its products.[3]

Critical forces converge to create new technologies. Understanding the forces driving technological development can help a manager anticipate, monitor, and manage technologies more effectively.

- There must be a *need*, or *demand*, for the technology. Without this need driving the process, there is no reason for technological innovation to occur.

- Meeting the need must be theoretically possible, and the *knowledge* to do so must be available from basic science.

- We must be able to *convert* the scientific knowledge into practice in engineering and economic terms. If doing something is theoretically possible but economically impractical, the technology cannot be expected to emerge.

- The *funding, skilled labor, time, space,* and *other resources* needed to develop the technology must be available.

- *Entrepreneurial initiative* must identify and pull all the necessary elements together.

This chapter discusses how technology can affect an organization's competitiveness and how managers identify which technologies an organization should adopt. Then we assess the primary ways in which organizations develop or acquire those technologies, including the leadership and management decisions that help new technology succeed. Of course, technology is not the only way organizations innovate and change. The remainder of the chapter looks more broadly at innovation, including change efforts aimed at achieving world-class status, the process of managing change, and efforts you can make to shape your own career.

L O 1 WHAT YOU NEED TO KNOW . . .
Can you summarize how to assess technology needs?

DECIDING TO ADOPT NEW TECHNOLOGY

Decisions about technology and innovation are strategic, and managers need to approach them systematically. In Chapter 4, we discussed two generic strategies a company can use to position itself in the market:[4]

1. *Low cost*—The company has an advantage from maintaining a lower cost than its competitors.

2. *Differentiation*—The advantage comes from offering a unique good or service for which customers are willing to pay a premium price.

For either strategy, managers must assess technology needs, decide whether to adopt a new technology, and if they adopt

---

DID YOU KNOW?

Executives at a majority of companies consider innovation a top priority, but only about half are satisfied with their company's return on innovation spending. Companies are most likely to measure innovation success in terms of customer satisfaction and growth in revenue, with only one out of five tracking the return on their investment in innovation.[5]

How would you rank innovation spending among other strategic priorities?

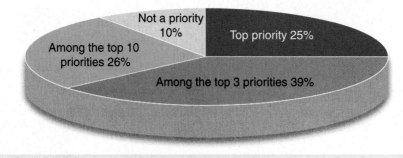

Not a priority 10%
Among the top 10 priorities 26%
Top priority 25%
Among the top 3 priorities 39%

> ## "The world hates change, yet that is the only thing that has brought progress."
> — Charles Kettering

Airborne networks—technology that NASA and the U.S. Air Force are developing—will create an "Internet in the sky" that could let planes fly safely without ground controllers. The U.S. Air Force plans to actively develop and test the network from 2008–2012.

the technology, determine the best method for developing or acquiring it.

Assess organizational needs for technologies

In today's increasingly competitive environment, failure to correctly assess the organization's technology needs can fundamentally impair the organization's effectiveness. Consider the biggest industry sector in the U.S. economy: health care services, where spending is soaring. One reason that health care costs so much is that the industry has been slow to adopt technology that can make operations more efficient. According to a RAND Corporation study, Americans could save $162 billion a year if health care providers made better investments in information technology. For example, less than one-fifth of hospitals use a complete bar code system for dispensing medicine, which could save money and reduce medication errors.[6]

To assess technology needs, managers measure current technologies and look for trends affecting the industry.

measuring current technologies To assist managers in understanding their current technology base, a technology audit helps clarify the key technologies on which an organization depends. One technique for measuring competitive value sorts technologies into several categories according to their competitive value:[7]

- *Emerging technologies* are still under development but may significantly alter the rules of competition in the future. Managers should monitor the development of emerging technologies but may not need to invest in them until they have been more fully developed.
- *Pacing technologies* have yet to prove their full value but have the potential to provide a significant advantage that alters the rules of competition. Managers should develop or invest in pacing technologies because of the competitive advantages they can provide.

- *Key technologies* have proved effective but offer a strategic advantage because not everyone uses them. Eventually, alternatives to key technologies can emerge. But until then, key technologies can give organizations a significant competitive edge and make it harder for new entrants to threaten the organization.
- *Base technologies* are commonplace in the industry; everyone must have them. They provide little competitive advantage, but managers have to invest to ensure their organization's continued competence in the technology.

Technologies can evolve rapidly through these categories. For example, electronic word processing was an emerging technology in the late 1970s. By the early 1980s, it could have been considered pacing, because its cost and capabilities restricted its usefulness to a few applications. With continued improvements and more powerful computer chips, electronic word processing quickly became a key technology. Its costs dropped, its usage spread, and it demonstrated the capacity to enhance productivity. By the late 1980s, it was a base technology in most applications, and now it is used so widely that it is routine in almost every office.

assessing external technological trends As with any planning, decisions about technology must balance internal capabilities (strengths and weaknesses) with external opportunities and threats. To understand how technology is changing within an industry, managers can use techniques we introduced in previous chapters:

- *Benchmarking* compares the organization's practices and technologies with those of other companies. Harley-Davidson recovered its reputation for manufacturing quality motorcycles after company executives toured Honda's plant and witnessed firsthand the relative weaknesses of Harley's manufacturing technologies and the vast potential for improvement. Competitors understandably are reluctant to share their secrets, but companies may be more willing to share their knowledge if they are not direct competitors and if the exchange of information might benefit both companies.
- *Environmental scanning* focuses on what can be done and what is being developed. It emphasizes identifying and monitoring the sources of new technologies for an industry. It also may include reading cutting-edge research journals and attending conferences and seminars. Organizations that operate closer to the cutting edge of technology rely more on scanning.

Japanese companies, such as Nissan, are often willing to show U.S. competitors their operations because they believe U.S. companies are unwilling or unable to use what they have learned.

L0 2 WHAT YOU NEED TO KNOW . . .

Can you identify the criteria on which to base technology decisions?

Base technology decisions on relevant criteria

After managers have thoroughly analyzed their organization's current technological position, they can plan how to develop or exploit emerging technologies. These plans must balance many interrelated factors, including the organization's competitive strategy, the technical abilities of its employees to deal with the new technology, the fit of the technology with the company's operations, and the company's ability to deal with the risks and ambiguities of adopting a new technology. All of these considerations jointly influence managers' decisions about technology innovations. A lack in even one of them can derail an otherwise promising project. Also, as we discuss later in this chapter, decisions go beyond whether to adopt a technology to include changes in the related factors—for example, improving the organization's capabilities and strategies, hiring or training employees, and changing internal policies and procedures.

anticipated market receptiveness The first consideration in developing a strategy around technological innovation is market potential. Many innovations are stimulated by external demand for new goods and services. For example, the share of Internet users who use a language other than English has been growing rapidly. This trend, along with the globalization of business, has fueled demand for the ability to search the Web in different languages. Companies are creating a variety of software innovations to meet this demand. Google will translate a searcher's query into a dozen languages and also translate Web pages to present results in the searcher's language. Yahoo! Answers will send queries to a native speaker of the user's language. It indexes those responses so that they can be searched by future users in that language.[8]

In assessing market receptiveness, executives need to make two determinations:

1. In the short run, the new technology should have an immediate, valuable application.

2. In the long run, the technology must be able to satisfy a market need or needs.

For example, when prescribing medicine, physicians view the traditional method of scribbling on a pad and handing the prescription to a patient or nurse as very simple to use. For the physicians to learn to use new technology for that purpose, it must be worthwhile to them. Hospitals that move to electronic management of drug distribution need to roll out entire systems, but those systems let doctors tap into information networks where they can look up drug interactions, side effects, and so on. When doctors see how the system helps them deliver better care and reduce errors, most are quick to embrace the new technology.[9]

Drawing on a decade of experience in designing computer games, Damion Schubert identified several important pitfalls to avoid if a game is to be well received by its market. Schubert, the lead combat designer for BioWare, says the first mistake is innovating too much. Trying to execute every new idea for a game confuses the message about what is exciting in that game, and it is probably impossible to do well. Instead, designers have to think about what they can accomplish well by their deadlines and then select innovations that users are most likely to enjoy.

Schubert learned of a team that was designing a multiplayer game and thought it would be interesting to allow players to set each others' houses on fire. However, that innovation did more to feed the designers' wish to try something new than it would add to players' enjoyment. Instead, Schubert says, designers need to ask gamers what *they* think would improve the game.

Similarly, Schubert says, game designers often confuse features with benefits. They might count the number of creatures, quests, or races in a game. Then they think of ways to add more creatures, quests, or races. But in most genres, the best games limit the number of such features, because genuine quality means that each choice is interesting, detailed, and well crafted. Thus, thorough testing to ensure that every innovation works well is more important than an abundance of new features. Gamers, Schubert insists, are looking not just for "something new" but rather for "something better."[10]

technological feasibility Managers also must consider whether technological innovations are feasible. Technical obstacles may represent barriers to progress. For example, the makers of computer chips face continual hurdles in developing newer and faster models. Since Intel brought the first microprocessor to market in 1971, chip makers have made dramatic advances in computing. The number of transistors on a chip, and its resulting performance, has doubled nearly every 18 to 24 months. But the frontier of microprocessor technology is restricted by the combined forces of physics and economics. The wires that run between transistors are 400 times thinner than a human hair, and the task of continually doubling the speed of electrons passing wires of near-zero width is tricky—and may become impossible at some point. To continue boosting processor speed economically, developers have had to be creative, using techniques such as shrinking components and embedding two or more processor cores on one microchip to shorten the distance data must travel between processors.[11]

Other industries face similar technological hurdles. In the oil industry, technological barriers prevent exploration and drilling in the deepest parts of the ocean. In medicine, scientists and doctors work continuously to identify the causes of and cures for diseases such as cancer and AIDS. Automakers' efforts to develop electric cars have been constrained by the difficulty of designing a battery that can power the long trips Americans love to take. General Motors' widely touted Volt has a range of 40 miles between charges, the same range as an experimental car being tested by Toyota for city driving.[12]

economic viability Apart from whether a firm can "pull off" a technological innovation, executives must consider whether there is a good financial incentive for doing so. The use of hydrogen-powered fuel-cell technology for automobiles is almost feasible technically, but its costs are still too high. Even if those costs were brought down to more acceptable levels, the absence of a supporting infrastructure—such as hydrogen refueling stations—represents another barrier to economic viability.

On a more practical level of economic feasibility, new technologies often require long-term commitment of substantial resources. And integrating them effectively in an organization

> "I have not failed. I've just found 10,000 ways that don't work."
>
> —Thomas Edison

can require a great deal of management time. For these reasons, managers must objectively analyze technology costs versus benefits. Of course, technology's benefits can be substantial. Fast-food restaurants can adopt a system called Hyperactive Bob. The system scans the parking lot to count vehicles that are arriving, compiles those data with information about time of day, cooking times, ordering patterns, and so on, and then issues orders to employees about which items and how many to begin cooking. Employees touch a screen to indicate

Hyperactive Bob applies robotics technology (computer vision and artificial intelligence) to fast-food operations to make them more efficient. Using this technology is economically feasible because it reduces waste, improves customer satisfaction, and reduces employee turnover.

when they accept a task and when they are finished. The system, made by Hyperactive Technologies, costs $5,000 to install and $3,000 a year for software licensing, but it saves thousands a year in reduced food waste plus much more in reduced employee turnover—because Bob is an alternative to being shouted at by an anxious supervisor.[13]

Conversion of paper medical records into electronic systems has been touted as a money-saving technological advance. Savings can come from recommending generic versions of medicines when available, keeping records in one centralized database rather than duplicating them in various locations, and avoiding errors from misreading handwritten orders or prescribing medicines that interact with other drugs the patient is already taking. The hurdle is how to pay for the conversion.

Managers of Midland Memorial Hospital wanted electronic medical records, because nurses were wasting time hunting for charts, squinting at messy handwriting, and filling out repetitive forms. But creating a computer system would cost as much as $20 million. Midland found the answer at the Veterans Health Administration. When VA facilities went electronic, they put the source code for their software in the public domain, so other programmers could use it, adding unique features for their clients. With the new system, Midland has lowered rates of infection and death and incurred fewer medication errors. The hospital also caught up on its billing backlog.

Doctors face a similar challenge. Fewer than two out of ten have computerized medical records, held back by the expense and a lack of computer experts on staff. The federal government has addressed the economic hurdle with incentives of about $40,000 for installing and using electronic-records systems. In New York City, the Primary Care Information Project developed software and helped more than 1,000 physicians implement it.

The project's head concludes that doctors will change but only if they have enough help—financial and technical.[14]

Patents and copyrights can help organizations recoup the costs of their investments in technological innovations. Without such protection, the investments in research and development might not be justifiable. Unfortunately, the growth in piracy and fakery of patented pharmaceuticals, software, and other products adds barriers to economic viability. Globalization has created a worldwide market for goods produced by low-cost counterfeiters and pirates. Pfizer's anti-impotence drug Viagra, Hewlett-Packard ink-jet cartridges, Intel computer chips, GM car designs, Coach handbags, Nike Air Jordan shoes, and countless music and movie recordings—all these and many more have been counterfeited or illegally copied and sold. Worldwide lost sales as a result of the theft of *intellectual property* have been estimated at more than $500 billion a year.

Some companies have taken action on this problem. Auto parts maker Bendix set up a team charged with enforcing intellectual property rights, used packaging that is harder to counterfeit, and educates customers by setting up trade show displays with side-by-side comparisons of its product and knock-offs. Other companies, including Pfizer, are using radio-frequency tags on their packages to track products more accurately during distribution. These measures are designed to help organizations maintain the economic viability of their innovations.[15]

anticipated competency development

Our advice that organizations base strategies on their core competencies applies to technology and innovation strategies. At Merck and Intel, core competencies in research and development lead to new technological innovations. By contrast, firms that are not technology oriented must develop new competencies to survive. For example, when Amazon.com changed the face of e-retailing in the 1990s, traditional brick-and-mortar bookstores had to adapt quickly. To regain competitiveness, they had to bolster their information technology competencies, which wasn't always easy for them to do.

The upshot is that while certain technologies may have tremendous market applicability, managers must have (or develop) the internal competencies to execute their technology strategies. In organizations without the skills needed to implement an innovation, even promising technological advances may prove disastrous.

organizational suitability The decision to adopt technological innovations also should take into account the culture of the organization, the interests of managers, and the expectations of stakeholders. With regard to technology adoption, we can consider three broad types of organizations:

- *Prospector firms*—These proactive "technology-push" innovators have cultures that are outward-looking and opportunistic. Examples include 3M and Google. Executives in these organizations give priority to developing and exploiting technological expertise, and decision makers have bold, intuitive visions of the future. Typically they have technology champions who articulate competitively aggressive, first-mover technological strategies. Executives tend to be more concerned about the opportunity costs of not taking action than they are about the potential to fail.

- *Defender firms*—These companies adopt a more circumspect posture toward innovation. They tend to operate in stable environments, so their strategies focus on deepening their capabilities through technologies that extend rather than replace their current ones. Strategic decisions are likely to be based on careful analysis and experience in the industry setting. In the United States, supermarkets have competed for decades by emphasizing low-cost distribution over large distances. That strategy has helped the companies survive low-cost pressure from Walmart but has not always translated well when U.S.-based supermarket chains have tried to expand into other parts of the world.[16]

- *Analyzer firms*—These hybrid organizations need to stay technologically competitive but tend to let others demonstrate solid demand in new arenas before responding. Such companies often adopt an early-follower strategy to grab a dominant position more from their strengths in marketing and manufacturing than from technological innovation. For example, Microsoft's Xbox game console, Office software, and Zune music player all contain innovations, but other companies pioneered the original path-breaking product concepts.

Every company has different capabilities to deal with new technology. *Early adopters* of new technologies tend to be larger, more profitable, and more specialized. As a result, they can absorb the risks associated with early adoption while profiting more from its advantages. In addition, the people involved in early adoption are more highly educated, have greater ability to deal with abstraction, can cope with uncertainty more effectively, and have strong problem-solving capabilities. Thus, early adopters can more effectively manage the difficulties and uncertainty of a less fully developed technology.[17]

Managers evaluating new technology also should consider its impact on employees. Often, new technology brings process changes that directly affect the organization's work environment. These changes may create anxiety and resistance among employees, making integration of the technology more difficult. But employees' cooperation is often a major factor in determining how difficult and costly the introduction of new technology

> ## "Almost everyone is more enthusiastic about change when the change is their own idea, and less enthusiastic if they feel the change is being imposed on them."
>
> —Maggie Bayless, managing partner, ZingTrain[18]

will be. We discuss the issue of managing change in more detail later in this chapter.

 3 WHAT YOU NEED TO KNOW . . .
What are the key ways of acquiring new technologies?

Know where to get new technologies

Developing new technology may conjure up visions of scientists and product developers working in research and development (R&D) laboratories. In many industries, the primary sources of new technology are the organizations that use it. More than three-fourths of scientific innovations are developed by the users of the scientific instruments being improved and subsequently may be licensed or sold to manufacturers or suppliers.[19] However, new technology can come from many sources, including suppliers, manufacturers, users, other industries, universities, the government, and overseas companies.

A decade ago, the German airline Deutsche Lufthansa developed route-mapping software for its own use, to calculate the most efficient routes for its flights. But the airline now sells versions of its Lido system to about 30 other carriers, including British Airways, Air Canada, Singapore Airlines, and Emirates Airlines.

The software tracks data such as weather, airport locations, runways, the weight and performance of aircraft, fixed air routes, and temporarily blocked airspace, and then searches through multiple scenarios to find the best route for each flight. British Airways estimates that the software saves the firm $15 million to $20 million a year. Air Canada reports similar results. So technology that was originally developed by one firm for its own internal use has become an option for purchase by many of its competitors.[20]

Essentially, the question of how to acquire new technology is a **make-or-buy decision**. In other words, should the organization develop the technology itself or acquire it from an outside source? That decision is not simple. There are many alternatives, and each has advantages and disadvantages. Here are some of the most common options:

- *Internal development*—Developing a new technology within the company can keep the technology proprietary—exclusive to the organization. However, internal development usually requires additional staff and funding for long periods. Even if the development succeeds, considerable time may elapse before practical benefits are realized. Intel balances these risks and benefits by operating research and development laboratories in several locations, including Oregon, Israel, India, and China. Engineers in these labs have come up with breakthrough ideas, and labs in offshore locations can get around legal restrictions on technology imports, as well as save money relative to the cost of hiring talent in the United States.[21]

- *Purchase*—Most technology already is available in products or processes that can be purchased. A bank that needs sophisticated information-processing equipment need not develop the technology itself. It can buy it from suppliers. In most situations, this is the simplest, easiest, and most cost-effective way to acquire new technology. However, the technology itself will not offer a competitive advantage.

- *Contracted development*—If the technology is not available and a company lacks the resources or time to develop it internally, it may contract the development from outside sources, such as other companies, independent research laboratories, and university and government institutions. Usually outside contracting involves an agreed-upon series of objectives and timetables for the project, with payments for completion of each.

- *Licensing*—Certain technologies that are not easily purchased can be licensed for a fee. Television producers license the right to install V-chips (paying a royalty of about $1 per TV set) because the U.S. government requires them so that parents can limit the content to which their children are exposed. Companies that develop videogames often license technology, including the software that models the physics behind the activities depicted in the game. The artwork, characters, and music for a particular game may be unique, but the basic laws of real-world physics apply to the action shown in most of today's sophisticated games, so there is no advantage to programming that aspect of each game. Licensing is more economical.[22]

- *Technology trading*—Some companies are willing to share ideas. Representatives from Scotsman Ice Systems have studied other manufacturers' information technology applications, learning from their experiences lessons that would have been expensive to learn from trial and error. Similarly, Mary Jo Cartwright, a director of manufacturing operations for Batesville Casket Company, toured a John Deere farm equipment plant and noted a technology called *visual management screens,* which display how-to information for production workers. Some time later, when Batesville became involved in more customization, the company introduced visual management screens to give workers detailed and understandable assembly instructions.[23] Not all industries are amenable to this kind of sharing, but technology trading is becoming increasingly common because of the high cost of developing advanced technologies independently.[24]

- *Research partnerships and joint ventures*—Research partnerships are arrangements for jointly pursuing specific new-technology development. Typically, each member contributes a different set of skills or resources, as when an established company contributes money and management know-how, and a start-up contributes technological expertise. Joint ventures are similar to research partnerships but generally are aimed at establishing entirely new companies.[25] An example is the strategic alliance formed by Tyson Foods, the giant meat producer, and ConocoPhillips, one of the big U.S. oil companies, to develop a renewable diesel fuel that includes beef, pork, and poultry fat discarded during meat processing. This alliance combines Tyson's knowledge in applying protein chemistry with Conoco's knowledge of refinery technology.[26]

- *Acquisition of a technology owner*—If a company lacks a technology but wishes to acquire ownership, it might purchase the company that owns the technology. This transaction can be an outright purchase of the entire company or a minority interest sufficient to gain access to the technology. For example, Motorola bought shares of Global Locate, which developed the technology for fast-working global positioning systems (GPSs). Customers are increasingly interested in GPS applications in cell phones and other mobile devices. A semiconductor supplier called Broadcom acquired Global Locate outright, so it could supply semiconductors featuring GPS navigation without having to license that technology or depend on an outside supplier.[27]

Choosing among these alternatives is simpler if managers ask a few basic questions:

1. Is it important (and possible) in terms of competitive advantage that the technology remain proprietary?

2. Are the time, skills, and resources for internal development available?

3. Is the technology readily available outside the company?

As Figure 14.1 illustrates, the answers to these questions guide the manager to the most appropriate technology acquisition option.

If the preferred decision is to acquire a company, managers take additional steps to ensure the acquisition will make sense for the long term. For example, they try to make sure that key employees will remain with the firm, instead of leaving and perhaps taking essential technical expertise with them. Similarly, as with any large investment, managers carefully assess whether the financial benefits of the acquisition will justify the purchase price.

FIGURE 14.1 Technology Acquisition Options

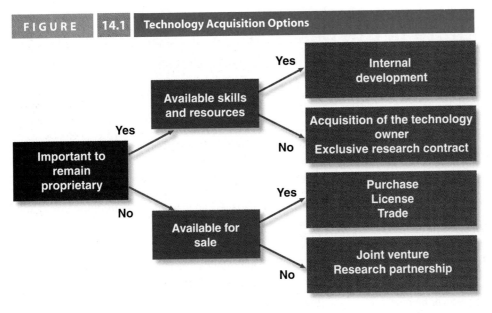

Important to remain proprietary

— Yes → Available skills and resources
— No → Available for sale

Available skills and resources
— Yes → Internal development
— No → Acquisition of the technology owner Exclusive research contract

Available for sale
— Yes → Purchase License Trade
— No → Joint venture Research partnership

L O 4 WHAT YOU NEED TO KNOW . . .

Can you describe the elements of an innovative organization?

ORGANIZING FOR INNOVATION

Successful innovation is a lot more than a great idea. A study by the Boston Consulting Group found that lack of good ideas is hardly ever the obstacle to profitable innovation. More often, ideas fail to generate financial returns because the organization isn't set up to innovate. The culture is risk averse, projects get bogged down, efforts aren't coordinated, and management can't figure out where to direct the company's money.[28]

In Chapter 6 we introduced the concept of *learning organizations*—companies that excel at solving problems, seeking and finding new approaches, and sharing new knowledge with all members of an organization. Learning organizations are particularly well positioned to carry out the two basic kinds of innovation:[29]

1. *Exploiting* existing capabilities, such as improving production speed or product quality

2. *Exploring* new knowledge—that is, seeking to develop new goods or services

Both innovation processes are necessary. Innovative learning organizations use their existing strengths to improve their operations—and their bottom lines. They also unleash people's creative energies and capabilities to develop new products and

processes that will ensure their long-term competitiveness. In this section we discuss some ways that managers organize for innovation.

Who is responsible for new technology innovations?

In organizations, technology was traditionally the responsibility of vice presidents for research and development, who oversaw corporate and divisional R&D laboratories. But companies today usually have the position of *chief information officer (CIO)* or *chief technology officer (CTO)*. The CIO is a corporate-level senior executive with broad responsibilities: coordinating the technological efforts of the business units, representing technology in the top management team, identifying ways that technology can support the company's strategy, supervising new-technology development, and assessing the technological implications of major strategic initiatives such as acquisitions, new ventures, and strategic alliances. CIOs also manage their organization's *information technology (IT)* group.[30]

Without the CIO's integrative role, an organization's departments could easily adopt different technology tools and standards, leading to much higher equipment and maintenance expense and difficulties in connecting the different parts of the organization. Their technical skills prepare them to supervise the organization's technology experts and help managers ensure that technology is aligned with the strategic goals of the organization.

Other people play critical roles in developing new technology. The *entrepreneur,* in an effort to exploit untried technologies, invents new products or finds new ways to produce old products. The entrepreneur opens up new possibilities that can change entire industries. For example, Steve Jobs started Apple Computer in his garage, helping to popularize the

Sophie Vandebroek, Chief Technology Officer of Xerox, has the goal of making Xerox's systems simpler, speedier, smaller, smarter, more secure, and socially responsible— what she calls the "six S's." Her own innovations include launching a research center on an island in the virtual world of Second Life so geographically separated employees can collaborate online.

personal computer and years later the MP3 music player.

In organizations, managers and employees may play key roles in acquiring and developing new technologies:[31]

- The *technical innovator* develops the new technology or has the skills needed to install and operate the technology. This person possesses technical skills but may lack the managerial skills needed to advance the idea and secure acceptance within the organization.

- The *product champion*—often at the risk of his or her position and reputation—promotes the idea throughout the organization, searching for support and acceptance. The champion can be a high-level manager but often is not. If the champion lacks the power and financial resources to make the required changes independently, she or he must convince people in authority to support the innovation. In other words, product champions must get sponsorship.

- Sponsorship comes from the *executive champion,* who has the status, authority, and financial resources to support the project and protect the product champion. This person's support and protection enable the new technology by making available the resources needed to develop the innovation and promoting the change.

To innovate, unleash creativity

Merck, 3M, Hewlett-Packard, and Rubbermaid have long histories of producing many successful new technologies and products. What sets these and other continuous innovators apart is an organizational culture that encourages innovation.[32]

Consider the 3M legend about inventor Francis G. Okie. In the early 1920s, Okie dreamed up the idea of using sandpaper instead of razor blades for shaving. The aim was to reduce the risk of nicks and avoid sharp instruments. The idea failed, but rather than punishing Okie for the failure, 3M encouraged him to champion other ideas, which included 3M's first blockbuster success: waterproof sandpaper. A culture that permits failure is crucial for fostering the creative thinking and risk taking required for innovation.

As strange as it may seem, *celebrating* failure can be vital to the innovation process.[34] Failure is the essence of learning, growing, and succeeding. In innovative companies, many people are trying many new ideas. A majority of the ideas

fail, but the few big hits that emerge can make a company an innovative star. Madison Mount, who leads the design work for food and beverage clients of IDEO, says, "If I'm not taking risks, I feel uncomfortable, because I'm not learning."[35] This type of attitude from a manager can foster creative thinking throughout the ranks.

To foster innovation, 3M uses a simple set of rules:[36]

- Set goals for innovation.
- Commit to research and development.
- Inspire intrapreneurship.
- Facilitate, don't obstruct.
- Focus on the customer.
- Tolerate failure.

These rules can be—and are—copied by other companies. But 3M has an advantage in that it has followed these rules since its inception and ingrained them in its culture.

Don't let bureaucracy squelch innovation

Bureaucracy is an enemy of innovation. Its main purpose is maintaining orderliness and efficiency, not pushing the creative envelope. Developing radically different technologies requires a fluid and flexible (organic) structure that does not restrict thought and action. However, such a structure can be chaotic and disruptive. Thus, although 3M has been admired for its culture of innovation, it became inefficient, with unpredictable profits and an unimpressive stock price. An efficiency drive beginning in 2001 impressed investors and drove up profits, but breakthrough innovations dried up.[37]

To balance innovation with other business goals, companies often establish special temporary project structures that are isolated from the rest of the organization and allowed to operate under different rules. These units go by many names, including "skunkworks," "greenhouses," and "reserves."

To foster a culture that values innovation, software maker Intuit set up a program called Innovation Lab. Adopting

Francis G. Okie of 3M's legend is a reminder that a culture that permits failure is crucial for fostering creative thinking, risk taking, and innovation.

a policy that Google made famous, the company allows employees to spend 10 percent of their time on unstructured activities aimed at generating and developing new ideas. They can choose an idea they feel passionate about or can devote the time to learning about new technologies. Intuit also sponsors "idea jams"—days set aside for employees with an idea to assemble a team to develop the idea. Idea jams are one-day events that take place every three months. Employees also have access to workgroup software called Brainstorm, which helps them share ideas and recruit team members to work on the ideas during the idea jams and their unstructured time. Review groups and mentors ensure that ideas are practical and successful. Intuit provides cash awards for winning ideas, but the excitement of Innovation Lab and idea jams is what really motivates Intuit employees to contribute to innovations such as the mobile version of QuickBooks Online.[38]

● **DEVELOPMENT PROJECT** A focused organizational effort to create a new product or process via technological advances.

● **SOCIOTECHNICAL SYSTEMS** An approach to job design that attempts to redesign tasks to optimize operation of a new technology while preserving employees' interpersonal relationships and other human aspects of the work.

(L)(O) 5 WHAT YOU NEED TO KNOW . . .

What are the characteristics of successful development projects?

Development projects can drive innovation

A powerful tool for managing technology and innovations is the **development project**.[39] A development project is a focused organizational effort to create a new product or process via technological advances. For example, when MTV launched MTV World, whose channels are aimed at various Asian American markets, the company used development projects embedded in a culture that values innovation. Nusrat Durani, general manager of MTV World, was among a group of employees drawn from various parts of the company. The development team members brought together a wide variety of backgrounds and experiences to create a successful plan for MTV World.[40]

Development projects typically feature a special cross-functional team that works together on an overall concept or idea. Like most cross-functional teams, its success depends on how well individuals work together to pursue a common vision. These teams interact with suppliers and customers, making their task more complex. Because of their urgency and strategic importance, most development projects are conducted under intense time and budget pressures.

Development projects have multiple benefits. Not only do they create new products and processes, but they also may cultivate skills and knowledge useful for future endeavors. Thus, the capabilities derived from a development project often can be turned into a source of competitive advantage. When Ford created a development project to design an air-conditioning compressor to outperform its Japanese rival, executives also discovered they had laid the foundation for new processes that Ford

TIP

Don't forget the human side of the technology equation.

could use in future projects. Their new capability in integrated design and manufacturing helped Ford reduce the costs and lead times for other product developments. Thus, *organizational learning* became equally important as a measure of the project's success.

For development projects to achieve their fullest benefit, they should build on core competencies, have a guiding vision about what must be accomplished and why, have a committed team, instill a philosophy of continuous improvement, and coordinate efforts across all units.

Job design and human resources make innovation possible

Adopting a new technology may require changes in the design of jobs. Often tasks are redefined to fit people to the demands of the technology. But this may fail to maximize total productivity, because it ignores the human part of the equation. Social relationships and human aspects of the task may suffer, lowering overall productivity.

The **sociotechnical systems** approach to work redesign specifically addresses this problem. This approach redesigns tasks in a way that jointly optimizes the social and technical efficiency of work. Beginning with studies on the introduction of new coal-mining technologies in 1949, the sociotechnical systems approach to work design focused on small, self-regulating work groups.[41] Later it was found that such work arrangements operated effectively only in an environment where bureaucracy was limited. Today's trends in bureaucracy bashing, lean and flat organizations, work teams, and workforce empowerment are logical extensions of the sociotechnical philosophy of work design. At the same time, the technologies of the information age—in which people at all organizational levels have access to vast amounts of information—make these leaner and less bureaucratic organizations possible.

Managers face choices in how to apply a new technology. Technology can be used to limit the tasks and responsibilities of workers and "de-skill" the workforce, turning workers into servants of the technology. Or managers can select and train workers to master the technology, using it to achieve great accomplishments and improve the quality of their lives. Technology, when managed effectively, can empower workers as it improves the organization's competitiveness.

As managers decide how to design jobs and manage employees, they need to consider how human resource systems can complement the introduction of new technology. For example, advanced manufacturing technology usually requires people with high levels of skill, a commitment to continuous learning, and ability to work in teams. Organizations can help this technology succeed by using pay systems that attract and reward people with the necessary qualities.[42] Examples include group incentives and skill-based pay. If a company's pay system is not aligned with the new technologies, it may not reward behavior that makes the changes work. Even worse, existing reward systems may reinforce counterproductive behaviors.

Taken as a whole, these ideas provide guidelines for managing the strategic and organizational issues associated with technology and innovation. To adapt to a dynamic marketplace, organizations may need to reshape themselves. Managing change and organizational learning are central elements of what it takes to become a world-class organization.

L O 6 WHAT YOU NEED TO KNOW . . .
What does it take to be world class?

BECOMING WORLD CLASS

Managers today want, or *should* want, their organizations to become world class.[43] Being *world class* requires applying the best and latest knowledge and ideas and having the ability to operate at the highest standards of any place anywhere.[44] Becoming world class is more than merely improving. It means becoming one of the very best in the world at what you do. To some people, world-class excellence seems a lofty, impossible, unnecessary goal. But this goal is essential to success in today's intensely competitive business world.

World-class companies create high-value products and earn superior profits over the long run. They demolish the obsolete methods, systems, and cultures of the past that impede progress and apply more effective and competitive organizational

strategies, structures, processes, and management of human resources. The result is an organization that can compete successfully on a global basis.[45]

Build organizations for sustainable, long-term greatness

Two Stanford professors, James Collins and Jerry Porras, studied 18 corporations that had achieved and maintained greatness for half a century or more.[46] The companies included Sony, American Express, Motorola, Marriott, Johnson & Johnson, Disney, 3M, Hewlett-Packard, Citicorp, and Walmart. Over the years, these companies have been widely admired as premier institutions in their industries and have made a real impact. Although every company experiences downturns, these companies have consistently prevailed across the decades. They turn in extraordinary performance over the long run, rather than fleeting greatness. This study is reported in the book called *Built to Last*—which is what these great organizations were and are.

The researchers sought to identify the essential characteristics of enduringly great companies. These great companies have strong core values in which they believe deeply, and they express and live the values consistently. They are driven by goals—not just incremental improvements or business-as-usual goals, but stretch goals (recall Chapter 10). They change continuously, driving for progress via adaptability, experimentation, trial and error, entrepreneurial thinking, and fast action. And they do not focus on beating the competition; they focus primarily on beating themselves. They continually ask, "How can we improve ourselves to do better tomorrow than we did today?"

Underneath the action and the changes, the companies' core values and vision remain steadfast. For example, Boeing's core values and mission include being on the leading edge of aeronautics technology, tackling huge challenges, maintaining product safety and quality; and behaving with integrity. Walt Disney's values and mission include fanatical attention to detail, continuous progress through creativity, commitment to preserving Disney's "magic" image, delivery of happiness and "wholesome American values," and a lack of cynicism. Note that the values are not all the same. In fact, no set of common values consistently predicted success. Instead, the critical factor is that the great companies *have* core values, *know* what they are and what they mean, and *live* by them—year after year.

Even small organizations can achieve greatness. Consider Neil Kelly Company (NKC), a home construction, remodeling, and repair firm that operates in Oregon. Under the leadership of Tom Kelly, son of the company's founder, Neil, the company meets difficult sales goals through creative marketing and maintains a strong culture based on a commitment to craftsmanship and environmentally friendly building practices.

Tom Kelly's passion for green construction led him to set up a "home performance" division, which conducts energy-efficiency audits, assesses indoor air quality, and fixes any problems that turn up in either assessment. The company also acquired a maker of "green" cabinets. NKC's concern for the environment is attractive to potential employees and prospective customers—especially in the Pacific Northwest, where environmental values are important to a sizable share of the population.

Along with his environmental ideals, Tom Kelly values creative marketing. Even when the economy took a sharp downturn, Kelly increased his marketing budget, building sales even as other companies were cutting back. For example, in a deal with a local television station, he did a series of stories about a green home-rebuilding project featuring NKC's new line of cabinetry, which gave the company media exposure while teaching consumers about green construction.[47]

Replace the "tyranny of the *or*" with the "genius of the *and*"

Many companies, and individuals, are plagued by what the authors of *Built to Last* call the "tyranny of the *or*"—the belief that things must be either A or B and cannot be both. The authors provide many common examples: beliefs that you must choose either change or stability, be conservative or bold, have control and consistency or creative freedom, do well in the short term or invest for the future, plan methodically or be opportunistic, create shareholder wealth or do good for the world, be pragmatic or idealistic.[48] However, beliefs that only one goal can be attained often are invalid.

An alternative to the "tyranny of the *or*" is the "genius of the *and*"—the ability to achieve multiple objectives at the same time.[49] It develops via the actions of many individuals throughout the organization. In earlier chapters we discussed the importance of delivering multiple competitive values to customers, performing all the management functions, reconciling hard-nosed business logic with ethics, and leading and empowering. Authors Collins and Porras have their own list:[50]

- Purpose beyond profit *and* pragmatic pursuit of profit
- Relatively fixed core values *and* vigorous change and movement
- Conservatism with the core values *and* bold business moves
- Clear vision and direction *and* experimentation
- Stretch goals *and* incremental progress
- Control based on values *and* operational freedom
- Long-term thinking and investment *and* demand for short-term results
- Visionary, futuristic thinking *and* daily, nuts-and-bolts execution

You have learned about all of these concepts throughout this course and should not lose sight of any—in your mind or in your actions. To achieve them requires the continuous and effective management of change.

Organization development systematically shapes success

How do organizations apply the "genius of the *and*" and move in the other positive directions described throughout this book? Several general approaches create positive change, and many of them can be incorporated into a formal process of organization development.

Organization development (OD) is a systemwide application of behavioral science knowledge to develop, improve, and reinforce the strategies, structures, and processes that lead to organization effectiveness.[51] Throughout this course, you have acquired knowledge about behavioral science and the strategies, structures, and processes that help organizations become more effective. The "systemwide" component of the definition means OD is not a narrow improvement in technology or operations but a broader approach to changing organizations, units, or people. The "behavioral science" component means OD is not focused directly on economic, financial, or technical aspects of the organization—although they may benefit, through changes in the behavior of the people in the organization. The other key part of the definition—to develop, improve, and reinforce—refers to the actual process of changing, for the better and for the long term.

Two features of organization development are important.[52] First, it aims to increase organizational effectiveness—improving the organization's ability to respond to customers, stockholders, governments, employees, and other stakeholders, which results in better-quality products, higher financial returns, and high quality of work life. Second, OD has an important underlying value orientation: it supports human potential, development, and participation in addition to performance and competitive advantage.

Many OD techniques fit under this philosophical umbrella.[53] There are four basic types:

The strategy of Cirque du Soleil is one of constant innovation: combining circus and theater and studying other industries like car design, fashion, and restaurants to find ideas for new shows.

1. *Strategic interventions,* including helping organizations conduct mergers and acquisitions, change their strategies, and develop alliances
2. *Technostructural interventions* relating to organization structure and design, employee involvement, and work design

3. *Human resources management interventions*, including attracting good people, setting goals, and appraising and rewarding performance

4. *Human process interventions*, including conflict resolution, team building, communication, and leadership.

You have learned about these topics throughout your management course. You also will learn more about the process of creating change in the rest of this chapter.

Certain management practices make organizations great

A study of 200 management techniques employed by 160 companies over 10 years identified the specific management practices that lead to sustained, superior performance.[54] The authors boiled their findings down to four key factors:

1. *Strategy* that is focused on customers, continually fine-tuned based on marketplace changes, and clearly communicated to employees.

2. *Execution* by good people, given decision-making authority on the front lines, who are doing quality work and cutting costs.

3. *Culture* that motivates, empowers people to innovate, rewards people appropriately (psychologically as well as economically), entails strong values, challenges people, and provides a satisfying work environment.

4. *Structure* that makes the organization easy to work in and easy to work with, characterized by cooperation and the exchange of information and knowledge throughout the organization.

You have been learning about these concepts throughout this course.

People are the key to successful change.[55] For an organization to be great, people have to care about its fate and know how they can contribute. But typically, leadership lies with a few people at the top. Too few take on the burden of change; too few care deeply and make innovative contributions. People throughout the organization need to take a greater interest and a more active role in helping the business as a whole. They have to identify with the entire organization, not just with their unit and close colleagues.

L O 7 WHAT YOU NEED TO KNOW . . .
How can you manage change effectively?

MANAGING CHANGE

Change happens, constantly and unpredictably. Any competitive advantage you may have depends on particular circumstances at a particular time, but circumstances change.[56] The economic environment shifts; new competitors pop up; markets emerge.

> "**During the last two to three years, we have experienced more change than this company has ever experienced.**"
>
> —Sharon Rues Pettid, human resource manager, Mutual of Omaha[59]

CompUSA Orders Up a Customer-Focused Future

Former electronics retailing giant CompUSA is making a marketplace comeback by using technology to put customers' interests first. Once one of the nation's "big three" electronics retailers (along with Best Buy and Circuit City), CompUSA filed for bankruptcy in 2007 after being squeezed out by competitors whose size enabled them to offer lower prices and wider selections.

But in 2008, CompUSA underwent a makeover. It closed its 200 stores nationwide and was sold for $30 million to electronics retailer Systemax, which also owns Tiger Direct. Systemax designed a new go-to-market strategy for CompUSA, which it dubbed "Retail 2.0." Along with leaner operations, aggressive prices, and remodeled stores, Retail 2.0's most innovative feature is that customers are encouraged to access the Internet from the merchandise displayed throughout the store.

Every screen on display in a CompUSA store is live and linked to the Internet. Not only can customers try a product before they buy it, they can familiarize themselves with product features, compare competitors' prices, identify whether the item is in stock—even check their Facebook and Twitter accounts. Most stores would hesitate to make comparison shopping easier, but CompUSA's expectation is that the ability to try out products will keep customers engaged.

CompUSA's idea is innovative but not unique. The company borrowed the merchandising idea from Apple stores, where customers can try out the Macs on display and surf the Web.

It doesn't hurt that CompUSA believes its prices will stand up to scrutiny. The company can keep prices low because its inventory is linked to that of sibling company Tiger Direct. Customers pay the same price for a product whether they buy it in the store or online.

According to Gilbert Fiorentino, chief executive of the Technology Products Group at Systemax, high-tech companies are constantly changing, but change comes much more slowly in retailing. He believes the Retail 2.0 strategy represents a big change for CompUSA customers: "Shoppers will get the online experience inside the store. They will know everything about the product before getting it home and unpackaged."

To accomplish the transformation, CompUSA's programmers wrote software that linked

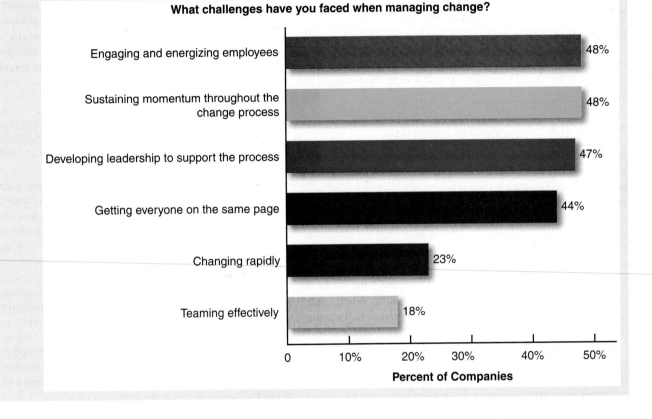

What challenges have you faced when managing change?

Challenge	Percent
Engaging and energizing employees	48%
Sustaining momentum throughout the change process	48%
Developing leadership to support the process	47%
Getting everyone on the same page	44%
Changing rapidly	23%
Teaming effectively	18%

Percent of Companies

computer monitors to the store's inventory. TVs were hooked up to hard drives and equipped with keyboards to make them Web-accessible. The conversion is pricey: between $50,000 and $100,000 per store. Yet CompUSA saw sales rise 14 percent in the first year of Retail 2.0, while Best Buy sales declined and Circuit City closed its doors.

Q: Discussion Questions

- Based on this description, in what areas has CompUSA embraced the "genius of the *and*"? Do you think giving shoppers access to the information of the Internet will make customers more loyal, or do you expect a trade-off between customer satisfaction and profits?
- How might this innovation at CompUSA affect the jobs of salespeople in the stores? If you were a store manager, how would you have wanted to help the employees prepare for the change?

SOURCES: Company Web site, http://www.compusa.com, accessed June 26, 2009; Reena Jana, "How CompUSA Made a Comeback," *BusinessWeek,* May 13, 2009, http://www.businessweek.com; David LaGesse, "Circuit City Name Is Pursued by Successful CompUSA Salvagers," *U.S. News & World Report,* April 14, 2009, http://www.usnews.com; Eric Krangel, "CompUSA Is Back, Taking Cues from Apple," *Business Insider,* April 10, 2009, http://www.businessinsider.com; and Priya Ganapati, "CompUSA Comes Back from the Dead," *Wired,* April 9, 2009, http://www.wired.com.

The challenge for organizations is not just to produce innovative new products but to balance a culture that is innovative and builds a sustainable business.[57] For individuals, the ability to cope with change is related to their job performance and the rewards they receive.[58]

The success of most change efforts requires *shared leadership;* people must be not just *supporters* of change but also *implementers.*[60] This shared responsibility for change is not unusual in start-ups and very small organizations, but it often is lost with growth and over time. In large, traditional corporations, it is all too rare. Organizations must rekindle individual creativity and responsibility, instituting true change in the behavior of people throughout the ranks. The essential task is to motivate people to keep changing in response to new business challenges.

Motivate people to change

People must be *motivated* to change. But often they resist changing. Some people resist change more than others, but managers tend to underestimate the amount of resistance they will encounter.[62]

People at all levels of their organizations, from entry-level workers to top executives, resist change. When Foremost Farms USA asked workers to switch goals—instead of making American cheese as fast as they could, they had to aim for getting each block to weigh precisely 640 pounds—the workers complied only as long as managers kept checking. When management's attention turned elsewhere, they reverted to the more familiar emphasis on speed.[63]

At IBM, many changes have been necessary to keep bureaucracy from stifling innovation, and all of them have been challenging. At one point, executives learned that lower-level managers were getting bogged down because they had to invest

Fear of the unknown and mistrust can prompt resistance to change. This scene shows thousands of protestors rallying against the federal government's Wall Street bailout policy in front of the New York Stock Exchange in September of 2008.

too much time and effort in obtaining approval from higher-ups. CEO Sam Palmisano announced that he would give first-level managers authority to spend $5,000 without prior approval—a daring move, considering that the authority applied to 30,000 managers. However, the managers felt uncomfortable with their new authority, and in the first year of the new program, they spent only $100,000 of the $150 million Palmisano had entrusted to them.[64] In other words, they were reluctant to change the way they worked, even though it could make their job easier.

To deal with such reactions and successfully implement positive change, managers must understand why people often resist change. Some reasons for resistance arise regardless of the actual content of the change:[65]

- *Inertia.* Usually people don't want to disturb the status quo. The old ways of doing things are comfortable and easy, so people don't want to try something new. For example, it is easier to keep living in the same apartment or house than to move to another.

- *Timing.* People often resist change because of poor timing. If managers or employees are unusually busy or under stress, or if relations between management and workers are strained, the timing is wrong for introducing new proposals. Where possible, managers should introduce change when people are receptive.

- *Surprise.* If a change is sudden, unexpected, or extreme, resistance may be the initial—almost reflexive—reaction. Suppose your university announced an increase in tuition, effective at the beginning of next term. Wouldn't you at least want more warning, so you can be prepared? Managers or others initiating a change often forget that others haven't given the matter much thought; the change leaders need to allow time for others to think about the change and prepare for it.

- *Peer pressure.* Sometimes work teams resist new ideas. Even if individual members do not strongly oppose a change suggested by management, the team may band together in opposition. If a group is highly cohesive and has anti-management norms, peer pressure will cause individuals to resist even reasonable changes. Of course, peer pressure can be a positive force, too. Change leaders who invite— and listen to—ideas from team members may find that peer pressure becomes a driving force behind the change's success.

Other causes of resistance arise from the specific nature of a proposed change:[66]

- *Self-interest.* Most people care less about the organization's best interest than they do about their own best interests. They will resist a change if they think it will cause them to lose something of value. What could people fear to lose? At worst, their jobs, if management is considering closing down a plant. A merger, reorganization, or technological change could create the same fear. Other possible fears include loss of the feeling of being competent in a familiar job, expectations that the job will become more difficult or time-consuming, uncertainty about whether enough training or other resources will be provided for succeeding at the change, and doubts about the organization's future success, given that management wasn't satisfied with the status quo.

- *Misunderstanding.* Even when management proposes a change that will benefit everyone, people may resist because they don't fully understand it. People may not see how the change fits with the firm's strategy, or they simply may not see the change's advantage over current practices.[67] One company met resistance to the idea of introducing flexible working hours, a system in which workers have some say regarding the hours they work. This system can benefit employees, but a false rumor circulated among plant employees that people would have to work evenings, weekends, or whenever their supervisors wanted. The employees' union demanded that management drop the idea. The president, caught off guard by this unexpected resistance, complied with the union's demand.

- *Different assessments.* Employees receive different—and usually less—information than management receives. Even within top management ranks, some executives know more than others do. Such discrepancies cause people to develop different assessments of proposed changes. Some may be aware that the benefits outweigh the costs, while others may see only the costs. This is a common problem when management announces a change in work procedures and doesn't explain to employees why the change is needed. Management expects increased efficiency, but workers may see the change as another arbitrary, ill-informed management rule that simply causes headaches for them.

- *Management tactics.* Sometimes a change that succeeds elsewhere is undertaken in a new location, and problems may arise during the transfer.[68] Management may try to force the change and fail to address concerns in order to develop employee commitment. Or it may not provide enough resources, knowledge, or leadership to help the change succeed. Sometimes a change receives so much exposure and glorification that employees resent it and resist. Managers who overpromise what they—or the change—can deliver may discover that the next time they want to introduce a change, they have lost credibility, so employees resist.

It is important to recognize that employees' assessments can be more accurate than management's; employees may know a change won't work even if management doesn't. In this case, resistance to change benefits the organization. Thus, even though management typically considers resistance

a challenge to overcome, it may actually represent an important signal that a proposed change requires further, more open-minded scrutiny.[69]

A three-stage model suggests ways to manage resistance

Motivating people to change often requires three basic stages, shown in Figure 14.2: unfreezing, moving to institute the change, and refreezing.[70]

unfreezing During the unfreezing stage, management realizes that its current practices are no longer appropriate and the company must break out of (unfreeze) its present mold by doing things differently. People must come to recognize that some of the past ways of thinking, feeling, and doing things are obsolete.[71] A direct and sometimes effective way to do this is to communicate the negative consequences of the old ways by comparing the organization's performance with that of its competitors. Management can also share with employees data about costs, quality, and profits.[72] Sometimes employees just need to understand the rationale for changing. In the earlier example of Foremost Farms, big competitors had made it impossible to win with a strategy of working efficiently and selling cheese at a low price. Management had decided to sell more profitable customized products, such as the 640-pound blocks of cheese that one customer planned to repackage in smaller sizes. After Foremost managers took the time to explain the situation to employees, the workers understood the new requirements and began minimizing size variations.[73]

When managers communicate a problem, they must take care not to arouse people's defensiveness. Managers tend to place employees on the defensive when they pin the blame for shortcomings directly and entirely on the workers[74] and when they bombard employees with

A+

TIP

Sometimes, it's the manager—not the employee—who resists change. As an employee trying to convince your boss that it's time to make a change for the good, you can offer background information that supports your idea, provide appropriate feedback during meetings, offer to schedule an expert guest speaker, and find a mentor who can help you gain influence with your own manager. Also perform your very best on the job; it will attract your boss's attention and establish your credibility. If you are the best at what you do, your opinion will carry more weight. However you approach it, though, always be tactful and respectful.[76]

FIGURE 14.2 **Motivating People to Change**

| Unfreezing (breaking from the old ways of doing things) | → | Moving (instituting the change) | → | Refreezing (reinforcing and supporting the new ways) |

- **PERFORMANCE GAP** The difference between actual performance and desired performance.

- **MOVING** Instituting the change.

- **FORCE-FIELD ANALYSIS** An approach to implementing Lewin's unfreezing/moving/refreezing model, involving identifying the forces that prevent people from changing and those that will drive people toward change.

- **REFREEZING** Strengthening the new behaviors that support the change.

facts aimed at inducing fear. When a problem seems huge, people often decide it is hopeless and withdraw from facing it. In *Change or Die*, journalist Alan Deutschman uses that pattern of behavior to explain why heart attack victims often fail to follow diet and exercise plans, even though doctors tell them they will literally die if they don't take care of themselves.[75] Deutschman sees a similar pattern playing out in companies where executives rely on threats of layoffs and corporate bankruptcy to motivate employees to adopt new work practices. In these difficult situations, leaders more effectively unfreeze negative behavior with a message of hope and a commitment to collaborate with others so that they can effect change together.

An important contributor to unfreezing is the recognition of a performance gap, which can precipitate major change. A **performance gap** is the difference between actual performance and the performance that should or could exist.[77] A gap typically implies poor performance, as when sales, profits, stock price, or other financial indicators are down. This situation attracts management's attention, and management introduces changes to try to correct things.

Another, very important form of performance gap occurs when performance is good but someone realizes it could be better. Thus, the gap is between what is and what *could be*. This realization is where entrepreneurs seize opportunities and companies gain a competitive edge. In the realm of change management, employees are best motivated by situations that combine the sense of urgency that comes from identifying a problem with the sense of excitement that comes from identifying an opportunity. Also, employees care about more than market share and revenues; they want to know how making a change can help them have a positive impact on their work group, their customers, their company, their community, and themselves. For example, a financial services company struggled to persuade employees that a change would enhance the company's competitive position. Employees got on board only after the change leaders started talking about how the change would help employees reduce errors, avoid duplication of effort, make jobs more interesting, and fulfill the organization's mission to deliver affordable housing.[78]

The Fox Valley Nursing Center, located northwest of Chicago in Elgin, Illinois, was struggling to maintain its certification several years ago when an early winter storm dropped 16 inches of snow in 24 hours. Roads were nearly impassable, and staff members were calling in to report they couldn't make it to work. CEO Jerry Rhoads learned of the staff

shortage in a phone call from the assistant director of nursing, and he told her she should simply list all the critical tasks that needed to be done for each resident, and the staff members should work in teams to get those tasks done. Rhoads was surprised by the result: staff members worked cheerfully and diligently for 72 hours, rotating through work and rest breaks so that no one became exhausted.

Rhoads saw an opportunity for meaningful change. He began reorganizing the nursing center's staff into teams handling specific processes. Under the new system, absenteeism and turnover fell, while morale and occupancy rates improved. Some people predicted that the snowstorm's effects had simply been an exception, but staff members told Rhoads that "they knew how to provide this level of care all along, but no one would let them do it." He adds, "I believed them, and they were the ones who made it work."[79]

moving The next step, **moving** to institute the change, begins with establishing a vision of where the company is heading. You learned about vision in the leadership chapter. The vision can be realized through strategic, structural, cultural, and individual change.

A technique that helps to manage the change process, **force-field analysis**, involves identifying the specific forces that prevent people from changing and the specific forces that will drive people toward change.[80] In other words, managers investigate forces acting in opposite directions at a particular time. Change leaders assess organizational strengths and select forces to add or remove in order to create change. Eliminating the restraining forces helps people unfreeze, and increasing the driving forces helps and motivates them to move forward.

Use of force-field analysis demonstrates that often a range of forces are pressing on an organization and its people at a particular time. This analysis can increase people's optimism that it is possible to strategize and plan for change. Kurt Lewin, who developed force-field analysis, theorized that although driving forces may be more easily affected, shifting them may increase opposition (tension and/or conflict) within the organization and add restraining forces. So, to create change, it may be more effective to remove restraining forces.

As part of an effort to change its organizational culture, the Wyoming State Penitentiary (WSP) instituted an awards program called the Doing It Right Employee Recognition Program. Under the program, which was designed to boost morale and close a performance gap, board members select employees of the month, quarter, and year. Any WSP employee may nominate any other employee for the award. For each award level, recipients receive some form of recognition: a certificate, photos displayed on the WSP Web site, an article about them in the organization's newsletter and/or the local newspaper, and at the highest award level, a gift certificate. After more than a year, employees and managers express enthusiasm for this program.

In addition, management at WSP launched an Employee Betterment Program designed to empower staff. Twice a year, employees are selected at random to attend an idea-generating session with upper managers. Typically, these meetings start out as gripe sessions until employees realize that top managers really want to hear their practical suggestions for improvement at the penitentiary. Some ideas are broad, such as examining the enforcement and application of rules; others are specific, like repaving the parking lot. Perhaps the most rewarding aspect of the Employee Betterment Program is the experience of seeing management implement their ideas.[81]

refreezing Finally, **refreezing** means strengthening the new behaviors that support the change. The changes must be diffused and stabilized throughout the company. Refreezing involves implementing control systems that support the change, applying corrective action when necessary, and reinforcing behaviors and performance that support the agenda. Management should consistently support and reward all evidence of movement in the right direction.[82]

In today's organizations, refreezing may not be the best third step if it creates new behaviors that are as rigid as the old ones. The ideal new culture is one of continuous change. Refreezing is appropriate when it permanently installs behaviors that maintain essential core values, such as a focus on important business results and the values maintained by companies that are "built to last." But refreezing should not create new rigidities that might become dysfunctional as the business environment continues to change.[83] The refrozen behaviors should promote continued adaptability, flexibility, experimentation, assessment of results, and continuous improvement. In other words, lock in key values, capabilities, and strategic mission, but not necessarily specific management practices and procedures.

Specific approaches can encourage cooperation

You can try to command people to change, but the key to long-term success is to use other approaches.[84] Developing true support is better than "driving" a program forward.[85] How, specifically, can managers motivate people to change?

Most managers underestimate the variety of ways they can influence people during a period of change.[86] Several effective approaches to managing resistance and enlisting cooperation are available, as summarized in Table 14.1.

- *Education and communication*—Management should educate people about upcoming changes before they occur. It should communicate the *nature* of the change and its *logic.* This

Lawrence Ellison, CEO of Oracle, is well versed in what it takes to convey a vision of change within his organization. Oracle has been acquiring other companies, which can bring tumultuous change for individual employees and managers.

process can include reports, memos, one-on-one discussions, and presentations to groups. Effective communication includes feedback and listening. Whenever Round Table Pizza introduces a new project or process, managers set up meetings with their employees to discuss the change and bring up any concerns they have.[87] That provides an environment in which management can explain the rationale for the change—and perhaps improve it.

- *Participation and involvement*—The people who are affected by a change should be involved in its design and implementation. For major, organizationwide change, participation in the process can extend from the top to the very bottom of the organization.[88] People who are involved in decisions understand them more fully and are more committed to them. Participation also allows for education and communication. Kate Peck, an administrative assistant with ZingTrain, the consulting arm of specialty-foods retailer Zingerman's, engaged others when she saw a need for change in the haphazard way office supplies were stored. Peck decided they should be arranged according to which items were used most often. But before she started moving supplies around, Peck sent an e-mail to the staff explaining what she planned to change and why, inviting feedback, and asking who else might need to be informed. One employee suggested that Peck improve on the change by making a diagram for the cabinets to help employees learn what each one contains. When Peck implemented the changes, her coworkers agreed she had improved the situation, and they found whatever they needed more quickly.[89]

- *Facilitation and support*—Management should make the change as easy as possible for employees and support their efforts. Facilitation involves providing the training and other resources people need to carry out the change and perform their jobs under the new circumstances. This step often includes decentralizing authority and empowering people. Offering support involves listening patiently to problems, being understanding if performance drops temporarily or the change is not perfected immediately, and generally being on the employees' side and showing consideration during a difficult period.

- *Negotiation and rewards*—When necessary, management can offer concrete incentives for cooperating with the change. Perhaps job enrichment is acceptable only with a higher wage rate, or a work rule change is resisted until management agrees to a concession on some other rule (say, about taking breaks). Even among higher-level managers, one executive might agree to another's idea for a policy change only in return for support on some other issue. Rewards such as bonuses, wages and salaries, recognition, job assignments,

TABLE 14.1 | Methods for Managing Resistance to Change

Approach	Situations Where Commonly Used	Advantages	Drawbacks
Education and communication	Where there is a lack of information or inaccurate information and analysis.	Once persuaded, people will often help with the implementation of the change.	Can be very time-consuming if lots of people are involved.
Participation and involvement	Where the initiators do not have all the information they need to design the change, and where others have considerable power to resist.	People who participate will be committed to implementing change, and any relevant information they have will be integrated into the change plan.	Can be very time-consuming if participators design an inappropriate change.
Facilitation and support	Where people are resisting because of adjustment problems.	No other approach works as well with adjustment problems.	Can be time-consuming and expensive, and still fail.
Negotiation and rewards	Where someone or some group will clearly lose out in a change, and where that group has considerable power to resist.	Sometimes it is a relatively easy way to avoid major resistance.	Can be too expensive in many cases if it alerts others to negotiate for compliance.
Manipulation and cooptation	Where other tactics will not work, or are too expensive.	It can be a relatively quick and inexpensive solution to resistance problems.	Can lead to future problems if people feel manipulated.
Explicit and implicit coercion	Where speed is essential, and the change initiators possess considerable power.	It is speedy and can overcome any kind of resistance.	Can be risky if it leaves people angry at the initiators.

SOURCE: Reprinted by permission of *Harvard Business Review*. From "Choosing Strategies for Change" by John P. Kotter and Leonard A. Schlesinger (March–April 1979). Copyright © 1979 by the Harvard Business School Publishing Corporation; all rights reserved.

and perks can be examined and perhaps restructured to reinforce the direction of the change.[90] Change is further facilitated by demonstrating that the change itself benefits people.[91] When a pharmaceutical company was trying to improve the way it managed its supply chain, the vice president in charge called a meeting at which participants were invited to share stories of their successes in carrying out their roles within the supply chain. Although suspicious at first, the participants gained enthusiasm and commitment before turning their energy toward making changes. The improvement was measurable: 20 days shaved off the product lead time, saving the company more than $250,000.[92] The participants not only saw themselves as effective problem solvers but also saw the dramatic improvement they could initiate in one meeting.

- *Manipulation and cooptation*— Sometimes managers use more subtle, covert tactics to implement change. One form of manipulation is cooptation, which involves giving a resisting individual a desirable role in the change process. The leader of a resisting group often is co-opted. For example, management might invite a union leader to be a member of an executive committee or ask a key member of an outside organization to join the company's board of directors. As a person becomes involved in the change, he or she may become less resistant to the actions of the co-opting group or organization.

- *Explicit and implicit coercion*—Some managers apply punishment or the threat of punishment to those who resist change. With this approach, managers use force to make people comply with their wishes. A manager might insist that subordinates cooperate with the change and threaten them with job loss, denial of a promotion, or an unattractive work assignment. Sometimes you just have to lay down the law.

Each approach to managing resistance has advantages and drawbacks and, like many of the other situational management approaches described in this book, each is useful in certain situations. Table 14.1 summarizes advantages, drawbacks, and appropriate circumstances for these approaches to managing resistance to change. Effective change managers are familiar with the various approaches and apply them according to the situation.

In the 1990s, when advertisers were wary of using the Internet, Yahoo! management hired someone it could trust as head of its sales force: Wenda Harris Millard. Millard was a 50-year-old veteran of the magazine industry. She taught her young and brash salespeople to work respectfully with their older ad agency clients, and she showed those clients that online ads could benefit them. Agency creative types loved TV ads but thought of Internet advertising as mainly boring pop-ups with a box saying "Click here." Yahoo! under Millard brought them together at educational summits and established the Yahoo Big Idea Chair award for the most creative online advertising. Seeing what innovative companies were doing, ad agency people became able to envision online advertising as a medium that allowed plenty of room for creativity—and Yahoo! began selling ads to big companies, reaching millions of Web visitors every day.[93]

Throughout the process, change leaders need to build in stability. Recall from the companies that were "built to last" that they share essential core characteristics and keep focused on them. In the midst of change, turmoil, and uncertainty, people need anchors onto which they can latch.[94] Making an organization's values and mission constant and visible can often serve this stabilizing function. In addition, strategic principles can be important anchors during change.[95] Managers also should maintain the visibility of key people, continue key assignments and projects, and make announcements about which organizational components will *not* change. Such anchors will reduce anxiety and help overcome resistance.

Managers have to harmonize multiple changes

There are no single-shot methods of changing organizations successfully. Single shots rarely hit a challenging target. Usually, many issues need simultaneous attention, and any single, small change will be absorbed by the prevailing culture and disappear. *Total organization change* involves introducing and sustaining multiple policies, practices, and procedures across multiple units and levels.[96] Such change affects the thinking and behavior of everyone in the organization, can enhance the organization's culture and success, and can be sustained over time.

A survey at a Harvard Business School conference found that the average attendee's company had five major change efforts going on at once.[97] The most common change programs were practices you have studied in this course: continuous improvement, quality programs, time-based competition, and creation of a learning organization, a team-based organization, a network organization, core competencies, and strategic alliances. The problem is, these efforts usually are simultaneous but not coordinated. As a result, changes get muddled; people lose focus.[98] The people involved suffer from confusion, frustration, low morale, and low motivation.

Because companies introduce new changes constantly, people complain about their companies' "flavor of the month"

approach to change. Employees often see change efforts as just the company's jumping on the latest bandwagon or fad. The more these fads come and go, the more cynical people become, and the harder it is to get them committed to making the change a success.[99]

One solution is to identify which change efforts are really worthwhile. Here are some specific questions to ask before embarking on a change project:[100]

- What is the evidence that the approach really can produce positive results?
- Is the approach relevant to your company's strategies and priorities?
- What are the costs and potential benefits?
- Does it really help people add value through their work?
- Does it help the company focus better on customers and what they value?
- Can you go through the decision-making process described in Chapter 4, understand what you're facing, and feel that you are taking the right approach?

The need for change was obvious when Janet Frank took the top job at California's State Compensation Insurance Fund, an agency with a state-appointed governing board and civil-service workers but no taxpayer funding. The State Fund, which provides workers' compensation insurance for many California companies, was in deep trouble. Several of its leaders were accused of conflict of interest in awarding contracts; two directors and two executives resigned. The government launched investigations and evaluated whether to press criminal charges.

The board of directors brought in Frank, then an executive with CNA Financial Corporation, to clean up. Given the mandate for change, the dilemma was where to begin. Frank had to satisfy angry citizens, legislators looking for evidence of better oversight, and business customers concerned about insurance costs. The state's insurance commissioner delivered 150 recommended changes during Frank's first two months on the job.

Frank started with governance and communication. She brought in a finance executive and a chief risk officer to lead audits. She began requiring the internal-audit department to report results directly to the board of directors, independent of management. She reorganized the communications department so it could deliver clearer messages to the agency's constituencies. She set up a public-records department to meet a new disclosure requirement. Communication efforts target employees worried about the future. In her frequent meetings with them, Frank not only shares goals but also listens.[101]

Management also needs to integrate the various efforts into a coherent picture that people can see, understand, and get behind.[102] You do this by understanding each change program and its goals, identifying similarities and differences of the programs, and dropping programs that don't meet priority goals or demonstrate clear results. Most important, you do it by

communicating to everyone concerned the common themes of the various programs: their common rationales, objectives, and methods. You show them how the parts fit the strategic big picture and how the changes will improve things for the company and its people. You must communicate these benefits thoroughly, honestly, and frequently.[103]

Managers must lead change

Successful change requires managers to actively lead it. The essential activities of leading change are summarized in Figure 14.3.

The companies that lead change most effectively *establish a sense of urgency*.[104] To do so, managers must examine current realities and pressures in the marketplace and the competitive arena, identify crises and opportunities, and be frank and honest about them. In this sense, urgency is a reality-based sense of determination, not just fear-based busyness. The immediacy of the need for change is important partly because so many large companies grow complacent. Complacency can arise from various sources:[105]

- Absence of a major and visible crisis
- Too many visible resources
- Organizational structures that focus employees on narrow functional goals
- Internal measurement systems that focus on the wrong performance indexes
- Lack of sufficient performance feedback from external sources
- Low-candor, low-confrontation culture ("kill the messenger of bad news")
- Human nature, with its capacity for denial, especially if people are already busy or stressed
- Too much happy talk from senior management

FIGURE 14.3 Leading Change

1 Establishing a sense of urgency

2 Creating the guiding coalition

3 Developing a vision and strategy

4 Communicating the change vision

5 Empowering broad-based action

6 Generating short-term wins

7 Consolidating gains and producing more change

8 Anchoring new approaches in the culture

To stop complacency and create urgency, a manager can talk candidly about the organization's weaknesses relative to competitors, making a point to back up statements with data. Other tactics include setting stretch goals, putting employees in direct contact with unhappy customers and shareholders, distributing worrisome information to all employees instead of merely engaging in management "happy talk," eliminating excessive perks, and highlighting the future opportunities that the organization so far has failed to pursue.

Ultimately, urgency is driven by compelling business reasons for change. Survival, competition, and winning in the marketplace are compelling; they provide a sense of direction and energy around change. Change becomes a business necessity.[106]

To *create a guiding coalition* means putting together a group with enough power to lead the change. Change efforts fail for lack of a powerful coalition.[107] Major organization change requires leadership from top management, working as a team. But over time, the support must expand outward and downward throughout the organization. Middle managers and supervisors are essential. Groups at all levels can hold change efforts together, communicate information about the changes, and provide the means for enacting new behaviors.[108]

Developing a vision and strategy, as discussed in earlier chapters, directs the change effort. This process involves determining the idealized, expected state of affairs after the change is implemented. Because confusion is common during major organizational change, this image of the future state must be as clear as possible and must be communicated to everyone.[109] This image, or vision, can clarify expectations, dispel rumors, and mobilize energies. Communication about it should include how the transition will occur, why the change is being implemented, and how people will be affected.

Communicating the change vision requires using every possible channel and opportunity to reinforce the vision and required new behaviors. It is said that aspiring change leaders undercommunicate the vision by a factor of 10,

100, or even 1,000, seriously undermining the chances of success.[110] In contrast, when Virginia Blood Services (VBS) launched an effort to improve its organizational culture in order to lower employee turnover and accident rates, communication was central to the change effort. The communication program at VBS includes employee meetings every three months, an employee newsletter distributed every two weeks, and messages from the president. In each site's break room, the organization replaced bulletin boards—where no one bothered to read the memos and government posters—with wall-mounted display cases featuring colorful posters and motivational, sometimes humorous messages about safety, quality, and teamwork. The items in the displays are changed every week to maintain interest. The communication program, which supports practical measures like safety training and new scheduling procedures, has helped to build support for the new organizational culture, motivating employees to stay safe and on the job.[111]

Empowering broad-based action means removing obstacles to success, including systems and structures that constrain rather than facilitate. Encourage risk taking and experimentation, and empower people by providing information, knowledge, authority, and rewards.

> ## "Change is a verb."
> —Mimi Silbert, founder, Delancey Street Foundation[113]

> ## "You do not lead by hitting people over the head—that's assault, not leadership."
> —Dwight D. Eisenhower

Generate short-term wins. Don't wait for the ultimate grand realization of the vision. You need results. As small victories accumulate, you make the transition from an isolated initiative to an integral part of the business.[112] Plan for and create small victories that show everyone that progress is being made. Recognize and reward the people who made the wins possible, doing it as visibly as you can so that people notice and the positive message permeates the organization.

Consolidate gains and produce more change. With the well-earned credibility of previous successes, keep changing things in ways that support the vision. Hire, promote, and develop people who will further the vision. Reinvigorate the organization and your change efforts with new projects and change agents.

Finally, *anchor new approaches in the culture.*[114] Highlight positive results, communicate the connections between the new behaviors and the improved results, and keep developing new change agents and leaders. Continually increase the number of people joining you in taking responsibility for change.[115]

L O 8 WHAT YOU NEED TO KNOW . . .
What are the tactics for creating a successful future?

SHAPING THE FUTURE

Most change is reactive. A better way to change is to be proactive. *Reactive change* means responding to pressure, after the problem has arisen. It implies being a follower. *Proactive change* means anticipating and preparing for an uncertain future. It implies being a leader and *creating* the future you want.

Think about the future

If you think only about the present or wallow in the uncertainties of the future, your future is just a roll of the dice. It is far better to exercise foresight, set an agenda for the future, and pursue it with everything you've got. So contemplate and envision the future.

BusinessWeek predicts that dramatic change will continue: "The global economy could be on the cusp of an age of innovation equal to that of the past 75 years. All the right factors are in place: Science is advancing rapidly, more countries are willing to devote resources to research and development and education, and corporate managers, too, are convinced of the importance of embracing change."[116]

Shoshana Zuboff and Jim Maxim, authors of *The Support Economy,* claim that the era of industrial capitalism is over, traditional business enterprises are disappearing, vast new markets exist, new kinds of companies are ready to be created, and the new business model hasn't yet emerged.[117] But new business concepts are always interesting to contemplate.

Two Chefs on a Roll is not a household name, nor is it meant to be. Still, the firm—founded more than 20 years ago by two chefs, Lori Daniel and Eliot Swartz—continues to be successful. Two Chefs is a private-label manufacturer of the highest-grade foods for restaurants and gourmet retailers. The owners do not name their clients, and their factories are shrouded in secrecy. When the two chefs started their company, they were exactly that. As the firm—and its customers—grew, the founders realized they needed to hire a CEO with experience in running large companies. So they recruited Jeffrey Goh, whose background includes serving as general manager of Frito-Lay in China and Hong Kong, where he introduced brands such as Head & Shoulders and Cheetos. Goh says the challenge was to take a company that was already successful and help it grow to the next level without losing quality and prestige: "A lot of success has already taken place, and you're trying to figure out what needs to change."

Goh was a perfect fit for the company, say Daniel and Swartz, because he was willing to take the time to understand Two Chefs before implementing change. "Other people seemed to think they could move us forward without asking how we had gotten here in the first place," explains Swartz. "Jeff wanted to understand the history." Once he had an understanding of the firm, Goh set about eliminating what he called "bad chaos" and nurturing what he termed "good chaos." He recruited an executive team with food experience, overhauled the human resource department, reorganized the research and development group, and borrowed money to build an agile manufacturing plant. Goh also developed ways to nurture the organization culture and innovation that made Two Chefs successful from the start.[118]

Create the future

As companies prepare to compete in an uncertain future, they can try different strategic postures. Adapters take the current industry structure and its future evolution as givens and choose where to compete. Most companies take this posture by conducting standard strategic analysis and choosing how to compete within given environments. In contrast, shapers try to change the structure of their industries, creating a future competitive landscape of their own design.[119]

Researchers studying corporate performance over a 10-year period found that 17 companies in the *Fortune* 1000 increased total shareholder return by 35 percent or more per year.[120] How? They completely reinvented industries. Harley-Davidson turned around by selling not just motorcycles, but nostalgia. Amgen broke the rules of the biotech industry by focusing not on what customers wanted, but on great science. Starbucks took a commodity and began selling it in trendy stores. CarMax and other companies reinvented the auto industry.

You need to create advantages. Rather than maintaining your position in the current competitive arena, the challenge is to create new competitive arenas, transform your industry, and imagine a future that others don't see. Creating advantage is better than playing catch-up. At best, working to catch up buys time; it cannot get you ahead of the pack

or buy world-class excellence.[121] To create new markets or transform industries—these are perhaps the ultimate forms of proactive change.[122]

Figure 14.4 illustrates the vast opportunity to create new markets. Articulated needs are those that customers acknowledge and try to satisfy. Unarticulated needs are those that customers have not yet experienced. Served customers are those to whom your company is now selling, and unserved customers are untapped markets.

While business as usual concentrates on the lower-left quadrant, the leaders who re-create the game are constantly trying to create new opportunities in the other three quadrants.[123] For example, you can pursue the upper-left quadrant by imagining how you can satisfy a larger proportion of your customers' total needs. Caterpillar appreciates that its customers want more than its heavy equipment; they also need excellent service so that they can use that equipment to meet their own customers' needs. As a result, if a customer anywhere in the world needs a Caterpillar part, the company will ship it there within 24 hours. And Lands' End expanded both its product offerings and number of served customers by offering customization—the ability to specify exact measurements when ordering jeans and other selected items of clothing.[124]

Other companies hope to meet unarticulated needs by developing and exploiting cutting-edge technology. The nanometer—one-billionth of a meter, 1/100,000 the width of a human hair, or about the size of 10 hydrogen atoms in a row—is the building block of a new industry, nanotechnology. Why is the nanometer so important?[125] Because matter of this size often behaves differently—transmitting light or electricity, or becoming harder than diamonds, or becoming powerful chemical catalysts. Early applications include coatings and light-emitting dots for more efficient semiconductors and nanoparticles that clean up polluted water by forming chemical bonds with contaminants.[126] Applications under development include 50-nanometer capsules containing vitamins and other nutrients that can be added to beverages without changing their taste or that can be activated by microwaves.[127]

As you've read, technological change is a central part of the changing landscape, and competition often arises between newcomers and established companies. All things considered, which should you and your firm do?

- Preserve old advantages or create new advantages?
- Lock in old markets or create new markets?
- Take the path of greatest familiarity or the path of greatest opportunity?

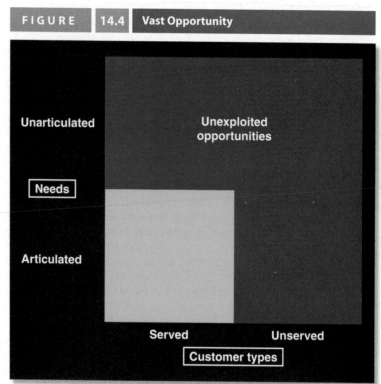

FIGURE 14.4 **Vast Opportunity**

SOURCE: Reprinted by permission of *Harvard Business Review*. From *Competing for the Future,* by Gary Hamel and C. K. Prahalad, Harvard School Press. Copyright © 1994 by the Harvard Business School Publishing Corporation; all rights reserved.

- Be only a benchmarker or a pathbreaker?
- Place priority on short-term financial returns or on making a real, long-term impact?

- Do only what seems doable or what is difficult and worthwhile?
- Change what is or create what isn't?
- Look to the past or live for the future?[128]

Shape your own future

If you are an organizational leader and your organization operates in traditional ways, your key goal should be to create a revolution, genetically reengineering your company before it becomes a dinosaur of the modern era.[129] What should be the goals of the revolution? You've been learning about them throughout this course.

But maybe you are not going to lead a revolution. Maybe you just want a successful career and a good life. You still

must deal with an economic environment that is increasingly competitive and fast-moving.[130] To create the future you want for yourself, you have to set high personal standards. Don't settle for mediocrity; don't assume that "good" is necessarily good enough—for yourself or for your employer. Think about how to exceed, not just meet, expectations; how to break free of apparent constraints that are unimportant, arbitrary, or imagined; and how to seize opportunities instead of letting them pass by.[131]

> Matthew Kirchner is chief executive of American Finishing Resources, a company that serves manufacturers by removing coatings (for example, from improperly painted parts) and by making customized fixtures used for applying coatings. While his industry may not seem glamorous, Kirchner is as buffeted as any manager by demands from his customers, regulators, bankers, and suppliers. In that situation, change could become something that just happens to his career and his company. Instead, Kirchner takes the reins of his career and his future by starting each day with a meeting scheduled for himself alone to plan for the changes he wants to see. During that hour, Kirchner reviews his personal mission statement (his expression of why he comes to work each day), the major efforts under way to land new business, basic measures of revenue and expenses, and schedules of work in process. By refreshing his view of the big picture, Kirchner starts his day focused on what he has determined is most important.[132]

You can continually add value to your employer—and also to yourself—as you upgrade your skills, ability to contribute, security with your current employer, and ability to find alternative employment if necessary. The most successful individuals take charge of their own development the way an entrepreneur takes charge of a business.[133] Here are some methods that help most people add value:[134]

"There is nothing wrong with change, if it is in the right direction."

—Winston Churchill

- Go beyond your job description: volunteer for projects, identify problems, and initiate solutions.
- Seek out others and share ideas and advice.
- Offer your opinions and respect those of others.
- Take an inventory of your skills every few months.
- Learn something new every week.
- Discover new ways to make a contribution.
- Engage in active thought and deliberate action.
- Take risks based on what you know and believe.
- Recognize, research, and pursue opportunity.
- Differentiate yourself.

More advice from the leading authors on career management:[135] Consciously and actively manage your own career. Develop marketable skills, and keep developing more. Make career choices based on personal growth, development, and learning opportunities. Look for positions that stretch you, and for bosses who develop their protégés. Seek environments that provide training and the opportunity to experiment and innovate. And know yourself—assess your strengths and weaknesses, your true interests, and ethical standards. If you are not already thinking in these terms and taking commensurate action, you should start now.

Additionally, become indispensable to your organization. Be happy and enthusiastic in your job and committed to doing great work, but don't be blindly loyal to one company. Be prepared to leave, if necessary. View your job as an opportunity to prove what you can do and increase what you can do, not as a comfortable niche for the long term.[136] Go out on your own if it meets your skills and temperament.

You need to maintain your options. More and more, contemporary careers include leaving a large organization and going entrepreneurial, becoming self-employed in the "postcorporate world."[137] In such a career, independent individuals make their own choices, responding quickly to demands and opportunities. Developing start-up ventures, consulting, accepting temporary employment, doing project work for one organization and then another, working in professional partnerships, being a constant deal maker—these can be the elements of a successful career. Ideally, this self-employed model balances working with living life at home and with family, because people have more control over their work activities and schedules.

This go-it-alone approach can sound ideal, but it also has downsides. Independence can be frightening, the future unpredictable. It can isolate "road warriors" who are always on the go, working from their cars and airports, and interfere with social and family life.[138] Effective self-management is needed to keep career and family obligations in perspective and in control. Coping with uncertainty and change is also easier if you develop resilience. To become more resilient, practice thinking of the world as complex but full of opportunities; expect change, but see it as interesting and potentially rewarding, even if changing is difficult. Also, keep a sense of purpose, set priorities for your time, be flexible when facing uncertainty or a need to change, and take an active role in the face of change, rather than waiting for change to happen to you.[139]

Learn and lead the way to your goals

Continuous learning is a vital route to renewable competitive advantage.[140] People in your organization—and you, personally—should constantly explore, discover, and take action,

repeating this cycle as you progress in your career:[141]

1. *Explore* your current reality, being as honest and open as possible about what is happening. Identify your problems and areas of opportunity. Gather data. Check with customers, suppliers, and other key stakeholders. Reveal hidden issues, and look for root causes. Rethink the issue, based on what you have learned.

2. *Discover* a deeper understanding of the current reality. The issues and choices should become clearer. Identify possible solutions or ways to take advantage of opportunities. Plan what to do, anticipating problems that may arise.

3. *Act* by testing solutions, implementing your plan, and evaluating the results. Recognize problems; that will prepare you for repeating the cycle. And be sure to celebrate your successes, too.

With this approach, you can learn what is effective and what is not and then adjust and improve accordingly. Continuous learning helps your company achieve lower cost, higher quality, better service, superior innovation, and greater speed—and helps you develop on a personal level.

Commit to lifelong learning. Be willing to seek new challenges, and reflect honestly on successes and failures.[142] Lifelong learning requires occasional risk taking. Move outside your comfort zone, honestly assess the reasons behind your successes and failures, ask for and listen to other people's information and opinions, and stay open to new ideas.

A leader—and this could include you—should be able to create an environment in which "others are willing to learn and change so their organizations can adapt and innovate [and] inspire diverse others to embark on a collective journey of continual learning and leading."[143] *Learning leaders* exchange knowledge freely; commit to their own continuous learning as well as to others'; commit to examining their own behaviors and defensiveness that may inhibit their learning; devote time to their colleagues, suspending their own beliefs while they listen thoughtfully; and develop a broad perspective, recognizing that organizations are an integrated system of relationships.[144]

Honored as one of the best management books of the year in Europe, *Leaning into the Future* gets its title from a combination of the words *leading* and *learning*.[145] The two perspectives, which may appear very different, are powerful and synergistic when pursued in complementary ways. A successful future derives from adapting to the world *and* shaping the future, being responsive to others' perspectives *and* being clear about what you want to change, encouraging others to change *while* recognizing what you need to change about yourself, understanding current realities *and* passionately pursuing your vision, learning *and* leading.

This is another example of an important concept from the beginning of the chapter. For yourself, as well as for your organization, live the genius of the *and*.

DIY

Build Your Skills

Practice and apply your knowledge by going online at

www.mhhe.com/ BatemanM2e

Chapter 1

1. Arnie Cooper, "Charging Ahead," *Popular Science,* December 15, 2008, http://www.popsci.com; Rebecca Buckman, "Tesla Cuts 20% of Workforce," *Forbes,* October 28, 2008, http://www.forbes .com; Fareed Zakaria, "A Tesla in Your Future?" *Newsweek,* July 21, 2008, http://www.newsweek.com.

2. Michael Abramowitz and Steve Vogel, "Apologies, Anger at Walter Reed Hearing," *Washington Post,* March 6, 2007, http://www. washingtonpost.com. See also Dana Priest and Anne Hull, "Soldiers Face Neglect, Frustration at Army's Top Medical Facility," *Washington Post,* February 18, 2007, http://www.washingtonpost .com.

3. John Christoffersen, "Global Ambition: GE Looks outside U.S. for Growth," *Cincinnati Post,* January 18, 2007, downloaded from Business & Company Resource Center, http://galenet.galegroup.com.

4. Ibid.

5. Nandini Lakshman, "Cisco's Grand India Ambitions," *Business-Week,* January 3, 2007, downloaded from Business & Company Resource Center, http://galenet.galegroup.com.

6. Gregory T. Huang, "Over the Border," *New Scientist,* January 20, 2007, downloaded from Business & Company Resource Center, http://galenet.galegroup.com (interview of Ethan Zuckerman).

7. Sue Shellenbarger, "Time-Zoned: Working around the Round-the-Clock Workday," *The Wall Street Journal,* February 15, 2007, http://online.wsj.com.

8. Stephanie Clifford, "How to Get Ahead in China," *Inc.,* May 2008, pp. 96–104.

9. S. Green, F. Hassan, J. Immelt, M. Marks, and D. Meiland, "In Search of Global Leaders," *Harvard Business Review,* August 2003, pp. 38–45.

10. Betsy Morris, "The Pepsi Challenge," *Fortune,* February 19, 2008, http://money.cnn.com.

11. T. Bisoux, "Corporate CounterCulture," *BizEd,* November/December 2004, pp. 16–20, quoted on p. 19.

12. G. Huber, *The Necessary Nature of Future Firms* (Thousand Oaks, CA: Sage, 2004).

13. Jay Greene and Cliff Edwards, "Desktops Are So Twentieth Century," *BusinessWeek,* December 8, 2006, http://www.businessweek.com.

14. F. Cairncross, *The Company of the Future* (Cambridge, MA: Harvard Business School Press, 2002).

15. George Avalos, "Shackled to Technology," *Contra Costa Times* (Walnut Creek, CA), January 14, 2007, downloaded from Business & Company Resource Center, http://galenet.galegroup.com.

16. Jean Chatzky, "Confessions of an E-Mail Addict," *Money,* March 2007, downloaded from Business & Company Resource Center, http://galenet.galegroup.com.

17. Ibid.

18. Robert Austin, "Managing Knowledge Workers," *Science,* July 21, 2006, accessed at ScienceCareers.org, http://sciencecareers .sciencemag.org.

19. David Raths, "Hospital IT Departments Prescribe Portals for Physicians," *KMWorld,* February 2007, downloaded from Business & Company Resource Center, http://galenet.galegroup.com.

20. M. Hansen and B. von Oetinger, "Introducing T-Shaped Managers: Knowledge Management's Next Generation," *Harvard Business Review,* March 2001, pp. 106–16.

21. John Teresko, "Toyota's Real Secret," *Industry Week,* February 2007, downloaded from Business & Company Resource Center, http://galenet.galegroup.com.

22. Ibid.

23. Bruce Horovitz, "Cranium Guys Have Their Inner Child on Speed Dial," *USA Today,* May 9, 2006, http://www.usatoday.com.

24. L. Willcocks and R. Plant, "Pathways to E-Business Leadership: Getting from Bricks to Clicks," *Sloan Management Review,* Spring 2001, pp. 50–59.

25. Suzanne Vranica, "P&G Boosts Social-Networking Efforts," *The Wall Street Journal,* January 8, 2007, http://online.wsj.com.

26. John D. Stoll, Monica Langley, and Sharon Terlep, "New GM CEO Says More Cuts Coming," *The Wall Street Journal,* March 31, 2009, http://online.wsj.com; Jeffrey McCracken, John D. Stoll, and Neil King Jr., "U.S. Threatens Bankruptcy for GM, Chrysler," *The Wall Street Journal,* March 31, 2009, http://online.wsj.com; and Mike Barris, "Auto Makers [sic] Sales Drop," *The Wall Street Journal,* April 1, 2009, http://online.wsj.com.

27. Adam Lashinsky, "Chaos by Design," *Fortune,* October 2, 2006, http://money.cnn.com.

28. Alexandria Sage, "Love Is Blind in Pitch Black Restaurant," Reuters, December 8, 2006, http://news.yahoo.com; Opaque–Dining in the Dark, "What Is Opaque?" http://www.opaque-events. com, accessed March 8, 2007; and Opaque–Dining in the Dark, "First Ever 'Dining in the Dark' Experience Coming to Los Angeles July 23," news release, n.d., accessed at http://www.opaque-events.com, March 8, 2007.

29. R. I. Sutton, "The Weird Rules of Creativity," *Harvard Business Review,* September 2001, pp. 94–103.

30. Laura Landro, "Hospitals Take Consumers' Advice," *The Wall Street Journal,* February 7, 2007, http://online.wsj.com.

31. Ibid.

32. O. Port, "The Kings of Quality," *BusinessWeek,* August 30, 2004, p. 20.

33. Karla Ward, "Attracting Opposites," *Lexington Herald-Leader,* December 12, 2006; and Lisa McTigue Pierce, "How to Do It 'My Way,'" *Food & Drug Packaging,* January 2007, both downloaded from Business & Company Resource Center, http://galenet.galegroup.com.

34. D. A. Garvin, "Manufacturing Strategic Planning," *California Management Review,* Summer 1993, pp. 85–106.

35. Reported in "Hospital Ratings May Not Be True Quality Measure," *Washington Post,* December 13, 2006, http://www.washingtonpost .com.

36. U.S. Census Bureau, *Statistical Abstract of the United States,* 2007, Table 650, p. 431, http://www.census.gov/prod/www/ statistical-abstract.html.

37. Ibid., Tables 607 and 608, pp. 394–95.

38. R. F. Maruca, "Voices: State of the New Economy," *Fast Company,* September 2000, pp. 105-44.

39. Mindy Fetterman, "Best Buy Gets in Touch with Its Feminine Side," *USA Today,* December 20, 2006, http://www.usatoday.com.

40. Sherri Begin, "The Art of Service," *Crain's Detroit Business,* February 12, 2007, downloaded from Business & Company Resource Center, http://galenet.galegroup.com.

41. Lashinsky, "Chaos by Design."

42. Teresko, "Toyota's Real Secret."

43. Ibid.

44. Gary McWilliams, "Wal-Mart's Radio-Tracked Inventory Hits Static," *The Wall Street Journal,* February 15, 2007, http:// online.wsj.com.

45. Kris Maher, "Wal-Mart Seeks New Flexibility in Worker Shifts," *The Wall Street Journal,* January 3, 2007, http://online.wsj.com.

46. Adam Bluestein, Leigh Buchanan, Max Chafkin, Jason Del Rey, April Joyner, and Ryan McCarthy, "The Ultimate Business Tune-Up for Times Like These," *Inc.,* January 2009, http://www.inc.com.

47. Julie Johnsson, "Jets Reach New Heights," *Chicago Tribune,* February 25, 2007, sec. 5, pp. 1, 4.

48. Adam Lashinsky, "Mark Hurd's Moment," *Fortune,* March 2, 2009, http://money.cnn.com, updated March 3, 2009.

49. Vanessa Fuhrmans, "A Novel Plan Helps Hospital Wean Itself off Pricey Tests," *The Wall Street Journal,* January 12, 2007, http://online.wsj.com.

50. "Avon Regains Some Allure," *BusinessWeek,* February 7, 2007, http://www.businessweek.com.

51. Claudia H. Deutsch, "A Chance to Save Their Skin," *New York Times,* January 19, 2007, downloaded from Business & Company Resource Center, http://galenet.galegroup.com.

52. J. W. Cortada, *21st Century Business* (London: Financial Times/ Prentice Hall, 2001).

53. D. Lepak, K. Smith, and M. S. Taylor, "Value Creation and Value Capture: A Multilevel Perspective," *Academy of Management Review* 23 (2007), pp. 180–94.

54. Randstad USA, "Focusing on Employees Can Pay Future Dividends," news release, October 20, 2008, http://www.us.ranstad .com/about/mediaRoom.html.

55. Julia Werdigier, "Chief's Bonus Is Cut at BP," *New York Times,* March 7, 2007, downloaded from Business & Company Resource Center, http://galenet.galegroup.com.

56. Rob Johnson, "Local Restaurants Check Their Peanut Butter," *Roanoke (Va.) Times,* February 24, 2007, downloaded from Business & Company Resource Center, http://galenet.galegroup.com; Joe Ruff, "FDA Finds Salmonella Strain at ConAgra Plant," *Omaha World-Herald,* March 2, 2007, http://galenet.galegroup.com; Centers for Disease Control and Prevention, "Salmonellosis—Outbreak Investigation, February 2007," news release, March 7, 2007, http://www.cdc.gov; Food and Drug Administration, "FDA Update on Peanut Butter Recall," news release, March 9, 2007, http:// www.fda.gov; and ConAgra Foods, "ConAgra Foods Presents Business Update at Consumer Conference," news release, February 20, 2007, http://investor.conagrafoods.com.

57. David R. Baker, "Electric Car Startup Downshifts for Rough Road," *San Francisco Chronicle,* December 28, 2008, http://www.sfgate .com; Buckman, "Tesla Cuts 20% of Workforce"; Claire Cain Miller, "Musk Unplugged: Tesla CEO Discusses Car Troubles," *New York Times,* October 24, 2008, http://bits.blogs.nytimes.com; Martin LaMonica, "Tesla Motors Replaces CEO, Plans Layoff," *CNET News,* October 15, 2008, http://news.cnet.com; Michael V. Copeland, "Tesla's Wild Ride," *Fortune,* July 11, 2008, http://money.cnn.com.

58. R. Webber, "General Management Past and Future," *Financial Times Mastering Management,* 1997.

59. Pui-Wing Tam, "CIO Jobs Morph from Tech Support into Strategy," *The Wall Street Journal,* February 20, 2007, http://online.wsj .com.

60. Ibid.

61. Q. N. Huy, "In Praise of Middle Managers," *Harvard Business Review,* September 2001, pp. 72–79.

62. L. A. Hill, "New Manager Development for the 21st Century," *Academy of Management Executive,* August 2004, pp. 121–26.

63. C. Bartlett and S. Goshal, "The Myth of the Generic Manager: New Personal Competencies for New Management Roles," *California Management Review* 40, no. 1 (1997), pp. 92–116.

64. L. R. Sayles, "Doing Things Right: A New Imperative for Middle Managers," *Organizational Dynamics,* Spring 1993, pp. 5–14.

65. H. Mintzberg, *The Nature of Managerial Work* (New York: Harper & Row, 1973).

66. R. Katz, "Skills of an Effective Administrator," *Harvard Business Review* 52 (September–October), pp. 90–102.

67. Hill, "New Manager Development for the 21st Century."

68. H. Mintzberg, "The Manager's Job: Folklore and Fact," *Harvard Business Review* 53 (July–August 1975), pp. 49–61.

69. Francesca Di Meglio, "Columbia Gets Personal," *BusinessWeek Online,* October 18, 2006 (interview with Michael Morris), downloaded from Business & Company Resource Center, http://galenet .galegroup.com.

70. "To Get That Job, Bring on the Charm," *Internet Week,* August 23, 2006, downloaded from Business & Company Resource Center, http://galenet.galegroup.com.

71. Di Meglio, "Columbia Gets Personal."

72. Colin Stewart, "Program Teaches Corporate Skills to Cure What Ails Them," *Orange County Register,* December 28, 2006, downloaded from Business & Company Resource Center, http://galenet .galegroup.com.

73. Hill, "New Manager Development for the 21st Century."

74. D. Goleman, R. Boyatzis, and A. McKee, *Primal Leadership: Realizing the Power of Emotional Intelligence* (Boston: Harvard Business School Press, 2002).

75. Debbie Kelley, "Rita Burns: Memorial Hospital's Public Voice," *(Colorado Springs) Gazette,* October 9, 2006, downloaded from Business & Company Resource Center, http://galenet.galegroup.com.

76. R. Boyatzis, "Get Motivated," *Harvard Business Review,* January 2004, p. 30.

77. W. George, "Find Your Voice," *Harvard Business Review,* January 2004, p. 35.

78. Stephen Xavier, "Control Yourself: What Role Does Emotional Intelligence Play in Executive Leadership?" *US Business Review,* March 2006, downloaded from Business & Company Resource Center, http://galenet.galegroup.com.

79. Ibid.

80. W. Kiechel III, "A Manager's Career in the New Economy," *Fortune,* April 4, 1994, pp. 68–72.

81. Elizabeth Garone, "Leading the Environmental Charge at Xerox," *The Wall Street Journal,* March 25, 2009, http://onlinewsj.com.

82. Lisa Takeuchi Cullen, "The Zeal for the Job," *Time,* March 19, 2007, http://www.time.com.

83. W. Kiechel III, "A Manager's Career in the New Economy," *Fortune,* April 4, 1994, pp. 68–72. Copyright © 1994 Times, Inc. All rights reserved. Reprinted by permission.

84. Diane Hess, "How I Got Where I Am Today: A Videogame Marketing Director," *CareerJournal.com,* May 11, 2006, http://www.careerjournal.com.

85. K. Inkson and M. B. Arther, "How to Be a Successful Career Capitalist," *Organizational Dynamics,* Summer 2001, pp. 48–60.

86. Geoffrey Colvin, "What It Takes to Be Great," *Fortune,* October 19, 2006, http://money.cnn.com.

87. L. M Roberts, J. Dutton, G. Spreitzer, E. Heaphy, and R. Quinn, "Composing the Reflected Best-Self Portrait: Building Pathways for Becoming Extraordinary in Work Organizations," *Academy of Management Review* 30 (2005), pp. 712–36.

88. L. M. Roberts, "Changing Faces: Professional Image Construction in Diverse Organizational Settings," *Academy of Management Review* 30 (2005), pp. 685–711.

89. M. E. P. Seligman, *Authentic Happiness: Using the New Positive Psychology to Realize Your Potential for Lasting Fulfillment* (New York: Free Press, 2002).

90. E. W. Morrison, "Newcomers' Relationships: The Role of Social Network Ties During Socialization," *Academy of Management Journal* 45 (2002), pp. 1149–60.

91. P. Adler and S. Kwon, "Social Capital: Prospects for a New Concept," *Academy of Management* Review 27 (2002), pp. 17–40.

92. Esther Shein, "Six Degrees of Irritation," *CFO,* March 2007, downloaded from Business & Company Resource Center, http://galenet.galegroup.com.

93. T. Peters, *Liberation Management* (New York: Alfred A. Knopf, 1992).

94. P. Drucker, "What Makes an Effective Executive?" *Harvard Business Review,* June 2004, pp. 58–63.

95. Marshall Goldsmith, "Three Obstacles to a Career Move," *BusinessWeek,* March 7, 2007, downloaded from Business & Company Resource Center, http://galenet.galegroup.com.

96. Bob Violino, Monica Sambataro, Eugene A. Demaitre, and John S. Webster, "The Making of an IT Career," *ComputerWorld,* December 11, 2006, downloaded from Business & Company Resource Center, http://galenet.galegroup.com.

Chapter 2

1. Company Web site and "Brewing a Better World," Corporate Social Responsibility Report, Fiscal Year 2007, http://www.greenmountaincoffee.com, accessed March 25, 2009; Rick Aristotle Munarriz, "Warm Up to Green Mountain Coffee Roasters," *The Motley Fool,* January 29, 2009, http://www.fool.com; "Green Mountain Coffee Roasters, Inc. Releases 'Brewing a Better World' Corporate Social Responsibility Report," *CSR Wire,* January 12, 2009, http://www.csrwire.com; Katy Marquardt, "Brewing Profits, a Cup at a Time," *U.S. News & World Report,* November 17/24, 2008, pp. 55–58; Paul Rolfes, "Green Mountain Coffee Roasters: Grounds for Growth," *Smallcapinvestor.com,* July 23, 2008, http://www.smallcapinvestor.com; Alliston Ackerman, "Retail Coffee Favored in Volatile Economy," *Consumer Goods Technology,* July 22, 2008, http://www.consumergoods.com; and "Green Mountain Coffee Roasters Founder Bob Stiller Will Step Down," *Automatic Merchandiser,* July 8, 2008, http://www.amonline.com.

2. Mike Hughlett, "Web Radio Fears Going Bust," *Chicago Tribune,* March 8, 2007; and "Recording Labels Should Negotiate Royalty System," *San Jose Mercury News,* March 14, 2007, both downloaded from Business & Company Resource Center, http://galenet.galegroup.com.

3. "CEO Dough," *USA Today,* January 20, 2006, http://www.usatoday.com.

4. Kate Galbraith, "Economy Shifts, and the Ethanol Industry Reels," *New York Times,* November 4, 2008, http://www.nytimes.com.

5. Kelly Evans, "Economy Dives as Goods Pile Up," *The Wall Street Journal,* January 31, 2009, http://online.wsj.com.

6. Joseph Fuller and Michael C. Jensen, "Just Say No to Wall Street," *Journal of Applied Corporate Finance* 14, no. 4 (Winter 2002), pp. 41–46.

7. Jad Mouawad, "Oil Innovations Pump New Life into Old Wells," *New York Times,* March 5, 2007, http://www.nytimes.com.

8. Bureau of Labor Statistics, "BLS Releases 2004–14 Employment Projections," news release, December 7, 2005, http://www.bls.gov.

9. Martha M. Hamilton, "Age 65 and Not Ready or Able to Go," *Washington Post,* January 14, 2007, http://www.washingtonpost.com.

10. Lori Aratani, "Teens Can Multitask, but What Are Costs?" *Washington Post,* February 26, 2007, http://www.washingtonpost.com.

11. Bureau of Labor Statistics, "Charting the U.S. Labor Market in 2005," June 2006, http://www.bls.gov/cps/labor2005/home.htm.

12. See, for example, Ben Arnoldy, "Too Prosperous, Massachusetts Is Losing Its Labor Force," *Christian Science Monitor,* January 9, 2007, http://www.csmonitor.com.

13. Mitra Toossi, "A New Look at Long-Term Labor Force Projections to 2050," *Monthly Labor Review,* November 2006, pp. 19–39.

14. Ibid.; and Bureau of Labor Statistics, "Charting the U.S. Labor Market."

15. "Gaming Goes for the Burn," *PR Week,* February 19, 2007, downloaded from Business & Company Resource Center, http://galenet.galegroup.com.

16. Michael Zitz, "Nintendo Winning Game System Red Hot," *Free Lance–Star (Fredericksburg, VA),* February 23, 2007, downloaded from Business & Company Resource Center, http://galenet.galegroup.com.

17. Charles J. Murray, "Fast and Cool," *Design News,* February 5, 2007, downloaded from Business & Company Resource Center, http://galenet.galegroup.com.

18. Matt Richtel, "Nintendo's Wii, Radiating Fun, Is Eclipsing Sony," *New York Times,* January 31, 2007, http://www.nytimes.com; "EA: Sony's Video Game Dominance Is Over," *ExtremeTech.com,* March 6, 2007, http://www.extremetech.com; and Kerry E. Grace, "Sony Cuts Price on PlayStation 2 to $99," *The Wall Street Journal,* March 31, 2009, http://online.wsj.com.

19. David J. Collis and Cynthia A. Montgomery, *Corporate Strategy: Resources and Scope of the Firm* (New York: McGraw-Hill/Irwin, 1997).

20. Adam Plowright, "New Wireless Internet Service Set to Leave Its Asian Niche," *Agence France Presse,* February 24, 2007, http://news.yahoo.com; and John Blau, "WiMax Likely Choice for 'Net Access in Emerging Markets,'" *InfoWorld,* February 14, 2007, http://www.infoworld.com.

21. John DeGaspari, "Pfizer Retrenches," *MMR,* February 12, 2007, downloaded from Business & Company Resource Center, http://galenet.galegroup.com.

22. Robert D. Hof, "Google Steps into Microsoft's Office," *BusinessWeek,* February 12, 2007, http://www.businessweek.com.

23. Aaron Ricadela, "Console Wars: Sony Fights Back," *BusinessWeek,* March 8, 2007, downloaded from Business & Company Resource Center, http://galenet.galegroup.com; and Grace, "Sony Cuts Price on Playstation 2 to $99."

24. Eric Gwinn, "Shootout at the Top," *Chicago Tribune,* February 27, 2007, downloaded from Business & Company Resource Center, http://galenet.galegroup.com.

25. Ricadela, "Console Wars."

26. "Looking Forward to the Next Level: Electronic Arts," *The Economist,* February 10, 2007, downloaded from Business & Company Resource Center, http://galenet.galegroup.com.

27. Yukari Iwatani Kane, "Look It's Mii—on Wii!" *The Wall Street Journal,* March 16, 2007, http://online.wsj.com.

28. Arthur Sherman, George Bohlander, and Scott Snell, *Managing Human Resources,* 11th ed. (Cincinnati, OH: South-Western Publishing, 1998).

29. Brian Bremner, "Nintendo Storms the Gaming World," *Business-Week,* January 29, 2007, downloaded from Business & Company Resource Center, http://galenet.galegroup.com.

30. Adapted from Hau L. Lee and Corey Billington, "The Evolution of Supply-Chain-Management Models and Practice at Hewlett-Packard," *Interfaces* 25, no. 5 (September–October 1995), pp. 42–63.

31. Tracy Maylett and Kate Vitasek, "For Closer Collaboration, Try Education," *Supply Chain Management Review,* January–February 2007, downloaded from Business & Company Resource Center, http://galenet.galegroup.com.

32. Don Tapscott and Anthony D. Williams, "Hack This Product, Please!" *BusinessWeek,* February 23, 2007, downloaded from Business & Company Resource Center, http://galenet.galegroup.com.

33. See, for example, "PS3 on Store Shelves at Wal-Mart," http://youtube.com/watch?v=thV53ZJlbng, added December 31, 2006; and "Wii60: Why Can't We Be Friends," http://youtube.com/watch?v=-mdAnzsnTy4, added May 18, 2006.

34. P. Kotler, *Marketing Management: Analysis, Planning, Implementation and Control,* 9th ed. (Englewood Cliffs, NJ: Prentice Hall, 1990).

35. Aaron A. Buchko, "Conceptualization and Measurement of Environmental Uncertainty: An Assessment of the Miles and Snow Perceived Environmental Uncertainty Scale," *Academy of Management Journal* 37, no. 2 (April 1994), pp. 410–25.

36. Abdalla F. Hagen, "Corporate Executives and Environmental Scanning Activities: An Empirical Investigation." *SAM Advanced Management Journal* 60, no. 2 (Spring 1995), pp. 41-47; Richard L. Daft. "Chief Executive Scanning, Environmental Characteristics, and Company Performance: An Empirical Study," *Strategic Management Journal* 9, no. 2 (March/April 1988), pp. 123–39; and Masoud Yasai-Ardekani, "Designs for Environmental Scanning Systems: Tests of a Contingency Theory," *Management Science* 42, no. 2 (February 1996), pp. 187–204.

37. Sumantra Ghoshal, "Building Effective Intelligence Systems for Competitive Advantage," *Sloan Management Review* 28, no. 1 (Fall 1986), pp. 49–58; and Kenneth D. Cory, "Can Competitive Intelligence Lead to a Sustainable Competitive Advantage?" *Competitive Intelligence Review* 7, no. 3 (Fall 1996), pp. 45–55.

38. Paul J. H. Schoemaker, "Multiple Scenario Development: Its Conceptual and Behavioral Foundation," *Strategic Management Journal* 14, no. 3 (March 1993), pp. 193–213.

39. Robin R. Peterson, "An Analysis of Contemporary Forecasting in Small Business," *Journal of Business Forecasting Methods & Systems* 15, no. 2 (Summer 1996), pp. 10–12; and Spyros Makridakis, "Business Forecasting for Management: Strategic Business Forecasting," *International Journal of Forecasting* 12, no. 3 (September 1996), pp. 435–37.

40. Dale Russakoff, "Building a Career Path Where There Was Just a Dead End," *Washington Post,* February 26, 2007, http://www.washingtonpost.com.

41. Bureau of Labor Statistics, "Contingent and Alternative Employment Arrangements, February 2005," news release, July 27, 2005, http://www.bls.gov/cps/.

42. Martin B. Meznar, "Buffer or Bridge? Environmental and Organizational Determinants of Public Affairs Activities in American Firms," *Academy of Management Journal* 38, no. 4 (August 1995), pp. 975–96.

43. David Lei, "Advanced Manufacturing Technology: Organizational Design and Strategic Flexibility," *Organization Studies* 17, no. 3 (1996), pp. 501–23; and James W. Dean Jr. and Scott A. Snell, "The Strategic Use of Integrated Manufacturing: An Empirical Examination," *Strategic Management Journal* 17, no. 6 (June 1996), pp. 459–80.

44. C. Zeithaml and V. Zeithaml, "Environmental Management: Revising the Marketing Perspective," *Journal of Marketing* 48 (Spring 1984), pp. 46–53.

45. "Washington Wire," *The Wall Street Journal,* March 16, 2007, http://blogs.wsj.com/washwire/.

46. Willem P. Burgers, "Cooperative Strategy in High Technology Industries," *International Journal of Management* 13, no. 2 (June 1996), pp. 127–34; and Jeffrey E. McGee, "Cooperative Strategy and New Venture Performance: The Role of Business Strategy and Management Experience," *Strategic Management Journal* 16, no. 7 (October 1995), pp. 565–80.

47. Zeithaml and Zeithaml, "Environmental Management."

48. Adam Bluestein, Leigh Buchanan, Max Chafkin, Jason Del Rey, April Joyner, and Ryan McCarthy, "The Ultimate Business Tune-Up for Times Like These," *Inc.,* January 2009, http://www.inc.com.

49. Center for Responsive Politics, "PACs by Industry," *OpenSecrets,* http://www.opensecrets.org, accessed April 6, 2009 (based on data from the Federal Election Commission, released March 2, 2009).

50. Richard A. D'Aveni, *Hypercompetition—Managing the Dynamics of Strategic Maneuvering* (New York: Free Press 1994); and Michael A. Cusumano, "Strategic Maneuvering and Mass-Market Dynamics: The Triumph of VHS over Beta," *Business History Review* 66, no. 1 (Spring 1992), pp. 51–94.

51. Model adapted from Zeithaml and Zeithaml, "Environmental Management: Revising the Marketing Perspective."

52. Bremner, "Nintendo Storms the Gaming World."

53. See, for example, Hiawatha Bray, "Analysis: IPod Likely to Be Apple's Strongest Player," *Boston Globe,* January 16, 2007, http://www.boston.com; Brian Garrity, "IWin," *Billboard,* December 23, 2006, http://www.billboard.com.

54. "Bayer to Axe 6,100 Jobs Worldwide after Schering Takeover," news release, March 2, 2007, *Agence France Presse,* http://www.afp.com.

55. Ricadela, "Console Wars."

56. Steve McGrath and John D. Stoll, "Ford to Sell Aston Martin Unit in Deal Valued at $848 Million," *The Wall Street Journal,* March 12, 2007, http://online.wsj.com.

57. R. Miles and C. Snow, *Organizational Strategy, Structure, and Process* (New York: McGraw-Hill, 1978).

58. Sarah E. Needleman, "Restaurateur Fights Online Mudslinging," *Startup Journal,* http://www.startupjournal.com, accessed October 24, 2006.

59. Sarah E. Needleman, "Tips on Safeguarding Your Online Reputation," *Startup Journal,* http://www.startupjournal.com, accessed October 24, 2006.

60. Ralph H. Kilmann, Mary J. Saxton, and Roy Serpa, *Gaining Control of the Corporate Culture* (San Francisco: Jossey-Bass, 1985); and Kim S. Cameron and Robert E. Quinn, *Diagnosing and Changing Organizational Culture: Based on the Competing Values Framework* (Englewood Cliffs, NJ: Addison-Wesley, 1998).

61. Jessica E. Vascellaro and Scott Morrison, "Google Gears Down for Tougher Times," *The Wall Street Journal,* December 3, 2008, http://online.wsj.com.

62. Carol Hymowitz, "In Deal-Making, Keep People in Mind," *The Wall Street Journal,* May 12, 2008, http://online.wsj.com.

63. Cameron and Quinn, *Diagnosing and Changing Organizational Culture.*

64. Sebastian Desmidt and Aime Heene, "Mission Statement Perception: Are We All on the Same Wavelength? A Case Study in a Flemish Hospital," *Health Care Management Review,* January–March 2007, downloaded from Business & Company Resource Center, http://galenet.galegroup.com.

65. Carmine Gallo, "How Ritz-Carlton Maintains Its Mystique," *BusinessWeek,* February 13, 2007, http://www.businessweek.com.

66. R. Leifer and P. K. Mills, "An Information Processing Approach for Deciding upon Control Strategies and Reducing Control Loss in Emerging Organizations," *Journal of Management* 22, no. 1 (1996), pp. 113–37; Scott A. Dellana and Richard D. Hauser, "Toward Defining the Quality Culture," *Engineering Management Journal* 11, no. 2 (June 1999), pp. 11–15; and Don Cohen and Lawrence Prusak, *In Good Company: How Social Capital Makes Organizations Work* (Cambridge, MA: Harvard Business School Press, 2001).

67. John Koob, "Early Warnings on Culture Clash," *Mergers & Acquisitions,* July 1, 2006, downloaded from Business & Company Resource Center, http://galenet.galegroup.com.

Chapter 3

1. N. Maestri, "Duke to Lead Wal-Mart as It Gains Clout," *Reuters,* November 21, 2008, http://www.reuters.com; J. Sturgeon, "Wal-Mart Seeks to Tie Low Prices, Sustainability," *Supermarket News,* October 10, 2008, http://supermarketnews.com; K. B. Connolly, "Wal-Mart's Scorecard Drives Sustainable Packaging," *Food Processing.com,* [no month] 2008, http://www.foodprocessing.com; C. Creno, "Wal-Mart's Sustainability Efforts Draw Praise," *Arizona Republic,* May 26, 2008, http://www.azcentral.com; and E. L. Plambeck, "The Greening of Wal-Mart's Supply Chain," *Supply Chain Management Review,* July 1, 2007, http://www.scmr.com.

2. V. Anand, B. Ashforth, and M. Joshi, "Business as Usual: The Acceptance and Perpetuation of Corruption in Organizations," *Academy of Management Executive,* May 2004, pp. 39–53.

3. Edelman, "Business More Trusted Than Media and Government in Every Region of the Globe," news release, January 22, 2007, *Trust Barometer 2007* pages of Edelman Web site, http://www.edelman.com/trust/2007/.

4. Kathy Gurchiek, "U.S. Workers Unlikely to Report Office Misconduct," *HRMagazine,* May 2006, downloaded from Business & Company Resource Center, http://galenet.galegroup.com.

5. Tom Zucco, "Ethics Issues? Check Goals," *St. Petersburg Times,* January 28, 2006, downloaded from Business & Company Resource Center, http://galenet.galegroup.com.

6. M. Banaji, M. Bazerman, and D. Chugh, "How (Un)Ethical Are You?" *Harvard Business Review,* December 2003, pp. 56–64.

7. S. L. Grover, "The Truth, the Whole Truth, and Nothing but the Truth: The Causes and Management of Workplace Lying," *Academy of Management Executive* 19 (May 2005), pp. 148–57.

8. D. Gelles, "Blogs That Spin a Web of Deception," *Financial Times,* February 12, 2009, downloaded from Business & Company Resource Center, http://galenet.galegroup.com.

9. B. L. Toffler, "Five Ways to Jump-Start Your Company's Ethics," *Fast Company,* October 2003, p. 36.

10. M. E. Guy, *Ethical Decision Making in Everyday Work Situations* (New York: Quorum Books, 1990).

11. O. C. Ferrell and J. Fraedrich, *Business Ethics: Ethical Decision Making and Cases,* 3rd ed. (Boston: Houghton Mifflin, 1997).

12. Ibid.

13. Guy, *Ethical Decision Making.*

14. Caux Round Table, "Principles for Business," http://www.cauxroundtable.org/documents/Principles%20for%20Business.PDF, adopted 1994, accessed July 31, 2007.

15. B. Sleeper, K. Schneider, and P. Weber, "Scale and Study of Student Attitudes toward Business Education's Role in Addressing Social Issues," *Journal of Business Ethics* 68 (2006), pp. 381–91; Y. J. Chen and T. L. P. Tang, "Attitude toward and Propensity to Engage in Unethical Behavior: Measurement Invariance across Major among University Students," *Journal of Business Ethics* 69 (2006), pp. 77–93; and B. A. Ritter, "Can Business Ethics Be Trained? A Study of the Ethical Decision-Making Process in Business Students," *Journal of Business Ethics* 68 (2006), pp. 153–64.

16. Ferrell and Fraedrich, *Business Ethics.*

17. John Hechinger and David Armstrong, "Universities Resolve Kickback Allegations," *The Wall Street Journal,* April 3, 2007, http://online.wsj.com; John Hechinger, "Probe into College-Lender Ties Widens," *The Wall Street Journal,* April 5, 2007, http://online.wsj.com; and Associated Press, "CIT Executives Placed on Leave Amid Student Loan Investigation," *The Wall Street Journal,* April 9, 2007, http://online.wsj.com.

18. Hechinger and Armstrong, "Universities Resolve Kickback Allegations"; and AP, "CIT Executives."

19. A. Spicer, T. Dunfee, and W. Biley, "Does National Context Matter in Ethical Decision Making? An Empirical Test of Integrative Social Contracts Theory," *Academy of Management Journal* 47 (2004), pp. 610–20.

20. Transparency International, "Persistently High Corruption in Low-Income Countries Amounts to an 'Ongoing Humanitarian Disaster,'" news release, September 23, 2008, http://www.transparency.org.

21. L. Kohlberg and D. Candee, "The Relationship of Moral Judgment to Moral Action" in *Morality, Moral Behavior, and Moral Development,* ed. W. M. Kurtines and J. L. Gerwitz (New York: John Wiley & Sons, 1984).

22. L. K. Trevino, "Ethical Decision Making in Organizations: A Person-Situation Interactionist Model," *Academy of Management Review,* 1992, pp. 601–17.

23. Ferrell and Fraedrich, *Business Ethics.*

24. J. Badarocco Jr. and A. Webb, "Business Ethics: A View from the Trenches," *California Management Review,* Winter 1995, pp. 8–28; and G. Laczniak, M. Berkowitz, R. Brookes, and J. Hale, "The Business of Ethics: Improving or Deteriorating?" *Business Horizons,* January–February 1995, pp. 39–47.

25. Brent Kallestad, "Survey: Bad Bosses Common, Problematic," Associated Press, January 1, 2007, http://news.yahoo.com.

26. M. Gunther, "God and Business," *Fortune,* July 9, 2001, pp. 58–80.

27. Anand, Ashforth, and Joshi, "Business as Usual"; and A. Bernstein, "Too Much Corporate Power?" *BusinessWeek,* September 11, 2000, pp. 146–47.

28. Brooks Barns, "Cartoon Network Chief Quits Over Boston Marketing Incident," *The Wall Street Journal,* February 9, 2007, http://online.wsj.com; and Jennifer Levitz and Emily Steel, "Boston Stunt Draws Legal, Ethical Fire," *The Wall Street Journal,* February 2, 2007, http://online.wsj.com.

29. Thompson Hine LLP, "U.S. Sentencing Commission Announces Stiffened Organization Sentencing Guidelines in Response to the Sarbanes-Oxley Act," advisory bulletin, June 1, 2004, last modified August 31, 2006, http://www.thompsonhine.com; and Robin J. Zablow, "Creating and Sustaining an Ethical Workplace," *Risk Management* 53, no. 9 (September 2006), downloaded from OCLC FirstSearch, http://firstsearch.oclc.org.

30. Jonathan Allard, "Ethics at Work," *CA Magazine* (Canadian Institute of Chartered Accountants), August 2006, downloaded from OCLC FirstSearch, http://firstsearch.oclc.org.

31. R. T. De George, *Business Ethics,* 3rd ed. (New York: Macmillan, 1990).

32. Ben W. Heineman Jr., "Avoiding Integrity Land Mines," *Harvard Business Review,* April 2007, pp. 100–108.

33. R. E. Allinson, "A Call for Ethically Centered Management," *Academy of Management Executive,* February 1995, pp. 73–76.

34. N. Adler, *International Dimensions of Organizational Behavior,* 2nd ed. (Boston: Kent, 1997).

35. R. A. Cooke, "Danger Signs of Unethical Behavior: How to Determine if Your Firm Is at Ethical Risk," *Journal of Business Ethics,* April 1991, pp. 249–53.

36. L. K. Trevino and M. Brown, "Managing to Be Ethical: Debunking Five Business Ethics Myths," *Academy of Management Executive,* May 2004, pp. 69–81.

37. Lynn Brewer, "Decisions: Lynn Brewer, Enron Whistleblower," *Management Today,* August 2006, downloaded from OCLC FirstSearch, http://firstsearch.oclc.org.

38. Ellen Nakashima, "Harsh Words Die Hard on the Web," *Washington Post,* March 7, 2007, http://www.washingtonpost.com.

39. Trevino and Brown, "Managing to Be Ethical."

40. Heineman, "Avoiding Integrity Land Mines."

41. S. Brenner and E. Molander, "Is the Ethics of Business Changing?" in *Ethics in Practice: Managing the Moral Corporation,* ed. K. Andrews (Cambridge, MA: Harvard Business School Press, 1989).

42. Trevino and Brown, "Managing to Be Ethical."

43. D. Messick and M. Bazerman, "Ethical Leadership and the Psychology of Decision Making," *Sloan Management Review,* Winter 1996, pp. 9–22.

44. C. Handy, *Beyond Uncertainty: The Changing Worlds of Organizations* (Boston: Harvard Business School Press, 1996).

45. J. Stevens, H. Steensma, D. Harrison, and P. Cochran, "Symbolic or Substantive Document? The Influence of Ethics Codes on Financial Executives' Decisions," *Strategic Management Journal* 26 (2005), pp. 181–95; and J. Weber, "Does It Take an Economic Village to Raise an Ethical Company?" *Academy of Management Executive* 19 (May 2005), pp. 158–59.

46. J. B. Ciulla, "Why Is Business Talking about Ethics? Reflections on Foreign Conversations," *California Management Review,* Fall 1991, pp. 67–80.

47. Zablow, "Creating and Sustaining an Ethical Workplace; Ethics Resource Center (ERC), "Code Construction and Content," *The Ethics Resource Center Toolkit,* http://www.ethics.org, accessed April 10, 2007; and Jerry Brown, "Ten Writing Tips for Creating an Effective Code of Conduct," Ethics Resource Center, http://www.ethics.org, accessed April 10, 2007.

48. Ethics Resource Center, "Performance Reviews Often Skip Ethics, HR Professionals Say," news release, June 12, 2008, http://www.ethics.org.

49. G. R. Weaver, L. K. Trevino, and P. L. Cochran, "Corporate Ethics Programs as Control Systems: Influences of Executive Commitment and Environmental Factors," *Academy of Management Journal* 42 (1999), pp. 41–57.

50. L. S. Paine, "Managing for Organizational Integrity," *Harvard Business Review,* March–April 1994, pp. 106–17.

51. F. Hall and E. Hall, "The ADA: Going beyond the Law," *Academy of Management Executive,* February 1994, pp. 7–13; and A. Farnham, "Brushing Up Your Vision Thing," *Fortune,* May 1, 1995, p. 129.

52. Luke O'Brien, "'Yahoo Betrayed My Husband," *Wired News,* March 15, 2007, http://www.wired.com.

53. G. R. Weaver, L. K. Trevino, and P. L. Cochran, "Integrated and Decoupled Corporate Social Performance: Management Commitments, External Pressures, and Corporate Ethics Practices" *Academy of Management Journal* 42 (1999), pp. 539–52.

54. Paine, "Managing for Organizational Integrity."

55. Trevino and Brown, "Managing to Be Ethical," p. 70.

56. Ibid.

57. Banaji, Bazerman, and Chugh, "How (Un)Ethical Are You?"

58. Anand, Ashforth, and Joshi, "Business as Usual."

59. A. Taylor, "Execs' Posh Retreat after Bailout Angers Lawmakers," *Yahoo News,* October 7, 2008, http://news.yahoo.com.

60. T. Thomas, J. Schermerhorn Jr., and J. Dienhart, "Strategic Leadership of Ethical Behavior in Business," *Academy of Management Executive,* May 2004, pp. 56–66.

61. L. T. Hosmer, *The Ethics of Management,* 4th ed. (New York: McGraw-Hill/Irwin, 2003).

62. Trevino and Brown, "Managing to Be Ethical."

63. "Ex-Aide at Coke Is Guilty in Plot to Steal Secrets," *The Wall Street Journal,* February 5, 2007, http://online.wsj.com.

64. Gurchiek, "U.S. Workers Unlikely to Report Office Misconduct."

65. Allard, "Ethics at Work."

66. M. Gundlach, S. Douglas, and M. Martinko, "The Decision to Blow the Whistle: A Social Information Processing Framework," *Academy of Management Review* 28 (2003), pp. 107–23.

67. Darren Dahl, "Learning to Love Whistleblowers," *Inc.,* March 2006, downloaded from OCLC FirstSearch, http://firstsearch.oclc.org.

68. Ibid.

69. Mark E. Schreiber and David R. Marshall, "Reducing the Risk of Whistleblower Complaints," *Risk Management* 53, no. 11 (November 2006), downloaded from OCLC FirstSearch, http://firstsearch.oclc.org.

70. L. Preston and J. Post, eds., *Private Management and Public Policy* (Englewood Cliffs, NJ: Prentice-Hall, 1975).

71. Ferrel and Fraedrich, *Business Ethics.*

72. A. Carroll, "Managing Ethically with Global Stakeholders: A Present and Future Challenge," *Academy of Management Executive,* May 2004, pp. 114–20.

73. Lauren Etter, "Smithfield to Phase Out Crates," *The Wall Street Journal,* January 25, 2007, http://online.wsj.com.

74. P. C. Godfrey, "The Relationship between Corporate Philanthropy and Shareholder Wealth: A Risk Management Perspective," *Academy of Management Review* 30 (2005), pp. 777–98.

75. R. Giacalone, "A Transcendent Business Education for the 21st Century," *Academy of Management Learning & Education,* 2004, pp. 415–20.

76. M. Witzel, "Not for Wealth Alone: The Rise of Business Ethics," *Financial Times Mastering Management Review,* November 1999, pp. 14–19.

77. D. C. Korten, *When Corporations Ruled the World* (San Francisco: BerrettKochler, 1995).

78. Handy, *Beyond Uncertainty.*

79. Dexter Roberts and Pete Engardio, "Secrets, Lies, and Sweatshops," *BusinessWeek,* November 17, 2006, http://www.businessweek.com.

80. D. Quinn and T. Jones, "An Agent Morality View of Business Policy," *Academy of Management Review* 20 (1995), pp. 22–42.

81. Betsy McKay, "Why Coke Aims to Slake Global Thirst for Safe Water," *The Wall Street Journal,* March 15, 2007, http://online.wsj.com.

82. Nicholas Varchaver, "Chemical Reaction," *Fortune,* April 2, 2007, downloaded from Business & Company Resource Center, http://galenet.galegroup.com.

83. D. Schuler and M. Cording, "A Corporate Social Performance–Corporate Financial Performance Behavioral Model for Consumers," *Academy of Management Review* 31 (2006), pp. 540–58.

84. D. Turban and D. Greening, "Corporate Social Performance and Organizational Attractiveness to Prospective Employees," *Academy of Management Journal* 40 (1997), pp. 658–72.

85. A. McWilliams and D. Siegel, "Corporate Social Responsibility: A Theory of the Firm Perspective," *Academy of Management Review* 26 (2001), pp. 117–27.

86. John Carey, "Hugging the Tree-Huggers," *BusinessWeek,* March 12, 2007, http://www.businessweek.com.

87. Michael E. Porter and Mark R. Kramer, "Strategy and Society: The Link between Competitive Advantage and Corporate Social Responsibility," *Harvard Business Review,* December 2006, pp. 78–92.

88. Ibid., p. 84.

89. S. L. Hart and M. B. Milstein, "Global Sustainability and the Creative Destructions of Industries," *Sloan Management Review,* Fall 1999, pp. 23–33.

90. P. M. Senge and G. Carstedt, "Innovating Our Way to the Next Industrial Revolution," *Sloan Management Review,* Winter 2001, pp. 24–38.

91. C. Holliday, "Sustainable Growth, the DuPont Way," *Harvard Business Review,* September 2001, pp. 129–34.

92. Marc Gunther, "Green Is Good," *Fortune,* March 22, 2007, http://money.cnn.com; and Martin LaMonica, "GE Chief: All Engines Go for Alternative Energy," *C/Net News.com,* March 12, 2007, http://news.com.com.

93. P. Shrivastava, "Ecocentric Management for a Risk Society," *Academy of Management Review* 20 (1995), pp. 118–37.

94. Ibid.

95. Ibid.

96. Donna Wright, "Lockheed Gets More Time," *Bradenton (Fla.) Herald,* March 7, 2006, downloaded from Business & Company Resource Center, http://galenet.galegroup.com.

97. Steve Raabe, "Asarco Closure Plan Cheers Globeville," *Denver Post,* July 13, 2006, downloaded from Business & Company Resource Center, http://galenet.galegroup.com.

98. Shrivastava, "Ecocentric Management."

99. Gunther, "Green Is Good."

100. J. O'Toole, "Do Good, Do Well: The Business Enterprise Trust Awards," *California Management Review* (Spring 1991), pp. 9–24.

101. A. Alter, "Yet Another 'Footprint' to Worry About: Water," *The Wall Street Journal,* February 17, 2009, http://www.online.wsj.com.

102. Ibid.; Shrivastava, "Ecocentric Management."

103. M. Russo and P. Fouts, "A Resource-Based Perspective on Corporate Environmental Performance and Profitability," *Academy of Management Journal* 40 (1997), pp. 534–59; R. D. Klassen and D. Clay Whybark, "The Impact of Environmental Technologies on Manufacturing Performance," *Academy of Management Journal* 42 (1999), pp. 599–615.

104. Martin LaMonica, "IBM Sees Green in Environmental Tech," *C/Net News.com,* March 6, 2007, http://news.com.com.

105. J. Ball, "Green Goal of 'Carbon Neutrality' Hits Limit," *The Wall Street Journal,* December 30, 2008, http://online.wsj.com; and Google Inc., "Going Green at Google," Corporate Overview: Green Initiatives, Google Corporate home page, http://www.google.com/corporate/green/, accessed April 21, 2009.

106. G. Pinchot and E. Pinchot, *The Intelligent Organization* (San Francisco: Berrett-Koehler, 1996).

107. S. L. Hart, "Beyond Greening: Strategies for a Sustainable World," *Harvard Business Review,* January–February 1997, pp. 66–76.

Chapter 4

1. Scott Moritz, "Nokia's Back on Its Feet," *TheStreet.com,* March 26, 2009, http://www.thestreet.com; Andrew Nusca, "How Nokia Ovi Store Will Trump Apple on Global Stage," *The Toy-Box,* March 25, 2009, http://blogs.zdnet.com; Elise Ackerman, "Mercury News Interview: Nokia CEO Maps Out U.S. Strategy," *San Jose Mercury News,* October 20, 2008, http://www.mercurynews.com; Dianne See Morrison, "Nokia Chief Olli-Pekka Kallasvuo: Hats Off to Apple, Jury Still Out on Google," *Yahoo! Finance,* October 2, 2008, http://biz.yahoo.com.

2. William M. Bulkeley, "How an IBM Lifer Built Software Unit into a Rising Star," *The Wall Street Journal,* April 2, 2007, http://online.wsj.com.

3. Jennifer Robison, "Are You Ready for Disaster?" *Las Vegas Review-Journal,* September 11, 2006, downloaded from Business &

Company Resource Center, http://galenet.galegroup.com. Data for companies with 500 or fewer workers.

4. Brent Bowers, "In Tough Times, Tackle Anxiety First," *New York Times,* November 13, 2008, downloaded from Business & Company Resource Center, http://galenet.galegroup.com.

5. Greg Farrell, "CEO Profile: Wells Fargo's Kovacevich Banks on Success as a One-Stop Shop," *USA Today,* March 26, 2007, http://www.usatoday.com.

6. Donald C. Hambrick and James W. Fredrickson, "Are You Sure You Have a Strategy?" *Academy of Management Executive* 19, no. 4 (2005), pp. 51–62.

7. Joseph L. Bower and Clark G. Gilbert, "How Managers' Everyday Decisions Create or Destroy Your Company's Strategy," *Harvard Business Review,* February 2007, pp. 72–79.

8. J. Lynn Lunsford, "Gradual Ascent: Burned by Last Boom, Boeing Curbs Its Pace," *The Wall Street Journal,* March 26, 2007, http://online.wsj.com; Boeing, "Boeing in Brief," About Us, http://www.boeing.com, February 2007; and Boeing, "Mission 2016," About Us, http://www.boeing.com/companyoffices/aboutus/mission, December 1, 2005.

9. Steven W. Floyd and Peter J. Lane, "Strategizing throughout the Organization: Management Role Conflict in Strategic Renewal," *Academy of Management Review* 25, no. 1 (January 2000), pp. 154–77.

10. Mission statements quoted from the corporate Web sites: McDonald's, "Student Research," http://www.mcdonalds.com; Microsoft, "Mission and Values," http://www.microsoft.com; and Allstate, Corporate Press Kit, http://www.allstate.com, accessed April 3, 2007.

11. Vision statements quoted from the organizations' Web sites: DuPont, "Our Company: DuPont Vision," http://www2.dupont.com; City of Redmond, "City of Redmond Vision Statement," http://www.ci.redmond.wa.us; and Great Lakes Naval Museum Association, "Vision Statement," http://www.greatlakesnavalmuseum.org, accessed April 3, 2007.

12. Andrew Martin, "The Happiest Meal: Hot Profits," *New York Times,* January 11, 2009, http://www.nytimes.com.

13. Boeing, "Mission 2016."

14. Arthur A. Thompson and A. J. Strickland III, *Strategic Management: Concepts and Cases,* 8th ed. (Burr Ridge, IL: Richard D. Irwin, 1995), p. 23.

15. Reyna Gobel, "Inspiring Innovation," *Success,* April 2009, pp. 24–26.

16. Michael Kanelios, "Full Steam Ahead for Nevada Solar Project," *CNet News.com,* March 20, 2007, http://news.com.com.

17. David Porter, "One Man's Garbage Becomes Another's Power Plant," *Yahoo! News,* October 28, 2008, http://www.news.yahoo.com.

18. David J. Collis and Cynthia A. Montgomery, *Corporate Strategy: A Resource-Based Approach,* 2nd ed. (New York, McGraw-Hill/Irwin, 2005).

19. Richard L. Priem, "A Consumer Perspective on Value Creation," *Academy of Management Review* 32, no. 1 (2007), pp. 219–35.

20. Farrell, "CEO Profile."

21. Adelaide Wilcox King, "Disentangling Interfirm and Intrafirm Causal Ambiguity: A Conceptual Model of Causal Ambiguity and Sustainable Competitive Advantage," *Academy of Management Review* 32, no. 1 (2007), pp. 156–78.

22. Steve Hamm and William C. Symonds, "Miskates Made on the Road to Innovation," *BusinessWeek,* November 27, 2006, http://www.businessweek.com.

23. Gautam Naik, "A Hospital Races to Learn Lessons of Ferrari Pit Stop," *The Wall Street Journal,* November 14, 2006, http://online.wsj.com.

24. "Moments of Truth: Global Executives Talk about the Challenges That Shaped Them as Leaders," *Harvard Business Review,* December 1, 2008, http://www.hbrideacast.org; Lionel Laurent, "Nokia's Trickle-Up Success," *Forbes,* June 16, 2008, http://www.forbes.com; Marguerite Reardon, "Nokia's Success Tied to Emerging Markets," *CNET News,* January 24, 2008, http://news.cnet.com.

25. Robert A. Guth, "Microsoft May Shift Strategy to Keep Up," *The Wall Street Journal,* March 29, 2007, http://online.wsj.com.

26. Robert A. Guth, Dennis K. Berman, and Kevin J. Delaney, "Google Joins Race to Buy DoubleClick," *The Wall Street Journal,* April 2, 2007, http://online.wsj.com.

27. Adam Bluestein, "The Success Gene," *Inc.,* April 2008, pp. 83–94.

28. P. Haspeslagh, "Portfolio Planning: Uses and Limits," *Harvard Business Review* 60, no.1 (1982), pp. 58–67; R. Hamermesh, *Making Strategy Work* (New York: John Wiley & Sons, 1986); and R. A. Proctor, "Toward a New Model for Product Portfolio Analysis," *Management Decision* 28, no. 3 (1990), pp. 14–17.

29. Avery Johnson, "Abbott's Makeover Attracts Investors," *The Wall Street Journal,* January 19, 2007, http://online.wsj.com.

30. M. Porter, *Competitive Advantage* (New York: Free Press, 1985), pp. 11–14.

31. Justin Ewers, "Making It Stick," *U.S. News & World Report,* February 5, 2007, pp. EE3–EE8.

32. Rajan Varadarajan, "Think Small," *The Wall Street Journal,* February 14, 2007, http://online.wsj.com.

33. Shaker A. Zahra, Sarah Nash, and Deborah J. Bickford, "Transforming Technological Pioneering in Competitive Advantage," *Academy of Management Executive* 9, no. 1 (1995), pp. 17–31; and Michael Sadowski and Aaron Roth, "Technology Leadership Can Pay Off," *Research Technology Management* 42, no. 6 (November/December 1999), pp. 32–33.

34. Masaaki Imai and Gemba Kaizen, *A Commonsense, Low-Cost Approach to Management* (New York: McGraw-Hill, 1997); and Masaaki Imai and Gemba Kaizen, *The Key to Japan's Competitive Success* (New York: McGraw-Hill, 1986).

35. A. Gary Shilling, "First-Mover Disadvantage," *Forbes,* June 18, 2007, downloaded from General Reference Center Gold, http://find.galegroup.com.

36. Fernando F. Suarez and Gianvito Lanzolla, "The Role of Environmental Dynamics in Building a First Mover Advantage Theory," *Academy of Management Review* 32, no. 2 (2007), pp. 377–92.

37. Bulkeley, "How an IBM Lifer Built Software Unit into a Rising Star"; and Farrell, "CEO Profile."

38. Justin Scheck and Paul Glader, "R&D Spending Holds Steady in Slump," *The Wall Street Journal,* April 6, 2009, http://online.wsj.com.

39. M. Beer and R. A. Eisenstat, "The Silent Killers of Strategy Implementation and Learning," *MIT Sloan Management Review,* no. 4 (Summer 2000), pp. 29–40.

40. R. A. Eisenstat, "Implementing Strategy: Developing a Partnership for Change," *Planning Review,* September–October 1993, pp. 33–36.

41. Daniel Michaels and J. Lyn Lunsford, "Lack of Seats, Galleys Delays Boeing, Airbus," *The Wall Street Journal,* August 8, 2008, http://online.wsj.com; and John Flowers, "Boeing Announces Further Delays to 787 Dreamliner Program," *The Wall Street Journal,* April 9, 2008, http://online.wsj.com.

42. M. Magasin and F. L. Gehlen, "Unwise Decisions and Unanticipated Consequences," *Sloan Management Review* 41 (1999), pp. 47–60; M. McCall and R. Kaplan, *Whatever It Takes: Decision Makers at Work* (Englewood Cliffs, NJ: Prentice-Hall, 1985); and Luda Kopeikina, "The Elements of a Clear Decision," *MIT Sloan Management Review* 47 (Winter 2006), pp. 19–20.

43. B. Bass, *Organizational Decision Making* (Homewood, IL: Richard D. Irwin, 1983).

44. J. Gibson, J. Ivancevich, and J. Donnelly Jr., *Organizations: Behavior, Structure, Processes,* 10th ed. (Burr Ridge, IL: McGraw-Hill, 2000). Copyright © 2000 by The McGraw-Hill Companies. Reproduced with permission of The McGraw-Hill Companies.

45. J. March, "Bounded Rationality, Ambiguity, and the Engineering of Choice," *Bell Journal of Economics* 9 (1978), pp. 587–608.

46. Susumu Ogawa and Frank T. Piller, "Reducing the Risks of New Product Development," *MIT Sloan Management Review* 47 (Winter 2006), pp. 65–71.

47. McCall and Kaplan, *Whatever It Takes.*

48. Max Chafkin, "Case Study: When the Bank Called in a Loan, Larry Cohen Had to Act Fast to Save the Family Business," *Inc.,* June 2006, pp. 58–60.

49. Del Jones, "Cisco CEO Sees Tech as Integral to Success," *USA Today,* March 19, 2007, p. 4B (interview of John Chambers).

50. K. MacCrimmon and R. Taylor, "Decision Making and Problem Solving," in *Handbook of Industrial and Organizational Psychology,* ed. M. D. Dunnette (Chicago: Rand McNally, 1976).

51. Chafkin, "Case Study," p. 58.

52. Q. Spitzer and R. Evans, *Heads, You Win! How the Best Companies Think* (New York: Simon & Schuster, 1997).

53. C. Gettys and S. Fisher, "Hypothesis Plausibility and Hypotheses Generation," *Organizational Behavior and Human Performance* 24 (1979), pp. 93–110.

54. E. R. Alexander, "The Design of Alternatives in Organizational Contexts: A Pilot Study," *Administrative Science Quarterly* 24 (1979), pp. 382–404.

55. A. R. Rao, M. E. Bergen, and S. Davis, "How to Fight a Price War," *Harvard Business Review,* March–April 2000, pp. 107–16.

56. Chafkin, "Case Study."

57. Ibid.

58. Joseph L. Bower and Clark G. Gilbert, "How Managers' Everyday Decisions Create or Destroy Your Company's Strategy," *Harvard Business Review,* February 2007, pp. 72–79.

59. Dana Mattioli and Sara Murray, "Employers Hit Salaried Staff with Furloughs," *The Wall Street Journal,* February 24, 2009, http://online.wsj.com.

60. "Is Executive Hubris Ruining Companies?" *Industry Week,* January 31, 2007, http://www.industryweek.com (interview of Matthew Hayward).

61. OfficeTeam, "On Your Best Behavior: Survey Shows the Boss' Assistant Can Influence the Hiring Decision," news release, *CNW Group,* March 19, 2009, downloaded from Business & Company Resource Center, http://galenet.galegroup.com.

62. Spitzer and Evans, *Heads, You Win!*

63. "Is Executive Hubris Ruining Companies?"

64. McCall and Kaplan, *Whatever It Takes.*

65. J. Pfeffer and R. Sutton, *The Knowing–Doing Gap* (Boston: Harvard Business School Press, 2000).

66. David Drickhamer, "By the Numbers," *Material Handling Management,* January 2006, downloaded from OCLC FirstSearch, http://firstsearch.oclc.org.

67. D. Siebold, "Making Meetings More Successful," *Journal of Business Communication* 16 (Summer 1979), pp. 3–20.

68. Chafkin, "Case Study."

69. J. W. Dean Jr. and M. Sharfman, "Does Decision Process Matter? A Study of Strategic Decision-Making Effectiveness," *Academy of Management Journal* 39 (1996), pp. 368–96.

70. R. Nisbett and L. Ross, *Human Inference: Strategies and Shortcomings* (Englewood Cliffs, NJ: Prentice-Hall, 1980).

71. D. Messick and M. Bazerman, "Ethical Leadership and the Psychology of Decision Making," *Sloan Management Review,* Winter 1996, pp. 9–22.

72. Phred Dvorak, "Dangers of Clinging to Solutions of the Past," *The Wall Street Journal,* March 2, 2009, http://online.wsj.com.

73. T. Bateman and C. Zeithaml, "The Psychological Context of Strategic Decisions: A Model and Convergent Experimental Findings," *Strategic Management Journal* 10 (1989), pp. 59–74.

74. Erin White, "Why Good Managers Make Bad Decisions," *The Wall Street Journal,* February 12, 2009, http://online.wsj.com.

75. Messick and Bazerman, "Ethical Leadership."

76. N. Adler, *International Dimensions of Organizational Behavior* (Boston: Kent, 1990).

77. Joann S. Lublin, "Recall the Mistakes of Your Past Bosses, So You Can Do Better," *The Wall Street Journal,* January 2, 2007, http://online.wsj.com.

78. K. M. Esenhardt, "Speed and Strategic Choice: How Managers Accelerate Decision Making," *California Management Review* 32 (Spring 1990), pp. 39–54.

79. Q. Spitzer and R. Evans, "New Problems in Problem Solving," *Across the Board,* April 1997, pp. 36–40.

80. G. W. Hill, "Group versus Individual Performance: Are *n* + 1 Heads Better Than 1?" *Psychological Bulletin* 91 (1982), pp. 517–39.

81. N. R. F. Maier, "Assets and Liabilities in Group Problem Solving: The Need for an Integrative Function," *Psychological Review* 74 (1967), pp. 239–49.

82. Ibid.

83. D. A. Garvin and M. A. Roberto, "What You Don't Know about Making Decisions," *Harvard Business Review,* September 2001, pp. 108–16.

84. A. Amason, "Distinguishing the Effects of Functional and Dysfunctional Conflict on Strategic Decision Making: Resolving a Paradox for Top Management Teams," *Academy of Management Journal* 39 (1996), pp. 123–48; and R. Dooley and G. Fyxell, "Attaining Decision Quality and Commitment from Dissent: The Moderating Effects of Loyalty and Competence in Strategic Decision-Making Teams," *Academy of Management Journal,* August 1999, pp. 389–402.

85. C. De Dreu and L. Weingart, "Task versus Relationship Conflict, Team Performance, and Team Member Satisfaction:

A Meta-Analysis," *Journal of Applied Psychology* 88 (2003), pp. 741–49.

86. K. Eisenhardt, J. Kahwajy, and L. J. Bourgeois III, "Conflict and Strategic Choice: How Top Management Teams Disagree," *California Management Review*, Winter 1997, pp. 42–62.

87. Ibid.

88. "Innovation from the Ground Up," *Industry Week*, March 7, 2007, http://www.industryweek.com (interview of Erika Andersen); A. Farnham, "How to Nurture Creative Sparks," *Fortune*, January 10, 1994, pp. 94–100; and T. M. Amabile, "A Model of Creativity and Innovation in Organizations," in *Research in Organizational Behavior*, ed. B. Straw and L. Cummings, vol. 10 (Greenwich, CT: JAI Press, 1988), pp. 123–68.

89. T. Amabile, C. Hadley, and S. Kramer, "Creativity under the Gun," *Harvard Business Review*, August 2002, pp. 52–61.

90. S. Farmer, P. Tierney, and K. Kung-McIntyre, "Employee Creativity in Taiwan: An Application of Role Identity Theory," *Academy of Management Journal* 46 (2003), pp. 618–30.

91. Mike Larson, "LEEDing by Example," *Western Builder*, April 6, 2009, downloaded from Business & Company Resource Center, http://galenet.galegroup.com.

Chapter 5

1. J. Timmons and S. Spinelli, *New Venture Creation: Entrepreneurship for the 21st Century*, 6th ed. (New York: McGraw-Hill/Irwin, 2004), p. 7; and Jeffrey Gangemi, "Where Are Last Year's Winners Now?" *BusinessWeek*, October 30, 2006, http://www.businessweek.com.

2. S. Shane and S. Venkataraman, "The Promise of Entrepreneurship as a Field of Research," *Academy of Management Review* 25 (2000), pp. 217–26.

3. J. A. Timmons, *New Venture Creation* (Burr Ridge, IL: Richard D. Irwin, 1994).

4. G. T. Lumpkin and G. G. Dess, "Clarifying the Entrepreneurial Orientation Construct and Linking It to Performance," *Academy of Management Review* 21 (1996), pp. 135–72.

5. Company Web site, http://www.virgin.com, accessed April 1, 2009; Sara Wilson, "Branson," *Entrepreneur*, November 2008, pp. 58–62; Emily Benammar, "Richard Branson Forced to Abandon Transatlantic Record Attempt," *Telegraph*, October 24, 2008, http://www.telegraph.co.uk; Jyoti Thottam, "Richard Branson's Flight Plan," *Time*, April 17, 2008, http://www.time.com; Alan Deutschman, "The Enlightenment of Richard Branson," *Fast Company*, December 19, 2007, http://www.fastcompany.com; Kane Farabaugh, "Virgin Group Founder Commits Billions of Dollars to Help Environment," *Voice of America*, March 19, 2007, http://voanews.com; and Michael Specter, "Branson's Luck," *New Yorker*, May 14, 2007, http://www.newyorker.com.

6. R. W. Smilor, "Entrepreneurship: Reflections on a Subversive Activity," *Journal of Business Venturing* 12 (1997), pp. 341–46.

7. W. Megginson, M. J. Byrd, S. R. Scott Jr., and L. Megginson, *Small Business Management: An Entrepreneur's Guide to Success*, 2nd ed. (Boston: Irwin McGraw-Hill, 1997).

8. Timmons and Spinelli, *New Venture Creation*, p. 3.

9. Timmons and Spinelli, *New Venture Creation*.

10. Angus Loten, "Start-Ups Key to States' Economic Success," *Inc.*, February 7, 2007, http://www.inc.com.

11. Timmons and Spinelli, *New Venture Creation*.

12. Ibid.

13. Ibid.

14. Adapted from J. A. Timmons and S. Spinelli, *New Venture Creation*, 6th ed., pp. 67–68. Copyright © 2004. Reproduced with permission of the authors.

15. D. Bricklin, "Natural-Born Entrepreneur," *Harvard Business Review*, September 2001, pp. 53–59, quoting p. 58.

16. Alexandra Levit, "'Insider' Entrepreners," *The Wall Street Journal*, April 6, 2009, http://online.wsj.com.

17. "For Zappos, the Next Trend Is More Customized Pages for Customers," *Internet Retailer*, February 12, 2009, http://www.internetretailer.com; and Max Chafkin, "How I Did It: Tony Hsieh, CEO, Zappos.com," *Inc.*, September 2006, http://www.inc.com.

18. Jeffrey Gangemi, "Young, Fearless, and Smart: Adnan Aziz, First Flavor," *BusinessWeek*, October 30, 2006, http://www.businessweek.com.

19. A. Marsh, "Promiscuous Breeding," *Forbes*, April 7, 1997, pp. 74–77; and Joe Nocera, "Fewer Eggs, More Baskets in the Incubator," *New York Times*, October 28, 2006, downloaded from Business & Company Resource Center, http://galenet.galegroup.com.

20. Larry Kanter, "The Eco-Advantage," *Inc.*, November 2006, pp. 78–103 (NaturaLawn example on p. 84).

21. H. Aldrich, *Ethnic Entrepreneurs: Immigrant Business in Industrial Societies* (Newbury Park, CA: Sage, 1990).

22. Raymund Flandez, "Immigrants Gain Edge Doing Business Back Home," *The Wall Street Journal*, March 20, 2007, http://online.wsj.com.

23. Gerrye Wong, "Lee's Sandwiches—Behind Every Success Story Stands a United Family," *Asian Week*, March 24, 2006, http://news.asianweek.com.

24. Leigh Buchanan, "Create Jobs, Eliminate Waste, Preserve Value," *Inc.*, December 2006, pp. 94–106.

25. Ibid.

26. Ibid., pp. 99–100.

27. Timmons and Spinelli, *New Venture Creation*.

28. Michael V. Copeland, "Products for the Other Three Billion," *Fortune*, April 1, 2009, http://money.cnn.com.

29. J. Collins and J. Porras, *Built to Last* (London: Century, 1996).

30. Michael V. Copeland, "Start Last, Finish First," *Business 2.0*, January–February 2006, downloaded from Business & Company Resource Center, http://galenet.galegroup.com.

31. Leigh Buchanan, "Share the Wealth," *Inc.*, June 2006, pp. 110–11.

32. Collins and Porras, *Built to Last*.

33. K. H. Vesper, *New Venture Mechanics* (Englewood Cliffs, NJ: Prentice Hall, 1993).

34. Kanter, "The Eco-Advantage," p. 87.

35. Vesper, *New Venture Mechanics*.

36. Kanter, "The Eco-Advantage," p. 84.

37. Joel Berg, "Entrepreneurs Develop Errand Service," *Patriot-News (Harrisburg, PA)*, January 23, 2007, http://galenet.galegroup.com.

38. Kanter, "The Eco-Advantage," p. 87.

39. Ibid., p. 84.

40. Gwendolyn Bounds, "Firms Jump on Trend to Broaden Use of Safety Gear," *The Wall Street Journal*, February 13, 2007, http://online.wsj.com.

41. Gwendolyn Bounds, "The Perils of Being First," *The Wall Street Journal,* March 19, 2007, http://online.wsj.com.

42. Timmons and Spinelli, *New Venture Creation.*

43. Patrick J. Sauer, "Serving Up Success," *Inc.,* January 2007, http://www.inc.com.

44. International Franchise Association, "Study Reveals Significant Growth of Franchising Sector," news release, February 23, 2007, http://www.franchise.org; and International Franchise Association, "The Profile of Franchising: 2006," August 3, 2006, http://www.franchise.org/IndustrySecondary.aspx?id=31604.

45. Kelly Spors, "Franchised versus Nonfranchised Businesses," *The Wall Street Journal,* February 27, 2007, http://online.wsj.com.

46. Timmons and Spinelli, *New Venture Creation.*

47. Richard Gibson, "Learning from Others' Mistakes," *The Wall Street Journal,* March 19, 2007, http://online.wsj.com.

48. Michael V. Copeland and Susanna Hamner, "The 20 Smartest Companies to Start Now," *Business 2.0,* September 2006, downloaded from General Reference Center Gold, http://find.galegroup.com.

49. Andy Pasztor, "Sharper Image Sells New Toy: Zero Gravity's Spacey Flights," *The Wall Street Journal,* March 28, 2007, http://online.wsj.com; and Benjamin Spillman, "Nothing to These Flights," *Las Vegas Review–Journal,* March 5, 2007, downloaded from Business & Company Resource Center, http://galenet.galegroup.com.

50. Wilson, "Branson;" Richard Branson, "In Defense of Capitalism," *Mail Online,* September 25, 2008, http://www.dailymail.co.uk; Peter Pae, "Richard Branson Unveils His Space Plane," *Newsday,* July 29, 2008, http://www.newsday.com; Deutschman, "The Enlightenment of Richard Branson"; and Farabaugh, "Virgin Group Founder Commits Billions of Dollars."

51. Anna Marie Kukec, "Two Start-Ups Get State Boost to Fight Terrorism," *Daily Herald (Arlington, IL),* January 10, 2006; and Tom Walsh, "State Venture Capital to Be Put to Work," *Detroit Free Press,* August 28, 2006, both downloaded from Business & Company Resource Center, http://galenet.galegroup.com.

52. J. E. Lange, "Entrepreneurs and the Continuing Internet: The Expanding Frontier," in Timmons and Spinelli, *New Venture Creation,* pp. 183–220.

53. Ibid.

54. Nielsen//NetRatings, "Resources: Free Data and Rankings," February 2007, http://www.nielsen-netratings.com, accessed April 24, 2007.

55. Jessica E. Vascellaro, "Selling Your Designs Online," *The Wall Street Journal,* April 5, 2007, http://online.wsj.com.

56. Alan Sipress, "The New Dot-Economy," *Washington Post,* December 5, 2006, http://www.washingtonpost.com.

57. Vesper, *New Venture Mechanics.*

58. Timmons, *New Venture Creation.*

59. J. R. Baum and E. A. Locke, "The Relationship of Entrepreneurial Traits, Skill, and Motivation to Subsequent Venture Growth," *Journal of Applied Psychology* 89 (2004), pp. 587–98.

60. Ellyn Pak, "Twenty-Something Entrepreneurs Are Helping Transform the Surf and Skate Industry," *Orange County Register (Santa Ana, CA),* February 23, 2007, downloaded from Business & Company Resource Center, http://galenet.galegroup.com.

61. Nocera, "Fewer Eggs, More Baskets."

62. M. Sonfield and R. Lussier, "The Entrepreneurial Strategy Matrix: A Model for New and Ongoing Ventures," *Business Horizons,* May–June 1997, pp. 73–77.

63. David J. Lynch, "Executive Suite—Today's Entrepreneur: Miami Magnate Gives City a Makeover," *USA Today,* March 11, 2007, http://www.usatoday.com.

64. Lange, "Entrepreneurs and the Continuing Internet."

65. S. Venkataraman and M. Low, "On the Nature of Critical Relationships: A Test of the Liabilities and Size Hypothesis," in *Frontiers of Entrepreneurship Research* (Babson Park, MA: Babson College, 1991), p. 97.

66. Timmons and Spinelli, *New Venture Creation.*

67. Peter Hoy, "Most Small Businesses Start without Outside Capital," *Inc.,* October 3, 2006, http://www.inc.com.

68. Rick Grant, "The Trade-Offs of Venture Capital," *Mortgage Banking,* February 2007, downloaded from Business & Company Resource Center, http://galenet.galegroup.com.

69. "Just the Facts," *Inc.,* September 2008, http://www.inc.com; and "Start-Up Capital," *Inc.,* September 2008, http://www.inc.com.

70. Cari Tuna, "Tough Call: Deciding to Start a Business," *The Wall Street Journal,* January 8, 2009, http://online.wsj.com.

71. Heidi Dietrich, "Worried about Future Viaduct Construction Woes, Sound Sports Is Planning Ahead," *Minneapolis–St. Paul Business Journal,* http://twincities.bizjournals.com, accessed June 14, 2006.

72. Buchanan, "Create Jobs."

73. "Dartmouth Incubator a Testament to Collaboration," *New Hampshire Business Review,* November 24, 2006, downloaded from Business & Company Resource Center, http://galenet.galegroup.com.

74. Michael V. Copeland, "A Studio System for Startups," *Business 2.0,* May 2007, downloaded from Business & Company Resource Center, http://galenet.galegroup.com.

75. "Dartmouth Incubator."

76. Norm Brodsky, "Street Smarts: Our Irrational Fear of Numbers," *Inc.,* January 2009, http://www.inc.com.

77. Chafkin, "How I Did It."

78. Anjali Cordeiro, "Sweet Returns," *The Wall Street Journal,* April 23, 2009, http://online.wsj.com.

79. Gibson, "Learning from Others' Mistakes."

80. Jacob Stokes, "University of Missouri: A New Life for Old Phones," *Inc.,* March 2009, http://www.inc.com.

81. D. McGinn, "Why Size Matters," *Inc.,* Fall 2004, pp. 32–36.

82. Leigh Buchanan, "Six Ways to Open an Office Overseas," *Inc.,* April 2007, pp. 120–21.

83. H. Sapienza, E. Autio, G. George, and S. Zahra, "A Capabilities Perspective on the Effects of Early Internationalization on Firm Survival and Growth," *Academy of Management Review* 31, no. 4 (2006), pp. 914–33.

84. B. Burlingham, "How Big Is Big Enough?" *Inc.,* Fall 2004, pp. 40–43.

85. Ibid.

86. Kanter, "The Eco-Advantage," p. 91.

87. Wendy Harris, "Team Players," *Black Enterprise,* January 2007, downloaded from Business & Company Resource Center, http://galenet.galegroup.com.

88. S. Finkelstein, "The Myth of Managerial Superiority in Internet Startups: An Autopsy," *Organizational Dynamics,* Fall 2001, pp. 172–85.

89. Gangemi, "Young, Fearless, and Smart."

90. Jim Melloan, "The Big Picture," *Inc.,* September 2006, http://www.inc.com.

91. Robert Weisman, "Bootstrappers Avoid Outside Money Ties," *Boston Globe,* February 5, 2007, downloaded from Business & Company Resource Center, http://galenet.galegroup.com.

92. Cordeiro, "Sweet Returns."

93. P. F. Drucker, "How to Save the Family Business," *The Wall Street Journal,* August 19, 1994, p. A10.

94. D. Gamer, R. Owen, and R. Conway, *The Ernst & Young Guide to Raising Capital* (New York: John Wiley & Sons, 1991).

95. Ibid.

96. A. Lustgarten, "Warm, Fuzzy, and Highly Profitable," *Fortune,* November 15, 2004, p. 194.

97. R. D. Hisrich and M. P. Peters, *Entrepreneurship: Starting, Developing, and Managing a New Enterprise* (Burr Ridge, IL: Irwin, 1994).

98. R. Hisrich and M. Peters, *Entrepreneurship: Starting, Developing, and Managing a New Enterprise,* p. 41. Copyright © 1998 by The McGraw-Hill Companies. Reproduced with permission of The McGraw-Hill Companies.

99. Ibid.

100. W. A. Sahlman, "How to Write a Great Business Plan," *Harvard Business Review,* July–August 1997, pp. 98–108.

101. Ibid.

102. Ibid.

103. Copeland, "Start Last, Finish First."

104. Robert D. Atkinson and Daniel K. Correa, *The 2007 State New Economy Index* (Ewing Marion Kauffman Foundation and Information Technology and Innovation Foundation, 2007), http://www.kauffman.org; and Jeffrey Gangemi, "Ranking the States for the New Economy," *BusinessWeek,* February 27, 2007, http://www.businessweek.com.

105. Sahlman, "How to Write a Great Business Plan."

106. Ibid.

107. M. Zimmerman and G. Zeitz, "Beyond Survival: Achieving New Venture Growth by Building Legitimacy," *Academy of Management Review* 27 (2002), pp. 414–21.

108. A. L. Stinchcombe, "Social Structure and Organizations," in J. G. March, ed., *Handbook of Organizations* (Chicago: Rand McNally, 1965), pp. 142–93.

109. Leslie Taylor, "Want Your Start-Up to Be Successful? Appearance Is Everything," *Inc.,* February 23, 2007, http://www.inc.com.

110. Ibid.

111. R. A. Baron and G. D. Markman, "Beyond Social Capital: How Social Skills Can Enhance Entrepreneurs' Success," *Academy of Management Executive,* February 2000, pp. 106–16.

112. J. Florin, M. Lubatkin, and W. Schulze, "A Social Capital Model of High-Growth Ventures," *Academy of Management Journal* 46 (2003), pp. 374–84.

113. Evan Ramstad, "In the Land of Conglomerates, Brian Ko Goes His Own Way," *CareerJournal.com,* January 4, 2007, http://www.careerjournal.com.

114. Leigh Buchanan, "How I Did It: Tim Litle, Chairman, Litle & Co.," *Inc.,* September 2006, http://www.inc.com.

115. Gangemi, "Young, Fearless, and Smart."

116. Ibid.

117. Harris, "Team Players."

118. Ibid.

119. John Markoff, "Searching for Michael Jordan? Microsoft Wants a Better Way," *New York Times,* March 7, 2007, downloaded from Business & Company Resource Center, http://galenet.galegroup.com; and "Microsoft Researchers Collaborate to Change the World," *Agence France Presse,* March 6, 2007, http://www.afp.com.

120. R. M. Kanter, *The Change Masters* (New York: Simon & Schuster, 1983).

121. D. Kuratko, R. D. Ireland, and J. Hornsby, "Improving Firm Performance through Entrepreneurial Actions: Acordia's Corporate Entrepreneurship Strategy," *Academy of Management Executive* 15 (2001), pp. 60–71.

122. Collins and Porras, *Built to Last.*

123. Rosabeth Moss Kanter, Cynthia Ingols, Erika Morgan, and Tobias K. Seggerman, "Driving Corporate Entrepreneurship," *Management Review* 76 (April 1987), pp. 14–16.

124. J. Argenti, *Corporate Collapse: The Causes and Symptoms* (New York: John Wiley & Sons, 1979).

125. Kanter et al., "Driving Corporate Entrepreneurship."

126. Yan Ling, Zeki Simsek, Michael Lubatkin, and John Veiga, "Transformational Leadership's Role in Promoting Corporate Entrepreneurship: Examining the CEO–TMT Interface," *Academy of Management Journal,* 2008, pp. 557–76.

127. G. T. Lumpkin and G. G. Dess, "Clarifying the Entrepreneurial Orientation Construct and Linking It to Performance," *Academy of Management Review* 21 (1996), pp. 135–72.

128. Stacy Perman, "Is There a Gene for Business?" *BusinessWeek,* October 30, 2006, http://www.businessweek.com.

129. T. Bateman and J. M. Crant, "The Proactive Dimension of Organizational Behavior," *Journal of Organizational Behavior,* 1993, pp. 103–18.

130. Sapienza et al., "A Capabilities Perspective."

131. Lumpkin and Dess, "Clarifying the Entrepreneurial Orientation Construct."

132. "Virgin Rebirth," *Economist,* September 25, 2008, http://www.economist.com; Pae, "Richard Branson Unveils His Space Plane"; "Virgin Launches Green Fund," *Environmental Leader,* January 21, 2008, http://www.environmentalleader.com; "Virgin to Test 747 on Biofuel," *Environmental Leader,* October 16, 2007, http://environmentalleader.com; "Richard Branson's Latest Venture," *BusinessWeek,* July 25, 2007, http://www.businessweek.com; Specter, "Branson's Luck"; "Virgin Trains Launches Green Marketing Blitz," *Environmental Leader,* March 28, 2007, http://www.environmentalleader.com; Farabaugh, "Virgin Group Founder Commits Billions of Dollars"; and "Virgin Group, NTR Form Virgin Bioverda," *Environmental Leader,* January 17, 2007, http://www.environmentalleader.com.

133. C. Pinchot and E. Pinchot, *The Intelligent Organization* (San Francisco: Barrett-Koehler, 1996).

Chapter 6

1. Company Web site, http://www.whirlpoolcorp.com, accessed April 8, 2009; Terry Waghorn, "Making Your Company an Innovation Machine," *Forbes,* January 8, 2009, http://www.forbes.com; Fara Warner, "Recipe for Growth," *Fast Company,* December 19, 2007, http://www.fastcompany.com; Kristen B. Frasch, "Best HR Ideas

for 2009," *Human Resource Executive Online,* March 2, 2009, http://www.hreonline.com; and Jill Rose, "Whirlpool: Nurturing Ideas," *American Executive,* September 30, 2008, http://www. americanexecutive.com.

2. T. Burns and G. Stalker, *The Management of Innovation* (London: Tavistock, 1961).

3. D. Krackhardt and J. R. Hanson, "Information Networks: The Company behind the Chart," *Harvard Business Review,* July–August 1993, pp. 104–11.

4. Ronald N. Ashkenas and Suzanne C. Francis, "Integration Managers: Special Leaders for Special Times," *Harvard Business Review* 78, no. 6 (November–December 2000), pp. 108–16.

5. Andrew West, "The Flute Factory: An Empirical Measurement of the Effect of the Division of Labor on Productivity and Production Cost," *American Economist* 43, no. 1 (Spring 1999), pp. 82–87.

6. P. Lawrence and J. Lorsch, *Organization and Environment* (Homewood, IL: Richard D. Irwin, 1969).

7. Ibid.; and Brad Lee Thompson, *The New Manager's Handbook* (New York: McGraw-Hill, 1994). See also S. Sharifi and K. S. Pawar, "Product Design as a Means of Integrating Differentiation," *Technovation* 16, no. 5 (May 1996), pp. 255–64; and W. B. Stevenson and J. M. Bartunek, "Power, Interaction, Position, and the Generation of Cultural Agreement in Organizations," *Human Relations* 49, no. 1 (January 1996), pp. 75–104.

8. Phanish Puranam, Harbir Singh, and Maurizio Zollo, "Organizing for Innovation: Managing the Coordination-Autonomy Dilemma in Technology Acquisitions," *Academy of Management Journal* 49, no. 2 (2006), pp. 263–80.

9. Susan F. Shultz, *Board Book: Making Your Corporate Board a Strategic Force in Your Company's Success* (New York: AMACOM, 2000); and Ralph D. Ward, *Improving Corporate Boards: The Boardroom Insider Guidebook* (New York: John Wiley & Sons, 2000).

10. "Board Membership Profiles Have Changed Sharply over the Past Decade," *Corporate Board,* January–February 2009, downloaded from Business & Company Resource Center, http://galenet .galegroup.com; and Spencer Stuart, *2008 Spencer Stuart Board Index,* November 2008, http://www.spencerstuart.com.

11. C. M. Daily and D. R. Dalton, "CEO and Board Chair Roles Held Jointly or Separately: Much Ado about Nothing?" *Academy of Management Executive* 11, no. 3 (August 1997), pp. 11–20.

12. Tony Simons, Lisa Hope Pelled, and Ken A. Smith, "Making Use of Difference: Diversity, Debate, and Decision Comprehensiveness in Top Management Teams," *Academy of Management Journal* 42, no. 6 (December 1999), pp. 662–73; and C. Carl Pegels, Yong I Song, and Baik Yang, "Management Heterogeneity, Competitive Interaction Groups, and Firm Performance," *Strategic Management Journal* 21, no. 3 (September 2000), pp. 911–21.

13. Abbas J. Ali, Robert C. Camp, and Manton Gibbs, "The Ten Commandments Perspective on Power and Authority in Organizations," *Journal of Business Ethics* 26, no. 4 (August 2000), pp. 351–61; and Robert F. Pearse, "Understanding Organizational Power and Influence Systems," *Compensation & Benefits Management* 16, no. 4 (Autumn 2000), pp. 28–38.

14. Shawnee Vickery, Cornelia Droge, and Richard Germain, "The Relationship between Product Customization and Organizational Structure," *Journal of Operations Management* 17, no. 4 (June 1999), pp. 377–91.

15. Joel Spolsky, "How Hard Could It Be? How I Learned to Love Middle Managers," *Inc.,* September 2008, http://www.inc.com.

16. Philippe Jehiel, "Information Aggregation and Communication in Organizations," *Management Science* 45, no. 5 (May 1999), pp. 659–69; and Ahnn Altaffer, "First-Line Managers: Measuring Their Span of Control," *Nursing Management* 29, no. 7 (July 1998), pp. 36–40.

17. "Span of Control vs. Span of Support," *Journal for Quality and Participation* 23, no. 4 (Fall 2000), p. 15; James Gallo and Paul R. Thompson, "Goals, Measures, and Beyond: In Search of Accountability in Federal HRM," *Public Personnel Management* 29, no. 2 (Summer 2000), pp. 237–48; and Clinton O. Longenecker and Timothy C. Stansfield, "Why Plant Managers Fail: Causes and Consequences," *Industrial Management* 42, no. 1 (January/February 2000), pp. 24–32.

18. Zhen Xiong Chen and Samuel Aryee, "Delegation and Employee Work Outcomes: An Examination of the Cultural Context of Mediating Processes in China," *Academy of Management Journal* 50, no. 1 (2007), pp. 226–38.

19. Ilan Brat, "Turning Managers into Takeover Artists," *The Wall Street Journal,* April 6, 2007, http://online.wsj.com.

20. "How to Delegate More Effectively," *Community Banker,* February 2009, p. 14; B. Nefer, "Don't Be Delegation-Phobic," *Supervision,* December 2008, downloaded from Business & Company Resource Center, http://galenet.galegroup.com; J. Mahoney, "Delegating Effectively," *Nursing Management* 28, no. 6 (June 1997), p. 62; and J. Lagges, "The Role of Delegation in Improving Productivity," *Personnel Journal,* November 1979, pp. 776–79.

21. G. Matthews, "Run Your Business or Build an Organization?" *Harvard Management Review* (March–April 1984), pp. 34–44.

22. Nicolaj Siggelkow and Jan W. Rivkin, "When Exploration Backfires: Unintended Consequences of Multi-level Organizational Search," *Academy of Management Proceedings* (2006), pp. BB1–BB6.

23. "More Than a Bicycle: The Leadership Journey at Harley-Davidson," *Harvard Business School Working Knowledge,* September 5, 2000, online; Clyde Fessler, "Rotating Leadership and Harley-Davidson: From Hierarchy to Interdependence," *Strategy & Leadership* 25, no. 4 (July/August 1997), pp. 42–43; and Jeffrey Young and Kenneth L. Murrell, "Harley-Davidson Motor Company Organizational Design: The Road to High Performance," *Organizational Development Journal* 16, no. 1 (Spring 1998), p. 65.

24. Russ Forrester, "Empowerment: Rejuvenating a Potent Idea," *Academy of Management Executive* 14, no. 3 (August 2000), pp. 67–80; and Monica L. Perry, Craig L. Pearce, and Henry P. Sims Jr., "Empowered Selling Teams: How Shared Leadership Can Contribute to Selling Team Outcomes," *Journal of Personal Selling & Sales Management* 19, no. 3 (Summer 1999), pp. 35–51.

25. Larry Gard, "Growth Trifecta," *Construction Today,* January 2009, downloaded from Business & Company Resource Center, http:// galenet.galegroup.com; and Environmental Systems Design, "About ESD," corporate Website, http://www.esdesign.com, accessed May 1, 2009.

26. E. E. Lawler III, "New Roles for the Staff Function: Strategic Support and Services," in *Organizing for the Future,* J. Galbraith, E. E. Lawler III, & Associates (San Francisco: Jossey-Bass, 1993).

27. Rob Cross and Lloyd Baird, "Technology Is Not Enough: Improving Performance by Building Organizational Memory," *Sloan Management Review* 41, no. 3 (Spring 2000), pp. 69–78; and R. Duncan, "What Is the Right Organizational Structure?" *Organizational Dynamics* 7 (Winter 1979), pp. 59–80.

28. George S. Day, "Creating a Market-Driven Organization," *Sloan Management Review* 41, no. 1 (Fall 1999), pp. 11–22.

29. George Strauss and Leonard R. Sayles, *Strauss and Sayles's Behavioral Strategies for Managers,* © 1980, p. 221. Reprinted by permission of Prentice-Hall, Inc., Englewood Cliffs, New Jersey.

30. R. Boehm and C. Phipps, "Flatness Forays," *McKinsey Quarterly* 3 (1996), pp. 128–43.

31. Bruce T. Lamont, V. Sambamurthy, Kimberly M. Ellis, and Paul G. Simmonds, "The Influence of Organizational Structure on the Information Received by Corporate Strategists of Multinational Enterprises," *Management International Review* 40, no. 3 (2000), pp. 231–52.

32. Linda A. Johnson, "Pfizer Planning to Redraw Its Battle Lines," *America's Intelligence Wire,* October 8, 2008, downloaded from Business & Company Resource Center, http://galenet.galegroup .com.

33. Morten T. Hansen, "When Internal Collaboration Is Bad for Your Company," *Harvard Business Review,* April 2009, pp. 83–88.

34. H. Kolodny, "Managing in a Matrix," *Business Horizons,* March–April 1981, pp. 17–24.

35. David Cackowski, Mohammad K. Najdawi, and Q. B. Chung, "Object Analysis in Organizational Design: A Solution for Matrix Organizations," *Project Management Journal* 31, no. 3 (September 2000), pp. 44–51; J. Barker, "Conflict Approaches of Effective and Ineffective Project Managers: A Field Study in a Matrix Organization," *Journal of Management Studies* 25, no. 2 (March 1988), pp. 167–78; G. J. Chambers, "The Individual in a Matrix Organization," *Project Management Journal* 20, no. 4 (December 1989), pp. 37–42, 50; and S. Davis and P. Lawrence, "Problems of Matrix Organizations," *Harvard Business Review,* May–June 1978, pp. 131–42.

36. Anthony Ferner, "Being Local Worldwide: ABB and the Challenge of Global Management Relations," *Industrielles* 55, no. 3 (Summer 2000), pp. 527–29; and C. Bartlett and S. Ghoshal, "Matrix Management: Not a Structure, a Frame of Mind," *Harvard Business Review* 68 (July–August 1990), pp. 138–45.

37. Jasmine Tata, Sameer Prasad, and Ron Thorn, "The Influence of Organizational Structure on the Effectiveness of TQM Programs," *Journal of Managerial Issues* 11, no. 4 (Winter 1999), pp. 440–53; and Davis and Lawrence, "Problems of Matrix Organizations."

38. R. E. Miles and C. C. Snow, *Fit, Failure, and the Hall of Fame* (New York: Free Press, 1994); and Gillian Symon, "Information and Communication Technologies and Network Organization: A Critical Analysis," *Journal of Occupational and Organizational Psychology* 73, no. 4 (December 2000), pp. 389–95.

39. Stephanie Clifford, "How I Did It: Morgan Lynch, CEO, Logoworks," *Inc.,* September 2006, http://www.inc.com.

40. Miles and Snow, *Fit, Failure, and the Hall of Fame.*

41. Sung-Choon Kang, Shad S. Morris, and Scott A. Snell, "Relational Archetypes, Organizational Learning, and Value Creation: Extending the Human Resource Architecture," *Academy of Management Review* 32, no. 1 (2007), pp. 236–56.

42. J. G. March and H. A. Simon, *Organizations* (New York: John Wiley & Sons, 1958); and J. D. Thompson, *Organizations in Action* (New York: McGraw-Hill, 1967).

43. Paul S. Adler, "Building Better Bureaucracies," *Academy of Management Executive* 13, no. 4 (November 1999), pp. 36–49.

44. Don Tapscott, "The Global Plant Floor," *BusinessWeek,* March 20, 2007, http://galenet.galegroup.com.

45. J. Galbraith, "Organization Design: An Information Processing View," *Interfaces* 4 (Fall 1974), pp. 28–36. See also S. A. Mohrman, "Integrating Roles and Structure in the Lateral Organization," in *Organizing for the Future,* ed. J. Galbraith, E. E. Lawler III, and Associates (San Francisco: Jossey-Bass, 1993); and Barbara B. Flynn and F. James Flynn, "Information-Processing Alternatives for Coping with Manufacturing Environment Complexity," *Decision Sciences* 30, no. 4 (Fall 1999), pp. 1021–52.

46. Galbraith, "Organization Design"; and Mohrman, "Integrating Roles and Structure."

47. Vauhini Vara, "After GE," *The Wall Street Journal,* April 12, 2007, http://online.wsj.com.

48. G. Hamel and C. K. Prahalad, "Competing for the Future," *Harvard Business Review,* July–August 1994, pp. 122–28.

49. G. Hamel and C. K. Prahalad, *Competing for the Future* (Boston: Harvard Business School Press, 1994).

50. David G. Sirmon, Michael A. Hitt, and R. Duane Ireland, "Managing Firm Resources in Dynamic Environments to Create Value: Looking inside the Black Box," *Academy of Management Review* 32, no. 1 (2007), pp. 273–92.

51. "Monster, NYT Form Online Jobs Alliance," *Reuters,* February 14, 2007, http://news.yahoo.com.

52. Gene Slowinski, Edward Hummel, Amitabh Gupta, and Ernest R. Gilmont, "Effective Practices for Sourcing Innovation," *Research-Technology Management,* January–February 2009, pp. 27–34.

53. Rachelle C. Sampson, "R&D Alliances and Firm Performance: The Impact of Technological Diversity and Alliance Organization on Innovation," *Academy of Management Journal* 50, no. 2 (2007), pp. 364–86.

54. Adapted and reprinted by permission of *Harvard Business Review.* From R. M. Kanter, "Collaborative Advantage: The Art of Alliances," July–August 1994, pp. 96–108. Copyright © 1994 by the Harvard Business School Publishing Corporation; all rights reserved.

55. Ibid.; John B. Cullen, Jean L. Johnson, and Tomoaki Sakano, "Success through Commitment and Trust: The Soft Side of Strategic Alliance Management," *Journal of World Business* 35, no. 3 (Fall 2000), pp. 223–40; and Prashant Kale, Harbir Singh, and Howard Perlmutter, "Learning and Protection of Proprietary Assets in Strategic Alliances: Building Relational Capital," *Strategic Management Journal* 21, no. 3 (March 2000), pp. 217–37.

56. P. Senge, *The Fifth Discipline* (New York: Doubleday Currency, 1990).

57. D. A. Garvin, "Building a Learning Organization," *Harvard Business Review,* July–August 1993, pp. 78–91; David A. Garvin, *Learning in Action: A Guide to Putting the Learning Organization to Work* (Boston: Harvard Business School Press, 2000); and Victoria J. Marsick and Karen E. Watkins, *Facilitating Learning Organizations: Making Learning Count* (Aldershot, Hampshire: Gower, 1999).

58. Ibid.; and N. Anand, Heidi K. Gardner, and Tim Morris, "Knowledge-Based Innovation: Emergence and Embedding of New Practice Areas in Management Consulting Firms," *Academy of Management Journal* 50, no. 2 (2007), pp. 406–28.

59. Robert J. Vandenberg, Hettie A. Richardson, and Lorrina J. Eastman, "The Impact of High Involvement Work Process on Organizational Effectiveness: A Second-Order Latent Variable Approach," *Group & Organization Management* 24, no. 3 (September 1999), pp. 300–39; Gretchen M. Spreitzer and Aneil K. Mishra, "Giving Up Control without Losing Control: Trust and Its Substitutes' Effects on Managers' Involving Employees in Decision Making," *Group & Organization Management* 24, no. 2 (June 1999), pp. 155–87; and

Susan Albers Mohrman, Gerald E. Ledford, and Edward E. Lawler III, *Strategies for High Performance Organizations—The CEO Report: Employee Involvement, TQM, and Reengineering Programs in Fortune 1000 Corporations* (San Francisco: Jossey-Bass, 1998).

60. Robin Pagnamenta, "Transformation That Could Rescue Unilever from the Slippery Slope," *The Times (London),* January 3, 2007; and "Unilever on Revival Track after Top Managers Culled," *Evening Standard (London),* May 3, 2007, both downloaded from Business & Company Resource Center, http://galenet.galegroup .com.

61. Bonnie Del Conte, "Manufacturing Plant as Classroom: Reinventing Continuous Learning," *Plant Engineering,* March 1, 2009, downloaded from Business & Company Resource Center, http://galenet .galegroup.com.

62. Wayne F. Cascio, "Downsizing: What Do We Know? What Have We Learned?" *Academy of Management Executive* 7 (February 1993), pp. 95–104; and Sarah J. Freeman, "The Gestalt of Organizational Downsizing: Downsizing Strategies as Package of Change," *Human Relations* 52, no. 12 (December 1999), pp. 1505–1541.

63. Ashlee Vance, "Microsoft Slashes Jobs as Sales Fall," *New York Times,* January 23, 2009, http://www.nytimes.com; Ashlee Vance, "Microsoft Profit Falls for First Time in 23 Years," *New York Times,* April 24, 2009, http://www.nytimes.com; and Peter Kafka, "Microsoft Starts the Layoff Machine Again with Thousands of Cuts," *All Things Digital,* May 5, 2009, http://mediamemo.allthingsd.com.

64. Wayne F. Cascio, "Strategies for Responsible Restructuring," *Academy of Management Executive* 19, no. 4 (2005), pp. 39–50; Cascio, "Downsizing"; and Jack Ciancio, "Survivor's Syndrome," *Nursing Management* 31, no. 5 (May 2000), pp. 43–45.

65. Cascio, "Strategies for Responsible Restructuring,"; Cascio, "Downsizing"; Freeman, "The Gestalt of Organizational Downsizing"; and M. Hitt, B. Keats, H. Harback, and R. Nixon, "Rightsizing: Building and Maintaining Strategic Leadership and Long-Term Competitiveness," *Organizational Dynamics,* Fall 1994, pp. 18–31.

66. Bill Creech, *The Five Pillars of TQM: How to Make Total Quality Management Work for You* (New York: Plume Publishing, 1995); and James R. Evans and William M. Lindsay, *Management and Control of Quality* (Cincinnati, OH: Southwestern College Publishing, 1998).

67. International Organization for Standardization, "ISO 9000/ISO 14000: Understand the Basics," http://www.iso.org, accessed May 7, 2007.

68. "UniFirst Manufacturing Facilities Awarded ISO 9001:2000 Certification," *Modern Uniforms,* February–March 2006, downloaded from Business & Company Resource Center, http://galenet .galegroup.com.

69. Joan Woodward, *Industrial Organization: Theory and Practice* (London: Oxford University Press, 1965).

70. James H. Gilmore and B. Joseph Pine, eds., *Markets of One: Creating Customer-Unique Value through Mass Customization* (Cambridge, MA: Harvard Business Review Press, 2000); and B. Joseph Pine, *Mass Customization: The New Frontier in Business Competition* (Cambridge, MA: Harvard Business School Press, 1992).

71. Funda Sahin, "Manufacturing Competitiveness: Different Systems to Achieve the Same Results," *Production and Inventory Management Journal* 41, no. 1 (First Quarter 2000), pp. 56–65.

72. Subhash Wadhwa and K. Srinivasa Rao, "Flexibility: An Emerging Meta-Competence for Managing High Technology," *International Journal of Technology Management* 19, no. 7–8 (2000), pp. 820–45.

73. Brett A. Peters and Leon F. McGinnis, "Strategic Configuration of Flexible Assembly Systems: A Single Period Approximation," *IIE Transaction* 31, no. 4 (April 1999), pp. 379–90.

74. Jeffrey K. Liker and James M. Morgan, "The Toyota Way in Services: The Case of Lean Product Development," *Academy of Management Perspectives* 20, no. 2 (May 2006), pp. 5–20; "Strategic Reconfiguration: Manufacturing's Key Role in Innovation," *Production and Inventory Management Journal,* Summer–Fall 2001, pp. 9–17; Stephen R. Morrey, "Learning to Think Lean: A Roadmap and Toolbox for the Lean Journey," *Automotive Manufacturing & Production* 112, no. 8 (August 2000), p. 147; and Funda Sahin, "Manufacturing Competitiveness: Different Systems to Achieve the Same Results," *Production and Inventory Management Journal* 41, no. 1 (First Quarter 2000), pp. 56–65.

75. Liker and Morgan, "The Toyota Way in Services"; and Hanah Cho, "Squeezing the Fat from Health Care," *Baltimore Sun,* September 17, 2006, downloaded from Business & Company Resource Center, http://galenet.galegroup.com.

76. Sahin, "Manufacturing Competitiveness"; and Gary S. Vasilash, "Flexible Thinking: How Need, Innovation, Teamwork & a Whole Bunch of Machining Centers Have Transformed TRW Tillsonburg into a Model of Lean Manufacturing," *Automotive Manufacturing & Production* 111, no. 10 (October 1999), pp. 64–65.

77. Chen H. Chung, "Balancing the Two Dimensions of Time for Time-Based Competition," *Journal of Managerial Issues* 11, no. 3 (Fall 1999), pp. 299–314; and Denis R. Towill and Peter McCullen, "The Impact of Agile Manufacturing on Supply Chain Dynamics," *International Journal of Logistics Management* 10, no. 1 (1999), pp. 83–96. See also George Stalk and Thomas M. Hout, *Competing against Time: How Time-Based Competition Is Reshaping Global Markets* (New York: Free Press, 1990).

78. M. Tucker and D. Davis, "Key Ingredients for Successful Implementation of Just-in-Time: A System for All Business Sizes," *Business Horizons,* May–June 1993, pp. 59–65; and Helen L. Richardson, "Tame Supply Chain Bottlenecks," *Transportation & Distribution* 41, no. 3 (March 2000), pp. 23–28.

79. See, for example, "Just-in-Time: Has Its Time Passed?" *Baseline,* September 11, 2006, downloaded from Business & Company Resource Center, http://galenet.galegroup.com.

80. John E. Ettlie, "Product Development—Beyond Simultaneous Engineering," *Automotive Manufacturing & Production* 112, no. 7 (July 2000), p. 18; Utpal Roy, John M. Usher, and Hamid R. Parsaei, eds. *Simultaneous Engineering: Methodologies and Applications* (Newark, NJ: Gordon and Breach, 1999); and Marilyn M. Helms and Lawrence P. Ettkin, "Time-Based Competitiveness: A Strategic Perspective," *Competitiveness Review* 10, no. 2 (2000), pp. 1–14.

81. Jeff Zygmont, "Detroit Faster on Its Feet," *Ward's Auto World,* July 1, 2006, downloaded from Business & Company Resource Center, http://galenet.galegroup.com.

Chapter 7

1. Company Web site, http://www.erac.com, accessed November 7, 2008; Enterprise Rent-A-Car, "Enterprise Rent-A-Car's Pam Nicholson Named to *Fortune*'s 50 Most Powerful Women in Business 2008," news release, September 29, 2008; "Breaking Barriers: Enterprise Rent-A-Car's Pam Nicholson," *The Wall Street Journal,* August 4, 2008, http://www.wsj.com; Alison Stein Wellner, "Nothing but Green Skies," *Inc.,* November 2007, http://www.inc .com; "Mentoring Is a Mission at Enterprise Rent-A-Car," *Diversity in Action,* April/May 2007, http://www.diversitycareers.com.

2. "HR's Impact on Shareholder Value," *Workforce Management,* December 11, 2006, downloaded from Business & Company Resource Center, http://galenet.galegroup.com.

3. Patrick M. Wright and Scott A. Snell, "Partner or Guardian? HR's Challenge in Balancing Value and Values," *Human Resource Management* 44, no. 2 (2005), pp. 177–82.

4. Elaine Pofeldt, "Empty Desk Syndrome: How to Handle a Hiring Freeze," *Inc.,* May 2008, pp. 39–40; and Cari Tuna, "Some Employers See Hiring Opportunity," *The Wall Street Journal,* April 3, 2009, http://online.wsj.com.

5. Peter Coy and Jack Ewing, "Where Are All the Workers?" *Business-Week,* April 9, 2007, http://www.businessweek.com.

6. Jim Hopkins, "Small Employers Struggle to Fill Jobs," *USA Today,* January 4, 2007, http://www.usatoday.com; "Most Employers Unprepared for Baby Boomer Retirements," *CCH Pension,* November 9, 2006, http://hr.cch.com; and David Ellwood, *Grow Faster Together, or Grow Slowly Apart* (Washington, DC: Aspen Institute, 2003), http://www.aspeninstitute.org.

7. Jessica Marquez, "Retrained and Ready," *Workforce Management,* May 7, 2007, http://galenet.galegroup.com.

8. Darin E. Hartley, *Job Analysis at the Speed of Reality* (Amherst, MA: HRD Press, 1999); Frederick P. Morgeson and Michael A. Campion, "Accuracy in Job Analysis: Toward an Inference-Based Model," *Journal of Organizational Behavior* 21, no. 7 (November 2000), pp. 819–27; and Jeffery S. Shippmann, Ronald A. Ash, Linda Carr, and Beryl Hesketh, "The Practice of Competency Modeling," *Personnel Psychology* 53, no. 3 (Autumn 2000), pp. 703–40.

9. Jeffery S. Schippmann, *Strategic Job Modeling: Working at the Core of Integrated Human Resources* (Mahwah, NJ: Lawrence Erlbaum Associates, 1999).

10. David E. Terpstra, "The Search for Effective Methods," *HR Focus,* May 1996, pp. 16–17; Herbert G. Heneman III and Robyn A. Berkley, "Applicant Attraction Practices and Outcomes among Small Businesses," *Journal of Small Business Management* 37, no. 1 (January 1999), pp. 53–74; and Jean-Marie Hiltrop, "The Quest for the Best: Human Resource Practices to Attract and Retain Talent," *European Management Journal* 17, no. 4 (August 1999), pp. 422–30.

11. Gina Ruiz, "Print Ads See Resurgence as Hiring Source," *Workforce Management,* March 26, 2007; and Gina Ruiz, "Recruiters Cite Referrals as Top Hiring Tool," *Workforce Management,* October 23, 2006, both downloaded from General Reference Center Gold, http://find.galegroup.com.

12. Fay Hansen, "Employee Referral Programs, Selective Campus Recruitment Could Touch Off Bias Charges," *Workforce Management,* June 26, 2006, downloaded from General Reference Center Gold, http://find.galegroup.com.

13. Ruiz, "Recruiters Cite Referrals," reporting data from a survey by ERE Media and Classified Intelligence.

14. Patricia Sellers, "Schooling Corporate Giants in Recruiting," *Fortune,* December 6, 2006, http://money.cnn.com.

15. Randy Myers, "Interviewing Techniques: Tips from the Pros," *Journal of Accountancy,* August 2006, downloaded from Business & Company Resource Center, http://galenet.galegroup.com; Michael McDaniel, Deborah L. Whetzel, Frank L. Schmidt, and Steven D. Maurer, "The Validity of Employment Interviews: A Comprehensive Review and Meta-Analysis," *Journal of Applied Psychology* 79, no. 4 (August 1994), pp. 599–616; Michael A. Campion, James E. Campion, and Peter J. Hudson Jr., "Structured Interviewing: A Note on Incremental Validity and Alternative Question Types," *Journal of Applied Psychology* 79, no. 6 (December 1994), pp. 998–1002; and R. A. Fear, *The Evaluation Interview* (New York: McGraw-Hill, 1984).

16. Myers, "Interviewing Techniques."

17. U.S. Merit Systems Protection Board, "The Federal Selection Interview: Unrealized Potential," February 2003, mspb.gov/studies/interview.htm.

18. Tamar Lewin, "Dean at M.I.T. Resigns, Ending a 28-Year Lie," *New York Times,* April 27, 2007, http://www.nytimes.com.

19. Christopher E. Stenberg, "The Role of Pre-Employment Background Investigations in Hiring," *Human Resource Professional* 9, no. 1 (January/February 1996), pp. 19–21; Paul Taylor, "Providing Structure to Interviews and Reference Checks," *Workforce,* May 1999, Supplement, pp. 7–10; "Fear of Lawsuits Complicates Reference Checks," *InfoWorld* 21, no. 5 (February 1, 1999), p. 73; and David E. Terpstra, R. Bryan Kethley, Richard T. Foley, and Wanthanee Limpaphayom, "The Nature of Litigation Surrounding Five Screening Devices," *Public Personnel Management* 29, no. 1 (Spring 2000), pp. 43–54.

20. Carolyn Bigda, "Web Widens Job-Search Connections," *Chicago Tribune,* March 4, 2007, http://www.chicagotribune.com.

21. See also M. R. Barrick and M. K. Mount, "The Big Five Personality Dimensions and Job Performance: A Meta-Analysis," *Personnel Psychology* 44 (1991), pp. 1–26; Daniel P. O'Meara, "Personality Tests Raise Questions of Legality and Effectiveness," *HRMagazine,* January 1994, pp. 97–100; and Lynn A. McFarland and Ann Marie Ryan, "Variance in Faking across Noncognitive Measures," *Journal of Applied Psychology* 85, no. 5 (October 2000), pp. 812–21.

22. Robert E. Ployhart, Jeff A. Weekley, and Kathryn Baughman, "The Structure and Function of Human Capital Emergence: A Multilevel Examination of the Attraction-Selection-Attrition Model," *Academy of Management Journal* 49, no. 4 (2006), pp. 661–77.

23. Patrick M. Wright, Michele K. Kacmar, Gary C. McMahan, and Kevin Deleeuw, "$P = f(M \times A)$: Cognitive Ability as a Moderator of the Relationship between Personality and Job Performance," *Journal of Management* 21, no. 6 (1995), pp. 1129–2063; Paul R. Sackett and Daniel J. Ostgaard, "Job-Specific Applicant Pools and National Norms for Cognitive Ability Tests: Implications for Range Restriction Corrections in Validation Research," *Journal of Applied Psychology* 79, no. 5 (October 1994), pp. 680–84; F. L. Schmidt and J. E. Hunter, "Tacit Knowledge, Practical Intelligence, General Mental Ability, and Job Knowledge," *Current Directions in Psychological Science* 2, no. 1 (1993), pp. 3–13; Mary Roznowski, David N. Dickter, Linda L. Sawin, Valerie J. Shute, and Sehee Hong, "The Validity of Measures of Cognitive Processes and Generability for Learning and Performance on Highly Complex Computerized Tutors: Is the G Factor of Intelligence Even More General?" *Journal of Applied Psychology* 85, no. 6 (December 2000), pp. 940–55; and Jose M. Cortina, Nancy B. Goldstein, Stephanie C. Payne, H. Krisl Davison, and Stephen W. Gilliland, "The Incremental Validity of Interview Scores over and above Cognitive Ability and Conscientiousness Scores," *Personnel Psychology* 53, no. 2 (Summer 2000), pp. 325–51.

24. Winfred Arthur Jr., David J. Woehr, and Robyn Maldegen, "Convergent and Discriminant Validity of Assessment Center Dimensions: A Conceptual and Empirical Reexamination of the Assessment Center Construct-Related Validity Paradox," *Journal of Management* 26, no. 4 (2000), pp. 813–35; and Raymond Randall, Eammon Ferguson, and Fiona Patterson, "Self-Assessment Accuracy and Assessment Center Decisions," *Journal of Occupational and Organizational Psychology* 73, no. 4 (December 2000), p. 443.

25. Lynn A. McFarland and Ann Marie Ryan, "Variance in Faking across Noncognitive Measures," *Journal of Applied Psychology* 85, no. 5 (October 2000), pp. 812–21; Terpstra et al., "The Nature of Litigation Surrounding Five Screening Devices."

26. D. S. Ones, C. Viswesvaran, and F. L. Schmidt, "Comprehensive Meta-Analysis of Integrity Test Validities: Findings and Implications for Personnel Selection and Theories of Job Performance," *Journal of Applied Psychology* 78 (August 1993), pp. 679–703.

27. Rocki-Lee DeWitt, "The Structural Consequences of Downsizing," *Organization Science* 4, no. 1 (February 1993), pp. 30–40; and Priti Pradhan Shah, "Network Destruction: The Structural Implications of Downsizing," *Academy of Management Journal* 43, no. 1 (February 2000), pp. 101–12.

28. See *Adair v. United States,* 2078 U.S. 161 (1908); and Deborah A. Ballam, "Employment-at-Will; The Impending Death of a Doctrine," *American Business Law Journal* 37, no. 4 (Summer 2000), pp. 653–87.

29. Paul Falcone, "Employee Separations: Layoffs vs. Terminations for Cause," *HRMagazine* 45, no. 10 (October 2000), pp. 189–96; and Paul Falcone, "A Blueprint for Progressive Discipline and Terminations," *HR Focus* 77, no. 8 (August 2000), pp. 3–5.

30. "James W. Bucking, "Employee Terminations: Ten Must-Do Steps When Letting Someone Go," *Supervision,* May 2008, downloaded from Business & Company Resource Center, http://galenet.galegroup.com; and Marie Price, "Employee Termination Process Is Tough for Those on Both Sides," *Journal Record* (Oklahoma City, OK), October 23, 2008, downloaded from Business & Company Resource Center, http://galenet.galegroup.com. Bullet points taken from S. Alexander, "Firms Get Plenty of Practice at Layoffs, but They Often Bungle the Firing Process," *The Wall Street Journal,* November 14, 1991, p. 31. Copyright © 1991 Dow Jones & Co., Inc. Reproduced with permission of Dow Jones & Co., Inc. via Copyright Clearance Center.

31. *Employer EEO Responsibilities* (Washington, DC: Equal Employment Opportunity Commission, U.S. Government Printing Office, 1996); and Nancy J. Edman and Michael D. Levin-Epstein, *Primer of Equal Employment Opportunity,* 6th ed. (Washington, DC: Bureau of National Affairs, 1994).

32. Robert Gatewood and Hubert Field, *Human Resource Selection,* 3rd ed. (Chicago: Dryden Press, 1994), pp. 36–49; and R. A. Baysinger, "Disparate Treatment and Disparate Impact Theories of Discrimination: The Continuing Evolution of Title VII of the 1964 Civil Rights Act," in *Readings in Personnel and Human Resource Management,* ed. R. S. Schuler, S. A. Youngblood, and V. L. Huber (St. Paul, MN: West Publishing, 1987).

33. "$56 Billion Budgeted for Formal Training," *Training,* December 2006, downloaded from General Reference Center Gold, http://find.galegroup.com.

34. George Anders, "Companies Find Online Training Has Its Limits," *The Wall Street Journal,* March 26, 2007, http://online.wsj.com.

35. Ibid.

36. Jack Gordon, "Building Brand Champions: How Training Helps Drive a Core Business Process at General Mills," *Training,* January–February 2007, downloaded from General Reference Center Gold, http://find.galegroup.com.

37. Phred Dvorak, "Simulation Shows What It's Like to Be Boss," *The Wall Street Journal,* March 31, 2008, http://online.wsj.com.

38. For more information, see Kenneth Wexley and Gary Latham, *Increasing Productivity through Performance Appraisal* (Reading, MA: Addison-Wesley, 1994).

39. Ginka Toegel and Jay Conger, "360 Degree Assessment: Time for Reinvention," *Academy of Management Learning and Education* 2, no. 3 (September 2003), p. 297; and Lauren Keller Johnson, "Retooling 360s for Better Performance," *Harvard Business School Working Knowledge,* February 23, 2004, online.

40. Mark Edwards and Ann J. Ewen, "How to Manage Performance and Pay with 360-Degree Feedback," *Compensation and Benefits Review* 28, no. 3 (May/June 1996), pp. 41–46. See also Mary N. Vinson, "The Pros and Cons of 360-Degree Feedback: Making It Work," *Training and Development* 50, no. 4 (April 1996), pp. 11–12; and R. S. Schuler, *Personnel and Human Resource Management* (St. Paul, MN: West Publishing, 1984).

41. Perri Capell, "When an Employee is a Problem Drinker," *Career Journal,* December 5, 2006, http;//www.careerjournal.com.

42. Carol Hymowitz, "Bosses Have to Learn How to Confront Troubled Employees," *The Wall Street Journal,* April 23, 2007, http://online.wsj.com.

43. George Bohlander, Scott Snell, and Arthur Sherman, *Managing Human Resources,* 12th ed. (Cincinnati, OH: South-Western, 2001).

44. Damon Darlin, "Using the Web to Get the Boss to Pay More," *New York Times,* March 3, 2007, http://www.nytimes.com.

45. Adrienne Colella, Ramona L. Paetzold, Asghar Zardkoohi, and Michael J. Wesson, "Exposing Pay Secrecy," *Academy of Management Review* 32, no. 1 (2007), pp. 55–71.

46. Garry M. Ritzky, "Incentive Pay Programs That Help the Bottom Line," *HRMagazine* 40, no. 4 (April 1995), pp. 68–74; Steven Gross and Jeffrey Bacher, "The New Variable Pay Programs: How Some Succeed, Why Some Don't," *Compensation and Benefits Review* 25, no. 1 (January–February 1993), p. 51; and G. T. Milkovich and J. M. Newman, *Compensation* (New York: McGraw-Hill/Irwin, 1999).

47. Kris Maher and Kris Hudson, "Wal-Mart to Sweeten Bonus Plans for Staff," *The Wall Street Journal,* March 22, 2007, http://online.wsj.com.

48. Theresa Welbourne and Luis Gomez-Mejia, "Gainsharing: A Critical Review and a Future Research Agenda," *Journal of Management* 21, no. 3 (1995), pp. 559–609; Luis P. Gomez-Mejia, Theresa M. Welbourne, and Robert M. Wiseman, "The Role of Risk Sharing and Risk Taking under Gainsharing," *Academy of Management Review* 25, no. 3 (July 2000), pp. 492–507; Denis Collins, *Gainsharing and Power: Lessons from Six Scanlon Plans* (Ithaca, NY: ILR Press, 1998); and P. K. Zingheim and J. R. Schuster, *Pay People Right!* (San Francisco: Jossey-Bass, 2000).

49. "Top Entry Level Employers," *CollegeGrad.com,* accessed November 7, 2008, http://www.collegegrad.com; David LaGesse, "A 'Stealth Company' No Longer," *U.S. News & World Report,* October 27, 2008, http://www.usnews.com; Patricia Sellers, "A Powerful Woman Revs Ahead at Enterprise," *Fortune,* August 4, 2008, http://www.fortune.com; Lindsey Edmonds Wickman, "Enterprise Rent-A-Car: Ahead of the Curve with Personalized Recruitment," *Talent Management* [no date], http://www.talentmgt.com; "Mentoring Is a Mission."

50. Edie Grossfield, "Superintendent Gets a Good Review and Partial Bonus," *Post-Bulletin* (Rochester, MN), July 13, 2006, downloaded from Business & Company Resource Center, http://galenet.galegroup.com. See also D. W. Meyers, *Human Management: Principles and Practice* (Chicago: Commerce Clearing House, 1986); and James P. Guthrie, "Alternative Pay Practices and Employee Turnover: An Organization Economics Perspective," *Group & Organization Management* 25, no. 4 (December 2000), pp. 419–39.

51. Rik Kirkland, "The Real CEO Pay Problem," *Fortune,* July 10, 2006, downloaded from Business & Company Resource Center, http://galenet.galegroup.com; Kevin Drawbaugh, "Soaring Executive Pay Meets Reforms," *Reuters,* March 9, 2007, http://news.yahoo.com; Robert Watts and Dan Roberts, "FTSE Pay Spirals out of Control," *Sunday Telegraph (London),* September 24, 2006, http://galenet.galegroup.com; "Study: Australian Execs Outstrip Workers," *UPI NewsTrack,* January 28, 2006, http://galenet. galegroup.com; and Martin Fackler and David Barboza, "In Asia, Executives Earn Much Less," *New York Times,* June 16, 2006, http://galenet.galegroup.com.

52. Martin J. Conyon, "Executive Compensation and Incentives," *Academy of Management Perspectives* 20, no. 1 (February 2006), pp. 25–44.

53. Ibid.

54. Jonathan D. Glater, "Stock Options Are Adjusted after Many Share Prices Fall," *New York Times,* March 27, 2009, http://www.nytimes.com; and David Nicklaus, "Worthless Options Worry Companies," *St. Louis Post-Dispatch,* April 3, 2009, downloaded from Business & Company Resource Center, http://galenet.galegroup.com.

55. U.S. Census Bureau, *Statistical Abstract of the United States,* 2007, p. 418; and Bureau of Labor Statistics, *Charting the U.S. Labor Market in 2005,* June 2006, http://www.bls.gov.

56. Alan Murray, "Why Taxpayers Should Take Note of Chrysler Deal," *The Wall Street Journal,* May 16, 2007, http://online.wsj.com; and Kathleen Kingsbury, "Pressure on Your Health Benefits," *Time,* November 6, 2006, downloaded from Business & Company Resource Center, http://galenet.galegroup.com.

57. Dennis Cauchon, "Pension Gap Divides Public and Private Workers," *USA Today,* February 21, 2007, http://www.usatoday.com.

58. Employee Benefit Research Institute, "Employer Spending on Health Insurance," in *EBRI Databook on Employee Benefits,* updated March 2009, http://www.ebri.org.

59. Ellen C. Kearns and Monica Gallagher, eds., *The Fair Labor Standards Act* (Washington, DC: Bureau of National Affairs, 1999).

60. Charles Fay and Howard W. Risher, "Contractors, Comparable Worth and the New OFCCP: Deja Vu and More," *Compensation and Benefits Review* 32, no. 5 (September/October 2000), pp. 23–33; and Gillian Flynn, "Protect Yourself from an Equal-Pay Audit," *Workforce* 78, no. 6 (June 1999), pp. 144–46.

61. Bohlander et al., *Managing Human Resources.*

62. Eileen Henry, "Wage-Bias Bill: Study Panel Proposed," *Arizona Business Gazette,* February 28, 2002, pp. 2–4; and Susan E. Gardner and Christopher Daniel, "Implementing Comparable Worth/Pay Equity: Experiences of Cutting-Edge States," *Public Personnel Management* 27, no. 4 (Winter 1998), pp. 475–89.

63. Pat Wingert and Arian Campo-Flores, "A Dark Place," *Newsweek,* January 16, 2006; and Alison Young, "Mining Regulators to Increase Fines for Safety Violations," *Knight Ridder Washington Bureau,* February 16, 2006, both downloaded from General Reference Center Gold, http://find.galegroup.com.

64. Mine Safety and Health Administration, "MSHA Fatality Statistics," http://www.msha.gov, accessed May 15, 2007.

65. "U.S. Teens Work Late, Long and in Danger, Study," *Reuters,* March 5, 2007, http://news.yahoo.com; and Carla K. Johnson, "Teens Tell about On-the-Job Dangers," *Chicago Tribune,* March 5, 2007, http://www.chicagotribune.com.

66. Linda Kahn, *Primer of Labor Relations,* 25th ed. (Washington, DC: Bureau of National Affairs Books, 1994); and A. Sloane and F. Witney, *Labor Relations* (Englewood Cliffs, NJ: Prentice Hall, 1985).

67. S. Premack and J. E. Hunter; "Individual Unionization Decisions," *Psychological Bulletin* 103 (1988), pp. 223–34; Leo Troy, *Beyond Unions and Collective Bargaining* (Armonk, NY: M. E. Sharpe, 1999); and John A. McClendon, "Members and Nonmembers: Determinants of Dues-Paying Membership in a Bargaining Unit," *Relations Industrielles* 55, no. 2 (Spring 2000), pp. 332–47.

68. Robert Sinclair and Lois Tetrick, "Social Exchange and Union Commitment: A Comparison of Union Instrumentality and Union Support Perceptions," *Journal of Organizational Behavior* 16, no. 6 (November 1995), pp. 669–79. See also Premack and Hunter, "Individual Unionization Decisions."

69. David Lewin and Richard B. Peterson, *The Modern Grievance Procedure in the United States* (Westport, CT: Quorum Books, 1998).

70. George Bohlander and Donna Blancero, "A Study of Reversal Determinants in Discipline and Discharge Arbitration Awards: The Impact of Just Cause Standards," *Labor Studies Journal* 21, no. 3 (Fall 1996), pp. 3–18.

Chapter 8

1. "No. 4: Marriott International," *DiversityInc.,* April 8, 2009, http://www.diversityinc.com; Company Web site, http://www.marriott.com, accessed January 7, 2009; Peter Haapaniemi, "Diversity Goes Global," *Capital Thinking,* Fall 2008, http://www.capitalthinkingmagazine.com; and Gillian Gaynair, "Marriott International Forms Diversity Position," *Washington Business Journal,* January 15, 2008, http://www.washington.bizjournals.com.

2. Bonnie Eisenberg and Mary Ruthsdotter, "Living the Legacy: The Women's Rights Movement 1848–1998," National Women's History Project, http://www.legacy98.org/move-hist.html.

3. Ibid.; and Bureau of Labor Statistics, "Labor Force Statistics from the Current Population Survey," http://www.bls.gov/cps, accessed May 18, 2007.

4. Bureau of Labor Statistics, "Household Data: Annual Averages," *Labor Force Statistics from the Current Population Survey,* last modified April 3, 2009, http://www.bls.gov/cps/demographics.htm; and Bureau of Labor Statistics, *Women in the Labor Force: A Databook,* Report 1011, December 2008, http://www.bls.gov/cps/wlf-databook-2008.pdf.

5. Carol Hymowitz, "Bend without Breaking: Women Executives Discuss the Art of Flex Schedules," *The Wall Street Journal,* March 6, 2007, http://online.wsj.com.

6. Bureau of Labor Statistics, *Charting the U.S. Labor Market in 2005* (Washington, DC: U.S. Department of Labor, June 2006), http://www.bls.gov; and Ellen Simon, "Women Make Less One Year after College," *Associated Press,* April 23, 2007, http://news.yahoo.com.

7. Carol Hymowitz, "The 50 Women to Watch," *The Wall Street Journal,* November 20, 2006, http://online.wsj.com; and Jenny Mero, "*Fortune* 500 Women CEOs," *Fortune,* April 30, 2007, http://money.cnn.com.

8. "50 Most Powerful Women in Business," *Fortune,* October 13, 2008, Rankings section, http://money.cnn.com/magazines/fortune.

9. C. Helfat, D. Harris, and P. Wolfson, "The Pipeline to the Top: Women and Men in the Top Executive Ranks of U.S. Corporations,"

Academy of Management Perspectives (November 2006), pp. 42–64.

10. Christine Larsen, "Top Companies 2007: Meet the Top Companies," National Association of Female Executives, http://www.nafe.com, accessed May 17, 2007.

11. Stephanie Armour, "Companies Try to Educate Teen Workers about Harassment," *USA Today,* October 19, 2006, http://www. usatoday .com.

12. George Bohlander, Scott Snell, and Arthur Sherman, *Managing Human Resources,* 12th ed. (Cincinnati, OH: South-Western Publishing, 2001) Copyright © 2001. Reprinted by permission of South-Western, a division of Thomson Learning, http://www. thomsonrights.com.

13. Bohlander et al., *Managing Human Resources;* and William Petrocelli and Barbara Kate Repa, *Sexual Harassment on the Job: What It Is and How to Stop It* (Berkeley, CA: Nolo Press, 1998).

14. Bureau of Labor Statistics, "Labor Force Characteristics of Foreign-Born Workers Summary," news release, April 25, 2007, http://www.bls.gov; and Jennifer Lee and Frank D. Bean, "America's Changing Color Lines," *Annual Review of Sociology,* 2004, pp. 221–43.

15. "The United States of Entrepreneurs," *The Economist,* March 14, 2009, accessed at http://www.kauffman.org.

16. Bureau of Labor Statistics, "Labor Force Statistics from the Current Population Survey," ftp://ftp.bls.gov, accessed May 21, 2007; and BLS, *Charting the U.S. Labor Market,* chart 4-7.

17. Marianne Bertrand and Sendhill Mullainathan, "Are Emily and Greg More Employable than Lakisha and Jamal?" NBER Working Paper No. 9873, July 2003, http://www.nber.org.

18. For these and other examples, see Sonia Alleyne, "The 40 Best Companies for Diversity," *Black Enterprise,* July 2006, downloaded from Business & Company Resource Center, http://galenet .galegroup.com; Nicole Voges, "Diversity in the Executive Suite," *Modern Healthcare,* April 10, 2006, http://galenet.galegroup.com; and National Association of Minority Media Executives, "Board of Directors," NAMME Web site, http://www.namme.org, accessed May 21, 2007.

19. "The 2009 DiversityInc Top 50 Companies for Diversity," Copyright © 2009, DiversityInc.com.

20. M. P. McQueen, "Workplace Disabilities Are on the Rise," *The Wall Street Journal,* May 1, 2007, http://online.wsj.com.

21. Census Bureau, "Facts for Features: Americans with Disabilities Act, July 26," news release, July 19, 2006, http://www.census.gov.

22. Equal Employment Opportunity Commission (EEOC), "Disability Discrimination," http://www.eeoc.gov, accessed May 12, 2009; EEOC, "Notice Concerning the Americans with Disabilities Act (ADA) Amendments Act of 2008," last modified March 10, 2009, http://www.eeoc.gov; and EEOC, "ADA Charge Data by Impairments/Bases: Resolutions, FY1997–FY2008," last modified March 11, 2009, http://www.eeoc.gov.

23. Bureau of Labor Statistics, *Charting the U.S. Labor Market in 2006,* last modified September 28, 2007, http://www.bls.gov/ cps/labor2006/; and Bureau of Labor Statistics, "Labor Force Characteristics of Foreign-Born Workers Summary," news release, April 25, 2007, http://www.bls.gov.

24. Nadira A. Hira, "Attracting the Twentysomething Worker," *Fortune,* May 15, 2007, http://money.cnn.com.

25. Thomas Hoffman, "Eight New Ways to Target Top Talent in '08," *Computerworld,* January 28, 2008, pp. 34, 36; and Alex Kingsbury,

"The CIA and NSA Want You to Be Their Friend on Facebook," *U.S. News & World Report Online,* February 5, 2009, downloaded from Business & Company Resource Center, http://galenet.galegroup .com.

26. Bill O. Driscoll, "Local Businesses Urged to Build Loyalty, Mentors," *Reno Gazette-Journal,* February 7, 2007, http://news .rgj.com.

27. Bureau of Labor Statistics, "BLS Releases 2004–14 Employment Projections," news release, December 7, 2005, http://www.bls .gov.

28. Census Bureau, "Minority Population Tops 100 Million," news release, May 17, 2007, http://www.census.gov.

29. Bureau of Labor Statistics, "Employment Projections: 2006–16," news release, December 4, 2007, http://www.bls.gov.

30. Census Bureau, *Statistical Abstract of the United States: 2007,* table 574, p. 373; and AARP, "Workforce Trends," Money and Work pages of AARP Web site, http://www.aarp.org, accessed May 21, 2007.

31. Driscoll, "Local Businesses Urged to Build Loyalty, Mentors."

32. Libby Tucker, "Portland Local and Oregon State Organizations Have Instituted Affirmative Action Programs," *Daily Journal of Commerce, Portland,* January 23, 2006, downloaded from Business & Company Resource Center, http://galenet.galegroup .com.

33. Kenneth Labich, "No More Crude at Texaco," *Fortune,* September 6, 1999, pp. 205–12; *Good for Business: Making Full Use of the Nation's Human Capital* (Washington, DC: Federal Glass Ceiling Commission, 1995); and Kimberly Weisul, "The Bottom Line on Women at the Top," *BusinessWeek,* January 26, 2004, http://www. businessweek.com.

34. Lisa Belkin, "Diversity Isn't Rocket Science, Is It?" *New York Times,* May 15, 2008, http://www.nytimes.com; Tara Weiss, "Science and the Glass Ceiling," *Forbes,* May 12, 2008, http://www. forbes.com; and Center for Work-Life Policy, "The Athena Factor: Reversing the Brain Drain in Science, Engineering, and Technology," news release, May 21, 2008, http://www.worklifepolicy .org.

35. N. Adler, *International Dimensions of Organizational Behavior,* 3rd ed. (Boston: PWS-Kent, 1997); and T. Cox and S. Blake, "Managing Cultural Diversity: Implications for Organizational Competitiveness," *Academy of Management Executive* 5 (August 1991), pp. 45–56.

36. Christine Larsen, "Top Companies 2007: Meet the Top Companies," National Association of Female Executives, http://www.nafe.com, accessed May 17, 2007; and Alleyne, "The 40 Best Companies for Diversity."

37. See, for example, Sarah Jane Tribble, "Cisco Accused of Bias in Hiring," *San Jose Mercury News,* May 10, 2007, http://www. mercurynews.com; Gail Appleson, "Baby Boomers, Often Targeted in Layoffs, Fight Age Discrimination," *St. Louis Post-Dispatch,* April 29, 2007, downloaded from Business & Company Resource Center, http://galenet.galegroup.com; "Class Action Suits in the Workplace Are on the Rise," *HR Focus,* April 2007, http://galenet.galegroup .com; and Mark Schoeff Jr., "Walgreen Suit Reflects EEOC's Latest Strategies," *Workforce Management,* March 26, 2007, http:// galenet.galegroup.com.

38. R. Roosevelt Thomas Jr., "From Affirmative Action to Affirming Diversity," *Harvard Business Review,* March–April 1990.

39. Kara Jesella, "Mom's Mad, and She's Organized," *New York Times,* February 22, 2007, http://www.nytimes.com.

40. George Avalos, "Study Looks at Diversity, Turnover," *Contra Costa Times (Walnut Creek, CA)*, October 13, 2006, downloaded from Business & Company Resource Center, http://galenet.galegroup.com.

41. Adler, *International Dimensions of Organizational Behavior;* and Cox and Blake, "Managing Cultural Diversity."

42. J. D. Nordell, "Positions of Power: How Female Ambition Is Shaped," *Slate,* November 21, 2006, http://www.slate.com.

43. Adler, *International Dimensions of Organizational Behavior.*

44. Karen A. Jehn, "Workplace Diversity, Conflict, and Productivity: Managing in the 21st Century," SEI Center for Advanced Studies in Management, Wharton School, University of Pennsylvania, *Diversity,* http://mktg-sun.wharton.upenn.edu/SEI/diversity.html.

45. Audrey J. Murrell, Faye J. Crosby, and Robin J. Ely, *Mentoring Dilemmas: Developmental Relationships within Multicultural Organizations* (Mahwah, NJ: Lawrence Erlbaum Associates, 1999). See a review of this book by Mark L. Lengnick-Hall, "Mentoring Dilemmas: Developmental Relationships within Multicultural Organizations," *Personnel Psychology* 53, no. 1 (Spring 2000), pp. 224–27.

46. Alexandra Kalev, Frank Dobbin, and Erin Kelly, "Best Practices or Best Guesses? Assessing the Efficacy of Corporate Affirmative Action and Diversity Policies," *American Sociological Review* 71 (2006), pp. 589–617.

47. Travis Reed, "NBA Has the Most Diverse Workforce," *Associated Press,* May 9, 2007, http://news.yahoo.com.

48. Robert Rodriguez, "Diversity Finds Its Place," *HRMagazine,* August 2006, downloaded from Business & Company Resource Center, http://galenet.galegroup.com.

49. Monica Yant Kinney, "Firm Makes a Case for Loyalty," *Philadelphia Inquirer,* April 5, 2009, downloaded from Business & Company Resource Center, http://galenet.galegroup.com; Robert Hightower, "Law Firm to Celebrate Employee's 50-Year Mark," *Philadelphia Tribune,* April 9, 2009, http://www.phillytrib.com; Caesar, Rivise, Bernstein, Cohen & Pokotilow, "About Us," http://www.crbcp.com, accessed May 12, 2009; Drexel University, "Drexel at a Glance," http://www.drexel.edu, accessed May 12, 2009; and Drexel University Earle Mack School of Law, "Diversity Initiatives," http://www.drexel.edu/law/diversity.asp, accessed May 12, 2009.

50. Adrienne Selko, "The Changing Faces of the Workplace," *Industry Week,* April 1, 2007, http://www.industryweek.com; and Mary Dean Lee, Shelley M. MacDermid, and Michelle L. Buck, "Organizational Paradigms of Reduced-Load Work: Accommodation, Elaboration, and Transformation," *Academy of Management Journal* 43, no. 6 (December 2000), pp. 1211–34.

51. Leslie E. Overmyer Day, "The Pitfalls of Diversity Training," *Training and Development* 49, no. 12 (December 1995), pp. 24–29; Sara Rynes and Benson Rosen, "A Field Survey of Factors Affecting the Adoption and Perceived Success of Diversity Training," *Personnel Psychology* 48, no. 2 (Summer 1995), pp. 247–70; Lynda Ford, "Diversity: From Cartoons to Confrontations," *Training & Development* 54, no. 8 (August 2000), pp. 70–71; and John M. Ivancevich and Jacqueline A. Gilbert, "Diversity Management: Time for a New Approach," *Public Personnel Management* 29, no. 1 (Spring 2000), pp. 75–92.

52. Michael Burkart, "The Role of Training in Advancing a Diversity Initiative," *Diversity Factor* 8, no. 1 (Fall 1999), pp. 2–5.

53. Alexandra Marks, "For Airport Screeners, More Training about Muslims," *Christian Science Monitor,* January 9, 2007, http://www.csmonitor.com.

54. "How Bad Is the Turnover Problem?" *HR Focus,* March 2007, downloaded from Business & Company Resource Center, http://galenet.galegroup.com; Barbara Thomas, "Black Entrepreneurs Win, Corporations Lose," *BusinessWeek,* September 20, 2006, General Reference Center Gold, http://find.galegroup.com; and Phyllis Shurn-Hannah, "Solving the Minority Retention Mystery," *The Human Resource Professional* 13, no. 3 (May/June 2000), pp. 22–27.

55. Lisa Bertagnoli, "Group Dynamics: Darden's Employee Networks," *Chain Leader,* September 1, 2008, http://www.chainleader.com; and David Farkas, "Talkin' 'bout Your Generations," *Chain Leader,* April 2009, pp. 38–41.

56. Alleyne, "The 40 Best Companies for Diversity"; and Mary Ellen Podmolik, "Mentor Match Found Online," *Chicago Tribune,* May 14, 2007, http://www.chicagotribune.com.

57. Carla K. Johnson, "Study: Fat Workers Cost Employers More," *Associated Press,* April 23, 2007, http://news.yahoo.com.

58. Rodriguez, "Diversity Finds Its Place."

59. Julie Jargon, "Kraft Reformulates Oreo, Scores in China," *The Wall Street Journal,* May 1, 2008, http://online.wsj.com.

60. Nancy J. Adler and Susan Bartholomew, "Managing Globally Competent People," *Academy of Management Executive* 6, no. 3 (1992), pp. 52–65; and Cecil G. Howard, "Profile of the 21st-Century Expatriate Manager," *HRMagazine,* June 1992, pp. 93–100.

61. "IBM's India Hiring Binge Continues," *Associated Press,* February 28, 2007, http://news.yahoo.com.

62. Traci Purdum, "Chasing the Sun," IndustryWeek.com, April 1, 2007, http://www.industryweek.com.

63. Aaron W. Andreason, "Expatriate Adjustment to Foreign Assignments," *International Journal of Commerce and Management* 13, no. 1 (Spring 2003), pp. 42–61.

64. Perri Capell, "Know before You Go: Expats' Advice to Couples," *Career Journal Europe,* May 2, 2006, http://www.careerjournaleurope.com.

65. Reyer A. Swaak, "Expatriate Failures: Too Many, Too Much Cost, Too Little Planning," *Compensation & Benefits Review,* November/December 1995, pp. 50–52.

66. Capell, "Know before You Go."

67. Gretchen M. Spreitzer, Morgan W. McCall, and Joan D. Mahoney, "Early Identification of International Executive Potential," *Journal of Applied Psychology* 82, no. 1 (1997), pp. 6–29; Ronald Mortensen, "Beyond the Fence Line," *HRMagazine,* November 1997, pp. 100–9; "Expatriate Games," *Journal of Business Strategy,* July/August 1997, pp. 4–5; and "Building a Global Workforce Starts with Recruitment," *Personnel Journal* (special supplement), March 1996, pp. 9–11.

68. Alan Paul, "How the Internet Shrinks the Distance between Us," *The Wall Street Journal,* March 16, 2007, http://online.wsj.com.

69. Geoffrey A. Fowler, "In China's Offices, Foreign Colleagues Might Get an Earful," *The Wall Street Journal,* February 13, 2007, http://online.wsj.com.

70. John Slocum, "Coming to America," *Human Resource Executive,* October 2, 2008, http://www.hrexecutive.com.

71. Emily Flitter, "Time Runs Differently in the Emirates," *The Wall Street Journal,* April 16, 2008, http://online.wsj.com.

72. Jeanne Brett, Kristin Behfar, and Mary C. Kern, "Managing Multicultural Teams," *Harvard Business Review,* November 2006, pp. 84–91.

73. David Stamps, "Welcome to America," *Training,* November 1996, pp. 23–30.

74. Linda K. Trevino and Katherine A. Nelson, *Managing Business Ethics: Straight Talk about How to Do It Right* (New York: John Wiley & Sons, 1995).

75. Transparency International, "Leading Exporters Undermine Development with Dirty Business Overseas," news release, October 4, 2006, http://www.transparency.org.

76. J. G. Longnecker, J. A. McKinney, and C. W. Moore, "The Ethical Issues of International Bribery: A Study of Attitudes among U.S. Business Professionals," *Journal of Business Ethics* 7 (1988), pp. 341–346.

77. Katharine Q. Seelye, "J&J Reveals Improper Payments," *New York Times,* February 13, 2007, downloaded from Business & Company Resource Center, http://galenet.galegroup.com.

78. Ashay B. Desai and Terri Rittenburg, "Global Ethics: An Integrative Framework for MNEs," *Journal of Business Ethics* 16 (1997), pp. 791–800; and Paul Buller, John Kohls, and Kenneth Anderson, "A Model for Addressing Cross-Cultural Ethical Conflicts," *Business & Society* 36, no. 2 (June 1997), pp. 169–93.

Chapter 9

1. Company Web site, http://www.rmi.org, accessed April 10, 2009; Kent Garber, "A Bright Light in the Field of New Energy," *U.S. News & World Report,* December 1–8, 2008, pp. 44–45; "Amory Lovins on Energy," CNN.com, October 16, 2008, http://www.edition.cnn .com; Lucy Siegle, "This Much I Know: Amory Lovins," *London Observer,* March 23, 2008, http://www.guardian.co.uk; Roger Fillion, "Energy-Efficient Visionary," *Rocky Mountain News,* February 9, 2008, http://www.rockymountainnews.com; Logan Warn, "Amory Lovins: Solving the Energy Crisis (and Bringing Wal-Mart)," *Popular Mechanics,* November 2007, http://www.popularmechanics.com; Rob Walton, "Heroes of the Environment: Amory B. Lovins," *Time,* October 25, 2007, http://www.time.com; Warren Karlenzig, "Rocky Mountain Institute Turns 25: The Distributed Generation of Amory Lovins' Brainpower," *Worldchanging Team,* August 15, 2007, http://www.worldchanging.com; David Roberts, "All You Need Is Lovins," *Grist,* July 26, 2007, http://www.grist.org.

2. W. Bennis and B. Nanus, *Leaders* (New York: Harper & Row, 1985), p. 27.

3. J. Petrick, R. Schere, J. Brodzinski, J. Quinn, and M. Fall Ainina, "Global Leadership Skills and Reputational Capital: Intangible Resources for Sustainable Competitive Advantage," *Academy of Management Executive,* February 1999, pp. 58–69.

4. Bennis and Nanus, *Leaders.*

5. Ibid., p. 144.

6. E. E. Lawler III, *Treat People Right! How Organizations and Individuals Can Propel Each Other into a Virtual Spiral of Success* (San Francisco: Jossey-Bass, 2003).

7. Beverly Kopf and Bobbie Birleffi, "Not Her Father's Chief Executive," *U.S. News and World Report,* October 22, 2006, http://www. usnews.com (interview with Marilyn Nelson).

8. Robert Half Finance and Accounting, "Survey: CFOs Cite Strong Leadership, Talent as Keys to Staying Ahead of the Competition," news release, April 8, 2009, http://www.roberthalffinance.com.

9. J. Kouzes and B. Posner, *The Leadership Challenge,* 2nd ed. (San Francisco: Jossey-Bass, 1995).

10. J. Kouzes and B. Posner, *The Leadership Challenge,* 1st ed. (San Francisco: Jossey-Bass, 1987).

11. Ibid.

12. Ibid.

13. J. Baum, E. A. Locke, and S. Kirkpatrick, "A Longitudinal Study of the Relation of Vision and Vision Communication to Venture Growth in Entrepreneurial Firms," *Journal of Applied Psychology* 83 (1998), pp. 43–54.

14. E. C. Shapiro, *Fad Surfing in the Boardroom* (Reading, MA: Addison-Wesley, 1995).

15. Kouzes and Posner, *The Leadership Challenge* (1995).

16. Ibid.

17. W. Bennis and R. Townsend, *Reinventing Leadership* (New York: William Morrow, 1995).

18. Ibid.

19. Alex Markels, "Turning the Tide at P&G," *U.S. News and World Report,* October 22, 2006, http://www.usnews.com.

20. Kouzes and Posner, *The Leadership Challenge* (1987).

21. J. A. Conger, "The Dark Side of Leadership," *Organizational Dynamics* 19 (Autumn 1990), pp. 44–55.

22. J. Conger, "The Vision Thing: Explorations into Visionary Leadership," in *Cutting Edge Leadership 2000,* ed. B. Kellerman and L. Matusak (College Park, MD: James MacGregor Burns Academy of Leadership, 2000).

23. Bill Wolpin, "The Tough Get Going," *American City and County,* November 1, 2008, downloaded from Business & Company Resource Center, http://galenet.galegroup.com; Mann Jackson, "Come-Back Kid," *American City and County,* November 1, 2008, http://galenet.galegroup.com; and Brett Zongker, "Museum Features Kansas Town That Went Green," Associated Press, *Yahoo News,* October 26, 2008, http://news.yahoo.com.

24. J. P. Kotter, "What Leaders Really Do," *Harvard Business Review* 68 (May–June 1990) pp. 103–11.

25. Mark E. Van Buren and Todd Safferstone, "Collective Quick Wins," *Computerworld,* January 26, 2009, pp. 24–25.

26. G. Yukl, *Leadership in Organizations,* 3rd ed. (Englewood Cliffs, NJ: Prentice Hall, 1994).

27. R. House and R. Aditya, "The Social Scientific Study of Leadership: Quo Vadis?" *Journal of Management* 23 (1997), pp. 409–73.

28. R. D. Ireland and M. A. Hitt. "Achieving and Maintaining Strategic Competitiveness in the 21st Century. The Role of Strategic Leadership," *Academy of Management Executive* (February 1999), pp. 43–57.

29. Julie Wood, "John Thompson III Named New Head Coach," *The Hoya,* http://www.thehoya.com, accessed March 26, 2007; and Dick Vitale, "Meet the Next Generation of Great Hoops Coaches, According to Dickie V," *USA Today,* February 13, 2007, http:// www.usatoday.com.

30. J. Gardner, "The Heart of the Matter: Leader–Constituent Interaction," in *Leading & Leadership,* ed. T. Fuller (Notre Dame, IN: University of Notre Dame Press, 2000), pp. 239–44, quote at p. 240.

31. R. E. Kelly, "In Praise of Followers," *Harvard Business Review* 66 (November–December 1988), pp. 142–48.

32. Bennis and Townsend, *Reinventing Leadership.*

33. Kelly, "In Praise of Followers."

34. J. R. P. French and B. Raven, "The Bases of Social Power," in *Studies in Social Power,* ed. D. Cartwright (Ann Arbor, MI: Institute for Social Research, 1959).

35. G. Yukl and C. Falbe, "Importance of Different Power Sources in Downward and Lateral Relations," *Journal of Applied Psychology* 76 (1991), pp. 416–23.

36. Yukl and Falbe, "Importance of Different Power Sources."

37. Ibid.

38. R. M. Stogdill, "Personal Factors Associated with Leadership: A Survey of the Literature," *Journal of Psychology* 25 (1948), pp. 35–71.

39. S. Kirkpatrick and E. Locke, "Leadership: Do Traits Matter?" *The Executive* 5 (May 1991), pp. 48–60.

40. G. A. Yukl, *Leadership in Organizations,* 2nd ed. (Englewood Cliffs, NJ: Prentice Hall, 1989).

41. R. Heifetz and D. Laurie, "The Work of Leadership," *Harvard Business Review,* January–February 1997, pp. 124–34.

42. T. Judge, J. Bono, R. Ilies, and M. Gerhardt, "Personality and Leadership: A Qualitative and Quantitative Review," *Journal of Applied Psychology* 87 (2002), pp. 765–80.

43. R. Foti and N. M. A. Hauenstein, "Pattern and Variable Approaches in Leadership Emergence and Effectiveness," *Journal of Applied Psychology* 92 (2007), pp. 347–55.

44. T. Fuller, ed., *Leading & Leadership, 2000* (Notre Dame, IN: University of Notre Dame Press, 2000), p. 243.

45. J. P. Kotter, *The General Managers* (New York: Free Press, 1982).

46. Gina Imperato, "The Adventurer: How I Did It," *Inc.,* May 2007, pp. 115–16.

47. S. Zaccaro, R. Foti, and D. Kenny, "Self-Monitoring and Trait-Based Variance in Leadership: An Investigation of Leader Flexibility across Multiple Group Situations," *Journal of Applied Psychology* 76 (1991), pp. 308–15.

48. D. Goleman, "Leadership That Gets Results," *Harvard Business Review,* March–April 2000, pp. 78–90.

49. J. Misumi and M. Peterson, "The Performance-Maintenance (PM) Theory of Leadership: Review of a Japanese Research Program," *Administrative Science Quarterly* 30 (June 1985), pp. 198–223.

50. T. Judge, R. Piccolo, and R. Ilies, "The Forgotten Ones? The Validity of Consideration and Initiating Structure in Leadership Research," *Journal of Applied Psychology* 89 (2004), pp. 36–51.

51. Misumi and Peterson, "The Performance-Maintenance (PM) Theory."

52. Judge, Piccolo, and Ilies, "The Forgotten Ones?"

53. Reprinted from Misumi and Peterson, "The Performance-Maintenance (PM) Theory of Leadership," by permission of *Administrative Science Quarterly,* © 1985 by Johnson Graduate School of Management, Cornell University.

54. G. Graen and M. Uhl-Bien, "Relationship-Based Approach to Leadership: Development of Leader-Member Exchange (LMX) Theory of Leadership over 25 Years: Applying a Multi-Level Multidomain Perspective," *Leadership Quarterly* 6, no. 2 (1995), pp. 219–47.

55. House and Aditya, "The Social Scientific Study of Leadership."

56. C. R. Gerstner and D. V. Day, "Meta-Analytic Review of Leader-Member Exchange-Theory: Correlates and Construct Issues," *Journal of Applied Psychology* 82 (1997), pp. 827–44.

57. Carmen Nobel, "The Smart Business of Diversity," *InfoWorld,* January 22, 2007, http://www.infoworld.com (interview with Carly Fiorina).

58. House and Aditya, "The Social Scientific Study of Leadership."

59. J. Wagner III, "Participation's Effect on Performance and Satisfaction: A Reconsideration of Research," *Academy of Management Review,* April 1994, pp. 312–30.

60. R. White and R. Lippitt, *Autocracy and Democracy: An Experimental Inquiry* (New York: Harper & Brothers, 1960).

61. J. Muczyk and R. Steel, "Leadership Style and the Turnaround Executive," *Business Horizons,* March–April 1999, pp. 39–46.

62. A. Tannenbaum and W. Schmidt, "How to Choose a Leadership Pattern," *Harvard Business Review* 36 (March–April 1958), pp. 95–101.

63. E. Fleishman and E. Harris, "Patterns of Leadership Behavior Related to Employee Grievances and Turnover," *Personnel Psychology* 15 (1962), pp. 43–56.

64. R. Likert, *The Human Organization: Its Management and Value* (New York: McGraw-Hill, 1967).

65. R. Blake and J. Mouton, *The Managerial Grid* (Houston: Gulf, 1964).

66. Misumi and Peterson, "The Performance-Maintenance (PM) Theory."

67. J. Wall, *Bosses* (Lexington, MA: Lexington Books, 1986), p. 103.

68. Tannenbaum and Schmidt, "How to Choose a Leadership Pattern."

69. V. H. Vroom, "Leadership and the Decision-Making Process," *Organizational Dynamics,* Spring 2000, pp. 82–93.

70. Vroom, "Leadership and the Decision-Making Process." Copyright © 2000 with permission from Elsevier Science.

71. Ibid.

72. F. E. Fiedler, *A Theory of Leadership Effectiveness* (New York: McGraw-Hill, 1967).

73. P. Hersey and K. Blanchard, *The Management of Organizational Behavior* (Englewood Cliffs, NJ: Prentice Hall, 1984).

74. Yukl, *Leadership in Organizations.*

75. R. J. House, "A Path Goal Theory of Leader Effectiveness," *Administrative Science Quarterly* 16 (1971), pp. 321–39.

76. J. Howell, D. Bowen, P. Dorfman, S. Kerr, and P. Podsakoff, "Substitutes for Leadership: Effective Alternatives to Ineffective Leadership," *Organizational Dynamics* 19 (Summer 1990), pp. 21–38.

77. R. G. Lord and W. Gradwohl Smith, "Leadership and the Changing Nature of Performance," in *The Changing Nature of Performance,* ed. D. R. Ilgen and E. D. Pulakos (San Francisco: Jossey-Bass, 1999).

78. S. Dionne, F. Yammarino, L. Atwater, and L. James, "Neutralizing Substitutes for Leadership Theory: Leadership Effects and Common-Source Bias," *Journal of Applied Psychology* 87 (2002), pp. 454–64.

79. B. M. Bass, *Leadership and Performance Beyond Expectations* (New York: Free Press, 1985).

80. Y. A. Nur, "Charisma and Managerial Leadership: The Gift That Never Was," *Business Horizons,* July–August 1998, pp. 19–26; and R. J. House, "A 1976 Theory of Charismatic Leadership," in *Leadership: The Cutting Edge,* ed. J. G. Hunt and L. L. Larson (Carbondale, IL: Southern Illinois University Press, 1977).

81. M. Brown and L. Trevino, "Socialized Charismatic Leadership, Values Congruence, and Deviance in Work Groups," *Journal of Applied Psychology* 91 (2006), pp. 954–62.

82. M. Potts and P. Behr, *The Leading Edge* (New York: McGraw-Hill, 1987).

83. J. Howell and B. Shamir, "The Role of Followers in the Charismatic Leadership Process: Relationships and Their Consequences," *Academy of Management Review* 30 (2005), pp. 96–112.

84. S. Yorges, H. Weiss, and O. Strickland, "The Effect of Leader Outcomes on Influence, Attributions, and Perceptions of Charisma," *Journal of Applied Psychology* 84 (1999), pp. 428–36.

85. Potts and Behr, *The Leading Edge.*

86. D. A. Waldman and F. J. Yammarino, "CEO Charismatic Leadership: Levels-of-Management and Levels-of-Analysis Effects," *Academy of Management Review* 24 (1999), pp. 266–85.

87. A. Fanelli and V. Misangyi, "Bringing Out Charisma: CEO Charisma and External Stakeholders," *Academy of Management Review* 31 (2006), pp. 1049–61.

88. House and Aditya, "The Social Scientific Study of Leadership."

89. D. A. Waldman, G. G. Ramirez, R. J. House, and P. Puranam, "Does Leadership Matter? CEO Leadership Attributes and Profitability under Conditions of Perceived Environmental Uncertainty," *Academy of Management Journal* 44 (2001), pp. 134–43.

90. B. Agle, N. Nagarajan, J. Sonnenfeld, and D. Srinivasan, "Does CEO Charisma Matter? An Empirical Analysis of the Relationships among Organizational Performance, Environmental Uncertainty, and Top Management Team Perceptions of CEO Charisma," *Academy of Management Journal* 49 (2006), pp. 161–74.

91. J. M. Howell and K. E. Hall-Merenda, "The Ties that Bind: The Impact of Leader-Member Exchange, Transformational and Transactional Leadership, and Distance on Predicting Follower Performance," *Journal of Applied Psychology* 84 (1999), pp. 680–94; and B. M. Bass, "Leadership: Good, Better, Best," *Organizational Dynamics,* Winter 1985, pp. 26–40.

92. F. J. Yammarino, F. Dansereau, and C. J. Kennedy, "A Multiple-Level Multidimensional Approach to Leadership: Viewing Leadership through an Elephant's Eye," *Organizational Dynamics,* Winter 2001, pp. 149–63.

93. D. I. Jung and B. J. Avolio, "Effects of Leadership Style and Followers' Cultural Orientation on Performance in Group and Individual Task Conditions," *Academy of Management Journal* 42 (1999), pp. 208–18.

94. Bass, *Leadership and Performance.*

95. Glenn Hall, "Unconventional Wisdom," *Orange County Register,* January 23, 2007, http://galennet.galegroup.com.

96. Bennis and Nanus, *Leaders.*

97. B. Bass, B. Avolio, and L. Goodheim, "Biography and the Assessment of Transformational Leadership at the World-Class Level," *Journal of Management* 13 (1987), pp. 7–20.

98. K. Albrecht and R. Zemke, *Service America* (Homewood, IL: Dow Jones Irwin, 1985).

99. T. A. Judge and J. E. Bono, "Five-Factor Model of Personality and Transformational Leadership," *Journal of Applied Psychology* 85 (2000), pp. 751–65; and B. Bass, "Does the Transactional-Transformational Paradigm Transcend Organizational and National Boundaries?" *American Psychologist* 22 (1997), pp. 130–42.

100. S. J. Shin and J. Zhou, "Transformational Leadership, Conservation, and Creativity: Evidence from Korea," *Academy of Management Journal* 46 (2003), pp. 703–14.

101. R. Piccolo and J. Colquitt, "Transormational Leadership and Job Behaviors: The Mediating Role of Core Job Characteristics," *Academy of Management Journal* 49 (2006), pp. 327–40.

102. A. Colbert, A. Kristof-Brown, B. Bradley, and M. Barrick, "CEO Transformational Leadership: The Role of Goal Importance Congruence in Top Management Teams," *Academy of Management Journal* 51 (2008), pp. 81–96.

103. T. Dvir, D. Eden, B. Avolio, and B. Shamir, "Impact of Transformational Leadership on Follower Development and Performance: A Field Experiment," *Academy of Management Journal* 45 (2002), pp. 735–44.

104. B. M. Bass, *Transformational Leadership: Industry, Military, and Educational Impact* (Mahwah, NJ: Lawrence Erlbaum Associates, 1998).

105. G. Spreitzer and R. Quinn, "Empowering Middle Managers to Be Transformational Leaders," *Journal of Applied Behavioral Science* 32 (1996), pp. 237–61.

106. J. Collins, "Level 5 Leadership," *Harvard Business Review* 1 (2001), pp. 66–76; and J. Kline Harrison and M. William Clough, "Characteristics of 'State of the Art' Leaders: Productive Narcissism versus Emotional Intelligence and Level 5 Capabilities," *Social Science Journal* 43 (2006), pp. 287–92.

107. D. Vera and M. Crossan, "Strategic Leadership and Organizational Learning," *Academy of Management Review* 29 (2004), pp. 222–40.

108. Esther Herlzfeld, "Leadership Leads to Growth," *Official Board Markets,* April 11, 2009, downloaded from Business & Company Resource Center, http://galenet.galegroup.com; and Barry-Wehmiller Web site, http://www.barry-wehmiller.com, accessed May 15, 2009.

109. F. Luthans, *Organizational Behavior,* 10th ed. (New York: McGraw-Hill/Irwin, 2005).

110. B. M. Bass, "Thoughts and Plans," in *Cutting Edge Leadership 2000,* ed. B. Kellerman and L. R. Matusak (College Park, MD: James MacGregor Burns Academy of Leadership, 2000), pp. 5–9.

111. N. Turner, J. Barling, O. Epitropaki, V. Butcher, and C. Milner, "Transformational Leadership and Moral Reasoning," *Journal of Applied Psychology* 87 (2002), pp. 304–11.

112. Bass, "Thoughts and Plans."

113. John Hersey, "Some SAGE Advice," *Hardware Retailing,* May 2009, downloaded from Business & Company Resource Center, http://galenet.galegroup.com.

114. W. Bennis, "The End of Leadership: Exemplary Leadership Is Impossible without Full Inclusion, Initiatives, and Cooperation of Followers," *Organizational Dynamics,* Summer 1999, pp. 71–79.

115. L. Spears, "Emerging Characteristics of Servant Leadership," in *Cutting Edge Leadership 2000,* ed. B. Kellerman and L. Matusak (College Park, MD: James MacGregor Burns Academy of Leadership, 2000); and Leigh Buchanan, "In Praise of Selflessness: Why the Best Leaders Are Servants," *Inc.,* May 2007, pp. 33–35.

116. Buchanan, "In Praise of Selflessness," p. 34.

117. J. Ciulla, "Bridge Leaders," in *Cutting Edge Leadership 2000,* ed. B. Kellerman and L. Matusak (College Park, MD: James MacGregor Burns Academy of Leadership, 2000), pp. 25–28.

118. C. L. Pearce, "The Future of Leadership: Combining Vertical and Shared Leadership to Transform Knowledge Work," *Academy of Management Executive,* February 2004, pp. 47–57.

119. J. Carson, P. Tesluk, and J. Marrone, "Shared Leadership in Teams: An Investigation of Antecedent Conditions and Performance," *Academy of Management Journal* 50 (2007), pp. 1217–34.

120. R. Fisher and A. Sharp, *Getting It Done* (New York: HarperCollins, 1998).

121. Alex Markels, "Guiding the Path to Mars," *U.S. News and World Report,* October 22, 2006, http://www.usnews.com.

122. Michael Useem, "Thinking Big, Lending Small," *U.S. News and World Report,* October 22, 2006, http://www.usnews.com.

123. P. Block, *The Empowered Manager* (San Francisco: Jossey-Bass, 1991).

124. Ibid.

125. Kouzes and Posner, *The Leadership Challenge* (1995).

126. Larry W. Boone and Monica S. Peborde, "Developing Leadership Skills in College and Early Career Positions," *Review of Business,* Spring 2008, downloaded from Business & Company Resource Center, http://galenet.galegroup.com.

127. Amanda Gaines, "Straight to the Top," *American Executive,* August 2008, downloaded from Business & Company Resource Center, http://galenet.galegroup.com; and Scott J. Allen and Nathan S. Hartman, "Leadership Development: An Exploration of Sources of Learning," *SAM Advanced Management Journal,* Winter 2008, pp. 10–19, 62–63.

128. M. McCall, *High Flyers* (Boston: Harvard Business School Press, 1998).

129. E. Van Velsor, C. D. McCauley, and R. Moxley, "Our View of Leadership Development," in *Center for Creative Leadership Handbook of Leadership Development,* ed. C. D. McCauley, R. Moxley, and E. Van Velsor (San Francisco: Jossey-Bass, 1998), pp. 1–25.

Chapter 10

1. Max Chafkin, "Everybody Loves Zappos," *Inc.,* May 2009, pp. 66–73; Lilly Rockwell, "Zappos Chief Speaks," *Austin American-Statesman,* March 13, 2009, http://www.austin360.com; Jeffrey M. O'Brien, "Zappos Knows How to Kick It," *Fortune,* January 22, 2009, http://money.cnn.com; Claire Cain Miller, "Making Sure the Shoe Fits at Zappos.com," *New York Times,* November 6, 2008, http://bits.blogs.nytimes.com; and Helen Coster, "A Step Ahead," *Forbes,* June 2, 2008, http://www.forbes.com.

2. R. Kreitner and F. Luthans, "A Social Learning Approach to Behavioral Management: Radical Behaviorists 'Mellowing Out,'" *Organizational Dynamics,* Autumn 1984, pp. 47–65.

3. D. Katz and R. L. Kahn, *The Social Psychology of Organizations* (New York: John Wiley & Sons, 1966).

4. C. A. Bartlett and S. Ghoshal, "Building Competitive Advantage through People," *Sloan Management Review,* Winter 2002, pp. 34–41.

5. Plante & Moran, "*Fortune* Announces 2007 List of 100 Best Companies to Work For," news release, January 8, 2007, http://www.plantemoran.com; and Karen Dybis, "Employees Embrace Family-Friendly Perks," *Detroit Free Press,* http://www.freep.com, accessed June 8, 2007.

6. Anne Fisher, "Loyalty Isn't Dead, Employers Have to Earn It," *Fortune,* January 16, 2007, http://money.cnn.com.

7. E. Locke, "Toward a Theory of Task Motivation and Incentives," *Organizational Behavior and Human Performance* 3 (1968), pp. 157–89.

8. W. F. Cascio, "Managing a Virtual Workplace," *Academy of Management Executive,* August 2000, pp. 81–90.

9. E. A. Locke, "Guest Editor's Introduction: Goal-Setting Theory and Its Applications to the World of Business," *Academy of Management Executive* 4 (November 2004), pp. 124–25.

10. G. P. Latham, "The Motivational Benefits of Goal-Setting," *Academy of Management Executive* 4 (November 2004), pp. 126–29.

11. E. A. Locke, "Linking Goals to Monetary Incentives," *Academy of Management Executive* 4 (November 2004), pp. 130–33.

12. E. E. Lawler III, *Treat People Right!* (San Francisco: Jossey-Bass, 2003).

13. Ibid.

14. J. Bono and T. Judge, "Self-Concordance at Work: Toward Understanding the Motivational Effects of Transformational Leaders," *Academy of Management Journal* 46 (2003), pp. 554–71.

15. R. H. Schaffer, "Demand Better Results—and Get Them," *Harvard Business Review* 69 (March–April 1991), pp. 142–49.

16. Amy Barrett, "Cracking the Whip at Wyeth," *BusinessWeek,* February 6, 2006, downloaded from Business & Company Resource Center, http://galenet.galegroup.com.

17. Brent Hunsberger, "Entrepreneurial Spirit Keeps Company Fired Up," *Seattle Times,* March 29, 2007, downloaded from Business & Company Resource Center, http://galenet.galegroup.com; and Paul Kaihla, "Best-Kept Secrets of the World's Best Companies," *Business 2.0,* April 2006, http://galenet.galegroup.com.

18. K. N. Shaw, "Changing the Goal-Setting Process at Microsoft," *Academy of Management Executive* 4 (November 2004), pp. 139–43.

19. S. Kerr and S. Laundauer, "Using Stretch Goals to Promote Organizational Effectiveness and Personal Growth: General Electric and Goldman Sachs," *Academy of Management Executive* 4 (November 2004), pp. 134–38.

20. Ibid.

21. Latham, "Motivational Benefits of Goal-Setting."

22. T. Mitchell and W. Silver, "Individual and Group Goals When Workers Are Interdependent: Effects on Task Strategies and Performance," *Journal of Applied Psychology* 75 (1990), pp. 185–93.

23. Latham, "Motivational Benefits of Goal-Setting."

24. Sarah Boehle, "The Games Trainers Play," *Training,* August 1, 2006, http://www.trainingmag.com; and M. P. McQueen, "Wellness Plans Reach Out to the Healthy," *The Wall Street Journal,* March 28, 2007, http://online.wsj.com.

25. M. Schweitzer, L. Ordonez, and B. Douma, "Goal Setting as a Motivator of Unethical Behavior," *Academy of Management Journal* 47 (2004), pp. 422–32.

26. Miguel A. Duran, "Norm-Based Behavior and Corporate Malpractice," *Journal of Economic Issues* 41, no. 1 (March 2007), downloaded from Business & Company Resource Center, http://galenet.galegroup.com; and Don Durfee, "Management or Manipulation?" *CFO,* December 2006, http://galenet.galegroup.com.

27. G. Seijts and G. Latham, "Learning versus Performance Goals: When Should Each Be Used?" *Academy of Management Executive* 19 (February 2005), pp. 124–31; P. C. Early, T. Connolly, and G. Ekegren, "Goals, Strategy Development, and Task Performance: Some Limits on the Efficacy of Goal Setting," *Journal of Applied Psychology* 74 (1989), pp. 24–33; and C. E. Shalley, "Effects of Productivity Goals, Creativity Goals, and Personal Discretion on Individual Creativity," *Journal of Applied Psychology* 76 (1991), pp. 179–85.

28. R. C. Litchfield, "Brainstorming Reconsidered: A Goal-Based View," *Academy of Management Review* 33 (2008), pp. 649–68.

29. R. Fisher and A. Sharp, *Getting It Done* (New York: HarperCollins, 1998).

30. E. Thorndike, *Animal Intelligence* (New York: Macmillan, 1911).

31. A. D. Stajkovic and F. Luthans, "Differential Effects of Incentive Motivators on Work Performance," *Academy of Management Journal* 44 (2001), pp. 580–90.

32. Adam Madison, "Positive Results," *Rock Products,* September 1, 2008, downloaded from Business & Company Resource Center, http://galenet.galegroup.com.

33. Anne Fisher, "Happy Employees, Loyal Employees," *Fortune,* "100 Best Companies to Work For," January 16, 2007, http://money.cnn.com.

34. K. Butterfield, L. K. Trevino, and G. Ball, "Punishment from the Manager's Perspective: A Grounded Investigation and Inductive Model," *Academy of Management Review* 39 (1996), pp. 1479–512.

35. Madison, "Positive Results."

36. T. Judge and R. Piccolo, "Transformational and Transactional Leadership: A Meta-Analytic Test of Their Relative Ability," *Journal of Applied Psychology* 89 (2004), pp. 755–68.

37. S. Kerr, "On the Folly of Rewarding *A* While Hoping for *B,*" *Academy of Management Journal* 18 (1975), pp. 769–83.

38. See Steve Lohr, "Science Finds Advantage in Focusing, Not Multitasking," *Chicago Tribune,* March 25, 2007, sec.1, p. 10.

39. Michael LeBoeuf, *The Greatest Management Principle in the World* (New York: Berkley Books, 1985).

40. E. E. Lawler III, *Rewarding Excellence* (San Francisco: Jossey-Bass, 2000).

41. Jacqueline Stenson, "Is Your Job Making You Fat?" *MSNBC,* February 6, 2007, http://www.msnbc.msn.com.

42. Michael Fitzgerald, "Thinks Big about the Little Guy," *New York Times,* February 4, 2007, downloaded from Business & Company Resource Center, http://galenet.galegroup.com.

43. "100 Best Companies to Work For 2007: Unusual Perks," *Fortune,* January 22, 2007, http://money.cnn.com.

44. Fisher, "Happy Employees, Loyal Employees."

45. Janet H. Cho, "Lessons in Employee Appreciation," *Star-Ledger (Newark, NJ),* February 8, 2007, downloaded from Business & Company Resource Center, http://galenet.galegroup.com.

46. Fitzgerald, "Thinks Big."

47. J. Pfeffer and R. Sutton, *The Knowing–Doing Gap* (Boston: Harvard Business School Press, 2000).

48. Joann S. Lublin, "Recall the Mistakes of Your Past Bosses, so You Can Do Better," *The Wall Street Journal,* January 2, 2007, http://online.wsj.com.

49. S. Moss and J. Sanchez, "Are Your Employees Avoiding You? Managerial Strategies for Closing the Feedback Gap," *Academy of Management Executive* 18, no. 1 (February 2004), pp. 32–44.

50. Lawler, *Treat People Right!*

51. Stanley B. Silverman, Corrie E. Pogson, and Alana B. Cober, "When Employees at Work Don't Get It: A Model for Enhancing Individual Employee Change in Response to Performance Feedback," *Academy of Management Executive* 19, no. 2 (May 2005), pp. 135–47; and J. Jackman and M. Strober, "Fear of Feedback," *Harvard Business Review,* April 2003, pp. 101–7.

52. V. H. Vroom, *Work and Motivation* (New York: John Wiley & Sons, 1964).

53. R. E. Wood, P. W. B. Atkins, and J. E. H. Bright, "Bonuses, Goals, and Instrumentality Effects," *Journal of Applied Psychology* 84 (1999), pp. 703–20.

54. Kerr, "Organizational Rewards."

55. Melanie Scarborough, "The Rewards of Recognition: Six Strategies for Successful Employee Programs," *Community Banker,* January 2009, pp. 24–27.

56. Vanessa Fuhrmans, "Training the Brain to Choose Wisely," *The Wall Street Journal,* April 28, 2009, http://online.wsj.com; and Laura Blue, "Making Good Health Easy," *Time,* February 23, 2009, Wellness 1–2.

57. A. H. Maslow, "A Theory of Human Motivation," *Psychological Review,* July 1943, pp. 370–96.

58. L. Mainicro and D. Gibson, "Managing Employee Trauma: Dealing with the Emotional Fallout from 9-11," *Academy of Management Executive,* August 2003, pp. 130–43.

59. M. Wahba and L. Birdwell, "Maslow Reconsidered: A Review of Research on the Need Hierarchy Theory," *Organizational Behavior and Human Performance* 15 (1976), pp. 212–40.

60. G. Dessler, "How to Earn Your Employees' Commitment," *Academy of Management Executive,* May 1999, pp. 58–67, quoted on p. 63.

61. Carol Hymowitz, "Managers Lose Talent When They Neglect to Coach Their Staffs," *The Wall Street Journal,* March 19, 2007, http://online.wsj.com.

62. Ibid.

63. C. Alderfer, *Existence, Relatedness, and Growth: Human Needs in Organizational Settings* (Glencoe, IL: Free Press, 1972).

64. Simona Covel, "Picking the Perks that Employees Value," *The Wall Street Journal,* April 9, 2007, http://online.wsj.com.

65. Lindsey Tanner, "Study: Napping Might Help Heart," *Yahoo News,* February 12, 2007, http://news.yahoo.com.

66. Carol Hymowitz, "When the Paycheck Isn't Optional, Ambition Is Less Complicated," *The Wall Street Journal,* April 26, 2007, http://online.wsj.com.

67. C. Pinder, *Work Motivation* (Glenview, IL: Scott, Foresman, 1984).

68. D. McClelland, *The Achieving Society* (New York: Van Nostrand Reinhold, 1961).

69. Quoted in Cho, "Lessons in Employee Appreciation."

70. D. McClelland and R. Boyatzis, "Leadership Motive Pattern and Long-Term Success in Management," *Journal of Applied Psychology* 67 (1982), pp. 737–43.

71. N. Adler, *International Dimensions of Organizational Behavior,* 2nd ed. (Boston: Kent, 1991); and G. Hofstede, *Cultures and Organizations* (London: McGraw-Hill, 1991).

72. Nancy R. Lockwood, "Leveraging Employee Engagement for Competitive Advantage: HR's Strategic Role," *HRMagazine,* March 2007, downloaded from Business & Company Resource Center, http://galenet.galegroup.com.

73. E. E. Lawler III and D. Finegold, "Individualizing the Organization: Past, Present, and Future," *Organizational Dynamics,* Summer 2000, pp. 1–15.

74. Ibid.

75. T. M. Amabile, "A Model of Creativity and Innovation in Organizations," in *Research in Organizational Behavior,* ed. B. M. Staw and L. L. Cummings (Greenwich, CT: JAI Press, 1988), pp. 10, 123–67.

76. C. M. Ford, "A Theory of Individual Creative Action in Multiple Social Domains," *Academy of Management Review* 21 (1996), pp. 1112–42.

77. G. Oldham and A. Cummings, "Employee Creativity: Personal and Contextual Factors at Work," *Academy of Management Journal* 39 (1996), pp. 607–34.

78. BlessingWhite, *The State of Employee Engagement, 2008: North American Overview,* 2008, http://www.blessingwhite.com/research.

79. T. Amabile, R. Conti, H. Coon, J. Lazenby, and M. Herron, "Assessing the Work Environment for Creativity," *Academy of Management Journal* 39 (1996), pp. 1154–84.

80. M. Campion and G. Sanborn. "Job Design," in *Handbook of Industrial Engineering,* ed. G. Salvendy (New York: John Wiley & Sons, 1991).

81. Lawler and Finegold, "Individualizing the Organization."

82. Rob Garretson, "Job Rotation Pays Dividends," *Network World,* February 26, 2007, downloaded from OCLC FirstSearch, http://firstsearch.oclc.org.

83. M. Campion and D. McClelland, "Interdisciplinary Examination of the Costs and Benefits of Enlarged Jobs: A Job Design Quasi-Experiment," *Journal of Applied Psychology* 76 (1991), pp. 186–98.

84. F. Herzberg, *Work and the Nature of Men* (Cleveland: World, 1966).

85. J. R. Hackman, G. Oldham, R. Janson, and K. Purdy, "A New Strategy for Job Enrichment," *California Management Review* 16 (Fall 1975), pp. 57–71.

86. Paula Lehman, "No. 5 Enterprise: A Clear Road to the Top," *BusinessWeek,* September 18, 2006, downloaded from General Reference Center Gold, http://find.galegroup.com.

87. R. Rechheld, "Loyalty-Based Management" *Harvard Business Review,* March–April 1993, pp. 64–73.

88. Kerry Miller, "Buying into the State Department Lifestyle," *BusinessWeek,* November 14, 2006, downloaded from General Reference Center Gold, http://find.galegroup.com.

89. Bill Trahant, "Recruiting and Engaging the Federal Workforce," *Public Manager,* Spring 2008, downloaded from Business & Company Resource Center, http://galenet.galegroup.com.

90. T. Peters and N. Austin, *A Passion for Excellence* (New York: Random House, 1985).

91. Kaihla, "Best-Kept Secrets."

92. Jeanna Bryner, "Survey Reveals Most Satisfying Jobs," *Yahoo News,* April 18, 2007, http://news.yahoo.com.

93. Campion and Sanborn, "Job Design."

94. S. Seibert, S. Silver, and W. A. Randolph, "Taking Empowerment to the Next Level: A Multiple-Level Model of Empowerment, Performance, and Satisfaction," *Academy of Management Journal* 47 (2004), pp. 332–49.

95. C. Argyris, "Empowerment: The Emperor's New Clothes," *Harvard Business Review,* May–June 1998, pp. 98–105.

96. R. Forrester, "Empowerment: Rejuvenating a Potent Idea," *Academy of Management Executive,* August 2000, pp. 67–80.

97. R. C. Liden, S. J. Wayne, and R. T. Sparrowe, "An Examination of the Mediating Role of Psychological Empowerment on the Relations between the Job, Interpersonal Relationships, and Work Outcomes," *Journal of Applied Psychology* 85 (2000), pp. 407–16.

98. Peters and Austin, *A Passion for Excellence.*

99. K. Thomas and B. Velthouse, "Cognitive Elements of Empowerment: An 'Interpretive' Model of Intrinsic Task Motivation," *Academy of Management Review* 15 (1990), pp. 666–81.

100. J. Kouzes and B. Posner, *The Leadership Challenge,* 2nd ed. Copyright © 1995 Jossey-Bass, Inc. This material is used by permission of Jossey-Bass, Inc., a subsidiary of John Wiley & Sons, Inc.

101. Price Waterhouse Change Integration Team, *Better Change* (Burr Ridge, IL: Richard D. Irwin, 1995).

102. E. E. Lawler III, *The Ultimate Advantage: Creating the High Involvement Organization* (San Francisco: Jossey-Bass, 1992).

103. O. Gadiesh and J. L. Gilbert, "Transforming Corner-Office Strategy into Frontline Action," *Harvard Business Review,* May 2001, pp. 72–79.

104. J. Kouzes and B. Posner, *The Leadership Challenge* (San Francisco: Jossey-Bass, 1995).

105. Price Waterhouse, *Better Change.*

106. J. Jasinowski and R. Hamrin, *Making It in America* (New York: Simon & Schuster, 1995).

107. Scott Morrison, "Google Searches for Staffing Answers," *The Wall Street Journal,* May 19, 2009, http://online.wsj.com; Michael Liedtke, "Ambitions Enough for Another 10 Years," *Houston Chronicle,* September 6, 2008, downloaded from Business & Company Resource Center, http://galenet.galegroup.com; and "Google's Lessons for Employers: Put Your Employees First," *HR Focus,* September 2008, http://galenet.galegroup.com.

108. W. A. Randolph and M. Sashkin, "Can Organizational Empowerment Work in Multinational Settings?" *Academy of Management Executive* 16 (2002), pp. 102–15.

109. J. Adams, "Inequality in Social Exchange," in *Advances in Experimental Social Psychology,* ed. L. Berkowitz (New York: Academic Press, 1965).

110. M. Bloom, "The Performance Effects of Pay Dispersion of Individuals and Organizations," *Academy of Management Journal* 42 (1999), pp. 25–40.

111. Gretchen Morgenson, "Peer Pressure: Inflating Executive Pay," *New York Times,* November 26, 2006, http://www.nytimes.com.

112. D. Skarlicki, R. Folger, and P. Tesluk, "Personality as a Moderator in the Relationships between Fairness and Retaliation," *Academy of Management Journal* 42 (1999), pp. 100–108.

113. Dunstan Prial, "Crunch Time for CPAs," *The Record (Bergen County, NJ),* April 17, 2007, downloaded from Business & Company Resource Center, http://galenet.galegroup.com.

114. J. Brockner, "Making Sense of Procedural Fairness: How High Procedural Fairness Can Reduce or Heighten the Influence of Outcome Favorability," *Academy of Management Review* 27 (2002), pp. 58–76; and D. De Cremer and D. van Knippenberg, "How Do Leaders Promote Cooperation? The Effects of Charisma and Procedural Fairness," *Journal of Applied Psychology* 87 (2002), pp. 858–66.

115. M. Kernan and P. Hanges, "Survivor Reactions to Reorganization: Antecedents and Consequences of Procedural, Interpersonal, and Informational Justice," *Journal of Applied Psychology* 87 (2002), pp. 916–28.

116. Lawler, *Treat People Right!*

117. Ann Pomeroy, "Company Is a Team, Not a Family," *HRMagazine,* April 2007, downloaded from Business & Company Resource Center, http://galenet.galegroup.com.

118. W. C. Kim and R. Mauborgne, "Fair Process: Managing in the Knowledge Economy," *Harvard Business Review,* July–August 1997, pp. 65–75.

119. T. Bateman and D. Organ, "Job Satisfaction and the Good Sold: The Relationship between Affect and Employee 'Citizenship,'" *Academy of Management Journal,* 1983, pp. 587–95.

120. D. Henne and E. Locke, "Job Dissatisfaction: What Are the Consequences?" *International Journal of Psychology* 20 (1985), pp. 221–40.

121. J. Barling, E. K. Kelloway, and R. Iverson, "High-Quality Work, Job Satisfaction, and Occupational Injuries," *Journal of Applied Psychology* 88 (2003), pp. 276–83.

122. D. Bowen, S. Gilliland, and R. Folger, "HRM and Service Fairness: How Being Fair with Employees Spills Over to Customers," *Organizational Dynamics,* Winter 1999, pp. 7–23.

123. J. Harter, F. Schmidt, and T. Hayes, "Business-Unit-Level Relationship between Employee Satisfaction, Employee Engagement, and Business Outcomes: A Meta-Analysis," *Journal of Applied Psychology* 87 (2002), pp. 268–79.

124. Tamara Schweitzer, "U.S. Workers Hate Their Jobs More than Ever," *Inc.,* March 6, 2007, http://www.inc.com.

125. T. Bisoux, "Corporate CounterCulture," *BizEd,* November/December 2004, pp. 16–20.

126. Fisher, "Happy Employees, Loyal Employees"; "100 Best Companies to Work for 2007," *Fortune* Rankings, January 22, 2007, http://money.cnn.com; First Horizon National Corp., "Careers" and "Our Benefits," http://www.firsthorizon.com, accessed June 5, 2007.

127. R. E. Walton, "Improving the Quality of Work Life," *Harvard Business Review,* May–June 1974, pp. 12, 16, 155.

128. E. E. Lawler III, "Strategies for Improving the Quality of Work Life," *American Psychologist* 37 (1982), pp. 486–93; and J. L. Suttle, "Improving Life at Work: Problems and Prospects," in *Improving Life at Work,* ed. J. R. Hackman and J. L. Suttle (Santa Monica, CA: Goodyear, 1977).

129. S. L. Robinson, "Trust and Breach of the Psychological Contract," *Administrative Science Quarterly* 41 (1996), pp. 574–99.

130. D. Rousseau, "Changing the Deal While Keeping the People," *Academy of Management Executive* 10 (1996), pp. 50–58.

131. E. E. Lawler III, *From the Ground Up* (San Francisco: Jossey-Bass 1996).

132. Ibid.

133. S. Ghoshal, C. Bartlett, and P. Moran, "Value Creation: The New Management Manifesto," *Financial Times Mastering Management Review,* November 1999, pp. 34–37.

134. Ram Charan, "Stop Whining, Start Thinking," *BusinessWeek,* August 14, 2008, http://www.businessweek.com.

Chapter 11

1. Oliver Marks, "From Command and Control to Collaboration and Teamwork," ZDNet.com, February 9, 2009, http://blogs.zdnet.com; Stephen Lawson, "Cisco to Shift Resources to Consumer Push," *PC World,* December 9, 2008, http://www.pcworld.com; Ellen McGirt, "How Cisco's CEO John Chambers Is Turning the Tech Giant Socialist," *Fast Company,* November 25, 2008, http://www.fastcompany.com; Bronwyn Fryer, "Cisco CEO John Chambers on Teamwork and Collaboration," *Harvard Business Review,* October 24, 2008, http://www.discussionleader.hbsp.com; "Reinventing Cisco Systems," *redOrbit,* January 27, 2008, http://www.redorbit.com; John Chambers, "Commentary," *Forbes,* January 23, 2008, http://www.forbes.com; and Susie Gharib, "One on One with John Chambers, Cisco Chairman and CEO, Shares Success Secrets," *Nightly Business Report,* November 7, 2007, http://www.pbc.org.

2. S. Cohen and D. Bailey, "What Makes Teams Work: Group Effectiveness Research from the Shop Floor to the Executive Suite," *Journal of Management* 23 (1997), pp. 239–90.

3. G. Chen, L. Donahue, and R. Klimoski, "Training Undergraduates to Work in Organizational Teams," *Academy of Management Learning and Education* 3 (2004), pp. 27–40.

4. Ken Blanchard Companies, "Client Spotlight: Summit Pointe," *Ignite!,* March 2007, http://www.kenblanchard.com/ignite.

5. K. Wexley and S. Silverman, *Working Scared* (San Francisco: Jossey-Bass, 1993).

6. Eric Fleischauer, "Nucor Manager Says Teamwork Key to Success; Q1 Earnings Up," *Decatur (AL) Daily,* April 20, 2007, http://www.decaturdaily.com.

7. E. E. Lawler, *From the Ground Up* (San Francisco: Jossey-Bass, 1996).

8. Kelley Holland, "How to Build Teamwork after an Awful Season," *New York Times,* December 28, 2008, downloaded from Business & Company Resource Center, http://galenet.galegroup.com.

9. D. Nadler, J. R. Hackman, and E. E. Lawler III, *Managing Organizational Behavior* (Boston: Little, Brown, 1979).

10. Holland, "How to Build Teamwork."

11. M. Cianni and D. Wnuck, "Individual Growth and Team Enhancement: Moving toward a New Model of Career Development," *Academy of Management Executive* 11 (1997), pp. 105–15.

12. Cohen and Bailey, "What Makes Teams Work."

13. J. Katzenbach and D. Smith, "The Discipline of Teams," *Harvard Business Review,* March–April 1993, pp. 111–20.

14. Matthew D. Sarrel, "SMB Boot Camp: Wicked Productive Wikis," *PC Magazine,* February 20, 2007, http://galenet.galegroup.com.

15. J. Zenger et al., *Leading Teams* (Burr Ridge, IL: Business One Irwin, 1994).

16. S. Cohen, "New Approaches to Teams and Teamwork," in J. Galbraith, E. E. Lawler III, and Associates, *Organizing for the Future* (San Francisco: Jossey-Bass, 1993).

17. Cohen and Bailey, "What Makes Teams Work."

18. Luke Mullins, "Integration Crew for Maryland Bank," *American Banker,* February 13, 2007, downloaded from General Reference Center Gold, http://find.galegroup.com.

19. Ibid.

20. C. Snow, S. Snell, S. Davison, and D. Hambrick, "Use Transnational Teams to Globalize Your Company," *Organizational Dynamics,* Spring 1996, pp. 50–67.

21. B. Kirkman, B. Rosen, C. Gibson, P. Tesluk, and S. McPherson, "Five Challenges to Virtual Team Success: Lessons from Sabre, Inc.," *Academy of Management Executive* 16 (2002), pp. 67–80.

22. A. Malhotra, A. Majchrzak, and B. Rosen, "Leading Virtual Teams," *Academy of Management Perspectives,* February 2007, pp. 60–70, table1.

23. R. Banker, J. Field, R. Schroeder, and K. Sinha, "Impact of Work Teams on Manufacturing Performance: A Longitudinal Field Study," *Academy of Management Journal* 39 (1996), pp. 867–90.

24. D. Yeatts, M. Hipskind, and D. Barnes, "Lessons Learned from Self-Managed Work Teams," *Business Horizons,* July–August 1994, pp. 11–18.

25. B. Kirkman and D. Shapiro, "The Impact of Cultural Values on Job Satisfaction and Organizational Commitment in Self-Managing Work Teams: The Mediating Role of Employee Resistance," *Academy of Management Journal* 44 (2001), pp. 557–69.

26. Ibid.

27. B. Kirkman and D. Shapiro, "The Impact of Cultural Values on Employee Resistance to Teams: Toward a Model of Globalized Self-Managing Work Team Effectiveness," *Academy of Management Review* 22 (1997), pp. 730–57.

28. B. Macy and H. Isumi, "Organizational Change, Design, and Work Innovation: A Meta-Analysis of 131 North American Field Studies—1961–1991," *Research in Organizational Change and Development* 7 (1993), pp. 235–313.

29. Ibid.

30. B. W. Tuckman, "Developmental Sequence in Small Groups," *Psychological Bulletin* 63 (1965), pp. 384–99.

31. S. Furst, M. Reeves, B. Rosen, and R. Blackburn, "Managing the Life Cycle of Virtual Teams," *Academy of Management Executive,* May 2004, pp. 6–20. Quotes in this paragraph are from pp. 11 and 12.

32. C. J. G. Gersick, "Time and Transition in Work Teams: Toward a New Model of Group Development," *Academy of Management Journal* 31 (1988), pp. 9–41.

33. J. R. Hackman, *Groups That Work (and Those That Don't)* (San Francisco: Jossey-Bass, 1990).

34. Zenger et al., *Leading Teams.*

35. R. Cross, "Looking before You Leap: Assessing the Jump to Teams in Knowledge-Based Work," *Business Horizons,* September–October 2000, pp. 29–36.

36. Ken Blanchard Companies, "The Critical Role of Teams," *Research Findings,* April 11, 2006, http://www.kenblanchard.com/thoughtleadership (reporting on a March 2006 survey of 962 HR, training, and operations leaders).

37. J. Case, "What the Experts Forgot to Mention," *Inc.,* September 1993, pp. 66–78.

38. A. Nahavandi and E. Aranda, "Restructuring Teams for the Reengineered Organization," *Academy of Management Executive,* November 1994, pp. 58–68.

39. B. Kirkman, B. Rosen, P. Tesluk, and C. Gibson, "The Impact of Team Empowerment on Virtual Team Performance: The Moderating Role of Face-to-Face Interaction," *Academy of Management Journal* 47 (2004), pp. 175–92.

40. Jon R. Katzenbach and Douglas K. Smith, *The Wisdom of Teams* (Boston: Harvard Business School Press, 1993).

41. Nadler et al., *Managing Organizational Behavior.*

42. T. Peters and N. Austin, *A Passion for Excellence* (New York: Random House, 1985).

43. Debra Wood, "Multidisciplinary Team Eliminates Inefficiencies in a Busy GYN Oncology Clinic," *Oncology Nursing News,* April 2009, downloaded from Business & Company Resource Center, http://galenet.galegroup.com.

44. Nadler et al., *Managing Organizational Behavior.*

45. Steve Adams, "Making All Your Teams into A-Teams," *Training Journal,* August 2008, downloaded from Business & Company Resource Center, http://galenet.galegroup.com.

46. David Clutterbuck, "How to Coach a Team in the Field: What Is Involved in Team Coaching and What Skills Are Required?" *Training Journal,* February 2007, downloaded from Business & Company Resource Center, http://galenet.galegroup.com.

47. Diane Coutu, "Why Teams Don't Work," *Harvard Business Review,* May 2009, pp. 99–105 (interview of J. Richard Hackman).

48. Katzenbach and Smith, "The Discipline of Teams."

49. Ibid.

50. L. Gibson, J. Mathieu, C. Shalley, and T. Ruddy, "Creativity and Standardization: Complementary or Conflicting Drivers of Team Effectiveness?" *Academy of Management Journal* 48 (2005), pp. 521–31.

51. C. Meyer, "How the Right Measures Help Teams Excel," *Harvard Business Review,* May–June 1994, pp. 95–103.

52. J. R. Katzenbach and J. A. Santamaria, "Firing Up the Front Line," *Harvard Business Review,* May–June 1999, pp. 107–17.

53. D. Knight, C. Durham, and E. Locke, "The Relationship of Team Goals, Incentives, and Efficacy to Strategic Risk, Tactical Implementation, and Performance," *Academy of Management Journal* 44 (2001), pp. 326–38.

54. B. L. Kirkman and B. Rosen, "Powering Up Teams," *Organizational Dynamics,* Winter 2000, pp. 48–66.

55. Lawler, *From the Ground Up.*

56. Avan Jassawalla, Hemant Sashittal, and Avinash Maishe, "Students' Perceptions of Social Loafing: Its Antecedents and Consequences in Undergraduate Business Classroom Teams", *Academy of Management Learning and Education,* 2009, 42–54.

57. M. Erez, "Is Group Productivity Loss the Rule or the Exception? Effects of Culture and Group-Based Motivation," *Academy of Management Journal* 39 (1996), pp. 1513–37.

58. Katzenbach and Smith, "The Discipline of Teams."

59. Matt Bolch, "Rewarding the Team," *HRMagazine,* February 2007, downloaded from General Reference Center Gold, http://find.galegroup.com; and P. Pascarelloa, "Compensating Teams," *Across the Board,* February 1997, pp. 16–22.

60. R. Wageman, "Interdependence and Group Effectiveness," *Administrative Science Quarterly* 40 (1995), pp. 145–80.

61. Bolch, "Rewarding the Team."

62. Lawler, *From the Ground Up.*

63. R. Wellins, R. Byham, and G. Dixon, *Inside Teams* (San Francisco: Jossey-Bass, 1994).

64. JoAnne Allen, "One 'Bad Apple' Does Spoil the Whole Office," *Reuters,* February 12, 2007, http://news.yahoo.com; and Joseph Wardy, "Don't Let One with Bad Attitude Infect Others," *Daily Record (Morris County, NJ),* April 23, 2007, http://www.dailyrecord.com.

65. Institute for Corporate Productivity, "Virtual Teams Now a Reality," news release, September 4, 2008, http://www.i4cp.com.

66. Abhishek Srivastava, Kathryn Bartol, and Edwin Locke, "Empowering Leadership in Management Teams: Effects on Knowledge Sharing, Efficacy, and Performance," *Academy of Management Journal,* 2006, pp. 1239–51.

67. J. M. Levine, E. T. Higgins, and H. Choi, "Development of Strategic Norms in Groups," *Organizational Behavior and Human Decision Processes* 82 (2000), pp. 88–101.

68. K. Jehn and E. Mannix, "The Dynamic Nature of Conflict: A Longitudinal Study of Intragroup Conflict and Group Performance," *Academy of Management Journal* 44 (2001), pp. 238–51.

69. J. O'Toole, *Vanguard Management: Redesigning the Corporate Future* (New York: Doubleday, 1985).

70. R. F. Bales, *Interaction Process Analysis: A Method for the Study of Small Groups* (Reading, MA: Addison-Wesley, 1950).

71. V. U. Druskat and J. Wheeler, "Managing from the Boundary: The Effective Leadership of Self-Managing Work Teams," *Academy of Management Journal* 46 (2003), pp. 435–57.

72. Katzenbach and Smith, *The Wisdom of Teams.*

73. Jay Carson, Paul Tesluk, and Jennifer Marrone, "Shared Leadership in Teams: An Investigation of Antecedent Conditions and Performance," *Academy of Management Journal,* 2007, pp. 1217–34.

74. C. Stoner and R. Hartman, "Team Building: Answering the Tough Questions," *Business Horizons,* September–October 1993, pp. 70–78.

75. S. E. Seashore, *Group Cohesiveness in the Industrial Work Group* (Ann Arbor: University of Michigan Press, 1954).

76. Greg Violin, "Teamwork Makes TV Show Go," *Orlando Sentinel,* April 8, 2007, http://www.orlandosentinel.com.

77. B. Mullen and C. Cooper, "The Relation between Group Cohesiveness and Performance: An Integration," *Psychological Bulletin* 115 (1994), pp. 210–27.

78. Banker et al., "Impact of Work Teams on Manufacturing Performance."

79. D. P. Forbes and F. J. Milliken, "Cognition and Corporate Governance: Understanding Boards of Directors as Strategic Decision-Making Groups," *Academy of Management Review* 24 (1999), pp. 489–505.

80. T. Simons, L. H. Pelled, and K. A. Smith, "Making Use of Difference: Diversity, Debate, and Decision Comprehensiveness in Top Management Teams," *Academy of Management Journal* 42 (1999), pp. 662–73.

81. Seashore, *Group Cohesiveness in the Industrial Work Group.*

82. B. Lott and A. Lott, "Group Cohesiveness as Interpersonal Attraction: A Review of Relationships with Antecedent and Consequent Variables," *Psychological Bulletin,* October 1965, pp. 259–309.

83. K. Dahlin, L. Weingart, and P. Hinds, "Team Diversity and Information Use," *Academy of Management Journal* 48 (2005), pp. 1107–23.

84. B. L. Kirkman and B. Rosen, "Beyond Self-Management: Antecedents and Consequences of Team Empowerment," *Academy of Management Journal* 42 (1999), pp. 58–74.

85. Hackman, *Groups That Work.*

86. W. Bennis, *Organizing Genius* (Reading, MA: Addison-Wesley, 1997).

87. Cianni and Wnuck, "Individual Growth and Team Enhancement."

88. K. Jehn, "A Multimethod Examination of the Benefits and Detriments of Intragroup Conflict," *Administrative Science Quarterly* 40 (1995), pp. 245–82.

89. Wellins et al., *Inside Teams.*

90. D. G. Ancona, "Outward Bound: Strategies for Team Survival in an Organization," *Academy of Management Journal* 33 (1990), pp. 334–65.

91. Ibid.

92. L. Sayles, *Leadership: What Effective Managers Really Do, and How They Do It* (New York: McGraw-Hill, 1979).

93. Ibid.

94. Patrick Lencioni, "How to Foster Good Conflict," *The Wall Street Journal,* November 13, 2008, http://online.wsj.com; and Debbie Schachter, "Learn to Embrace Opposition for Improved Decision Making," *Information Outlook,* October 2008, downloaded from Business & Company Resource Center, http://galenet.galegroup.com.

95. J. Chatman and F. Flynn, "The Influence of Demographic Heterogeneity on the Emergence and Consequences of Cooperative Norms in Work Teams," *Academy of Management Journal* 44 (2001), pp. 956–74; and R. T. Keller, "Cross-Functional Project Groups in Research and New Product Development: Diversity, Communications, Job Stress, and Outcomes," *Academy of Management Journal* 44 (2001), pp. 547–55.

96. Ranjini Manian, "Teamwork, Sweat and Tears," *Business Line,* March 23, 2009, downloaded from Business & Company Resource Center, http://galenet.galegroup.com.

97. "Managing Multicultural Teams: Winning Strategies from Teams around the World," *Computerworld,* November 20, 2006, http://find.galegroup.com.

98. D. Tjosvold, *Working Together to Get Things Done* (Lexington, MA: Lexington Books, 1986).

99. C. Tinsley and J. Brett, "Managing Workplace Conflict in the United States and Hong Kong," *Organizational Behavior and Human Decision Processes* 85 (2001), pp. 360–81.

100. K. W. Thomas, "Conflict and Conflict Management," in *Handbook of Industrial and Organizational Psychology,* ed. M. D. Dunnette (Chicago: Rand McNally, 1976).

101. Joann S. Lublin, "How Best to Supervise Internal Runner-Up for the Job You Got," *The Wall Street Journal,* January 30, 2007, http://online.wsj.com.

102. Ibid.

103. K. W. Thomas, "Toward Multi-Dimensional Values in Teaching: The Example of Conflict Behaviors," *Academy of Management Review,* 1977, pp. 484–89.

104. C. O. Longenecker and M. Neubert, "Barriers and Gateways to Management Cooperation and Teamwork," *Business Horizons,* September–October 2000, pp. 37–44.

105. P. S. Nugent, "Managing Conflict: Third-Party Interventions for Managers," *Academy of Management Executive* 16 (2002), pp. 139–54.

106. M. Blum and J. A. Wall Jr., "HRM: Managing Conflicts in the Firm," *Business Horizons,* May–June 1997, pp. 84–87.

107. Vickie Elmer, "Stressed Out," *The Washington Post,* October 19, 2006, http://www.washingtonpost.com.

108. J. A. Wall Jr., and R. R. Callister, "Conflict and Its Management," *Journal of Management* 21 (1995), pp. 515–58.

109. J. Polzer, C. B. Crisp, S. Jarvenpaa, and J. Kim, "Extending the Faultline Model to Geographically Dispersed Teams: How Collocated Subgroups Can Impair Group Functioning," *Academy of Management Journal* 49 (2006), pp. 679–92.

110. M. Montoya-Weiss, A. Massey, and M. Song, "Getting It Together: Temporal Coordination and Conflict Management in Global Virtual Teams," *Academy of Management Journal* 44 (2001), pp. 1251–62.

111. R. Standifer and J. A. Wall Jr., "Managing Conflict in B2B Commerce," *Business Horizons,* March–April 2003, pp. 65–70.

Chapter 12

1. L. Penley, E. Alexander, I. E. Jernigan, and C. Henwood, "Communication Abilities of Managers: The Relationship to Performance," *Journal of Management* 17 (1991), pp. 57–76.

2. W. V. Haney, "A Comparative Study of Unilateral and Bilateral Communication," *Academy of Management Journal* 7 (1964), pp. 128–36.

3. Jared Sandberg, "What Exactly Was It That the Boss Said? You Can Only Imagine," *The Wall Street Journal,* September 19, 2006, http://online.wsj.com.

4. M. McCormack, "The Illusion of Communication," *Financial Times Mastering Management Review,* July 1999, pp. 8–9.

5. Jared Sandberg, "Not Communicating with Your Boss? Count Your Blessings," *The Wall Street Journal,* May 22, 2007, http://online.wsj.com.

6. R. Cross and S. Brodt, "How Assumptions of Consensus Undermine Decision Making," *Sloan Management Review* 42 (2001), pp. 86–94.

7. S. Mohammed and E. Ringseis, "Cognitive Diversity and Consensus in Group Decision Making: The Role of Inputs, Processes, and Outcomes," *Organizational Behavior and Human Decision Processes* 85 (2001), pp. 310–35.

8. S. Parker and C. Axtell, "Seeing Another Viewpoint: Antecedents and Outcomes of Employee Perspective Taking," *Academy of Management Journal* 44 (2001), pp. 1085–100.

9. D. Tannen, "The Power of Talk: Who Gets Heard and Why," *Harvard Business Review,* September–October 1995, pp. 138–48.

10. Ibid.

11. Ibid.

12. L. K. Larkey, "Toward a Theory of Communicative Interactions in Culturally Diverse Workgroups," *Academy of Management Review,* April 1996, pp. 463–91.

13. Nancy J. Adler, *International Dimensions of Organizational Behavior.* Copyright © 1986. Reprinted with permission of South-Western College Publishing, a division of Thomson Learning.

14. C. Argyris, "Good Communication That Blocks Learning," *Harvard Business Review,* July–August 1994, pp. 77–85.

15. Eric Krell, "The Unintended Word," *HRMagazine,* August 2006, downloaded from General Reference Center Gold, http://find.galegroup.com.

16. C. Deutsch, "The Multimedia Benefits Kit," *New York Times,* October 14, 1990, sec. 3, p. 25.

17. T. W. Comstock, *Communicating in Business and Industry* (Albany, NY: Delmar, 1985).

18. J. Taylor and W. Wacker, *The 500 Year Delta: What Happens after What Comes Next* (New York: HarperCollins, 1997).

19. Michael Totty, "Rethinking the Inbox," *The Wall Street Journal,* March 26, 2007, http://online.wsj.com.

20. Kate Lorenz, "WAN2CHAT? 10 Tips for IM-ing at Work," *AOL Jobs,* December 15, 2006, http://jobs.aol.com.

21. Totty, "Rethinking the Inbox."

22. Susan J. Leandri, "Five Ways to Improve Your Corporate Blogs," *Information Outlook,* January 2007, downloaded from Business & Company Resource Center, http://galenet.galegroup.com.

23. Robert D. Hof, "Web 2.0: The New Guy at Work," *BusinessWeek,* June 19, 2006, downloaded from Business & Company Resource Center, http://galenet.galegroup.com.

24. Jessica Dye, "Collaboration 2.0: Make the Web Your Workspace," *EContent,* January–February 2007, downloaded from General Reference Center Gold, http://find.galegroup.com.

25. Ellen Lee, "The Maze Meltdown: Crash May Virtually Change Commuting," *San Francisco Chronicle,* May 6, 2007, http://www.sfgate.com.

26. S. S. K. Lam and J. Schaubroeck, "Improving Group Decisions by Better Pooling Information: A Comparative Advantage of Group Decision Support Systems," *Journal of Applied Psychology* 85 (2000), pp. 565–73.

27. M. Schrage, "If You Can't Say Anything Nice, Say It Anonymously," *Fortune,* December 6, 1999, p. 352; and Brad Stone, "A Call for Manners in the World of Nasty Blogs," *New York Times,* April 9, 2007, http://www.nytimes.com.

28. C. Naquin and G. Paulson, "Online Bargaining and Interpersonal Trust," *Journal of Applied Psychology* 88 (2003), pp. 113–20.

29. B. Baltes, M. Dickson, M. Sherman, C. Bauer, and J. LaGanke, "Computer-Mediated Communication and Group Decision Making: A Meta-Analysis," *Organizational Behavior and Human Decision Processes* 87 (2002), pp. 156–79.

30. R. Rice and D. Case, "Electronic Message Systems in the University: A Description of Use and Utility," *Journal of Communication* 33 (1983), pp. 131–52; and C. Steinfield, "Dimensions of Electronic Mail Use in an Organizational Setting," *Proceedings of the Academy of Management,* San Diego, 1985.

31. Marilyn Gardner, "You've Got Mail: 'We're Letting You Go,'" *Christian Science Monitor,* September 18, 2006, http://www.csmonitor.com; and Linton Weeks, "Read the Blog: You're Fired," *National Public Radio,* December 8, 2008, http://www.npr.org.

32. Leandri, "Five Ways to Improve Your Corporate Blogs."

33. Reuters, "Is That Really What Your E-mail Meant to Say?" *Yahoo News,* February 14, 2007, http://news.yahoo.com.

34. B. Glassberg, W. Kettinger, and J. Logan, "Electronic Communication: An Ounce of Policy Is Worth a Pound of Cure," *Business Horizons,* July–August 1996, pp. 74–80.

35. A. Joyce, "Never Out of IM Reach," *Washington Post,* December 26, 2004, p. F5; and Gina Hughes, "Quick Guide to IM-ing at Work," *Yahoo Tech,* January 24, 2007, http://tech.yahoo.com.

36. Totty, "Rethinking the Inbox"; Reuters, "BlackBerrys, Laptops Blur Work/Home Balance: Poll," *Yahoo News,* April 5, 2007, http://news.yahoo.com; and Margaret Locher, "BlackBerry Addiction Starts at the Top," *PC World,* March 6, 2007, http://www.pcworld.com.

37. Caroline McCarthy, "Americans Mixed about Constant Net Access, Poll Finds," *CNet News,* April 16, 2007, http://news.com.com.

38. Taylor and Wacker, *The 500 Year Delta;* Locher, "BlackBerry Addiction"; and Hughes, "Quick Guide to IM-ing."

39. Locher, "BlackBerry Addiction."

40. Eric Horng, "No E-mail Fridays Transform Office," *ABC News,* March 10, 2007, http://abcnews.go.com.

41. Ibid.

42. V. Govindarajan and A. Gupta, "Building an Effective Global Team," *Organizational Dynamics* 42 (2001), pp. 63–71.

43. N. B. Kurland and D. E. Bailey, "Telework: The Advantages and Challenges of Working Here, There, Anywhere, Anytime," *Organizational Dynamics,* Autumn 1999, pp. 53–68; and Ben Van Der Meer, "Realty Companies Making Internet Home," *Modesto (CA) Bee,* December 15, 2006, downloaded from General Reference Center Gold, http://find.galegroup.com.

44. "ALA Washington Opens Virtual Office," *American Libraries,* March 2007, downloaded from General Reference Center Gold, http://find.galegroup.com.

45. Van Der Meer, "Realty Companies Making Internet Home."

46. Teresa Mackintosh, "Is This the Year You Move to a Virtual Office?" *Accounting Technology,* May 2007, downloaded from General Reference Center Gold, http://find.galegroup.com.

47. E. M. Hallowell, "The Human Moment at Work," *Harvard Business Review,* January–February 1999, pp. 58–66.

48. Jessica Marquez, "Connecting a Virtual Workforce," *Workforce Management,* September 22, 2008, downloaded from Business & Company Resource Center, http://galenet.galegroup.com.

49. R. Lengel and R. Daft, "The Selection of Communication Media as an Executive Skill," *Academy of Management Executive* 2 (1988), pp. 225–32.

50. J. R. Carlson and R. W. Zmud, "Channel Expansion Theory and the Experiential Nature of Media Richness Perceptions," *Academy of Management Journal* 42 (1999), pp. 153–70.

51. L. Trevino, R. Daft, and R. Lengel, "Understanding Managers' Media Choices: A Symbolic Interactionist Perspective," in *Organizations and Communication Technology,* ed. J. Fulk and C. Steinfield (London: Sage, 1990).

52. J. Fulk and B. Boyd, "Emerging Theories of Communication in Organizations," *Journal of Management* 17 (1991), pp. 407–46.

53. From *Communicating for Managerial Effectiveness* by P. G. Clampitt. Copyright © 1991 by Sage Publications, Inc. Reprinted by permission of Sage Publications, Inc.

54. L. Bossidy and R. Charan, *Confronting Reality: Doing What Matters to Get Things Right* (New York: Crown Business, 2004).

55. M. McCall, M. Lombardo, and A. Morrison, *The Lessons of Experience: How Successful Executives Develop on the Job* (Lexington, MA: Lexington, 1988).

56. J. A. Conger, "The Necessary Art of Persuasion," *Harvard Business Review,* May–June 1998, pp. 84–95.

57. Nick Morgan, "How to Become an Authentic Speaker," *Harvard Business Review,* November 2008, pp. 115–19.

58. N. Nohria and B. Harrington, *Six Principles of Successful Persuasion* (Boston: Harvard Business School Publishing Division, 1993).

59. Justin Ewers, "Making It Stick," *U.S. News & World Report,* January 29–February 5, 2007, pp. EE2–EE8 (review of *Made to Stick* by Chip Heath and Dan Heath).

60. Lynn Hamilton, class handout (with permission).

61. H. K. Mintz, "Business Writing Styles for the 70's," *Business Horizons,* August 1972. Cited in *Readings in Interpersonal and Organizational Communication,* ed. R. C. Huseman, C. M. Logue, and D. L. Freshley (Boston: Allyn & Bacon, 1977).

62. C. D. Decker, "Writing to Teach Thinking," *Across the Board,* March 1996, pp. 19–20.

63. M. Forbes, "Exorcising Demons from Important Business Letters," *Marketing Times,* March–April 1981, pp. 36–38.

64. W. Strunk Jr. and E. B. White, *The Elements of Style,* 3rd ed. (New York: Macmillan, 1979); and H. R. Fowler and J. E Aaron, *The Little, Brown Handbook,* 10th ed. (New York: Longman, 2006).

65. Jessica Tsai, "Spiff Up Your Site!" *CRM Magazine,* December 2008, downloaded from Business & Company Resource Center, http://galenet.galegroup.com.

66. Del Jones, "Cisco CEO Sees Tech as Integral to Success," *USA Today,* March 19, 2007, p. 4B (interview with John Chambers).

67. G. Ferraro, "The Need for Linguistic Proficiency in Global Business," *Business Horizons,* May–June 1996, pp. 39–46.

68. P. C. Early and E. Mosakowski, "Creating Hybrid Team Cultures: An Empirical Test of Transnational Team Functioning," *Academy of Management Journal* 43 (2000), pp. 26–49.

69. Ferraro, "The Need for Linguistic Proficiency."

70. C. Chu, *The Asian Mind Game* (New York: Rawson Associates, 1991).

71. Ferraro, "The Need for Linguistic Proficiency."

72. Joann S. Lublin, "Improv Troupe Teaches Managers How to Give Better Presentations," *Career Journal,* February 7, 2007, http://www.careerjournal.com.

73. Comstock, *Communicating in Business and Industry.*

74. M. Korda, *Power: How to Get It, How to Use It* (New York: Random House, 1975).

75. A. Mehrabian, "Communication without Words," *Psychology Today,* September 1968, p. 52. Cited in M. B. McCaskey, "The Hidden Message Managers Send," *Harvard Business Review,* November–December 1979, pp. 135–48.

76. Ferraro, "The Need for Linguistic Proficiency."

77. *Business Horizons,* May–June 1993. Copyright 1993 by the Foundation for the School of Business at Indiana University. Used with permission.

78. Ann Therese Palmer, "Art of Listening Picked Up Young," *Chicago Tribune,* April 29, 2007, sec. 5, p. 3.

79. Ibid.

80. A. Athos and J. Gabarro, *Interpersonal Behavior* (Englewood Cliffs, NJ: Prentice-Hall, 1978).

81. Ralph G. Nichols, "Listening Is a 10-Part Skill," *Nation's Business* 45 (July 1957), pp. 56–60. Cited in R. C. Huseman, C. M. Logue, and D. L. Freshley, eds., *Readings in Interpersonal and Organizational Communication* (Boston: Allyn & Bacon, 1977).

82. Mary K. Pratt, "Five Ways to Drive Your Best Workers out the Door," *Computerworld,* August 25, 2008, pp. 26–27, 30.

83. J. Kouzes and B. Posner, *The Leadership Challenge* (San Francisco: Jossey-Bass, 1995).

84. G. Graham, J. Unruh, and P. Jennings, "The Impact of Nonverbal Communication in Organizations: A Survey of Perceptions," *Journal of Business Communications* 28 (1991), pp. 45–62.

85. Ibid.

86. D. Upton and S. Macadam, "Why (and How) to Take a Plant Tour," *Harvard Business Review,* May–June 1997, pp. 97–106.

87. N. Adler, *International Dimensions of Organizational Behavior,* 2nd ed. (Boston: Kent, 1991).

88. Chu, *The Asian Mind Game.*

89. Alex Pentland, "How Social Networks Network Best," *Harvard Business Review,* February 2009, p. 37.

90. A. Smidts, A. T. H. Pruyn, and C. B. M. van Riel, "The Impact of Employee Communication and Perceived External Prestige on Organizational Identification," *Academy of Management Journal* 49 (2001), pp. 1051–62.

91. J. W. Koehler, K. W. E. Anatol, and R. L. Applebaum, *Organizational Communication: Behavioral Perspectives* (Orlando, FL: Holt, Rinehart & Winston, 1981).

92. Krell, "The Unintended Word."

93. J. Waldroop and T. Butler, "The Executive as Coach," *Harvard Business Review,* November–December 1996, pp. 111–17.

94. D. T. Hall, K. L. Otazo, and G. P. Hollenbeck, "Behind Closed Doors: What Really Happens in Executive Coaching," *Organizational Dynamics,* Winter 1999, pp. 39–53.

95. T. Judge and J. Cowell, "The Brave New World of Coaching," *Business Horizons,* July–August 1997, pp. 71–77; E. E. Lawler III, *Treat People Right!* (San Francisco: Jossey-Bass, 2003); and

L. A. Hill, "New Manager Development for the 21st Century," *Academy of Management Executive,* August 2004, pp. 121–26.

96. J. Gutknecht and J. B. Keys, "Mergers, Acquisitions, and Take-overs: Maintaining Morale of Survivors and Protecting Employees," *Academy of Management Executive,* August 1993, pp. 26–36.

97. D. Schweiger and A. DeNisi, "Communication with Employees Following a Merger: A Longitudinal Field Experiment," *Academy of Management Journal* 34 (1991), pp. 110–35.

98. J. Case, "The Open-Book Managers," *Inc.,* September 1990, pp. 104–13.

99. J. Case, "Opening the Books," *Harvard Business Review,* March–April 1997, pp. 118–27.

100. T. R. V. Davis, "Open-Book Management: Its Promise and Pitfalls," *Organization Dynamics,* Winter 1997, pp. 7–20.

101. B. Burlingham, "Jack Stack, SRC Holdings," *Inc.,* April 2004, pp. 134–35.

102. R. Aggarwal and B. Simkins, "Open Book Management: Optimizing Human Capital," *Business Horizons* 44 (2001), pp. 5–13.

103. W. V. Ruch, *Corporate Communications* (Westport, CT: Quorum, 1984).

104. Jared Sandberg, "Working for a Boss Who Only Manages Up Can Be a Real Downer," *The Wall Street Journal,* May 16, 2006, http://online.wsj.com.

105. Krell, "The Unintended Word."

106. J. Gardner, "The Heart of the Matter: Leader-Constituent Interaction," in *Leading and Leadership,* ed. T. Fuller (Notre Dame, IN: Notre Dame University Press, 2000), pp. 239–44.

107. Yukari Watani Kane and Phred Dvorak, "Howard Stringer, Japanese CEO," *The Wall Street Journal,* March 3, 2007, http://online.wsj.com; and "We're All Criss-Crossing," *The Wall Street Journal,* March 3, 2007, http://online.wsj.com.

108. R. Ashkenas, D. Ulrich, T. Jick, and S. Kerr, *The Boundaryless Organization* (San Francisco: Jossey-Bass, 1995).

109. Ruch, *Corporate Communications.*

110. Pete Bach, "Staying in Touch a Changing Picture," *Post-Crescent (Appleton, WI),* April 18, 2006, downloaded from General Reference Center Gold, http://find.galegroup.com.

111. Mark Fitzgerald, "The Earl of Florida," *Editor & Publisher,* February 1, 2007, downloaded from General Reference Center Gold, http://find.galegroup.com.

112. Linda Dulye, "Get Out of Your Office," *HRMagazine,* July 2006, downloaded from General Reference Center Gold, http://find.galegroup.com.

113. A. Hutton, "Four Rules for Taking Your Message to Wall Street," *Harvard Business Review,* May 2001, pp. 125–32.

114. Koehler et al., *Organizational Communication.*

115. William Atkinson, "Let's Work Together Right Now," *Collections & Credit Risk,* May 2006, downloaded from Business & Company Resource Center, http://galenet.galegroup.com.

116. Janet Pogue, "Working around the Water Cooler," *Employee Benefit News,* February 1, 2009, downloaded from Business & Company Resource Center, http://galenet.galegroup.com; Gensler, "Gensler Survey Measures Connection between Workplace Design and Business Performance," news release, October 23, 2008, http://www.gensler.com; and Gensler, *2008 Workplace Survey: United States,* 2008, http://www.gensler.com.

117. Ashkenas et al., *The Boundaryless Organization.*

118. D. K. Denton, "Open Communication," *Business Horizons,* September–October 1993, pp. 64–69.

119. N. B. Kurland and L. H. Pelled, "Passing the Word: Toward a Model of Gossip and Power in the Workplace," *Academy of Management Review* 25 (2000), pp. 428–38.

120. L. Abrams, R. Cross, E. Lesser, and D. Levin, "Nurturing Interpersonal Trust in Knowledge-Sharing Networks," *Academy of Management Executive* 17 (November 2003), pp. 64–77.

121. R. L. Rosnow, "Rumor as Communication: A Contextual Approach," *Journal of Communication* 38 (1988), pp. 12–28.

122. L. Burke and J. M. Wise, "The Effective Care, Handling, and Pruning of the Office Grapevine," *Business Horizons,* May–June 2003, pp. 71–76.

123. K. Davis, "The Care and Cultivation of the Corporate Grapevine," *Dun's Review,* July 1973, pp. 44–47.

124. N. Difonzo, P. Bordia, and R. Rosnow, "Reining in Rumors," *Organizational Dynamics,* Summer 1994, pp. 47–62.

125. "Office Politics Is on the Rise According to a Survey by Accountemps," *Bradenton (FL) Herald,* October 25, 2008, downloaded from Business & Company Resource Center, http://galenet.galegroup.com; and Alan M. Wolf, "A Morale Boost," *Raleigh (NC) News & Observer,* March 15, 2009, http://galenet.galegroup.com.

126. Difonzo et al., "Reining in Rumors."

127. Ashkenas et al., *The Boundaryless Organization.*

128. R. M. Hodgetts, "A Conversation with Steve Kerr," *Organizational Dynamics,* Spring 1996, pp. 68–79.

129. R. M. Fulmer, "The Evolving Paradigm of Leadership Development," *Organizational Dynamics,* Spring 1997, pp. 59–72.

130. General Electric, "GE Shares Skills, Intellectual Capital with CommonBond Communities," news release, December 4, 2006, http://www.genewscenter.com.

131. Ashkenas et al., *The Boundaryless Organization.*

Chapter 13

1. Company Web site, http://www.legalseafoods.com, accessed April 22, 2009; Leigh Buchanan, "The Way I Work: Roger Berkowitz," *Inc.,* July 2008, pp. 84–87; and Elissa Elan, "Roger Berkowitz: Legal Sea Foods Leader Fosters Collaboration in Menu Development," *Nation's Restaurant News,* May 5, 2008, http://findarticles.com.

2. "BlackBerry Outage Explained," *Chicago Tribune,* April 21, 2007, sec. 3, p. 2; and Nancy Weil, "BlackBerry Service Restored, Slow Response Irks Users," *InfoWorld,* April 18, 2007, http://www.infoworld.com.

3. W. G. Ouchi, "Markets, Bureaucracies, and Clans," *Administrative Science Quarterly* 25 (1980), pp. 129–41.

4. James C. Collins, and Jerry I. Porras, *Built to Last: Successful Habits of Visionary Companies* (New York: HarperBusiness, 1994).

5. Robert Simons, Antonio Davila, and Robert S. Kaplan, *Performance Measurement & Control Systems for Implementing Strategy* (Englewood Cliffs, NJ: Prentice Hall, 2000); W. G. Ouchi, "A Conceptual Framework for the Design of Organizational Control Mechanisms," *Management Science* 25 (1979), pp. 833–48; W. G. Ouchi, "Markets, Bureaucracies, and Clans," *Administrative Science Quarterly* 25 (1980), pp. 129–41; and Richard D. Robey and C. A. Sales, *Designing Organizations* (Burr Ridge, IL: Richard D. Irwin, 1994).

6. Elaine D. Pulakos, Sharon Arad, Michelle A. Donovan, and Kevin E. Plamondon, "Adaptability in the Workplace: Development of a Taxonomy of Adaptive Performance," *Journal of Applied Psychology* 85, no. 4 (August 2000), pp. 12–24; and John H. Sheridan, "Lean Sigma Synergy," *Industry Week* 249, no. 17 (October 16, 2000), pp. 81–82.

7. Elizabeth Gardner, "High-Quality Information," *Modern Healthcare,* March 5, 2007, downloaded from General Reference Center Gold, http://find.galegroup.com.

8. Michael S. Rosenwald, "Chocolate Purists Alarmed by Proposal to Fudge Standards," *Washington Post,* April 27, 2007, http://www.washingtonpost.com.

9. J. T. Burr, "Keys to a Successful Internal Audit," *Quality Progress* 30, no. 4 (April 1997), pp. 75–77; and John Zorabedian, "Uniform Security," *American Executive,* June 2008, downloaded from Business & Company Resource Center, http://galenet.galegroup.com.

10. Leigh Buchanan, "Leadership: Armed with Data," *Inc.,* March 2009, http://www.inc.com.

11. Rosabeth Moss Kanter, "The Matter with the Mainstream," *U.S. News & World Report,* October 30, 2006, downloaded from General Reference Center Gold, http://find.galegroup.com.

12. "Quality Leadership 100," *Quality,* September 2006, downloaded from Business & Company Resource Center, http://galenet.galegroup.com.

13. Erin White, "How Surveying Workers Can Pay Off," *The Wall Street Journal,* June 18, 2007, http://online.wsj.com.

14. Bill Roberts, "Stay ahead of the Technology Use Curve," *HRMagazine,* October 2008, downloaded from Business & Company Resource Center, http://galenet.galegroup.com; and Kathy Ames Carr, "Broaching Body Art," *Crain's Cleveland Business,* September 29, 2008, http://galenet.galegroup.com.

15. Tom Hals, "Beware the Pitfalls of Office Romance," *Yahoo News,* February 13, 2007, http://news.yahoo.com; and Molly Selvin, "'Love Contract'? It's Office Policy," *Los Angeles Times,* February 13, 2007, http://www.latimes.com.

16. "McDonald's Sales Rise 7.1%," *CNNMoney,* February 9, 2009, http://money.cnn.com; and "CEOs Who Don't Get Out Often Enough, and Some Who Do," *24/7 Wall Street,* May 7, 2008, http://247wallst.com.

17. Vanessa Urch Druskat, "Effects and Timing of Developmental Peer Appraisals in Self-Managing Work Groups," *Journal of Applied Psychology* 84, no. 1 (February 1999), p. 58.

18. Tracy Cox, "Finding the Real MVPs in the Business," *Industry Week,* January 17, 2007, http://www.industryweek.com.

19. Sandra Waddock and Neil Smith, "Corporate Responsibility Audits: Doing Well by Doing Good," *Sloan Management Review* 41, no. 2 (Winter 2000), pp. 75–83; Lynn L. Bergeson, "OSHA Gives Incentives for Voluntary Self-Audits," *Pollution Engineering* 32, no. 10 (October 2000), pp. 33–34; and Tom Rancour and Mike McCracken, "Applying 6 Sigma Methods for Breakthrough Safety Performance," *Professional Safety* 45, no. 10 (October 2000), pp. 29–32.

20. Shaun Aghili, "A Six Sigma Approach to Internal Audits," *Strategic Finance,* February 2009, downloaded from Business & Company Resource Center, http://galenet.galegroup.com.

21. See, for example, Brian Hindo, "At 3M, a Struggle between Efficiency and Creativity," *BusinessWeek,* June 11, 2007, downloaded from General Reference Center Gold, http://find

.galegroup.com; Brian Hindo and Brian Grow, "Six Sigma; So Yesterday?" *BusinessWeek,* June 11, 2007, http://find.galegroup.com; and Jeneanne Rae, "Viewpoint: Have It Both Ways," *BusinessWeek,* June 11, 2007, http://find.galegroup.com.

22. Shaunessy Everett, "Do More, Better, for Less," *Library Journal,* September 15, 2006, http://galenet.galegroup.com.

23. Rancour and McCracken, "Applying 6 Sigma Methods for Breakthrough Safety Performance;" and George Eckes, "Making Six Sigma Last," *Ivey Business Journal,* January–February 2002, p. 77.

24. Janet L. Colbert, "The Impact of the New External Auditing Standards," *Internal Auditor* 5, no. 6 (December 2000), pp. 46–50.

25. Aghili, "A Six Sigma Approach"; Yves Giard and Yves Nadeau, "Improving the Processes," *CA Magazine,* December 2008, downloaded from Business & Company Resource Center, http://galenet.galegroup.com; and Glenn Cheney, "Connecting the Dots to the Next Crisis," *Financial Executive,* April 2009, pp. 30–33.

26. Jonathan D. Glater, "The Better the Audit Panel, the Higher the Stock Price," *New York Times,* April 8, 2005, p. C4.

27. Bill Roberts, "Data-Driven Human Capital Decisions," *HRMagazine,* March 2007, downloaded from General Reference Center Gold, http://find.galegroup.com.

28. P. C. Brewer and L. A. Vulinec, "Harris Corporation's Experiences with Using Activity-Based Costing," *Information Strategy: The Executive's Journal* 13, no. 2 (Winter 1997), pp. 6–16; and Terence P. Pare, "A New Tool for Managing Costs," *Fortune,* June 14, 1993, pp. 124–29.

29. K. Merchant, *Control in Business Organizations* (Boston: Pitman, 1985); C. W. Chow, Y. Kato, and K. A. Merchant, "The Use of Organizational Controls and Their Effects on Data Manipulation and Management Myopia," *Accounting, Organizations, and Society* 21, nos. 2/3 (February/April 1996), pp. 175–92.

30. E. E. Lawler III and J. Rhode, *Information and Control in Organizations* (Pacific Palisades, CA: Goodyear, 1976); Anthony Ferner, "The Underpinnings of 'Bureaucratic' Control Systems: HRM in European Multinationals," *Journal of Management Studies* 37, no. 4 (June 2000), pp. 521–39; and Marilyn S. Fenwick, "Cultural and Bureaucratic Control in MNEs: The Role of Expatriate Performance Management," *Management International Review* 39 (1999), pp. 107–25.

31. Hindo, "At 3M, a Struggle between Efficiency and Creativity."

32. David H. Freedman, "Go Ahead, Make a Mess," *Inc.,* December 2006, pp. 120–25.

33. J. Veiga and J. Yanouzas, *The Dynamics of Organization Theory,* 2nd ed. (St. Paul, MN: West, 1984).

34. Pedro Ruz Gutierrez, "Airport Workers Report Breach," *Orlando Sentinel,* May 26, 2007, downloaded from General Reference Center Gold, http://find.galegroup.com.

35. David Kiley, "The New Heat on Ford," *BusinessWeek,* June 4, 2007, http://www.businessweek.com.

36. Marcia Gelbart, "L&I Gets Ritz-Carlton Image Tips," *Philadelphia Inquirer,* March 10, 2009, http://www.philly.com.

37. Scott Leibs, "Measuring Up," *CFO,* June 2007, downloaded from General Reference Center Gold, http://find.galegroup.com.

38. Joe Fleischer, "New Methods to Measure Performance," *Call Center,* February 1, 2007, downloaded from General Reference Center Gold, http://find.galegroup.com.

39. Michael Hammer, "The Seven Deadly Sins of Performance Measurement and How to Avoid Them," *MIT Sloan Management Review* 48, no. 3 (Spring 2007), pp. 19–28.

40. Lawler and Rhode, *Information and Control in Organizations;* and J. A. Gowan Jr. and R. G. Mathieu, "Critical Factors in Information System Development for a Flexible Manufacturing System," *Computers in Industry* 28, no. 3 (June 1996), pp. 173–83.

41. Jennifer Robison, "How the Ritz-Carlton Manages the Mystique," *Gallup Management Journal,* December 11, 2008, downloaded from Business & Company Resource Center, http://galenet.galegroup .com.

42. Wendy Leavitt, "Twenty-First Century Driver Training," *Fleet Owner,* January 1, 2006, downloaded from Business & Company Resource Center, http://galenet.galegroup.com.

43. Robert S. Kaplan and David P. Norton, *The Balanced Scorecard: Translating Strategy into Action* (Boston: Harvard Business School Press, 1996); and Andra Gumbus and Robert N. Lussier, "Entrepreneurs Use a Balanced Scorecard to Translate Strategy into Performance Measures," *Journal of Small Business Management* 44, no. 3 (July 2006), downloaded from General Reference Center Gold, http://find.galegroup.com.

44. Gumbus and Lussier, "Entrepreneurs Use a Balanced Scorecard."

45. Marcia A. Reed-Woodard, "The Business of Nonprofit," *Black Enterprise,* June 2007, downloaded from General Reference Center Gold, http://find.galegroup.com.

46. Randy Myers, "Going Away," *CFO,* May 2007, downloaded from General Reference Center Gold, http://find.galegroup.com.

47. Ken Moores and Joseph Mula, "The Salience of Market, Bureaucratic, and Clan Controls in the Management of Family Firm Transitions: Some Tentative Australian Evidence," *Family Business Review* 13, no. 2 (June 2000), pp. 91–106; and Anthony Walker and Robert Newcombe, "The Positive Use of Power on a Major-Construction Project," *Construction Management and Economics* 18, no. 1 (January/February 2000), pp. 37–44.

48. Peter H. Fuchs, Kenneth E. Mifflin, Danny Miller, and John O. Whitney, "Strategic Integration: Competing in the Age of Capabilities," *California Management Review* 42, no. 3 (Spring 2000), pp. 118–47; Mary Ann Lando, "Making Compliance Part of Your Organization's Culture," *Healthcare Executive* 15, no. 5 (September/October 1999), pp. 18–22; and Kenneth A. Frank and Kyle Fahrbach, "Organization Culture as a Complex System: Balance and Information in Models of Influence and Selection," *Organization Science* 10, no. 3 (May/June 1999), pp. 253–77.

49. "100 Best Companies to Work For, 2009," *Fortune,* February 2, 2009, http://money.cnn.com.

50. Gerald H. B. Ross, "Revolution in Management Control," *Management Accounting,* November 1990, pp. 23–27. Reprinted with permission.

Chapter 14

1. Robert A. Burgelman, Modesto A. Maidique, and Steven C. Wheelwright, *Strategic Management of Technology and Innovation* (New York: McGraw-Hill, 2000).

2. Donna C. L. Prestwood and Paul A. Schumann Jr., "Revitalize Your Organization," *Executive Excellence* 15, no. 2 (February 1998), p. 16; Carliss Y. Baldwin and Kim B. Clark, "Managing in an Age of Modularity," *Harvard Business Review* 75, no. 5 (September–October 1997), pp. 84–93; Shanthi Gopalakrishnan, Paul Bierly, and Eric H. Kessler, "A Reexamination of Product and Process Innovations Using a Knowledge-Based View," *Journal of High Technology Management Research* 10, no. 1 (Spring 1999), pp. 147–66; and John Pullin, "Bombardier Commands Top Marks," *Professional Engineering* 13, no. 3 (July 5, 2000), pp. 40–46.

3. Mohanbir Sawhney, Robert C. Wolcott, and Inigo Arroniz, "The 12 Different Ways for Companies to Innovate," *MIT Sloan Management Review* 47, no. 3 (Spring 2006), pp. 75–81.

4. M. E. Porter, *Competitive Strategy* (New York: Free Press, 1980).

5. J. P. Andrew, K. Haanæs, D. C. Michael, H. L. Sirkin, and A. Taylor, *Innovation 2009: Making Hard Decisions in the Downturn,* Boston Consulting Group Senior Management Survey, http://www.bcg .com.

6. Geoff Colvin, "McKesson: Wiring the Medical World," *Fortune,* February 5, 2007, http://money.cnn.com.

7. Ronald E. Oligney and Michael I. Economides, "Technology as an Asset," *Hart's Petroleum Engineer International* 71, no. (September 1998), p. 27.

8. Jessica E. Vascellaro, "Found in Translation," *The Wall Journal,* May 24, 2007, http://online.wsj.com.

9. Colvin, "McKesson."

10. Damion Schubert, "Focusing Your Innovation," *oper,* February 1, 2009, downloaded from Bus Resource Center, http://galenet.galegroup.com

11. See, for example, Ben Ames, "IBM Spe Memory," *PC World,* February 14, 2C com; Scott Ferguson, "Intel Plans P Markets," *eWeek,* May 3, 2007, httr Ferguson, "AMD's Next-Gen Mob Power," *eWeek,* May 18, 2007,

12. Alex Taylor III, "The Great E 2009, http://money.cnn.co

13. Michael Kanellos, "For *News,* March 26, 20C

14. Laura Landro, " Records," *The wsj.com; and Records a Re nytimes.com.

15. Jill Jusko, "F from Genera

16. "Fresh, bu downloade .galegroup

17. Rajiv De Internet-Journal 2000), sion," Everet 1995

18. Mage Reta ter

19. Eri Ur K (

20.

21. Tom Krazit, "Intel R&D on Slow Boat to China," *CNet News,* April 16, 2007, http://news.com.com.

22. Ken MacQueen, "Cashing in His V-Chips," *Maclean's,* June 11, 2007, downloaded from General Reference Center Gold, http://find.galegroup.com; and "Online Gaming's Netscape Moment?" *The Economist,* June 9, 2007, http://find.galegroup.com.

23. Traci Purdum, "Benchmarking outside the Box: Best Practices Can Rise from Where You Least Expect Them," *Industry Week,* March 2007, downloaded from General Reference Center Gold, http://find.galegroup.com.

24. Von Hippel, *The Sources of Innovation;* and Leonard, *Wellsprings of Knowledge.*

25. John Hagedoorn, Albert N. Link, and Nicholas S. Vonortas, "Research Partnerships," *Research Policy* 29, no. 4/5 (April 2000), pp. 567–86; and Sang-Seung Yi, "Entry, Licensing and Research Joint Ventures," *International Journal of Industrial Organization* 17, no. 1 (January 1999), pp. 1–24.

26. Robert Dorn, "Chicken, Pork or Beef?" *Fleet Equipment,* May 2007, downloaded from General Reference Center Gold, http://find.galegroup.com; and "One of the Nation's Largest Producers of Animal Fat and a Major Oil Company Have Decided to Make Diesel Fuel Together," *Diesel Progress,* North American ed., May 2007, http://find.galegroup.com.

27. "Broadcom Acquires GPS Specialist Global Locate for $146 Million," *Information Week,* June 12, 2007, downloaded from General Reference Center Gold, http://find.galegroup.com.

Andrew et al., *Innovation 2009,* p. 11.

G. March, "Exploration and Exploitation in Organizational [Lea]rning," *Organization Science* 2, no. 1 (1991), pp. 71–87.

[Tho]mas Hoffman, "Change Agents," *ComputerWorld,* April 23, [200]7, downloaded from General Reference Center Gold, http://find. [galegr]oup.com; Center for CIO Leadership, "Center for CIO Leader[ship Un]veils 2008 Survey Results," news release, November 18, [http://www.](http://www).marketwire.com; and Center for CIO Leadership, [Lea]dership Survey Executive Summary," abstract, 2008, www.cioleadershipcenter.com, accessed June 3, 2009; and [Car]nthes, "The CIO/CTO Balancing Act," *ComputerWorld* (June 19, 2000), pp. 50–51.

"Raising Radicals: Different Processes for Champi[on]ing Corporate Ventures," *Organization Science* 5, [(19]94), pp. 148–72; Clifford Siporin, "Want Speedy [...] Hire a 'Product Champion," *Medical Marketing &* [...] 1993, pp. 22–28; Clifford Siporin, "How You Can [...] [Pha]se 3B," *Medical Marketing & Media,* October [...] Eric H. Kessler, "Tightening the Belt: Methods [...] [Devel]opment Costs Associated with New Product [...] *of Engineering and Technology Management* [...] 0), pp. 59–92.

[3]M, a Struggle between Efficiency and [We]ek, June 11, 2007, http://www.busi[ness-we]ek.com; "Creativity on Demand"; Edgar Figueroa [...] Rethinking the Innovation Process in [...] Case Study of 3M," *Journal of Engi[neering and Technology] Management* 17, no. 1 (March 2000), [...] [P]owell, "No Such Thing as a Daft [...] *[Engineeri]ng* 13, no. 4 (February 23, 2000),

[Mac]coby, "Embracing Risk to Grow [...] May 16, 2007, http://www.

34. David A. Fields, "How to Stop the Dumbing Down of Your Company," *Industry Week,* March 7, 2007, http://www.industry-week.com; Lisa K. Gundry, Jill R. Kickul, and Charles W. Prather, "Building the Creative Organization," *Organizational Dynamics* 22, no. 2 (Spring 1994), pp. 22–36; and Thomas Kuczmarski, "Inspiring and Implementing the Innovation Mind-Set," *Planning Review,* September–October 1994, pp. 37–48.

35. Ibid.

36. Company reports; R. Mitchell, "Masters of Innovation: How 3M Keeps Its New Products Coming," *BusinessWeek,* April 10, 1989, pp. 58–63; T. Katauskas, "Follow-Through: 3M's Formula for Success," *R&D,* November 1990; and Thomas J. Martin, "Ten Commandments for Managing Creative People," *Fortune,* January 16, 1995, pp. 135–36.

37. Hindo, "At 3M, a Struggle."

38. Doug Tsuruoka, "Intuit Innovation Lab, 'Idea Jams' Aim to Spur Creativity," *Investor's Business Daily,* April 14, 2009, downloaded from Business & Company Resource Center, http://galenet.galegroup.com.

39. H. Kent Bowen, Kim B. Clark, Charles A. Holloway, and Steven C. Wheelwright, "Development Projects: The Engine of Renewal," *Harvard Business Review,* September–October 1994, pp. 110–20; C. Eden, T. Williams, and F. Ackermann, "Dismantling the Learning Curve: The Role of Disruptions on the Planning of Development Projects," *International Journal of Project Management* 16, no. 3 (June 1998), pp. 131–38; and Mohan V. Tatikonda and Stephen R. Rosenthal, "Technology Novelty, Project Complexity, and Product Development Project Execution Success: A Deeper Look at Task Uncertainty in Product Innovation," *IEEE Transactions on Engineering Management* 47, no. 1 (February 2000), pp. 74–87.

40. Brad Nemer, "How MTV Channels Innovation," *BusinessWeek,* November 6, 2006, downloaded from General Reference Center Gold, http://find.galegroup.com.

41. E. Trist, "The Evolution of Sociotechnical Systems as a Conceptual Framework and as an Action Research Program," in *Perspectives on Organizational Design and Behavior,* ed. A. Van de Ven and W. F. Joyce, pp. 19–75 (New York: John Wiley & Sons, 1981); and Alfonso Molina, "Insights into the Nature of Technology Diffusion and Implementation: The Perspective of Sociotechnical Alignment," *Technovation* 17, nos. 11/12 (November/December 1997), pp. 601–26.

42. Scott A. Snell and James W. Dean Jr., "Strategic Compensation for Integrated Manufacturing: The Moderating Effects of Jobs and Organizational Inertia," *Academy of Management Journal* 37 (1994), pp. 1109–40.

43. C. Giffi, A. Roth, and G. Seal, *Competing in World-Class Manufacturing: America's 21st Century Challenge* (Homewood, IL: Business One Irwin, 1990).

44. R. M. Kanter, *World Class: Thriving Locally in the Global Economy* (New York: Touchstone, 1995).

45. Giffi, Roth, and Seal, *Competing in World-Class Manufacturing.*

46. J. Collins and J. Porras, *Built to Last* (London: Century, 1996).

47. Michael R. Morris, "The Dean of Green," *Professional Remodeler,* November 1, 2008, downloaded from Business & Company Resource Center, http://galenet.galegroup.com.

48. Collins and Porras, *Built to Last.*

49. C. Gibson and J. Birkinshaw, "The Antecedents, Consequences, and Mediating Role of Organizational Ambidexterity," *Academy of Management Journal* 47 (2004), pp. 209–26.

50. Collins and Porras, *Built to Last.*

51. T. Cummings and C. Worley, *Organization Development and Change,* 8th ed. (Mason, OH: Thomson/South-Western, 2005).

52. Ibid.

53. Ibid.

54. N. Nohria, W. Joyce, and B. Roberson, "What Really Works," *Harvard Business Review,* July 2003, pp. 42–52.

55. Daryl R. Conner, *Managing at the Speed of Change* (New York: Random House, 2006); and R. Teerlink, "Harley's Leadership U-Turn," *Harvard Business Review,* July-August 2000, pp. 43–48.

56. C. M. Christensen, "The Past and Future of Competitive Advantage," *Sloan Management Review,* Winter 2001, pp. 105–9.

57. M. Schrage, "Getting Beyond the Innovation Fetish," *Fortune,* November 13, 2000, pp. 225–32.

58. T. A. Judge, C. J. Thoresen, V. Pucik, and T. M. Welbourne, "Managerial Coping with Organizational Change: A Dispositional Perspective," *Journal of Applied Psychology* 84 (1999), pp. 107–22.

59. Nancy Hatch Woodward, "To Make Changes, Manage Them," *HRMagazine,* May 2007, downloaded from General Reference Center Gold, http://find.galegroup.com.

60. E. E. Lawler III, *Treat People Right!* (San Francisco: Jossey-Bass, 2003).

61. Pat Zigarmi and Judd Hoekstra, "Leadership Strategies for Making Change Stick," *Perspectives* (Ken Blanchard Companies, 2008), http://www.kenblanchard.com, accessed May 22, 2009.

62. Conner, *Managing at the Speed of Change;* and S. Oreg, "Resistance to Change: Developing an Individual Differences Measure," *Journal of Applied Psychology* (2003), pp. 680–93.

63. Phred Dvorak, "How Understanding the 'Why' of Decisions Matters," *The Wall Street Journal,* March 19, 2007, http://online.wsj.com.

64. Alan Deutschman, *Change or Die* (Los Angeles: Regan, 2007), pp. 164–78.

65. J. Stanislao and B. C. Stanislao, "Dealing with Resistance to Change," *Business Horizons,* July–August 1983, pp. 74–78.

66. J. P. Kotter and L. A. Schlesinger, "Choosing Strategies for Change," *Harvard Business Review,* March–April 1979, pp. 106–14.

67. D. Zell, "Overcoming Barriers to Work Innovations: Lessons Learned at Hewlett-Packard," *Organizational Dynamics,* Summer 2001, pp. 77–85.

68. Ibid.

69. E. B. Dent and S. Galloway Goldberg, "Challenging Resistance to Change," *Journal of Applied Behavioral Science,* March 1999, pp. 25–41.

70. G. Johnson, *Strategic Change and the Management Process* (New York: Basil Blackwell, 1987); and K. Lewin, "Frontiers in Group Dynamics," *Human Relations* 1 (1947), pp. 5–41.

71. E. H. Schein, "Organizational Culture: What It Is and How to Change It," in *Human Resource Management in International Firms,* ed. P. Evans, Y. Doz, and A. Laurent (New York: St. Martin's Press, 1990).

72. M. Beer, R. Eisenstat, and B. Spector, *The Critical Path to Corporate Renewal* (Cambridge, MA: Harvard Business School Press, 1990).

73. Dvorak, "How Understanding the 'Why' of Decisions Matters."

74. E. E. Lawler III, "Transformation from Control to Involvement," in *Corporate Transformation,* ed. R. Kilmann and T. Covin (San Francisco: Jossey-Bass, 1988).

75. Deutschman, *Change or Die,* pp. 1–15.

76. Paul Willax, "Getting the Boss to Embrace Change Requires Tact, Ingenuity," *New Hampshire Business Review,* May 11, 2007, http://find.galegroup.com.

77. D. Hellriegel and J. W. Slocum Jr., *Management,* 4th ed. (Reading, MA: Addison-Wesley, 1986).

78. Carolyn Aiken and Scott Keller, "The Irrational Side of Change Management," *McKinsey Quarterly,* April 2009, http://www.mckinseyquarterly.com.

79. Jerry L. Rhoads, "A Storm-Inspired Makeover," *Contemporary Long Term Care,* April–May 2007, downloaded from General Reference Center Gold, http://find.galegroup.com.

80. Lewin, "Frontiers in Group Dynamics."

81. Larry Hubbell and Scott Abbot, "Cultural Change in a Maximum Security Prison," *Public Manager* 35, no. 2 (Summer 2006), http://galenet.galegroup.com.

82. Schein, "Organizational Culture."

83. E. E. Lawler III, *From the Ground Up* (San Francisco: Jossey-Bass, 1995).

84. Q. Nguyen Huy, "Time, Temporal Capability, and Planned Change," *Academy of Management Review* 26 (2001), pp. 601–23.

85. B. Sugarman, "A Learning-Based Approach to Organizational Change: Some Results and Guidelines," *Organizational Dynamics,* Summer 2001, pp. 62–75.

86. Kotter and Schlesinger, "Choosing Strategies for Change."

87. Woodward, "To Make Changes, Manage Them."

88. R. H. Miles, "Beyond the Age of Dilbert: Accelerating Corporate Transformations by Rapidly Engaging All Employees," *Organizational Dynamics,* Spring 2001, pp. 313–21.

89. Bayless, "A Recipe for Effective Change."

90. D. A. Nadler, "Managing Organizational Change: An Integrative Approach," *Journal of Applied Behavioral Science* 17 (1981), pp. 191–211.

91. D. Rousseau and S. A. Tijoriwala, "What's a Good Reason to Change? Motivated Reasoning and Social Accounts in Promoting Organizational Change," *Journal of Applied Psychology* 84 (1999), pp. 514–28.

92. Ed Oakley, "Leading Change without Authority," *Material Handling Management,* May 2007, downloaded from General Reference Center Gold, http://find.galegroup.com.

93. Deutschman, *Change or Die,* pp. 187–93.

94. C. F. Leana and B. Barry, "Stability and Change as Simultaneous Experiences in Organizational Life," *Academy of Management Review* 25 (2000), pp. 753–59.

95. O. Gadiesh and J. Gilbert, "Transforming Corner-Office Strategy into Frontline Action," *Harvard Business Review,* May 2001, pp. 72–79.

96. B. Schneider, A. Brief, and R. Guzzo, "Creating a Climate and Culture for Sustainable Organizational Change," *Organizational Dynamics,* Spring 1996, pp. 7–19.

97. Price Waterhouse Change Integration Team, *Better Change: Best Practices for Transforming Your Organization* (Burr Ridge, IL: Irwin, 1995).

98. M. Beer and N. Nohria, "Cracking the Code of Change," *Harvard Business Review,* May–June 2000, pp. 133–41.

99. N. Nohria and J. Berkley, "Whatever Happened to the Take-Charge Manager?" *Harvard Business Review,* January–February 1994, pp. 128–37.

100. D. Miller, J. Hartwick, and I. Le Breton-Miller, "How to Detect a Management Fad—and Distinguish It from a Classic," *Business Horizons,* July–August 2004, pp. 7–16.

101. Cari Tuna, "Repairing an Agency's Credibility," *The Wall Street Journal,* March 22, 2009, http://online.wsj.com; and State Compensation Insurance Fund, "Testimony of Janet Frank, President, State Compensation Insurance Fund, to the Senate Banking, Finance and Insurance Committee," February 6, 2008, http://www.scif.com.

102. Price Waterhouse Change Integration Team, *Better Change.*

103. Ibid.

104. Ellen M. Heffes, "You Need Urgency Now!" *Financial Executive,* January–February 2009, downloaded from Business & Company Resource Center, http://galenet.galegroup.com (interview with John P. Kotter).

105. John P. Kotter, *Leading Change* (Boston: Harvard Business School Press, 1996).

106. Lawler, *From the Ground Up.*

107. Kotter, *Leading Change.*

108. Schneider, Brief, and Guzzo, "Creating a Climate and Culture."

109. R. Beckhard and R. Harris, *Organizational Transitions* (Reading, MA: Addison-Wesley, 1977).

110. Kotter, *Leading Change.*

111. Eleanor Boens, "Positive Communication," *Industrial Safety and Hygiene News,* June 2006, downloaded from General Reference Center Gold, http://find.galegroup.com.

112. G. Hamel, "Waking Up IBM," *Harvard Business Review,* July–August 2000, pp. 137–46; and Deutschman, *Change or Die.*

113. Deutschman, *Change or Die,* p. 202.

114. Kotter, *Leading Change.*

115. D. Smith, *Taking Charge of Change* (Reading, MA: Addison-Wesley, 1996).

116. M. J. Mandel, "This Way to the Future," *BusinessWeek,* October 11, 2004, pp. 92–98, quoting p. 93.

117. Shoshana Zuboff and James Maxim, *The Support Economy* (New York: Penguin, 2004).

118. Two Chefs on a Roll Web site, http://www.twochefsonaroll.com, accessed March 2, 2007; and Leigh Buchanan, "Recipe for Success," *Inc.,* August 2006, pp. 101–7.

119. H. Courtney, J. Kirkland, and P. Viguerie, "Strategy under Uncertainty," *Harvard Business Review,* November–December 1997, pp. 66–79.

120. J. O'Shea and C. Madigan, *Dangerous Company: The Consulting Powerhouses and the Business They Save and Ruin* (New York: Times Books, 1997).

121. G. Hamel and C. K. Prahalad, *Competing for the Future* (Boston: Harvard Business School Press, 1994).

122. Ibid.

123. Ibid.

124. Robert D. Hof, "How to Hit a Moving Target," *BusinessWeek,* August 21, 2006, downloaded from General Reference Center Gold, http://find.galegroup.com.

125. Scott E. Rickert, "Taking the NanoPulse: Sizing Up Nanotechnology," *Industry Week,* May 9, 2007, http://www.industryweek.com; Mark David, "Into the Nano Frontier—Closer than You Might Think," *Electronic Design,* May 10, 2007, downloaded from General Reference Center Gold, http://find.galegroup.com; and S. Baker and A. Aston, "The Business of Nanotech," *BusinessWeek,* February 14, 2005, pp. 569–70.

126. David, "Into the Nano Frontier"; and Melanie Haiken, "Eight Nanotech Takes on Water Pollution," *Business 2.0,* July 2007, downloaded from General Reference Center Gold, http://find.galegroup.com.

127. Michael C. Bellas, "Very Small and Unfathomably Huge," *Beverage World,* June 15, 2007, downloaded from General Reference Center Gold, http://find.galegroup.com.

128. Hamel and Prahalad, *Competing for the Future.*

129. J. Kotter, *The New Rules: How to Succeed in Today's Post-Corporate World* (New York: Free Press, 1995).

130. Ibid.

131. T. Bateman and C. Porath, "Transcendent Behavior," in *Positive Organizational Scholarship,* ed. K. Cameron, J. Dutton, and R. Quinn (San Francisco: Barrett-Koehler, 2003).

132. Matthew Kirchner, "One Hour a Day," *Products Finishing,* September 2008, downloaded from Business & Company Resource Center, http://galenet.galegroup.com.

133. L. A. Hill, "New Manager Development for the 21st Century," *Academy of Management Executive,* August 2004, pp. 121–26.

134. List compiled from C. Hakim, *We Are All Self-Employed* (San Francisco: Barrett-Koehler, 1994).

135. Lawler, *From the Ground Up;* and Kotter, *The New Rules.*

136. Lawler, *Treat People Right!*

137. M. Peiperl and Y. Baruck, "Back to Square Zero: The Post-Corporate Career," *Organizational Dynamics,* Spring 1997, pp. 7–22.

138. Ibid.

139. Conner, *Managing at the Speed of Change,* pp. 235–45.

140. J. W. Slocum Jr., M. McGill, and D. Lei, "The New Learning Strategy Anytime, Anything, Anywhere," *Organizational Dynamics,* Autumn 1994, pp. 33–37.

141. George Binney and Colin Williams, *Leaning into the Future: Changing the Way People Change Organizations* (London: Nicholas Brealey, 1997).

142. Kotter, *The New Rules.*

143. Hill, "New Manager Development for the 21st Century," p. 125.

144. J. A. Raelin, "Don't Bother Putting Leadership into People," *Academy of Management Executive,* August 2004, pp. 131–35.

145. Binney and Williams, *Leaning into the Future.*

CREDITS

Chapter 1

Page 2 left, Andy Resek; Page 2 right, Andy Resek; Page 3, © Photodisc/Getty Images/DAL; Page 5, © Royalty-Free/Corbis/DAL; Page 6 top, © AP Photo/Marcio Jose Sanchez; Page 6 bottom, © Bethean/Corbis/DAL; Page 8, © AP Photo/Elaine Thompson; Page 9, © AP Photo/Laurent Rebours; Page 11, © The McGraw-Hill Companies, Inc./Ken Cavanagh, photographer/DAL; Page 13 top, © Royalty-Free/Corbis; Page 13 bottom, © AP Photo/Richard Drew; Page 14, Courtesy of Google.com; Page 20, © BananaStock/PictureQuest/DAL; Page 21, Courtesy of Xerox Corporation; Page 23, © Royalty-Free/Corbis/DAL; Page 25, © Javier Pierini/Getty Images/DAL.

Chapter 2

Page 26, © Comstock/PunchStock/DAL; Page 27 left, Andy Resek; Page 27 right, Andy Resek; Page 30, © AP Photo/David Zalubowski; Page 32, © Photodisc/Getty Images/DAL; Page 35, © AP Photo/Eckehard Schulz; Page 41 left, © Ryan McVay/Getty Images/DAL; Page 41 right, © AP Photo/M. Spencer Grant; Page 43 top, Public Domain/DAL; Page 43 bottom, © Chris Keigan/The McGraw-Hill Companies, Inc./DAL; Page 46, Courtesy of Nordstrom, Inc; Page 47, © Skip Nall/Getty Images/DAL; Page 49 top, © Royalty-Free/Corbis/DAL; Page 49 bottom, © Stockbyte/Getty Images/DAL.

Chapter 3

Page 50 left, Andy Resek; Page 50 right, Donna Callais; Page 51, © Imagesource/PictureQuest/DAL; Page 52, © Michael Newman/PhotoEdit; Page 55, © Royalty-Free/Corbis/DAL; Page 57, © AP Photo/Lisa Poole; Page 58 top, © DynamicGraphics/Jupiterimages/DAL; Page 58 bottom, © David D. Banfield; Page 60, © Royalty-Free/Corbis; Page 62, Courtesy of NovaCare; Page 63, © AP Photo/Pat Sullivan; Page 67, © AP Photo/Dawn Villella; Page 68, © Jonathan Nourok/Photo Edit; Page 70, © Jack Star/PhotoLink/Getty Images/DAL.

Chapter 4

Page 72, © Imagesource/AP Images/RF; Page 73 left, Andy Resek; Page 73 right, Andy Resek; Page 77 top, © Richard Cummins/Corbis; Page 77 bottom, © Digital Vision/Getty Images/DAL; Page 80, © The McGraw-Hill Companies, Inc./John Flournoy, photographer/DAL; Page 83, © Erica Simone Leeds 2007/DAL; Page 85, © Robert Maass/Corbis; Page 87, Courtesy of Nordstrom, Inc; Page 89 top, © Royalty-Free/Corbis; Page 89 bottom, Courtesy of Toyota Motor North America, Inc; Page 93, © AP Photo/Fiona Hanson; Page 95, © Comstock/PunchStock/DAL; Page 97, © Ryan McVay/Getty Images/DAL.

Chapter 5

Page 100 left, Andy Resek; Page 100 right, Andy Resek; Page 101, © Doug Menuez/Getty Images/DAL; Page 102, © AP Photo/The News-Gazette, Heather Coit; Page 104, Courtesy of Zappos.com. © 2009 Zappos.com, Inc. Page 107, © Dominic Lipinski/PA Wire/AP Images; Page 110, Courtesy of Scaled Composites; Page 111 top, © Library of Congress, Prints and Photographs Division; Page 111 bottom, © John Lee/Aurora Photos; Page 112, © AP Photo/Pat Sullivan; Page 114, © AP Photo/Reed Saxon; Page 118, Courtesy of Amie Street; Page 123, © Don Farrall/Photodisc/Getty Images/RF; Page 125, © Stockbyte/PunchStock Images/DAL.

Chapter 6

Page 126, © Photodisc/Getty Images/DAL; Page 127 left, Andy Resek; Page 127 right, Andy Resek; Page 130, © Eric Audra/PhotoAlto/PictureQuest/DAL; Page 131, © Chris Goodenow/Reuters/Corbis; Page 134, © AP Photo/Nati Harnik; Page 139, Courtesy of NASA; Page 140, © Gary Reyes/MCT/Landov; Page 142, ©1997 IMS Communications LTD/Capstone Design. All rights reserved./DAL; Page 143 top, Courtesy of Seven Cycles; Page 143 bottom, © Royalty-Free/Corbis; Page 144, © Paul J. Richards/AFP/Getty Images; Page 145, © Joe Raedle/Getty Images; Page 146, © Ryan McVay/Getty Images/DAL; Page 150, © AP Photo/Paul Sakuma; Page 151, © Royalty Free/Corbis/DAL; Page 152, © David Graham/Time Life Pictures/Getty Images.

Chapter 7

Page 154 left, Andy Resek; Page 154 right, Andy Resek; Page 155, © PunchStock Images/Digital Vision/DAL; Page 156, © NBAE/Getty Images; Page 160, © Tim Boyle/Getty Images; Page 162, © Ryan McVay/Getty Images/DAL; Page 164 top, © Bettmann/Corbis; Page 164 bottom, © AP Photo/Uwe Lein; Page 167, Courtesy of Persuasive Games; Page 174, Courtesy of Tersiguel's; photo by Vickie Goeller; Page 177, © Robyn Beck/AFP/Getty Images; Page 178, © Photodisc Collection/Getty Images/DAL; Page 179, © PhotoLink/Getty Images/DAL.

Chapter 8

Page 180, © Doug Menuez/Getty Images/DAL; Page 181 left, Andy Resek; Page 181 right, Andy Resek; Page 182, © Library of Congress, Prints and Photographs Division, LC-U9-10364-37; Page 186, © AP Photo/Thibault Camus; Page 187, © AP Photo/Advantica; Page 190, © The McGraw-Hill Companies, Inc./David Planchet/DAL; Page 194, © Alan Einstein/NBAE/Getty Images; Page 196 top, © Royalty-Free/Corbis; Page 196 bottom, © Jodi Hilton/Corbis; Page 198, © AP Photo/Williams Perry; Page 199, © John Neubauer/PhotoEdit; Page 202, © AP Photo/Ling long-Imaginechina; Page 204, © arabianEye/PunchStock/DAL; Page 205, © Flying Colours Ltd./Getty Images/DAL.

Chapter 9

Page 206 left, Andy Resek; Page 206 right, Andy Resek; Page 207, © Jupiterimages/Comstock/Alamy/DAL; Page 209,

INDEX

A

Abbott Laboratories, 86, 198
ABC Supply, 105, 114
Abrams, Rhonda, 105
A.C. Moore, 285
Accenture, 185, 282–283
Accommodation, 198, 268–269
Accountability, 132–133, 198
Accounting audits, 305
AccuRadio, 28–29
Accurate Perforating, 91–92, 94, 95
Achievement, need for, 240
Achievement-oriented leadership, 220
Acquisitions, 44
Action Fast Print, 225
Activity-based costing, 305–306
Adapters, 343
Adapting at the core, 41–42
Adapting to the environment, 40–42
Adhocracy, 47
Adidas, 32
Adjourning stage, 258
Adler, Nancy J., 193, 276
Adverse impact, 167
Advertising support model, 110
Advisory boards, 121
Advisory relationships, 267
Aéropostale, 37
Aetna Life & Casualty, 12, 60, 191, 195
Affiliate model, 110
Affiliation, need for, 240
Affirmative action, 189–193; *See also*
    Diversity
Affordable Internet Services Online, 107
Aflac, 197
Agility, organizational, 144–152
Air Canada, 325–326
Albert, Sarah, 2, 252
Alderfer's ERG theory, 239–240
Alexander, Whit, 8
Allen, Paul, 100
Alliances, strategic, 42, 145–146, 326
Allied Signal, 301
Allison, Mary Ann, 157
Allstate, 80, 249
Amazon, 6, 8, 83, 223, 229, 324
American Arbitration Association, 270
American Bank, 256
American Express, 42, 330
American Finishing Resources, 344
American International Group (AIG), 63
American Library Association, 282
American Management Association, 52
Americans with Disabilities Act (ADA),
    62, 167, 188

Amica Mutual, 238
Amie Street, 118
Analysis, environmental, 38–40, 81–82
Analyzer firms, 325
Anderson, Brad, 131
Anderson, Erika, 240
Anticipated competency development,
    324–325
Anticipated market receptiveness,
    322–323
AOL Radio, 29
Apple, 44, 45, 73, 83, 92, 100, 118,
    145, 157, 197, 212, 327
Applications, for jobs, 161
Arbitration, 178–179
Archer Daniels Midland, 185
Arnold, Bill, 172
Asarco, 69
Ash, Mary Kay, 241
Ashcroft, John, 234
Asiala, Laura, 4
Assessment centers, 164
Assets, 306
Association of Certified Fraud Examiners,
    58, 65
Astex Therapeutics, 107
Aston, Adam, 223
Astroturfing, 53
At-will employment, 165
ATI Technologies, 37
AT&T, 21, 76, 188, 199, 225, 286
Attractive environment, 39
Audit relationships, 267
Audits, 302–303, 305, 321
Authentic leadership, 224–225
Authoritarianism, 220
Authority, 130–132
AutoAdmit, 59
Autocratic leadership, 214–215
Autonomous work groups, 257
Autonomy, 244
Aviles, Alvin, 187
Avoidance, of conflict, 268–269
Avon, 12, 186, 195
A&W, 106
Awareness building, 196–197
Aziz, Adnan, 104

B

Babcock, D., 71
Background checks, 162
Bailey, Steve, 286
Balance sheets, 306, 307
Balanced scorecard, 313
Ballmer, Steve, 147

Banatao, Desi, 108
Banatao, Rey, 108, 109
Bank of America, 68
Banker, R., 257
Barber, Donna, 107
Bargaining, collective, 177–178
Barnes, Brenda, 185
Barnes & Noble, 6
Barriers to entry, 35
Barry, Nancy, 226
Barry-Wehmiller Companies, 224
BARS, 170
Bartlett, C., 18
Base technologies, 321
Bateman, T., 219, 238
Batesville Casket Company, 326
Baxter Healthcare, 290
Bayer Corporation, 44, 108
Bayer MaterialScience, 108
Bayless, Maggie, 325
BCG matrix, 85–86
BeadforLife, 16–17
Beaumont, Claudine, 279
Behavior modification, 234
Behavioral appraisals, 170
Behavioral approach to leadership,
    214–216
Behavioral description interview, 162
Behrens, Rick, 37
Beloit Corporation, 105, 114
Ben & Jerry's, 231
Benchmarking, 40, 84, 321
Bendix, 324
Benefits, employee, 175–176
Benkow, Kenneth, 247
Berdovsky, Peter, 57
Berg, Shari L., 17
Berke, Howard, 106, 107
Berkowitz, George, 294
Berry, Ben, 287
Bertken, Dennis, 107–108
Best, David, 67
Best Buy, 10–11, 131, 332
Best-case scenario, 39
Best-in-class, 40
Bezos, Jeff, 223
Biden, Joe, 30
Bierce, Ambrose, 102
Bigari, Steven T., 235
BioWare, 322
Black, Ryan, 108
Blake, Robert R., 216
Blake and Mouton's Leadership Grid,
    215–216
Blanchard, Ken, 316
Blockbuster, 35

IN A NUTSHELL

Management is the process of working with people and resources to accomplish organizational goals. Effective managers help their organizations achieve their goals and remain competitive in the changing global marketplace.

The following questions will test your take-away knowledge from this chapter. How many can you answer?

LO.1. Can you summarize the major challenges of managing in the new competitive landscape?

LO.2. Can you describe the sources of competitive advantage for a company?

LO.3. How are the functions of management evolving in today's business environment?

LO.4. How does the nature of management vary at different organizational levels?

LO.5. Can you define the skills you need to be an effective manager?

LO.6. Can you identify the principles that will help you manage your career?

Did your answers include the following important points?

LO.1. Can you summarize the major challenges of managing in the new competitive landscape?

- Four major challenges are the globalization of business, technological change, knowledge workers and their ideas, and the need for collaboration.

LO.2. Can you describe the sources of competitive advantage for a company?

- Innovation in goods and services keeps an organization ahead of its competitors, and service focuses on satisfying customers.
- Quality must continuously improve for a firm to be successful.
- Speed in response or delivery gives a company a leg up in the marketplace, and cost competitiveness attracts customers.

LO.3. How are the functions of management evolving in today's business environment?

- Planning sets goals for an individual, group, work unit, or the entire organization—of delivering strategic value.
- Organizing the human, financial, physical, informational, and other resources of a firm builds its flexibility and adaptiveness.
- A manager's skills in leading other employees stimulates them to become high performers.
- Controlling—monitoring performance and making needed changes—ensures goal achievement.

LO.4. How does the nature of management vary at different organizational levels?

- Top-level managers set and communicate organizational strategy.
- Middle-level managers devise the tactics to implement the strategy.
- Frontline managers provide the vital operational link between employees and the strategies.

LO.5. Can you define the skills you need to be an effective manager?

- A manager's technical skill is the ability to perform a specialized task.
- Interpersonal and communication skills help managers interact effectively with their employees.
- Conceptual and decision skills help managers identify and solve problems.

LO.6. Can you identify the principles that will help you manage your career?

- Emotional intelligence helps you understand and manage yourself and deal effectively with others.
- By being both a specialist—an expert at something—and a generalist—a person with broad knowledge—you can advance your career.
- Being self-reliant gives you power over yourself, your actions, and your career.
- Building social capital fosters goodwill with your organization and allows you to survive and thrive in your career.

Practical Application

LO.1.

- The competitive landscape of today's business has moved from local to _____ and increasingly uses _____, such as the Internet.
- _____ is the set of practices aimed at discovering and harnessing an organization's intellectual resources.
- Toyota develops products by bringing together design engineers and manufacturing employees; Toyota is using _____ in its product development.

LO.2.

- Google keeps introducing new goods and services for its customers, valuing _____ to remain competitive.
- Miguel comments on the excellence of his latte and the efficiency and politeness of the barista in providing it; he is commenting on the _____ and _____ of the coffee shop.
- Walmart is known for its low prices, practicing _____ in its strategy.

LO.3.

- The process of working with people and resources to accomplish organizational goals is known as _____.
- Laura needs to set goals for her team; she needs to _____.
- The CEO comments on Jason's ability to motivate his team to surpass their performance goals; he is noticing his _____.

LO.4.

- Amanda has been hired as the senior executive of a local bank and needs to set its strategy; she is the _____ manager of the firm.
- A _____ is responsible for direct supervision of employees.
- Devon has been promoted to department head and assumes a _____ manager role.

LO.5.

- An ad on a software company's Web site is asking for applicants with computer programming expertise; it needs someone with _____ skill.
- _____ skills involve the ability to identify and resolve problems for the benefit of the organization and its members.
- Lori's manager gives great speeches and everyone seems to love her. Lori's manager obviously must have _____ skills.

LO.6.

- If you understand yourself, can manage yourself, and deal effectively with others, you have _____.
- During his performance review, Len's manager encourages him to learn more about the other departments in his manufacturing firm, not just focus on his expertise as a production manager. Len's manager wants him to become more of a _____.
- Goodwill stemming from your social relationships is known as _____.

IN A NUTSHELL

An organization's external environment, such as its macroenvironment and competitive environment, influences how it works to achieve its goals and the success it has against its rivals. The strength of an organization's culture also profoundly shapes its responses and effectiveness.

The following questions will test your take-away knowledge from this chapter. How many can you answer?

LO.1. How do environmental forces influence organizations, and how can organizations influence their environments?

LO.2. Can you distinguish between the macroenvironment and the competitive environment?

LO.3. Why should managers and organizations attend to economic and social developments?

LO.4. Can you identify elements of the competitive environment?

LO.5. Can you summarize how organizations respond to environmental uncertainty?

LO.6. Can you define elements of an organization's culture?

LO.7. How does an organization's culture affect its response to its external environment?

Did your answers include the following important points?

LO.1. How do environmental forces influence organizations, and how can organizations influence their environments?

- Organizations are open systems, so they both affect and are affected by their external environment.
- Organizations take inputs such as goods and services from their environment and create outputs such as products and services.

LO.2. Can you distinguish between the macroenvironment and the competitive environment?

- The macroenvironment includes governments, economic conditions, and other fundamental factors in the general environment.
- The competitive environment is the immediate environment surrounding a firm, including suppliers, customers, and rivals.

LO.3. Why should managers and organizations attend to economic and social developments?

- They should pay attention to economic and social developments because these changes affect managers' ability to function and their strategic choices.
- Demographic factors influence not only customer attitudes and characteristics but also those of the workforce.

LO.4. Can you identify elements of the competitive environment?

- Rivalry among current competitors
- New entrants in the marketplace
- Substitute and complementary products
- Suppliers
- Customers

LO.5. Can you summarize how organizations respond to environmental uncertainty?

- Managers can practice environmental scanning, formulate competitive intelligence, make forecasts, and benchmark other firms to reduce uncertainty.
- Three basic responses to the environment include adapting to the environment, influencing the environment, and selecting a new environment.

LO.6. Can you define elements of an organization's culture?

- Elements of organizational culture include assumptions about the organization and its goals and practices that members share.
- A company's organizational culture is reflected in its mission statement and goals; business practices; symbols, rites, and ceremonies; and the stories people tell.

LO.7. How does an organization's culture affect its response to its external environment?

- The firm's culture affects whether it emphasizes flexibility or control and whether its focus is internal or external to the organization.
- Four general types of organizational culture are group, hierarchical, rational, and adhocracy.

Practical Application

LO.1.
- Because organizations are open systems, they are affected by and in turn affect their _____.
- Organizations take _____ like goods and services from their environment and use them to create _____.

LO.2.
- The general environment, including legal, political, economic, technological, demographic, and social factors, is called the _____.
- To set a strategy for his restaurant, Avram is seeking information about his rivals, customers, suppliers, and their products. Avram is gathering information about his _____ environment.
- Zora is concerned about the effects of tax law changes and a possible recession on her customers' buying power. She is concerned about elements in her _____.

LO.3.
- Inflation rates, interest rates, and the stock market are part of an organization's _____ environment.
- _____ are measures of various characteristics of the people who make up groups or other social units.
- Some major demographic trends affecting today's workforce are aging, _____, and _____.

LO.4.
- Elements of the competitive environment, as developed by Michael Porter, include rivalry among current competitors, _____, substitute and complementary products, suppliers, and customers.
- Conditions that prevent new companies from entering an industry are called _____.

- The downturn in the housing market has reduced the demand for major appliances. Homes and appliances can be considered _____.

LO.5.
- Complexity and dynamism add to the _____ for managers.
- Orlando is scanning his environment and gathering information about his competitors, customers, and suppliers. He is gathering _____ to help his firm.
- The process of comparing an organization's practices and technologies with those of other companies is called _____.
- Nokia recently bought a digital mapping company. This is an example of a/an _____.

LO.6.
- _____ is the set of important assumptions about the organization and its goals and practices that members share.
- For evidence of a company's culture, you can look at its _____ and official goals.
- The daily Ritz-Carlton "wow story," where employees relate an example of an employee's extraordinary service, is an example of a company _____.

LO.7.
- An organization that is internally oriented and is flexible has a/an _____.
- Arletta complains that her company and manager are "control freaks" and are afraid of change. Arletta's company most likely has a/an _____.
- Companies that are entrepreneurial and take risks are examples of _____.

ANSWERS LO1• external environment • inputs/outputs LO2• macroenvironment • competitive • macroenvironment LO3• economic • Demographics • education/immigration LO4• new entrants • barriers to entry • complements or complementary products LO5• environmental uncertainty • competitive intelligence • benchmarking • acquisition LO6• Organizational culture • mission statement • ritual or ceremony LO7• group culture • hierarchical culture • adhocracies

active review card

Ethics and Corporate Social Responsibility

chapter three

IN A NUTSHELL

When managers formulate strategies or make decisions based on the concept of moral right and wrong, they are considering ethics. Corporate social responsibility encompasses both business ethics and concern for the natural environment.

The following questions will test your take-away knowledge from this chapter. How many can you answer?

LO.1. How do different ethical perspectives guide decision making?

LO.2. How can companies influence their ethics environments?

LO.3. Can you outline a process for making ethical decisions?

LO.4. What are the important issues surrounding corporate social responsibility?

LO.5. Can you summarize how organizations respond to environmental uncertainty?

LO.6. Can you identify actions managers can take to manage with the environment in mind?

Did your answers include the following important points?

LO.1. How do different ethical perspectives guide decision making?

- Universalism emphasizes certain values that society needs to function.
- Egoism seeks to maximize benefits for the individual.
- Utilitarianism's overriding concern is finding the greatest good for the greatest number of people.
- Relativism bases judgments of ethical behavior on the opinions and actions of relevant other people.
- Virtue ethics views what is moral as what a mature person with good moral character would deem right.

LO.2. How can companies influence their ethics environments?

- Organizations can evaluate their ethical climate, the processes by which decisions are made on the basis of right and wrong.
- They can look for danger signs such as excessive emphasis on short-term over long-term goals, quick-fix solutions, a focus solely on financial costs, or a concern only for legalities or public relations.
- They can develop written ethics codes and standards to guide conduct.

LO.3. Can you outline a process for making ethical decisions?

- Moral awareness is the realization that an issue has ethical implications.
- Moral judgment involves knowing what actions are morally defensible.

- Moral character is the strength and persistence to act according to your ethics, despite challenges.

LO.4. What are the important issues surrounding corporate social responsibility?

- Economic responsibilities are the obligations of the business to produce goods and services that society wants at a price that perpetuates the firm and satisfies its investors.
- Legal responsibilities are the requirements to follow laws.
- Ethical responsibilities are meeting other social expectations.
- Philanthropic responsibilities are additional behaviors that society finds desirable and that the values of the business support.

LO.5. Can you summarize how organizations respond to environmental uncertainty?

- Companies consider the environment to satisfy consumer demand, react to competitors, meet requests from customers or suppliers, comply with guidelines, and create a competitive advantage.

LO.6. Can you identify actions managers can take to manage with the environment in mind?

- Managers can develop an ecocentric management philosophy, which creates sustainable economic development and improves the quality of life worldwide.
- Managers can focus on sustainable growth, which meets present needs without harming the needs of future generations.

Practical Application

LO.1.

- Principles, rules, and values people use in deciding what is right or wrong make up a/an _____.
- Julia is self-centered and only concerned about how she can get ahead in her career. She is functioning under the ethical system called _____.
- In considering raises, your boss is focused on providing the biggest pay increases for the greatest number of his staff. He is operating under a/an _____ philosophy.

LO.2.

- In response to such corporate scandals as Enron and WorldCom, Congress passed the _____ to improve investor confidence.
- An organization's _____ is the processes by which decisions are evaluated and made on the basis of right and wrong.
- Corporate ethics programs range from _____, designed by corporate lawyers to prevent, detect, and punish legal violations, to _____, which are designed to instill a personal responsibility for ethical behavior.

LO.3.

- Making ethical decisions requires three things: _____, _____, and _____.
- The Level-3 (worst) costs of unethical behavior related to customers are _____ and _____.
- Giovanni has repeatedly brought a serious ethical problem to his manager's attention but has been ignored. He decides that his only

course of action is to notify authorities of the wrongdoing; this is called _____.

LO.4.

- The obligation toward society assumed by business is called _____.
- Legal responsibilities are concerned with _____, while ethical responsibilities are focused on meeting _____.
- Empathy, generativity, mutuality, civil aspiration, and intolerance of ineffective humanity are the five higher goals that characterize a/an _____.

LO.5.

- General Electric's "ecomagination" program was developed out of concern for the _____.
- Acid rain is an example of _____.

LO.6.

- _____ has the goal of creating sustainable economic development and improving the quality of life worldwide for all organizational stakeholders.
- Josh is trying to prepare a plan for his organization that allows it to grow in the present without harming future generations. He is concerned with _____.
- Analyzing all inputs and outputs, through a "cradle-to-grave" life of a product, to determine its environmental impact is called _____.

IN A NUTSHELL

An organization's strategy sets its course and fine-tunes its direction. Managers at all levels plan and make decisions that contribute to the achievement of goals.

The following questions will test your take-away knowledge from this chapter. How many can you answer?

LO.1. What are the basic steps in any planning process?

LO.2. How should strategic planning be integrated with tactical and operational planning?

LO.3. Can you describe how strategy is based on analysis of the external environment and the firm's strengths and weaknesses?

LO.4. How can companies achieve competitive advantage through business strategy?

LO.5. Can you identify the keys to effective strategy implementation?

LO.6. How can you make effective decisions as a manager?

LO.7. What are the principles for group decision making?

Did your answers include the following important points?

LO.1. What are the basic steps in any planning process?

- The formal planning steps are analyzing the situation, generating alternatives, evaluating them, selecting goals and plans, implementing them, and monitoring and controlling performance.

LO.2. How should strategic planning be integrated with tactical and operational planning?

- Strategic planning sets the long-term direction for a firm.
- Tactical planning translates broad strategic goals into specific plans for a particular part of the organization.
- Operational planning identifies specific procedures and processes for lower levels of the organization.

LO.3. Can you describe how strategy is based on analysis of the external environment and the firm's strengths and weaknesses?

- Managers analyze the organization's external opportunities and threats to formulate a strategy.
- Internal strengths and weaknesses of the organization determine its resources and core competencies.

LO.4. How can companies achieve competitive advantage through business strategy?

- Low-cost strategies allow a company to build a competitive advantage by being efficient and offering standard, no-frills products.

- Differentiation strategies foster a competitive advantage by distinguishing a firm as unique in its industry.

LO.5. Can you identify the keys to effective strategy implementation?

- Keys to effective strategy implementation are defining strategic tasks, assessing organization capabilities, developing an implementation agenda, and creating an implementation plan.

LO.6. How can you make effective decisions as a manager?

- Managers can determine which decisions are programmed and which nonprogrammed, reduce uncertainty, and manage risks.
- Formal decision making has six stages: identifying and diagnosing the problem, generating alternatives, evaluating alternatives, making the choice, implementing the decision, and evaluating it.

LO.7. What are the principles for group decision making?

- Groups are effective decision makers when they have more information, consider a greater number of perspectives, provide intellectual stimulation, help more people understand the decision, and generate commitment to the decision.
- Groups are ineffective decision makers when one member dominates the discussion, they settle for a solution that is less than optimal, they pressure members to avoid disagreement, or they displace original goals with less important ones.

Practical Application

LO.1.
- The hallmark of effective goals is the acronym SMART, which stands for _____.
- _____ are the actions or means the manager intends to use to achieve goals.
- Erica's manager has asked her to develop different _____, or narratives that describe a particular set of future conditions, during her planning.

LO.2.
- An organization's CEO is most likely to be involved in _____ planning to set long-term goals.
- To help support the company's overall profitability goals, Chen Lu has been asked to come up with specific goals and plans for the accounting department. She needs to develop _____.
- As a frontline manager, Ross needs to develop specific procedures and processes for his engineers. Ross needs to do _____.

LO.3.
- Strategic planning involves developing a/an _____, a/an _____, and goals for the organization.
- _____ are groups and individuals who affect and are affected by the achievement of an organization's mission, goals, and strategies.
- Comparison of an organization's strengths, weaknesses, opportunities, and threats is called _____.

LO.4.
- Southwest Airlines routinely advertises its bargain fares. Southwest is using a/an _____ business strategy.

- Apple continually tries to outdo its competitors by offering unique products that stand out in the marketplace. Apple uses a _____ business strategy.

LO.5.
- Defining strategic tasks, assessing organizational capabilities, developing an agenda, and creating a plan are the four steps in strategy _____.
- A/An _____ is a system designed to support managers in evaluating the organization's progress on its strategy and taking corrective action, when needed.

LO.6.
- Louis needs to determine how many beverages to keep in his convenience store's inventory. This decision is an example of a/an _____ decision.
- Chloe is trying to decide where to relocate her hair salon after her lease expires. She needs to make a/an _____ decision.
- Jennifer's boss tells her, "I don't care how long it takes you to find the best alternative to increase sales! Just do it!" Jennifer's boss wants her to practice _____ in her decision making.

LO.7.
- "Two heads are better than one" is the philosophy behind _____.
- All staff members were most concerned with pleasing their department head during a brainstorming session, so they didn't disagree or raise objections to his proposals. The team is demonstrating _____.
- Consuela was assigned the job of criticizing every idea during a group decision making session. Consuela is playing the role of _____.

ANSWERS LO1• Specific, measurable, attainable, relevant, time-bound • Plans • scenarios **LO2•** strategic • tactical plans • operational planning **LO3•** mission/vision • Stakeholders • SWOT analysis **LO4•** low-cost • differentiation **LO5•** implementation • strategic control system **LO6•** programmed • nonprogrammed • maximizing **LO7•** group decision making • groupthink • devil's advocate

active review card

IN A NUTSHELL

Entrepreneurs are a great source of innovation and creativity in today's business world. Large corporations also develop new business ideas through intrapreneurship.

The following questions will test your take-away knowledge from this chapter. How many can you answer?

LO.1. Why do people become entrepreneurs, and what does it take, personally?

LO.2. How do you assess opportunities to start new businesses?

LO.3. Can you identify common causes of success and failure?

LO.4. What are the common management challenges?

LO.5. How can you increase your chances of success, including good business planning?

LO.6. How can managers of large companies foster entrepreneurship?

Did your answers include the following important points?

LO.1. Why do people become entrepreneurs, and what does it take, personally?

- Entrepreneurs start their own firms because of the challenge, profit potential, satisfaction, and better quality of life.
- Entrepreneurs like being independent and building something from nothing and seeing it succeed.
- Entrepreneurs are innovators who also have good knowledge and skills in management, business, and networking.

LO.2. How do you assess opportunities to start new businesses?

- New businesses often start from an innovative idea a person has.
- Opportunities in the marketplace, such as technological discoveries, demographic changes, lifestyle and taste changes, economic dislocations, calamities, and government initiatives and rule changes, can spur the idea for a new business.
- Franchising and trial and error also present opportunities.

LO.3. Can you identify common causes of success and failure?

- Personal characteristics that often lead to success include commitment and determination; leadership; opportunity obsession; tolerance of risk, ambiguity, and uncertainty; creativity, self-reliance, and ability to adapt; and motivation to excel.
- Factors that contribute to failure include risk, economic environment and uncertain financing, and management-related hazards.

LO.4. What are the common management challenges?

- Management challenges of entrepreneurship include the possibility that you might not enjoy it, along with the facts that survival is difficult, growth can create problems, delegation can be hard, funds could be misused, controls may be lacking, and you may become ill or die.

LO.5. How can you increase your chances of success, including good business planning?

- Good planning, including a formal business plan, can increase the chances of success.
- Nonfinancial resources—including a perception of legitimacy in the minds of the public; strong social networks; and top managers, advisory boards, and partners—also contribute to long-term success.

LO.6. How can managers of large companies foster entrepreneurship?

- Managers in big companies can bring their ideas to life by building support among others in their organizations.
- Managers can foster intrapreneurship by building an entrepreneurial culture at the heart of the corporate strategy.
- Managers can also create separate entrepreneurial efforts within the organization, such as skunkworks and bootlegging.

Practical Application

LO.1.

- An individual who establishes a new organization without the benefit of corporate sponsorship is called a/an _____.
- _____ are new-venture creators working inside big companies.
- A/An _____ has fewer than 100 employees, is independently owned and operated, is not dominant in its field, and is not characterized by many innovations; in contrast, a/an _____ has growth and high profitability as primary objectives.

LO.2.

- Entrepreneurs need two things to start a business: a/an _____ and the _____.
- Pizza Hut and Dunkin' Donuts are examples of _____.
- Five successful models for e-commerce are the transaction fee model, _____, intermediary model, affiliate model, and subscription model.

LO.3.

- His friends say Toby has an "entrepreneurial personality"; Toby likely has these characteristics: commitment, _____, opportunity obsession, tolerance of risk and uncertainty, creativity and self-reliance, and _____.
- Two reasons for new-business failure are _____ and _____.
- Protected environments for new, small businesses are known as _____.

LO.4.

- Suzanne is a micromanager; she finds it hard to _____.
- Record keeping is a form of _____.
- John says he is "going public" with his company; he is planning a/an _____.

LO.5.

- A/An _____ is a formal planning step that focuses on the entire venture and describes all the elements in starting it.
- Five key factors in a good business plan are the _____, the opportunity, the _____, the context, and the risk and reward.
- People's judgment of a company's acceptance, appropriateness, and desirability is called _____.

LO.6.

- Helen works in a big company and has an idea for a new product. To build support for her idea, she is looking for a top executive who will assist her, otherwise known as a/an _____.
- A/An _____ is a project team designated to produce a new, innovative product.
- Informal work on projects that employees choose to do outside their official projects is called _____.

IN A NUTSHELL

An organization's structure is one of the most important factors in determining whether its strategy can be carried out. Today's organizations are implementing structures that allow them more flexibility to adapt to change.

The following questions will test your take-away knowledge from this chapter. How many can you answer?

LO.1. What are the characteristics of organization structure?

LO.2. Can you summarize how authority operates and who generally holds top authority in a company?

LO.3. How does span of control affect structure and managerial effectiveness?

LO.4. Can you explain how to delegate effectively?

LO.5. Can you distinguish between centralized and decentralized organizations?

LO.6. What are the basic types of organization structures, and what are their strengths?

LO.7. Can you describe important mechanisms used to coordinate work?

LO.8. How can organizations improve their agility?

Did your answers include the following important points?

LO.1. What are the characteristics of organization structure?

- Organizations can be characterized as either organic or mechanistic; structures vary in terms of differentiation and integration.

LO.2. Can you summarize how authority operates and who generally holds top authority in a company?

- Authority is formally invested in job positions.
- The ultimate authority in an organization rests with the owner or owners.
- Stockholders in a corporation hold the top authority, and they elect a board of directors to oversee the organization.

LO.3. How does span of control affect structure and managerial effectiveness?

- Differences in the span of control affect the shape: narrow spans build tall structures, and wide spans create flat ones.
- An optimal span of control is narrow enough to permit managers to maintain control over subordinates but not so narrow that it leads to overcontrol and an excessive number of managers.

LO.4. Can you explain how to delegate effectively?

- Managers should define their goals; select the person for the task; solicit the subordinate's views about the task; give the subordinate the authority, time, and resources; check to ensure progress is being made; and discuss progress at appropriate intervals.

LO.5. Can you distinguish between centralized and decentralized organizations?

- When responsibility and authority are delegated, decision making is decentralized.
- When important decisions are made by top managers, the organization is centralized.

LO.6. What are the basic types of organization structures, and what are their strengths?

- Line departments deal directly with the organization's primary goods and services, and staff departments provide support for line departments.
- Functional organizations foster efficiency, and divisional organizations focus on specific customer segments, products, or geographic regions.
- Matrix organizations ideally combine the best of both functional and divisional organizations.

LO.7. Can you describe important mechanisms used to coordinate work?

- Organizations coordinate work through standardization, formalization, coordination by plan, and coordination by mutual adjustment.

LO.8. How can organizations improve their agility?

- Organizations can improve their agility through their strategy, their commitment to customers, and their technology.

Practical Application

LO.1.

- A/an _____ depicts the reporting structure and division of labor in an organization.
- A/an _____ is a formal structure that seeks to maximize internal efficiency; a/an _____ is an organizational form that emphasizes flexibility.
- _____ and _____ are characteristics of differentiation in an organization.
- _____ is a mark of integration in an organization.

LO.2.

- In organizations, the legitimate right to make decisions and to tell other people what to do is called _____.
- Members of the board of directors who are also top executives of the firm are known as _____.
- The _____ is at the top of the organizational pyramid.

LO.3.

- Allen wants to increase the number of people reporting to him; he wants to increase his _____.
- A/an _____ organization has many reporting levels; a/an _____ organization has few reporting levels.

LO.4.

- Lilly's manager constantly checks on her progress; her manager has problems with _____ authority.
- The assignment of a task that an employee is supposed to carry out is called _____.

LO.5.

- All of the managers in Robert's organization have to get approval for changes they want to make; this organization is a/an _____ one.

- Harley-Davidson changed its structure to push decisions about products down to its frontline supervisors and their employees. Harley became more _____.

LO.6.

- Madison works as a pastry chef in a restaurant. She works in a/an _____ department.
- Jeff is the head of the human resource department for an automobile manufacturer. Jeff works in a/an _____ department.
- PepsiCo has separate units for each of the geographic regions in which it operates; it is characterized by a/an _____ organization.

LO.7.

- _____ establishes common routines and procedures that apply uniformly to everyone.
- When interdependent units are free to modify and adapt their actions, as long as they meet their deadlines and targets, they are operating according to _____.
- When units interact with one another to come to flexible solutions, they are operating according to _____.

LO.8.

- The ability to act quickly to meet customer needs and respond to other outside pressures is known as _____.
- Some major airlines have banded together to provide common ground services such as ticketing, check-in, and baggage handling. This relationship is known as a/an _____.
- Dell pioneered the idea of producing varied, individually customized computers at a low cost; this type of flexible manufacturing is called _____.

IN A NUTSHELL

A company's human resources can be a significant source of competitive advantage. Organizations need to ensure that they manage their human resources well.

The following questions will test your take-away knowledge from this chapter. How many can you answer?

LO.1. How do companies use human resources management to gain competitive advantage?

LO.2. Why do companies recruit both internally and externally for new hires?

LO.3. What are the various methods for selecting new employees?

LO.4. What is the importance of spending on training and development?

LO.5. Can you explain alternatives for who appraises an employee's performance?

LO.6. Can you describe the fundamental aspects of a reward system?

LO.7. How do unions and labor laws influence human resources management?

Did your answers include the following important points?

LO.1. How do companies use human resources management to gain competitive advantage?

- Organizations create a competitive advantage by possessing or developing resources that are valuable, rare, inimitable, and organized.
- Since people create value, talent is rare, motivated people are difficult to imitate, and they can be organized for success, the human resources function is directly involved in creating a competitive advantage for an organization.

LO.2. Why do companies recruit both internally and externally for new hires?

- Companies recruit internally because existing employees are already familiar with their organizations and the opportunity to move up in their firms encourages them to work hard and stay with the company.
- External recruiting brings in new ideas and talents that can inspire innovation.

LO.3. What are the various methods for selecting new employees?

- Organizations solicit applications and résumés, conduct interviews, check applicants' backgrounds, and perform a variety of tests to select new employees.
- Organizations use layoffs and termination to let employees go.

LO.4. What is the importance of spending on training and development?

- Continual improvement in employee skills increases organizational effectiveness.

- Spending on training and development indicates the importance organizations place on their employees.

LO.5. Can you explain alternatives for who appraises an employee's performance?

- Managers and supervisors typically appraise employee performance.
- Other people who may contribute during performance appraisals are peers and team members, subordinates, internal and external customers, and the employee himself or herself.

LO.6. Can you describe the fundamental aspects of a reward system?

- The primary method of rewarding employees is through their pay.
- Employees also receive fringe benefits, which are a significant part of their reward packages.

LO.7. How do unions and labor laws influence human resources management?

- Labor laws protect employees' right to unionize and their right to free speech in the workplace, define unfair labor practices by unions, and curb union abuses and corruption.
- Unions recruit members and collect dues to ensure that employees are treated fairly with respect to wages, working conditions, and other issues.

Practical Application

LO.1.

- The term for formal systems for the management of people within an organization is _____.
- The three stages of organizational staffing are _____, _____, and _____.
- _____ is a tool for determining what is done on a given job and what should be done on that job.

LO.2.

- _____ is the development of a pool of applicants for jobs in an organization.
- A job-posting system on a company bulletin board is an example of _____.
- _____ methods often include employee referrals, Internet job boards, and employment agencies.

LO.3.

- A/an _____ is a selection technique that involves asking all applicants the same questions and comparing their responses with a standardized set of answers.
- Two types of checks that an HR staff member may conduct on an applicant are _____ and _____ checks.
- When Jodie went in for her interview, the HR interviewer asked her to do a number of activities and exercises that her new job would require; this type of performance test is called a/an _____.
- The legal concept that an employee may be terminated for any reason is known as _____.

LO.4.

- An analysis that identifies the jobs, people, and departments for which training is necessary is called a/an _____.
- On his first day on the job, Charles watched a video and heard a presentation about company policies and procedures. The term for such a session is _____.
- _____ provides employees with the skills and perspectives they need to collaborate with others.

LO.5.

- Performance appraisals can assess three basic categories of employee performance: traits, _____, and _____.
- Michelle hears that her supervisor is an advocate of MBO; this means that he believes in _____.
- During his performance appraisal, Cliff received feedback from subordinates, coworkers, and supervisors; Cliff had a/an _____.

LO.6.

- Three types of decisions are crucial for designing an effective pay plan: _____, pay structure, and individual pay decisions.
- Two types of group incentive pay plans are _____ and _____.
- About 30 percent of an employer's payroll costs are from _____.

LO.7.

- The system of relations between workers and management is called _____.
- When a labor dispute arises and the parties call in a neutral third party to resolve it, this is known as _____.
- A company that requires employees to join the union after a set period time is called a/an _____.

ANSWERS LO1 • human resources management • planning/programming/evaluating • Job analysis **LO2.** Recruitment • internal recruiting • External recruiting **LO3.** structured interview • reference/background • assessment center • employment-at-will **LO4.** needs assessment • orientation or orientation training • Team training **LO5.** behaviors/results • management by objectives • 360-degree appraisal **LO6.** pay level • gainsharing/profit sharing • employee benefits **LO7.** labor relations • arbitration • union shop

IN A NUTSHELL

The U.S. working population is becoming more diverse in terms of gender, racial and ethnic differences, age, and many other factors. Companies are also increasingly doing business globally. Today's managers need to prepare themselves to work with employees from many backgrounds.

The following questions will test your take-away knowledge from this chapter. How many can you answer?

LO.1. How do changes in the U.S. workforce make diversity a critical organizational and managerial issue?

LO.2. Can you distinguish between affirmative action and managing diversity?

LO.3. How can diversity, if well managed, give organizations a competitive edge?

LO.4. What are the challenges associated with managing a diverse workforce?

LO.5. Can you define monolithic, pluralistic, and multicultural organizations?

LO.6. What steps can managers and their organizations take to cultivate diversity?

LO.7. Can you summarize the skills and knowledge managers need to manage globally?

LO.8. What are the ways in which cultural differences across countries influence management?

Did your answers include the following important points?

LO.1. How do changes in the U.S. workforce make diversity a critical organizational and managerial issue?

- Women make up nearly half the workforce.
- Immigration and the growth of minorities have increased their proportion of the population.
- Ages of employees, people with mental and physical disabilities, and differing educational levels also contribute to diversity.

LO.2. Can you distinguish between affirmative action and managing diversity?

- Affirmative action focuses on correcting the past exclusion of women and minorities from the workplace.
- Managing diversity moves beyond legislated mandates to be proactive and value people's differences.

LO.3. How can diversity, if well managed, give organizations a competitive edge?

- A diverse and inclusive organization can reap economic benefits.
- Organizations that appreciate diversity can attract and retain motivated employees, meet diverse customer needs, be more creative in problem solving, and enhance their flexibility.

LO.4. What are the challenges associated with managing a diverse workforce?

- Some challenges are unexamined assumptions, lower cohesiveness, communication problems, mistrust and tension, and stereotyping.

LO.5. Can you define monolithic, pluralistic, and multicultural organizations?

- Monolithic organizations have highly homogeneous employees.
- Pluralistic organizations have relatively diverse employee populations.
- Multicultural organizations value diversity and seek to utilize and encourage it.

LO.6. What steps can managers and their organizations take to cultivate diversity?

- Organizations can cultivate a diverse workforce by securing top management's commitment, assessing progress toward goals, attracting and retaining employees, and training employees in diversity.

LO.7. Can you summarize the skills and knowledge managers need to manage globally?

- Global managers need knowledge of other countries' customs and cultures to succeed, interest in other cultures, and flexibility.

LO.8. What are the ways in which cultural differences across countries influence management?

- Global managers need to consider not only the difficulties employees might have adjusting to a foreign assignment but also the basic differences between the two cultures to manage effectively.
- Global managers may also need to adjust their assumptions about work to meet foreign employees' needs.

Practical Application

LO.1.

- _____ refers to differences in religious affiliation, age, disability status, military experience, sexual orientation, economic class, educational level, lifestyle, gender, race, ethnicity, and nationality.
- A metaphor for the invisible barrier that makes it difficult for women and minorities to rise above a certain level is known as the _____.
- _____ is conduct of a sexual nature that has negative consequences for employment.

LO.2.

- The term for special efforts to recruit and hire qualified members of groups that have been discriminated against in the past is _____.
- Embracing a proactive business philosophy of valuing the richness that diverse employees bring to an organization is known as _____.

LO.3.

- Work team diversity increases _____ and _____ in problem solving.
- Because a diverse workforce encompasses many different points of view, it gives an organization a better _____.

LO.4.

- The term for how tightly knit a group is and the degree to which they see and act the same way is _____.
- The tendency to see all members of a group as alike is called _____.

LO.5.

- A monolithic organization, which has a highly homogeneous employee population, is also said to have little _____.

- A company that has a relatively diverse employee population and tries to involve people from different backgrounds but in which employees are still clustered in certain functions is called a/an _____.
- An organization that has fully integrated minority members, both formally and informally, into its workforce could be called a/an _____.

LO.6.

- The first step in cultivating a diverse workforce involves _____.
- Two components of diversity training are _____ and _____.
- A/an _____ is a higher-level manager who helps ensure that high-potential people are introduced to top management and socialized into the norms and values of the organization.

LO.7.

- Individuals from the company's parent country who are sent on overseas assignments are called _____.
- When an organization hires natives of the country in which the overseas division is located, these employees are called _____.
- A/an _____ is a foreign national brought in to work at a parent company.

LO.8.

- _____ is the tendency to judge others by the standards of one's group or culture, which are seen as superior.
- Soon after Emily was sent to Asia to work, she experienced disorientation and stress. Emily was suffering from _____.
- The extent to which a society accepts the unequal distribution of power in organizations is called _____.

IN A NUTSHELL

Strong and effective leadership can set an organization on the path to success. Leaders draw on many personal traits and skills, but they must modify their approaches to fit the needs of the situation and the organization.

The following questions will test your take-away knowledge from this chapter. How many can you answer?

LO.1. What do people want and organizations need from their leaders?

LO.2. How does a good vision help you be a better leader?

LO.3. What are the similarities and differences between leading and managing?

LO.4. Can you identify sources of power in organizations?

LO.5. What are the personal traits and skills of effective leaders?

LO.6. Can you describe behaviors that will make you a better leader and identify when the situation calls for them?

LO.7. What are the differences between charismatic and transformational leaders?

LO.8. Can you describe types of opportunities to be a leader in an organization?

LO.9. How can you further your own leadership development?

Did your answers include the following important points?

LO.1. What do people want and organizations need from their leaders?

- People want help in achieving their goals, such as pay, promotions, personal development, and fair treatment.
- Organizations need people at all levels to be leaders—to help implement and sometimes to create strategic direction.

LO.2. How does a good vision help you be a better leader?

- Vision is a fundamental component of leadership, providing a view of future possibilities and the entire business.

LO.3. What are the similarities and differences between leading and managing?

- Management deals with ongoing, day-to-day complexities of organizations; leadership orchestrates change by setting a direction and inspiring people.

LO.4. Can you identify sources of power in organizations?

- Power comes from the authority to tell others what to do, the ability to provide rewards, the authority to punish, the possession of personal characteristics that appeal to others, and the possession of expertise or knowledge.

LO.5. What are the personal traits and skills of effective leaders?

- Effective leaders have drive, leadership motivation, integrity, self-confidence, and knowledge of the business.

LO.6. Can you describe behaviors that will make you a better leader and identify when the situation calls for them?

- The behavioral approach to leadership tries to identify what good leaders do, such as achieve goals and maintain relationships.
- The situational approach to leadership states that the most effective way to lead depends on the situation.

LO.7. What are the differences between charismatic and transformational leaders?

- Charismatic leaders are dominant, are exceptionally self-confident, and have a strong conviction in their beliefs.
- Transformational leaders motivate people to transcend their personal interests for the good of the group.

LO.8. Can you describe types of opportunities to be a leader in an organization?

- In addition to heading firms, effective leaders develop leadership in others so they can figure out what needs to be done and do it well.

LO.9. How can you further your own leadership development?

- You can develop skills by watching other leaders, practicing, reading about other leaders, and making mistakes and learning from them.

Practical Application

LO.1.
- One who influences others to attain goals is called a/an _____.
- The best leaders, according to Kouzes and Posner, do five things: challenge the process, _____, enable others to act, _____, and encourage the heart.

LO.2.
- A/an _____ is a mental image of a possible and desirable future state of the organization.
- The best visions are both _____ and _____.

LO.3.
- Behavior that provides guidance, support, and corrective feedback is called _____, as opposed to strategic leadership.
- _____ gives purpose and meaning to organizations by anticipating and envisioning a viable future for the organization and working with others to initiate changes that create such a future.

LO.4.
- A leader who has control over punishments has _____ power.
- _____ power is the power a leader has when he or she has personal characteristics that appeal to others.

LO.5.
- A leadership perspective that attempts to determine the personal characteristics that great leaders share is called the _____.
- A set of characteristics that reflect a high level of effort, high need for achievement, constant striving for improvement, ambition, energy, tenacity, and initiative is called _____.

LO.6.
- _____ behaviors are the leader's efforts to ensure that the work unit or organization reaches its goals; _____ behaviors are actions taken to ensure the satisfaction of members, to develop and maintain harmonious work relationships, and to preserve social stability.
- The Vroom model of leadership and path-goal theory are two examples of the _____ approach to leadership.

LO.7.
- John F. Kennedy and Martin Luther King Jr. are examples of _____ leaders.
- _____ leaders use their legitimate, reward, and coercive powers to give commands and exchange rewards for services rendered. In contrast, _____ leaders motivate people to transcend their personal interests for the good of the group.

LO.8.
- A leader who serves others' needs while strengthening the organization is known as a/an _____.
- _____ leadership is rotating leadership, in which people rotate through the leadership role based on which person has the most relevant skills at a particular time.

LO.9.
- The most effective leadership development experiences have three components: assessment, _____, and support.
- _____ includes information that helps you understand where you are now, what your strengths are, and what your primary development needs are.

IN A NUTSHELL

Organizations need motivated employees to accomplish their goals. Managers can examine the outcomes employees receive and the jobs they do to help motivate their workforces.

The following questions will test your take-away knowledge from this chapter. How many can you answer?

LO.1. What kinds of behaviors do managers need to motivate in people?

LO.2. What are the principles for setting goals that motivate employees?

LO.3. How can you reward good performance effectively?

LO.4. Can you describe the key beliefs that affect people's motivation?

LO.5. What are the ways in which people's individual needs affect their behavior?

LO.6. How can you create jobs that motivate?

LO.7. How do people assess and achieve fairness?

LO.8. Can you identify causes and consequences of a satisfied workforce?

Did your answers include the following important points?

LO.1. What kinds of behaviors do managers need to motivate in people?

- Managers need to motivate employees to join and remain with the organization, come to work regularly, perform their duties, and exhibit good citizenship.

LO.2. What are the principles for setting goals that motivate employees?

- Well-crafted goals are meaningful, challenging but attainable, specific, and quantifiable.

LO.3. How can you reward good performance effectively?

- Reinforcement of behavior provides rewards for performance.
- Behavior that is followed by positive consequences probably will be repeated.

LO.4. Can you describe the key beliefs that affect people's motivation?

- If people believe that their efforts will lead to a certain outcome, and if they value that outcome, they will try harder to achieve it.

LO.5. What are the ways in which people's individual needs affect their behavior?

- People have different needs that energize and motivate them.
- The extent to which and the ways in which a person's needs are met or not met at work affect his or her behavior on the job.

LO.6. How can you create jobs that motivate?

- Managers can make the job itself more varied and interesting, which can lead to high motivation, high-quality performance, high satisfaction, and low absenteeism and turnover.
- Enriched jobs provide skill variety, task identity, task significance, autonomy, and feedback.

LO.7. How do people assess and achieve fairness?

- People measure their contributions and their outcomes against those of other people.
- When people feel they have been treated inequitably, they try to even the balance.

LO.8. Can you identify causes and consequences of a satisfied workforce?

- Some causes of workforce satisfaction are adequate compensation, a safe work environment, jobs that develop skills and enhance personal growth, a positive social environment, a workplace that upholds employee rights, jobs that minimize infringement on personal and family time, and an organization that acts in a socially responsible manner.
- Some consequences of a satisfied workforce are low employee turnover and absenteeism, fewer destructive behaviors, fewer injuries and better health, good customer service, and higher productivity and profits.

Practical Application

LO.1.

- Forces that energize, direct, and sustain a person's efforts are called _____.
- Performance on a job means that employees work hard to achieve _____ and _____.

LO.2.

- A motivation theory stating that people have conscious goals that energize them and direct their thoughts and behaviors toward a particular end is called _____.
- _____ are targets that are particularly demanding, sometimes thought to be impossible.

LO.3.

- Thorndike's law of effect states that behavior that is followed by _____ will likely be repeated.
- Removing or withholding an undesirable consequence is called _____.
- _____ is the term for withdrawing or failing to provide a reinforcing consequence.

LO.4.

- _____ is a theory proposing that people will behave based on their perceived likelihood that their effort will lead to a certain outcome and on how highly they value that outcome.
- Bill believes that if he studies hard, he'll perform well on the test; he has a high _____.
- The perceived likelihood that performance will be followed by a particular outcome is called _____.

LO.5.

- Maslow's need hierarchy organizes needs into five general categories: physiological, _____, social, ego, and _____.
- Alderfer's ERG theory postulates that people have three sets of needs: _____, _____, and _____.
- McClelland theorized that people have some basic needs that guide them; they are the need for achievement, the need for _____, and the need for power.

LO.6.

- _____ are rewards given to a person by the boss, company, or another person; _____ are rewards a worker derives directly from performing the job.
- Antoine's production employees were getting bored doing the same job over and over. To alleviate their boredom, he had them switch jobs every other day, which is called _____.
- Herzberg's two-factor theory identified two factors that affect people's work motivation and satisfaction: _____ and motivators.

LO.7.

- Equity theory states that people assess how fairly they have been treated according to two key factors: _____ and _____.
- People who believe they have been treated inequitably have four options: reducing their inputs, _____, decreasing others' outcomes, and increasing others' inputs.

LO.8.

- Stealing, sabotage, and vandalism are signs of _____.
- A/An _____ is a set of perceptions of what employees owe their employers and what their employers owe them.

ANSWERS LO1• motivation • high output (productivity)/high quality **LO2•** goal-setting theory • Stretch goals **LO3•** positive consequences • negative reinforcement • Extinction **LO4•** Expectancy theory • expectancy • instrumentality **LO5•** safety or security/self-actualization • existence/relatedness/growth • affiliation **LO6•** Extrinsic rewards/intrinsic rewards • Job rotation • hygiene factors **LO7•** outcomes/inputs • increasing their outcomes **LO8•** job dissatisfaction • psychological contract

active review card

Teamwork

IN A NUTSHELL

Teams are transforming the ways companies do business. Nearly all companies now use teams to produce goods and services, manage projects, and make decisions.

The following questions will test your take-away knowledge from this chapter. How many can you answer?

LO.1. How can teams contribute to an organization's effectiveness?

LO.2. Can you distinguish between the new team environment and that of traditional work groups?

LO.3. How do groups become teams?

LO.4. Why do groups sometimes fail?

LO.5. How is an effective team built?

LO.6. What are the methods for managing a team's relationships with other teams?

LO.7. Can you identify ways to manage conflict?

Did your answers include the following important points?

LO.1. How can teams contribute to an organization's effectiveness?

- Teams can serve as a building block for organization structure.
- Teams can also increase productivity, improve quality, reduce costs, enhance speed, and foster innovation and change.

LO.2. Can you distinguish between the new team environment and that of traditional work groups?

- Organizations have been using groups for a long time, but groups are different from teams.
- In today's true team environment, people are more involved, they are better trained, cooperation is higher, and the culture is one of learning as well as producing.

LO.3. How do groups become teams?

- Groups must successfully navigate the various stages of team development: forming, storming, norming, and performing.
- Groups enter critical periods in their formative stages.

LO.4. Why do groups sometimes fail?

- Groups sometimes fail because they never become a cohesive unit.

- Groups can also fail to develop enough autonomy to make real decisions.

LO.5. How is an effective team built?

- Effective teams are built by using team-building activities or working with an outside coach.

LO.6. What are the methods for managing a team's relationships with other teams?

- Teams must understand the nature of their lateral relationships with other teams.
- To develop relationships with other teams, some team members need to manage outward and coordinate their activities with other teams' activities.

LO.7. Can you identify ways to manage conflict?

- Some conflict is natural in organizations and can be constructive, but when it interferes with goal achievement, it must be managed.
- People deal with conflict through avoidance, accommodation, compromise, competing, and collaboration.

Practical Application

LO.1.

- Some organizations use _____ as building blocks for organization structure.
- Effective use of teams can benefit an organization's competitiveness, increasing productivity, improving _____, reducing costs, enhancing speed, and fostering _____.

LO.2.

- _____ teams are teams that make or do things like manufacture, assemble, sell, or provide service; _____ teams are teams that work on long-term projects but disband once the work is completed.
- Erica's new-product team members are located in different offices, communicate mostly by e-mail, and conduct meetings via teleconference. Erica's team is an example of a/an _____ team.
- Self-managed teams have more _____ than traditional work groups.

LO.3.

- The first stage in team development, when members lay the ground rules, is called _____.
- _____ and _____ are the second and third stages of team development.
- The last stage of team development, prior to adjourning or declining, in which the team is operating at highest efficiency, is called _____.

LO.4.

- Some teams fail because they receive little _____ or support.
- Some teams are never allowed to make important decisions; in other words, they are not _____.

LO.5.

- _____ is working less and being less productive when in a group.
- Shared beliefs about how people should think and behave are called _____.
- Sanjay's team has surpassed all its performance goals, and its members enjoy working with each other and want to remain on the team to tackle new challenges. Sanjay's team exhibits _____.

LO.6.

- A team member who keeps abreast of current developments and provides the team with relevant information is known as a/an _____.
- A/an _____ strategy entails making decisions with the team and then telling outsiders of the team's intentions.
- A team strategy that requires members to interact frequently with outsiders, diagnose their needs, and experiment with solutions is called a/an _____ strategy.

LO.7.

- A reaction to conflict that involves ignoring the problem by doing nothing at all or deemphasizing the disagreement is called _____.
- Mary Ellen is trying to resolve a conflict between herself and another team member by cooperating with the other person and not being assertive about her own interests. Mary Ellen is demonstrating _____.
- _____ is a style of dealing with conflict involving moderate attention to both parties' concerns; in contrast, _____ involves a strong focus on one's own goals with little or no concern for the other person's goals.
- A style of dealing with conflict that emphasizes both cooperation and assertiveness in order to maximize both parties' satisfaction is called _____.

IN A NUTSHELL

Communication within an organization ensures that all members receive the information they need to do their jobs well. Managers should select the best channels to convey their messages.

The following questions will test your take-away knowledge from this chapter. How many can you answer?

LO.1. What are the important advantages of two-way communication?

LO.2. Can you identify communication problems to avoid?

LO.3. When and how should you use the various communication channels?

LO.4. How can you become a better "sender" and "receiver" of information?

LO.5. How can you improve downward, upward, and horizontal communication?

LO.6. How can you work with the company grapevine?

LO.7. Can you describe the boundaryless organization and its advantages?

Did your answers include the following important points?

LO.1. What are the important advantages of two-way communication?

- True two-way communication is more accurate than one-way communication because it allows people to ask questions and make modifications.
- Fewer mistakes occur and fewer problems arise with two-way communication.

LO.2. Can you identify communication problems to avoid?

- Problems in perception and filtering can hinder communication.
- Communication can also be more difficult when the sender and receiver are from two different cultures.

LO.3. When and how should you use the various communication channels?

- Oral communication should be used when the message is complex, is critically important, or involves difficult or emotional situations.
- Written communication should be used when time and distance prevent face-to-face communication, cost is a factor, the message needs to convey factual details, or a permanent record needs to be made.

LO.4. How can you become a better "sender" and "receiver" of information?

- Senders can improve their communication by polishing their presentation skills, improving their writing skills, and being aware of nonverbal signals.
- Receivers can improve their listening, reading, and observational skills.

LO.5. How can you improve downward, upward, and horizontal communication?

- You can avoid information overload, be open with colleagues, and make sure the information is accurate and not just what others want to hear.

LO.6. How can you work with the company grapevine?

- To work effectively with the company grapevine, you should develop a good network of people who are willing and able to help.

LO.7. Can you describe the boundaryless organization and its advantages?

- If no boundaries separate people, jobs, processes, and places, then ideas, information, decisions, and actions can move to where they are most needed.

Practical Application

LO.1.

- _____ is the transmission of information and meaning from one party to another through the use of shared symbols.
- A billboard posted on a highway advertising a vacation spot is an example of _____ -way communication.
- Teresa sent an e-mail to her manager about a proposed meeting time, and her manager replied to the message that she was free then. This is an example of _____.

LO.2.

- The process of receiving and interpreting information is called _____.
- Joshua was afraid to give his supervisor the bad news that nationwide sales were much lower than expected. Instead, he told his supervisor that Western Division sales were up 1 percent. This is an example of _____ in communication.
- Verbal communication between people from different cultures can be improved by using clear, slow speech, _____, simple sentences, and active verbs.

LO.3.

- Telephone conversations and speeches, as compared with written documents, are examples of _____.
- _____ is the term for a set of Internet-based applications that encourage user-provided content and collaboration.
- The degree to which a communication channel conveys information is called _____.

LO.4.

- To make your reports and memos readable and interesting, you should strive for _____, organization, readability, and _____.

- Body language, compared with the spoken word, is a type of _____.
- A process by which a person states what he or she believes the other person is saying is called _____.

LO.5.

- Information that flows from higher to lower levels in the organization's hierarchy is called _____; information that flows from lower to higher levels in the organization's hierarchy is called _____.
- _____ is dialogue with a goal of helping another be more effective and achieve his or her full potential on the job.
- The practice of sharing with employees at all levels of the organization vital information previously meant for management's eyes only is known as _____.
- The department heads met to discuss the changes in employee benefits; such a meeting is an example of _____.

LO.6.

- Official, organization-sanctioned episodes of information transmission are called _____.
- An informal communication network is known as the _____.

LO.7.

- An organization in which there are no barriers to information flow is called a/an _____.
- GE's Workout program, in which employees hold a series of meetings across multiple hierarchical levels and have extremely frank, tough discussions, is an example of breaking down _____.

IN A NUTSHELL

Managerial control goes hand in hand with planning. It ensures that employees know what is expected of them and that their progress will be checked to correct problems and reward accomplishments.

The following questions will test your take-away knowledge from this chapter. How many can you answer?

LO.1. Why do companies develop control systems for employees?

LO.2. Can you summarize how to design a basic bureaucratic control system?

LO.3. What are the purposes for using budgets as a control device?

LO.4. Can you define basic types of financial statements and financial ratios used as controls?

LO.5. What are the procedures for implementing effective control systems?

LO.6. Can you identify ways in which organizations use market control mechanisms?

LO.7. How is clan control used in an empowered organization?

Did your answers include the following important points?

LO.1. Why do companies develop control systems for employees?

- Companies develop control systems so employees know what is expected of them and that their progress will be checked.
- Control systems allow organizations to ensure that they are meeting planned goals.

LO.2. Can you summarize how to design a basic bureaucratic control system?

- To develop a bureaucratic control system, an organization needs to set performance standards, measure performance, compare performance against the standards and determine deviations, and take action to correct problems and reinforce success.

LO.3. What are the purposes for using budgets as a control device?

- Budgetary control is one of the most widely recognized and commonly used methods of managerial control.
- Budgetary control finds out what is being done and compares the results with data in the plans to verify accomplishments or remedy differences.

LO.4. Can you define basic types of financial statements and financial ratios used as controls?

- Balance sheets show the financial picture of a company at a given time and itemize assets, liabilities, and stockholders' equity.

- Profit and loss statements itemize the income and expenses of a company's operations.
- Key financial ratios, such as liquidity, leverage, and profitability ratios, suggest a company's strengths and weaknesses.

LO.5. What are the procedures for implementing effective control systems?

- Managers can implement effective control systems by ensuring that the systems are based on valid performance standards, communicate adequate information to employees, are acceptable to employees, use multiple approaches, and recognize the relationship between empowerment and control.

LO.6. Can you identify ways in which organizations use market control mechanisms?

- Organizations use market controls to determine prices and profits through supply and demand.

LO.7. How is clan control used in an empowered organization?

- Clan control relies on frontline decision making and strong relationships developed as a result of the organization's culture to direct today's employees.

Practical Application

LO.1.

- Lax management and an absence of policies are signs that a company lacks _____.
- Any process that directs the activities of individuals toward the achievement of goals is called _____.

LO.2.

- A/an _____ is expected performance for a given goal.
- A managerial principle stating that control is enhanced by concentrating on the significant deviations from the expected result or standard is called the _____.
- Ely thinks it is important to set policies, procedures, and rules before operations begin to ensure that plans are carried out properly. Ely believes in _____.
- An evaluation conducted by one organization, such as a CPA firm, on another is known as a/an _____.

LO.3.

- _____ is the process of investigating what is being done and comparing the results with corresponding financial data to verify accomplishments or remedy differences.
- Procedures used to verify accounting reports and statements are called _____.
- _____ is a method of cost accounting designed to identify streams of activity and then to allocate costs across particular business processes according to the amount of time employees devote to particular activities.

LO.4.

- A report that shows the financial picture of a company at a given time and itemizes assets, liabilities, and stockholders' equity is called a/an _____.

- _____ are the values of the various items the corporation owns; _____ are the amounts a corporation owes to various creditors.
- Alice's manager only cares about short-term earnings, not long-term strategic obligations. You could say Alice's manager has _____.

LO.5.

- Valid performance standards are expressed in quantitative terms, are _____, and are difficult to sabotage or fake.
- The seven "deadly sins" of performance measurement to avoid are vanity, provincialism, narcissism, _____, pettiness, inanity, and _____.
- A/an _____ is a control system that combines four sets of performance measures: financial, customer, business process, and learning and growth.

LO.6.

- Control based on the use of pricing mechanisms and economic information to regulate activities within organizations is called _____.
- A/an _____ is a price charged by one unit for a good or service provided to another unit within the organization.

LO.7.

- _____ is control based on the norms, values, shared goals, and trust among group members.
- Bureaucratic and market controls are insufficient to direct today's workforce because employees' jobs have changed, the nature of management has changed, and _____.

IN A NUTSHELL

Innovative organizations are those that seek to explore and exploit new technologies and capabilities. Managers can either lead changes or react to them; either way, they must manage them well.

The following questions will test your take-away knowledge from this chapter. How many can you answer?

LO.1. Can you summarize how to assess technology needs?

LO.2. Can you identify the criteria on which to base technology decisions?

LO.3. What are the key ways of acquiring new technologies?

LO.4. Can you describe the elements of an innovative organization?

LO.5. What are the characteristics of successful development projects?

LO.6. What does it take to be world class?

LO.7. How can you manage change effectively?

LO.8. What are the tactics for creating a successful future?

Did your answers include the following important points?

LO.1. Can you summarize how to assess technology needs?

- In assessing the need for technology, managers first need to consider the organization's competitive strategy to see whether technology furthers those goals.
- Managers also need to measure current technologies and look for trends that affect the industry in which they compete.

LO.2. Can you identify the criteria on which to base technology decisions?

- Criteria on which to base technology decisions include the market potential of the technology, its technological feasibility, its economic viability, the organization's core competency, and the suitability of the technology to the organization.

LO.3. What are the key ways of acquiring new technologies?

- The most common options for acquiring new technology are internal development, purchase, contracted development, licensing, technology trading, research partnerships and joint ventures, and acquisition of a technology owner.

LO.4. Can you describe the elements of an innovative organization?

- Innovative organizations either exploit existing capabilities, such as production speed or product quality, or explore new knowledge, such as seeking to develop new goods or services.

LO.5. What are the characteristics of successful development projects?

- Successful development projects build on core competencies in the organization, have a guiding vision, have a committed team, instill a philosophy of continuous improvement, and coordinate efforts across all units.

LO.6. What does it take to be world class?

- Being world class requires an organization to apply the best and latest knowledge and to have the ability to operate at the highest standards of any place anywhere.
- Becoming world class is more than merely improving; it means becoming one of the very best in the world at what you do.

LO.7. How can you manage change effectively?

- Successful change requires shared leadership; people must be implementers of change, not just supporters.
- People must be motivated to change, and managers must lead change.

LO.8. What are the tactics for creating a successful future?

- To create a successful future, you must be proactive, not reactive.
- Successful managers are those who think about the future, envision how they want it to be, and then work to bring their goals to life.

Practical Application

LO.1.

- The process of clarifying the key technologies on which an organization depends is called a/an _____.
- _____ technologies are still under development but may significantly alter the rules of competition in the future.
- Technologies that have proved effective but offer a strategic advantage because not everyone uses them are known as _____ technologies.

LO.2.

- _____ firms are "technology-push" innovators having cultures that are outward-looking and opportunistic.
- Companies that adopt a more circumspect posture toward innovation are known as _____ firms.

LO.3.

- The question an organization asks itself about whether to acquire new technology from an outside source or develop it itself is known as the _____.
- Partnerships between two or more organizations to form a new company that will pursue new technology development are called _____.

LO.4.

- In acquiring or developing new technology, the _____ role develops the new technology or has the skills needed to install and operate the technology.
- The person who promotes the new technology throughout the organization, often at the risk of his or her reputation, to gain support and acceptance is called the _____.

LO.5.

- A focused organizational effort to create a new product or process via technological advances is called a/an _____.
- The benefits of development projects include the development of new products and processes and the cultivation of skills and knowledge for future endeavors, which is called _____.

LO.6.

- In companies that have enduring greatness, their core _____ remain steadfast.
- The "tyranny of the *or* " means that _____; the "genius of the *and* " means that _____.
- The term for the systemwide application of behavioral science knowledge to develop, improve, and reinforce the strategies, structures, and processes that lead to organizational effectiveness is _____.

LO.7.

- The three-stage model for motivating people to change is _____, _____, and _____.
- The difference between actual performance and desired performance is called a/an _____.
- _____ involves identifying the forces that prevent people from changing and those that will drive people toward change.

LO.8.

- _____ means responding to pressure; in contrast, _____ means anticipating and preparing for an uncertain future.
- _____ are companies that try to change the structure of their industries, creating a future competitive landscape of their own design.